The Classic 1000
Seafood Recipes

Everyday Eating made more exciting

The Classic 1000 Seafood Recipes

by
Carolyn Humphries

foulsham
LONDON • NEW YORK • TORONTO • SYDNEY

foulsham
The Publishing House, Bennetts Close,
Cippenham, Berkshire SL1 5AP, England

ISBN 978-0-572-02696-7

Cover photograph by Peter Howard Smith

Printed in Great Britain by Creative Print & Design (Wales), Ebbw Vale

Contents

Introduction

Fish and other seafood make great eating – from simple everyday fare to spectacular special-occasion meals. They have so many terrific attributes and are so versatile that many varieties can be served at any meal of the day.

Seafood is also highly nutritious. It is an excellent source of protein and vitamins A and D. We now also know that fish oils – unlike meat fat – are good for you as they are high in polyunsaturated omega-3 fatty acids, which can help prevent heart disease.

All fish and seafood are quick to cook and easy to digest. And, most of all, there are so many fabulous varieties – some economical, some expensive and luxurious – that you will always be spoilt for choice. This book will tell you everything you need to know about fish and seafood, with every tasty, creative, sumptuous recipe you could ever dream of.

TYPES OF FISH

Fish can be divided into various categories, and each member of each group shares similar characteristics.

White fish

This group comprises sea fish with white flesh whose oil is stored only in the liver. There are two types: round fish and flat fish. Skate is also a flat fish but only the wings, not the main body, are eaten.

Round fish include cod, coley, haddock, whiting, hake, bream and bass.

Flat fish include plaice, Dover sole, lemon sole, halibut, turbot, brill and flounder.

Oily fish

These have coarser, oily flesh in a variety of colours from beige to red. Some are caught at sea, others are freshwater fish caught in rivers and lakes and some are now farmed.

Seawater fish include conger eel, red and grey mullet, mackerel, herring, pilchard, sprat, snapper, tuna, swordfish and marlin. There are also the small fry like whitebait (baby herring) and sardines (young pilchards).

Freshwater fish include salmon, rainbow and brown trout, carp, pike, perch and eel.

Shellfish

There are two types: crustaceans and molluscs.

Crustaceans are creatures with jointed shells and include various types of crab, lobster, crawfish, brown and pink shrimps, prawns (shrimp), Dublin Bay prawns (also known as saltwater crayfish and scampi, especially when sold peeled), langoustines (or Norway lobster), crayfish (also known as freshwater lobster) and king or tiger prawns (jumbo shrimp).

Molluscs are soft-bodied creatures that are usually, although not always, encased in a hard shell. This group includes mussels, oysters, scallops, clams, whelks, winkles and cockles and also creatures like squid and cuttlefish, which do not have a hard shell.

Other sea creatures

There are many other marine creatures from all round the world that are considered to be delicacies. These include octopus, sea urchins, sea anemones and sea cucumbers.

Smoked fish

There are two types: cold-smoked and hot-smoked.

Cold-smoked fish are still raw after smoking, and you can buy cod, haddock, kippers (herrings), salmon and trout. Cold-smoked salmon and trout are sold thinly sliced and served raw. The others should be cooked before eating.

Hot-smoked fish are cooked as they are smoked, so they do not need cooking before eating. These include buckling (herring), mackerel, trout and some salmon. Smoked oysters and mussels are also sold in cans.

Arbroath smokies are small whole haddock, split, salted and hot-smoked over oak or birch wood. To eat, they are boned, spread with butter and sprinkled with pepper, closed up again and briefly grilled (broiled) just until hot through.

Cod's roe is also smoked, salted and pressed. It can be served sliced as a starter or made into taramasalata, the creamy Greek dip.

Smoked eel fillets are served like smoked salmon, with brown bread and butter and lemon juice, or with scrambled egg.

Some smoked fish such as cod, haddock and kippers may have colouring added to deepen the colour. I prefer the undyed varieties. Red herrings are small whole herrings that have been dried, salted, smoked and dyed red. They have a very strong, salty flavour.

Salt fish

Salted anchovies need brief soaking in cold water before use. Fillets can also be bought preserved in oil in cans or jars.

Bombay duck is dried, cured bommaloe fish fillets. It smells very strong but tastes great. It is not soaked before cooking. Grill (broil) it until crispy and serve as an appetiser or crumble over rice dishes.

Caviare is the salted roes of various fish. Beluga is one of the most famous – and will become even rarer and more expensive as continued unregulated overfishing depletes the sturgeon stocks – but other roe like sevuga and osetra are also used. Keta is the red, salted roe of salmon. Lumpfish roe is really pink but is dyed black or red and is known as Danish or German caviare. It is an inexpensive alternative and good for serving as a starter with blinis, soured (dairy sour) cream and chopped onion, or used to garnish smoked salmon or prawns (shrimp).

Dried salt cod fillet should be soaked in several changes of cold water for 24 hours before cooking. It is usually then gently simmered in water for about 20 minutes until tender before use.

Dried salt herrings are sold whole. They should be soaked in several changes of cold water for 12 hours before use.

Dried sharks' fin looks like a dried old man's beard. Soak it in several changes of cold water until it becomes a firm jelly. It is used in oriental soups and stews.

Pickled fish

Bismark herrings are steeped whole in vinegar, then filleted, split and layered in a dish with onions, carrots and peppercorns. They are served with potatoes and soured (dairy sour) cream.

Gravadlax (sometimes called gravlax) is salmon pickled raw with dill (dill weed), salt, sugar, peppercorns and sometimes brandy.

Rollmops are herring fillets rolled up with sliced onions and peppercorns, then placed in jars and preserved in vinegar. Dill (dill weed) is also sometimes used for flavouring.

Soused mackerel or herring are rolled fillets cooked in vinegar with onions and spices and served hot or cold.

Canned and frozen fish

Both canned and frozen fish are highly nutritious and very versatile. Fish, unlike meat, can be cooked successfully from frozen. Follow the packet instructions. Canned fish can make many tasty meals and it is worth keeping a supply in the storecupboard.

Choosing and Storing Fish

CHOOSING FISH

All fresh, whole fish should have a slippery, shiny skin, bright in colour with firm but elastic flesh. The eyes should be bright and prominent with clear, black pupils. Stale fish have grey, sunken eyes with red rims. The gills should be bright red and clean. Fish and shellfish should always smell pleasant. Fishy, yes: offensive, no.

Crustaceans should feel heavy, and when shaken there should be no sound of water inside. Raw lobsters, crabs and prawns (shrimp) are greenish blue, not pink or red (they change colour when cooked). Lobsters and prawns can be bought raw to cook yourself; crabs tend to be sold ready cooked. If buying a raw lobster, choose one that feels heavy and is lively. Avoid very large ones as the meat may be tough.

Molluscs should be clean and intact. Avoid batches with lots of barnacles or broken shells and any that are open.

Thawed, frozen fish should have the appearance of fresh fish. Dull, flabby flesh is a sign that it has been thawed badly and should be avoided.

STORING FISH

Frozen fish should be taken home and placed in the freezer straight away. NEVER freeze fresh fish unless you have just caught it or bought it straight off a trawler or it is clearly marked in the supermarket as suitable for home freezing. Most fish you buy may already have been frozen. On the whole, domestic freezers can't freeze fish fast enough to prevent ice crystals forming between the flesh, which damages the texture.

Fresh or thawed, frozen fish should be eaten on the day of purchase or, at most, kept in the fridge overnight.

Preparing Fish

TO SKIN FISH FILLETS

1. Place the fillet on a board, skin-side down.
2. Make a small cut at one end between the flesh and skin.
3. Hold the flap of skin firmly between your finger and thumb (dip your fingers in salt first to help you grip), then ease the flesh away from the skin with a large, sharp knife, pulling the skin as you go. It should come away fairly easily.

TO SKIN WHOLE FLAT FISH

This isn't as easy as for fillets and if you prefer you can ask your fishmonger to do it for you. It is usually necessary to skin only the dark side of the fish. White skin is soft and pleasant to eat.

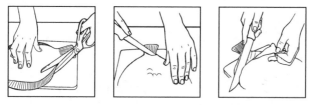

1. Trim the fish for grilling (broiling) or frying (sautéing) (page 12).
2. Make a snick with a knife at the tail end. Loosen a flap of skin.
3. Dip your fingers in salt to help you grip and gently pull the skin back, easing with a sharp knife as you go until you reach the head end. Trim off with scissors if necessary.

TO SKIN WHOLE ROUND FISH

1. Cook the fish first. Place on a board and, using a sharp knife, gently ease the skin away from behind the head, then pull it gently, scraping with the knife if necessary to remove it completely.
2. Gently turn the fish over and repeat on the other side.

TO SCALE FISH

1. Hold the fish by the tail.
2. Scrape away the scales with the back of a knife, working firmly from the tail to the head.

TO BONE WHOLE FISH SUCH AS MACKEREL

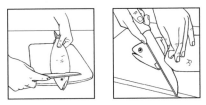

1. Cut off the head and tail.
2. Open out the cleaned fish and lay it skin-side up on a board.
3. Run your thumb firmly up and down the backbone several times.
4. Turn the fish over and lift off the backbone and any loose bones.

TO FILLET FLAT FISH

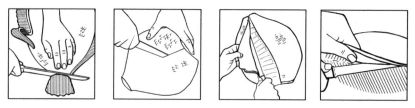

1. Trim the fins and tail and cut off the head.
2. Make a slit along the length of the backbone (down the centre of the fish) from the head to the tail.
3. Slice one fillet away from the backbone, cutting towards the outer edge, gently pulling the fillet free with your other hand. Repeat with the other fillet on that side.
4. Turn the fish over and fillet the other side in the same way.

TO FILLET ROUND FISH

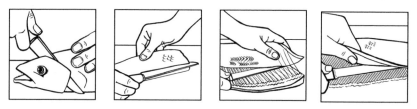

1. Cut off the head and tail.
2. Make a cut all the way along the backbone (opposite the slit where the fish was cleaned) from the head to the tail.
3. Gently slide the knife between the flesh and the bones, carefully easing it away as you go, lifting the fillet with your other hand.
4. Turn the fish over and repeat on the other side.

TO PREPARE WHOLE FLAT FISH FOR GRILLING (BROILING) OR FRYING (SAUTÉING)

1. Use scissors to square off the tails.
2. Trim the fins to within 5 mm/¼ in of the flesh on each side.
3. Leave the heads intact.

TO VANDYKE THE TAIL

This is named after the small pointed beard worn by Anthony Van Dyck, the seventeenth-century artist.
1. Hold the fish firmly in one hand.
2. Using kitchen scissors, cut an acute V-shape out of the tail, making two distinct points each side.

TO CLEAN MUSSELS

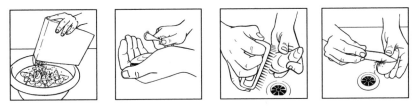

1. If you have time, place the mussels in a large bowl and cover with water. Sprinkle with rolled oats or oatmeal. This will help clean the mussels on the inside.
2. Discard any that are damaged or open or won't close when tapped sharply.
3. Scrub under running water and cut off any barnacles.
4. Pull off the beard hanging down from each mussel.

TO SHUCK OYSTERS

1. Hold the oyster firmly in one hand, protected by a cloth or oven glove. Insert a sharp, pointed knife between the two shells near the hinge.
2. Push the knife against the hinge, twisting until the hinge breaks.
3. Carefully open the oyster without losing the juice and loosen it from its shell with the knife.

TO OPEN AND CLEAN SCALLOPS

1. Lever the two halves of the shell apart with a large, sharp knife.
2. Cut under the scallop where it is attached to the round shell to remove it. Pull off the round shell. Peel off the filmy membrane covering the scallop. Rinse under cold water.
3. Still keeping the scallop in its half shell underwater, carefully cut away the black intestines, holding the rest of the scallop with your thumb.

TO CLEAN SQUID

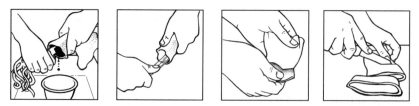

1. Reach inside the body and pull away the head and tentacles. Cut off the tentacles and reserve (these can be chopped and cooked too). Discard the head.
2. Pull out the transparent quill from inside the body. Peel the skin off the body.
3. Pull away the side flaps, then cut them up (they can be cooked too).
4. Thoroughly rinse inside and out, then cut the body into rings or leave whole for stuffing.

TO KILL LOBSTERS

I prefer to buy a very freshly cooked lobster, but many foodies maintain that you can only appreciate the flavour if you cook it yourself.

1. Hold the lobster flat on a board. Put a cloth over its tail.
2. Hold it firmly behind the head.
3. Insert the point of a large, sharp, pointed chopping knife in the little cross mark on the centre of the head. The lobster is killed instantly.

TO BOIL RAW LOBSTERS

Bring a pan of water to the boil with a wineglass of white wine, an onion and a few peppercorns. Drop in the lobster. Cover, reduce the heat and simmer gently for 20 minutes for a lobster weighing about 450 g/1 lb, 30 minutes for a 700 g/1½ lb one. If any larger, cook for 45 minutes. Leave it to cool in the liquid.

TO PREPARE LOBSTER OR CRAWFISH

This is suitable for raw or cooked lobster or crawfish.

 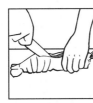  

1. Twist off the legs and claws. Crack them open and extract the meat.
2. Using a large, sharp knife, split the lobster in half down the back of the head, then along the centre of the back.
3. Remove the gills from behind the head and the black intestine that runs along the length of the body.
4. The red coral, black roe and green tomalley are edible.

TO PEEL PRAWNS (SHRIMP)

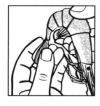 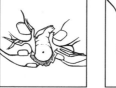

1. Hold the prawn firmly in the middle and pull off the head, then the tail.
2. Turn it upside-down and peel back the legs and body shell. It will slide off over the back of the prawn.
3. Remove the dark vein that runs the length of the body.

TO PREPARE A COOKED CRAB

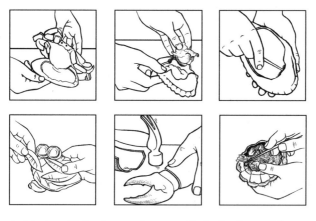

1. Twist off the large claws. Pull the body and legs away from the top shell. Remove the legs.
2. Remove the bundle of intestines that is either stuck in the shell or clinging to the body. Scrape it to remove any dark meat still clinging to it, then discard the bundle.
3. Scoop out the dark meat from the shell.
4. Discard the gills (dead men's fingers) from the body.
5. Crack open the large claws and legs and pick out the white meat.
6. Pick out the little bits of white meat from the body (this is fiddly).

TO PREPARE WHELKS AND WINKLES

  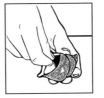 

1. If raw, scrub well in several changes of cold water.
2. Cook in plenty of boiling, salted water for 20 minutes. Drain and leave to cool.
3. Discard the flat, black disc that covers the fish at the opening of the shell.
4. Serve cold with vinegar, pepper and bread and butter. Use cocktail sticks (toothpicks) or tiny forks to pick the fish from the shells.

TO PREPARE COCKLES OR CLAMS

Shelled and ready cooked

Wash thoroughly to remove any sand and serve with vinegar, pepper and bread and butter.

Still in their shells

1. Scrub well and place in a saucepan with about 300 ml/½ pt/ 1¼ cups of water. Cover, bring to the boil and cook for about 3–4 minutes until the shells open, shaking the pan occasionally.
2. Discard any that remain closed.
3. Remove the fish from their shells and use as required.

COOK'S TIPS

- ✿ The bones in canned fish are very soft and should be eaten where appropriate as they are high in calcium.
- ✿ In most cases it is a good idea to drain off all brine or oil before using canned fish. Anchovy oil, however, is often used to drizzle over the dish or as part of a dressing.
- ✿ Don't overcook fish or it will become dry.
- ✿ Oily fish can be grilled (broiled) without extra fat.

Cooking Fish

GRILLING (BROILING)

Fish fillets
1. Place on foil on a grill (broiler) rack.
2. Drizzle with oil or dot with butter or margarine and sprinkle with lemon juice. Season lightly.
3. Cook quickly under a preheated grill for about 3–5 minutes until golden and just tender, when the fish flakes easily when tested with a knife. Do not turn over. You can cook salmon and other oily fish without fat if you prefer.

Fish steaks or cutlets
Prepare as above but cook for 4–6 minutes, turning once during cooking.

Whole fish such as mackerel or trout
1. Wipe inside and out with kitchen paper (paper towels).
2. Make several slashes with a sharp knife through to the bone on each side, then prepare as above and cook for 5–8 minutes, turning once during cooking.

FRYING (SAUTÉING)

Fillets, steaks and cutlets
1. Heat a little butter or margarine and/or oil in a non-stick frying pan (skillet).
2. Dip the fish in seasoned plain (all-purpose) flour, if liked, or season lightly with salt and pepper. Sprinkle with lemon juice.
3. Fry (sauté) for 3–6 minutes, depending on thickness, turning once, until golden brown and just cooked through.
4. Drain on kitchen paper (paper towels) before serving.

Whole fish
1. Wipe inside and out with kitchen paper (paper towels).
2. Make several slashes in the flesh through to the bone on each side.
3. Season and cook for 5–8 minutes, depending on size, turning once, until just cooked through and golden brown.

DEEP-FRYING

Fillets

1. Heat the oil for deep-frying in a deep-fat fryer or saucepan to 190°C/375°F on a universal thermometer or until a cube of day-old bread browns in 30 seconds.
2. Dust with seasoned plain (all-purpose) flour, then dip in egg and breadcrumbs. Alternatively, dip in a batter made by mixing self-raising (self-rising) flour and a pinch of salt with just enough water to form a thick batter that will just drop off the spoon.
3. Lower into the hot oil and cook for about 4–5 minutes until golden brown.
4. Drain on kitchen paper (paper towels) before serving.

Small-fry such as whitebait

1. Dip in milk, then seasoned plain (all-purpose) flour, and cook for about 2 minutes until crisp and golden.
2. Drain on kitchen paper (paper towels) before serving.

BAKING

1. Wrap in buttered foil or greaseproof (waxed) paper, or cover with a sauce.
2. Bake in a preheated oven at 190°C/375°F/gas mark 5 for 10–25 minutes, depending on thickness, until just tender. Do not overcook.

POACHING

Fillets and steaks or cutlets

1. Place in a frying pan (skillet) with a lid or a flameproof casserole dish (Dutch oven).
2. Add just enough water, milk or stock to cover. Add flavourings to taste, for example a bay leaf or a sprig of fresh herbs or a bouquet garni sachet and/or a few slices of onion and a little salt and pepper.
3. Bring the liquid just to the boil, cover, reduce the heat and simmer gently for about 3–8 minutes, depending on thickness, until the fish is just tender.
4. Carefully lift out of the liquid with a fish slice. Use the strained cooking liquid to make a sauce, if appropriate.

Large whole fish

1. Wipe the fish inside and out with kitchen paper (paper towels). Remove the head, if preferred.
2. Place on a large sheet of foil and add flavourings of your choice (see Fillets, page 19). Wrap in the foil, leaving extra foil at each end for lifting the fish.
3. Place in a fish kettle, if you have one, or a large flameproof container that will hold the fish comfortably. Pour in just enough water to cover, adding 300 ml/½ pt/1¼ cups white wine or cider if liked.
4. Bring the liquid just to the boil, cover, reduce the heat and poach for 4 minutes per 450 g/1 lb.
5. Leave to stand for 10 minutes in the liquid if serving hot, or leave to cool completely in the liquid if serving cold. Lift out of the liquid and remove the foil and flavourings.
6. Peel off the skin, if preferred, and garnish with parsley, watercress or cucumber slices.

BRAISING

This is best for large whole fish.
1. Wipe inside and out with kitchen paper (paper towels). Stuff if liked.
2. Place on a bed of chopped carrots, onions and celery, first blanched in boiling water for 3 minutes and drained.
3. Pour 300 ml/½ pt/1¼ cups water or stock and/or white wine or cider round the fish and add a bouquet garni sachet. Season, then cover and cook in a preheated oven at 160°C/325°F/gas mark 3 for 15 minutes per 450 g/1 lb or until the fish can be eased away from the bone easily with the point of a knife.
4. The juices can be strained for serving or the vegetables puréed with the stock to serve as a thick sauce.

MICROWAVING

Fillets and steaks or cutlets

1. Place in a microwave-safe container with a lid, with the tails pointing towards the centre for fillets or in a circle round the dish for steaks or cutlets.
2. Add 60 ml/4 tbsp milk, water or a mixture of wine or cider and water.
3. Add flavourings of your choice (see Poaching, page 19).
4. Cook on High (100 per cent power) for 3–6 minutes per 450 g/ 1 lb until the fish is just opaque. The exact time will depend on the thickness of the fish and the output of your microwave. Do not overcook. Leave to stand for 2 minutes to finish cooking before serving.

Whole fish such as mackerel

1. Wipe inside and out with kitchen paper (paper towels).
2. Make several slashes on each side and lay head-to-tail in a suitable container.
3. Add 60 ml/4 tbsp milk, water or a mixture of wine or cider and water.
4. Add flavourings of your choice (see Poaching, page 19).
5. Cook on High (100 per cent power) for 4–6 minutes per 450 g/ 1 lb, turning carefully after 3 minutes, until just cooked through (check by looking inside the body opening of the fish; the flesh should look just opaque). Leave to stand for 2 minutes before serving.

Notes on the Recipes

❀ All ingredients are given in imperial, metric and American measures. Follow one set only in a recipe. American terms are given in brackets.

❀ All spoon measures are level: 1 tsp = 5 ml; 1 tbsp = 15 ml.

❀ Eggs are medium unless otherwise stated.

❀ Always wash, peel, core and seed, if necessary, fresh produce before use.

❀ Seasoning and the use of strongly flavoured ingredients such as garlic or chillies are very much a matter of personal taste. Adjust seasonings to suit your own palate.

❀ Always use fresh herbs unless dried are specifically called for. If you wish to substitute dried for fresh, use only half the quantity or less as they are very pungent. Frozen, chopped varieties have a better flavour than the dried ones.

❀ All can sizes are approximate as they vary from brand to brand. For example, if I call for a 400 g/14 oz/1 large can of tomatoes, a 397 g can is fine.

❀ I have given the choice of butter or margarine in the recipes. Use a different spread if you prefer but check that it is suitable for general cooking, not just for spreading.

❀ Cooking times will depend on the thickness of the fish, so those given are approximate and should be used only as a guide. Always check that the fish is cooked through before serving. It should look opaque and separate easily into flakes. Do not overcook, though, or it will dry out.

❀ All frozen fish and seafood should be thawed and dried on kitchen paper (paper towels) unless otherwise stated.

Soups

Rich, hearty, nutritious, colourful – all these and many more adjectives can describe glorious fish soups. Not a bit of goodness or flavour is lost when you serve up any of these delicious dishes. Many are substantial enough for a main meal, with just crusty bread to accompany. Then perhaps you could follow with a little cheese, more bread and a green salad to create a simple but stunning meal.

Simple fish stock

MAKES ABOUT 1 LITRE/1¾ PTS/4¼ CUPS

Use this in any recipe that calls for stock.

1 kg/2¼ lb fish trimmings, e.g. heads,
  tails, bones, skin
1 onion, roughly chopped
1 carrot, roughly chopped
2 outer celery sticks, roughly chopped
1 bouquet garni sachet
6 black peppercorns
1 litre/1¾ pts/4¼ cups water
150 ml/¼ pt/⅔ cup white wine or cider
Salt

Put all the ingredients in a large saucepan, adding salt to taste. Bring to the boil, reduce the heat, part-cover and simmer gently for 40 minutes. Strain through a very fine sieve (strainer). Leave to cool. Store in an airtight container in the fridge or freeze in small, measured portions.

Spicy tomato and prawn soup

SERVES 4

1 large onion, finely chopped
15 g/½ oz/1 tbsp butter or margarine
15 ml/1 tbsp plain (all-purpose) flour
5 ml/1 tsp paprika
1.5 ml/¼ tsp cayenne
450 ml/¾ pt/2 cups passata (sieved
  tomatoes)
600 ml/1 pt/2½ cups fish or chicken
  stock
10 ml/2 tsp tomato purée (paste)
1 bouquet garni sachet
A pinch of ground cloves
120 ml/4 fl oz/½ cup medium-dry
  sherry
100 g/4 oz cooked peeled prawns
  (shrimp)

Fry (sauté) the onion in the butter or margarine for 3 minutes, stirring, until soft but not brown. Stir in the flour and cook for 1 minute. Stir in the paprika and cayenne. Remove from the heat and blend in the passata, stock and tomato purée. Return to the heat and bring to the boil, stirring. Add the bouquet garni and cloves and simmer for 20 minutes. Add the sherry and prawns and heat through for about 3 minutes. Serve hot.

New-age partan bree

SERVES 6

1 large cooked crab, prepared (page 16)
50 g/2 oz/¼ cup brown rice
600 ml/1 pt/2½ cups milk
450 ml/¾ pt/2 cups chicken stock
5 ml/1 tsp anchovy essence (extract)
10 ml/2 tsp tomato purée (paste)
Salt and freshly ground white pepper
150 ml/¼ pt/⅔ cup crème fraîche
15 ml/1 tbsp chopped parsley, to serve

Slice the meat from the large claws neatly and put to one side. Put the rice and milk in a saucepan. Bring to the boil, reduce the heat and simmer for about 40 minutes, stirring occasionally, until the rice is tender. Transfer to a blender or food processor with the brown and white meat from the body and legs, the green tomalley and any coral. Purée until smooth.

Return to the saucepan and stir in the stock, anchovy essence and tomato purée. Season with a pinch of salt and pepper to taste. Reheat until almost boiling, then stir in the crème fraîche and the sliced claw meat. Taste and re-season if necessary. Ladle into warm bowls and sprinkle with the parsley to serve.

Traditional partan bree

SERVES 6

Prepare as for New-age Partan Bree, but use white long-grain rice instead of brown and simmer for 15 minutes until tender. Substitute single (light) cream for the crème fraîche.

Chilled consommé with caviare

SERVES 6

3 × 295 g/10½ oz/medium cans of condensed beef consommé
60 ml/4 tbsp medium-dry sherry
A few drops of Tabasco sauce
150 ml/¼ pt/⅔ cup soured (dairy sour) cream
50 g/2 oz/1 small jar of Danish lumpfish roe

Empty the contents of the cans of consommé into a bowl. Stir in the sherry and Tabasco and chill until jellied. Spoon into soup bowls, top each with a spoonful of soured cream, then a spoonful of lumpfish roe and serve immediately.

Chilled consommé with prawns

SERVES 6

Prepare as for Chilled Consommé with Caviare, but substitute crème fraîche for the soured (dairy sour) cream and cooked, peeled prawns (shrimp) for the Danish lumpfish roe. Garnish the side of each bowl with a cooked, unpeeled prawn.

Clam bisque

SERVES 4

1 onion, finely chopped
1 celery stick, finely chopped
15 g/½ oz/1 tbsp butter or margarine
30 ml/2 tbsp plain (all-purpose) flour
300 ml/½ pt/1¼ cups fish or chicken stock
150 ml/¼ pt/⅔ cup milk
150 ml/¼ pt/⅔ cup crème fraîche
210 g/7½ oz/1 small can of minced (ground) clams
30 ml/2 tbsp chopped parsley
Salt and freshly ground black pepper
60 ml/4 tbsp finely grated Cheddar cheese

Fry (sauté) the onion and celery very gently in the butter or margarine, stirring, for 5 minutes until soft but not brown. Blend in the flour. Remove from the heat and gradually blend in the stock and milk. Return to the heat, bring to the boil and simmer gently for 3 minutes. Stir in the crème fraîche, the contents of the can of clams, the parsley and seasoning to taste. Simmer gently for 1 minute. Ladle into warm bowls and top with the cheese before serving.

Wontons in garlic soup

SERVES 6

*50 g/2 oz cooked peeled prawns
(shrimp), chopped*
50 g/2 oz cup minced (ground) pork
*50 g/2 oz/½ cup cooked chicken,
chopped*
5 ml/1 tsp soy sauce
*1 bunch of spring onions (scallions),
chopped*
½ garlic bulb, cloves crushed
Salt
*100 g/4 oz/1 cup plain (all-purpose)
flour, sifted*
2 eggs, beaten
15 ml/1 tbsp sunflower oil
1 onion, finely chopped
1.75 litres/3 pts/7½ cups chicken stock

Mix the prawns with the pork,
chicken, soy sauce, half the spring
onions, one of the garlic cloves and
a pinch of salt. Put the flour in a
bowl. Add the eggs and work with
the fingers into a firm but not sticky
dough, adding a little cold water, if
necessary. Knead gently on a lightly
floured surface and roll out thinly.
Cut into 7.5 cm/3 in triangles.
Divide half the prawn and meat
mixture between the triangles. Fold
in the two side points and roll up.
   Heat the oil in a large saucepan or
wok. Fry (sauté) the remaining
garlic and the chopped onion until
lightly golden. Add the remaining
filling and fry, stirring, for 3 minutes.
Add the stock and season to taste
with salt. Bring to the boil, drop in
the dumplings, reduce the heat,
cover and simmer for about
15 minutes. Sprinkle the remaining
spring onions into the pot just before
serving ladled into warm soup
bowls.

Summer salmon bisque

SERVES 6

1 small red (bell) pepper
1 onion, chopped
1 garlic clove, crushed
1 potato, finely diced
15 g/½ oz/1 tbsp butter or margarine
*2 tomatoes, skinned, seeded and
chopped*
*300 ml/½ pt/1¼ cups fish or chicken
stock*
225 g/8 oz salmon tail, skinned
1.5 ml/¼ tsp cayenne
5 ml/1 tsp dried dill (dill weed)
300 ml/½ pt/1¼ cups milk
30 ml/2 tbsp brandy
150 ml/¼ pt/⅔ cup double (heavy) cream
Salt and freshly ground black pepper
6 tiny watercress sprigs

Cut six thin rings off the pepper.
Plunge the rings in boiling water for
1 minute, drain, rinse with cold
water and drain again. Dry on
kitchen paper (paper towels) and
reserve. Chop the remaining pepper
and place in a pan with the onion,
garlic, potato and butter or
margarine. Fry (sauté), stirring, for
2 minutes until softened but not
browned. Add the tomatoes and
stock, bring to the boil, reduce the
heat and simmer for 10 minutes until
the vegetables are soft.
   Add the salmon, cayenne and dill
and simmer for 5 minutes or until
the fish is tender. Stir in a little of
the milk to cool the soup slightly.
Turn into a blender or food
processor and purée until smooth.
Pour into a bowl, stir in the
remaining milk and leave until cold.
Stir in the brandy, cream and
seasoning to taste. Chill well. Pour
into soup bowls, float a pepper ring
on top and garnish each with a tiny
sprig of watercress.

Scottish salmon trimmings soup

It's worth asking your fishmonger for the 'bits' if you aren't buying whole fish.

1 salmon head and end of tail
1 plaice or sole head and bones
1.5 litres/2½ pts/6 cups water
1 bouquet garni sachet
Salt and freshly ground black pepper
1 large carrot, finely diced
1 bunch of spring onions (scallions), chopped
1 celery stick, chopped
1 potato, chopped
2 large ripe tomatoes, skinned, seeded and chopped
300 ml/½ pt/1¼ cups milk
15 ml/1 tbsp cornflour (cornstarch)
75 ml/5 tbsp double (heavy) cream
30 ml/2 tbsp whisky

Put the fish, water, bouquet garni and some salt and pepper in a large saucepan. Bring to the boil, skim the surface, reduce the heat, cover and simmer gently for 1 hour. Strain and return the stock to the rinsed-out saucepan. Pick all the meat off the heads and tails and add to the pan. Add all the prepared vegetables, bring to the boil, then reduce the heat and simmer for 30 minutes until really tender. Purée in a blender or food processor and return to the pan. Blend the milk with the cornflour and stir in. Bring to the boil, reduce the heat and simmer for 1 minute, stirring. Stir in the cream and whisky, taste and re-season if necessary. No garnish is needed.

Fragrant haddock and tomato soup

2 onions, chopped
25 g/1 oz/2 tbsp butter or margarine
400 g/14 oz/1 large can of chopped tomatoes
300 ml/½ pt/1¼ cups fish or chicken stock
10 ml/2 tsp chopped rosemary
50 g/2 oz/¼ cup long-grain rice
350 g/12 oz haddock fillet, skinned and diced
50 g/2 oz/½ cup frozen peas
150 ml/¼ pt/⅔ cup single (light) cream
Salt and freshly ground black pepper

Fry (sauté) the onions in the butter or margarine for 2 minutes, stirring. Add the tomatoes, stock, rosemary and rice and simmer for 15 minutes until the rice is really tender. Stir in the fish and peas and simmer for 5 minutes. Add the cream and salt and pepper to taste, and reheat but do not boil. Ladle into warm soup bowls and serve.

Cypriot fish soup with egg and lemon

SERVES 6

450 g/1 lb any cheap white fish fillet, skinned
1.2 litres/2 pts/5 cups fish or chicken stock
2 onions
20 ml/4 tsp olive oil
6 courgettes (zucchini), chopped
6 carrots, chopped
4 celery sticks, chopped
½ bunch of parsley, chopped
Salt and freshly ground black pepper
A good pinch of ground cinnamon
90 ml/6 tbsp long-grain rice
Juice of 2 small lemons
2 eggs

Place the fish in a pan with 1 litre/ 1¾ pts/4¼ cups of the stock. Add the onions, bring to the boil, reduce the heat, cover and simmer until the fish is tender. Lift out the fish with a draining spoon. Add the olive oil, vegetables, parsley, a little salt and pepper and the cinnamon to the stock. Simmer until the vegetables are tender. Purée the fish, vegetables and stock and return to the saucepan.

Meanwhile, simmer the rice in the remaining stock until tender. Add to the purée and heat through. Beat together the lemon juice and eggs. Add a spoonful of soup to the egg mixture and whisk well. Pour this mixture into the soup and stir. Heat but do not allow to boil. Ladle into soup bowls and serve hot.

Winter haddock soup

SERVES 4

1 large onion, finely chopped
25 g/1 oz/2 tbsp butter or margarine
400 g/14 oz/1 large can of chopped tomatoes
300 ml/½ pt/1¼ cups milk
150 ml/¼ pt/⅔ cup fish stock
15 ml/1 tbsp chopped thyme
50 g/2 oz/¼ cup long-grain rice
100 g/4 oz broccoli, cut into tiny florets
350 g/12 oz haddock fillet, skinned and diced
Salt and freshly ground black pepper
Croûtons (page 395), to garnish

Fry (sauté) the onion in the butter or margarine in a saucepan for 2 minutes until softened but not browned. Add the tomatoes, milk, stock, thyme and rice. Bring to the boil, reduce the heat, cover and simmer for 10 minutes. Stir, add the broccoli and simmer for 3 minutes. Add the fish and a little salt and pepper and cook for a further 3–5 minutes or until the fish is tender but still holds its shape. Taste and re-season if necessary. Ladle into soup bowls and garnish with Croûtons before serving.

Mussel chowder

SERVES 4–6

1.25 kg/2½ lb fresh mussels in their
shells, cleaned (page 13)
150 ml/¼ pt/⅔ cup dry white wine
25 g/1 oz/2 tbsp butter or margarine
4 streaky bacon rashers (slices), rinded
and chopped
1 onion, finely chopped
1 small green (bell) pepper, finely diced
1 celery stick, chopped
1 large potato, diced
Salt and freshly ground black pepper
1 bay leaf
300 ml/½ pt/1¼ cups water
25 g/1 oz/¼ cup plain (all-purpose)
flour
600 ml/1 pt/2½ cups milk
15 ml/1 tbsp chopped parsley
150 ml/¼ pt/⅔ cup single (light) cream

Put the mussels in a large saucepan
with the wine. Cover, bring to the
boil and cook for 3 minutes, shaking
the pan occasionally. Drain through
a colander over a bowl, reserving
the liquid. Leave until cool enough
to handle, then remove the mussels
from their shells and reserve. Melt
the butter or margarine in the
rinsed-out saucepan. Add the bacon,
onion, green pepper, celery, potato
and seasoning and fry (sauté) for
2 minutes, stirring. Add the bay leaf
and water and simmer for about
15 minutes until the vegetables are
really tender.

Blend the flour with a little of the
milk. Stir into the pan with the
remaining milk and the reserved
mussel liquid. Bring to the boil and
cook for 2 minutes, stirring all the
time. Return the mussels to the pan,
add the parsley and simmer for
2 minutes. Discard the bay leaf and
stir in the cream. Taste and re-
season, if necessary, then reheat but
do not boil. Serve hot.

Simple corn and tuna soup

SERVES 4

475 g/1 lb 1 oz/1 very large can of
creamed sweetcorn (corn)
185 g/6½ oz/1 small can of tuna,
drained
450 ml/¾ pt/2 cups milk
1.5 ml/¼ tsp ground mace
Salt and freshly ground black pepper
2 streaky bacon rashers (slices), rinded
15 ml/1 tbsp chopped parsley

Mix the corn, tuna, milk and mace
in a saucepan and heat through.
Season to taste. Meanwhile, grill
(broil) or dry-fry the bacon until
crisp and snip into pieces with
scissors. Ladle the soup into bowls,
scatter the bacon and parsley on top
and serve straight away.

Mussel brose

SERVES 4

For a richer soup, use half milk and half buttermilk and add 15 ml/ 1 tbsp whisky just before serving.

1.75 kg/4 lb mussels, cleaned
(page 13)
300 ml/½ pt/1¼ cups water
30 ml/2 tbsp fine oatmeal
600 ml/1 pt/2½ cups milk
1 small onion, finely chopped
15 g/½ oz/1 tbsp butter or margarine
Salt and freshly ground black pepper
30 ml/2 tbsp chopped parsley

Place the mussels in a large saucepan with the water. Cover, bring to the boil, reduce the heat and cook for 5 minutes, shaking the pan occasionally. Discard any mussels that have not opened. Strain the cooking liquid into a bowl. Remove the mussels from their shells and add to the liquor. Toast the oatmeal in a separate pan until golden. Add the milk, bring to the boil, reduce the heat and simmer for 5 minutes, stirring. Fry (sauté) the onion in the butter or margarine in the rinsed-out mussel saucepan for 3 minutes until soft but not brown. Add the mussels in their liquor and bring to the boil. Stir in the oatmeal milk. Season to taste and serve sprinkled with the parsley.

Chardonnay mussel soup

SERVES 4

1 onion, finely chopped
25 g/1 oz/2 tbsp butter or margarine
1 large garlic clove, crushed
900 g/2 lb mussels, cleaned (page 13)
1 bouquet garni sachet
300 ml/½ pt/1¼ cups Chardonnay
750 ml/1¼ pts/3 cups fish stock
15 ml/1 tbsp cornflour (cornstarch)
15 ml/1 tbsp milk
2 egg yolks
45 ml/3 tbsp double (heavy) cream
Salt and freshly ground black pepper
15 ml/1 tbsp chopped parsley

Fry (sauté) the onion in the butter or margarine in a large saucepan for 2 minutes, stirring. Add the garlic, the prepared mussels, the bouquet garni and the Chardonnay. Cover and cook for about 5 minutes, shaking the pan occasionally, until the mussels open.

Remove the mussels from their shells and reserve. Discard the shells and strain the cooking liquor. Return to the rinsed-out pan and add the stock. Blend the cornflour with the milk and stir into the pan. Bring to the boil and cook for 1 minute, stirring. Beat the yolks with the cream and stir in. Do not allow to boil. Return the mussels to the soup and heat through, again without boiling. Season to taste and sprinkle with the parsley before serving.

Italian mussel soup

SERVES 4

1 red onion, finely chopped
1 garlic clove, crushed
60 ml/4 tbsp olive oil
400 g/14 oz/1 large can of chopped
    tomatoes
750 ml/1¼ pts/3 cups fish stock
900 g/2 lb mussels, cleaned (page 13)
250 ml/8 fl oz/1 cup dry vermouth
1 bouquet garni sachet
1 thick lemon slice
30 ml/2 tbsp fresh white breadcrumbs
15 ml/1 tbsp chopped flatleaf parsley

Cook the onion and garlic in the oil
for 2 minutes, stirring. Add the
tomatoes and stock, bring to the
boil, reduce the heat and simmer for
15 minutes until pulpy. Meanwhile,
put the mussels in a large pan with
the vermouth, bouquet garni and
lemon slice. Bring to the boil, cover
and cook for 5 minutes, shaking the
pan occasionally, until the mussels
open. Strain the mussels, reserving
the cooking liquor. Remove the
mussels from their shells and add to
the soup with the strained liquor
and the breadcrumbs. Simmer for
5 minutes, then serve garnished with
the parsley.

Brittany mussel bisque

SERVES 4

1 kg/2¼ lb fresh mussels, cleaned
    (page 13)
600 ml/1 pt/2½ cups water
300 ml/½ pt/1¼ cups dry cider
2 celery sticks, finely chopped
1 onion, finely chopped
45 ml/3 tbsp chopped parsley
Salt and freshly ground black pepper
50 g/2 oz/¼ cup long-grain rice
1 large tomato, skinned, seeded and
    finely chopped
10 ml/2 tsp lemon juice

Put the mussels in a large pan with
the water, cider, celery, onion and
half the parsley. Season with salt
and pepper and bring to the boil.
Cover and cook for 5 minutes.
Remove the mussels with a draining
spoon and discard any that have not
opened. Take the mussels out of
their shells and reserve. Meanwhile,
add the rice and tomato to the
cooking liquor, bring to the boil and
cook for 10 minutes or until the rice
is tender. Stir in the lemon juice and
mussels and reheat. Taste and
re-season if necessary. Serve in soup
bowls, garnished with the remaining
parsley.

Clam chowder

SERVES 4

175 g/6 oz salt pork, finely diced
30 ml/2 tbsp olive oil
1 large onion, finely chopped
2 large potatoes, cubed
2 beefsteak tomatoes, skinned, seeded
  and chopped
300 ml/½ pt/1¼ cups passata (sieved
  tomatoes)
600 ml/1 pt/2½ cups fish stock
295 g/10½ oz/1 medium can of clams
A few drops of Tabasco sauce
Salt and freshly ground black pepper
90 ml/6 tbsp double (heavy) cream
Paprika, to garnish

Fry (sauté) the pork in the oil until
brown and crisp all over. Remove
from the pan with a draining spoon
and reserve. Add the onion to the
pan and fry for 3 minutes until
lightly golden. Add the potatoes,
tomatoes, passata and stock. Bring
to the boil, reduce the heat, part-
cover and simmer for about
10 minutes or until the potatoes are
tender but still hold their shape. Add
the pork, the clams with their juice,
the Tabasco and salt and pepper to
taste. Simmer for 5 minutes. Ladle
into warm bowls and serve with a
swirl of cream and a dusting of
paprika on each.

Smoked haddock and butter bean chowder

SERVES 4–6

4 streaky bacon rashers (slices), rinded
  and finely chopped
1 onion, finely chopped
600 ml/1 pt/2½ cups chicken stock
50 g/2 oz short-cut macaroni
225 g/8 oz smoked haddock fillet
450 ml/¾ pt/2 cups milk
200 g/7 oz/1 small can of butter
  (lima) beans, drained
Salt and freshly ground pepper
150 ml/¼ pt/⅔ cup single (light) cream
30 ml/2 tbsp chopped parsley

Fry (sauté) the bacon in a large
saucepan, stirring, until the fat runs.
Add the onion and fry for 2 minutes.
Add the stock and pasta, bring to
the boil, reduce the heat and simmer
for 15 minutes. Meanwhile, poach
the fish in the milk for 5 minutes or
until it flakes easily with a fork.
Remove the skin, flake the fish and
add it to the soup with the cooking
milk. Stir in the beans and a little
salt and pepper. Bring to the boil,
reduce the heat and simmer for a
further 5 minutes. Remove from the
heat. Stir in the cream and serve
straight away garnished with the
parsley.

Cullen skink

SERVES 6

This is traditionally made with whole Finnan Haddies but I prefer to use fillet, which is much more readily available.

450 g/1 lb smoked haddock fillet
1 large onion, chopped
450 ml/³⁄₄ pt/2 cups milk
600 ml/1 pt/2½ cups chicken stock
2 leeks, chopped
1 large potato, very finely diced
50 g/2 oz/¼ cup butter or margarine, diced
300 ml/½ pt/1¼ cups single (light) cream
1 egg yolk
Salt and white pepper
15 ml/1 tbsp chopped parsley

Put the fish in a saucepan with the onion and milk. Bring to the boil, reduce the heat and simmer gently for 8 minutes or until the fish is tender. Lift out the fish. Remove the skin and any bones and return the skin and bones to the milk. Simmer for a further 10 minutes. Strain the liquid, then return it to the rinsed-out saucepan. Discard the skin, bones and onion. Add the stock, leeks and potato to the milk. Bring to the boil, reduce the heat and simmer for 10 minutes or until the leeks and potato are tender.

Mash with a potato masher so the potato thickens the liquid slightly. Whisk in the butter or margarine. Stir in the fish. Whisk together the cream and egg yolk and stir in. Heat again but do not allow to boil. Season to taste and stir in the parsley. Serve hot.

American chowder

SERVES 6

2 large onions, thinly sliced
30 ml/2 tbsp sunflower oil
350 g/12 oz lean belly pork, rinded, boned and finely diced
700 g/1½ lb potatoes, diced
600 ml/1 pt/2½ cups chicken stock
225 g/8 oz turbot fillet, skinned and cubed
150 ml/¼ pt/⅔ cup dry white wine
30 ml/2 tbsp tomato purée (paste)
5 ml/1 tsp caster (superfine) sugar
1 bouquet garni sachet
Salt and freshly ground black pepper
30 ml/2 tbsp chopped parsley

Fry (sauté) the onions in the oil in a large saucepan for 2 minutes, stirring. Remove from the pan with a draining spoon. Add the pork and fry for about 10 minutes, stirring, until golden and tender. Pour off any excess fat. Add the potatoes, onions and stock. Bring to the boil, reduce the heat, part-cover and simmer until the potatoes are really tender, then mash into the liquid. Add all the remaining ingredients except the parsley. Bring to the boil, cover, reduce the heat and simmer gently for 10 minutes. Taste and re-season if necessary. Discard the bouquet garni and sprinkle with the parsley before serving.

Winter fish chowder

SERVES 4

25 g/1 oz/2 tbsp butter or margarine
1 large onion, thinly sliced
2 celery sticks, thinly sliced
1 large carrot, diced
2 large potatoes, diced
750 ml/1¼ pts/3 cups fish or chicken
  stock
Salt and freshly ground black pepper
1 bay leaf
450 g/1 lb white fish fillet, skinned
  and cut into small pieces
150 ml/¼ pt/⅔ cup single (light) cream
150 ml/¼ pt/⅔ cup milk
15 ml/1 tbsp chopped parsley

Melt the butter or margarine in a
saucepan. Add the onion, celery and
carrot and fry (sauté) for 3 minutes,
stirring. Add the potatoes and stock,
some salt and pepper and the bay
leaf. Bring to the boil, reduce the
heat and simmer for 10 minutes.
Add the fish and cook for a further
5 minutes until everything is tender.
Stir in the cream and milk. Discard
the bay leaf. Heat through, taste and
re-season if necessary. Ladle into
warm bowls and sprinkle with the
parsley.

Lobster bisque

SERVES 4–6

1 cooked lobster, about 450 g/1lb
125 g/4½ oz/generous ½ cup unsalted
  (sweet) butter
30 ml/2 tbsp sunflower oil
2 spring onions (scallions), finely
  chopped
150 ml/¼ pt/⅔ cup dry vermouth
1.2 litres/2 pts/5 cups fish or chicken
  stock
40 g/1½ oz/⅓ cup plain (all-purpose)
  flour
Salt and freshly ground black pepper
150 ml/¼ pt/⅔ cup crème fraîche

Prepare the lobster (page 15),
reserving the green tomalley and the
coral separately. Mash the coral with
40 g/1½ oz/3 tbsp of the butter, roll
into a small sausage shape, wrap in
greaseproof (waxed) paper and chill.
Chop up all the lobster meat.
    Meanwhile, melt 40 g/1½ oz/
3 tbsp of the remaining butter in a
saucepan with the oil and fry (sauté)
the spring onions gently until
softened. Add the green tomalley
from the lobster, the vermouth and
stock and simmer for 5 minutes. Put
the lobster meat in a blender or food
processor with 60 ml/4 tbsp of the
soup and purée until smooth.
    Melt the remaining butter in a
clean saucepan. Stir in the flour and
cook for 1 minute, stirring.
Gradually add the remaining stock
mixture, then bring to the boil and
simmer, stirring, for 2 minutes. Stir
in the lobster purée, season with salt
and pepper and stir in the crème
fraîche. Reheat and ladle into warm
soup bowls. Slice the chilled coral
butter and float a piece on top of
each. Serve straight away.

Green eel soup

SERVES 6

1.2 litres/2 pts/5 cups fish or chicken
stock
1.5 ml/¼ tsp grated nutmeg
1 lemon slice
1 bouquet garni sachet
450 g/1 lb small eels, or larger eels cut
into chunks
Salt and freshly ground black pepper
50 g/2 oz/¼ cup unsalted (sweet)
butter
1 large onion, finely chopped
1 leek, finely chopped
20 g/¾ oz/3 tbsp plain (all-purpose)
flour
150 ml/¼ pt/⅔ cup milk
1.5 ml/¼ tsp caster (superfine) sugar
1 egg yolk
150 ml/¼ pt/⅔ cup single (light) cream
45 ml/3 tbsp chopped parsley
15 ml/1 tbsp chopped thyme

Put the stock, nutmeg, lemon slice,
bouquet garni and the eels in a large
saucepan. Season lightly. Bring to
the boil, reduce the heat, part-cover
and simmer gently for 30 minutes or
until the flesh is coming away from
the bones of the eels. Strain the
liquid into a bowl. Remove all flesh
from the bones. Discard the bones
and cut the flesh into neat pieces.

Melt the butter in the rinsed-out
saucepan. Add the onion and leek,
cover and cook very gently for
10 minutes, stirring occasionally,
until completely soft but not brown.
Stir in the flour and cook for
1 minute. Remove from the heat and
gradually blend in the cooking stock
and the milk. Return to the heat,
bring to the boil, then reduce the
heat and simmer for 2 minutes,
stirring. Add the eels, sugar and salt
and pepper to taste and simmer for
2 minutes.

Whisk the egg yolk and stir in
30 ml/2 tbsp of the hot stock. Whisk
in the cream and return the whole
lot to the pan with the herbs.
Reheat, but do not allow to boil.
Taste and re-season if necessary,
then ladle into warm bowls and
serve.

Rustic fish soup with rosemary

SERVES 4

25 g/1 oz/2 tbsp unsalted (sweet)
butter
1 onion, finely chopped
400 g/14 oz/1 large can of chopped
tomatoes
300 ml/½ pt/1¼ cups fish or chicken
stock
5 ml/1 tsp chopped rosemary
50 g/2 oz/¼ cup brown rice
100 g/4 oz French (green) beans,
chopped
350 g/12 oz cod, skinned and diced
Salt and freshly ground black pepper
150 ml/¼ pt/⅔ cup crème fraîche

Melt the butter in a saucepan and
fry (sauté) the onion for 2 minutes,
stirring, until soft but not brown.
Add the tomatoes, stock, rosemary
and rice, bring to the boil, cover,
reduce the heat and simmer gently
for 30 minutes. Add the remaining
ingredients and simmer for
5 minutes. Season to taste and serve.

Rich prawn bisque

SERVES 6

1 large onion, finely chopped
1 potato, cut into small pieces
25 g/1 oz/2 tbsp unsalted (sweet)
  butter
200 g/7 oz/1 small can of pimientos,
  chopped
1 kg/2¼ lb ripe tomatoes, skinned,
  seeded and chopped
15 ml/1 tbsp tomato purée (paste)
1.5 litres/2½ pts/6 cups fish or chicken
  stock
1 bouquet garni sachet
175 g/6 oz cooked peeled prawns
  (shrimp)
Salt and freshly ground black pepper
150 ml/¼ pt/⅔ cup crème fraîche

Cook the onion and potato gently in
the butter for 2 minutes, stirring,
until slightly softened but not
browned. Add the pimientos,
tomatoes, tomato purée, stock and
bouquet garni. Bring to the boil,
reduce the heat, cover and simmer
gently for 30 minutes. Discard the
bouquet garni and purée the mixture
and all but six of the prawns in a
blender or food processor. Return to
the pan and season to taste. Stir in
all but 30 ml/2 tbsp of the crème
fraîche and reheat. Ladle into warm
bowls, top each with a swirl of
reserved crème fraîche and a
reserved prawn and serve hot.

Crab and potato bisque

SERVES 4

25 g/1 oz/2 tbsp butter or margarine
1 large potato, finely chopped
1 carrot, finely chopped
1 small onion, finely chopped
40 g/1½ oz/1 very small can of dressed
  crab
45 ml/3 tbsp plain (all-purpose) flour
900 ml/1½ pts/3¾ cups fish, chicken or
  vegetable stock
5 ml/1 tsp celery salt
30 ml/2 tbsp dry sherry
150 ml/¼ pt/⅔ cup milk
150 ml/¼ pt/⅔ cup single (light) cream
170 g/6 oz/1 small can of white
  crabmeat
Chopped parsley, to garnish

Melt the butter or margarine in a
saucepan. Add the potato, carrot and
onion. Stir, then cover and cook very
gently for 5 minutes until softened
but not browned. Stir in the dressed
crab and flour and cook for 1 minute.
Remove from the heat and gradually
blend in the stock. Bring to the boil,
stirring, reduce the heat and simmer
for 10 minutes, stirring occasionally.
Stir in the remaining ingredients and
heat through. Sprinkle with parsley
before serving.

Bouillabaisse

SERVES 4–6

It is impossible to create a totally authentic version of this soup away from its native shores of France, simply because some of the essential fish are not available. But a pretty good imitation is possible with this easy recipe.

1 large onion, finely chopped
1 leek, chopped
1 fennel stick, chopped
30 ml/2 tbsp olive oil
3 tomatoes, skinned and chopped
2 large garlic cloves, crushed
1 thick orange slice
1 bouquet garni sachet
1.2 litres/2 pts/5 cups boiling water
15 ml/1 tbsp saffron powder
1.5 kg/3 lb mixed fish such as red mullet, john dory, bass, conger eel, raw tiger prawns (jumbo shrimp), whiting and rock salmon
Salt and freshly ground black pepper
30 ml/2 tbsp chopped parsley
Rouille (page 374), French bread, Aioli (page 372) and plain potatoes, to serve

Fry (sauté) the onion, leek and fennel in the oil in a large saucepan for 3 minutes, stirring, to soften. Add the tomatoes and garlic and cook, stirring, for a further 1 minute. Add the orange slice, bouquet garni, boiling water and saffron and boil for 2 minutes, stirring rapidly. Add the fish, starting with the thickest pieces only, and simmer for 5 minutes. Add the remaining fish, season with salt and pepper and simmer gently for a further 10 minutes until all the fish pieces are cooked but still holding their shape.

Carefully lift all the fish out of the pan. Remove any skin and bones, keeping the fish in large pieces. Transfer to a warm serving dish. Strain the soup, taste and re-season if necessary, and add a ladleful to the fish. Sprinkle with half the parsley, cover and keep warm. Ladle the remaining soup into warm soup bowls. Sprinkle with the remaining parsley and serve with Rouille and French bread. When the soup is finished, serve the fish with plain potatoes and the Aioli.

French mushroom prawn and herb soup

SERVES 6

2 × 295 g/10½ oz/medium cans of condensed cream of mushroom soup
Milk
100 g/4 oz cooked peeled prawns (shrimp)
15 ml/1 tbsp chopped tarragon
45 ml/3 tbsp cognac
A little single (light) cream

Empty the cans of soup into a saucepan. Blend in four canfuls of milk, the prawns, 10 ml/2 tsp of the tarragon and the cognac. Heat through, stirring, until almost boiling. Ladle into soup bowls and garnish each with a swirl of cream and a sprinkling of the remaining tarragon.

Salmon and prawn bisque

SERVES 4

300 g/11 oz/1 medium can of creamed
  sweetcorn (corn)
300 ml/½ pt/1¼ cups chicken stock
300 ml/½ pt/1¼ cups milk
200 g/7 oz/1 small can of pink salmon
50 g/2 oz cooked peeled prawns
  (shrimp)
15 ml/1 tbsp brandy
60 ml/4 tbsp double (heavy) cream
15 ml/1 tbsp chopped parsley
Salt and freshly ground black pepper

Blend the sweetcorn with the stock
and milk in a saucepan. Drain in the
liquid from the can of salmon.
Discard the skin and bones from the
salmon, then add the salmon and
prawns to the saucepan. Stir in the
brandy, cream and half the parsley.
Heat through gently until piping hot.
Season to taste. Ladle into warm
bowls and top each with a
sprinkling of the remaining parsley.

Peanut, corn and cod chowder

SERVES 6

½ bunch of spring onions (scallions),
  chopped
15 ml/1 tbsp butter or margarine
45 ml/3 tbsp smooth peanut butter
600 ml/1 pt/2½ cups vegetable stock
45 ml/3 tbsp dried milk powder (non-
  fat dry milk)
25 g/1 oz/2 tbsp light brown sugar
100 g/4 oz/1 cup salted roasted
  peanuts
200 g/7 oz/1 small can of sweetcorn
  (corn) with (bell) peppers
225 g/8 oz cod fillet, skinned and cut
  into small chunks
Salt and freshly ground black pepper
225 g/8 oz/2 cups Cheddar cheese,
  grated
Croûtons (page 395), to garnish

Fry (sauté) the spring onions in
the butter or margarine for about
3 minutes until soft and lightly
golden. Stir in the peanut butter and
a little of the stock until smooth.
Blend in the dried milk and
remaining stock, the sugar, nuts and
sweetcorn. Bring to the boil, stirring,
then reduce the heat and simmer for
5 minutes. Add the fish, season to
taste and cook for a further
5 minutes. Stir in the cheese gently
until melted. Ladle the soup into
warm bowls and sprinkle the
Croûtons over before serving.

Chinese chicken, prawn and sweetcorn soup

SERVES 4

100 g/4 oz/1 cup cooked chicken, diced
100 g/4 oz cooked peeled prawns (shrimp)
900 ml/1½ pts/3¾ cups chicken stock
5 ml/1 tsp grated fresh root ginger
200 g/7 oz/1 small can of sweetcorn (corn)
15 ml/1 tbsp soy sauce
Salt and freshly ground black pepper
15 ml/1 tbsp cornflour (cornstarch)
30 ml/2 tbsp dry sherry
2 spring onions (scallions), finely chopped

Place all the ingredients except the cornflour, sherry and spring onions in a saucepan. Bring to the boil and simmer for 1 minute. Blend the cornflour with the sherry. Stir into the soup and simmer for 1 minute until slightly thickened. Ladle into warm bowls and sprinkle with the spring onions before serving.

Chinese crab, mushroom and sweetcorn soup

SERVES 4

Prepare as for Chinese Chicken, Prawn and Sweetcorn Soup, but simmer 100 g/4 oz sliced shiitake mushrooms, stalks removed, in the stock with the ginger for 10 minutes or until tender before adding the remaining ingredients. Omit the chicken and prawns and add 170 g/6 oz/1 small can of white crabmeat and a 2.5 cm/1 in piece of cucumber, finely chopped, instead.

Creamy white onion and haddock soup

SERVES 4

2 large onions, chopped
1 large potato, diced
50 g/2 oz/¼ cup butter or margarine
450 ml/¾ pt/2 cups chicken stock
1 bouquet garni sachet
228 g/8 oz haddock fillet, skinned and all bones removed
40 g/1½ oz/⅓ cup plain (all-purpose) flour
300 ml/½ pt/1¼ cups milk
150 ml/¼ pt/⅔ cup single (light) cream
Salt and white pepper
Snipped chives, to garnish

Fry (sauté) the onions and potato gently in the butter or margarine for 3 minutes, stirring all the time, until softened but not browned. Stir in the stock and add the bouquet garni sachet. Bring to the boil, reduce the heat, cover and simmer gently for 5 minutes. Add the haddock and simmer for a further 5 minutes or until the fish and vegetables are tender. Allow to cool slightly.

Discard the bouquet garni, then purée in a blender or food processor. Return to the saucepan. Blend the flour with a little of the milk. Stir in the remaining milk, then add to the pan. Bring to the boil and cook for 2 minutes, stirring all the time. Stir in the cream and season to taste. Ladle into soup bowls and garnish with snipped chives.

39

Baked garlic, egg and prawn soup

SERVES 4

45 ml/3 tbsp olive oil
1 large garlic clove, finely chopped
225 g/8 oz/4 cups fresh white
  breadcrumbs
15 ml/1 tbsp paprika
250 ml/8 fl oz/1 cup chicken stock
Salt and freshly ground black pepper
100 g/4 oz cooked peeled prawns
  (shrimp)
4 eggs
Grated Parmesan cheese, for sprinkling
  (optional)

Heat the oil in a frying pan (skillet).
Add the garlic and fry (sauté) gently
until brown. Stir in the breadcrumbs
and cook gently over a low heat
until lightly golden. Stir in the
paprika and stock, season to taste
and simmer for 2 minutes. Ladle
into four ovenproof dishes and add
the prawns. Break an egg into each
and bake in the oven at 180°C/
350°F/gas mark 4 for about
10 minutes or until the eggs are
cooked. Serve sprinkled with grated
Parmesan, if liked.

Garlic, egg, cod and pancetta soup

SERVES 4

Prepare as for Baked Garlic, Egg and
Prawn Soup, but omit the prawns
(shrimp). Add 50 g/2 oz chopped
pancetta with the breadcrumbs and
stir in 175 g/6 oz cod fillet, skinned
and cut into small pieces, when you
add the stock. Simmer for 1 minute
before ladling into the dishes.
Sprinkle the eggs with a little
chopped basil before baking.

Curried prawn soup

SERVES 4

25 g/1 oz/2 tbsp butter or margarine
25 g/1 oz/¼ cup plain (all-purpose)
  flour
10 ml/2 tsp curry powder
900 ml/1½ pts/3¾ cups fish stock
1 celery stick, cut into very thin strips
225 g/8 oz/1 small can of bamboo
  shoots, cut into thin strips
1 small carrot, cut into fine
  matchsticks
50 g/2 oz mangetout (snow peas), cut
  into very thin strips
100 g/4 oz cooked peeled prawns
  (shrimp)
Finely grated rind and juice of
  ½ lemon
A few drops of Tabasco sauce
15 ml/1 tbsp soy sauce
Salt and freshly ground black pepper
90 ml/6 tbsp crème fraîche

Melt the butter or margarine in a
saucepan. Add the flour and curry
powder and cook for 1 minute,
stirring. Blend in the stock and bring
to the boil, stirring. Add the celery,
bamboo shoots and carrot and
simmer for 10 minutes. Add the
mangetout, prawns and lemon rind
and juice and simmer for 2 minutes.
Stir in a few drops of Tabasco sauce,
the soy sauce and salt and pepper to
taste. Add the crème fraîche and
heat through. Ladle into warm bowls
and serve.

Salmon chowder

SERVES 4–6

*400 g/14 oz/1 large can of pink
  salmon*
600 ml/1 pt/2½ cups milk
*300 g/11 oz/1 medium can of creamed
  sweetcorn (corn)*
*200 g/7 oz/1 small can of sweetcorn
  with (bell) peppers*
15 ml/1 tbsp mayonnaise
15 ml/1 tbsp chopped parsley
5 ml/1 tsp lemon juice
Salt and freshly ground black pepper

Drain the can of salmon, discard the
skin and bones and break the fish
into chunks. Put the milk in a
saucepan and bring to the boil.
Add the salmon and all the
remaining ingredients and stir gently
until piping hot. Ladle into warm
bowls and serve.

Salmon and pimento bisque

SERVES 4–6

Prepare as for Salmon Chowder, but
add 275 g/10 oz/1 small can of new
potatoes, cut into small chunks, and
omit the creamed sweetcorn (corn).
Add 200 g/7 oz/1 small can of
pimientos, drained and finely diced,
just before serving.

Bacon, cheese and tuna soup

SERVES 4

*4 streaky bacon rashers (slices), rinded
  and chopped*
15 g/½ oz/1 tbsp butter or margarine
1 onion, finely chopped
1 carrot, finely diced
1 celery stick, chopped
30 ml/2 tbsp plain (all-purpose) flour
300 ml/½ pt/1¼ cups fish stock
450 ml/¾ pt/2 cups milk
*85 g/3½ oz/1 very small can of tuna,
  drained*
75 g/3 oz/¾ cup Cheddar cheese, grated
Salt and freshly ground black pepper
15 ml/2 tbsp chopped parsley

Put the bacon in a saucepan and
cook over a gentle heat until the fat
runs. Add the butter or margarine,
the onion, carrot and celery and
cook, stirring, for 5 minutes. Stir in
the flour and cook for 1 minute.
Remove from the heat and blend in
the stock and milk. Return to the
heat and bring to the boil, stirring.
Reduce the heat and simmer for
15 minutes. Stir in the tuna and heat
through for 2 minutes. Add the
cheese and stir until melted. Season
to taste. Sprinkle with the parsley
before serving.

Mushroom, prawn and pasta chowder

SERVES 4

25 g/1 oz/2 tbsp butter or margarine
1 onion, chopped
100 g/4 oz pancetta, diced
1 garlic clove, crushed
100 g/4 oz button mushrooms, sliced
15 ml/1 tbsp plain (all-purpose) flour
600 ml/1 pt/2½ cups fish stock
150 ml/¼ pt/⅔ cup milk
50 g/2 oz soup pasta
150 ml/¼ pt/⅔ cup single (light) cream
50 g/2 oz cooked peeled prawns (shrimp)
Salt and freshly ground black pepper
15 ml/1 tbsp chopped parsley

Melt the butter or margarine in a saucepan. Add the onion, pancetta, garlic and mushrooms and fry (sauté) for 2 minutes, stirring. Add the flour and cook for 1 minute. Remove from the heat and blend in the stock and milk. Return to the heat and bring to the boil. Add the pasta and simmer for 10 minutes. Add the cream and prawns and season to taste. Heat through but do not allow to boil. Ladle into warm bowls and sprinkle with the parsley.

Swiss olive and prawn soup

SERVES 4

25 g/1 oz/2 tbsp butter or margarine
2 large onions, finely chopped
½ fennel bulb, finely chopped
750 ml/1¼ pts/3 cups fish stock
100 g/4 oz stuffed olives, sliced
100 g/4 oz cooked peeled prawns (shrimp)
Freshly ground black pepper
4 slices of French bread
75 g/3 oz/¾ cup Emmental (Swiss) cheese, grated

Melt the butter or margarine in a saucepan. Add the onions and fennel and cook gently, stirring, for 5 minutes until lightly golden. Add the stock and olives, bring to the boil, reduce the heat and simmer gently for 30 minutes. Add the prawns and season with pepper. Meanwhile, toast the French bread. Ladle the soup into warm, flameproof bowls. Float a slice of bread on each and sprinkle with the cheese. Flash under a hot grill (broiler) to melt the cheese.

Chinese mock seaweed soup

SERVES 4

225 g/8 oz curly kale
1.2 litres/2 pts/5 cups fish stock
5 ml/1 tsp anchovy essence (extract)
1 bunch of spring onions (scallions),
* chopped*
15 ml/1 tbsp sunflower oil
45 ml/3 tbsp soy sauce
1.5 ml/¼ tsp ground ginger
30 ml/2 tbsp dry sherry
Freshly ground black pepper
1 egg white
A pinch of salt
15 ml/1 tbsp snipped chives

Discard any thick stalks from the kale and shred. Bring the stock and anchovy essence to the boil, add the kale and cook for 5 minutes. Meanwhile, fry (sauté) the spring onions in the oil for 3 minutes, stirring. Add to the kale and stock and simmer for a further 30 minutes. Purée in a blender or food processor.

Return to the pan and stir in the soy sauce, ginger, sherry and lots of pepper. Reheat. Whisk the egg white with the salt until stiff. Fold in the chives. Ladle the soup into flameproof bowls and put a spoonful of the egg white on top of each. Flash under a preheated grill (broiler) for about 2 minutes to brown and set the egg white. Serve straight away.

Haricot bean, cod and ratatouille soup

SERVES 6

1 onion, finely chopped
1 garlic clove, crushed
15 ml/1 tbsp olive oil
1 aubergine (eggplant), diced
1 red (bell) pepper, diced
1 green pepper, diced
1 courgette (zucchini), diced
425 g/15 oz/1 large can of haricot
* (navy) beans, drained and*
* thoroughly rinsed*
400 g/14 oz/1 large can of chopped
* tomatoes*
1 vegetable stock cube
15 ml/1 tbsp tomato purée (paste)
2.5 ml/½ tsp dried mixed herbs
A pinch of salt
Freshly ground black pepper
225 g/8 oz cod fillet, skinned and cut
* into small cubes*

Fry (sauté) the onion and garlic in the oil in a large saucepan for 2 minutes, stirring. Add all the remaining ingredients except the fish. Fill the tomato can with water and add to the pan. Repeat with a second canful of water. Bring to the boil, reduce the heat, part-cover and simmer for 25 minutes until the vegetables are really tender. Add the fish and cook for a further 5 minutes. Ladle into warm bowls and serve.

Salt cod, aubergine and red pepper soup with green rouille

SERVES 6

2 aubergines (eggplants)
1 red (bell) pepper
1 green pepper
1 red onion, chopped
2 garlic cloves, crushed
2 tomatoes, skinned, seeded and
   chopped
90 ml/6 tbsp olive oil
90 ml/6 tbsp sunflower oil
600 ml/1 pt/2½ cups chicken or fish
   stock
225 g/8 oz piece of salt cod, soaked for
   24 hours and cooked (page 8)
Salt and freshly ground black pepper
1 green chilli, seeded and chopped
1 slice of white bread, crusts removed
1 egg yolk

Grill (broil) the aubergines and peppers for about 20 minutes, turning, until the skins are blackened. Place the peppers in a plastic bag (this helps to loosen the skins). Hold the aubergines until cold running water and peel off the skins. Chop the flesh and place in a saucepan. Remove the skins from the peppers. Chop the red one and add to the aubergines with the onion, one of the garlic cloves, the tomatoes and 30 ml/2 tbsp of each of the olive and sunflower oils.

Cook over a moderate heat for 5 minutes, stirring occasionally, until sizzling. Cover, reduce the heat and cook for a further 15 minutes, stirring occasionally. Add the stock and fish and season to taste. Bring to the boil, cover, reduce the heat and simmer for a further 15 minutes.

Purée the soup in a blender or food processor and return to the pan. Taste and re-season if necessary.

Meanwhile, roughly chop the green pepper and put in a blender or food processor with the chilli, the remaining garlic, the bread and egg yolk. Add a sprinkling of salt and pepper. Run the machine until smooth, stopping and scraping down the sides as necessary. With the machine running, add the remaining oils in a thin trickle until the mixture is thick and glossy and has the consistency of mayonnaise. Taste and re-season if necessary. Turn into a small bowl, cover in clingfilm (plastic wrap) and chill until required. Ladle the soup into warm bowls, add a spoonful of the rouille to each and serve.

Chinese bean curd and seafood soup

SERVES 4

1 litre/1¾ pts/4¼ cups chicken or fish
   stock
250 g/9 oz/1 block of firm tofu,
   drained and cut into very small
   cubes
170 g/6 oz/1 small can of white
   crabmeat, drained
100 g/4 oz cooked peeled prawns
   (shrimp)
½ × 225 g/8 oz/small can of bamboo
   shoots, chopped
5 ml/1 tsp soy sauce
15 ml/1 tbsp snipped chives

Put the stock in a pan with the tofu. Bring to the boil, reduce the heat and simmer for 10 minutes. Add the remaining ingredients and simmer for 5 minutes. Ladle into bowls and serve.

Danish pea and smoked cod soup

75 g/3 oz/½ cup yellow split peas
75 g/3 oz/scant ½ cup pearl barley
15 ml/1 tbsp olive oil
1 large onion, finely chopped
1.2 litres/2 pts/5 cups vegetable or
  chicken stock
Freshly ground black pepper
225 g/8 oz smoked cod fillet, skinned
  and cut into small cubes
A good pinch of pimenton (optional)
10 ml/2 tsp tomato purée (paste)
150 ml/¼ pt/⅔ cup milk
15 ml/1 tbsp snipped chives
15 ml/1 tbsp chopped parsley

Soak the peas and barley in cold water overnight. Drain. Heat the oil in a saucepan and cook the onion gently, stirring, for 3 minutes until soft but not brown. Add the stock, peas and barley and a good grinding of pepper. Bring to the boil, skim the surface, part-cover, reduce the heat and simmer gently for 1½ hours. Add the fish and pimenton, if using, for the last 5 minutes of cooking. Purée in a blender or food processor with the tomato purée. Return to the saucepan and season to taste. Stir in the milk and chives and heat through. Ladle into warm bowls and sprinkle with the parsley before serving.

Rich mushroom and tuna soup

1 small onion, chopped
350 g/12 oz button mushrooms,
  roughly chopped
15 g/½ oz/1 tbsp butter or margarine
150 ml/¼ pt/⅔ cup chicken or vegetable
  stock
30 ml/2 tbsp plain (all-purpose) flour
450 ml/¾ pt/2 cups milk
185 g/6½ oz/1 small can of tuna,
  drained and flaked
Salt and freshly ground black pepper
30 ml/2 tbsp finely chopped parsley
30 ml/2 tbsp fromage frais

Cook the onion and mushrooms in the butter or margarine gently for 3 minutes, stirring, until soft but not brown. Add the stock, stir and cover. Reduce the heat and simmer gently for 10 minutes, stirring occasionally, until tender. Blend the flour with a little of the milk, then stir into the mushrooms with the remaining milk. Bring to the boil and cook for 2 minutes, stirring. Purée in a blender or food processor with the tuna and return to the saucepan. Season with a pinch of salt and pepper to taste, then stir in the parsley and fromage frais. Reheat but do not allow to boil. Ladle into warm soup bowls and serve straight away.

Cod-a-leekie soup

SERVES 6

2 large leeks, thinly sliced
75 g/3 oz/scant ½ cup pearl barley
1 bouquet garni sachet
1.75 litres/3 pts/7½ cups chicken stock
A pinch of salt
Freshly ground black pepper
350 g/12 oz cod fillet
8 prunes, quartered and stoned
    (pitted)
30 ml/2 tbsp chopped parsley

Put all the ingredients except the fish, prunes and parsley in a large saucepan. Bring to the boil, reduce the heat, part-cover and simmer gently for 1¼ hours. Add the fish and prunes and cook for a further 10 minutes until the barley and fish are tender. Lift the fish out of the soup. Remove the skin and flake into large chunks. Return to the pan and simmer for a further 2 minutes. Taste and re-season if necessary. Discard the bouquet garni. Sprinkle with the parsley and serve.

Golden root and haddock soup

SERVES 8

1 onion, chopped
25 g/1 oz/2 tbsp butter or margarine,
    plus extra for spreading
½ small swede (rutabaga), diced
1 potato, diced
1 small parsnip, diced
1 large carrot, diced
½ small celeriac (celery root), diced
1.5 litres/2½ pts/6 cups vegetable stock
1 bay leaf
A pinch of salt
Freshly ground black pepper
225 g/8 oz smoked haddock fillet
2 slices of wholemeal bread
5 ml/1 tsp paprika
30 ml/2 tsp chopped parsley

Fry (sauté) the onion in the butter or margarine for 2 minutes, stirring, until soft but not brown. Add the remaining vegetables, the stock, bay leaf, salt and a little pepper. Bring to the boil, part-cover, reduce the heat and simmer for 25 minutes. Add the fish and cook for a further 5 minutes or until the fish flakes easily with a fork. Lift the fish out and remove the skin and any bones. Discard the bay leaf. Purée the fish and vegetable mixture in a blender or food processor. Return to the pan and re-season if necessary. Heat through.

Meanwhile, butter the bread and cut into small cubes. Dust with the paprika. Dry-fry in a frying pan (skillet), tossing until crisp and brown. Ladle the soup into warm bowls, sprinkle with the parsley and serve with the croûtons handed separately.

Easy tomato, carrot, orange and whiting soup

SERVES 4

275 g/10 oz/1 small can of carrots,
    drained
400 g/14 oz/1 large can of tomatoes
150 ml/¼ pt/⅔ cup pure orange juice
5 ml/1 tsp dried basil
Salt and freshly ground black pepper
175 g/6 oz whiting fillet, skinned and
    cut into small cubes
20 ml/4 tsp plain yoghurt

Put the carrots and tomatoes in a
blender or food processor and blend
until smooth. Add the orange juice,
basil and some salt and pepper and
blend again. Tip into a saucepan
and add the fish. Simmer gently for
about 5 minutes until the fish is
tender. Ladle into warm soup bowls
and top each with a spoonful of
yoghurt.

Broad bean, spinach and haddock soup

SERVES 6

1 onion, finely chopped
15 g/½ oz/1 tbsp butter or margarine
225 g/8 oz shelled fresh or frozen
    broad (fava) beans
450 g/1 lb fresh or frozen spinach,
    chopped
900 ml/1½ pts/3¾ cups fish stock
175 g/6 oz haddock fillet
Salt and freshly ground black pepper
A good pinch of grated nutmeg
15 ml/1 tbsp snipped chives

Fry (sauté) the onion in the butter or
margarine, stirring, for 3 minutes.
Add the beans, spinach and stock.
Bring to the boil, reduce the heat
and simmer gently for 20 minutes.
Add the fish and cook for a further
5 minutes. Remove the fish and

discard the skin an[...]
Purée the fish and [...]
or food processor [...]
saucepan. Season[...]
and the nutmeg. [...]
warm bowls and spr[...]
chives.

Thick red lentil, tuna and tomato soup

SERVES 4

1 large onion, chopped
1 large potato, chopped
1 carrot, chopped
15 g/½ oz/1 tbsp butter or margarine
175 g/6 oz/1 cup red lentils
750 ml/1¼ pts/3 cups fish stock
400 g/14 oz/1 large can of tomatoes
1 bay leaf
Salt and freshly ground black pepper
185 g/6½ oz/1 small can of tuna,
    drained
30 ml/2 tbsp chopped parsley

Fry (sauté) the onion, potato and
carrot in the butter or margarine,
stirring, for 2 minutes until slightly
softened but not browned. Add all
the remaining ingredients except the
tuna and parsley and bring to the
boil. Part-cover, reduce the heat and
simmer gently for 20 minutes. Add
the tuna and continue simmering
until everything is really tender.
Discard the bay leaf. Purée in a
blender or food processor and return
to the pan. Taste and re-season if
necessary. Serve hot, sprinkled with
the parsley.

...ch tomato, rice and rock salmon soup

SERVES 6

Give this a Mediterranean flavour by adding 30 ml/2 tbsp chopped basil just before serving.

1 onion, finely chopped
2 carrots, finely chopped
1 celery stick, finely chopped
25 g/1 oz/2 tbsp butter or margarine
50 g/2 oz/¼ cup long-grain rice
1.2 litres/2 pts/5 cups fish stock
1 small garlic clove, crushed
700 g/1½ lb tomatoes, skinned and chopped
15 ml/1 tbsp tomato purée (paste)
15 ml/1 tbsp caster (superfine) sugar
Salt and freshly ground black pepper
175 g/6 oz piece of rock salmon
150 ml/¼ pt/⅔ cup crème fraîche

Fry (sauté) the onion, carrots and celery in the butter or margarine for 3 minutes, stirring, until softened but not browned. Stir in the rice and cook for 1 minute. Blend in the stock and add all the remaining ingredients except the crème fraîche. Bring to the boil, reduce the heat and simmer for 20 minutes. Lift out the fish and flake the flesh, discarding the bones. Return to the pan, stir in the crème fraîche and heat through. Taste and re-season if necessary. Ladle into warm bowls and serve hot.

Marine minestrone

SERVES 6

1 large onion, halved and thinly sliced
2 carrots, chopped
1 turnip, chopped
15 g/½ oz/1 tbsp butter or margarine
400 g/14 oz/1 large can of chopped tomatoes
1 bay leaf
2 fish stock cubes
5 ml/1 tsp anchovy essence (extract)
50 g/2 oz short-cut macaroni
425 g/15 oz/1 large can of haricot (navy) beans, drained
¼ small green cabbage, shredded
175 g/6 oz cod fillet
Salt and freshly ground black pepper
Grated Parmesan cheese, to serve

Fry (sauté) the onion, carrots and turnip in the butter or margarine in a large saucepan for 3 minutes, stirring. Stir in the tomatoes. Fill the can with water and add. Repeat with a second canful of water. Add the bay leaf and stock cubes, bring to the boil, reduce the heat and simmer gently for 30 minutes.

Discard the bay leaf and add the remaining ingredients, putting the fish in last. Bring back to the boil, reduce the heat and simmer for a further 10 minutes until everything is really tender. Lift out the fish, discard the skin and cut into small pieces. Return to the pan. Taste and re-season if necessary. Ladle into warm bowls and serve with grated Parmesan cheese.

Smooth lettuce, prawn and parsley soup

SERVES 6

This is delicious hot or cold.

1 bunch of spring onions (scallions), chopped
20 g/³/₄ oz/1½ tbsp butter or margarine
20 g/³/₄ oz/3 tbsp cornflour (cornstarch)
600 ml/1 pt/2½ cups fish stock
1 round lettuce, shredded
50 g/2 oz parsley, chopped
150 ml/¼ pt/⅔ cup milk
100 g/4 oz cooked peeled prawns (shrimp)
60 ml/4 tbsp single (light) cream
Salt and freshly ground black pepper

Fry (sauté) the spring onions in the butter or margarine for 2 minutes, stirring, until softened but not browned. Add the cornflour, then remove from the heat and blend in the stock. Return to the heat and bring to the boil, stirring. Add the lettuce and all but 30 ml/2 tbsp of the parsley and simmer for 15 minutes. Purée in a blender or food processor and return to the pan. Stir in the milk, prawns and half the cream. Season to taste. Either reheat and serve hot, or cool, then chill, before serving in soup bowls, garnished with the remaining cream and parsley.

Gazpacho with prawns

SERVES 6

2 slices of white bread, crusts removed
150 ml/¼ pt/⅔ cup cold water
30 ml/2 tbsp olive oil
15 ml/1 tbsp white wine vinegar
1 garlic clove, crushed
2 × 400 g/14 oz /large cans tomatoes
30 ml/2 tbsp tomato purée (paste)
1 red (bell) pepper, chopped
5 cm/2 in piece of cucumber, roughly chopped
Salt and freshly ground black pepper
18 cooked unpeeled prawns (shrimp)
6 lemon slices

Soak the bread in the water for 2 minutes. Place in a blender or food processor with all the remaining ingredients except the seasoning, prawns and lemon slices. Purée until smooth. Season to taste and chill. To serve, pour into deep soup cups and hang three prawns over the rim of each. Add a slice of lemon and serve.

Chilled tomato and tuna soup

SERVES 4

185 g/6½ oz/1 small can of tuna, drained
400 g/14 oz/1 large can of tomatoes
15 ml/1 tbsp tomato purée (paste)
15 ml/1 tbsp red wine vinegar
15 ml/1 tbsp olive oil
1 spring onion (scallion), roughly chopped
1 small green (bell) pepper, roughly chopped
Salt and freshly ground black pepper
5 ml/1 tsp caster (superfine) sugar
150 ml/¼ pt/⅔ cup iced water
15 ml/1 tbsp snipped chives

Put all the ingredients except the water and chives in a blender or food processor and run the machine until as smooth as possible. Pour into a container and chill until ready to serve. Thin with a little iced water and serve very cold, garnished with the chives.

Iced prawn bisque

SERVES 6

Prepare as for Rich Prawn Bisque (page 36), but use whipped cream instead of crème fraîche. When puréed, tip the mixture into a bowl, cover, cool and then chill. When ready to serve, fold in all but 30 ml/ 2 tbsp of the whipped cream and sharpen slightly with lemon juice. Spoon into chilled dishes and top each with a small spoonful of whipped cream and a prawn.

Chilled avocado, prawn and pimiento soup

SERVES 4–6

2 ripe avocados, peeled and stoned (pitted)
10 ml/2 tsp lemon juice
450 ml/¾ pt/2 cups cold vegetable stock
2 spring onions (scallions), roughly chopped
300 ml/½ pt/1¼ cups plain Greek yoghurt
15 ml/1 tbsp Worcestershire sauce
200 g/7 oz/1 small can of pimientos
Salt and freshly ground black pepper
1.5 ml/¼ tsp chilli powder (optional)
100 g/4 oz cooked peeled prawns (shrimp)
150 ml/¼ pt/⅔ cup cold milk
15 ml/1 tbsp snipped chives

Place all the ingredients except the prawns, milk and chives in a blender or food processor. Blend until smooth. Stir in the prawns and thin to taste with cold milk. Chill for at least 1 hour to allow the flavours to develop. Ladle into bowls and garnish with the chives.

Creamy cheese, salmon and cucumber soup

SERVES 4

15 g/½ oz/1 tbsp butter or margarine
175 g/6 oz salmon fillet, skinned and
* cut into pieces*
15 g/½ oz/2 tbsp plain (all-purpose)
* flour*
300 ml/½ pt/1¼ cups milk
1 bay leaf
50 g/2 oz/½ cup Cheddar cheese, grated
50 g/2 oz/½ cup Parmesan cheese,
* grated*
300 ml/½ pt/1¼ cups chicken stock
½ cucumber, roughly chopped
Salt and freshly ground black pepper
150 ml/¼ pt/⅔ cup single (light) cream
6 cooked peeled prawns (shrimp), to
* garnish (optional)*

Melt the butter or margarine in a saucepan. Add the salmon and fry (sauté) for about 5 minutes, stirring, until cooked through. Remove from the pan with a fish slice. Stir the flour into the pan, then gradually blend in the milk and add the bay leaf. Bring to the boil and cook for 2 minutes, stirring all the time. Stir in the cheeses, then blend in the stock. Leave to cool, then remove the bay leaf.

Turn the mixture into a blender or food processor and add the cucumber and salmon, a little salt and pepper and all but 15 ml/ 1 tbsp of the cream. Run the machine until smooth. Taste and re-season if necessary. Chill. Ladle into soup bowls and garnish each with a swirl of the remaining cream and top with a prawn before serving, if liked.

Chilled prawn with cucumber soup

SERVES 4

1 cucumber, grated
Salt and freshly ground black pepper
1 spring onion (scallion), finely
* chopped*
5 ml/1 tsp dried dill (dill weed)
100 g/4 oz cooked peeled prawns
* (shrimp)*
300 ml/½ pt/1¼ cups plain yoghurt
300 ml/½ pt/1¼ cups ice-cold milk

Sprinkle the cucumber with salt in a colander. Leave to drain for 30 minutes. Squeeze as dry as possible, then put the cucumber in a large bowl. Stir in the spring onion, dill, prawns and yoghurt and chill until ready to serve. Season with pepper and stir in the milk. Ladle into cold bowls and serve.

Chilled guacamole soup with prawns

SERVES 6

2 large ripe avocados
1 shallot, grated
15 ml/1 tbsp lemon juice
15 ml/1 tbsp olive oil
10 ml/2 tsp Worcestershire sauce
1.5 ml/¼ tsp Tabasco sauce
300 ml/½ pt/1¼ cups cold fish stock
450 ml/¾ pt/2 cups milk
5 cm/2 in piece of cucumber, very
  finely chopped
2 tomatoes, finely chopped
100 g/4 oz cooked peeled prawns,
  chopped
Freshly ground black pepper
6 cooked unpeeled prawns
30 ml/2 tbsp snipped chives

Peel the avocados, remove the stones (pits) and place in a blender or food processor with the shallot, lemon juice and oil. Run the machine until smooth. Add the Worcestershire and Tabasco sauces and the cooled stock. Run the machine again. Turn the mixture into a bowl and stir in all the remaining ingredients except the unpeeled prawns and the chives. Chill. When ready to serve, ladle into soup bowls, place a whole prawn on the edge of each bowl and sprinkle the soup with snipped chives before serving.

Jellied bortsch with rollmops

SERVES 4

2 celery sticks, grated, discarding any
  strings
1 large carrot, grated
1 onion, grated
3 plain cooked beetroot (red beets),
  grated
900 ml/1½ pts/3¾ cups fish stock
15 ml/1 tbsp red wine vinegar
Salt and freshly ground black pepper
15 ml/1 tbsp powdered gelatine
30 ml/2 tbsp plain yoghurt
1 rollmop, cut into 8 thin slices
15 ml/1 tbsp snipped chives

Put the celery, carrot, onion, beetroot, stock and wine vinegar in a saucepan and bring to the boil. Part-cover, reduce the heat and simmer for 20 minutes until everything is soft. Season to taste and stir in the gelatine until completely dissolved. Leave to cool, then chill until softly set. Ladle into soup bowls and top each with a spoonful of yoghurt, two slices of rollmop and a sprinkling of chives.

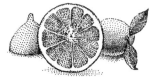

Starters

There are probably more fish starters than any other kinds of appetiser. Teamed up with salad stuffs, vegetables, eggs, or simply prepared and served with bread and butter, they are always popular. Many of the recipes here can be prepared well in advance; others are very quick to cook just before your guests sit down and some need hardly any preparation at all! Serving fish or other seafood as a first course is also a great opportunity to enjoy some of the more expensive and exotic varieties because you don't need so much of them. But, having said that, I must add that most of the recipes here make delicious lunch or supper dishes too.

Tuna and walnut stuffed pears with creamy tarragon dressing

SERVES 6

6 ripe pears
85 g/3½ oz/1 very small can of tuna,
  drained and flaked
50 g/2 oz/½ cup walnuts, finely
  chopped
150 ml/¼ pt/⅔ cup crème fraîche
Salt and freshly ground black pepper
Lettuce leaves
30 ml/2 tbsp sunflower oil
10 ml/2 tsp lemon juice
30 ml/2 tbsp chopped tarragon
5 ml/1 tsp caster (superfine) sugar
12 walnut halves and paprika,
  to garnish

Peel, halve and core the pears.
Mix the tuna and walnuts with
15–30 ml/1–2 tbsp of the crème
fraîche to bind and season to taste.
Spoon into the pear cavities. Arrange
the lettuce leaves on six plates and
place the pears, rounded-sides up,
on top. Blend the remaining crème
fraîche with the oil, lemon juice,
tarragon, sugar and a little salt and
pepper. Spoon the dressing over the
pears. Garnish with the walnut
halves and a dusting of paprika and
serve.

Avocados with tuna salsa

SERVES 6

185 g/6½ oz/1 small can of tuna,
  drained
2 ripe tomatoes, seeded and finely
  chopped
1 shallot, finely chopped
1 small green (bell) pepper, finely
  diced
1 small green or red chilli, seeded and
  finely diced
Freshly ground black pepper
A dash of Worcestershire sauce
3 ripe avocados
Lemon juice
1 black olive, cut into 6 slices
6 tiny parsley sprigs

Mash the tuna thoroughly in a bowl.
Mix in the tomatoes, shallot, green
pepper and chilli. Season with
pepper and Worcestershire sauce.
Halve the avocados, remove the
stones (pits) and peel off all the skin
with your fingers rather than a knife
to leave a smooth shape. Brush all
over with lemon juice. Spread out
the salsa on six plates. Lay an
avocado half, rounded-side up, on
each. Top each round with a slice of
olive and place a tiny sprig of
parsley in the centre of each slice.

Egg pizza salad

SERVES 4

4 beefsteak tomatoes, each cut into
  6 slices
4 hard-boiled (hard-cooked) eggs,
  sliced
2 × 125 g/4½ oz buffalo Mozzarella
  cheeses, each cut into 6 slices
50 g/2 oz/1 small can of anchovies,
  drained and split lengthways
12 stoned (pitted) black olives
8 basil leaves, torn
30 ml/2 tbsp olive oil
15 ml/1 tbsp red wine vinegar
Freshly ground black pepper

Arrange the tomato, egg and cheese
slices overlapping each other
attractively on four serving plates
with the anchovies. Scatter the
olives and basil over. Drizzle the oil
and vinegar over the salads and
sprinkle with pepper.

Poor man's caviare with smoked salmon

SERVES 4

1 large aubergine (eggplant)
1 shallot, finely chopped
1 small garlic clove, crushed
2 ripe tomatoes, skinned and chopped
30–45 ml/2–3 tbsp olive oil
Lemon juice
Salt and freshly ground black pepper
4 little gem lettuce leaves
15 ml/1 tbsp chopped parsley
4 slices of smoked salmon
Wholemeal toast, to serve

Grill (broil) the aubergine, turning
occasionally until the skin is
blackened and the aubergine feels
soft when squeezed. Allow to cool
slightly, then cut in half and scoop
out the flesh. Chop it finely and

place in a bowl. Add the shallot,
garlic and tomatoes and mix well.
Beat in enough of the oil, a drop at a
time, until the mixture is glistening
but not runny. Add lemon juice and
seasoning to taste. Spoon into the
lettuce leaves on four small plates
and sprinkle with the parsley. Roll
the salmon slices and arrange
alongside. Serve with wholemeal
toast.

Lentil and tuna vinaigrette

SERVES 4

100 g/4 oz/⅔ cup brown or green
  lentils, rinsed
185 g/6½ oz/1 small can of tuna,
  drained
1 small onion, sliced and separated
  into rings
1 small green (bell) pepper, diced
1 garlic clove, crushed
30 ml/2 tbsp olive oil
15 ml/1 tbsp white wine vinegar
5 ml/1 tsp chopped thyme
A pinch of salt
Freshly ground black pepper
15 ml/1 tbsp chopped parsley
Tomato slices, to garnish

Cook the lentils in plenty of boiling
water for about 30 minutes or until
tender. Drain thoroughly and leave
to cool. Place in a bowl with the
tuna, onion and green pepper.
Whisk together all the remaining
ingredients except the parsley. Pour
over the lentil mixture and toss
gently. Cover and chill for 1 hour to
allow the flavours to develop. Spoon
on to small plates and sprinkle with
the parsley. Garnish with tomato
slices before serving.

Warm scallop, Parma ham and apple salad

SERVES 4

1 head of chicory (Belgian endive)
50 g/2 oz rocket leaves
1 radicchio lettuce, torn into pieces
2 plum tomatoes, sliced
100 g/4 oz radishes, sliced
1 small red onion, thinly sliced and
  separated into rings
45 ml/3 tbsp olive oil
1 small onion, finely chopped
4 thin slices of Parma ham, chopped
1 small red eating (dessert) apple,
  cored and diced
8 large shelled scallops, quartered
60 ml/4 tbsp cider
15 ml/1 tbsp snipped chives
Freshly ground black pepper
30 ml/2 tbsp cider vinegar
15 ml/1 tbsp water
Chopped parsley, to garnish

Cut a cone-shaped section out of the core of the chicory and discard. Break the remainder into pieces. Arrange with the rocket and radicchio on four plates. Scatter the tomatoes, radishes and red onion rings over.

Heat the oil in a large frying pan (skillet). Add the chopped onion, ham and apple and fry (sauté) for 1 minute. Add the scallops and cook, stirring, for 2–3 minutes. Add the cider, chives and pepper and simmer for 2 minutes. Lift the scallop and ham mixture out of the pan with a draining spoon and place on the salads. Quickly add the vinegar, water and another good grinding of pepper to the juices in the pan and bring just to the boil. Spoon over the salads and sprinkle with chopped parsley before serving straight away.

Italian crostini

SERVES 4 OR 8

8 large diagonal slices of ciabatta loaf
1 large garlic clove
175 g/6 oz button mushrooms, finely
  chopped
30 ml/2 tbsp olive oil
15 ml/1 tbsp dry vermouth
Freshly ground black pepper
50 g/2 oz/⅓ cup stoned (pitted) black
  olives
5 ml/1 tsp lemon juice
15 ml/1 tbsp chopped basil
50 g/2 oz/1 small can of anchovies,
  drained and rolled

Lay the slices of bread on a baking (cookie) sheet. Cut the garlic clove in half and rub one half over all the surfaces of the bread. Then crush it with the remaining half and reserve. Bake the bread in a preheated oven at 180°C/350°F/gas mark 4 for about 20 minutes until golden. Meanwhile, put the crushed garlic in a saucepan with the mushrooms, half the olive oil and the vermouth. Add a good grinding of pepper. Cook gently for 5 minutes, stirring occasionally, until soft.

Meanwhile, purée the olives with the remaining oil in a blender or food processor, stopping the machine and scraping down the sides if necessary. Sharpen to taste with the lemon juice. Remove the bread from the oven, spread with the olive paste and top with the mushroom mixture. Sprinkle with the basil and top with an anchovy roll. Serve straight away.

Creamy scallops with oyster mushrooms

SERVES 4

If you can get scallops in their shells, open and clean them (page 14) scrub the deep halves of the shells and use them to serve this dish instead of individual flameproof dishes.

450 g/1 lb potatoes, peeled and cut
  into small pieces
30 ml/2 tbsp butter or margarine
275 ml/9 fl oz/scant 1¼ cups milk
4 shelled scallops
1 bay leaf
1 onion slice
100 g/4 oz oyster mushrooms, sliced
30 ml/2 tbsp cornflour (cornstarch)
60 ml/4 tbsp crème fraîche
Salt and freshly ground black pepper
30 ml/2 tbsp grated Parmesan cheese
30 ml/2 tbsp fresh white breadcrumbs
4 small parsley sprigs, to garnish

Boil the potatoes in lightly salted water until really tender. Drain thoroughly, mash, then beat in half the butter or margarine and 30 ml/ 2 tbsp of the milk until light and fluffy. Either spoon around the edge of four individual flameproof serving dishes or use to fill a piping bag fitted with a large star tube (tip) and pipe in a border around each dish. Rinse the scallops and cut into quarters. Bring all but 30 ml/2 tbsp of the remaining milk to the boil with the bay leaf and onion and simmer for 3 minutes. Strain into a clean pan. Add the mushrooms, cover and cook gently for 4 minutes. Add the scallops and cook for a further 3 minutes. Lift out the scallops and mushrooms with a draining spoon and place in the centres of the prepared dishes.

Blend the cornflour with the remaining milk and add to the cooking milk. Bring to the boil and cook for 1 minute, stirring, until thickened. Stir in the crème fraîche and salt and pepper to taste. Spoon over the scallops and mushrooms. Melt the remaining butter or margarine and mix with the Parmesan and breadcrumbs. Spoon over the tops. Place the dishes under a preheated moderate grill (broiler) and cook for a few minutes until lightly browning. Garnish each with a sprig of parsley and serve hot.

Smoked mackerel with watercress and orange

SERVES 6

1 bunch of watercress
2 oranges
15 ml/1 tbsp olive oil
15 ml/1 tbsp pure orange juice
10 ml/2 tsp lemon juice
Freshly ground black pepper
5 ml/1 tsp horseradish relish
6 cooked smoked mackerel fillets

Trim off the feathery stalks of the watercress and separate into sprigs. Place in a bowl. Hold the oranges over the bowl to catch the juice and cut off all the rind and pith. Cut the orange into segments and add to the bowl. Squeeze the membranes over to extract any juice. Whisk together the oil, pure orange and lemon juice, lots of pepper and the horseradish. Pour over the watercress and orange and toss gently. Lay the mackerel on serving plates and arrange the salad to one side of each. Drizzle any remaining dressing over the mackerel and serve.

Marinated mushrooms with prawns

SERVES 6

1 bunch of spring onions (scallions), chopped, reserving the green tops for garnish
1 garlic clove, crushed
30 ml/2 tbsp olive oil
300 ml/½ pt/1¼ cups red wine
A pinch of salt
Freshly ground black pepper
2.5 ml/½ tsp dried oregano
450 g/1 lb button mushrooms
400 g/14 oz/1 large can of chopped tomatoes
5 ml/1 tsp finely grated lemon rind
A pinch of caster (superfine) sugar
175 g/6 oz cooked peeled prawns (shrimp)
Round lettuce leaves
6 lemon slices

Put the spring onions in a large saucepan with the garlic and oil. Cook gently for 2 minutes, stirring. Add all the remaining ingredients except the prawns, lettuce leaves and lemon slices and bring to the boil. Reduce the heat and simmer for 20 minutes until the mushrooms are cooked and bathed in sauce. Leave until cold, then stir in the prawns and chill. When ready to serve, line six bowls with lettuce leaves and spoon in the mushroom mixture. Top each with a slice of lemon. Chop the reserved spring onion tops and sprinkle over.

Asparagus with tuna vinaigrette

SERVES 6

700 g/1½ lb asparagus spears
Salt
75 ml/5 tbsp white wine vinegar
30 ml/2 tbsp sunflower oil
15 ml/1 tbsp walnut oil
30 ml/2 tbsp water
85 g/3½ oz/1 very small can of tuna, drained
Freshly ground black pepper
2.5 ml/½ tsp caster (superfine) sugar
15 ml/1 tbsp chopped tarragon
15 ml/1 tbsp chopped parsley

Trim off any thick woody ends of the asparagus and tie in two bundles. Stand the bundles in a large pan of boiling water with a pinch of salt added. Bring back to the boil, cover with a lid (or use foil if the bunches are too tall) and simmer for 10 minutes. Drain (reserve the liquid for soup or stock if liked). Rinse the asparagus with cold water, drain again and leave until completely cold. Chill. Meanwhile, put the remaining ingredients in a blender or food processor with a pinch of salt and run the machine until the mixture is thick and creamy. Chill. When ready to serve, lay the asparagus on serving plates. Whisk the dressing again and spoon across the stems. Serve cold.

Whitebait

SERVES 4

450 g/1 lb whitebait
45 ml/3 tbsp plain (all-purpose) flour
Salt and freshly ground black pepper
5 ml/1 tsp paprika
Oil, for deep-frying
Lemon wedges and parsley sprigs, to garnish

Spread out the whitebait on kitchen paper (paper towels). Pick over to remove any weed and discard any fish that are not whole. Do not wash. Mix the flour with a little salt and pepper and the paprika. Toss the fish gently in this. Heat the oil until a cube of day-old bread browns in 30 seconds, then deep-fry the fish in small batches for about 2–3 minutes until golden and crisp. Drain on kitchen paper and keep warm while cooking the remainder. Serve hot, garnished with lemon wedges and parsley sprigs.

Gambas a la plancha

SERVES 4

Make sure you provide finger bowls to rinse the hands. You can make this with cooked prawns (shrimp) but the flavour won't be quite as good.

24 raw unpeeled king prawns (jumbo shrimp)
Salt
Olive oil
Lemon wedges

Sprinkle the prawns with salt. Brush a griddle or heavy-based frying pan (skillet) with oil. When really hot, add the prawns and toss for 2–3 minutes until pink and piping hot. Serve straight away with lemon wedges.

Crispy sole pecorino

SERVES 4–6

1 large parsnip
700 g/1½ lb lemon sole fillets, cut into thick strips
30 ml/2 tbsp plain (all-purpose) flour
Salt and freshly ground black pepper
40 g/1½ oz/¾ cup fresh white breadcrumbs
45 ml/3 tbsp grated Pecorino cheese
1 large egg, beaten
75 g/3 oz/⅓ cup butter
90 ml/6 tbsp olive oil
Parsley sprigs, to garnish

Thinly pare the parsnip into strips with a potato peeler, then place in a bowl of cold water. Toss the sole in the flour, seasoned with a little salt and pepper. Mix together the breadcrumbs and cheese. Dip the fish strips in the egg, then in the crumb mixture to coat completely. Melt 50 g/2 oz/¼ cup of the butter and half the oil in a large frying pan (skillet), add the fish and cook until crisp and golden, turning occasionally. Drain on kitchen paper (paper towels) and keep warm. Drain the strips of parsnip and dry on kitchen paper. Wipe out the pan, then heat the remaining butter and oil. Add the parsnip strips and toss until golden. Drain on kitchen paper. Serve the sole with the parsnip strips, garnished with parsley sprigs.

Dublin Bay prawns with garlic butter

SERVES 4

You'll definitely need finger bowls with this dish!

24 raw unpeeled Dublin Bay prawns (saltwater crayfish)
Salt
100 g/4 oz/½ cup unsalted (sweet) butter
2 small garlic cloves, crushed
30 ml/2 tbsp chopped parsley
Lemon wedges, to garnish

Sprinkle the prawns with salt. Melt 15 g/½ oz/1 tbsp of the butter in a heavy-based frying pan (skillet), add the prawns and toss until just pink. Add the remaining butter, the garlic and parsley and allow to sizzle until melted. Toss gently to coat. Pile on to warm plates and garnish with lemon wedges.

Gravadlax

SERVES 8–12

This is also known as gravlax.

2 salmon tail fillets, each about 450 g/1 lb
30 ml/2 tbsp salt
30 ml/2 tbsp granulated sugar
5 ml/1 tsp coarsely ground black pepper
15 ml/1 tbsp chopped dill (dill weed)
Dill sprigs, to garnish
Rye bread and unsalted (sweet) butter and Dill and Mustard Sauce (page 373), to serve

Scrape any scales off the skin of the fish using a round-bladed knife. Wipe with kitchen paper (paper towels). Mix together the salt, sugar, pepper and chopped dill. Sprinkle a quarter of the mixture in a dish long enough to hold the fish, then lay one fillet in the dish. Sprinkle two-thirds of the remaining dill mixture on the flesh and lay the other fillet on top, skin-side up. Sprinkle with the remaining mixture and cover with foil. Weigh down with heavy weights or cans of food and chill for 24 hours. Drain off the liquid, trim any dried edges, then slice the fish across the flesh, as for smoked salmon. Serve thinly sliced, garnished with dill sprigs with rye bread and unsalted butter and Dill and Mustard Sauce.

Seafood cocktail

SERVES 6

1 small iceberg lettuce, shredded
170 g/6 oz/1 small can of white crabmeat, drained
250 g/9 oz/1 medium can of mussels in brine, drained
185 g/6½ oz/1 small can of tuna, drained
175 g/6 oz cooked peeled prawns (shrimp)
6 celery sticks, chopped
90 ml/6 tbsp olive oil
45 ml/3 tbsp white wine vinegar
15 ml/1 tbsp chopped parsley
15 ml/1 tbsp chopped thyme
Salt and freshly ground black pepper
5 ml/1 tsp caster (superfine) sugar

Divide the lettuce between six glass sundae dishes or large wine goblets. Mix together all the fish in a bowl with the celery. Whisk together the remaining ingredients and pour over the fish. Toss gently, then pile on to the lettuce.

Tuna cocktail

SERVES 4

60 ml/4 tbsp mayonnaise
30 ml/2 tbsp crème fraîche
15 ml/1 tbsp tomato purée (paste)
5 ml/1 tsp Worcestershire sauce
A few drops of Tabasco sauce
A pinch of caster (superfine) sugar
Freshly ground black pepper
185 g/6½ oz/1 small can of tuna,
    drained
1 small round lettuce, shredded
4 lemon slices and paprika, to garnish
Brown bread and butter, to serve

Mix the mayonnaise with the crème
fraîche, tomato purée and
Worcestershire and Tabasco sauces,
the sugar and a good grinding of
pepper. Fold in the fish. Divide the
lettuce between four wine goblets
and top with the fish mixture.
Garnish each with a slice of lemon
and a dusting of paprika and serve
with brown bread and butter.

Tuna and mushroom cocktail

SERVES 6

Prepare as for Tuna Cocktail, but
add 50 g/2 oz thinly sliced baby
button mushrooms to the sauce.

Prawn cocktail

SERVES 4

Prepare as for Tuna Cocktail, but
substitute 225 g/8 oz cooked, peeled
prawns (shrimp) for the tuna. Put
them on the lettuce and spoon the
sauce over, rather than mixing
together. Garnish each with a
cooked, unpeeled prawn hung over
the side of each glass with the
lemon and paprika.

Prawn and artichoke rosa

SERVES 4

Prepare as for Prawn Cocktail, but
use only 100 g/4 oz cooked, peeled
prawns (shrimp) and add 425 g/
15 oz/1 large can of artichoke
hearts, drained and quartered.

Potted salmon

SERVES 6

225 g/8 oz salmon tail fillet, skinned
A pinch of ground mace
A pinch of ground cloves
1 small bay leaf
Salt and freshly ground black pepper
175 g/6 oz/¾ cup unsalted (sweet)
    butter, diced
Lemon wedges and parsley sprigs, to
    garnish
Hot toast, to serve

Put the fish in a small ovenproof
dish and add the spices, bay leaf and
some salt and pepper. Dot with the
butter, then cover with a lid or foil.
Bake in a preheated oven at
180°C/350°F/gas mark 4 for about
15 minutes or until the fish is just
cooked through. Do not overcook.
Discard the bay leaf, then process
the fish and buttery juices in a
blender or food processor until the
mixture forms a paste. Pack into a
small pot and chill until firm.
Garnish with lemon wedges and
parsley sprigs and serve with hot
toast.

Potted crab

SERVES 4

1 cooked crab, all meat removed
  (page 16)
5 ml/1 tsp red chilli sauce
A pinch of ground mace
Juice of ½ large lemon
30 ml/2 tbsp double (heavy) cream
Salt and freshly ground black pepper
175 g/6 oz/¾ cup unsalted (sweet)
  butter, melted
Shredded lettuce, cucumber slices,
  tomato wedges, olive oil and
  balsamic vinegar, to garnish
Hot toast, to serve

Mix together the dark and light
crabmeat. Stir in the chilli sauce,
mace, lemon juice and cream,
adding salt and pepper to taste. Pack
into ramekins (custard cups). Pour
over just enough of the melted
butter to soak the ingredients. Place
the ramekins in a baking tin (pan)
with enough boiling water to come
halfway up the sides of the dishes.
Bake in a preheated oven at 160°C/
325°F/gas mark 3 for 15 minutes.
Pour the rest of the butter over,
leave to cool, then chill until firm.

When ready to serve, turn out on
to serving plates. Arrange some
shredded lettuce, cucumber slices
and tomato wedges to one side and
sprinkle them with olive oil and
balsamic vinegar and a good
grinding of pepper before serving
with hot toast.

Potted trout

SERVES 4

4 trout, filleted
Salt and freshly ground black pepper
2.5 ml/½ tsp grated nutmeg
225 g/8 oz/1 cup unsalted (sweet)
  butter
4 small tarragon sprigs, to garnish
Lemon wedges and granary bread, to
  serve

Season the trout fillets with salt,
pepper and the nutmeg. Sandwich
together in pairs and leave
overnight. The next day, melt 50 g/
2 oz/¼ cup of the butter in a
flameproof casserole (Dutch oven).
Add the fish. Cut the remaining
butter into slices and lay over the
fish. Cover with a lid and bake in a
preheated oven at 150°C/300°F/gas
mark 2 for 1¼ hours until really
tender.

Carefully transfer the fish to a
plate and pull off the skin. Lay
another plate over the fish and
invert, then pull off the skin from
the other sides. Leave to cool. Strain
the butter into a small pan. When
the fish is completely cold, transfer
to individual serving dishes and lay
a small sprig of tarragon on each.
Melt the butter again, if necessary,
and pour over the fish. Leave until
cold, then chill overnight before
serving with lemon wedges and
granary bread.

Old-fashioned potted shrimps

SERVES 4

225 g/8 oz/1 cup unsalted (sweet)
   butter
450 g/1 lb cooked peeled shrimps
1.5 ml/¼ tsp ground mace
A few drops of Tabasco sauce
Salt and freshly ground black pepper
Crusty bread, to serve

Put half the butter in a saucepan
and melt. Add half the shrimps and
cook gently for 2 minutes until hot
through. Purée in a blender or food
processor. Stir in the remaining
shrimps and season with the mace,
a few drops of Tabasco sauce and
salt and pepper. Pack into a small
pot. Melt the remaining butter and
pour over the surface. Leave to cool,
then chill until firm. Serve with
crusty bread.

Whole potted shrimps

SERVES 4

Prepare as for Old-fashioned Potted
Shrimps, but heat all the shrimps in
the butter and do not purée any but
leave them all whole. Take care not
to let the fish boil or they will
become tough.

Potted prawns

SERVES 4

Prepare as for either style of potted
shrimps but use cooked, peeled
prawns (shrimp) instead.

Creamy prawn pots

SERVES 4

50 g/2 oz/¼ cup unsalted (sweet)
   butter, softened
30 ml/2 tbsp plain (all-purpose) flour
350 g/12 oz cooked peeled prawns
   (shrimp)
150 ml/¼ pt/⅔ cup dry white wine
150 ml/¼ pt/⅔ cup fish stock
5 ml/1 tsp white wine vinegar
1 egg yolk
15 ml/1 tbsp single (light) cream
Grated nutmeg
Salt and freshly ground black pepper
15 ml/1 tbsp chopped parsley
4 slices of toast, cut into triangles

Mash together the butter and flour
until smooth. Put the prawns in a
saucepan with the wine, stock and
vinegar. Bring just to the boil. Add
the butter mixture a small piece at a
time, stirring with a wooden spoon
all the time until thickened and
smooth. Whisk the egg yolk and
cream in a small bowl. Whisk in a
little of the sauce, then stir this back
into the pan over a low heat. Do not
allow to boil, but stir until slightly
thicker. Season to taste with nutmeg,
salt and pepper. Spoon into small
pots on plates and sprinkle with the
parsley. Arrange the toast triangles
round the edges of the plates and
serve straight away.

Creamy mussel and prawn pots

SERVES 4

Prepare as for Creamy Prawn Pots,
but substitute 250 g/9 oz/
1 medium can of mussels in brine,
drained, for half the prawns
(shrimp).

Greek stuffed eggs

SERVES 6

6 hard-boiled (hard-cooked) eggs
175 g/6 oz smoked cod's roe
50 g/2 oz/¼ cup unsalted (sweet)
  butter, softened
Thinly pared rind and juice of 1 lemon
300 ml/½ pt/1¼ cups mayonnaise
120 ml/4 fl oz/½ cup passata (sieved
  tomatoes)
15 ml/1 tbsp powdered gelatine
450 g/1 lb plum tomatoes, sliced
2.5 ml/½ tsp caster (superfine) sugar
60 ml/4 tbsp olive oil
Salt and freshly ground black pepper
Cayenne, for dusting

Shell and halve the eggs and put the yolks into a bowl. Split open the cod's roe and scoop into the bowl. Pound with the end of a rolling pin. Add the butter and work until smooth. Add 5 ml/1 tsp of the lemon juice and 30 ml/2 tbsp of the mayonnaise and beat with a wooden spoon. Spoon into the egg whites and sandwich together in pairs.

Put 30 ml/2 tbsp of the passata in a bowl and sprinkle the gelatine over. Leave to soften for 5 minutes, then stand the bowl in a pan of hot water and stir until dissolved or heat briefly in the microwave. Stir in the remaining passata and mayonnaise and leave until beginning to set.

Place the eggs on plates to one side and spoon the mayonnaise mixture over. Arrange the tomato slices on the plates and sprinkle with a few grains of sugar.

Whisk together the oil and 20 ml/1½ tbsp of the lemon juice with a little salt and pepper. Thinly shred the lemon rind and boil in water for 2 minutes. Drain, rinse with cold water and drain again. Pour the dressing over the tomatoes and scatter the lemon rind over. Dust the eggs very lightly with cayenne and chill until ready to serve.

Baked eggs with prawns and caviare

SERVES 4

15 g/½ oz/1 tbsp butter
100 g/4 oz cooked peeled prawns
  (shrimp)
4 eggs
60 ml/4 tbsp single (light) cream
Salt and freshly ground black pepper
50 g/2 oz/1 small jar of Danish
  lumpfish roe

Grease four ramekins (custard cups) with the butter. Put the prawns in the dishes and break an egg into each. Top each with a spoonful of cream and a little salt and pepper. Place them in a roasting tin (pan) and add enough boiling water to come halfway up the sides of the dishes. Bake in a preheated oven at 180°C/350°F/gas mark 4 for about 12 minutes until the whites are set but the yolks runny. Cook a little longer for firmer eggs. Top each with a spoonful of lumpfish roe and serve.

Baked eggs with smoked salmon

SERVES 4

Prepare as for Baked Eggs with Prawns and Caviare but substitute smoked salmon trimmings, neatly chopped, for the prawns (shrimp).

Baked stuffed eggs with prawns

SERVES 4

175 g/6 oz cooked peeled prawns
(shrimp)
4 hard-boiled (hard-cooked) eggs
40 g/1½ oz/3 tbsp butter or margarine
2.5 ml/½ tsp pimenton or paprika
Salt and freshly ground black pepper
15 ml/1 tbsp chopped parsley
225 g/8 oz small thin asparagus spears
1 quantity of Béchamel Sauce
(page 376)
20 ml/1½ tbsp grated Parmesan cheese

Finely chop 50 g/2 oz of the prawns and place in a bowl. Shell and halve the eggs and scoop the yolks into the bowl. Mash together thoroughly, then work in the butter or margarine and pimenton or paprika. Season to taste and work in the parsley. Spoon into the hollows of the egg whites. Cook the asparagus in a little lightly salted, boiling water for about 4 minutes until just tender but the heads are still intact. Drain and arrange in a shallow ovenproof dish. Arrange the stuffed eggs on top. Scatter the remaining prawns over, then cover with the Béchamel Sauce. Sprinkle with the Parmesan and bake in a preheated oven at 200°C/400°F/gas mark 6 for 15 minutes until golden brown. Serve hot.

Baked stuffed eggs with anchovies

SERVES 4

Prepare as for Baked Stuffed Eggs with Prawns, but substitute 50 g/2 oz/1 small can of anchovies, drained and chopped, for the prawns (shrimp) and lay the eggs on a bed of 450 g/1 lb spinach, cooked with no extra water for 5 minutes and drained, instead of the asparagus.

Crab pâté

SERVES 6

1 large cooked crab
175 g/6 oz/¾ cup unsalted (sweet)
butter
1.5 ml/¼ tsp pimenton or paprika
2 egg yolks
45 ml/3 tbsp crème fraîche
Salt and freshly ground black pepper
A few drops of Tabasco sauce
½ cucumber, thinly sliced
Lemon juice
Oatcakes, to serve

Pick all the meat out of the crab (page 16) and place in a bowl with 50 g/2 oz/¼ cup of the butter. Stand the bowl over a pan of hot water and cook gently, stirring, for 5 minutes. Beat in the pimenton or paprika, the egg yolks and crème fraîche. Continue to cook, stirring, until the mixture thickens but do not let it boil or the egg yolks may curdle. Remove the bowl from the pan. Beat thoroughly again, then season to taste with salt, pepper and Tabasco sauce. Turn into a small container. Melt the remaining butter and pour over the surface. Leave to cool completely, then chill until firm. Serve with the cucumber slices, tossed in lemon juice and sprinkled with lots of black pepper, and oatcakes.

pâté

SERVES 6

fillets
oz/1 cup unsalted (sweet)
butter
Juice of 1 small lemon
Salt and freshly ground black pepper
White toast, to serve

Put the fish in a saucepan and just cover with water. Bring to the boil, reduce the heat, cover and cook gently for about 6 minutes or until the fish flakes easily with a fork. Lift out of the water. Remove the skin and any remaining bones. Place the fish in a blender or food processor with half the butter and half the lemon juice. Season to taste and add more of the lemon juice, if liked. Pack into a small pot. Melt the remaining butter and pour over. Chill until firm. Serve with white toast.

Smoked haddock pâté

SERVES 6

Prepare as for Kipper Pâté, but substitute 350 g/12 oz smoked haddock fillet for the kippers.

Smoked trout pâté

SERVES 6

Prepare as for Kipper Pâté, using smoked trout. There is no need to cook the fish first. Simply remove the skin, then place in a blender or food processor and continue as before, adding 5 ml/1 tsp grated horseradish to the mixture.

Smoked mackerel pâté

SERVES 6

Prepare as for Smoked Trout Pâté, but substitute smoked mackerel for the smoked trout.

Smoked salmon pâté

SERVES 6

Prepare as for Smoked Trout Pâté, but substitute smoked salmon trimmings for the smoked trout. There is no need to skin. Simply place the fish in a blender or food processor and continue as before.

Pike and beancurd pâté

SERVES 6

450 g/1 lb pike fillet
250 g/9 oz silken tofu
15 ml/1 tbsp tomato purée (paste)
5 ml/1 tsp anchovy essence (extract)
5 ml/1 tsp grated fresh root ginger
10 ml/2 tsp soy sauce
3 eggs
½ bunch of spring onions (scallions), finely chopped
30 ml/2 tbsp chopped parsley
15 ml/1 tbsp chopped coriander (cilantro)
Salt and freshly ground black pepper
Lettuce leaves, to garnish
Horseradish Creme (page 381), to serve

Skin the pike fillet, remove all the bones and cut the flesh into pieces. With a blender or food processor running, drop in the pieces of fish. Add the tofu, tomato purée, anchovy essence, ginger and soy sauce and run the machine again. Add the eggs and blend once more. Stir in the spring onions and herbs and season with salt and pepper. Turn into an oiled and lined 450 g/1 lb loaf tin (pan). Cover with oiled foil and stand the tin in a roasting tin containing 2.5 cm/1 in boiling water. Bake in a preheated oven at 160°C/325°F/gas mark 3 for 45 minutes or until set. Remove from the water and leave to cool, then chill overnight. Serve sliced on a bed of lettuce with Horseradish Creme.

Prawns and pimientos in aspic

SERVES 6

900 ml/1½ pts/3¾ cups fish stock
45 ml/3 tbsp powdered gelatine
150 ml/¼ pt/⅔ cup dry white wine
175 g/6 oz cooked peeled prawns
    (shrimp)
200 g/7 oz/1 small can of pimientos,
    drained and cut into strips
2 tomatoes, skinned, seeded and cut
    into 6 wedges
Watercress, to garnish
Thousand Island Dip (page 375),
    to serve

Spoon 75 ml/5 tbsp of the stock
into a small bowl. Sprinkle the
gelatine over and leave to soften for
5 minutes. Stand the bowl in a pan
of hot water and stir until the
gelatine is completely dissolved.
Alternatively, heat briefly in the
microwave. Stir into the remaining
stock with the wine and leave until
the consistency of raw egg white.
   Spoon a layer of the aspic in a
very lightly oiled 1.2 litre/2 pt/5 cup
ring mould and chill until set.
Arrange a ring of a third of the
prawns on top, then spoon on just
enough aspic to cover the prawns.
Chill again until set. Top with a layer
of pimiento strips, then spoon on
more aspic and chill until set. Repeat
the prawn and pimiento layers once
more, adding aspic and chilling to
set in between. Add the tomato
wedges, more aspic and set again.
Finally, add the last of the prawns
and the rest of the aspic and chill
until ready to serve.
   To serve, dip the mould very
briefly in hot water, place a serving
plate on top, invert, shake and
remove the mould. Fill the centre
with watercress and serve with
Thousand Island Dip.
   Note: if the unused aspic begins
to set too firmly, stand the container
briefly in hot water and stir.

Seviche

SERVES 4

750 g/1¾ lb very fresh turbot, skinned
    and boned
1 red (bell) pepper, diced
1 green pepper, diced
1 small green chilli, seeded and
    chopped
Finely grated rind and juice of 1 large
    lemon
Salt and freshly ground black pepper
Lettuce leaves
8 tomatoes, thinly sliced
1 red onion, thinly sliced and
    separated into rings
10 ml/2 tsp olive oil
Hot French bread, to serve

Slice the turbot thinly with a sharp
knife, then cut the slices into narrow
strips. Place in a bowl with all the
peppers, the chilli and lemon rind
and juice, a sprinkling of salt and a
good grinding of pepper. Toss gently
and chill for 1–2 hours until the fish
is opaque. Arrange lettuce leaves on
four plates. Arrange the tomato
slices and onion rings alternately in
a ring around the edge and spoon
the fish mixture into the centre.
Sprinkle a few drops of olive oil on
each and serve with hot French
bread.

Salmon seviche

SERVES 4

Prepare as for Seviche, but substitute
fresh salmon for the turbot, and lime
rind and juice for lemon.

Cebiche

SERVES 4

This is another version of Seviche (page 67).

450 g/1 lb very fresh white fish fillet such as cod or haddock, skinned and cubed
1 onion, thinly sliced and separated into rings
Salt and freshly ground black pepper
15 ml/1 tbsp chopped coriander (cilantro)
50 ml/2 fl oz/¼ cup lemon juice
1 small green chilli, seeded, if preferred, and finely chopped
15 ml/1 tbsp chopped parsley
2 corn cobs, each cut into 4 pieces
2 sweet potatoes, cut into wedges
Lettuce leaves
50 g/2 oz/¼ cup unsalted (sweet) butter

Put the fish and onion rings in a shallow dish and season well. Sprinkle with the coriander and then the lemon juice, chilli and parsley. Leave to marinate for 2 hours until the fish is opaque. Meanwhile, boil the corn and sweet potato wedges in lightly salted, boiling water until tender. Drain. Arrange lettuce leaves on four plates and pile the fish on top. Serve with the corn pieces and sweet potato wedges, dotted with the butter.

Very simple seviche

SERVES 4

This is the easiest of all the marinated raw fish recipes.

450 g/1 lb very fresh firm white fish fillet, skinned and cubed
1 onion, sliced and separated into rings
1 green (bell) pepper, diced
1 green chilli, seeded and chopped
Salt and freshly ground black pepper
75 ml/5 tbsp fresh lime or lemon juice
Lollo rosso leaves
15 ml/1 tbsp chopped parsley

Put the fish in a shallow dish. Add the onion, green pepper and chilli. Season with salt and pepper and drizzle the lime or lemon juice over. Toss lightly and leave to stand for 2 hours or until the fish turns pure white (as if it's cooked). Spoon on to a bed of lollo rosso leaves and sprinkle with the parsley before serving.

Squid seviche

SERVES 4

Prepare as for Very Simple Seviche, but substitute baby squid, cleaned and cut into rings, for some or all of the white fish (page 14).

Prawn seviche

SERVES 4

Prepare as for Very Simple Seviche, but substitute cooked, peeled, large prawns (shrimp) for half the white fish.

Caveached mackerel

SERVES 4

This is an old English version of
Seviche. You can also use herrings
with this method, but make sure
they are very fresh.

40 g/1½ oz/3 tbsp coarse sea salt
15 ml/1 tbsp coarsely crushed black
  peppercorns
5 ml/1 tsp grated nutmeg
2.5 ml/½ tsp ground allspice
1.5 ml/¼ tsp ground cloves
15 ml/1 tbsp demerara sugar
4 small mackerel, filleted and cut into
  5 cm/2 in pieces
Sunflower oil
Malt vinegar
Brown bread and butter, to serve

Mix together the dry ingredients and
rub all over the fish. Leave to
marinate for 4 hours. Heat a little oil
in a frying pan (skillet) and fry
(sauté) the fish quickly on both
sides to brown. Drain on kitchen
paper (paper towels) and leave until
cold. Pack into a clean, large screw-
topped jar and pour in enough
vinegar to come 2.5 cm/1 in above
the fish. Pour a 5 mm/¼ in layer of
sunflower oil over the top. Screw the
lid on tightly and store in the fridge
for 1 week before eating with brown
bread and butter. It will keep for
several months if the oil is left
undisturbed.

Elegant smoked salmon

SERVES 4

225 g/8 oz small thin asparagus spears
Salt and freshly ground black pepper
75 g/3 oz/⅓ cup fromage frais
45 ml/3 tbsp milk
Finely grated rind of ½ lemon
15 ml/1 tbsp chopped tarragon
8 thin slices of smoked salmon
Lemon wedges, to garnish
Brown bread and butter, to serve

Trim the base of the stalks of the
asparagus, if necessary. Lay them in
a shallow pan and add enough water
to cover and a good pinch of salt.
Bring to the boil, reduce the heat,
cover and cook very gently for
4 minutes only. The asparagus
should be almost tender but still
with a little bite. Carefully lift out
with a fish slice and drain on
kitchen paper (paper towels). Leave
to cool.

Mix the fromage frais with the
milk, lemon rind, tarragon and salt
and pepper to taste. Add a little
more milk, if necessary, to give a
thick, pouring consistency. When
ready to serve, lay the salmon in
overlapping slices on four plates and
arrange the asparagus neatly to one
side. Pour the fromage frais sauce
over the centres of the asparagus
stalks. Garnish with lemon wedges
and serve with brown bread and
butter.

Spinach and smoked salmon rolls

SERVES 6

12 large spinach leaves
200 g/7 oz/scant 1 cup medium-fat soft
  cheese
15 ml/1 tbsp chopped parsley
15 ml/1 tbsp chopped dill (dill weed)
Finely grated rind of 1 lemon
10 ml/2 tsp anchovy essence (extract)
Freshly ground black pepper
6 slices of smoked salmon
For the dressing:
45 ml/3 tbsp olive oil
15 ml/1 tbsp lemon juice
5 ml/1 tsp balsamic vinegar
2.5 ml/½ tsp caster (superfine) sugar
15 ml/1 tbsp chopped dill
A pinch of salt
A few mixed salad leaves, to garnish

Trim away the stalks from the spinach and plunge the leaves in boiling water for 1 minute. Drain, rinse with cold water and drain again. Pat dry on kitchen paper (paper towels). Mash the cheese with the herbs, lemon rind and anchovy essence. Season to taste with pepper. Halve the salmon slices lengthways and gently spread each piece with the cheese mixture. Carefully roll up. Lay each on a spinach leaf, fold in the sides, then roll up tightly. Place in an airtight container and chill until ready to serve.

Put the dressing ingredients in a screw-topped jar with a good grinding of pepper. Shake well. To serve, put two rolls on each of six plates and slice them attractively. Garnish with salad leaves. Shake the dressing and spoon a little over the slices before serving.

Crisp-fried smoked salmon and aubergine sandwiches

SERVES 6

4 aubergines (eggplants), sliced
Salt
100 g/4 oz smoked salmon slices
5 ml/1 tsp dried dill (dill weed)
30 ml/2 tbsp plain (all-purpose) flour
15 ml/1 tbsp water
10 ml/2 tsp white wine vinegar
1 egg, beaten
Oil, for deep-frying
Parsley sprigs and lemon wedges, to
  garnish

Put the aubergine slices in a colander. Sprinkle with salt and leave to stand for 15 minutes. Rinse thoroughly and pat dry on kitchen paper (paper towels). Sandwich the slices of aubergine together with the salmon and a sprinkling of dill. Beat together the flour, water, vinegar, egg and a pinch of salt. Heat the oil until a cube of day-old bread browns in 30 seconds. Dip the sandwiches in the batter and deep-fry for 3–4 minutes until golden brown. Drain on kitchen paper and arrange on warm plates. Garnish with parsley sprigs and lemon wedges and serve.

Baby smoked salmon blinis

MAKES 24

For the blinis:
350 g/12 oz/3 cups plain (all-purpose) flour
10 ml/2 tsp easy-blend dried yeast
A pinch of salt
10 ml/2 tsp caster (superfine) sugar
375 ml/13 fl oz/1½ cups hand-hot water
25 g/1 oz/2 tbsp butter or margarine, melted
2 eggs, separated
300 ml/½ pt/1¼ cups hand-hot milk
Oil, for shallow-frying
For the filling:
200 g/7 oz/scant 1 cup cream cheese
100 g/4 oz smoked salmon trimmings, finely chopped
Lemon juice
Freshly ground black pepper
50 g/2 oz/1 small jar of Danish lumpfish roe

To make the blinis, sift the flour into a bowl and stir in the yeast, salt and sugar. Mix with the water to form a thick batter. Cover and leave to rise in a warm place for 30 minutes. Whisk together the melted butter or margarine, egg yolks and milk and whisk into the batter. Whisk the egg whites until stiff and fold in with a metal spoon. Heat a little oil in a frying pan (skillet) and make three or four pancakes using 10 ml/2 tsp of the batter for each one. Cook for about 1 minute on each side until golden brown. Wrap in a clean cloth while making the remaining blinis.

To make the filling, beat the cheese until smooth, then mix in the salmon. Spike with lemon juice to taste and season with pepper. Divide the mixture between the centres of the blinis and top each with a little lumpfish roe. Carefully lift up the opposite edges of each blini to form a boat and secure with a cocktail stick (toothpick).

Large blinis with smoked salmon

SERVES 4–6

350 g/12 oz/3 cups plain (all-purpose) flour
10 ml/2 tsp easy-blend dried yeast
A pinch of salt
10 ml/2 tsp caster (superfine) sugar
375 ml/13 fl oz/1½ cups hand-hot water
25 g/1 oz/2 tbsp butter or margarine, melted
2 eggs, separated
300 ml/½ pt/1¼ cups hand-hot milk
Oil, for shallow-frying
175 g/6 oz smoked salmon trimmings
Crème fraîche, lemon wedges and parsley sprigs, to garnish

To make the blinis, sift the flour into a bowl and stir in the yeast, salt and sugar. Mix with the water to form a thick batter. Cover and leave to rise in a warm place for 30 minutes. Whisk together the melted butter or margarine, egg yolks and milk and whisk into the batter. Whisk the egg whites until stiff and fold in with a metal spoon. Heat a little oil in a frying pan (skillet) and spoon in enough of the batter to make a 10 cm/4 in diameter pancake. Cook for about 1 minute on each side until golden brown. Wrap in a clean cloth while making the remaining blinis.

Put the blinis on individual plates and place a small pile of salmon to one side. Add a good spoonful of crème fraîche to each plate and garnish with lemon wedges and parsley sprigs.

Blinis with caviare

SERVES 4–6

Prepare as for Large Blinis with Smoked Salmon (page 71), but omit the salmon and use 50 g/2 oz/ 1 small jar of Danish lumpfish roe (or a better-quality caviare if you can afford it!) instead. Garnish with chopped onion and crème fraîche.

Blinis with egg and caviare

SERVES 4–6

Prepare as for Blinis with Caviare, but use only 25 g/1 oz/1 very small jar of Danish lumpfish roe and add 1 hard-boiled (hard-cooked) egg, sliced, per serving. Garnish with mayonnaise instead of onion and crème fraîche.

Avocado with prawns

SERVES 4

2 ripe avocados
Lemon juice
100 g/4 oz cooked peeled prawns
  (shrimp)
45 ml/3 tbsp mayonnaise
15 ml/1 tbsp tomato ketchup (catsup)
2.5 ml/½ tsp Worcestershire sauce
A few drops of Tabasco sauce
Salt and freshly ground black pepper
Parsley sprigs and lemon wedges, to
  garnish

Halve the avocados, discard the stones (pits) and brush the cut surfaces with lemon juice. Place in individual serving dishes and put the prawns in the cavities. Mix together the remaining ingredients and spoon over. Garnish with parsley sprigs and lemon wedges and serve.

Rustic-style avocado

SERVES 4

1 green (bell) pepper, cut into small
  diamond shapes
3 spring onions (scallions), diagonally
  cut into small pieces
1 small smoked mackerel fillet,
  skinned
Salt and freshly ground black pepper
2 large avocados, halved
Lemon juice
8 stoned (pitted) black olives, halved
  and cut lengthways into strips
30 ml/2 tbsp white wine vinegar
90 ml/6 tbsp olive oil
5 ml/1 tsp caster (superfine) sugar
15 ml/1 tbsp chopped parsley

Blanch the green pepper and spring onions in boiling water for 1 minute. Drain, rinse with cold water and drain again. Shred the mackerel between two forks and season with pepper. Halve the avocados, remove the stones (pits) and brush the cut surfaces with lemon juice. Place in shallow dishes and spoon the fish into the cavities. Mix the green pepper and spring onions with the olives. Whisk together all the remaining ingredients except the parsley with a little salt and pepper and add to the pepper mixture. Toss. Pile on top of the mackerel, allowing the dressing to run down the sides. Sprinkle with the parsley and serve.

Crunchy tuna and prawn salad

SERVES 6

The discarded outer celery sticks can be stored in the fridge and used for any cooked recipe that requires chopped or sliced celery.

1 small head of celery
185 g/6½ oz/1 small can of tuna, drained and flaked
100 g/4 oz cooked peeled prawns
45 ml/3 tbsp olive oil
15 ml/1 tbsp white wine vinegar
2.5 ml/½ tsp Dijon mustard
5 ml/1 tsp chopped parsley
5 ml/1 tsp chopped basil
Salt and freshly ground black pepper
Round lettuce leaves, to serve

Separate the celery and discard two or three of the thick outer sticks. Cut the rest into 4 cm/1½ in lengths, then cut each piece into thin shreds. Place in a bowl and add the tuna and prawns. Whisk together all the remaining ingredients and pour over. Toss gently and chill. Serve on a bed of lettuce leaves on individual plates.

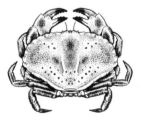

Crab-stuffed aubergines

SERVES 4

2 aubergines (eggplants)
1 large onion, thinly sliced
60 ml/4 tbsp olive oil
225 g/8 oz/1 small can of chopped tomatoes
15 ml/1 tbsp tomato purée (paste)
2.5 ml/½ tsp dried mixed herbs
15 ml/1 tbsp paprika
1 small green chilli, seeded and chopped
170 g/6 oz/1 small can of white crabmeat, drained
Salt and freshly ground black pepper
30 ml/2 tbsp grated Parmesan cheese

Halve the aubergines, discarding the stalks. Boil in lightly salted water for about 8 minutes or until just tender. Drain, rinse with cold water and drain again. Scoop out most of the flesh into a bowl, leaving a border all round the inside of the skin. Chop the flesh. Fry (sauté) the onion in half the oil until soft and lightly golden. Add the tomatoes, tomato purée, herbs, paprika and chilli. Bring to the boil, stirring. Add the aubergine flesh, reduce the heat and simmer for about 5 minutes until really pulpy. Remove from the heat and stir in the crabmeat. Season to taste.

Put the aubergine shells in a lightly oiled, ovenproof dish and spoon in the filling. Sprinkle with the cheese, then drizzle the remaining olive oil over. Bake in a preheated oven at 220°C/425°F/gas mark 7 for 10 minutes until browned on top and piping hot. Serve hot.

Baked avocado with crab

SERVES 4

25 g/1 oz/2 tbsp butter or margarine
2 spring onions (scallions), finely
  chopped
2 celery sticks, finely chopped
15 ml/1 tbsp cornflour (cornstarch)
150 ml/¼ pt/⅔ cup milk
170 g/6 oz/1 small can of white
  crabmeat, drained
30 ml/2 tbsp mayonnaise
15 ml/1 tbsp plain yoghurt
Salt and freshly ground black pepper
2 avocados
Lemon juice
50 g/2 oz/1 cup fresh white
  breadcrumbs

Melt half the butter or margarine in
a saucepan. Add the spring onions
and celery and cook, stirring, for
3 minutes until softened but not
browned. Remove from the heat and
blend in the cornflour, then the
milk. Return to the heat, bring to the
boil and cook for 1 minute, stirring
all the time. Stir in the crab,
mayonnaise and yoghurt and season
to taste. Halve the avocados, discard
the stones (pits) and brush the cut
surfaces with lemon juice. Place in
individual ovenproof dishes and
spoon the crab mixture into each.
Melt the remaining butter or
margarine, add the breadcrumbs and
toss thoroughly. Spoon over the
avocados and bake in a preheated
oven at 200°C/400°F/gas mark 6 for
15 minutes until golden brown.
Serve hot.

Baked avocado with prawns and fennel

SERVES 4

Prepare as for Baked Avocado with
Crab, but substitute cooked peeled
prawns (shrimp) for the crab. Omit
the celery and add half a fennel
bulb, chopped. Garnish with the
reserved fennel fronds before
serving.

Crab and avocado cream

SERVES 6

2 ripe avocados, halved and stoned
  (pitted)
15 ml/1 tbsp lemon juice
2 × 40 g/1½ oz/very small cans of
  dressed crab
1 small red (bell) pepper, diced
1 small green pepper, diced
30 ml/2 tbsp mayonnaise
A few drops of Tabasco sauce
100 ml/3½ fl oz/scant ½ cup double
  (heavy) cream, lightly whipped
Salt and freshly ground black pepper
Lettuce leaves
Lemon slices and 30 ml/2 tbsp
  chopped parsley, to garnish
Wholemeal toast, to serve

Scoop the avocado flesh into a bowl
and mash with the lemon juice. Beat
in the crab, then stir in the peppers,
mayonnaise and Tabasco sauce to
taste. Fold in the cream and season
to taste with salt and pepper. Pile on
to a bed of lettuce on six plates,
garnish with lemon slices and the
parsley and serve with wholemeal
toast.

Prawn and goat's cheese parcels

SERVES 6

Prepare as for Crab and Camembert Parcels (right), but substitute goat's cheese for the Camembert and prawns (shrimp) for the crabmeat. Serve with a spoonful of cranberry sauce, blended with an equal quantity of mayonnaise instead of (or as well as) the French dressing.

Tiger prawns with light garlic mayonnaise

SERVES 4

24 raw unpeeled tiger prawns (jumbo shrimp), heads removed
30 ml/2 tbsp olive oil
15 ml/1 tbsp lemon juice
1 large rosemary sprig
Freshly ground black pepper
45 ml/3 tbsp mayonnaise
45 ml/3 tbsp plain yoghurt
1 large garlic clove, crushed
15 ml/1 tbsp chopped parsley
Lemon wedges and rosemary sprigs, to garnish

Lay the prawns in a shallow dish. Whisk together the oil and lemon juice and pour over the prawns. Add the large rosemary sprig and a good grinding of pepper. Cover and chill for 2–3 hours, turning occasionally. Mix the mayonnaise, yoghurt, garlic, parsley and a good grinding of pepper. Turn into a bowl, cover and chill. Thread the marinated prawns on to four soaked, wooden skewers. Grill (broil) for about 4 minutes until pink, turning occasionally and brushing with any remaining marinade. Garnish with lemon wedges and rosemary sprigs and serve with the garlic mayonnaise.

Camembert and crab parcels

SERVES 6

6 rectangular sheets of filo pastry (paste)
50 g/2 oz/¼ cup butter or margarine, melted
2 × 170 g/6 oz/small cans of white crabmeat, drained
1 whole Camembert cheese
90 ml/6 tbsp crème fraîche
30 ml/2 tbsp dried dill (dill weed)
Salt and freshly ground black pepper
A few mixed salad leaves
2 small avocados, peeled, stoned (pitted), sliced and tossed in lemon juice
French dressing

Lay a sheet of filo on the work surface and brush with a little melted butter or margarine. Fold in half widthways and brush with a little more butter. Repeat with the remaining sheets of pastry. Divide the crabmeat between the centres of the pastry. Cut the cheese into six wedges, then cut each in half horizontally. Lay two pieces on each portion of crab and spoon the crème fraîche over. Sprinkle with the dill and season lightly. Fold the pastry neatly over the filling to form parcels.

Transfer to a lightly greased baking (cookie) sheet and brush with a little more butter or margarine. Bake in a preheated oven at 190°C/375°F/gas mark 5 for about 15 minutes until crisp and golden. Transfer to individual serving plates and arrange a few salad leaves and avocado slices attractively to one side. Spoon a little French dressing over the garnish and serve.

Portuguese prawn rissoles

SERVES 4

200 g/7 oz/1¾ cups plain (all-purpose)
   flour
Salt and freshly ground black pepper
250 ml/8 fl oz/1 cup water
50 g/2 oz/¼ cup butter or margarine
250 ml/8 fl oz/1 cup milk
100 g/4 oz cooked peeled prawns
   (shrimp), roughly chopped
2.5 ml/½ tsp anchovy essence (extract)
Lemon juice, to taste
15 ml/1 tbsp chopped parsley
15 ml/1 tbsp chopped coriander
   (cilantro)
1 egg, beaten
75 g/3 oz/1½ cups fresh white
   breadcrumbs
Oil, for deep-frying
Lemon wedges and coriander or
   parsley sprigs, to garnish

Sift 150 g/5 oz/1¼ cups of the flour
into a bowl with a pinch of salt and
a good grinding of pepper. Put the
water and 25 g/1 oz/2 tbsp of the
butter or margarine in a saucepan
and heat until the fat melts, then
bring to the boil. Add the seasoned
flour all at once and beat with a
wooden spoon until the mixture
leaves the sides of the pan clean.
Cook, stirring, for a further
2 minutes, then turn out on to a
plate. Leave to cool while making
the filling.

Melt the remaining butter or
margarine in a clean saucepan. Stir
in the remaining flour and cook for
1 minute. Remove from the heat and
blend in the milk. Return to the heat
and bring to the boil, stirring all the
time, until thick. Cook for a further
2 minutes, stirring all the time.
Remove from the heat and stir in the

prawns, anchovy essence, lemon
juice to taste and the herbs. Leave to
cool.

Roll out the dough thinly on a
lightly floured surface. Cut into
rounds using a 7.5 cm/3 in biscuit
(cookie) cutter, then roll out the
rounds to 10 cm/4 in across. They
should now be very thin but not
transparent. Divide the filling
between the rounds, brush the edges
with the egg and fold the pastry over
to form semicircular parcels. Press
the edges together to seal. Brush all
over with egg and coat in the
breadcrumbs. Chill for at least
1 hour. Deep-fry in hot oil for about
4 minutes until golden brown. Drain
on kitchen paper (paper towels) and
serve straight away, garnished with
lemon wedges and coriander or
parsley sprigs.

Artichoke and prawn Moskova

SERVES 4

425 g/15 oz/1 large can of artichoke
   hearts, drained and roughly chopped
175 g/6 oz cooked peeled prawns
   (shrimp)
45 ml/3 tbsp olive oil
15 ml/1 tbsp white wine vinegar
Salt and freshly ground black pepper
150 ml/¼ pt/⅔ cup soured (dairy sour)
   cream
50 g/2 oz/1 small jar of Danish
   lumpfish roe

Mix together the artichoke hearts
and prawns. Sprinkle the oil, vinegar
and some salt and pepper over and
toss gently. Spoon into four wine
goblets. Top each with a good
spoonful of soured cream and chill.
Spoon the lumpfish roe on top just
before serving.

Sizzling chilli prawns

SERVES 6

Use the largest prawns (shrimp) you can lay your hands on and don't forget to remind your guests not to eat the chillies.

18 unpeeled raw king prawns (jumbo shrimp)
6 very small red chillies
3 large garlic cloves, cut into very thin slivers
About 450 ml/¾ pt/2 cups olive oil
Coarse sea salt and freshly ground black pepper
Crusty bread, to serve

Pack the prawns into six ramekins (custard cups), curling them round to fit. Push a chilli and a few slivers of garlic in the centre of each dish. Pour over enough oil to cover the prawns and season well with sea salt and pepper. Leave to marinate for several hours, if time allows. Place on a baking (cookie) sheet and cook in a preheated oven at 230°C/450°F/gas mark 8 for 10 minutes until bubbling and turning golden on top. Leave to stand for a few minutes, then serve with lots of crusty bread to mop up every bit of the chilli and garlic-flavoured oil.

Sizzling chilli scallops

SERVES 6

Prepare as for Sizzling Chilli Prawns, but use 30 queen scallops instead of the prawns. Sprinkle with the finely grated rind of 1 orange before baking.

Dreamy fish mousse

SERVES 4–6

225 g/8 oz white fish fillet
2 eggs, separated
15 ml/1 tbsp powdered gelatine
30 ml/2 tbsp water
60 ml/4 tbsp mayonnaise
65 g/2½ oz/1 small can of dressed crab
10 ml/2 tsp tomato purée (paste)
Salt and freshly ground black pepper
30 ml/2 tbsp chopped parsley
Crisp crackers, to serve

Put the fish in a saucepan and cover with water. Bring to the boil and cook for 5 minutes. Slide the egg yolks into the pan and continue cooking for 4 minutes. Gently lift the hard-boiled (hard-cooked) egg yolks out of the pan and put to one side. Lift out the fish and discard any skin or bones. Put the fish in a bowl and mash with a fork. Sprinkle the gelatine over the measured water in a small bowl. Leave to soften for 5 minutes, then stand the bowl in a pan of hot water and stir until completely dissolved, or heat briefly in the microwave.

Mix the mayonnaise into the fish with the crab, tomato purée and salt and pepper to taste. Stir in the gelatine. Whisk the egg whites until stiff and fold in with a metal spoon. Turn into an attractive serving dish and chill until set. Push the egg yolks through a sieve (strainer) and sprinkle over the mousse with the parsley. Serve with crisp crackers.

Cod and mushroom soufflé

SERVES 4

25 g/1 oz/2 tbsp butter or margarine,
  plus extra for greasing
30 ml/2 tbsp dried breadcrumbs
225 g/8 oz cod fillet
Oil, for brushing
100 g/4 oz button mushrooms, finely
  chopped
1 onion, finely chopped
25 g/1 oz/¼ cup plain (all-purpose)
  flour
150 ml/¼ pt/⅔ cup milk
2.5 ml/½ tsp Dijon mustard
5 ml/1 tsp dried fennel or dill (dill
  weed)
Salt and freshly ground black pepper
3 eggs, separated
Hot Chilli Salsa (page 378), to serve

Grease a 1.2 litre/2 pt/5 cup soufflé
dish and sprinkle with the
breadcrumbs. Brush the fish with
a little oil and grill (broil) for
8 minutes until cooked through.
Flake with a fork, discarding any
skin. Cook the mushrooms and
onion in the butter or margarine for
3 minutes, stirring. Remove from the
heat and blend in the flour, then the
milk. Return to the heat, bring to the
boil and cook for 2 minutes until
thick, stirring all the time. Stir in the
fish, mustard, fennel or dill and
some salt and pepper. Beat in the
egg yolks. Whisk the egg whites
until stiff, then fold in with a metal
spoon. Turn into the soufflé dish and
bake in a preheated oven at 190°C/
375°F/gas mark 5 for 35 minutes
until well risen and golden brown.
Serve straight away, with the Hot
Chilli Salsa served separately.

Individual smoked trout soufflés

SERVES 4

Prepare as for Cod and Mushroom
Soufflé, but use flaked, cooked,
smoked trout fillets, skinned and
boned instead of the cod. Turn the
mixture into individual soufflé
dishes and bake for about
20 minutes or until risen and set.
Serve with Horseradish Creme (page
381) instead of the Hot Chilli Salsa.

Piri piri prawns

SERVES 4

24 raw peeled tiger prawns (jumbo
  shrimp), tails left on
1 green chilli, seeded and chopped
2.5 ml/½ tsp salt
Juice of 1 lime
Olive oil, for shallow-frying
Lime wedges, to garnish

Place the prawns in a shallow dish.
Mix the chilli with the salt and lime
juice and sprinkle over. Toss and
leave to marinate for 1 hour. Heat
the oil in a large frying pan (skillet).
Add the prawns and toss until pink.
Do not overcook. Spoon on to warm
plates and garnish with lime wedges.

Crusted prawn and avocado mousse

SERVES 6–8

For the mousse:
30 ml/2 tbsp powdered gelatine
150 ml/¼ pt/⅔ cup boiling chicken
  stock
30 ml/2 tbsp dry vermouth
30 ml/2 tbsp water
175 g/6 oz cooked peeled prawns
  (shrimp)
5 thin lemon slices
2 ripe avocados, stoned (pitted)
15 ml/1 tbsp lemon juice
1.5 ml/¼ tsp Tabasco sauce
15 ml/1 tbsp Worcestershire sauce
15 ml/1 tbsp anchovy essence (extract)
15 ml/1 tbsp grated onion
3 eggs, separated
150 ml/¼ pt/⅔ cup mayonnaise
150 ml/¼ pt/⅔ cup whipping cream,
  whipped
Salt and freshly ground black pepper
For the case (pie shell):
6 slices of white bread, crusts removed
75 g/3 oz/⅓ cup butter or margarine,
  melted
Parsley sprigs, to garnish

To make the mousse, dissolve the gelatine in the stock. Spoon 30 ml/2 tbsp of this mixture into the base of an oiled 18 cm/7 in soufflé dish. Stir in the vermouth and water. Arrange 8 prawns attractively in the liquid with the lemon slices and leave to set.

Meanwhile, mash the avocado flesh with 10 ml/2 tsp of the lemon juice until smooth. Beat in the Tabasco and Worcestershire sauces, the anchovy essence, grated onion and egg yolks. Chop the remaining prawns and add. Stir in the remaining gelatine mixture, then the mayonnaise and cream. Finally, whisk the egg whites until stiff and fold in with a metal spoon. Season to taste. Spoon into the prepared dish and chill until set.

To make the case, brush the bread with the melted butter or margarine to coat both sides completely. Arrange five slices in a 20 cm/8 in loose-bottomed flan tin (pie pan) with a corner of each slice pointing up out of the tin. Press the final slice in the base. Press down well and bake in a preheated oven at 190°C/375°F/gas mark 5 for about 25 minutes until crisp and golden brown. Remove from the oven and leave to cool. Place on a plate.

Stand the base of the soufflé dish of mousse in hot water for 30 seconds. Invert over the baked case and, holding the plate and dish, give a firm shake to loosen the mousse. Lift off the soufflé dish. Garnish with parsley sprigs before serving.

Prawn and egg mousse

SERVES 6

15 ml/1 tbsp powdered gelatine
30 ml/2 tbsp water
25 g/1 oz/¼ cup plain (all-purpose)
  flour
150 ml/¼ pt/⅔ cup fish stock
150 ml/¼ pt/⅔ cup milk
25 g/1 oz/2 tbsp butter or margarine
Tabasco sauce
Salt and freshly ground black pepper
175 g/6 oz cooked peeled prawns
  (shrimp)
2 hard-boiled (hard-cooked) eggs,
  chopped
2 egg whites
A small parsley sprig, to garnish
Lemon wedges and hot toast, to serve

Sprinkle the gelatine over the water in a small bowl and leave to soften for 5 minutes. Stand the bowl in a pan of hot water and stir until dissolved. Alternatively, heat briefly in the microwave. Blend the flour with the stock in a saucepan. Stir in the milk and add the butter or margarine. Bring to the boil and cook for 2 minutes, stirring all the time. Season to taste with Tabasco sauce, salt and pepper and stir in the gelatine. Leave until cool but not set. Stir in 150 g/5 oz of the prawns and one of the hard-boiled eggs. Whisk the egg whites until stiff and fold in with a metal spoon. Turn into an attractive serving dish and chill until set. Garnish the top with the remaining prawns and hard-boiled egg, then finish with the parsley. Serve with lemon wedges and hot toast.

Melon and prawn cocktail with herby cheese slices

SERVES 6

1 honeydew melon
225 g/8 oz cooked peeled prawns
  (shrimp)
45 ml/3 tbsp olive oil
15 ml/1 tbsp lemon juice
5 ml/1 tsp dried mint
Salt and freshly ground black pepper
6 cooked unpeeled prawns (shrimp)
1 small French stick, sliced into
  12 pieces
80 g/3¼ oz/scant ½ cup garlic and herb
  soft cheese
50 g/2 oz/¼ cup butter or margarine,
  softened

Halve the melon. Discard the seeds, then scoop out the flesh using a melon baller. Alternatively, cut off the rind and cut the flesh into cubes. Place in a bowl and add the prawns. Whisk the oil and lemon juice with the mint and some salt and pepper. Pour over the melon and prawns and toss gently. Chill. When ready to serve, spoon into six wine goblets and hang an unpeeled prawn over each rim. Toast the French bread slices on one side. Mash the cheese and butter or margarine together and spread over the untoasted sides of the bread. Grill (broil) until melted and bubbling. Serve with the cocktail.

Prawn choux balls

MAKES 30

For the pastry (paste):
65 g/2½ oz/scant ¾ cup plain (all-purpose) flour
A pinch of salt
25 g/1 oz/2 tbsp butter or margarine
150 ml/¼ pt/⅔ cup water
1 egg, beaten
For the filling:
100 g/4 oz cooked peeled prawns (shrimp), roughly chopped
60 ml/4 tbsp mayonnaise
A pinch of cayenne
5 ml/1 tsp anchovy essence (extract)
Freshly ground black pepper
150 ml/¼ pt/⅔ cup whipping cream

To make the pastry, sift the flour and salt on to a sheet of kitchen paper (paper towel). Heat the butter or margarine and water in a pan until it has melted, then bring to the boil. Add the flour all in one go and beat with a wooden spoon until the mixture is smooth and leaves the sides of the pan clean. Remove from the heat. Beat for 1 minute to cool, then gradually beat in the egg, beating well after each addition, until smooth and glossy and the mixture holds its shape. Spoon into 30 small balls on a greased baking (cookie) sheet.

Bake in a preheated oven at 220°C/425°F/gas mark 7 for 7 minutes, then reduce the heat to 190°C/375°F/gas mark 5 and cook for a further 15 minutes until golden brown and crisp. Transfer to a wire rack and leave to cool.

To make the filling, mix the prawns with the mayonnaise, cayenne, anchovy essence and pepper to taste. Whip the cream until peaking and fold into the mixture with a metal spoon. Make a small slit in the side of each choux ball and spoon the mixture inside.

Smoked mussel choux balls

MAKES 30

Prepare as for Prawn Choux Balls, but substitute 100 g/4 oz/1 small can of smoked mussels, drained and finely chopped, for the prawns (shrimp). Add the finely grated rind of 1 small lemon to the filling.

Smoked salmon choux balls

MAKES 30

Prepare as for Prawn Choux Balls but substitute 100 g/4 oz smoked salmon trimmings, chopped, and 2.5 ml/½ tsp grated onion for the prawns (shrimp). Use fromage frais instead of whipped cream.

Chillied crab mangetout

MAKES ABOUT 36

175 g/6 oz mangetout (snow peas)
170 g/6 oz/1 small can of white crabmeat, drained
15 ml/1 tbsp mayonnaise
5 ml/1 tsp tomato purée (paste)
1 small green chilli, seeded and finely chopped
Salt and freshly ground black pepper
A few drops of lemon juice

Plunge the mangetout into boiling water for 1 minute. Drain, rinse with cold water and drain again. Dry on kitchen paper (paper towels) and carefully make a slit in the side of each one to form a pocket. Mash together the remaining ingredients and spoon into the mangetout. Chill until ready to serve.

Moules à la marinière

SERVES 4

40 g/1½ oz/3 tbsp butter or margarine
1 large onion, finely chopped
1 garlic clove, crushed
1 celery stick, finely chopped
1.75 kg/4 lb mussels in their shells,
  cleaned (page 13)
250 ml/8 fl oz/1 cup white wine
120 ml/4 fl oz/½ cup water
Freshly ground black pepper
30 ml/2 tbsp chopped parsley

Melt the butter or margarine in a
large saucepan. Add the onion,
garlic and celery, cover and cook
gently for 3 minutes without
browning. Add the mussels, wine
and water and a good grinding of
pepper. Cover and cook for about
5 minutes, shaking the pan
occasionally, until the mussels open.
Discard any that remain closed.
Ladle into warm bowls and sprinkle
with the parsley.

Moules à la crème

SERVES 4–6

Prepare as for Moules à la Marinière,
but once cooked remove the fish
from their shells completely. Strain
the cooking liquid, stir in 30 ml/
2 tbsp plain (all-purpose) flour
blended with 30 ml/2 tbsp milk and
15 ml/1 tbsp brandy, bring to the
boil and cook for 2 minutes. Stir in
75 ml/5 tbsp single (light) cream
and season to taste. Serve in large,
shallow soup bowls.

Creamy chilli mussels

SERVES 4–6

15 g/½ oz/1 tbsp butter or margarine
1 onion, finely chopped
2 celery sticks, finely chopped
90 ml/6 tbsp dry white wine
5 ml/1 tsp cumin seeds, coarsely
  crushed
1 kg/2¼ lb mussels in their shells,
  cleaned (page 13)
5 ml/1 tsp grated fresh root ginger
1 red chilli, seeded and finely chopped
1 tomato, skinned, seeded and
  chopped
5 ml/1 tsp tomato purée (paste)
150 ml/¼ pt/⅔ cup crème fraîche
Lemon juice, to taste
Freshly ground black pepper
Warm garlic and coriander (cilantro)
  naan breads, to serve

Melt the butter or margarine in a
large saucepan. Add the onion and
celery and fry (sauté) for 2 minutes,
stirring, until softened but not
browned. Add the wine and cumin
and bring to the boil. Add the
mussels, cover and cook for
4–5 minutes, shaking the pan
occasionally.

Tip the mussels into a colander
over a bowl, then strain the cooking
liquid back into the rinsed-out
saucepan. Add the ginger, chilli and
chopped tomato. Boil the liquid until
reduced by half, then stir in the
tomato purée and crème fraîche.
Add lemon juice and pepper to taste.
Remove the mussels from their
shells and return to the sauce. Heat
through. Spoon into small, warm
bowls and serve with wedges of
warm garlic and coriander naan
bread.

Sizzling oysters with chilli salsa

SERVES 6

1 red chilli, seeded
3 ripe tomatoes, skinned
200 g/7 oz/1 small can of pimientos,
    drained
15 ml/1 tbsp tomato purée (paste)
15 ml/1 tbsp red wine vinegar
5 ml/1 tsp clear honey
Salt and freshly ground black pepper
18 fresh oysters in their shells

Put all the ingredients except the salt
and pepper and oysters in a blender
or food processor. Run the machine
until fairly smooth. Season to taste.
Turn into a small saucepan and heat
through. Shuck the oysters (page
13), remove the top shells and add a
good grinding of pepper to the
oysters. Put the oysters in their
shells on the grill (broiler) rack,
taking care not to spill the juices,
and cook for about 3 minutes until
the oysters sizzle. Lift on to serving
plates, spoon a little salsa over each
and serve.

Tiger eye mussels with fiery cucumber salsa

SERVES 6

These large mussels are sold ready-
cooked in their half shells.

1 quantity of Fiery Cucumber Salsa
    (page 379)
18 large cooked tiger eye mussels
Freshly ground black pepper
75 ml/5 tbsp olive oil
Lime wedges, to garnish

Make the salsa and heat in a small
saucepan. Put the mussels in their
shells on the grill (broiler) rack. Add
a good grinding of pepper to the
oysters and drizzle each with olive
oil. Grill (broil) for about 2 minutes
until hot. Lift on to serving plates,
spoon a little salsa over each and
serve garnished with lime wedges.

Canny creamed mussels

SERVES 6

1 onion, finely chopped
1 garlic clove, crushed
15 g/½ oz/1 tbsp butter or margarine
2 × 250 g/9 oz/medium cans of
    mussels in brine
150 ml/¼ pt/⅔ cup white wine
150 ml/¼ pt/⅔ cup water
15 ml/1 tbsp cornflour (cornstarch)
150 ml/¼ pt/⅔ cup single (light) cream
Freshly ground black pepper
30 ml/2 tbsp chopped parsley
Hot French bread, to serve

Fry (sauté) the onion and garlic in
the butter or margarine in a
saucepan for 2 minutes, stirring,
until soft but not brown. Drain one
of the cans of mussels and add them
to the onion. Add the second can,
including its juice, and the wine.
Blend the water with the cornflour
and stir in. Bring to the boil and
cook for 1 minute, stirring, until
thickened. Stir in the cream and
season to taste with pepper. Heat
through but do not allow to boil.
Add the parsley, spoon into warm
bowls and serve with hot French
bread.

Oysters au naturel

SERVES 4

Some people like to add a dash of Tabasco sauce before eating for an extra kick.

24 oysters in their shells
Cracked ice
Lemon wedges
Parsley sprigs
Thin brown bread and butter, to serve

Shuck the oysters (page 13), taking care not to spill the juice. Lay them in their half shells on a bed of crushed ice. Garnish with lemon wedges and parsley sprigs and serve with thin brown bread and butter.

Grilled oysters with cream

SERVES 4

16 oysters in their shells
Freshly ground black pepper
90 ml/6 tbsp double (heavy) cream
90 ml/6 tbsp freshly grated Parmesan cheese

Shuck the oysters (page 13), taking care not to spill the juices. Put them in the grill (broiler) pan and season with pepper. Grill (broil) for 2–3 minutes until sizzling. Top each with a spoonful of cream and cheese and return to the grill just until bubbling. Serve straight away.

Oyster loaves

SERVES 4

These were made when oysters were the food of the poor but they are so fabulous they are worth indulging in for a treat! They were made with soured (dairy sour) and double (heavy) cream; I prefer to use crème fraîche. Another version of this dish can be found on page 124.

16 oysters in their shells
4 large or 8 small brioches
175 g/6 oz/¾ cup unsalted (sweet) butter
150 ml/¼ pt/⅔ cup crème fraîche
Salt and freshly ground black pepper
A few drops of Tabasco sauce
A few drops of Worcestershire sauce

Shuck the oysters (page 13) and tip into a sieve (strainer) over a bowl to catch all the juices. Slice the top off each of the brioches and scoop out most of the dough inside, leaving a wall all round. Melt 150 g/5 oz/ ⅔ cup of the butter and brush all over the bread shells and the 'lids'. Place on a baking (cookie) sheet and bake in a preheated oven at 200°C/ 400°F/gas mark 6 for about 10 minutes until crisp.

Meanwhile, melt the remaining butter in a frying pan (skillet). Add the oysters and toss for just 45 seconds until opaque. Remove from the pan with a draining spoon and slice in half through the middle. Add the oyster juices and crème fraîche to the frying pan, stir well and boil for 1 minute. Season to taste with salt, pepper and the Tabasco and Worcestershire sauces. Return the oysters to the pan and heat through. Put the brioches on warm plates and spoon in the oyster cream. Top with the lids and serve.

Mediterranean slippers

SERVES 6

3 even-sized aubergines (eggplants)
45 ml/3 tbsp olive oil, plus extra for
  brushing
Salt and freshly ground black pepper
2 Spanish onions, chopped
1 garlic clove, crushed
150 ml/¼ pt/⅔ cup passata (sieved
  tomatoes)
5 ml/1 tsp caster (superfine) sugar
30 ml/2 tbsp pine nuts
50 g/2 oz/1 small can of anchovy
  fillets, drained and chopped
12 stoned (pitted) black olives,
  quartered
5 ml/1 tsp ground cinnamon
15 ml/1 tbsp chopped parsley

Trim off the stalks from the
aubergines and discard. Boil the
aubergines in lightly salted water for
10 minutes. Drain and plunge into
cold water. When cool enough to
handle, drain and halve lengthways.
Scoop out most of the flesh, leaving
the 'shells' intact. Chop the flesh
and reserve. Brush a baking tin
(pan) with oil. Lay the shells in it
and brush each with a little more
oil. Season with salt and pepper.
Bake in a preheated oven at
180°C/350°F/gas mark 4 for
30 minutes. Remove from the oven.
   Meanwhile, heat the oil in a
saucepan. Add the chopped
aubergine, onions and garlic and fry
(sauté), stirring, for 3 minutes to
soften. Add all the remaining
ingredients except the parsley. Bring
to the boil and simmer for about
10 minutes until the onions are soft
and the mixture is bathed in sauce.
Season to taste and leave to cool.
Spoon into the aubergine shells,
sprinkle with the parsley and chill
until ready to serve.

Angels on horseback

SERVES 1

Multiply the quantities given here
according to the number of people
you are serving. You can use canned
oysters if you prefer.

4 oysters, shucked (page 13)
2 rindless streaky bacon rashers
  (slices), rinded and halved
1 slice of wholemeal toast, crusts
  removed and lightly buttered
5 ml/1 tsp chopped parsley

Roll up each oyster in half a rasher
of bacon. Secure with cocktail sticks
(toothpicks), if necessary. Grill
(broil), turning once, for about
4–5 minutes until golden brown. Cut
the toast into quarters, put a bacon
roll on each and sprinkle with the
parsley before serving.

Butterfly prawns

SERVES 4

700 g/1½ lb raw peeled tiger prawns
  (jumbo shrimp), tails left on
1 large egg
15 ml/1 tbsp cornflour (cornstarch)
2.5 ml/½ tsp salt
Freshly ground black pepper
Oil, for deep-frying
Lemon or lime wedges, to garnish

Split the prawns along their backs
and flatten out. Lightly beat the egg
with the cornflour, salt and some
pepper. Dip the prawns in this,
then deep-fry in hot oil for about
3 minutes until golden. Drain on
kitchen paper (paper towels) and
garnish with lemon or lime wedges.

Plaice georgette

SERVES 4

This is a very substantial starter that can also be served as a light lunch or supper dish.

4 large even-sized potatoes, scrubbed
4 white-skinned plaice fillets
150 ml/¼ pt/⅔ cup dry white wine
75 ml/5 tbsp water
1 small bay leaf
Salt and freshly ground black pepper
40 g/1½ oz/3 tbsp butter or margarine
20 g/¾ oz/3 tbsp plain (all-purpose) flour
75 ml/5 tbsp single (light) cream
100 g/4 oz cooked peeled prawns (shrimp)
15 ml/1 tbsp milk
50 g/2 oz/½ cup Cheddar cheese, grated

Prick the potatoes all over with a fork. Bake in a preheated oven at 180°C/350°F/gas mark 4 for 2 hours or until soft when squeezed. Meanwhile, fold the plaice fillets into three. Place in an ovenproof dish with the wine, water, bay leaf, a pinch of salt and a little pepper. Cover and bake below the potatoes for about 15 minutes until just opaque. Carefully lift the fish out of the dish and reserve. Melt half the butter or margarine in a saucepan. Stir in the flour and cook for 1 minute. Remove from the heat and strain in the fish cooking liquid. Return to the heat, bring to the boil and cook for 2 minutes, stirring, until very thick. Stir in the cream and prawns and season to taste.

When the potatoes are cooked, remove from the oven and increase the temperature to 200°C/400°F/gas mark 6. Cut a slice off the top of each potato and scoop out the flesh into a bowl. Mash with the remaining butter or margarine and the milk and season lightly. Beat well until smooth. Place the potato shells on individual ovenproof dishes. Spoon half the prawn mixture into each shell and top with a plaice fillet. Add the remaining prawn mixture. Pipe or spoon the potato round the edge of each and sprinkle with the cheese. Return to the oven and bake for about 15–20 minutes until golden brown. Serve hot.

Pilchard creams

SERVES 4

425 g/15 oz/1 large can of pilchards in tomato sauce
30 ml/2 tbsp mayonnaise
15 ml/1 tbsp tomato purée (paste)
120 ml/4 fl oz/½ cup crème fraîche
5 ml/1 tsp red wine vinegar
Salt and freshly ground black pepper
A few drops of Tabasco sauce
15 ml/1 tbsp snipped chives
Rye bread, to serve

Mash the pilchards in a bowl (ideally mash the bones too, for calcium). Beat in the mayonnaise, tomato purée, crème fraîche, wine vinegar, some salt and pepper and Tabasco to taste. Spoon into small pots and sprinkle with the chives. Chill until ready to serve with rye bread.

Plaice with egg and parsley sauce

SERVES 8

4 plaice fillets, halved lengthways
10 ml/2 tsp lemon juice
Salt and freshly ground black pepper
65 g/2½ oz/scant ⅓ cup butter or
  margarine, plus extra for greasing
30 ml/2 tbsp sunflower oil
8 slices of ciabatta bread
30 ml/2 tbsp plain (all-purpose) flour
150 ml/¼ pt/⅔ cup milk
1 bay leaf
45 ml/3 tbsp single (light) cream
2 hard-boiled (hard-cooked) eggs,
  chopped
15 ml/1 tbsp chopped parsley
8 small parsley sprigs, to garnish

Remove any black skin from the
plaice fillets. Sprinkle each with
lemon juice and a little salt and
pepper. Roll up and place on a plate.
Cover with foil or a lid and place the
plate over a pan of gently simmering
water for 10–15 minutes until
cooked through.

Meanwhile, heat 50 g/2 oz/¼ cup
of the butter or margarine and the
oil in a large frying pan (skillet). Fry
(sauté) the ciabatta slices until
golden brown on each side. Drain on
kitchen paper (paper towels) and
keep warm. Whisk the flour with the
milk in a saucepan. Add the
remaining butter or margarine and
the bay leaf, bring to the boil and
cook for 2 minutes, whisking all the
time. Remove the bay leaf, stir in the
cream, eggs and parsley and season
to taste. Put a slice of fried (sautéed)
bread on each warm plate. Top each
with a plaice roll, then spoon a little
sauce over. Garnish each with a
small sprig of parsley and serve
straight away.

Italian plaice

SERVES 4

4 plaice fillets
150 ml/¼ pt/⅔ cup water
1 small bay leaf
5 ml/1 tsp lemon juice
Salt and freshly ground black pepper
2 beefsteak tomatoes, skinned and
  halved
120 ml/4 fl oz/½ cup olive oil
30 ml/2 tbsp red wine vinegar
150 ml/¼ pt/⅔ cup passata (sieved
  tomatoes)
A good pinch of caster (superfine)
  sugar
1 small garlic clove, crushed
15 ml/1 tbsp chopped basil
15 ml/1 tbsp chopped parsley
50 g/2 oz/1 small can of anchovy
  fillets, drained
4 stuffed olives, sliced

Remove any black skin from the
plaice. Fold in three and place in a
frying pan (skillet) with the water,
bay leaf, lemon juice, a pinch of salt
and a good grinding of pepper. Bring
to the boil, reduce the heat, cover
and poach for 4 minutes or until
cooked through. Lift out with a fish
slice and drain on kitchen paper
(paper towels). Leave to cool.

Meanwhile, fry (sauté) the tomato
halves in 30 ml/2 tbsp of the oil for
2 minutes only. Transfer to a serving
platter and top each with a cooked
plaice fillet. Whisk the remaining oil
with the vinegar, passata, sugar,
garlic, herbs and a little salt and
pepper. Spoon over the fish. Garnish
with a criss-cross of anchovy fillets
and scatter the olive slices over.
Chill until ready to serve.

Chinese prawn spring rolls

MAKES 12

If you can't find spring roll wrappers, use three sheets of filo pastry (paste), each cut into four.

225 g/8 oz cooked peeled prawns (shrimp), chopped
225 g/8 oz minced (ground) pork or chicken
50 g/2 oz button mushrooms, finely chopped
3 spring onions (scallions), finely chopped
50 g/2 oz beansprouts
30 ml/2 tbsp dry sherry
5 ml/1 tsp grated fresh root ginger
1 small garlic clove, crushed
10 ml/2 tsp soy sauce
Freshly ground black pepper
A pinch of Chinese five-spice powder
12 spring roll wrappers
30 ml/2 tbsp water
5 ml/1 tsp cornflour (cornstarch)
Oil, for deep-frying

Thoroughly mix together all the ingredients except the wrappers, water and cornflour. Divide the mixture between the wrappers, laying it across one corner. Mix together the water and cornflour and use to brush the edges of each wrapper. Fold and roll up to form parcels. Deep-fry for 4–5 minutes until crisp and golden. Drain on kitchen paper (paper towels) and serve hot.

Crisp fried whiting

SERVES 6

450 g/1 lb whiting fillets, skinned
30 ml/2 tbsp plain (all-purpose) flour
Salt and freshly ground black pepper
2 eggs, beaten
100 g/4 oz/2 cups fresh white breadcrumbs
Sunflower oil, for deep-frying
Parsley sprigs and lemon wedges, to garnish
Piquant Dip (page 372), to serve

Cut the fish into 5 cm/2 in long strips, about 1 cm/½ in wide. Mix the flour with a little salt and pepper and use to coat the fish. Dip the strips in the egg, then the breadcrumbs. Heat the oil until a cube of day-old bread browns in 30 seconds. Deep-fry the fish for about 2 minutes until golden brown. Drain on kitchen paper (paper towels). Pile on to warm plates, garnish with parsley and lemon wedges and serve with Piquant Dip.

Crisp fried plaice

SERVES 6

Prepare as for Crisp Fried Whiting, but substitute plaice for the whiting. Dip in dry parsley and thyme stuffing mix instead of breadcrumbs and serve with Barbecue Sauce (page 380).

Crisp fried sole

SERVES 6

Prepare as for Crisp Fried Whiting, but substitute lemon sole fillets for the whiting and dip in dry sage and onion stuffing mix instead of breadcrumbs. Serve with Orange and Mango Salsa (page 381).

Tuna bean dip

SERVES 6

*425 g/15 oz/1 large can of cannellini
   beans, drained*
1 garlic clove, crushed
*85 g/3½ oz/1 very small can of tuna,
   drained*
30 ml/2 tbsp sunflower oil
15 ml/1 tbsp lemon juice
A good pinch of cayenne
15 ml/1 tbsp chopped parsley
Pitta bread fingers, to serve

Put all the ingredients except the
parsley in a blender or food
processor and run the machine until
smooth, stopping and scraping down
the sides if necessary. Spoon on to
plates, garnish with the parsley and
serve with pitta bread fingers.

Salmon and flageolet dip

SERVES 6

Prepare as for Tuna Bean Dip, but
substitute 200 g/7 oz/1 small can of
pink salmon, drained and all skin
removed, for the tuna and flageolet
beans for the cannellini beans. Add
10 ml/2 tsp tomato purée (paste) to
the mixture to enhance the colour
and 5 ml/1 tsp anchovy essence
(extract) to pick up the flavour.

Simple tuna dip

SERVES 4–6

*185 g/6½ oz/1 small can of tuna,
   drained*
60 ml/4 tbsp mayonnaise
45 ml/3 tbsp plain yoghurt
15 ml/1 tbsp tomato ketchup (catsup)
5 ml/1 tsp lemon juice
1.5 ml/¼ tsp chilli powder
Tortilla chips, to serve

Beat together all the ingredients until
smooth. Turn into a small pot and
serve with tortilla chips.

Simple pilchard dip

SERVES 4–6

Prepare as for Simple Tuna Dip, but
substitute 155 g/5¼ oz/1 small can
of pilchards in tomato sauce for the
tuna and add tomato relish instead
of ketchup (catsup).

Tuna cheese

SERVES 4–6

*185 g/6½ oz/1 small can of tuna,
   drained*
*200 g/7 oz/scant 1 cup medium-fat soft
   cheese*
15 ml/1 tbsp lemon juice
1.5 ml/¼ tsp cayenne
Salt and freshly ground black pepper
15 ml/1 tbsp chopped parsley
*Mixed salad leaves and lemon slices,
   to garnish*
Hot toast, to serve

Thoroughly beat together the
tuna and cheese, then beat in the
remaining ingredients. Shape into
a roll on a sheet of greaseproof
(waxed) pepper. Wrap and chill.
Cut the roll into 12 slices, arrange
on four or six plates and garnish
with salad leaves and lemon slices.
Serve with hot toast.

Sardine pâté

SERVES 6

2 × 120 g/4½ oz/small cans of
  sardines, drained
75 g/3 oz/⅓ cup unsalted (sweet)
  butter, melted
150 ml/¼ pt/⅔ cup plain yoghurt
5 ml/1 tsp lemon juice
A good pinch of cayenne
Salt and freshly ground black pepper
6 large round lettuce leaves
3 hard-boiled (hard-cooked) eggs,
  sliced
2 red onions, thinly sliced and
  separated into rings
30 ml/2 tbsp chopped parsley
Melba toast, to serve

Put the sardines in a blender or food
processor. Run the machine, then
gradually blend in the melted butter.
Add the yoghurt, lemon juice,
cayenne and a little salt and pepper
and run the machine again until well
blended. Arrange the lettuce leaves
on individual plates and spoon the
sardine mixture on top. Top with the
egg slices and onion rings and
sprinkle with the parsley. Serve with
melba toast.

Sardine and tomato salad

SERVES 6

2 × 120 g/4½ oz/small cans of
  sardines, drained
450 g/1 lb tomatoes, skinned and sliced
½ bunch of spring onions (scallions),
  finely chopped
30 ml/2 tbsp capers
45 ml/3 tbsp olive oil
15 ml/1 tbsp red wine vinegar
2.5 ml/½ tsp Dijon mustard
2.5 ml/½ tsp caster (superfine) sugar
30 ml/2 tbsp chopped coriander
  (cilantro)

Carefully halve the sardines and
remove the bones. Put the tomato
slices in the base of six shallow
individual dishes and sprinkle the
spring onions over. Top with the
sardines, then the capers. Whisk
together all the remaining
ingredients except the coriander and
pour over. Chill for 30 minutes to
allow the flavours to develop.
Sprinkle with the coriander before
serving.

Bagna cauda

SERVES 4

Have a container of breadsticks on
the table for dipping, too.

1 fennel bulb, trimmed and cut into
  strips
2 carrots, cut into strips
1 red (bell) pepper, cut into strips
1 green or yellow pepper, cut into
  strips
¼ large cucumber, cut into strips
2 celery sticks, cut into strips
2 × 50 g/2 oz/small cans of anchovies
150 ml/¼ pt/⅔ cup olive oil
3 garlic cloves, crushed
50 g/2 oz/¼ cup unsalted (sweet)
  butter

Chill the vegetables for at least
1 hour. Drain the anchovy oil from
the cans into a saucepan and add
the olive oil and garlic. Chop the fish
finely and add. Simmer gently for
5 minutes until the fish have
'melted' into the oil. Beat in the
butter, a little at a time, until the
mixture is glistening. Spoon into
four small pots. Serve straight away
with the very cold vegetables to dip
into the hot fishy oil, stirring up the
sediment every time.

Marinated kipper fillets

SERVES 6

2 × 175 g/6 oz/small packets of kipper
* fillets*
1 small onion, thinly sliced and
* separated into rings*
1 large bay leaf
90 ml/6 tbsp olive oil
30 ml/2 tbsp white wine vinegar
5 ml/1 tsp Dijon mustard
2.5 ml/½ tsp caster (superfine) sugar
Salt and freshly ground black pepper
30 ml/2 tbsp chopped parsley
Brown bread and butter, to serve

Pull the skin off the fish fillets and
discard, then lay the kippers in a
large, shallow dish. Scatter the onion
rings over, break the bay leaf in half
and add. Whisk together all the
remaining ingredients except the
parsley and pour over. Leave in a
cool place to marinate for at least
3 hours or overnight, turning
occasionally, until the fish feels
tender when pierced with a knife.
Remove the bay leaf pieces. Fold the
fillets and arrange in six shallow
dishes. Spoon the marinade over and
arrange the onion rings on top.
Sprinkle with the parsley and serve
with brown bread and butter.

Marinated herring fillets

SERVES 6

Prepare as for Marinated Kipper
Fillets, but substitute fresh herring
fillets for the kippers and add 5 ml/
1 tsp dried dill (dill weed) to the oil
and vinegar mixture.

Calamares a la parilla

SERVES 4

8 baby squid, cleaned (page 14) and
* tentacles reserved*
1 garlic clove, crushed
60 ml/4 tbsp fresh white breadcrumbs
45 ml/3 tbsp chopped parsley
Salt and freshly ground black pepper
5 ml/1 tsp lemon juice
5 ml/1 tsp finely grated lemon rind
60 ml/4 tbsp olive oil
Lemon wedges, to garnish

Rinse the squid and pat dry on
kitchen paper (paper towels). Finely
chop the tentacles and mix with the
garlic, breadcrumbs, 30 ml/2 tbsp of
the parsley, a little salt, lots of
pepper, the lemon juice and rind.
Moisten with half the olive oil.
Spoon this mixture into the squid
and secure the ends with soaked,
wooden cocktail sticks (toothpicks).
Brush with more of the oil and cook
under a preheated grill (broiler) or
barbecue for 6 minutes, turning
once, until the squid is turning
golden at the edges. Remove the
cocktail sticks, sprinkle with the
remaining parsley and serve
garnished with lemon wedges.

Calamares a la plancha

SERVES 4

120 ml/4 fl oz/½ cup olive oil
450 g/1 lb baby squid, cleaned
  (page 14) and sliced
2 garlic cloves, crushed
Juice of ½ lemon
Salt and freshly ground black pepper
30 ml/2 tbsp chopped parsley
Crusty bread, to serve

Heat the oil in a large frying pan
(skillet). Add the squid and garlic
and fry (sauté), stirring, for
2 minutes until turning opaque.
Cover the pan and continue cooking
gently for 10 minutes until the squid
is really tender and turning slightly
pink. Add the lemon juice, some salt
and pepper and the parsley to the
pan. Spoon into shallow bowls and
serve with crusty bread to mop up
the juices.

Baby octopus with fragrant herb dressing

SERVES 4

6–8 cooked baby octopus, chopped
¼ cos (romaine lettuce), cut into chunks
1 shallot, finely chopped
30 ml/2 tbsp chopped parsley
15 ml/1 tbsp chopped thyme
15 ml/1 tbsp chopped dill (dill weed)
45 ml/3 tbsp olive oil
15 ml/1 tbsp white wine vinegar
2.5 ml/½ tsp caster (superfine) sugar
1.5 ml/¼ tsp pimenton or 4 slices of
  chorizo sausage, chopped
Salt and freshly ground black pepper
Aioli (page 372) and seeded bread,
  to serve

Mix the octopus with the lettuce,
shallot and herbs. Whisk together
the remaining ingredients and pour
over. Toss and pile on four plates.
Serve with Aioli and seeded bread.

Scallops mornay

SERVES 4

4 scallops in their shells
200 ml/7 fl oz/scant 1 cup milk
1 lemon slice
40 g/1½ oz/3 tbsp butter or margarine
25 g/1 oz/¼ cup plain (all-purpose)
  flour
150 ml/¼ pt/⅔ cup crème fraîche
75 g/3 oz/¾ cup Cheddar cheese, grated
Salt and freshly ground black pepper
5 ml/1 tsp Dijon mustard
50 g/2 oz/1 cup fresh white
  breadcrumbs

Open and clean the scallops (page
14). Scrub the deep shells and
reserve. Put the fish and the corals
in a saucepan with the milk and
slice of lemon. Simmer gently for
about 3 minutes until just tender.
Lift out and cut into quarters.
Reserve the milk, discarding the
lemon.

Melt 25 g/1 oz/2 tbsp of the
butter or margarine in a separate
saucepan and stir in the flour. Cook
for 1 minute, stirring. Remove from
the heat and gradually blend in the
reserved scallop cooking milk.
Return to the heat, bring to the boil
and cook for 2 minutes, stirring. Stir
in the crème fraîche, 50 g/2 oz/
½ cup of the cheese and salt and
pepper to taste. Beat in the mustard.

Spoon a little of the sauce into
each of the reserved shells. Top with
the scallop quarters and corals, then
the remaining sauce. Melt the
remaining butter or margarine and
stir in the breadcrumbs. Scatter over
the surface of each. Bake in a
preheated oven at 190°C/375°F/gas
mark 5 for about 20 minutes until
golden and bubbling. Serve hot.

Coquilles St Jacques Dulgère

SERVES 4

If you can't get scallops in their shells, put the prepared mixture in small, shallow, ovenproof dishes instead.

450 g/1 lb potatoes, cut into chunks
25 g/1 oz/2 tbsp butter or margarine
15 ml/1 tbsp single (light) cream or full-cream milk
300 ml/½ pt/1¼ cups milk
1 slice of onion
1 bay leaf
6 peppercorns
4 scallops in their shells
15 g/½ oz/2 tbsp plain (all-purpose) flour
10 ml/2 tsp chopped parsley
A squeeze of lemon juice
Salt
45 ml/3 tbsp dried breadcrumbs

Boil the potatoes in lightly salted water until tender. Drain and pass through a sieve (strainer), then beat well with 15 g/½ oz/1 tbsp of the butter or margarine and the cream or full-cream milk. Put the milk, onion slice, bay leaf and peppercorns in a saucepan. Bring to the boil, turn off the heat and leave to infuse for 5 minutes. Strain and return the milk to the pan.

Open and clean the scallops (page 14) and reserve the deep shells. Cut off the corals and cut the white parts into quarters. Put in the flavoured milk. Bring just to the boil, reduce the heat, cover and cook gently for 3 minutes. Scrub the reserved shells well. Lift the scallops out of the milk and transfer to the shells. Mash the remaining butter or margarine with the flour. Gradually whisk into the hot milk over a moderate heat, whisking all the time, until thick and smooth. Cook for a further 1 minute. Add the parsley and lemon juice and salt to taste. Spoon over the scallops. Pipe or spoon the potato around the edges of the shells. Sprinkle the breadcrumbs over the sauce in the centre. Place on a baking (cookie) sheet and cook in a preheated oven at 200°C/400°F/gas mark 6 for 15 minutes until lightly golden. Serve hot.

Baked scallops with bacon

SERVES 6

6 large shelled scallops
30 ml/2 tbsp melted unsalted (sweet) butter
Salt and freshly ground black pepper
Finely grated rind and juice of ½ lime or ½ small lemon
90 ml/6 tbsp double (heavy) cream
45 ml/3 tbsp fresh wholemeal breadcrumbs
15 ml/1 tbsp grated Parmesan cheese
6 smoked streaky bacon rashers (slices), rinded and halved

Quarter the scallops, separating the corals. Put 5 ml/1 tsp of the butter in each of six ramekins (custard cups). Add the scallop quarters and corals to each. Sprinkle with salt, pepper and lime or lemon rind and juice. Spoon the cream over. Mix the breadcrumbs with the remaining butter and scatter over with the cheese. Bake in a preheated oven at 190°C/375°F/gas mark 5 for 10 minutes until cooked through and golden. Meanwhile, roll up the halved bacon rashers and grill (broil) or dry-fry until brown all over. Put two on top of each ramekin and serve hot.

Scallops with rosé and oyster mushrooms

SERVES 4

8 baby new potatoes, scrubbed and thinly sliced
4 large scallops, cleaned (page 14) and shells reserved
150 ml/¼ pt/⅔ cup water
1 lemon slice
1 small bay leaf
50 g/2 oz/¼ cup butter or margarine
1 onion, finely chopped
100 g/4 oz oyster mushrooms, sliced
1 small garlic clove, crushed
30 ml/2 tbsp cornflour (cornstarch)
150 ml/¼ pt/⅔ cup rosé wine
150 ml/¼ pt/⅔ cup fish stock
5 ml/1 tsp anchovy essence (extract)
Salt and freshly ground black pepper
60 ml/4 tbsp dried breadcrumbs

Boil the potato slices in lightly salted water for 3–4 minutes until just tender but still holding their shape. Drain, rinse with cold water and drain again. Quarter the scallops, separating the corals. Put in a pan with the water, slice of lemon and bay leaf. Bring almost to the boil, reduce the heat and cook gently for 3 minutes. Drain, reserving the liquid. Put the scallops in the scrubbed deep shells.

Melt half the butter or margarine in a saucepan. Add the onion and cook gently for 3 minutes until softened but not browned. Add the mushrooms and garlic, cover and stew gently for 5 minutes. Stir in the cornflour, then blend in the wine, stock and anchovy essence. Bring to the boil and cook for 1 minute, stirring. Thin with the reserved cooking water to give a thick, pouring sauce. Season to taste and spoon over the scallops. Sprinkle the centres with the breadcrumbs and

lay the potato slices round the edges. Melt the remaining butter or margarine and brush over the potatoes. Cook under a hot grill (broiler) until the potatoes are turning golden. Serve hot.

Scallop tartlets with pesto

SERVES 6

1 sheet of ready-rolled puff pastry (paste)
1 egg, beaten
45 ml/3 tbsp Pesto (page 377 or use bought)
1 ripe tomato, skinned and cut into 6 slices
15 ml/1 tbsp olive oil
6 shelled scallops with their corals
45 ml/3 tbsp Pernod
45 ml/3 tbsp crème fraîche
Salt and freshly ground black pepper
6 oakleaf lettuce leaves, to garnish

Cut six rounds out of the pastry using a 7.5 cm/3 in biscuit (cookie) cutter. Place on a dampened baking (cookie) sheet and brush with the egg to glaze. Bake in a preheated oven at 200°C/400°F/gas mark 6 for 10–15 minutes until puffy and golden. Spread with the pesto and top each with a slice of tomato. Keep warm in a low oven.

Meanwhile, heat the oil in a frying pan (skillet), add the scallops and fry (sauté) for 2 minutes on each side until just cooked through. Add the Pernod and bring to the boil. Stir in the crème fraîche and season to taste. Put the pastry rounds on warm plates. Top each with a scallop and spoon the pan juices over. Garnish each with an oakleaf lettuce leaf and serve warm.

Traditional taramasalata

SERVES 6

Use smoked cod's roe if you can't find grey mullet roe. If you don't want the hard slog, put the mixture in a blender or food processor.

225 g/8 oz smoked grey mullet's roe
1 thick slice of white bread
2 garlic cloves, crushed
Juice of 1 small lemon
90 ml/6 tbsp olive oil, plus extra for
  sprinkling
Freshly ground black pepper
15 ml/1 tbsp chopped parsley
Lemon wedges and hot pitta breads,
  to serve

Split the skin of the mullet roe, then scrape the contents into a bowl or a large mortar. Cover the bread with cold water, then squeeze it to remove the water. Add to the bowl with the garlic and pound with a pestle or the end of a rolling pin until it forms a smooth paste. Beat in a little of the lemon juice, then a few drops of the olive oil. Continue until all the lemon juice and oil are blended in and the mixture forms a smooth, creamy dip. Season with pepper and spoon into a serving bowl. Trickle a little oil over the surface and sprinkle with the parsley. Serve with lemon wedges and hot pitta breads.

Creamy taramasalata

SERVES 4–6

3 slices of white bread, crusts removed
45 ml/3 tbsp milk
1 garlic clove, crushed
100 g/4 oz smoked cod's roe, skin
  removed
15 ml/1 tbsp lemon juice
30 ml/2 tbsp single (light) cream
150 ml/¼ pt/⅔ cup sunflower oil
Freshly ground black pepper
A few black olives, to garnish
Warm pitta breads, to serve

Break up the bread and place in a food processor. Add the milk and leave to soak for 10 minutes. Add the garlic, cod's roe, lemon juice and cream and run the machine until smooth. With the machine running, gradually add the oil in a thin trickle until the mixture is thick and creamy. Season to taste with pepper. Spoon into a small pot and chill. When ready to serve, garnish with olives and serve with warm pitta breads.

Danish salted sprats

SERVES 6

300 g/11 oz coarse sea salt
5 ml/1 tsp coarsely crushed black
  pepper
8 juniper berries, crushed
5 ml/1 tsp powdered bay leaves or
  3 dried bay leaves, crushed
900 g/2 lb sprats, cleaned and heads
  and tails removed
Blinis (page 71, or use bought)
300 ml/½ pt/1¼ cups soured (dairy
  sour) cream
A few whole chives

Mix the salt with the pepper, juniper
berries and bay leaves. Put a layer in
the base of a large stone or glass
wide-necked jar, then add a layer of
fish. Repeat the layers finishing with
a layer of the salt mixture. Tap the
jar firmly on the work surface to
settle the contents. Cover with a
double thickness of greaseproof
(waxed) paper, then cover with a
saucer that fits snugly inside the jar
and press down firmly on top. Cover
the jar with a lid and store in the
fridge for at least 1 week or up to
1 month before eating. To serve, lift
the fish out of the jar and dry on
kitchen paper (paper towels). Pile on
to plates and serve with a plate of
blinis and the soured cream in a
dish. Throw a few whole chives over
the sprats to garnish.

Golden scampi in yeast batter

SERVES 4–6

Use strips of monkfish instead of
scampi for an equally delicious
result.

175 g/6 oz/1½ cups plain (all-purpose)
  flour
5 ml/1 tsp easy-blend dried yeast
15 ml/1 tbsp sunflower oil
300 ml/½ pt/1¼ cups hand-hot water
Salt and freshly ground black pepper
Oil, for deep-frying
450 g/1 lb raw peeled scampi
Lemon wedges and parsley sprigs, to
  garnish
Alabama Dressing (page 386), to serve

Sift the flour in a bowl, then stir in
the yeast and oil. Gradually beat in
the water to form a smooth batter.
Add a pinch of salt and a good
grinding of pepper and leave
to stand in a warm place for
30 minutes. Heat the oil until a
cube of day-old bread browns in
30 seconds. Dip the scampi in the
batter and deep-fry until golden
brown. Drain on kitchen paper
(paper towels). Pile on warm plates,
garnish with lemon wedges and
parsley sprigs and serve with
Alabama Dressing.

Tiger prawns in yeast batter

SERVES 4–6

Prepare as for Golden Scampi in
Yeast Batter, but use raw, peeled
tiger prawns (jumbo shrimp) with
their tails left on instead of the
scampi. Hold the fish by the tails to
dip them in the batter.

Scampi in breadcrumbs

SERVES 4–6

30 ml/2 tbsp plain (all-purpose) flour
Salt and freshly ground black pepper
450 g/1 lb raw peeled scampi
1 large egg
15 ml/1 tbsp milk
75 g/3 oz/1½ cups fresh white
  breadcrumbs
Oil, for deep-frying
Lemon wedges and parsley sprigs,
  to garnish
Tartare Sauce (page 372), to serve

Mix the flour with a little salt and
pepper. Toss the scampi in this. Beat
together the egg and milk and put
the breadcrumbs in a separate dish.
Dip the fish in the egg mixture, then
in the breadcrumbs to coat completely.
Chill, if time allows, then deep-fry in
hot oil until crisp and golden. Drain
on kitchen paper (paper towels) and
pile on to warm plates. Garnish with
lemon wedges and parsley sprigs
and serve with Tartare Sauce.

Dublin Bay prawns with aioli

SERVES 4

600 ml/1 pt/2½ cups fish stock
150 ml/¼ pt/⅔ cup dry white wine
1 small bay leaf
6 peppercorns
450 g/1 lb raw unpeeled Dublin Bay
  prawns (saltwater crayfish)
Aioli (page 372)
Lemon wedges and parsley sprigs,
  to garnish
Warm French bread, to serve

Put the stock, wine, bay leaf and
peppercorns in a saucepan and bring
just to the boil. Add the prawns and
simmer gently for 10 minutes. Lift
out of the stock and leave to cool.
Lightly crack the claws to allow for

easier removal of the meat. Spoon
the Aioli into small dishes. Place the
shellfish and dishes of Aioli on
plates and garnish with lemon
wedges and parsley sprigs. Serve
with warm French bread and
provide small forks or lobster picks
to remove the meat from the shells,
and finger bowls to clean the hands.

Swiss sole mornay

SERVES 6

6 double lemon sole fillets
1 small onion, sliced
1 small bay leaf
300 ml/½ pt/1¼ cups milk
20 g/¾ oz/3 tbsp plain (all-purpose)
  flour
25 g/1 oz/2 tbsp butter or margarine
A pinch of salt
Freshly ground black pepper
100 g/4 oz button mushrooms, sliced
45 ml/3 tbsp grated Gruyère (Swiss)
  cheese

Roll up the sole fillets and place in a
frying pan (skillet). Add the onion,
bay leaf and all but 45 ml/3 tbsp of
the milk. Cover and cook gently
until tender. Carefully lift out the
fillets and place in six small,
shallow, ovenproof dishes. Discard
the onion and bay leaf from the
cooking liquid. Blend the remaining
milk with the flour and stir into the
liquid. Add half the butter or
margarine. Bring to the boil and
cook for 2 minutes, stirring, until
thickened. Add the salt and pepper
to taste. Melt the remaining butter or
margarine in a saucepan, add the
mushrooms and cook gently,
stirring, for 3 minutes until softened.
Stir into the sauce. Taste and re-
season if necessary. Pour over the
fish, sprinkle with the cheese and
place under a hot grill (broiler) until
golden and bubbling.

Turbot with saffron mayonnaise

SERVES 6

700 g/1½ lb turbot
Juice of ½ lemon
Salt and freshly ground black pepper
Butter or margarine, for greasing
½ cucumber, peeled and finely diced
5 ml/1 tsp chopped parsley
5 ml/1 tsp chopped mint
5 ml/1 tsp chopped thyme
1 shallot, very finely chopped
5 ml/1 tsp white wine vinegar
1.5 ml/¼ tsp saffron powder
15 ml/1 tbsp boiling water
150 ml/¼ pt/⅔ cup mayonnaise
Round lettuce leaves
1 hard-boiled (hard-cooked) egg, finely chopped
50 g/2 oz/1 small can of anchovies, drained and halved lengthways

Put the fish in a shallow dish, sprinkle with the lemon juice and some salt and just cover with cold water. Leave to soak for 30 minutes. Drain and pat dry with kitchen paper (paper towels). Place in a greased ovenproof dish. Cover with foil and bake in a preheated oven at 180°C/350°F/gas mark 4 for 20 minutes. Remove from the oven and leave to cool, then flake with two forks, discarding the skin and any bones.

Meanwhile, mix the cucumber with a little salt and leave to stand for 30 minutes. Rinse, squeeze out the moisture and place the cucumber in a bowl. Stir in the herbs, shallot, wine vinegar and a good grinding of pepper. Mix the saffron with the water and stir into the mayonnaise. Lay the lettuce leaves on six individual plates. Top with the cucumber mixture, then the fish. Spoon the saffron mayonnaise over. Sprinkle each with a little chopped egg, then garnish with the anchovy halves.

Cheese and anchovy cups

SERVES 4

2 slices of bread, cut into small cubes
25 g/1 oz/2 tbsp butter or margarine, plus extra for greasing
15 ml/1 tbsp olive oil
1 small garlic clove, halved
50 g/2 oz/1 small can of anchovy fillets, drained and finely chopped
2 eggs
300 ml/½ pt/1¼ cups milk
Salt and freshly ground black pepper
50 g/2 oz/½ cup Gruyère (Swiss) cheese, grated
Paprika, for dusting

Fry (sauté) the bread in the butter or margarine and oil with the garlic added until golden all over. Drain on kitchen paper (paper towels) and discard the garlic. Grease four ramekins (custard cups). Put some fried bread cubes and anchovy pieces in the base of each. Beat together the eggs and milk and season with salt and pepper. Divide the cheese between the ramekins and pour the egg mixture over. Place the dishes in a baking tin (pan). Add enough boiling water to the pan to come halfway up the sides of the ramekins. Bake in a preheated oven at 190°C/375°F/gas mark 5 for 20 minutes until set and golden. Dust with a little paprika to garnish and serve straight away.

Brill with cucumber and dill

SERVES 6

6 small brill fillets, about 700 g/
1½ lb in all
Finely grated rind and juice of
½ lemon
150 ml/¼ pt/⅔ cup fish stock
Salt and freshly ground black pepper
1 cucumber, peeled and diced
15 ml/1 tbsp chopped dill (dill weed)
15 ml/1 tbsp cornflour (cornstarch)
15 ml/1 tbsp milk
150 ml/¼ pt/⅔ cup buttermilk
30 ml/2 tbsp grated Parmesan cheese
6 dill sprigs, to garnish

Fold the fish into thirds and place in a shallow pan with the lemon rind and juice and the stock. Season lightly. Bring to the boil, reduce the heat, cover and poach gently for about 6 minutes until tender.

Meanwhile, boil the cucumber in lightly salted water for 3 minutes until almost tender. Drain, sprinkle with the dill and keep warm. Lift the fish out of the pan and place in individual warm, shallow, flameproof dishes. Blend the cornflour with the milk and stir into the pan with the buttermilk. Bring to the boil and simmer for 1 minute, stirring. Season to taste. Spoon over the fish and sprinkle with the cheese. Flash under a hot grill (broiler) to brown. Top with the cucumber and garnish each with a sprig of dill.

Brandade

SERVES 4

450 g/1 lb salt cod, soaked and cooked
(page 8)
250 ml/8 fl oz/1 cup olive oil
1 small garlic clove, halved
1 quantity of Béchamel Sauce (page
376), made using 25 g/1 oz/
2 tbsp butter or margarine and
25 g/1 oz/¼ cup flour with the given
quantity of milk
Salt and freshly ground black pepper
Grated nutmeg
8 triangles of fried (sautéed) bread
8 black and 8 green stoned (pitted)
olives

Put the fish in a blender or food processor and run the machine until smooth, stopping and scraping down the sides as necessary. Heat the oil in a saucepan. Add the garlic and fry (sauté) until golden. Remove and discard the garlic. Add half the sauce to the fish and run the machine again. When blended, add 30 ml/ 2 tbsp of the oil and run the machine again until blended. Repeat, blending the sauce and oil until it is all incorporated. Season to taste with salt (if necessary), pepper and the nutmeg. Spoon into a serving dish and arrange the triangles of fried bread around interspersed with the olives.

Salmon antipasto

SERVES 6

170 g/6 oz thinly sliced smoked salmon
1 small honeydew melon, peeled,
seeded and cut into 6 wedges
6 stoned (pitted) black olives, sliced
6 stuffed green olives, sliced

Arrange the salmon slices on small plates with a wedges of melon to one side of each. Scatter the olive slices over and serve chilled.

Seafood gratin

SERVES 4

450 g/1 lb cod fillet, skinned and cut
  into strips
100 g/4 oz cooked peeled prawns
  (shrimp)
295 g/10½ oz/1 small can of clams,
  drained
50 g/2 oz button mushrooms, thinly
  sliced
5 ml/1 tsp lemon juice
Salt and freshly ground black pepper
15 ml/1 tbsp chopped parsley
1 quantity of Béchamel Sauce
  (page 376)
30 ml/2 tbsp freshly grated Parmesan
  cheese

Divide the cod, prawns and clams
between four individual, shallow,
ovenproof dishes. Sprinkle with the
mushrooms, lemon juice, salt,
pepper and the parsley. Spoon the
Béchamel Sauce over and sprinkle
with the cheese. Bake in a preheated
oven at 180°C/350°F/gas mark 4 for
25 minutes until golden brown and
bubbling. Serve hot.

Spicy crab pots

SERVES 4

200 g/7 oz/scant 1 cup medium-fat soft
  cheese
30 ml/2 tbsp crème fraîche
½ small green chilli, seeded and
  chopped, or 1.5 ml/¼ tsp chilli
  powder
15 ml/1 tbsp tomato ketchup (catsup)
170 g/6 oz/1 small can of white
  crabmeat, drained
Lemon juice
Salt and freshly ground black pepper
¼ cucumber, finely chopped
Tortilla chips, to serve

Mash the cheese with the crème
fraîche until smooth. Stir in the chilli
or chilli powder, ketchup and crab
and add lemon juice, salt and
pepper to taste. Spoon into small
pots and chill until ready to serve.
Cover each with a layer of finely
chopped cucumber and serve
surrounded by tortilla chips.

Nutty cheese, anchovy and olive roll

SERVES 6

225 g/8 oz/2 cups Cheddar cheese,
  grated
25 g/1 oz stuffed olives, chopped
3 hard-boiled (hard-cooked) eggs,
  chopped
4 anchovy fillets, drained and chopped
2.5 ml/½ tsp Dijon mustard
30 ml/2 tbsp single (light) cream
30 ml/2 tbsp mayonnaise
30 ml/2 tbsp snipped chives
Salt and freshly ground black pepper
45 ml/3 tbsp chopped mixed nuts,
  toasted
Lettuce leaves
Tomato wedges and cucumber slices,
  to garnish
Crackers or crisp toast, to serve

Mix together all the ingredients
except the nuts and lettuce in a bowl
until well blended. Shape into a roll
on a sheet of greaseproof (waxed)
paper, roll up firmly and chill for
2 hours. Unwrap and roll in the
nuts. Cut into slices and arrange on
lettuce leaves. Garnish with tomato
wedges and cucumber slices before
serving with crackers or crisp toast.

Crab and avocado cocktail

SERVES 4

1 large ripe avocado, peeled and
stoned (pitted)
Lemon juice
170 g/6 oz/1 small can of white
crabmeat, drained
45 ml/3 tbsp mayonnaise
10 ml/2 tsp Worcestershire sauce
15 ml/1 tbsp tomato purée (paste)
30 ml/2 tbsp single (light) cream
Salt and freshly ground black pepper
Shredded lettuce
Paprika, for dusting
4 lemon slices

Dice the avocado and toss in lemon
juice to prevent browning. Add the
crab and toss gently. Blend the
mayonnaise with the Worcestershire
sauce, tomato purée, cream and a
little salt and pepper until smooth.
Place some shredded lettuce in four
wine goblets and top with the crab
and avocado mixture. Spoon the
dressing over and dust each with a
little paprika. Place a lemon slice on
the side of each glass and chill, if
time, before serving.

Cottage avocado with prawns

SERVES 4

2 ripe avocados, halved and stoned
(pitted)
Lemon juice
225 g/8 oz/1 cup cottage cheese with
prawns (shrimp)
20 ml/4 tsp tomato chutney
15 ml/1 tbsp chopped parsley
4 lemon wedges
Prawn crackers, to serve

Place the avocado halves in avocado
dishes or small bowls and brush
with lemon juice to prevent
browning. Spoon the cheese into
the cavities and top each with
5 ml/1 tsp of the tomato chutney.
Sprinkle with the parsley. Add a
wedge of lemon to the side of each
and serve with a dish of prawn
crackers

Cheesy salmon avocado

SERVES 4

Prepare as for Cottage Avocado with
Prawns, but substitute cottage
cheese with salmon for the cottage
cheese with prawns (shrimp). Top
with cucumber relish and serve with
spicy tortilla chips.

Avocado, tuna and pepper salad

SERVES 6

2 ripe avocados, peeled and stoned
(pitted)
185 g/6½ oz/1 small can of tuna,
drained and roughly flaked
1 red (bell) pepper, cut into rings
1 yellow pepper, cut into rings
1 green pepper, cut into rings
1 small onion, sliced and separated
into rings
45 ml/3 tbsp olive oil
15 ml/1 tbsp white wine vinegar
Salt and freshly ground black pepper
15 ml/1 tbsp chopped parsley
6 black olives
Hot ciabatta bread

Slice the avocados and place in a
bowl with the tuna, peppers and
onion. Whisk the oil and vinegar
with a little salt and pepper and
pour over. Toss gently. Spoon on to
small plates and sprinkle with the
parsley. Garnish each with an olive
before serving with hot ciabatta
bread.

Prawn pâté

SERVES 4

2 slices of white bread, crusts removed
100 g/4 oz cooked peeled prawns
  (shrimp)
150 ml/¼ pt/⅔ cup sunflower oil
10 ml/2 tsp anchovy essence (extract)
Lemon juice
Salt and freshly ground black pepper
15 ml/1 tbsp chopped parsley
Lemon wedges, to garnish
Warm pitta breads, to serve

Soak the bread in water for
1 minute. Squeeze out and place in a
blender or food processor. Add the
prawns and run the machine until
smooth. With the machine still
running, add the oil in a thin trickle,
stopping and scraping down the
sides from time to time, until a thick,
smooth paste is formed. Add the
anchovy essence and lemon juice to
taste. Season lightly. Spoon on to
plates, sprinkle with chopped parsley
and garnish with lemon wedges.
Serve with warm pitta breads.

French-style mushrooms with eggs

SERVES 4

1 onion, chopped
15 g/½ oz/1 tbsp butter or margarine
225 g/8 oz button mushrooms, sliced
1 garlic clove, crushed
150 ml/¼ pt/⅔ cup chicken stock
185 g/6½ oz/1 small can of tuna,
  drained
10 ml/2 tsp chopped tarragon
15 ml/1 tbsp chopped parsley
Salt and freshly ground black pepper
4 eggs
45 ml/3 tbsp single (light) cream
French bread, to serve

Fry (sauté) the onion in the butter or
margarine for 3 minutes in a large
frying pan (skillet) until soft but not
brown. Add the mushrooms, garlic
and stock. Bring to the boil and
simmer gently for 10 minutes. Stir in
the tuna, herbs and a little salt and
pepper. Make four 'wells' in the
mushroom mixture and break an egg
into each. Drizzle the cream over.
Cover with foil or a lid and cook for
5–10 minutes or until the eggs are
cooked to your liking. Serve straight
from the pan with lots of crusty
French bread.

Potted garlic mushrooms with prawns

SERVES 4

100 g/4 oz/½ cup butter
1 onion, chopped
450 g/1 lb open mushrooms, peeled
  and sliced
15 ml/1 tbsp chopped parsley
1 large garlic clove, crushed
Salt and freshly ground black pepper
100 g/4 oz cooked peeled prawns
  (shrimp)

Melt half the butter in a saucepan.
Add the onion and fry (sauté) for
2 minutes, stirring. Stir in the
mushrooms, parsley and garlic and
season lightly. Cover and cook gently
for 10 minutes, stirring occasionally,
until the mushrooms are really
tender and the juices have run. Turn
into a blender or food processor and
run the machine briefly to finely
chop the mushrooms and onion. Do
not purée. Taste and re-season if
necessary. Turn into four ramekins
(custard cups) and level the surfaces.
Leave to cool, then chill until firm.
Arrange a layer of prawns over the
top of the mushrooms. Melt the
remaining butter and pour over the
mushroom mixture. Chill until the
butter is firm.

Smoked haddock and quail's egg salad

SERVES 6

350 g/12 oz smoked haddock fillet
12 quail's eggs
100 g/4 oz smoked lardons (finely
  diced bacon)
100 g/4 oz baby asparagus spears
100 g/4 oz baby spinach leaves
50 g/2 oz rocket leaves
2 spring onions (scallions), finely
  chopped
For the dressing:
60 ml/4 tbsp olive oil
10 ml/2 tsp balsamic vinegar
30 ml/2 tbsp lemon juice
5 ml/1 tsp Dijon mustard
5 ml/1 tsp caster (superfine) sugar
75 ml/5 tbsp single (light) cream
Salt and freshly ground black pepper

Put the fish in a frying pan (skillet)
with just enough water to cover.
Bring to the boil, cover, reduce the
heat and simmer gently for about
5 minutes or until it flakes easily
with a fork. Leave to cool in the
cooking liquid. Put the eggs in a
saucepan and cover with cold water.
Bring to the boil and cook for
3 minutes. Drain, cover with cold
water and leave to cool. Dry-fry the
lardons until crisp and golden, then
drain on kitchen paper (paper
towels) and leave to cool. Cook the
asparagus in a little lightly salted,
boiling water for 3 minutes until just
tender but still with a little 'bite'.
Drain, rinse with cold water and
drain again.

Mix together the spinach and
rocket leaves and place in six
shallow serving dishes or plates.
Drain the fish and pat dry on
kitchen paper. Remove the skin and
break the flesh into small pieces,
discarding any bones. Scatter over
the leaves. Shell and halve the eggs
and arrange four halves, cut-side up,
on each portion. Sprinkle the
lardons and spring onions on the
salads and arrange the asparagus
attractively round the edge.

To make the dressing, whisk
together all the ingredients,
seasoning to taste with salt and
pepper. Spoon over the salads and
serve.

Egg and smoked salmon mayonnaise

SERVES 6

6 hard-boiled (hard-cooked) eggs,
  halved
100 g/4 oz thinly sliced smoked
  salmon
90 ml/6 tbsp mayonnaise
Freshly ground black pepper
30 ml/2 tbsp milk
1 box of salad cress
Paprika, for dusting

Scoop the yolks from the eggs into a
bowl and mash with a fork. Finely
chop half the salmon and stir into
the yolks with 15 ml/1 tbsp of the
mayonnaise. Season with pepper
and pile back into the whites.
Sandwich back together again in
pairs. Mix the remaining mayonnaise
with the milk to give a thick, coating
consistency. Use the cress to line six
small serving plates. Put a stuffed
whole egg on each plate and spoon
the mayonnaise over. Cut the
remaining salmon into strips and
pile on top. Dust with paprika and
serve.

Baked quail's eggs with tuna

SERVES 6

15 g/½ oz/1 tbsp butter or margarine
185 g/6½ oz/1 small can of tuna,
  drained
30 ml/2 tbsp chopped parsley
12 quail's eggs
Salt and freshly ground black pepper
90 ml/6 tbsp single (light) cream
Parsley sprigs, to garnish

Grease six ramekins (custard cups) with the butter or margarine. Flake the tuna and divide it between the dishes. Sprinkle with the chopped parsley. Break two quail's eggs into each dish. Season with salt and pepper and top each with 15 ml/ 1 tbsp of the cream. Bake in a preheated oven at 180°C/350°F/gas mark 4 for about 5 minutes or until cooked to your liking. Garnish with parsley sprigs and serve hot.

Buckling pâté

SERVES 4

1 good-sized buckling
100 g/4 oz/½ cup unsalted (sweet)
  butter
30 ml/2 tbsp chopped parsley
15 ml/1 tbsp horseradish relish
5 ml/1 tsp balsamic vinegar
10 ml/2 tsp lemon juice
Freshly ground black pepper
4 large lettuce leaves
Lemon wedges, to garnish
Wholemeal toast, to serve

Put the buckling in a shallow dish. Pour boiling water over and leave to stand for 2 minutes. Drain and pat dry with kitchen paper (paper towels). Pull off the skin and remove the flesh from the bones. Flake with a fork into a large bowl. Beat in the butter, parsley, horseradish, vinegar and lemon juice. Season to taste with pepper. Arrange the lettuce leaves on four plates and pile the fish mixture on top. Garnish with lemon wedges and serve with wholemeal toast.

Crunchy scallops

SERVES 4

8 large shelled scallops
Salt and freshly ground black pepper
15 ml/1 tbsp lemon juice
45 ml/3 tbsp cornflour (cornstarch)
2 eggs, beaten
100 g/4 oz/2 cups fresh white
  breadcrumbs
30 ml/2 tbsp sunflower oil
25 g/1 oz/2 tbsp butter or margarine
Lemon wedges and parsley sprigs, to
  garnish

Rinse the scallops and pat dry with kitchen paper (paper towels). Cut into quarters and season with salt and pepper. Sprinkle with the lemon juice and toss well. Coat in the cornflour, then dip in the egg, then the breadcrumbs. Coat again in the egg and breadcrumbs, then chill for at least 30 minutes. Heat the oil and butter or margarine in a large frying pan (skillet) and fry (sauté) the scallops for about 2 minutes, tossing, until golden brown. Drain on kitchen paper and serve hot, garnished with lemon wedges and parsley sprigs.

Pan-fried oysters

SERVES 4

24 small oysters, shucked (page 13)
2 small eggs, beaten
30 ml/2 tbsp crème fraîche
Salt and freshly ground black pepper
A few drops of Tabasco sauce
100 g/4 oz/2 cups fresh white
  breadcrumbs
75 g/3 oz/⅓ cup unsalted (sweet) butter
45 ml/3 tbsp olive oil
Lemon wedges and parsley sprigs, to
  garnish

Pat the oysters dry with kitchen paper (paper towels). Beat the eggs with the crème fraîche and season with salt, pepper and the Tabasco sauce. Coat the oysters in the egg mixture, then the breadcrumbs. Repeat the coating, then chill for 20 minutes. Heat the butter and oil in a large frying pan (skillet) or wok. Add the oysters and fry (sauté) for 3–4 minutes, turning occasionally, until crisp and golden. Drain on kitchen paper and serve hot, garnished with lemon wedges and parsley sprigs.

Spicy prawns in crème fraîche

SERVES 4

50 g/2 oz/¼ cup butter or margarine
350 g/12 oz cooked peeled prawns
  (shrimp)
5 ml/1 tsp lemon juice
1 green chilli, seeded and finely
  chopped
5 ml/1 tsp garam masala
60 ml/4 tbsp crème fraîche
2 egg yolks
Salt and freshly ground black pepper
4 small naan breads with garlic and
  coriander (cilantro)
15 ml/1 tbsp chopped coriander

Heat the butter or margarine gently in a large frying pan (skillet). Add the prawns, lemon juice, chilli and garam masala and heat through, tossing gently, for 2–3 minutes. Beat together the crème fraîche and egg yolks and stir into the pan. Heat very gently, stirring, until thickened. Do not allow to boil. Season to taste. Meanwhile, warm the naan breads under the grill (broiler) or in the microwave. Place on warm plates and top with the prawns. Garnish with the coriander and serve.

Crab tartare

SERVES 4

1 quantity of Caper Sauce (page 377)
3 gherkins (cornichons), finely
  chopped
30 ml/2 tbsp double (heavy) cream
350 g/12 oz cooked crabmeat
Salt and freshly ground black pepper
30 ml/2 tbsp fresh white breadcrumbs
25 g/1 oz/2 tbsp butter or margarine,
  melted
Parsley sprigs, to garnish

Make the Caper Sauce, then stir in the gherkins, cream and crabmeat and season to taste. Heat through. Spoon into individual flameproof dishes. Mix the breadcrumbs with the butter or margarine and scatter over. Place under a hot grill (broiler) for about 3–4 minutes until golden brown and bubbling. Serve hot, garnished with parsley sprigs.

Thai king prawns in rice noodles

SERVES 6

200 g/7 oz rice noodles
18 raw peeled tiger prawns (jumbo
*   shrimp), tails left on*
Salt and freshly ground black pepper
4 egg whites, lightly beaten
Oil, for deep-frying
Thai Chilli Ginger Sauce (page 382),
*   to serve*

Soak the noodles according to the packet directions. Drain and squeeze out as much moisture as possible and place in a shallow bowl. Season the prawns lightly with salt and pepper. Dip them in the egg whites, drain off the excess, then coat in the rice noodles. Deep-fry in hot oil for about 2 minutes until crisp and golden. Drain on kitchen paper (paper towels) and serve straight away with Thai Chilli Ginger Sauce for dipping.

Sashimi

SERVES 4–6

This Japanese raw fish speciality must be made with the freshest fish.

1 bunch of spring onions (scallions)
1 carrot, cut into thin ribbons with a
*   potato peeler*
1 white salsify or winter white radish,
*   cut into thin shreds*
450 g/1 lb mixed fresh fish such as
*   trout, bass and monkfish*
225 g/8 oz shelled scallops
30 ml/2 tbsp grated fresh root ginger
225 g/8 oz raw peeled tiger prawns
*   (jumbo shrimp), tails left on*
Light soy sauce (preferably Japanese)
Lemon slices

Trim the spring onions to 7.5 cm/ 3 in from the white ends. Make several 2.5 cm/1 in cross cuts in the white bulbs of the onions and place in a bowl of iced water to open. Put the carrot and salsify in separate bowls of iced water to crisp and curl. Slice all the fish fillets very thinly using a large, very sharp knife. Slice the scallops thinly. Squeeze the ginger into a ball. Arrange the fish attractively on a large, preferably black lacquered, platter with the ball of ginger and piles of the drained, crisp vegetables. Pour soy sauce into small individual bowls and serve with the fish and the lemon wedges. Guests add ginger to the soy sauce to taste and dip in the raw fish and vegetables.

Western-cooked sashimi

SERVES 4–6

Prepare exactly as for Sashimi, but poach the thin fish pieces and scallops in hot fish stock for 30 seconds or until just turning opaque and the prawns (shrimp) for 1–2 minutes until just pink before arranging on the platter. Leave everything until cold before serving.

Italian aubergines

SERVES 4

1 aubergine (eggplant), sliced
Olive oil, for shallow frying
Salt and freshly ground black pepper
120 ml/4 fl oz/½ cup passata (sieved
  tomatoes)
5 ml/1 tsp dried basil
100 g/4 oz/1 cup Mozzarella cheese,
  grated
50 g/2 oz/1 small can of anchovies,
  drained

Fry (sauté) the aubergine slices in
hot oil until golden on both sides.
Drain on kitchen paper (paper
towels), then arrange in four
individual gratin dishes. Sprinkle
with salt and pepper. Spoon the
passata over and sprinkle with the
basil. Top with the Mozzarella, then
the anchovies in a lattice pattern.
Grill (boil) until the cheese is melted
and bubbling. Serve straight away.

Sea urchins au naturel

SERVES 4

If you are lucky enough to come
across these, this is the gourmet's
way to enjoy them – raw!

4 or 8 black or green sea urchins
2 lemons, halved
Freshly ground black pepper
Fresh crusty bread

With a thickly gloved hands, use a
heavy, sharp knife (unless you have
a coupe-oursin – a special tool to do
the job) to cut the urchins in half.
Lay the halves on serving plates,
each with half a lemon. Squeeze the
lemon over, sprinkle with pepper
and scoop out the pink or orange
roes with a hunk of bread.

Grilled sea urchin and crab diamonds

SERVES 4

You may come across canned urchin
roes in a speciality food shop. If not,
you'll have to find fresh ones and
scoop out the roes yourself.

1 egg, separated
170 g/6 oz/1 small can of white
  crabmeat, drained
5 ml/1 tsp dry sherry
5 ml/1 tsp anchovy essence (extract)
Salt and freshly ground black pepper
Oil, for greasing
4 black or green sea urchins, halved
  and the roes removed (see Sea
  Urchins au Naturel, left)
15 ml/1 tbsp poppy seeds
15 ml/1 tbsp sesame seeds
Spring onion (scallion) flowers (see
  Sashimi, page 106)
150 ml/¼ pt/⅔ cup light soy sauce
5 ml/1 tsp grated fresh root ginger
1 small garlic clove, crushed

Lightly beat the egg white and mix
with the crabmeat, sherry, anchovy
essence and a little salt and pepper.
Turn into a well-oiled, small,
shallow, square baking tin (pan).
Mash the sea urchin roes and spread
over. Brush with the egg yolk several
times to give a thick coating. Place
in the grill (broiler) pan (not on the
rack) and grill (broil) for about
5 minutes until set and glazed.
Sprinkle with the poppy and sesame
seeds and grill again for 1 minute
until golden. Leave to cool, then
chill. Cut into small diamond shapes
and triangles. Arrange attractively on
four plain plates and garnish with
spring onion flowers. Mix the soy
sauce with the ginger and garlic. Tip
into small bowls and serve as a dip
with the grilled urchin.

Sandwiches and other snacks

Canned fish, frozen fish, pickled fish and cooked leftover fish all make quick, tasty bites for either lunchtime or in the evening. Some of the recipes in this chapter are very simple, others smart enough to impress your friends. All are nutritious and tasty and all can be prepared with very little effort. Most of the ideas have a starchy food included such as bread in one form or another, potatoes or crackers; a few are speedy, throw-together grills or oven bakes that would benefit from just a hunk of bread to accompany them.

\

Hot mushroom and anchovy rolls

SERVES 4

These are also good cut into slices (pinwheels) before baking to serve as an appetiser with drinks.

8 slices of bread, crusts removed
Butter or margarine, for spreading
170 g/6 oz/1 small can of creamed mushrooms
50 g/2 oz/1 small can of anchovy fillets, drained
5 ml/1 tsp dried oregano
Carrot, celery and cucumber, cut into matchsticks, to serve

Spread the bread on one side only with butter or margarine. Place, buttered-sides down, on a baking (cookie) sheet and spread with the mushrooms. Lay an anchovy fillet on each and sprinkle with the oregano. Roll up, making sure the sealed edge is underneath. Bake in a preheated oven at 190°C/375°F/gas mark 5 for about 10 minutes or until crisp and golden. Serve hot with carrot, celery and cucumber sticks.

Italian snackwiches

SERVES 4

4 canned anchovy fillets
45 ml/3 tbsp milk
1 garlic clove, halved
15 ml/1 tbsp pine nuts
5 ml/1 tsp lemon juice
45 ml/3 tbsp olive oil
4 thick slices of ciabatta bread, cut diagonally
4 ripe tomatoes, sliced
Freshly ground black pepper
8 basil leaves, torn

Soak the anchovies in the milk for 15 minutes. Drain. With the machine running, drop them in a blender or food processor with the garlic, pine nuts and lemon juice, stopping and scraping down the sides as necessary. Run the machine again and trickle in 30 ml/2 tbsp of the olive oil to form a paste. Brush one side of the bread slices with the remaining oil. Grill (broil) until toasted on that side. Turn the bread over and spread with the paste. Top with the tomatoes and a good grinding of pepper. Grill again until the tomatoes are soft and the paste is bubbling. Scatter the basil over and serve.

Hot salmon special

SERVES 2–4

200 g/7 oz/1 small can of pink or red salmon
30 ml/2 tbsp mayonnaise
10 ml/2 tsp capers, chopped
2.5 cm/1 in piece of cucumber, chopped
4 slices of wholemeal bread
Butter or margarine, for spreading
50 g/2 oz/½ cup Mozzarella cheese, grated
Freshly ground black pepper

Drain the fish, discarding any skin, and mash well. Remove the bones if you like but they are very good for you. Mix in the mayonnaise, capers and cucumber. Toast the bread on both sides. Leave on the grill (broiler) rack and spread one side with butter or margarine, then top with the salmon mixture. Sprinkle the cheese over and add a good grinding of pepper. Grill (broil) under a moderate heat until the cheese melts and bubbles. Serve straight away.

Egg, smoked salmon and mushroom milk toasts

SERVES 4

4 large flat mushrooms
50 g/2 oz/¼ cup butter or margarine,
  plus extra for spreading
1 garlic clove, chopped
Salt and freshly ground black pepper
4 small eggs
10 ml/2 tsp lemon juice
4 round slices of milk bread
4 small or 2 large thin slices of smoked
  salmon
Chopped parsley, to garnish

Peel the mushrooms and discard the
stalks. Melt the butter or margarine
in a frying pan (skillet), add the
mushrooms, sprinkle with the garlic
and season lightly. Fry (sauté) for
2 minutes, then cover with a lid,
reduce the heat and cook for about
5 minutes until just tender.
Meanwhile, poach the eggs in gently
simmering water to which the lemon
juice has been added. Toast the
bread and spread with a little butter
or margarine. Place on individual
plates and top each with a small
whole slice or half a large slice of
smoked salmon. Top with a
mushroom, then a poached egg and
sprinkle with chopped parsley.

Tuna crunchy corn pittas

SERVES 4

85 g/3½ oz/1 very small can of tuna,
  drained
200 g/7 oz/1 small can of sweetcorn
  (corn), drained
1 celery stick, finely chopped
15 ml/1 tbsp toasted pine nuts
30 ml/2 tbsp tomato relish
4–6 pitta breads

Mix together the tuna, sweetcorn,
celery, pine nuts and tomato relish.
Warm the pittas under the grill
(broiler) or briefly in the microwave
until they start to puff up. Halve
widthways, gently open to form
pockets and spoon in the filling.

Greek pittas

SERVES 4

4 pitta breads
225 g/8 oz taramasalata (page 95 or
  use bought)
Shredded lettuce
15 ml/1 tbsp sliced stoned (pitted)
  black olives
½ lemon
Freshly ground black pepper
15 ml/1 tbsp olive oil

Warm the pitta breads under the
grill (broiler) or briefly in the
microwave. Halve widthways and
gently open to form pockets. Fill
with the taramasalata, some
shredded lettuce and the olives. Add
a squeeze of lemon, a good grinding
of pepper and a dash of olive oil to
each and serve.

Sautéed bacon, tomato, mussel and lettuce sandwiches

SERVES 4

4 smoked back bacon rashers (slices), rinded
2 tomatoes, sliced
250 g/9 oz/1 medium can of mussels in brine
8 slices of wholemeal bread
45 ml/3 tbsp mayonnaise
Shredded lettuce
Freshly ground black pepper

Grill (broil) the bacon for 2 minutes. Add the tomato slices and cook for a further 1–2 minutes until the bacon is golden and the tomato slices are hot through. Meanwhile, heat the mussels in a saucepan and drain thoroughly. Spread the bread with the mayonnaise and cover four slices with a little shredded lettuce. Top with a bacon rasher, the slices of tomato and the mussels. Add a good grinding of pepper and top with the other slices of bread. Cut into halves and serve.

Egg, cress and prawn sandwiches

SERVES 4

2 hard-boiled (hard-cooked) eggs, chopped
15 ml/1 tbsp mayonnaise
75 g/3 oz cooked peeled prawns (shrimp)
Freshly ground black pepper
8 slices of granary bread
Butter or margarine, for spreading
½ box of salad cress

Mash the eggs with the mayonnaise. Fold in the prawns and some pepper. Spread the bread with the butter or margarine. Spread half the slices with the egg mixture, top with the cress, then the other slices. Cut into halves and serve.

Salmon tartare sandwiches

SERVES 4

75 g/3 oz/⅓ cup butter or margarine
100 g/4 oz/1 very small can of pink salmon, drained and skin removed
30 ml/2 tbsp tartare sauce (page 372, or use bought)
Salt and freshly ground black pepper
8 slices of wholemeal bread

Mash the butter or margarine with a fork. Mash in the fish (discarding the bones, if preferred, but they are very good for you). Work in the tartare sauce and a little salt and pepper. Spread over the slices of bread and sandwich together in pairs. Cut into triangles and serve.

Smoked salmon and soft cheese sandwiches

SERVES 4

100 g/4 oz/½ cup medium-fat soft cheese
8 slices of brown bread
4 small slices of smoked salmon
Freshly ground black pepper
A little lemon juice

Spread the cheese on the bread. Top four slices with the salmon slices, season with pepper and add a sprinkling of lemon juice. Cover with the remaining bread and cut off the crusts, if preferred. Cut into triangles and serve.

Smoked mackerel, orange and fromage frais deckers

SERVES 4

1 smoked mackerel fillet, skinned
60 ml/4 tbsp fromage frais
Freshly ground black pepper
300 g/11 oz/1 medium can of
   mandarin oranges, drained
8 slices of granary bread
Butter or margarine, for spreading
30 ml/2 tbsp salad cress

Mash the mackerel, discarding any bones. Work in the fromage frais and season with pepper. Drain the oranges thoroughly on kitchen paper (paper towels). Spread the bread with a little butter or margarine. Top four slices with the mackerel mixture, then the mandarins, then a sprinkling of cress. Cover with the remaining bread, cut into quarters and serve.

Smoked salmon, cucumber and soft cheese bagels

SERVES 2 OR 4

2 slices of smoked salmon
2 bagels, split in half
30 ml/2 tbsp medium-fat soft cheese
Cucumber slices
A little lemon juice
Freshly ground black pepper
4 small parsley sprigs

Halve the slices of salmon, then halve again and roll up. Spread the bagels with the cheese and top each with cucumber slices, then two salmon rolls. Sprinkle with lemon juice and add a good grinding of pepper. Garnish each with a sprig of parsley and serve.

Mozzarella, tomato and anchovy bagels

SERVES 4

30 ml/2 tbsp tomato purée (paste)
5 ml/1 tsp water
2 bagels, split in half and lightly
   toasted
50 g/2 oz/½ cup Mozzarella cheese,
   grated
4 cherry tomatoes, sliced
50 g/2 oz/1 small can of anchovies,
   drained
5 ml/1 tsp dried oregano

Blend the tomato purée with the water and spread over the cut surfaces of the bagels. Place on the grill (broiler) rack and sprinkle the cheese over. Arrange the tomato slices on top, then lay the anchovies in a criss-cross pattern over. Sprinkle with the oregano. Grill (broil) until the cheese melts and bubbles and serve straight away.

Smoked mackerel and soft cheese bagels

SERVES 2 OR 4

2 smoked mackerel fillets
2 bagels, split in half
30 ml/2 tbsp medium-fat soft cheese
10 ml/2 tsp horseradish relish
A little lemon juice
Freshly ground black pepper
½ box of salad cress

Cut the mackerel into small pieces, discarding the skin, if preferred. Spread the bagels with the cheese and top with a thin spreading of horseradish relish, then the mackerel. Sprinkle with lemon juice and add a good grinding of pepper. Top with salad cress and serve.

Smoked oyster cottage pittas

SERVES 4

25 g/1 oz/2 tbsp butter or margarine
1 small onion, finely chopped
100 g/4 oz/1 small can of smoked
*   oysters*
225 g/8 oz/1 cup cottage cheese with
*   chives*
2 tomatoes, finely chopped
Salt and freshly ground black pepper
4 pitta breads
Shredded lettuce

Melt the butter or margarine in a pan and add the onion. Fry (sauté), stirring, for 3 minutes. Stir in the oysters, cheese and tomatoes and season to taste. Heat through gently. Meanwhile, warm the pittas under the grill (broiler) or briefly in the microwave. Halve widthways and gently open to form pockets. Spoon in the warm cheese mixture, add some shredded lettuce and serve straight away.

Nutty smoked mussel cottage pittas

SERVES 4

Prepare as for Smoked Oyster Cottage Pittas, but substitute smoked mussels for the oysters and add 15 ml/1 tbsp toasted pine nuts.

Spicy sardine and bean pittas

SERVES 4

120 g/4½ oz/1 small can of sardines in
*   tomato sauce*
1 small garlic clove, crushed
1 small red chilli, seeded and finely
*   chopped, or 1.5 ml/¼ tsp chilli powder*
225 g/8 oz/1 small can of butter
*   (lima) beans, drained and mashed*
Salt and freshly ground black pepper
Shredded lettuce
Cucumber slices
4 wholemeal pitta breads

Mash the sardines, preferably including the bones. Add the garlic, chilli and mashed beans and season to taste. Warm the pittas under the grill (broiler) or briefly in the microwave. Halve widthways and gently open to form pockets. Spoon in the sardine mixture, add some shredded lettuce and cucumber slices and serve.

Smoked salmon with scrambled egg

SERVES 4

8 eggs
30 ml/2 tbsp milk
A good knob of butter or margarine
100 g/4 oz smoked salmon trimmings
4 large slices of wholemeal toast
Parsley sprigs, to garnish

Beat the eggs in a pan with the milk. Add the butter or margarine and a very little salt and lots of pepper. Cook, stirring gently, over a very low heat until the egg scrambles but is still creamy. Break up the salmon and stir with the eggs just long enough to heat through. Pile on to the toast, garnish with parsley sprigs and serve hot.

Kippers with scrambled egg

SERVES 4

Prepare as for Smoked Salmon with Scrambled Egg (page 113), but use two boil-in-the-bag kippers instead of the salmon. Cook the kippers as directed on the packet, drain and cut into pieces. Add to the scrambled egg when cooked but still creamy and serve straight away.

Toasted baked bean, tuna and cheese sandwiches

SERVES 4

8 slices of bread, buttered
20 ml/4 tsp brown table sauce
85 g/3½ oz/1 very small can of tuna, drained and flaked
50 g/2 oz/½ cup Cheddar cheese, grated

Lay four slices of the bread buttered-side down on a board. Spread lightly with the brown sauce. Divide the beans between the sandwiches and spread out all round but not too near the edges. Top with the tuna and sprinkle the cheese over. Top with the remaining bread slices, buttered-sides up. Cook in a sandwich toaster or place on a grill (broiler) rack with a cooling rack pressed firmly over the top and grill (broil) until the tops are golden brown. With oven-gloved hands, invert the grill rack so the cooling rack is under the sandwiches and return to the grill to toast the other sides. Alternatively, fry (sauté) in a frying pan (skillet), pressing down firmly from time to time with a fish slice, until the base is golden, then carefully turn over and brown the other sides.

Aberdeen toasties

SERVES 4

This is also good made with plain haddock. For a non-fluffy version, simply beat the whole egg and stir into the sauce with the cheese and seasoning.

175 g/6 oz smoked haddock fillet, skinned
175 ml/6 fl oz/¾ cup milk
15 g/½ oz/2 tbsp plain (all-purpose) flour
25 g/1 oz/¼ cup strong hard cheese, grated
1 egg, separated
Salt and freshly ground black pepper
4 slices of toast, buttered

Put the haddock and 150 ml/¼ pt/ ⅔ cup of the milk in a saucepan. Bring to the boil, reduce the heat, cover and cook for about 5 minutes or until it flakes easily with a fork. Lift out the fish and flake. Blend the flour with the remaining milk and stir into the milk in the saucepan. Bring to the boil and cook for 2 minutes, stirring, until thick. Stir in the cheese, the egg yolk, fish and salt and pepper to taste and heat through. Whisk the egg white until stiff and fold in with a metal spoon. Put the toast on the grill (broiler) rack, spoon the fish mixture on top and grill (broil) until lightly browned. Serve straight away.

Toasted tuna, cranberry and mayo sandwiches

SERVES 4

8 slices of granary bread, buttered
185 g/6½ oz/1 small can of tuna,
  drained and flaked
15 ml/1 tbsp cranberry sauce
30 ml/2 tbsp mayonnaise
Salt and freshly ground black pepper

Lay four of the slices of bread buttered-side down on a board. Mix the tuna, cranberry sauce and mayonnaise with a little salt and pepper and spread over the bread. Top with the remaining slices, buttered-sides up. Cook as for Toasted Baked Bean, Tuna and Cheese Sandwiches (page 114).

Barking mad hot dogs

SERVES 4

25 g/1 oz/2 tbsp butter or margarine
1 large onion, chopped
50 g/2 oz/1 small can of anchovy
  fillets, drained and chopped
8 hot dog sausages, canned or from a
  packet
8 finger rolls, warmed
45 ml/3 tbsp mild chilli relish

Melt the butter or margarine in a small saucepan. Add the onion and fry (sauté) for 2 minutes, stirring. Add the anchovies. Cover and cook gently for 5 minutes or until the onions are tender. Remove the lid and cook, stirring, until the anchovies have formed a paste. Meanwhile, heat the hot dogs according to the instructions. Split the rolls and spread one cut surface with the chilli relish. Spoon in the onion and anchovy mixture, add a hot dog to each and serve straight away.

Toasted curried tuna sandwiches

SERVES 4

8 slices of wholemeal bread, buttered
20 ml/4 tsp mango or peach chutney
185 g/6½ oz/1 small can of tuna,
  drained and flaked
45 ml/3 tbsp mayonnaise
5–10 ml/1–2 tsp curry paste
Salt and freshly ground black pepper

Lay four slices of bread buttered-side down on a board. Spread with the chutney. Mix the tuna with the mayonnaise and curry paste to taste. Season lightly. Spread over the bread, not quite to the edges. Top with the remaining slices, buttered-side up. Cook as for Toasted Baked Bean, Tuna and Cheese Sandwiches (page 114).

Cheese, pineapple and sild toasts

SERVES 4

Sild are very small sardines.

4 slices of bread
Butter or margarine, for spreading
225 g/8 oz/1 small can of pineapple
  pieces, drained and finely chopped
4 slices of Leerdammer or Gruyère
  (Swiss) cheese
120 g/4½ oz/1 small can of sild,
  drained
1 tomato, cut into 4 slices
Dried basil

Toast the bread on both sides and spread lightly with butter or margarine. Top each with a layer of pineapple, then a slice of cheese, then the sild. Top with a slice of tomato and sprinkle with a pinch of basil. Grill (broil) until the cheese melts and serve straight away.

Neapolitan pizza rolls

SERVES 4

4 soft rolls
225 g/8 oz/1 small can of chopped
tomatoes, drained thoroughly
5 ml/1 tsp dried basil
50 g/2 oz/1 small can of anchovy
fillets, rolled up
100 g/4 oz/1 cup Mozzarella or
Cheddar cheese, grated

Cut a shallow 'lid' off the top of
each roll, not quite removing the
slice. Pull out the soft centre, leaving
a thick wall. Spoon in the tomatoes
and sprinkle with the basil. Add the
anchovies and cheese. Wrap each
roll in foil and steam in a steamer or
colander, covered with a lid, over a
pan of simmering water for
10 minutes until the cheese is
melted. Alternatively, place in the
oven at 220°C/425°F/gas mark 7 for
10 minutes. They may also be
heated in the microwave, unwrapped
and placed in a microwave-safe dish
with a lid; microwave for 2 minutes,
rearrange and cook a little longer,
depending on the output of your
microwave. Do not overcook or they
will be tough.

Prawn pizza rolls

SERVES 4

Prepare exactly as for Neapolitan
Pizza Rolls, but substitute 50 g/2 oz
cooked peeled prawns (shrimp) for
the anchovies and use dried oregano
instead of basil.

Tuna mornay

SERVES 2–4

2 onions, thinly sliced
40 g/1½ oz/3 tbsp butter or margarine
20 g/¾ oz/3 tbsp plain (all-purpose)
flour
300 ml/½ pt/1¼ cups milk
50 g/2 oz/½ cup Cheddar cheese, grated
Salt and freshly ground black pepper
185 g/6½ oz/1 small can of tuna,
drained and flaked
Hot toast, to serve

Fry (sauté) the onions in the butter
or margarine for 3 minutes, stirring,
until softened. Stir in the flour and
cook for 1 minute. Remove from the
heat and blend in the milk. Return
to the heat, bring to the boil and
cook for 2 minutes, stirring. Stir in
half the cheese and season to taste.
Place the tuna in a shallow
ovenproof dish. Pour the sauce over
and sprinkle with the remaining
cheese. Place under a moderate
preheated grill (broiler) for about
6 minutes until golden, bubbling and
hot through. Serve with hot toast.

Tuna and egg mornay

SERVES 2–4

Prepare as for Tuna Mornay, but
arrange 2–4 sliced, hard-boiled
(hard-cooked) eggs over the tuna
before pouring on the sauce. Heat
through for a few minutes longer,
covering loosely with foil if
necessary to prevent over-browning,
to make sure it is piping hot
throughout.

Soft roes on toast

SERVES 4

You can use canned roes for this, but it is much more tasty made with roes fresh from the fishmonger.

8 pairs of soft roes
40 g/1½ oz/⅓ cup plain (all-purpose)
  flour
Salt and freshly ground black pepper
5 ml/1 tsp cayenne
15 ml/1 tbsp chopped parsley, plus
  extra for garnish
150 g/5 oz/⅔ cup butter or margarine
4 slices of bread
A dash of lemon juice

Separate the roes and wipe with kitchen paper (paper towels). Season the flour well with salt and pepper and add the cayenne and parsley. Melt 100 g/4 oz/½ cup of the butter or margarine in a large frying pan (skillet) and fry (sauté) the roes for about 2 minutes on each side until just cooked and creamy coloured. Do not overcook. Drain on kitchen paper. Meanwhile, toast the bread and spread with the remaining butter or margarine. Top with the roes, add a dash of lemon juice, sprinkle with parsley and serve.

Gentleman's soft roes

SERVES 4

Prepare as for Soft Roes on Toast, but spread the bread with a scraping of Gentleman's Relish before topping with the roes.

Cheesy soft roes

SERVES 4

Prepare as for Soft Roes on Toast, but add 30 ml/2 tbsp grated Parmesan cheese to the flour mixture and substitute snipped chives for the parsley.

Sardine and horseradish sandwiches

SERVES 4

120 g/4½ oz/1 small can of sardines in
  oil, drained
50 g/2 oz/¼ cup butter or margarine,
  softened
30 ml/2 tbsp lemon juice
15 ml/1 tbsp horseradish relish
Salt and freshly ground black pepper
8 slices of wholemeal bread
½ cucumber, sliced

Mash the sardines with a fork. Beat in the butter or margarine, lemon juice and horseradish until well blended, then season to taste. Spread on the bread and sandwich together in pairs with cucumber slices. Cut into quarters and serve.

Sardines on toast

SERVES 1 OR 2

2 slices of wholemeal bread
15 g/½ oz/1 tbsp butter or margarine,
  softened
10 ml/2 tsp horseradish relish
120 g/4½ oz/1 small can of sardines,
  drained
Lemon juice
Freshly ground black pepper
15 ml/1 tbsp chopped parsley

Toast the bread on both sides under a grill (broiler). Mash the butter or margarine with the horseradish and spread on the toast. Top with the sardines and return to the grill to heat through. Sprinkle with lemon juice, pepper and the parsley and serve straight away.

Pilchard pots

SERVES 4

This recipe also makes a delicious sandwich filling, with slices of tomato, cucumber or some shredded lettuce.

425 g/15 oz/1 large can of pilchards in tomato sauce
30 ml/2 tbsp mayonnaise
15 ml/1 tbsp tomato purée (paste)
90 ml/6 tbsp plain yoghurt
5 ml/1 tsp red wine vinegar
1.5 ml/¼ tsp cayenne
15 ml/1 tbsp snipped chives
Toast, to serve

Empty the pilchards into a bowl and mash thoroughly (including the bones). Add the remaining ingredients and beat well. Turn into ramekins (custard cups) and chill, if time. Sprinkle with snipped chives and serve with toast.

Family cheese and tuna slices

SERVES 4–6

750 g/1¾ lb/1 large uncut wholemeal loaf
175 g/6 oz/¾ cup butter or margarine, softened
200 g/7 oz/scant 1 cup medium-fat soft cheese
1 carrot, grated
185 g/6½ oz/1 small can of tuna, drained
2 sun-dried tomatoes, finely chopped
15 ml/1 tbsp snipped chives
6 tomatoes, sliced
3 dill pickles, sliced
5 ml/1 tsp dried dill (dill weed)

Cut the loaf lengthways into seven slices. Spread each slice with a very little of the butter or margarine. Mash the cheese with the carrot and half the remaining butter or margarine until well blended. Work in the tuna. Mash the remaining butter or margarine with the sun-dried tomatoes and chives. Spread the base slice of bread with a third of the cheese mixture and top with some of the tomato slices. Sprinkle with a little dill. Spread the next with a third of the tomato butter mixture and top with dill pickle slices. Repeat the layers twice, then top with the buttered top crust. Wrap tightly in foil and chill for at least 1 hour. Cut carefully into thick slices to serve.

Minted sardine pittas

SERVES 4

120 g/4½ oz/1 small can of sardines in oil
2 tomatoes, finely chopped
¼ cucumber, finely chopped
2 spring onions (scallions), finely chopped
15 ml/1 tbsp chopped mint
15 ml/1 tbsp chopped parsley
A good pinch of cayenne
Finely grated rind and juice of ½ lemon
Salt and freshly ground black pepper
4 wholemeal pitta breads

Drain the fish, reserving the oil. Mash thoroughly (preferably including the bones). Mix in the tomatoes, cucumber, spring onions, herbs and cayenne. Stir in the lemon rind and juice and moisten a little with some of the fish oil, if liked. Season with salt and pepper. Warm the pittas in a toaster, under the grill (broiler) or briefly in the microwave. Make a slit along one long edge of each and gently open to form a packet. Pack with the fish mixture and serve.

Dace and bacon batons

SERVES 4

You can use any small, flat fish fillets for this recipe. Ready-prepared crispy bacon rashers for sandwiches are wonderful in this recipe – and there's no need to cook them of course!

4 dace fillets
Salt and freshly ground black pepper
15 ml/1 tbsp olive oil
8 thin streaky bacon rashers (slices), rinded
4 batons or other long oval rolls
4 thin slices of Cheddar cheese
2 tomatoes, sliced
30 ml/2 tbsp mayonnaise

Place the fish on foil on a grill (broiler) rack and season to taste. Brush the fish with the oil and grill (broil) for 4 minutes or until golden and tender. Dry-fry the bacon until crisp. Open the rolls, lay a fish fillet on each roll and top with a slice of cheese. Heat under the grill until the cheese melts. Top with the bacon, tomatoes and mayonnaise. Fold over the top of the roll and serve straight away.

Egg and anchovy baps

SERVES 4

You can vary the quantity of anchovies to taste.

75 g/3 oz/⅓ cup butter or margarine, softened
3 eggs
15 ml/1 tbsp milk
10 ml/2 tsp snipped chives
Salt and freshly ground black pepper
4 canned anchovies, finely chopped
4 soft white baps
A little salad cress

Melt 50 g/2 oz/¼ cup of the butter or margarine in a saucepan. Beat together the eggs and milk and stir into the pan. Cook, stirring, over a gentle heat until scrambled but do not allow to boil. Stir in the chives and a little salt and pepper and leave to cool. Meanwhile, mash the remaining butter with the anchovies. Split the baps and spread with the anchovy butter. Fill with the cold egg and a little cress and serve.

Anchovy and Mozzarella rolls

SERVES 4

Vary the quantity of anchovies according to taste.

25 g/1 oz/2 tbsp butter or margarine, softened
4 canned anchovy fillets, finely chopped
4 ciabatta rolls
100 g/4 oz Mozzarella cheese, sliced
2 plum tomatoes, sliced
Freshly ground black pepper
A few torn basil leaves

Mash the butter or margarine with the anchovy fillets. Split the rolls and spread with the anchovy butter. Top with slices of Mozzarella and tomato and sprinkle with pepper. Add a few torn basil leaves and serve.

Piperade with tuna

SERVES 2–4

15 g/½ oz/1 tbsp butter or margarine
15 ml/1 tbsp olive oil
2 onions, sliced
1 green (bell) pepper, sliced
1 red pepper, sliced
4 ripe tomatoes, roughly chopped
1 garlic clove, crushed
185 g/6½ oz/1 small can of tuna,
    drained and roughly flaked
4 eggs, beaten
Salt and freshly ground black pepper

Heat the butter or margarine and oil in a large frying pan (skillet). Add the onions, peppers, tomato and garlic and cook, stirring, for 5 minutes until soft. Add the tuna, then the eggs and some salt and pepper and cook over a gentle heat, stirring, until scrambled. Serve straight from the pan.

Tomato and Leerdammer bites

SERVES 4

4 slices of white bread, crusts removed
1 large egg
200 ml/7 fl oz/scant 1 cup milk
Salt and freshly ground black pepper
50 g/2 oz/¼ cup butter or margarine
30 ml/2 tbsp sunflower oil
10 ml/2 tsp Gentlemen's Relish
100 g/4 oz Leerdammer cheese, thinly
    sliced
4 ripe tomatoes, sliced
5 ml/1 tsp chopped rosemary

Cut each slice of bread into three pieces. Beat the egg and milk with a little salt and pepper. Soak the bread in this. Heat the butter or margarine and oil in a large frying pan (skillet). Add the bread and fry (sauté) slowly until golden underneath. Turn over and fry the other sides. Drain on kitchen paper (paper towels). Spread each with a little Gentlemen's Relish and place in a large, shallow, flameproof container. Top with the Leerdammer, trimmed to fit each slice, then with the tomatoes. Sprinkle with the rosemary. Place under a hot grill (broiler) until the cheese melts and bubbles. Serve straight away.

Smoky jackets

SERVES 4

4 large potatoes, scrubbed
25 g/1 oz/2 tbsp butter or margarine
225 g/8 oz/1 cup medium-fat soft
    cheese
100 g/4 oz/1 small can of smoked
    mussels, drained
15 ml/1 tbsp chopped parsley
A little lemon juice
Salt and freshly ground black pepper

Prick the potatoes all over and boil in water for about 20 minutes or until tender. Alternatively, bake in a preheated oven at 180°C/350°F/gas mark 4 for 1½ hours or until tender when squeezed, or wrap the potatoes in kitchen paper (paper towels) and microwave on High for about 4 minutes per potato until soft when squeezed. Halve the cooked potatoes and scoop out most of the flesh into a bowl. Mash with the butter or margarine and the cheese. Add the mussels, either whole or roughly cut up. Add the parsley and lemon juice, salt and pepper to taste. Pack back into the shells. Place under a hot grill (broiler) for about 5 minutes to heat through and brown the tops.

Tuna and mayo jackets

SERVES 4

4 large potatoes, scrubbed
25 g/1 oz/2 tbsp butter or margarine
185 g/6½ oz/1 small can of tuna,
  drained
45 ml/3 tbsp mayonnaise
15 ml/1 tbsp snipped chives
Salt and freshly ground black pepper

Cook the potatoes as for Smoky Jackets (page 120). Halve and scoop out most of the potato into a bowl. Mash with the butter or margarine, the tuna, half the mayonnaise, the chives and a little salt and pepper. Pack back into the shells and place under a hot grill (broiler) for about 5 minutes until hot and lightly golden. Top with the remaining mayonnaise and serve.

Sardine jackets

SERVES 4

Prepare as for Smoky Jackets (page 120), but substitute 120 g/4½ oz/ 1 small can of sardines, drained and mashed, for the mussels.

Pimiento and anchovy jackets with Mozzarella

SERVES 4

Prepare as for Smoky Jackets (page 120), but substitute 200 g/7 oz/ 1 small can of pimientos, drained and diced, and 50g/2 oz/1 small can of anchovies, drained and soaked in a little milk for 10 minutes before chopping, for the mussels. After packing back in the skins, top each potato half with 10 ml/2 tsp grated Mozzarella cheese before grilling (broiling) and garnish with a few torn basil leaves.

Salmon and cucumber jackets

SERVES 4

Prepare as for Smoky Jackets (page 120), but substitute 200 g/7 oz/ 1 small can of pink or red salmon, drained and flaked and skin discarded, for the mussels and add a 5 cm/2 in piece of finely chopped cucumber and 5 ml/1 tsp dried dill (dill weed).

Smoked mackerel jackets with horseradish mayo

SERVES 4

Prepare as for Smoky Jackets (page 120), but substitute 1 smoked mackerel fillet, skinned and flaked, for the mussels. Mix 30 ml/2 tbsp mayonnaise with 10 ml/2 tsp horseradish relish and a good grinding of pepper and spoon on top of the grilled (broiled) jackets.

Pilchard and sun-dried tomato jackets

SERVES 4

Prepare as for Smoky Jackets (page 120), but substitute 155 g/5¼ oz/ 1 small can of pilchards in tomato sauce, mashed, for the mussels and add two drained sun-dried tomatoes, finely chopped, with the parsley.

Cheesy tuna jackets

SERVES 4

Prepare as for Smoky Jackets (page 120), but substitute 185 g/6½ oz/ 1 small can of tuna, drained, for the mussels. After packing back into the skins, top each potato half with 10 ml/2 tsp grated Cheddar cheese and a sprinkling of Worcestershire sauce before grilling (broiling).

Cheesy corn and tuna jackets

SERVES 4

Prepare as for Smoky Jackets (page 120), but substitute 85 g/3½ oz/1 very small can of tuna, drained, for the mussels and add 200 g/7 oz/1 small can of sweetcorn (corn), drained, to the mixture. Top each potato half with 10 ml/2 tsp grated Cheddar cheese before grilling (boiling).

Prawn and mayo jackets

SERVE 4

Prepare as for Tuna and Mayo Jackets (page 120), but substitute 175 g/6 oz cooked peeled prawns (shrimp) for the tuna. Add a few drops of Tabasco sauce to the mixture with the salt and pepper.

Soft roe and blue cheese jackets

SERVES 4

Prepare as for Smoky Jackets (page 120), but use 100 g/4 oz/1 small can of soft roes, drained, instead of the smoked mussels and substitute 100 g/ 4 oz/½ cup of the soft cheese with a creamy blue cheese.

Prawn cocktail jackets

SERVES 4

4 large potatoes, scrubbed
4 knobs of butter or margarine
45 ml/3 tbsp mayonnaise
15 ml/1 tbsp tomato ketchup (catsup)
5 ml/1 tsp Worcestershire sauce
5 ml/1 tsp soy sauce
A few drops of Tabasco sauce
Salt and freshly ground black pepper
175 g/6 oz cooked peeled prawns
  (shrimp)
Paprika and lemon wedges, to garnish

Cook the potatoes as for Smoky Jackets (page 120). Make a cross cut in the top of each one, squeeze gently and add a knob of butter or margarine. Meanwhile, mix the mayonnaise with the ketchup, Worcestershire, soy and Tabasco sauces. Season to taste and stir in the prawns. Spoon on top of the hot, cooked potatoes and garnish with a sprinkling of paprika and lemon wedges.

Luxury smoked salmon and crème fraîche jackets

SERVES 4

Prepare as for Prawn Cocktail Jackets (left), but after cutting and squeezing the potatoes and adding a knob of butter, top each with a good spoonful of smoked salmon trimmings, a large dollop of crème fraîche, a squeeze of lemon juice and a good grinding of black pepper.

American-style fish fingers

SERVES 2

8 fish fingers
2 soft baps
2 slices of Cheddar cheese or processed cheese
30 ml/2 tbsp Tartare Sauce (page 372 or use bought)
Shredded lettuce

Grill (broil) or fry (sauté) the fish fingers. Split the rolls and lay the fish fingers inside. Top with the cheese and flash under a hot grill (broiler) to melt the cheese. Add the tartare sauce and a little shredded lettuce, then top with the lids of the rolls.

Fish finger fingers

SERVES 2

20 g/¾ oz/1½ tbsp butter or margarine
15 ml/1 tbsp tomato ketchup (catsup)
5 ml/1 tsp capers, chopped
6 fish fingers
2 slices of wholemeal bread

Mash the butter or margarine with
the tomato ketchup and capers. Grill
(broil) the fish fingers and the bread
on both sides until the fish is cooked
and the bread is golden, removing
the bread if toasted before the fish.
Spread the toast with the butter
mixture. Cut each slice into three
fingers, top each with a fish finger
and serve.

Chilli fingers

SERVES 4

4 small baguettes, split
Butter or margarine, for spreading
30 ml/2 tbsp tomato chutney
30 ml/2 tbsp mayonnaise
Hot chilli sauce, to taste
10 fish fingers
Shredded lettuce

Split the baguettes and spread with
butter or margarine. Mix the chutney
with the mayonnaise and spice up
with hot chilli sauce to taste. Grill
(broil) or fry (sauté) the fish fingers.
Divide between the baguettes. Top
with the spicy mayonnaise and push
in some shredded lettuce. Serve
while still hot.

Prawn and chilli mayo wraps

SERVES 4

60 ml/4 tbsp mayonnaise
15 ml/1 tbsp chilli relish
175 g/6 oz cooked peeled prawns
(shrimp)
2 tomatoes, seeded and chopped
5 cm/2 in piece of cucumber
4 flour tortillas
A few lettuce leaves, shredded

Mix the mayonnaise with the chilli
relish. Stir in the prawns, tomatoes
and cucumber. Sprinkle the tortillas
with lettuce. Spread on the prawn
mixture, fold in the sides, then fold
over to form filled pockets.

Curried prawn baguettes

SERVES 2

30 ml/2 tbsp mayonnaise
5 ml/1 tsp curry paste
5 ml/1 tsp tomato purée (paste)
10 ml/2 tsp sultanas (golden raisins)
1 tomato, finely chopped
5 cm/2 in piece of cucumber, finely
chopped
100 g/4 oz cooked peeled prawns
(shrimp)
Salt and freshly ground black pepper
4 small baguettes, split and buttered
Shredded lettuce

Mix the mayonnaise with the curry
paste, tomato purée, sultanas,
tomato and cucumber. Fold in the
prawns and season to taste. Spread
in the split baguettes and fill with
shredded lettuce.

Oyster baguette slices

SERVES 4

This is another version of Oyster Loaves given on page 84. Use the bread you remove to make breadcrumbs.

1 French stick
50 g/2 oz/¼ cup butter or margarine, melted
24 small oysters, shucked (page 13)
30 ml/2 tbsp cornflour (cornstarch)
Salt and freshly ground black pepper
30 ml/2 tbsp olive oil
A few drops of Tabasco sauce
5 ml/2 tsp lemon juice
¼ lettuce, shredded
45 ml/3 tbsp mayonnaise
Avocado Cream (page 372), or avocado slices, tossed in lemon juice, to serve

Split the French stick lengthways, not quite right through. Pull out the soft bread from the bottom half of the loaf. Open out as flat as possible without breaking the loaf. Brush inside and out with the butter or margarine. Bake in a preheated oven at 200°C/400°F/gas mark 6 for 15 minutes or until crisp and golden.

Meanwhile, toss the oysters in the cornflour, seasoned with a little salt and pepper. Fry (sauté) quickly in the oil for about 2 minutes until golden, then drain on kitchen paper (paper towels). Sprinkle with Tabasco and lemon juice and pack into the hollow in the French bread. Top with shredded lettuce. Spread the top cut side with mayonnaise and sandwich the loaf back together again. Slice thickly and serve with Avocado Cream or slices of avocado, tossed in lemon juice.

Prawn and avocado rolls

SERVES 2 OR 4

1 ripe avocado, peeled, halved, stoned (pitted) and chopped
5 ml/1 tsp lemon juice
A few drops of Tabasco sauce
75 g/3 oz cooked peeled prawns (shrimp)
4 large granary baps
30 ml/2 tbsp mayonnaise
Freshly ground black pepper

Toss the avocado with the lemon juice to prevent browning. Add a few drops of Tabasco and the prawns and toss again. Split the baps and spread generously with the mayonnaise. Fill with the prawn and avocado mixture and add a good grinding of pepper.

Cheese and tuna croissants

SERVES 4

These are also good cold without grilling (broiling).

4 large croissants
185 g/6½ oz/1 small can of tuna, drained
15 ml/1 tbsp mayonnaise
Freshly ground black pepper
50 g/2 oz Cheddar cheese, thinly sliced

Make a split in the side of each croissant. Mix the tuna with the mayonnaise and pepper to taste and use to fill the croissants. Add the cheese slices and grill gently, turning once, until the cheese melts and the tuna mixture is hot.

Tuna and avocado chunkies

SERVES 2 OR 4

Prepare as for Prawn and Avocado Rolls (page 124), but substitute 185 g/6½ oz/1 small can of tuna, drained, for the prawns. Spoon on to four thick slices of lightly buttered wholemeal bread and top with some shredded lettuce. Cover with four more slices of buttered bread, cut into halves and serve.

Fried fish sangers

SERVES 4

4 fresh or frozen breaded cod or
  haddock fillets
30 ml/2 tbsp tomato ketchup (catsup)
25 g/1 oz/2 tbsp butter or margarine,
  softened
8 thick slices of crusty white bread
Lemon juice
Salt and freshly ground black pepper

Fry (sauté) the fish fillets as directed on the packet. Meanwhile, mash the ketchup into the butter or margarine. Spread on the bread. Put four of the slices on serving plates. Top with a cooked fish fillet, sprinkle with lemon juice, salt and pepper and top with the remaining slices of tomato buttered bread. Halve and serve hot.

Fish and chip butties

SERVES 4

Prepare as for Fried Fish Sangers, but use thinner slices of bread (or the butties are impossible to eat!). While the fish is frying, grill (broil) two good handfuls of oven chips (fries), turning occasionally until crisp and golden. Put in the sandwiches with the fish and sprinkle with vinegar instead of lemon juice.

Fish and chip butties with pea butter

SERVES 4

200 g/7 oz/1 small can of garden peas,
  thoroughly drained
25 g/1 oz/2 tbsp butter or margarine,
  softened
8 slices of white bread
4 fresh or frozen breaded cod or
  haddock fillets
2 handfuls of oven chips (fries)
Tomato ketchup (catsup), optional
Salt (optional)

Mash the peas thoroughly into the butter or margarine. Use this mixture to spread on the bread. Fry (sauté) the fish fillets as directed on the packet and grill (broil) the oven chips until golden, turning occasionally. Put the fish and chips on four of the slices of bread, add a little ketchup and salt, if liked, and cover with the remaining bread slices. Cut into halves and serve.

Cockleshell Bay specials

SERVES 4

225 g/8 oz cooked shelled cockles
5 cm/2 in piece of cucumber, thinly
  sliced
30 ml/2 tbsp malt vinegar
Freshly ground black pepper
8 slices of wholemeal bread, buttered

Rinse the cockles thoroughly in several changes of cold water. Drain and dry on kitchen paper (paper towels). Place in a bowl with the cucumber and vinegar. Toss gently and season well with pepper. Leave to marinate for 15 minutes, then drain off all excess vinegar. Spoon on to four slices of the bread and top with the remaining slices. Cut into halves and serve straight away.

Rollmop and cream cheese open sandwiches

SERVES 4

2 rollmops, sliced
4 rye crispbreads
30 ml/2 tbsp cream cheese
Small dill (dill weed) sprigs

Drain the rollmop slices on kitchen paper (paper towels). Spread the crispbreads with the cheese. Lay the rollmop slices on top and garnish with dill sprigs.

Egg and caviare open sandwiches

SERVES 4

4 rye crispbreads
Butter or margarine
3 hard-boiled (hard-cooked) eggs, sliced
20 ml/4 tsp Danish lumpfish roe
15 ml/1 tbsp snipped chives

Spread the crispbreads with butter or margarine and lay the egg slices on top. Add 5 ml/1 tsp of the lumpfish roe to each and sprinkle with the snipped chives.

Sardine pâté crispers

SERVES 4

120 g/4½ oz/1 small can of sardines, drained
40 g/1½ oz/3 tbsp butter or margarine
75 ml/5 tbsp plain yoghurt
2.5 ml/½ tsp lemon juice
A few drops of Tabasco sauce
Salt and freshly ground black pepper
8 rye crispbreads
1 small onion, thinly sliced and separated into rings
15 ml/1 tbsp chopped parsley

Put all the ingredients except the crispbreads, onion and parsley in a blender or food processor and run the machine until smooth. Spread thickly on the crispbreads and top with the onion rings and parsley.

Smoked salmon and fromage frais open sandwiches

SERVES 4

4 slices from a wholemeal batch loaf
30 ml/2 tbsp fromage frais
2 slices of smoked salmon, halved
4 cucumber slices
Freshly ground black pepper

Spread the bread with the fromage frais. Make the salmon into small rolls and put one on each slice. Garnish with the cucumber slices and add a good grinding of black pepper.

Smoked salmon and horseradish on rye

SERVES 4

40 g/1½ oz/3 tbsp butter or margarine, softened
15 ml/1 tbsp horseradish relish
5 ml/1 tsp Dijon mustard
A few drops of lemon juice
Salt and freshly ground black pepper
4 slices of rye bread
100 g/4 oz smoked salmon trimmings, cut into neat pieces
Parsley sprigs, to garnish

Mash the butter or margarine with the horseradish, mustard and lemon juice and season to taste. Spread on the rye bread. Top with the salmon and garnish each with a sprig of parsley.

Anchovy toasts

SERVES 4

8 slices of bread
1 quantity of Anchovy Butter
  (page 384)
30 ml/2 tbsp chopped parsley

Toast the bread on both sides and spread with the anchovy butter. Cut into fingers and dip one end of each finger in the parsley.

Asparagus and smoked salmon in the fingers

SERVES 4

4 eggs
60 ml/4 tbsp cold water
Salt and freshly ground black pepper
5 ml/1 tsp dried oregano
25 g/1 oz/2 tbsp butter or margarine
4 thin slices of smoked salmon
295 g/10½ oz/1 medium can of
  asparagus spears, drained

Beat one of the eggs in a bowl with 15 ml/1 tbsp of the water, a little salt and pepper and a quarter of the oregano. Heat 10 ml/2 tsp/¼ oz of the butter or margarine in a small non-stick frying pan (skillet). Add the egg mixture and fry (sauté), lifting the edge of the mixture to allow the uncooked egg to run underneath. When the base is set and golden, slide out of the pan, then invert back in the pan and cook for a further 1 minute to set the top. Slide out and leave to cool while cooking the remaining three eggs in the same way. Lay a salmon slice on each omelette. Divide the asparagus spears between the four omelettes, roll up and eat in the fingers.

Tortilla with tuna

SERVES 4

2 large potatoes, very thinly sliced
1 large onion, very thinly sliced
45 ml/3 tbsp olive oil
6 eggs
Salt and freshly ground black pepper
185 g/6½ oz/1 small can of tuna,
  drained and flaked

Fry (sauté) the potatoes and onion very gently in the olive oil for about 8–10 minutes until soft but not brown, stirring and turning frequently. Spread out evenly in the pan. Beat the eggs with a little salt and pepper and the tuna and pour into the pan. Cook gently, lifting the edge to allow the uncooked egg to run underneath, until set and golden on the base. Place the pan under a moderate preheated grill (broiler) and cook until set. Serve hot or cold, cut into wedges.

Gentlemen's crumpets

SERVES 4

4 crumpets
15 g/½ oz/1 tbsp unsalted (sweet)
  butter
10 ml/2 tsp Gentlemen's Relish
1 hard-boiled (hard-cooked egg), cut
  into 4 slices, discarding the ends
4 parsley sprigs

Toast the crumpets. Spread with the butter and a thin scraping of Gentlemen's Relish. Top each with a slice of egg and a sprig of parsley and serve.

Blushing butter beans with tuna

SERVES 4

1 onion, chopped
30 ml/2 tbsp olive oil
1 garlic clove, crushed
225 g/8 oz/1 small can of chopped
    tomatoes
A pinch of caster (superfine) sugar
Salt and freshly ground black pepper
425 g/15 oz/1 large can of butter
    (lima) beans, drained
15 ml/1 tbsp snipped chives
Crusty bread, to serve

Cook the onion gently in the oil for 3 minutes until soft but not brown. Add all the remaining ingredients except the chives, stir gently and simmer for 5 minutes. Sprinkle with the chives and serve hot with crusty bread.

Tofu and prawn cakes

SERVES 4

75 g/3 oz firm tofu, drained and finely
    chopped
75 g/3 oz cooked peeled prawns
    (shrimp), chopped
1 large potato, grated
1 small onion, finely grated
30 ml/2 tbsp chopped parsley
30 ml/2 tbsp sunflower oil, plus extra
    for shallow-frying
Salt and freshly ground black pepper
75 g/3 oz/¾ cup self-raising (self-
    rising) wholemeal flour
150 ml/¼ pt/⅔ cup milk
Mayonnaise and chilli relish, to serve

Mix together all the ingredients except the milk in a bowl. Gradually beat in the milk to form a batter.

Heat a little oil a large, heavy-based frying pan (skillet) and drop in spoonfuls of the batter. Fry (sauté) until cooked through and golden brown on both sides. Drain on kitchen paper (paper towels). Keep warm while cooking the remainder. Serve hot with mayonnaise and chilli relish.

Mackerel dogs

SERVES 4

Make the mackerel 'sausages' in advance and store in the fridge or freezer until ready to use.

2 smoked mackerel fillets, about
    350 g/12 oz in all, skinned and
    cut into pieces
2 thick slices of white bread, torn into
    pieces
75 g/3 oz button mushrooms
Finely grated rind of ½ lemon
10 ml/2 tsp horseradish relish
Salt and freshly ground black pepper
1.5 ml/¼ tsp chilli powder (optional)
1 egg, beaten
4 finger rolls
Tomato chutney, to serve

With the machine running, drop the pieces of the fish into a food processor or blender. With the machine still running, add the bread and the mushrooms, then the lemon rind, horseradish and some salt and pepper. Blend in the chilli powder, if using, then mix with the egg to bind. Shape into four rolls about 13 cm/5 in long. Chill until ready to cook. Grill (broil) the sausages until golden on all sides and hot through. Place in the finger rolls and serve with tomato chutney.

Sautées and Stir-fries

Frying (sautéing) is a very rapid method of cooking, suitable for most types of fish. Use shellfish and firm-fleshed varieties for stir-frying or they will break up too much when being tossed in the pan. The more delicate whole fish or fillets, like plaice, should be browned quickly on one side, then gently turned over to complete cooking because if they are cooked too long on one side they are likely to break up on turning. There are delicious recipes here for everything from quick suppers to elegant feasts. Deep- or shallow-fried, stir-fried or sautéed in a very little fat, they are all succulent, sumptuous, quick and thoroughly rewarding to cook.

Sole meunière

SERVES 1

1 Dover sole, trimmed
15 ml/1 tbsp plain (all-purpose) flour
Salt and freshly ground black pepper
50 g/2 oz/¼ cup unsalted (sweet) butter
15 ml/1 tbsp chopped parsley
15 ml/1 tbsp lemon juice

Skin the fish, if preferred (I usually don't bother). Mix the flour with a pinch of salt and a good grinding of pepper and dust all over the fish. Melt half the butter in a frying pan (skillet). Add the fish and fry (sauté) for about 3–5 minutes on each side, depending on thickness, until it is cooked through and the flesh can easily be removed from the bones. Transfer to a warm plate. Add the remaining butter, the parsley and lemon juice to the pan and swirl round until the fat melts and colours a little. Season lightly, then pour over the fish and serve.

Sole fillets meunière

SERVES 4

Prepare as for Sole Meunière, but use four sole fillets, halved lengthways, and double the quantity of the remaining ingredients. Also, add the finely grated rind of half a lemon to the flour.

Trout meunière

SERVES 1

Prepare as for Sole Meunière, but use cleaned trout instead of sole. Don't bother to skin the fish before cooking as it forms a lovely brown crust.

Sole meunière aux moules

SERVES 4

Prepare as for Sole Fillets Meunière, but before cooking the fish prepare 900 g/2 lb mussels (page 13) and cook them in 150 ml/¼ pt/⅔ cup water in a covered pan for 5 minutes until they open. Discard any that remain closed. Remove from their shells and add to the pan with the remaining butter before adding the parsley and lemon juice. Serve garnished with lemon wedges.

Plaice meunière

SERVES 1

Prepare as for Sole Meunière, but use a trimmed plaice instead of a sole. Try using lime juice instead of lemon for a delicious change.

Simple pan swordfish

SERVES 4

4 swordfish steaks
Salt and freshly ground black pepper
25 g/1 oz/2 tbsp butter or margarine
30 ml/2 tbsp chopped parsley
Lemon wedges and parsley sprigs, to garnish
Baby new potatoes and French (green) beans, to serve

Cut the skin off the fish. Season lightly. Heat the butter or margarine in a frying pan (skillet), add the fish and fry (sauté) for 4–5 minutes on each side until cooked through and golden. Sprinkle with the parsley, then transfer with the juices to warm plates. Garnish with lemon wedges and parsley sprigs and serve with baby new potatoes and French beans.

Simple pan tuna

SERVES 4

Prepare as for Simple Pan Swordfish, but substitute tuna steaks for the swordfish. Sprinkle with a mixture of chopped coriander (cilantro) and parsley instead of all parsley, and add the finely grated rind of half a lemon.

Haddock creole

SERVES 4

4 haddock fillets, about 175g/6 oz each, skinned
30 ml/2 tbsp plain (all-purpose) flour
Salt and freshly ground black pepper
1 small green chilli, seeded and finely chopped
25 g/1 oz/2 tbsp butter or margarine
2 green bananas, thickly sliced
10 ml/2 tsp lime juice
Lime wedges and coriander (cilantro) sprigs, to garnish
Wild Rice Mix for Fish (page 394) and Orange and Mango Salsa (page 381), to serve

Wipe the fish with kitchen paper (paper towels). Season the flour with salt and pepper and add the chilli. Use to coat the fish. Heat half the butter or margarine in a non-stick frying pan (skillet), add the fish and fry (sauté) for 3 minutes. Turn over and fry the other sides for 3 minutes. Carefully slide out of the pan and keep warm. Melt the remaining butter or margarine in the pan, add the banana slices with the lime juice and toss over a fairly high heat until softening slightly. Transfer the fish to warm plates and spoon the bananas on top. Garnish with lime wedges and coriander sprigs and serve with Wild Rice Mix and Orange and Mango Salsa.

Sole colbert

SERVES 4

4 small sole, about 225 g/8 oz each, skinned and trimmed
30 ml/2 tbsp plain (all-purpose) flour
Salt and freshly ground black pepper
1 egg, beaten
75 g/3 oz/³⁄₄ cup dried breadcrumbs
Oil, for deep-frying
Maître d'Hôtel Butter (page 384) and lemon wedges, to serve

Using a sharp knife make a slit along the backbone of the white-skinned side of the fish. Using short strokes, lift the fish away from the bones down to the fins but do not cut them off. Dust the fish in the flour, seasoned with a little salt and pepper, both inside the cut fillets and outside. Brush the surface with the egg, then coat in the breadcrumbs.

Heat the oil until a cube of day-old bread browns in 30 seconds. Fry (sauté) the fish one or two at a time for about 6 minutes until crisp and golden. Drain on kitchen paper (paper towels). Snip the backbone with scissors just behind the head and at the tail end, then gently pull out the bone. Transfer to ovenproof plates. Put slices of Maître d'Hôtel Butter along the centre where the bones were. Heat in a preheated oven at 190°C/375°F/gas mark 5 for 3 minutes, then serve garnished with lemon wedges.

Hake a la gallega

SERVES 4

*900 g/2 lb potatoes, cut into small,
even-sized pieces*
*225 g/8 oz French (green) beans,
trimmed but left whole*
*4 pieces of hake fillet, about 175 g/
6 oz each*
2 bay leaves
Salt and freshly ground black pepper
2 Spanish onions, chopped
60 ml/4 tbsp olive oil
5 ml/1 tsp pimenton

Cook the potatoes and beans
separately in lightly salted, boiling
water until tender. Drain.
Meanwhile, put the fish in a frying
pan (skillet) with the bay leaves, a
little salt and pepper and just
enough water to cover. Bring to the
boil, reduce the heat, cover and
simmer gently for about 6 minutes
or until the fish flakes easily with a
fork. In a separate frying pan, gently
fry (sauté) the onions in the oil for
8 minutes, stirring, until softened
and lightly golden. Stir in the
pimenton, then immediately remove
from the heat. Spoon the potatoes
and beans on to warm plates.
Remove the fish from the pan with a
fish slice and place on the potatoes.
Spoon the onion mixture on top and
serve straight away.

Mediterranean hake

SERVES 4

*4 pieces of hake fillet, about 175 g/
6 oz each*
45 ml/3 tbsp olive oil
1 onion, chopped
2 garlic cloves, crushed
1 red (bell) pepper, sliced
1 yellow pepper, sliced
1 green pepper, sliced
4 ripe tomatoes, skinned and chopped
2.5 ml/½ tsp caster (superfine) sugar
Salt and freshly ground black pepper
6 black olives, sliced
30 ml/2 tbsp chopped parsley
Noodles, tossed in olive oil, to serve

Wipe the fish with kitchen paper
(paper towels). Heat half the oil in a
large frying pan (skillet), add the
fish, skin-side up, and fry (sauté)
for 3 minutes. Carefully turn the
fish over and cook for a further
3 minutes until tender and cooked
through. Carefully lift out of the pan
and keep warm. Heat the remaining
oil in the pan. Add the onion and fry
for 2 minutes, stirring. Add the
garlic, peppers, tomatoes, sugar and
a little salt and pepper. Cook,
stirring, for about 8 minutes until
pulpy. Stir in the olives and parsley.
Transfer the fish to warm serving
plates, spoon the tomato mixture
over and serve hot with noodles
tossed in olive oil.

Trout with cashew nuts

SERVES 4

4 trout, cleaned and heads removed, if
preferred
Salt and freshly ground black pepper
75 g/3 oz/⅓ cup butter or margarine
50 g/2 oz/½ cup raw cashew nuts
15 ml/1 tbsp lemon juice
30 ml/2 tbsp chopped parsley
New potatoes and French (green)
beans, to serve

Wipe the fish inside and out with
kitchen paper (paper towels). Make
several slashes on each side and
season with salt and pepper. Heat
the butter or margarine in a large
frying pan (skillet), add the fish and
fry (sauté) for 3–4 minutes until
golden brown underneath.

Turn over and add the nuts. Fry
for a further 3 minutes until golden
and cooked through. Carefully
transfer the fish to warm plates,
leaving the nuts in the pan. Add the
lemon juice and parsley to the pan
with a little more salt and pepper.
Heat through, stirring. Spoon over
the fish and serve hot with new
potatoes and French beans.

Trout with Pernod, fennel and mushrooms

SERVES 4

1 fennel bulb
4 trout fillets
25 g/1 oz/2 tbsp butter or margarine
175 g/6 oz button mushrooms, sliced
1 garlic clove, crushed
45 ml/3 tbsp Pernod
120 ml/4 fl oz/½ cup crème fraîche
Salt and freshly ground black pepper
Plain potatoes, to serve

Trim off the feathery fronds from the
fennel and reserve. Slice the bulb
and boil in lightly salted water for
about 8 minutes until just tender.
Drain and reserve. Wipe the fish
with kitchen paper (paper towels).
Melt half the butter or margarine in
a large non-stick frying pan (skillet),
add the fish, skin-side up, and
brown for 2 minutes. Turn the
fish over and cook for a further
3 minutes until tender. Carefully lift
out of the pan and keep warm.

Heat the remaining butter or
margarine in the pan. Add the
mushrooms and stir for 2 minutes.
Add the fennel slices, garlic and
Pernod, cover with foil or a lid and
cook gently for 4 minutes. Stir in the
crème fraîche and season to taste.
Bring to the boil and boil, stirring,
for 2 minutes. Transfer the trout to
warm plates. Spoon the sauce over,
garnish with the reserved fronds and
serve with plain boiled potatoes.

Crisp fried trout

SERVES 4

4 trout, cleaned
60 ml/4 tbsp soy sauce
15 ml/1 tbsp dry sherry
15 ml/1 tbsp plain (all-purpose) flour
5 ml/1 tsp ground ginger
Salt and freshly ground black pepper
1 egg, beaten
75 g/3 oz/1½ cups fresh white
  breadcrumbs
Oil, for shallow-frying

Wipe the trout thoroughly with kitchen paper (paper towels) and lay them in a shallow dish. Mix the soy sauce with the sherry and pour over. Rub well into each side of the fish, inside and out, and leave to marinate for 1 hour. Mix the flour with the ginger and a little salt and pepper. Drain the trout, pat dry on kitchen paper, then coat in the flour mixture, then the egg, then breadcrumbs. Heat the oil and shallow-fry for 5 minutes on each side until golden and cooked through. Drain on kitchen paper and serve hot.

Simple trout with almonds

SERVES 4

4 trout, cleaned
Salt and freshly ground black pepper
25 g/1 oz/2 tbsp butter or margarine
30 ml/2 tbsp toasted flaked (slivered)
  almonds
Lemon juice
15 ml/1 tbsp chopped parsley

Slash the trout in several places on both sides. Season with salt and pepper. Fry (sauté) in the butter or margarine for 4–5 minutes on each side until golden brown and cooked through. Sprinkle with the almonds

and lemon juice to taste. Transfer to warm plates and spoon the juices over. Sprinkle with the parsley and serve.

Speciality trout with almonds

SERVES 4

15 g/½ oz/1 tbsp butter or margarine
4 rainbow trout, cleaned and heads
  removed, if preferred
120 ml/4 fl oz/½ cup medium-sweet
  cider
30 ml/2 tbsp toasted flaked (slivered)
  almonds
15 ml/1 tbsp chopped parsley
15 ml/1 tbsp snipped chives
Freshly ground black pepper
New potatoes, boiled in their skins,
  and broccoli, to serve

Melt the butter or margarine in a large, non-stick frying pan (skillet). Add the trout and fry (sauté) for 5 minutes on each side until cooked through. Lift out of the pan with a fish slice and transfer to warm plates. Keep warm. Add the cider to the juices in the pan and boil, stirring, until reduced by half. Add the nuts and herbs and a good grinding of pepper. Stir well, then spoon over the trout. Serve straight away with new potatoes in their skins and broccoli.

Carp soy

SERVES 4

700 g/1½ lb carp, filleted
Freshly ground black pepper
30 ml/2 tbsp soy sauce
10 ml/2 tsp Worcestershire sauce
15 ml/1 tbsp lemon juice
100 g/4 oz/2 cups fresh wholemeal
*   breadcrumbs*
5 ml/1 tsp dried onion granules
50 g/2 oz/½ cup plain (all-purpose)
*   flour*
2 eggs, beaten
Oil, for deep-frying
Ginger Dipping Sauce (page 381), and
*   Chinese egg noodles, to serve*

Cut the fish into 2.5 cm/1 in thick
slices and place in a shallow dish.
Season with pepper. Mix together
the soy sauce, Worcestershire sauce
and lemon juice. Pour over the fish
and toss gently. Leave to marinate
for 1 hour. Mix the breadcrumbs
with the onion granules. Dip the
pieces of fish in the flour, then the
eggs, then the breadcrumbs. Deep-
fry the pieces in hot oil for about
4 minutes until crisp and golden
brown. Drain on kitchen paper
(paper towels). Serve with Ginger
Dipping Sauce and Chinese egg
noodles.

Creamed turbot in cider

SERVES 4

2 spring onions (scallions), finely
*   chopped*
25 g/1 oz/2 tbsp butter or margarine
4 slices of turbot, about 2 cm/¾ in
*   thick*
Salt and freshly ground black pepper
300 ml/½ pt/1¼ cups dry cider
15 ml/1 tbsp brandy
2 egg yolks
150 ml/¼ pt/⅔ cup crème fraîche
Lemon juice
15 ml/1 tbsp snipped chives
Sauté Potatoes (page 389) and
*   mangetout (snow peas), to serve*

Fry (sauté) the spring onions in the
butter or margarine for 2 minutes,
stirring, until soft but not brown.
Remove from the pan with a
draining spoon. Add the fish to the
pan and season with salt and
pepper. Cook for 2 minutes on each
side. Add the cider and brandy and
bring to the boil. Cover, reduce the
heat and cook gently for 10 minutes
until the fish feels tender when
pierced with a knife. Transfer with a
draining spoon to a serving dish and
keep warm.

Bring the cooking liquid to the
boil and boil until reduced by half.
Whisk together the egg yolks and
crème fraîche and stir into the sauce.
Cook gently, stirring, until
thickened. Do not allow to boil. Add
lemon juice, salt and pepper to taste.
Spoon over the turbot and sprinkle
with the chives. Serve hot with
Sauté Potatoes and mangetout.

Salmon with mixed vegetable stir-fry

SERVES 4

30 ml/2 tbsp sunflower oil
15 ml/1 tbsp chopped fresh root ginger
1 small garlic clove, crushed
100 g/4 oz broccoli, cut into tiny florets
1 large carrot, cut into thin
  matchsticks
100 g/4 oz baby corn cobs
100 g/4 oz mangetout (snow peas)
¼ small red cabbage, finely shredded
50 g/2 oz button mushrooms, thinly
  sliced
50 g/2 oz beansprouts
4 pieces of salmon fillet, about
  175 g/6 oz each
10 ml/2 tsp lemon juice
Salt and freshly ground black pepper
15 ml/1 tbsp soy sauce
1 bunch of spring onions (scallions),
  finely chopped
15 ml/1 tbsp chopped coriander
  (cilantro)
5 ml/1 tsp sesame oil
Plain Rice for Fish (page 392), to serve

Heat half the sunflower oil in a wok or large frying pan (skillet). Add 5 ml/1 tsp of the ginger and the garlic and cook for 10 seconds. Add the broccoli, carrot, corn cobs, mangetout, cabbage, mushrooms and beansprouts. Stir-fry for 6 minutes.

Meanwhile, place the fish under the grill (broiler), sprinkle with the lemon juice and some salt and pepper and grill (broil) for about 6 minutes until tender. Mix the soy sauce into the vegetables, then spoon on to warm plates. Place the salmon to one side and keep warm. Heat the remaining sunflower oil and ginger, the spring onions, coriander and sesame oil in a small saucepan with a good grinding of pepper. Spoon over the salmon and serve with rice.

Pan salmon with rocket

SERVES 4

4 salmon tail fillets, about 175 g/6 oz
  each
25 g/1 oz/2 tbsp unsalted (sweet)
  butter
15 ml/1 tbsp brandy
60 ml/4 tbsp crème fraîche
Salt and freshly ground black pepper
A good pinch of caster (superfine)
  sugar
50 g/2 oz rocket leaves
Lime wedges, to garnish
Sauté Potatoes (page 389), to serve

Fry (sauté) the salmon in the butter, flesh-side down, for 4 minutes. Turn the fish over and continue to fry until tender and just cooked through. Remove from the pan and keep warm. Stir the brandy into the pan and ignite. When the flames have died down, stir in the crème fraîche, some salt and pepper and the sugar. Put the rocket on four warm plates, top with a salmon fillet and spoon a little sauce over each. Garnish with lime wedges and serve with Sauté Potatoes.

Birthday salmon

SERVES 4

I like to remove the bones and skin for easy eating, but the fish does keep its shape better if you leave them in. The choice is yours.

4 salmon steaks
Salt and freshly ground black pepper
15 ml/1 tbsp olive oil
5 ml/1 tsp dried dill (dill weed)
100 g/4 oz small thin asparagus spears
100 g/4 oz mangetout (snow peas)
175 g/6 oz/¾ cup unsalted (sweet) butter
1 onion, finely chopped
4 tomatoes, skinned and quartered
10 ml/2 tsp capers
A good pinch of caster (superfine) sugar
4 shelled scallops
200 g/7 oz raw peeled tiger prawns (jumbo shrimp)
30 ml/2 tbsp mayonnaise
Lemon juice
15 ml/1 tbsp chopped thyme
15 ml/1 tbsp chopped oregano
15 ml/1 tbsp chopped parsley
A few drops of Tabasco sauce
A few whole chives, to garnish
New potatoes, to serve

Carefully remove the skin and bones from the fish, if preferred. Overlap the two thin flaps of flesh at the front of each steak to form a circle and secure with cocktail sticks (toothpicks). Place in a non-stick frying pan (skillet). Season with a little salt and pepper, the oil and dill and leave to stand while preparing the rest of the dish.

Cook the asparagus and mangetout together in lightly salted, boiling water for 3 minutes until just tender but still with some 'bite'. Drain, rinse with cold water and drain again. Melt 15 g/½ oz/1 tbsp of the butter in the saucepan.

Add the onion and fry (sauté) for 3 minutes to soften. Add the cooked vegetables, the tomatoes, capers, sugar and a little salt and pepper and toss gently until the tomatoes soften. Add 60 ml/4 tbsp water to the fish. Cover and cook gently for 6 minutes or until the fish is just cooked through.

Meanwhile, melt 15 g/½ oz/1 tbsp of the remaining butter in a separate frying pan. Add the scallops and prawns and cook, tossing gently, for about 3 minutes until the prawns are pink and the scallops are just firm. Stir in the mayonnaise, spike with lemon juice and season to taste. Melt the remaining butter and stir in the herbs, 5 ml/1 tsp lemon juice, the Tabasco and a little salt and pepper. Spoon the vegetable mixture in a pile on four warm plates. Top each with a salmon steak and remove the cocktail sticks. Spoon the scallop mixture in the centres and drizzle the herb butter round the edge of the plates. Lay a few whole chives in a criss-cross pattern round the edge of each plate and serve with new potatoes.

Creamy pan scallops with Cointreau

SERVES 4

Thinly pared rind of 1 orange, cut into thin strips
2 streaky bacon rashers (slices), rinded and finely chopped
2 onions, finely chopped
25 g/1 oz/2 tbsp unsalted (sweet) butter
16 shelled scallops, halved widthways
30 ml/2 tbsp Cointreau
150 ml/¼ pt/⅔ cup fish stock
150 ml/¼ pt/⅔ cup double (heavy) cream
A dash of lemon juice
Salt and freshly ground black pepper
Plain Rice for Fish (page 392), to serve
15 ml/1 tbsp chopped parsley, to garnish

Boil the orange rind in water for 2 minutes, drain, rinse with cold water, drain again and reserve. Fry (sauté) the bacon and onion in the butter for 3 minutes, stirring, until soft but not brown. Add the scallops and cook, turning once, for about 3 minutes until tender. Remove from the pan with a draining spoon and keep warm. Add the Cointreau to the pan and ignite. Shake the pan until the flames subside, then stir in the stock and boil until syrupy and reduced by half. Stir in the cream and lemon juice and bubble for 2 minutes. Return the scallop mixture to the pan and season to taste. Heat through for 2 minutes, then serve on a bed of rice, sprinkled with the parsley.

Pan casserole of whiting

SERVES 4

900 g/2 lb potatoes, cut into chunks
2 carrots, sliced
450 g/1 lb whiting fillets, skinned and cut into chunks
30 ml/2 tbsp soy sauce
A few drops of Tabasco sauce
2 large onions, thinly sliced
2 leeks, thinly sliced
30 ml/2 tbsp sunflower oil
400 g/14 oz/1 large can of chopped tomatoes
15 ml/1 tbsp tomato purée (paste)
5 ml/1 tsp anchovy essence (extract)
Finely grated rind and juice of ½ orange
1 garlic clove, crushed
1 bay leaf
Salt and freshly ground black pepper
Plain Rice for Fish (page 392), to serve

Boil the potatoes and carrots in lightly salted water for 4 minutes until almost tender. Drain. Toss the fish in the soy and Tabasco sauces. In a large frying pan (skillet), fry (sauté) the onions and leeks in the oil for 5 minutes, stirring. Add the tomatoes, tomato purée, anchovy essence, orange rind and juice, the garlic and bay leaf. Bring to the boil, add the potatoes and carrots, reduce the heat and simmer for 5 minutes. Add the fish and any juices and simmer for a further 5 minutes or until everything is tender. Discard the bay leaf. Taste and season if necessary. Serve piping hot on a bed of rice.

Salmon with cucumber and dill

SERVES 4

4 salmon tail fillets, about 175 g/6 oz
  each
50 g/2 oz/¼ cup unsalted (sweet)
  butter
Salt and freshly ground black pepper
½ cucumber, skinned and finely diced
300 ml/½ pt/1¼ cups soured (dairy
  sour) cream
5 ml/1 tsp dried dill (dill weed)

Fry (sauté) the salmon, skin-side up, in the butter for 1½ minutes. Turn the fish over and cook on the other side for a further 1½ minutes. Season well. Add the cucumber, soured cream and dill, cover and simmer for 5 minutes. Serve straight from the pan.

Freddie's prawns

SERVES 4

1 large onion, finely chopped
45 ml/3 tbsp olive oil
10 ml/2 tsp curry paste
250 ml/8 fl oz/1 cup passata (sieved
  tomatoes)
10 ml/2 tsp tomato purée (paste)
Salt and freshly ground black pepper
45 ml/3 tbsp tomato chutney
450 g/1 lb raw peeled tiger prawns
  (jumbo shrimp)
½ head of celery, cut into small
  matchsticks
45 ml/3 tbsp cornflour (cornstarch)
Oil, for deep-frying
Plain Rice for Fish (page 392), to serve

Fry (sauté) the onion in the olive oil for 3 minutes until lightly golden. Stir in the curry paste and cook for 1 minute. Add the passata, tomato purée and a little salt and pepper. Simmer for 5 minutes. Remove from the heat and stir in the chutney.

Meanwhile, toss the prawns and celery in the cornflour, seasoned with a little salt and pepper. Deep-fry in hot oil until golden. Drain on kitchen paper (paper towels). Pile on to a bed of rice and spoon the sauce over. Serve straight away.

Golden fish, corn and potato fry

SERVES 4

15 g/½ oz/1 tbsp butter or margarine
15 ml/1 tbsp sunflower oil
450 g/1 lb potatoes, grated
Salt and freshly ground black pepper
350 g/12 oz smoked haddock fillet,
  skinned and cubed, discarding any
  bones
200 g/7 oz/1 small can of sweetcorn
  (corn), drained
300 ml/½ pt/1¼ cups passata (sieved
  tomatoes)
A good pinch of caster (superfine)
  sugar
Leaf spinach, to serve

Melt the butter or margarine in a frying pan (skillet) and add the oil. Add half the potato and press down well. Sprinkle with salt and pepper. Scatter the fish and sweetcorn over the top, then add the remaining potato. Press down well again and season lightly. Cover with foil or a lid and cook for 30 minutes until cooked through. Meanwhile, heat the passata with the sugar. Turn the fishcake out on to a warm plate. Cut into wedges and serve with the passata and leaf spinach.

Smoked mackerel rosti

SERVES 4

1 lemon
25 g/1 oz/2 tbsp butter or margarine
450 g/1 lb potatoes, grated
Salt and freshly ground black pepper
350 g/12 oz smoked mackerel fillet,
    skinned and cut into small pieces
15 ml/1 tbsp chopped parsley
300 ml/½ pt/1¼ cups passata (sieved
    tomatoes)
5 ml/1 tsp chopped basil

Halve the lemon. Grate the rind from one half and cut the other into wedges. Melt the butter or margarine in a frying pan (skillet). Add half the potato and press down well. Season with salt and pepper. Add the fish in an even layer and sprinkle with the parsley, lemon rind and a little seasoning. Top with the remaining potato, press down well again and season lightly. Cover with foil or a lid and cook gently for 30 minutes until cooked through. Meanwhile, heat the passata with the basil in a small saucepan. Turn the fishcake out on to a warm serving plate. Garnish with the lemon wedges, then cut into quarters and serve with the tomato sauce.

Cod rosti

SERVES 4

Prepare as for Smoked Mackerel Rosti, but substitute cod fillet for the smoked mackerel, omit the lemon and flavour the passata with dried, mixed herbs instead of basil.

John dory in cider and calvados

SERVES 4

4 John Dory fillets
Salt and freshly ground black pepper
2 spring onions (scallions), finely
    chopped
25 g/1 oz/2 tbsp unsalted (sweet)
    butter
300 ml/½ pt/1¼ cups medium-sweet
    cider
50 g/2 oz baby button mushrooms,
    thinly sliced
30 ml/2 tbsp calvados
2 egg yolks
150 ml/¼ pt/⅔ cup crème fraîche
Lemon juice
15 ml/1 tbsp chopped parsley
Plain potatoes and sautéed courgettes
    (zucchini), to serve

Wipe the fish with kitchen paper (paper towels) and season with salt and pepper. Fry (sauté) the spring onions in the butter for 3 minutes until softened. Add the fish, flesh-side down, and cook for 1 minute. Turn over and add the cider and mushrooms. Bring to the boil, reduce the heat, cover and cook gently for 8 minutes or until the fish is tender. Carefully lift the fish and mushrooms out of the pan and keep warm.

Boil the cider rapidly until reduced by half. Add the calvados, ignite and shake the pan until the flames subside. Whisk the egg yolks with the crème fraîche and stir into the pan. Cook, stirring, until thickened but do not allow to boil or it will curdle. Add lemon juice, salt and pepper to taste. Spoon over the fish and garnish with the parsley. Serve with plain potatoes and sautéed courgettes.

Mackerel in oatmeal with horseradish mayonnaise

SERVES 4

4 mackerel, cleaned and boned
Salt and freshly ground black pepper
100 g/4 oz/1 cup oatmeal
50 g/2 oz/¼ cup butter or margarine
30 ml/2 tbsp olive oil
60 ml/4 tbsp mayonnaise
10 ml/2 tsp horseradish relish
Lemon wedges

Season the mackerel with salt and pepper and coat thoroughly in the oatmeal. Heat the butter or margarine and oil in a large frying pan (skillet) and fry (sauté) the fish for 5 minutes on each side until crisp, golden and cooked through. Drain on kitchen paper (paper towels) and transfer to warm plates. Mix the mayonnaise with the horseradish and season to taste. Put a spoonful to the side of each mackerel and garnish the plates with lemon wedges.

Mackerel with mushrooms and tomatoes

SERVES 4

4 mackerel, cleaned
25 g/1 oz/2 tbsp butter or margarine
1 garlic clove, crushed
4 tomatoes, skinned and chopped
100 g/4 oz button mushrooms, sliced
15 ml/1 tbsp chopped parsley
15 ml/1 tbsp snipped chives
5 ml/1 tsp tomato purée (paste)
A good pinch of caster (superfine) sugar
Salt and freshly ground black pepper
Plain potatoes, to serve

Slash the fish several times on each side. Heat the butter or margarine in a large frying pan (skillet), add the fish and brown for 2 minutes on each side. Add the garlic, tomatoes and mushrooms, cover the pan and cook for 5–8 minutes until the fish is cooked and the tomatoes are pulpy. Lift out the fish and keep warm. Add the herbs, tomato purée, sugar and some salt and pepper to the pan. Simmer, stirring, for 2 minutes. Spoon over the fish and serve with plain potatoes.

Cod's roe fritters

SERVES 4

2 × 200 g/7 oz/small cans of pressed cod's roe
50 g/2 oz/½ cup wholemeal flour
Salt and freshly ground black pepper
1.5 ml/¼ tsp cayenne
30 ml/2 tbsp chopped parsley
Sunflower oil, for shallow-frying
Lemon wedges and parsley sprigs, to garnish
Sauté Potatoes (page 389) and peas, to serve

Slice each can of roe into six pieces. Mix the flour with some salt and pepper, the cayenne and parsley and use to coat the slices. Heat enough oil to cover the base of a frying pan (skillet) and fry (sauté) the slices for about 3 minutes on each side until golden. Drain on kitchen paper (paper towels) and transfer to warm plates. Garnish with lemon wedges and parsley sprigs and serve with Sauté Potatoes and peas.

Brittany cod

SERVES 4

4 potatoes, cut into 4 or 6 pieces
15 button (pearl) onions, peeled but
left whole
75 g/3 oz/⅓ cup unsalted (sweet)
butter
700 g/1½ lb cod fillet, skinned and cut
into large chunks
Salt and freshly ground black pepper
30 ml/2 tbsp sunflower oil
5 ml/1 tsp caster (superfine) sugar
½ lemon
15 ml/1 tbsp chopped parsley

Cook the potatoes in lightly salted,
boiling water for 4 minutes until
almost tender. Drain. Boil the onions
separately for 3 minutes. Drain. Melt
25 g/1 oz/2 tbsp of the butter in a
frying pan (skillet), add the fish,
season, cover and cook very gently
for 10 minutes, basting once or twice
as the juices run. Meanwhile, melt
half the remaining butter and the oil
in the potato saucepan. Add the
potatoes and fry (sauté), turning
occasionally, until golden brown all
over and cooked through. In the
onion pan, melt the remaining butter
and fry the onions until golden.
Sprinkle the sugar over, cover and
cook for a further 3–4 minutes until
browned and tender, shaking the
pan occasionally to prevent sticking.
Transfer the fish and all the juices to
the middle of a warm serving platter.
Put the potatoes down one side and
the onions down the other. Squeeze
the lemon over the fish and sprinkle
with the parsley before serving.

Cod croquettes

SERVES 4–6

Butter or margarine, for greasing
450 g/1 lb cod fillet
Salt and freshly ground black pepper
Juice of ½ lemon
1 quantity of Béchamel Sauce (page
376), made with twice the amount
of flour and butter or margarine
7.5 ml/1½ tsp powdered gelatine
15 ml/1 tbsp hot water
2 eggs, beaten
15 ml/1 tbsp snipped chives
45 ml/3 tbsp plain (all-purpose) flour
25 g/1 oz/½ cup fresh white
breadcrumbs
Oil, for deep-frying
All-year Tomato Sauce (page 379),
to serve

Grease an ovenproof dish. Add the
fish and season with salt, pepper
and the lemon juice. Cover with
greased foil and bake in a preheated
oven at 160°C/325°F/gas mark 3 for
10 minutes. Remove the skin and
flake the fish. Make up the very
thick sauce and beat in the fish.
Dissolve the gelatine in the hot
water and stir in. Beat in one of the
eggs and the chives and re-season to
taste. Turn the mixture into a
shallow square or rectangular dish
and leave to cool, then chill until
firm. Cut into oblongs about
7.5 cm/3 in long and 2.5 cm/1 in
wide. Roll into sausage shapes, then
dust in the flour, seasoned with salt
and pepper. Brush with the
remaining egg, then roll gently in
the breadcrumbs. Deep-fry in hot oil
for about 4 minutes until golden
brown. Drain on kitchen paper
(paper towels). Serve hot with All-
year Tomato Sauce.

Salmon croquettes

SERVES 4–6

Prepare as for Cod Croquettes, but substitute salmon fillet for the cod and chopped dill (dill weed) for the chives. Serve hot with Dill and Mustard Sauce (page 373) instead of All-year Tomato Sauce.

Smoked haddock croquettes

SERVES 4–6

Prepare as for Cod Croquettes, but substitute smoked haddock for the cod.

Curried fish croquettes

SERVES 4

350 g/12 oz white fish fillet
100 g/4 oz/½ cup mashed potato
100 g/4 oz/1 cup cooked long-grain rice
1 small onion, grated
10 ml/2 tsp curry powder
10 ml/2 tsp mango chutney
Salt and freshly ground black pepper
1 egg, beaten
25 g/1 oz/½ cup fresh white breadcrumbs
Oil, for deep-frying
Lemon wedges, to garnish

Put the fish in a pan with just enough water to cover. Cook gently for 10 minutes until tender. Drain, discard the skin and any bones and flake the fish. Mix with the potato, rice, onion, curry powder, chutney and salt and pepper to taste. Shape into eight small rolls. Coat with the egg, then the breadcrumbs. Heat the oil to 190°C/375°F or until a cube of day-old bread browns in 30 seconds. Fry (sauté) until crisp and golden. Drain on kitchen paper (paper towels) and serve garnished with lemon wedges.

Trout with lemon and tarragon

SERVES 4

4 trout, cleaned
25 g/1 oz/2 tbsp butter or margarine
120 ml/4 fl oz/½ cup dry white wine
1 small lemon, thinly sliced
1 small onion, finely chopped
15 ml/1 tbsp chopped tarragon
30 ml/2 tbsp chopped parsley
Salt and freshly ground black pepper
150 ml/¼ pt/⅔ cup double (heavy) cream
Buttered Rice (page 392) and broccoli, to serve

Brown the fish in the butter or margarine quickly on both sides in a large frying pan (skillet), then pour the wine over. Cover with the lemon slices, the onion, tarragon and half the parsley. Season lightly, bring to the boil, cover and cook gently for 8–10 minutes until the trout are tender and cooked through. Carefully transfer to warm plates and keep warm. Boil the cooking liquid until reduced by half. Stir in the cream and simmer for 2 minutes. Season to taste. Spoon over the fish, sprinkle with the remaining parsley and serve with Buttered Rice and broccoli.

Seaside pancakes

SERVES 4

For the pancakes:
*100 g/4 oz/1 cup plain (all-purpose)
 flour*
A pinch of salt
1 egg
150 ml/¼ pt/⅔ cup milk
150 ml/¼ pt/⅔ cup water
Oil, for shallow-frying
For the filling:
15 g/½ oz/1 tbsp butter or margarine
*225 g/8 oz cod fillet, skinned and
 finely diced*
*295 g/10½ oz/1 medium can of
 condensed mushroom soup*
*200 g/7 oz/1 small can of sweetcorn
 (corn) with (bell) peppers, drained*
Freshly ground black pepper
75 g/3 oz/¾ cup Cheddar cheese, grated
Cucumber slices, to garnish

To make the pancakes, sift the flour
and salt into a bowl. Make a well in
the centre and break in the egg. Add
half the milk and half the water and
beat well until smooth. Stir in the
remaining milk and water. Heat a
little oil in a frying pan (skillet).
Pour off any excess. Add just enough
batter to cover the base when
swirled round. Cook until the
underside is golden. Toss the
pancake or turn over with a palette
knife or fish slice and cook the other
side. Slide on to a plate, cover and
keep warm over a pan of hot water
while making the remaining seven
pancakes.

 To make the filling, melt the
butter or margarine in a saucepan.
Add the fish and cook gently,
tossing, for about 4 minutes until
just cooked. Gently stir in the soup,
corn and pepper to taste. Heat
through until bubbling. Use the
mixture to fill the pancakes, roll up
and place in a flameproof serving
dish. Sprinkle with the cheese and
place under a preheated grill
(broiler) to brown. Garnish with
cucumber slices before serving.

Tuna and sweetcorn
pancakes

SERVES 4

*1 quantity of pancakes (see Seaside
 Pancakes, left)*
1 quantity of Cheese Sauce (page 376)
*185 g/6½ oz/1 small can of tuna,
 drained*
*200 g/7 oz/1 small can of sweetcorn
 (corn), drained*
30 ml/2 tbsp chopped parsley
50 g/2 oz/½ cup Cheddar cheese, grated
*Sliced cucumber and tomatoes in
 French dressing, to serve*

Make up the pancakes and keep
warm. Make the cheese sauce, stir in
the tuna, sweetcorn and parsley and
heat through. Divide between the
pancakes and roll up. Place in a
shallow, flameproof dish. Sprinkle
with the cheese and place under a
preheated grill (broiler) until golden
and bubbling. Serve hot with
cucumber and tomatoes, tossed in
French dressing.

Bacalhau a bras

SERVES 4

This is probably one of the most famous Portuguese fish dishes.

450 g/1 lb salt cod, soaked and cooked (page 8)
Oil, for deep-frying
450 g/1 lb potatoes, peeled and cut into thick matchsticks
75 g/3 oz/⅓ cup unsalted (sweet) butter
45 ml/3 tbsp olive oil
2 large onions, thinly sliced
1 garlic clove, crushed
6 eggs, beaten
Salt and freshly ground black pepper
15 ml/1 tbsp sliced black olives
30 ml/2 tbsp chopped parsley
Crusty bread, to serve

Drain the cooked cod, remove the skin and separate the fish into large flakes. Heat the oil until a cube of day-old bread browns in 30 seconds. Add the potatoes and cook just until they are beginning to turn golden but are still soft, not crisp. Remove with a draining spoon. Drain on kitchen paper (paper towel).

Heat half the butter and the olive oil in a very large frying pan (skillet) or wok. Add the onions and fry (sauté) gently for 5 minutes until soft and a pale golden brown. Add the garlic and cook for a further 1 minute. Stir in the fish and toss gently for 3 minutes. Lift out with a draining spoon and reserve.

Melt the remaining butter in the pan. Add the almost-cooked potatoes and toss for 1 minute. Add the fish mixture and toss again. Season the eggs with salt and pepper and pour into the pan. Keep turning over the mixture with a spatula or fish slice until the mixture is creamy and lightly scrambled. Pile on to warm plates and sprinkle with the olives and parsley. Serve straight away with lots of crusty bread.

Roman-style cod

SERVES 4

Experiment using soaked and cooked salt cod (page 8) instead of fresh for a very traditional dish.

120 ml/4 fl oz/½ cup olive oil
1 large onion, halved and thinly sliced
2 green (bell) peppers, cut into thin strips
1 red pepper, cut into thin strips
400 g/14 oz/1 large can of chopped tomatoes
15 ml/1 tbsp tomato purée (paste)
A pinch of caster (superfine) sugar
Salt and freshly ground black pepper
700 g/1½ lb cod fillet, skinned and cut into large chunks
30 ml/2 tbsp plain (all-purpose) flour
5 ml/1 tsp paprika
15 ml/1 tbsp chopped basil

Heat 60 ml/4 tbsp of the oil in a frying pan (skillet). Add the onion and peppers and fry (sauté) quickly for 3 minutes. Add the tomatoes, tomato purée, sugar and a little salt and pepper and simmer for 5 minutes or until soft and pulpy. Meanwhile, toss the fish in the flour, mixed with the paprika and a little salt and pepper. Heat the remaining oil and fry (sauté) the cod on all sides until golden and tender. Drain on kitchen paper (paper towels). Add to the sauce and simmer for a further 3 minutes. Taste and re-season if necessary, then sprinkle with the basil and serve.

Smoked haddock stuffed pancakes

SERVES 4

For the filling:
225 g/8 oz undyed smoked haddock, skinned
100 g/4 oz button mushrooms, sliced
350 ml/12 fl oz/1⅓ cups milk
60 ml/4 tbsp plain (all-purpose) flour
5 ml/1 tsp lemon juice
30 ml/2 tbsp chopped parsley
Freshly ground black pepper
For the pancakes:
100 g/4 oz/1 cup wholemeal flour
A pinch of salt
1 egg
300 ml/½ pt/1¼ cups milk
15 g/½ oz/1 tbsp butter or margarine, melted
Oil, for shallow-frying
Lemon wedges and parsley sprigs, to garnish
Mangetout (snow peas) and baby carrots, to serve

To make the filling, poach the fish and mushrooms in 300 ml/½ pt/ 1¼ cups of the milk for 6 minutes or until the fish flakes easily with a fork. Lift the fish out of the milk and reserve. Blend the flour with the remaining milk. Stir into the fish milk, bring to the boil and cook for 2 minutes, stirring, until thickened. Add the lemon juice, parsley and pepper to taste. Flake the fish and fold in gently.

To make the pancakes, sift the flour and salt into a bowl. Make a well in the centre and add the egg and half the milk. Beat well until smooth. Stir in the remaining milk and the butter or margarine. Heat a little oil in a frying pan (skillet). Pour off the excess. Add enough batter to coat the base of the pan when swirled round. Cook until the underside is golden. Toss the pancake or turn over with a palette knife or fish slice and cook the other side. Slide on to a plate, cover and keep warm over a pan of hot water while making the remainder. Reheat the fish mixture, stirring gently, until piping hot. Divide the mixture between the pancakes, roll up and arrange on warm plates. Garnish with lemon wedges and parsley sprigs and serve straight away with mangetout and baby carrots.

Squid with pesto

SERVES 4

15 ml/1 tbsp olive oil
16 baby squid, cleaned (page 14) and sliced
Pesto (page 377 or use bought)
1 wineglass of dry white wine
Crusty bread and a tomato and rocket salad, to serve

Heat the oil in a frying pan (skillet). Add the squid and toss over a moderate heat for 3 minutes until turning opaque. Add the Pesto and wine and simmer for about 10 minutes, stirring occasionally, until the squid is tender. Serve with lots of crusty bread and a tomato and rocket salad.

Katie's hija tuna

SERVES 4

4 tuna steaks
5 ml/1 tsp pimenton
Salt and freshly ground black pepper
75 ml/5 tbsp olive oil
3 large potatoes, coarsely grated
1 onion, finely chopped
6 (bell) peppers, of various colours,
  each cut into 8 wedges
1 garlic clove, finely chopped
Lemon wedges and coriander
  (cilantro) leaves, to garnish

Wipe the tuna with kitchen paper (paper towels) and place in a dish. Sprinkle with half the pimenton and some salt and pepper. Drizzle with 15 ml/1 tbsp of the oil. Turn over, sprinkle with the remaining pimenton, more salt and pepper and another 15 ml/1 tbsp of the oil. Leave to marinate while preparing the remaining ingredients.

Heat 15 ml/1 tbsp of the remaining oil in a fairly small frying pan (skillet). Squeeze the grated potato to remove excess moisture. Mix in the onion and some salt and pepper and press into the frying pan. Cover and cook over a moderate heat for about 8 minutes until golden underneath. Turn the cake over and turn down the heat. Cover again and cook gently for a further 20 minutes until golden underneath and cooked through.

Meanwhile, heat the remaining oil in a separate frying pan and add the peppers, garlic and some salt and pepper. Fry (sauté), stirring, for about 10 minutes until just tender and lightly browning. Heat a separate pan. Add the tuna and their juices and fry for about 3 minutes on each side until cooked through and lightly golden. Cut the potato cake into quarters. Place on warm plates and top each with a tuna steak. Put a pile of the peppers to one side and serve garnished with lemon wedges and coriander leaves.

Rangoon haddock

SERVES 4

450 g/1 lb haddock fillet, skinned
450 ml/¾ pt/2 cups milk
25 g/1 oz/2 tbsp unsalted (sweet) butter
1 onion, finely chopped
1 garlic clove, crushed
2.5 cm/1 in piece of cinnamon stick
5 ml/1 tsp grated fresh root ginger
2 cardamom pods, split
8 button mushrooms, sliced
25 g/1 oz/¼ cup plain (all-purpose)
  flour
150 ml/¼ pt/⅔ cup crème fraîche
Salt and freshly ground black pepper
Lemon juice
Plain Rice for Fish (page 392), to serve

Put the fish in a frying pan (skillet) with the milk. Bring to the boil, reduce the heat, cover and cook gently for about 5 minutes or until cooked through. Transfer the fish to a bowl and flake with a fork. Pour off the milk and reserve. Rinse the frying pan and wipe dry with kitchen paper (paper towels). Melt the butter in the pan and fry (sauté) the onion, garlic and spices for 2 minutes, stirring. Add the mushrooms and cook for a further 1 minute. Stir in the flour and cook for 1 minute. Remove from the heat and blend in the fish milk. Return to the heat, bring to the boil and cook for 2 minutes, stirring, until thick and smooth. Remove the cinnamon and cardamom pods. Stir in the fish and crème fraîche. Season to taste with salt, pepper and lemon juice and heat through. Spoon on to a bed of rice and serve.

Funky fishcakes

SERVES 4

Serve with canned plum tomatoes instead of the poached ones, if you prefer.

2 potatoes, cut into chunks
225 g/8 oz white fish fillet, skinned
  and any bones removed
100 g/4 oz bacon pieces, rinded
25 g/1 oz/2 tbsp butter or margarine
15 ml/1 tbsp snipped chives
Salt and freshly ground black pepper
3 eggs
75 g/3 oz/¾ cup dried breadcrumbs
8 tomatoes
60 ml/4 tbsp water
1 mint sprig
Oil, for shallow-frying
Peas, to serve

Put the potatoes in a saucepan of lightly salted water and bring to the boil. Place the fish in a steamer or colander over the pan of potatoes. Cover and cook for about 10 minutes until the fish and potatoes are tender. Remove the fish. Drain the potatoes and place in a bowl. Add the fish and mash the potatoes and fish together.

Meanwhile, fry (sauté) the bacon in the butter or margarine for 2 minutes. Snip into small pieces with scissors, then add with the fat in the pan to the potato mixture. Add the chives and a little salt and pepper and mix well. Beat one of the eggs and add to the mixture to bind. Beat the remaining eggs in a shallow dish. Put the breadcrumbs in a separate dish. With well-floured hands, shape the mixture into eight fish-shaped cakes. Dip the cakes in the beaten egg, then the breadcrumbs, until thoroughly coated. Chill for at least 30 minutes, if possible.

Cut a cross in the top of each tomato. Place in a saucepan with the water and mint. Bring to the boil, reduce the heat, cover and cook very gently for about 5 minutes until the tomatoes are soft but still hold their shape.

Fry (sauté) the fishcakes in hot oil for about 2 minutes on each side until golden brown. Drain on kitchen paper (paper towels). Transfer the fishcakes to warm plates, put two tomatoes to the side of each and serve with peas.

Tuna fishcakes

SERVES 4

2 potatoes, cut into chunks
A knob of butter or margarine
185 g/6½ oz/1 small can of tuna,
  drained
15 ml/1 tbsp chopped parsley
Salt and freshly ground black pepper
2 eggs
45 ml/3 tbsp plain (all-purpose) flour
60 ml/4 tbsp dried breadcrumbs
Oil, for shallow-frying
Lemon wedges and parsley sprigs, to
  garnish

Cook the potatoes in lightly salted, boiling water until tender. Drain and mash with the butter or margarine. Beat in the tuna, parsley and salt and pepper to taste. Beat one of the eggs and stir in to bind. Divide the mixture into eight equal pieces and shape into small cakes. Coat in the flour. Beat the other egg and dip the cakes in this, then in the breadcrumbs, to coat completely. Fry (sauté) in hot oil for 3 minutes on each side until golden brown. Drain on kitchen paper (paper towels) and serve hot, garnished with lemon wedges and parsley sprigs.

White fishcakes

SERVES 4

Prepare as for Tuna Fishcakes, but substitute 225 g/8 oz any white fish fillet, skinned and poached (page 19), for the tuna.

Curried fishcakes

SERVES 4

Prepare as for White Fishcakes, but add 10 ml/2 tsp curry paste to the potatoes and serve with mango chutney.

Salmon fishcakes

SERVES 4

Prepare as for Tuna Fishcakes, but substitute 200 g/7 oz/1 small can of salmon, drained and skin removed, for the tuna. Remove the bones, if preferred, or simply mash them up with the fish.

Smoked haddock fishcakes

SERVES 4

Prepare as for Tuna Fishcakes, but substitute 225 g/8 oz smoked haddock fillet, skinned and poached (page 19), for the tuna, and snipped chives for the parsley.

Smoked haddock and cheese fishcakes

SERVES 4

Prepare as for Tuna Fishcakes, but substitute 225 g/8 oz smoked haddock fillet, skinned and poached (page 19), for the white fish. Add 50 g/2 oz/½ cup Cheddar cheese, grated, to the potato and omit the butter or margarine.

Sardine fishcakes

SERVES 4

Prepare as for Tuna Fishcakes, but substitute 2 × 125 g/4½ oz/small cans of sardines, drained and thoroughly mashed, for the tuna, and spike with 10 ml/2 tsp lemon juice. Serve with fried (sautéed) tomatoes to offset the richness.

Severn eels

SERVES 4

450 g/1 lb elvers
30 ml/2 tbsp salt
25 g/1 oz/2 tbsp dripping
8–12 smoked streaky bacon rashers (slices), rinded
4 eggs
15 ml/1 tbsp single (light) cream
Salt and freshly ground black pepper
15 ml/1 tbsp chopped parsley
Warm crusty bread and butter, to serve

Put the elvers in a large bowl. Cover with cold water and add the salt. Stir well with a wooden spoon to clean the fish. Tip them into a colander and rinse thoroughly under cold, running water for a good minute, tossing and shaking them to clean thoroughly. Pat dry on kitchen paper (paper towels). Melt the dripping in a large frying pan (skillet). Add the bacon and fry (sauté) until crisp. Remove from the pan with a draining spoon and keep warm. Add the elvers to the pan and toss gently for a few minutes until white. Beat the eggs with the cream and a little salt and pepper. Add to the frying pan and stir gently until lightly scrambled but still creamy. Pile the elver mixture on to warm plates. Top with the rashers of bacon and scatter the parsley over. Serve with warm crusty bread and butter.

Traditional fish and chips

SERVES 4

700 g/1½ lb cod or haddock fillet
100 g/4 oz/1 cup plain (all-purpose)
  flour
Salt and freshly ground black pepper
1 kg/2¼ lb potatoes
15 ml/1 tbsp sunflower oil
120 ml/4 fl oz/½ cup tepid water
1 large egg white
Oil, for deep-frying
Vinegar, tomato ketchup (catsup) and
  peas, to serve

Skin the fish, cut into four equal pieces and wipe with kitchen paper (paper towels). Toss in 25 g/1 oz/ ¼ cup of the flour, seasoned with salt and pepper. Cut the potatoes into thick slices, then each slice into thick fingers. Place in a bowl of cold water. Mix the remaining flour with a pinch of salt. Add the measured oil and the water and beat until smooth. Whisk the egg white until stiff and fold in with a metal spoon. Drain the potatoes and dry on kitchen paper.

Heat the oil for deep-frying until a cube of day-old bread browns in 30 seconds. Add about a quarter of the chips (fries) and fry (sauté) for about 3 minutes until soft but not brown. Drain on kitchen paper and cook the remaining chips in the same way. Dip the fish in the batter to coat completely. Deep-fry for 5–6 minutes until golden brown and cooked through. Drain on kitchen paper and keep warm. Reheat the oil, put all the chips back in and cook until crisp and golden. Drain on kitchen paper. Serve the fish and chips with vinegar, tomato ketchup and peas.

Curried fish croquettes

SERVES 4

350 g/12 oz white fish fillet
2 potatoes, cut into small pieces
15 g/½ oz/1 tbsp butter or margarine
1 small onion, grated
10 ml/2 tsp curry powder
15 ml/1 tbsp mango chutney
Salt and freshly ground black pepper
1 egg, beaten
25 g/1 oz/½ cup fresh white
  breadcrumbs
Oil, for shallow-frying
Mango chutney, sliced bananas, cherry
  tomatoes, sliced cucumber and green
  leaf salad, to serve

Put the fish in a saucepan and cover with water. Cook for 6–8 minutes until tender. Drain and remove the skin. Flake the fish in a bowl. Meanwhile, cook the potatoes in lightly salted, boiling water until tender. Drain and mash with the butter or margarine. Stir in the fish, onion, curry powder, chutney and salt and pepper to taste. Shape into eight rolls about 7.5 cm/3 in long. Dip in the egg, then the breadcrumbs, and chill until ready to cook. Heat about 1 cm/½ in of oil in a large frying pan (skillet). Add the croquettes and fry (sauté) for about 4 minutes, turning occasionally, until golden brown all over. Drain on kitchen paper (paper towels) and serve with mango chutney, sliced bananas, cherry tomatoes, sliced cucumber and a green leaf salad.

Lobster Newburg

SERVES 4

1 large cooked lobster
25 g/1 oz/2 tbsp butter or margarine
90 ml/6 tbsp medium-dry sherry
30 ml/2 tbsp lemon juice
2 egg yolks
150 ml/¼ pt/⅔ cup single (light) cream
A good pinch of cayenne
Salt and freshly ground black pepper
Plain Rice for Fish (page 392), to serve
Paprika, for dusting

Split the lobster and remove all the meat (page 15). Cut the meat into neat pieces. Melt the butter or margarine in a frying pan (skillet). Add the lobster and toss over a gentle heat for 3–4 minutes until piping hot but not brown. Add the sherry and lemon juice and boil rapidly until reduced by half. Beat the egg yolks with the cream, cayenne and a little salt and pepper. Pour into the pan and cook over a gentle heat until thickened. Do not allow to boil. Spoon on to a bed of rice and dust with paprika before serving.

Prawns Newburg

SERVES 4

Prepare as for Lobster Newburg, but substitute 350 g/12 oz raw, peeled tiger prawns (jumbo shrimp) for the lobster meat.

Devilled lobster

SERVES 4

2 cooked lobsters
1 small onion, very finely chopped
15 g/½ oz/1 tbsp butter or margarine
30 ml/2 tbsp Worcestershire sauce
15 ml/1 tbsp mushroom ketchup
  (catsup)
15 ml/1 tbsp soy sauce
5 ml/1 tsp anchovy essence (extract)
5 ml/1 tsp tomato purée (paste)
5 ml/1 tsp red wine vinegar
1 garlic clove, crushed
1 bay leaf
1 thick lemon slice
150 ml/¼ pt/⅔ cup red wine
150 ml/¼ pt/⅔ cup fish stock
225 g/8 oz/1 small can of chopped
  tomatoes
5 ml/1 tsp caster (superfine) sugar
Salt and freshly ground black pepper
A pinch of chilli powder
30 ml/2 tbsp snipped chives
Wild Rice Mix for Fish (page 394) and
  green salad, to serve

Halve the lobsters and remove all the meat (page 15). Cut the meat into neat pieces. Clean the shells and heat through in a very low oven. Fry (sauté) the onion in the butter or margarine in a large frying pan (skillet), stirring, for 2 minutes. Add all the remaining ingredients except the chives. Bring to the boil, reduce the heat and simmer for 10 minutes, stirring occasionally, until pulpy. Add the lobster meat and heat through for 3 minutes. Pile into the shells, sprinkle liberally with the chives and serve with Wild Rice Mix and a green salad.

Sautéed spiced crab with green bananas

SERVES 4

1 large cooked crab, prepared
  (page 16)
50 g/2 oz/¼ cup butter or margarine
1 bunch of spring onions (scallions),
  finely chopped
15 ml/1 tbsp grated Parmesan cheese
60 ml/4 tbsp double (heavy) cream
5 ml/1 tsp anchovy essence (extract)
1 small green chilli, seeded and finely
  chopped
5 ml/1 tsp Worcestershire sauce
225 g/8 oz/1 small can of chopped
  tomatoes
Salt and freshly ground black pepper
2 green bananas, thickly sliced
  diagonally
30 ml/2 tbsp plain (all-purpose) flour
30 ml/2 tbsp sunflower oil
Plain Rice for Fish (page 392), to serve
Coriander (cilantro) sprigs, to garnish

Mix the dark and light crabmeat
together. Melt half the butter or
margarine in a frying pan (skillet)
and add the spring onions. Cook,
stirring, for 3 minutes until softened.
Add the cheese, cream, anchovy
essence, chilli, Worcestershire sauce
and tomatoes. Bring to the boil and
bubble for 3–4 minutes. Stir in the
crab and season to taste.

Meanwhile, toss the bananas in
the flour, seasoned with a little salt
and pepper. Melt the remaining
butter or margarine with the oil in a
separate pan. Add the bananas and
fry (sauté) until golden on both
sides. Drain on kitchen paper (paper
towels). Spoon the crab mixture on
to a bed of rice, put the bananas to
one side and garnish with coriander
sprigs.

Scampi à la crème

SERVES 4

450 g/1 lb raw peeled scampi
25 g/1 oz/2 tbsp unsalted (sweet)
  butter
5 ml/1 tsp paprika
1.5 ml/¼ tsp cayenne
120 ml/4 fl oz/½ cup medium-dry
  sherry
2 egg yolks
300 ml/½ pt/1¼ cups crème fraîche
2 beefsteak tomatoes, skinned, seeded
  and chopped
Salt and freshly ground black pepper
Plain Rice for Fish (page 392), to serve
30 ml/2 tbsp chopped parsley, to
  garnish

Fry (sauté) the scampi in the butter
for 2–3 minutes until pink. Add the
paprika, cayenne and sherry and
boil rapidly until the liquid is
reduced by half. Blend together the
egg yolks and crème fraîche and stir
into the pan. Cook very gently,
stirring, until the sauce thickens.
Do not allow to boil. Add the
tomatoes and cook gently for a
further 1 minute. Season to taste.
Serve on a bed of rice, garnished
with the parsley.

Scampi Provençal

SERVES 4

2 large onions, sliced
2 green (bell) peppers, diced
1 garlic clove, crushed
30 ml/2 tbsp olive oil
400 g/14 oz/1 large can of chopped
   tomatoes
15 ml/1 tbsp tomato purée (paste)
5 ml/1 tsp dried mixed herbs
5 ml/1 tsp anchovy essence (extract)
350 g/12 oz raw peeled scampi
Salt and freshly ground black pepper
12 stoned (pitted) black olives, halved
Plain Rice for Fish (page 392), to serve

Fry (sauté) the onions, peppers and
garlic in the oil for 3 minutes,
stirring. Add the tomatoes, tomato
purée, herbs and anchovy essence.
Boil rapidly for about 5 minutes,
stirring occasionally, until pulpy.
Add the scampi and simmer, stirring,
for 5 minutes. Season to taste and
stir in the olives. Spoon on to a bed
of rice and serve very hot.

Egg foo yung

SERVES 2 OR 4

6 eggs
Soy sauce
Salt and freshly ground black pepper
2 spring onions (scallions), finely
   chopped
30 ml/2 tbsp cooked frozen peas
175 g/6 oz cooked peeled prawns
   (shrimp)
A pinch of Chinese five-spice powder
30 ml/2 tbsp sunflower oil

Beat the eggs lightly in a bowl with
a dash of soy sauce and a little salt
and pepper. Stir in the spring
onions, peas, prawns and spice. Heat
the oil in a frying pan (skillet). Add
the egg mixture and cook gently,
lifting and stirring, until golden

brown underneath and almost set.
Turn the omelette over and cook the
other side. Roll up and transfer to a
warm serving dish. Sprinkle with
soy sauce and serve cut into slices.

Corn and tuna fritters

SERVES 4

These are also good for breakfast or
served with Aioli (page 372) as a
starter and they are also wonderful
as a side dish with any grilled
(broiled), fried (sautéed) or baked
fish. Try using mushrooms, blanched
broccoli or cauliflower florets or
leftover mixed, cooked vegetables
instead of sweetcorn (corn), too.

75 g/3 oz/⅓ cup plain (all-purpose)
   flour
A good pinch of salt
15 ml/1 tbsp baking powder
120 ml/4 fl oz/½ cup water
75 g/3 oz frozen sweetcorn
85 g/3½ oz/1 very small can of tuna,
   thoroughly drained
Oil, for shallow-frying
Mixed salad and Cooling Cheese and
   Onion Dip (page 382), to serve

Mix the flour with the salt and
baking powder. Stir in enough of the
water to form a thick, creamy batter.
Stir in the sweetcorn and tuna. Heat
the oil in a frying pan (skillet) and
drop in spoonfuls of the batter. Fry
(sauté) until golden brown
underneath. Turn over and cook
until golden and crisp. Drain on
kitchen paper (paper towels) and
serve hot with a mixed salad and
Cooling Cheese and Onion Dip.

Omelette Arnold Bennett

SERVES 2

175 g/6 oz smoked haddock fillet,
* skinned*
150 ml/¼ pt/⅔ cup water
50 g/2 oz/¼ cup unsalted (sweet)
* butter*
150 ml/¼ pt/⅔ cup double (heavy)
* cream*
Salt and freshly ground black pepper
4 eggs, separated
45 ml/3 tbsp freshly grated Parmesan
* cheese*
Parsley sprigs, to garnish

Put the fish in a frying pan (skillet)
with the water. Bring to the boil,
reduce the heat, cover and poach
gently for about 5 minutes or until
the fish flakes easily with a fork.
Drain and tip the fish into a bowl.
Dry the pan with kitchen paper
(paper towels). Flake the fish with a
fork. Melt half the butter in the
frying pan and add the fish and
cream. Toss gently for 2 minutes and
season lightly with pepper. Beat the
egg yolks with 15 ml/1 tbsp of the
cheese and a little salt and pepper.
Tip in the haddock mixture and half
the cheese and stir gently. Whisk the
egg whites until stiff and fold in
with a metal spoon.

 Wipe out the frying pan with
kitchen paper. Melt the remaining
butter in the pan, add the fish
mixture and cook until golden on
the underside and almost set.
Sprinkle with the remaining cheese.
Place under a preheated grill
(broiler) to brown the top. Cut in
half, slide on to warm plates and
garnish with parsley sprigs.

Edward VII's favourite omelette

SERVES 4

1 small lobster, about 350 g/12 oz
175 g/6 oz button mushrooms, sliced
75 g/3 oz/⅓ cup unsalted (sweet)
* butter*
30 ml/2 tbsp brandy
30 ml/2 tbsp port
60 ml/4 tbsp double (heavy) cream
Salt and freshly ground black pepper
1 quantity of Béchamel Sauce
* (page 376)*
75 ml/5 tbsp freshly grated Parmesan
* cheese*
8 eggs
30 ml/2 tbsp water

Remove and dice all the meat from
the lobster body and large claws
(page 15), but reserve the legs for
garnish. Fry (sauté) the mushrooms
in half the butter for 2 minutes. Add
the brandy and port and boil until
reduced by half. Stir in the cream, a
little salt and pepper and the lobster
meat. Heat through, stirring, and
allow to bubble until the mixture
forms a thick sauce. Make the
Béchamel Sauce and stir in 30 ml/
2 tbsp of the cheese.

 Melt the remaining butter in a
large frying pan (skillet). Beat
together the eggs and water with a
little salt and pepper and pour into
the pan. Cook, lifting and stirring,
until the omelette is golden
underneath and almost set but still
creamy on top. Spread the lobster
mixture over. Roll up and slide on to
a flameproof plate. Spoon the
Béchamel Sauce over and sprinkle
with the remaining cheese. Brown
quickly under a preheated grill
(broiler) and serve piping hot,
garnished with the lobster legs.

Prawn omelette

SERVES 1

2 eggs
15 ml/1 tbsp water
Salt and freshly ground black pepper
5 ml/1 tsp butter or margarine
50 g/2 oz cooked peeled prawns
 (shrimp)
15 ml/1 tbsp chopped parsley
10 ml/2 tsp tomato ketchup (catsup)
A few drops of Worcestershire sauce

Beat the eggs and water with a little salt and pepper. Melt the butter or margarine in a small omelette pan. Add the egg mixture and cook, lifting and stirring gently, until the base is golden and the egg mixture is almost set. Mix the prawns with the parsley, ketchup, and a few drops of Worcestershire sauce. Spoon over half the omelette. Heat through for a few minutes. Sprinkle with a little more Worcestershire sauce and fold the omelette over the filling. Slide on to a warm plate and serve.

Creamy prawn omelette

SERVES 1

Prepare as for Prawn Omelette, but mix 15 ml/1 tbsp crème fraîche into the prawn mixture and use snipped chives instead of chopped parsley.

Madame Bovary's omelette

SERVES 4

1 small onion, finely chopped
150 g/5 oz/⅔ cup butter or margarine
2 × 100 g/4 oz/small cans of soft cod's
 roes, drained
85 g/3½ oz/1 very small can of tuna,
 drained
8 eggs, beaten
Salt and freshly ground black pepper
15 ml/1 tbsp chopped parsley
5 ml/1 tsp dried mixed herbs
A little lemon juice
Hot French bread, to serve

Fry (sauté) the onion in 50 g/ 2 oz/¼ cup of the butter or margarine for 3 minutes, stirring, until softened but not browned. Mix the roes and tuna into the onion, then stir into the eggs and season well. Melt a small knob of the remaining butter or margarine in a frying pan (skillet), add a quarter of the egg mixture and cook, lifting and stirring gently, until the base is golden brown and the omelette is almost set but still slightly creamy. Fold, slide out of the pan on to a plate and keep warm in a low oven while making three more omelettes. Melt the remaining butter or margarine in a saucepan. Add the herbs and lemon juice and a good grinding of pepper. Pour a little over each omelette and serve with hot French bread.

Spicy prawn fajitas

SERVES 4

1 red onion, chopped
1 large garlic clove, crushed
200 g/4 oz button mushrooms, sliced
30 ml/2 tbsp olive oil
1 red chilli, seeded and chopped
400 g/14 oz/1 large can of chopped
   tomatoes
30 ml/2 tbsp tomato purée (paste)
5 ml/1 tsp caster (superfine) sugar
Salt and freshly ground black pepper
225 g/8 oz raw peeled tiger prawns
   (jumbo shrimp)
A few drops of Tabasco sauce
   (optional)
8 large flour tortillas
¼ iceberg lettuce, finely shredded
5 cm/2 in piece of cucumber, finely
   chopped
1 small red (bell) pepper, finely
   chopped
90 ml/6 tbsp plain yoghurt

Fry (sauté) the onion, garlic and
mushrooms in the oil in a large
frying pan (skillet) for 3 minutes,
stirring, until soft but not brown.
Add the chilli, tomatoes, tomato
purée, sugar and a little salt and
pepper, bring to the boil and boil
fairly rapidly for about 5 minutes,
stirring occasionally, until really
thick and pulpy. Add the prawns and
continue to bubble until the prawns
are pink. Taste and re-season, adding
a few drops of Tabasco, if liked.
   Meanwhile, warm the tortillas
according to the packet directions.
Divide the lettuce, cucumber and
pepper between the tortillas, top
with the prawn mixture and spoon a
little yoghurt over. Roll up and serve.

Spicy cod fajitas

SERVES 4

Prepare as for Spicy Prawn Fajitas,
but substitute 350 g/12 oz thick cod
fillet, skinned and cubed, for the
prawns. Take care not to overcook
the cod; it should be just opaque
but still holding its shape. Add
5 ml/1 tsp anchovy essence (extract)
to the sauce.

Eggs romaine

SERVES 4

700 g/1½ lb spinach, well washed and
   torn into pieces
50 g/2 oz/¼ cup butter or margarine
1 quantity of Béchamel Sauce
   (page 376)
15 ml/1 tbsp double (heavy) cream
Salt and freshly ground black pepper
8 eggs
30 ml/2 tbsp olive oil
50 g/2 oz/1 small can of anchovy
   fillets, drained

Cook the spinach in a saucepan with
no extra water for about 5 minutes
or until soft, pressing down
occasionally during cooking. Drain
in a colander and chop with
scissors. Heat half the butter or
margarine in the saucepan until
lightly golden, then add the spinach
and toss. When piping hot, turn into
four individual dishes and keep
warm. Meanwhile, make the sauce
and stir in the cream. Season to taste
and spoon over the spinach. Fry
(sauté) the eggs in the remaining
butter or margarine and the oil. Slide
on top of the sauce and garnish with
the anchovies. Serve straight away.

Skate with black butter

SERVES 2

2 skate wings
15 ml/1 tbsp lemon juice
600 ml/1 pt/2½ cups fish stock
1 onion, finely chopped
Salt and freshly ground black pepper
50 g/2 oz/¼ cup butter or margarine
5 ml/1 tsp white wine vinegar
15 ml/1 tbsp capers
15 ml/1 tbsp chopped parsley

Wash the skate and place in a large
frying pan (skillet). Cover with
water and add the lemon juice.
Bring to the boil, reduce the heat,
cover and simmer for 6 minutes. Lift
out and remove the membrane
surrounding the flesh. Heat the stock
and onion in the pan. Add a little
salt and pepper. Bring to the boil,
slide in the skate, cover and turn off
the heat. Leave for 15 minutes, then
transfer to warm plates and keep
warm. Melt the butter or margarine
in a separate frying pan and cook
until golden, but do not let it burn.
Add the wine vinegar and season.
Pour over the fish, sprinkle with
capers and parsley and serve very
hot.

Neapolitan salt cod

SERVES 4

This is also good made with
unsalted cod (there's no need to
soak and cook it, of course).

90 ml/6 tbsp olive oil
1 red (bell) pepper, cut into thin strips
2 large garlic cloves, crushed
2 beefsteak tomatoes, skinned and
*   chopped*
Salt and freshly ground black pepper
5 ml/1 tsp caster (superfine) sugar
A good pinch of cayenne
15 ml/1 tbsp capers
5 ml/1 tsp caper vinegar
15 stoned (pitted) green olives
700 g/1½ lb salt cod, soaked and
*   cooked (page 8)*
30 ml/2 tbsp plain (all-purpose) flour
Buttered Noodles for Fish (page 394),
*   to serve*

Heat 30 ml/2 tbsp of the oil in a
saucepan. Add the red pepper, garlic,
tomatoes, some salt and pepper, the
sugar, cayenne, capers, vinegar and
olives. Simmer, stirring, for about
5 minutes until pulpy. Meanwhile,
cut the cooked salt cod into large
chunks. Toss in the flour. Fry (sauté)
for a few minutes, turning
occasionally, until golden. Drain on
kitchen paper (paper towels) and
place in a warm serving dish. Spoon
the sauce over and serve hot with
Buttered Noodles for Fish.

Fritto misto di mare

SERVES 6

If you buy whole, unprepared squid, use 350 g/12 oz and prepare as on page 14.

100 g/4 oz/1 cup plain (all-purpose) flour
20 ml/1½ tbsp olive oil
A good pinch of salt
300 ml/½ pt/1¼ cups lukewarm water
1 egg white
Oil, for deep-frying
225 g/8 oz baby squid tubes, cut into rings
225 g/8 oz raw peeled tiger prawns (jumbo shrimp)
225 g/8 oz monkfish, cut into small cubes
225 g/8 oz whitebait
Lemon wedges and parsley sprigs, to garnish

Put the flour in a bowl and add the olive oil and salt. Gradually work in the water to form a thick, smooth batter. Whisk the egg white until stiff and fold in with a metal spoon. Heat the oil for deep-frying until a cube of day-old bread browns in 30 seconds. Dip each piece of one type of fish in the batter using tongs or a fork and drop into the oil. Fry (sauté) until crisp and golden brown. Drain on kitchen paper (paper towels) and keep warm while cooking the remainder. Pile on to warm plates, garnish with lemon wedges and parsley sprigs and serve hot.

Mackerel with bacon and mustard

SERVES 4

8 smoked streaky bacon rashers (slices), rinded
4 mackerel, cleaned, heads removed and boned
Salt and freshly ground black pepper
30 ml/2 tbsp Dijon mustard
50 g/2 oz/1 cup fresh white breadcrumbs
30 ml/2 tbsp mayonnaise
30 ml/2 tbsp lemon juice
60 ml/4 tbsp sunflower oil
Lemon wedges and parsley sprigs, to garnish
Plain potatoes, to serve

Stretch each rasher of bacon with the back of a knife. Lay the mackerel on a board and season with salt and pepper. Mix together the mustard, breadcrumbs, mayonnaise and lemon juice and spread on the fish. Reshape the fish and wrap in the bacon rashers. Heat the oil in a large frying pan (skillet). Add the fish and fry (sauté) for about 5 minutes on each side until golden brown and cooked through. Garnish with lemon wedges and parsley sprigs and serve with plain potatoes.

Japanese prawn tempura

SERVES 4–6

50 g/2 oz/½ cup cornflour (cornstarch)
50 g/2 oz/½ cup self-raising (self-rising) flour
2.5 ml/½ tsp baking powder
2.5 ml/½ tsp salt
1 egg, beaten
200 ml/7 fl oz/scant 1 cup iced water
300 ml/½ pt/1¼ cups dashi or fish stock
30 ml/2 tbsp Japanese soy sauce
45 ml/3 tbsp dry sherry
5 ml/1 tsp light brown sugar
10 ml/2 tsp grated fresh root ginger
Oil, for deep-frying
450 g/1 lb raw peeled tiger prawns (jumbo shrimp), tails left on
16 mangetout (snow peas)
6 large cup mushrooms, sliced
1 large courgette (zucchini), cut into short fingers
1 bunch of spring onions (scallions), trimmed to 5 cm/2 in from the white end
Shredded carrot, white salsify or winter white radish and flatleaf parsley leaves, to garnish

Sift the cornflour and flour together with the baking powder and salt in a bowl. Make a well in the centre and beat in the egg and half the water. Beat well until smooth. Whisk in the remaining water and place in the fridge until ready to cook. Put the dashi or fish stock in a saucepan with the soy sauce, sherry and sugar and heat until almost boiling, stirring until the sugar is completely dissolved. Stir in the ginger and keep hot.

Heat the oil until a cube of day-old bread browns in 30 seconds. Dip the prawns and vegetables, a few pieces at a time, in the batter and deep-fry until golden. Drain on kitchen paper (paper towels) and keep warm while cooking the remainder. Pile on to warm plates, garnish with shredded carrot and salsify or white radish and a few flatleaf parsley leaves. Pour the hot dipping sauce into small bowls and serve straight away.

Japanese mixed seafood tempura

SERVES 4–6

Prepare as for Japanese Prawn Tempura, but omit the vegetables and use 225 g/8 oz squid rings, 225 g/8 oz cubed monkfish and 225 g/8 oz shelled scallops, halved widthways, in addition to the prawns.

Herrings in oatmeal

SERVES 4

4 small herrings, cleaned, heads removed, scaled and boned
Salt and freshly ground black pepper
45 ml/3 tbsp milk
60 ml/4 tbsp medium oatmeal
50 g/2 oz/¼ cup butter or margarine
30 ml/2 tbsp sunflower oil
Lemon wedges and parsley sprigs, to garnish

Rinse and dry the herrings on kitchen paper (paper towels). Season all over with salt and pepper and reshape. Dip in the milk, then the oatmeal, to coat completely. Melt the butter or margarine and oil in a large frying pan (skillet) and fry (sauté) the fish for about 5 minutes on each side until golden and cooked through. Drain on kitchen paper and garnish with lemon wedges and parsley sprigs before serving.

Mackerel in millet

SERVES 4

4 mackerel, cleaned, heads removed
and boned
75 g/3 oz/¾ cup millet flakes
30 ml/2 tbsp chopped parsley
5 ml/1 tsp paprika
Salt and freshly ground black pepper
1 egg, beaten
60 ml/4 tbsp sunflower oil
Lemon wedges and parsley sprigs, to
garnish
New potatoes, broad (fava) beans and
Parsley Sauce (page 377), to serve

Rinse the fish and dry on kitchen paper (paper towels). Mix the millet with the parsley, paprika and a little salt and pepper. Dip the fish in the egg, then the millet mixture, to coat completely. Brush a baking (cookie) sheet with some of the oil. Add the fish, skin-side down, and drizzle with the remaining oil. Bake towards the top of a preheated oven at 190°C/ 375°F/gas mark 5 for about 25 minutes until golden and cooked through. Transfer to warm plates, garnish with lemon wedges and parsley sprigs and serve with new potatoes, broad beans and Parsley Sauce.

Perch with sage and onions

SERVES 4

4 perch, filleted
2 onions, thinly sliced
50 g/2 oz/¼ cup unsalted (sweet)
butter
Salt and freshly ground black pepper
300 ml/½ pt/1¼ cups crème fraîche
15 ml/1 tbsp chopped sage
15 ml/1 tbsp chopped parsley
Plain potatoes and peas, to serve

Rinse the perch under cold water and dry on kitchen paper (paper towels). Fry (sauté) the onions in the butter for 3 minutes until softened but not browned. Remove from the pan with a draining spoon. Add the perch fillets, season and fry (sauté) for 3 minutes on each side until golden and cooked through. Remove from the pan and keep warm. Return the onions to the pan. Add the crème fraîche, herbs and seasoning to taste. Bring to the boil, stirring, and bubble for several minutes until thickening slightly. Transfer the perch to warm plates, spoon the sauce over and serve with plain potatoes and peas.

Portuguese fishcakes

SERVES 4

2 potatoes, cut into small chunks
A knob of butter or margarine
2 × 120 g/4½ oz/small cans of
sardines, drained, boned and
mashed
2 spring onions (scallions), very finely
chopped
15 ml/1 tbsp chopped parsley
10 ml/2 tsp lemon juice
Salt and freshly ground black pepper
1.5 ml/¼ tsp cayenne
1 egg, beaten
75 g/3 oz/¾ cup dried breadcrumbs
Oil, for shallow-frying

Cook the potatoes in lightly salted, boiling water until tender. Drain and mash with the butter or margarine. Mix in the fish, onions, parsley, lemon juice, a little salt and pepper and the cayenne. Shape into eight flat cakes. Dip in the egg, then the breadcrumbs. Shallow-fry in hot oil on each side until crisp and golden brown. Drain on kitchen paper (paper towels) and serve hot.

Fried snapper with round chips

SERVES 4

2 large potatoes, cut into thin round
    slices
450 g/1 lb snapper fillets
30 ml/2 tbsp plain (all-purpose) flour
Salt and freshly ground black pepper
120 ml/4 fl oz/½ cup olive oil
60 ml/4 tbsp red wine vinegar
1 garlic clove, crushed
10 ml/2 tsp Dijon mustard
15 ml/1 tbsp chopped parsley
2.5 ml/½ tsp caster (superfine) sugar
Oil, for shallow-frying
Mixed salad, to serve

Put the potato slices in ice-cold
water for 15 minutes. Drain and dry
in a clean tea towel (dish cloth).
Wipe the fish with kitchen paper
(paper towels) and coat in the flour,
seasoned with a little salt and
pepper. Put the olive oil, vinegar,
garlic, mustard, parsley, sugar and
some salt and pepper in a screw-
topped jar and shake vigorously
until well blended.

Heat two large frying pans
(skillets). Add 2.5 cm/1 in oil to one
and 5 mm/¼ in to the other and
heat until smoking. Slide the dried
potato slices into the deeper oil and
fry (sauté) until golden. Drain on
kitchen paper. Lay the fish in the
shallower oil and fry for 3 minutes
on each side until golden and
cooked through. Drain on kitchen
paper. Lay the fish on warm plates
with the potatoes to one side.
Sprinkle the potatoes with salt.
Shake the dressing and trickle over
the fish. Serve hot with a mixed
salad.

Salmon with vegetable and cashew nut sauce

SERVES 4

4 dried shiitake mushrooms
75 ml/5 tbsp warm water
2 carrots, thinly sliced
1 bunch of spring onions (scallions),
    cut into short lengths
60 ml/4 tbsp sunflower oil
8 baby corn cobs, cut into short lengths
45 ml/3 tbsp soy sauce
Salt and freshly ground black pepper
50 g/2 oz/½ cup raw cashew nuts
4 salmon tail fillets, about
    175 g/6 oz each
45 ml/3 tbsp cornflour (cornstarch)
225 g/8 oz cellophane noodles, to serve

Soak the mushrooms in the water
for 15 minutes. Drain, reserving the
water. Discard the tough stalks and
slice the caps. Fry (sauté) the carrots
and spring onions in half the oil for
2 minutes, stirring. Add the
mushrooms, corn cobs, the
mushroom soaking water and the
soy sauce. Simmer for 5 minutes.
Add the nuts and season to taste.

Meanwhile, toss the fish in the
cornflour, seasoned with a little salt
and pepper, and fry in the remaining
oil for 2 minutes on each side until
just cooked. Drain on kitchen paper
(paper towels). Cook the noodles
according to the packet directions.
Drain and pile on to warm plates.
Top with the salmon fillets and
spoon the sauce over. Serve hot.

Smelts with hazelnuts

SERVES 4

16 smelts
90 ml/6 tbsp milk
45 ml/3 tbsp plain (all-purpose) flour
Salt and freshly ground black pepper
5 ml/1 tsp paprika
100 g/4 oz/½ cup unsalted (sweet) butter
15 ml/1 tbsp olive oil
50 g/2 oz/½ cup chopped hazelnuts
   (filberts)
A good squeeze of lemon juice
Parsley sprigs, to garnish

Cut off the heads from the smelts and gently squeeze the bodies to clean out the insides. Carefully rinse and dry on kitchen paper (paper towels). Dip in the milk, then in the flour seasoned with salt, pepper and the paprika. Melt half the butter in a frying pan (skillet) with the oil. Fry (sauté) the smelts for about 3 minutes on each side until golden brown. Drain on kitchen paper and keep warm. Add the remaining butter to the pan and stir in the hazelnuts. Cook until turning golden. Add the lemon juice and pour over the smelts. Serve straight away, garnished with parsley sprigs.

Thai-style tuna

SERVES 4

4 tuna steaks
Freshly ground black pepper
30 ml/2 tbsp cornflour (cornstarch)
Oil, for shallow-frying
90 ml/6 tbsp soy sauce
½ cucumber, skinned and thinly sliced
6 tomatoes, skinned and thinly sliced
½ bunch of spring onions (scallions),
   finely chopped
A few torn coriander (cilantro) leaves
Thai Fragrant Rice (page 392), to serve

Wipe the fish with kitchen paper (paper towels) and season with

pepper. Dust all over with the cornflour. Heat the oil in a frying pan (skillet) and shallow-fry the fish for 2 minutes on each side until crisp and golden. Do not overcook – the fish should still be slightly pink in the centre. Lay on plates and sprinkle with the soy sauce. Lay the cucumber and tomato slices to one side and sprinkle the fish with the spring onions and a few torn coriander leaves. Serve with Thai Fragrant Rice.

Prawn jalfrezi

SERVES 4

350 g/12 oz raw peeled tiger prawns
   (jumbo shrimp)
100 g/4 oz button mushrooms,
   quartered
10 ml/2 tsp garlic powder
5 ml/1 tsp chilli powder
5 ml/1 tsp ground ginger
25 g/1 oz/2 tbsp butter or margarine
1 onion, very finely chopped
30 ml/2 tbsp curry paste
2 green (bell) peppers, cut into thin strips
30 ml/2 tbsp water
4 mild green chillies, seeded and
   chopped
60 ml/4 tbsp chopped coriander
   (cilantro)
Salt and sugar, to taste
Plain Rice for Fish (page 392), to serve

Put the prawns and mushrooms in a shallow dish and sprinkle with the garlic and chilli powders and the ginger. Heat the butter or margarine in a large frying pan (skillet). Add the onion and fry (sauté), stirring, for 2 minutes. Add the curry paste, prawns, mushrooms and peppers and stir-fry for 3 minutes. Add the water, chillies and coriander and toss for 2 minutes. Season to taste with salt and sugar and serve on a bed of rice.

Creamed Italian-style tuna with peppers

SERVES 4

450 g/1 lb potatoes, cut into equal-
  sized chunks
1 celeriac, cut into equal-sized chunks
30 ml/2 tbsp milk
15 g/½ oz/1 tbsp butter or margarine
4 tuna steaks
Salt and freshly ground black pepper
1 red (bell) pepper, halved and thinly
  sliced
1 green pepper, halved and thinly
  sliced
1 yellow pepper, halved and thinly
  sliced
1 green chilli, seeded and finely
  chopped
2 red onions, halved and thinly sliced
90 ml/6 tbsp olive oil
1 large garlic clove, crushed
60 ml/4 tbsp white wine
150 ml/¼ pt/⅔ cup double (heavy)
  cream

Cook the potatoes and celeriac in
lightly salted, boiling water for about
20 minutes until tender. Drain and
mash thoroughly with the milk and
butter or margarine, then beat
thoroughly with a wooden spoon
until light and fluffy. Keep warm.
  Meanwhile, wipe the fish with
kitchen paper (paper towels) and
season lightly. Fry (sauté) the
peppers, chilli and onions in 60 ml/
4 tbsp of the oil, stirring, for
5 minutes until soft and only very
lightly golden. Add the garlic and
cook for a further 1 minute. Remove
the vegetables from the pan with a
draining spoon. Heat the remaining
oil in the pan, add the fish and fry
for no longer than 3 minutes on
each side. Remove from the pan and
keep warm. Return the pepper
mixture to the pan and add the

wine. Allow to bubble until reduced
by half. Stir in the cream and bubble
for a further 2 minutes. Taste and
re-season. Pile the celeriac and
potato mash on to four warm plates
and top each with a tuna steak.
Spoon the sauce over and serve
straight away.

Rock salmon with garlic and herbs

SERVES 4

4 pieces of rock salmon, about
  225 g/8 oz each
Salt and freshly ground black pepper
50 g/2 oz/¼ cup unsalted (sweet)
  butter
1 bunch of spring onions (scallions),
  finely chopped
1 large garlic clove, crushed
15 ml/1 tbsp chopped thyme
15 ml/1 tbsp chopped parsley
Finely grated rind and juice of
  ½ lemon
1 large bay leaf
Green Hollandaise (page 371), to serve

Wipe the fish with kitchen paper
(paper towels) and season with salt
and pepper. Melt half the butter in a
frying pan (skillet), add the spring
onions and fry (sauté) for 2 minutes
until slightly softened. Stir in the
garlic. Remove from the pan with a
draining spoon. Melt the remaining
butter in the pan, add the rock
salmon and brown quickly on both
sides. Return the onions to the pan.
Sprinkle with the herbs, lemon rind
and juice and add the bay leaf.
Cover and cook gently for
10 minutes or until the fish is really
tender. Transfer to warm plates,
discard the bay leaf and serve hot
with Green Hollandaise.

Steamed, Poached, Casseroled and Curried

This section covers all recipes you cook in a saucepan, steamer or casserole dish (Dutch oven). Poaching and steaming are particularly suitable for delicate fish as they cook gently in moist heat without damaging and drying the flesh. Casseroling and currying are more suitable for coarser-textured, firmer varieties, which can take the higher temperatures and more robust flavouring. All the dishes in this chapter are bathed in delicious juices or sauces and all are colourful and nutritious. Many are one-pot meals: others need the addition of some rice, pasta, potatoes or crusty bread to complete the meal.

Mixed seafood pot

SERVES 4–6

1 large onion, halved and thinly sliced
1 large garlic clove, crushed
10 g/¼ oz/2 tsp butter or margarine
30 ml/2 tbsp white wine vinegar
10 ml/2 tsp clear honey
300 ml/½ pt/1¼ cups dry white wine
300 ml/½ pt/1¼ cups water
400 g/14 oz/1 large can of chopped
*   tomatoes*
1 aubergine (eggplant), quartered and
*   sliced*
1 courgette (zucchini), sliced
1 green (bell) pepper, sliced
2.5 ml/½ tsp dried mixed
*   Mediterranean herbs*
1 kg/2¼ lb mussels in their shells,
*   cleaned (page 13)*
450 g/1 lb white fish fillet, cut into
*   large cubes*
225 g/8 oz baby squid, cleaned and
*   cut into rings (page 14)*
Salt and freshly ground black pepper
Chopped parsley and lemon wedges, to
*   garnish*
Crusty bread, to serve

Fry (sauté) the onion and garlic in
the butter or margarine in a large
saucepan for 2 minutes, stirring. Add
the wine vinegar, honey, wine,
water, tomatoes, prepared vegetables
and herbs and cook gently for
5 minutes. Add the mussels, white
fish and squid, cover and simmer for
a further 5 minutes. Season with salt
and lots of pepper and stir gently.
Sprinkle with parsley, garnish with
lemon wedges and serve straight
from the pan with fresh crusty
bread.

Cod and flageolet pot

SERVES 4

Prepare as for Mixed Seafood Pot,
but use four pieces of cod fillet
instead of all the different seafood
and add 425 g/15 oz/1 large can of
flageolet beans, drained and rinsed,
with the other vegetables.

Monkfish and lentil casserole

SERVES 4

4 pieces of monkfish fillet, about
*   700 g/1½ lb in all*
30 ml/2 tbsp olive oil
1 large onion, chopped
1 carrot, chopped
1 large garlic clove, crushed
450 ml/¾ pt/2 cups passata (sieved
*   tomatoes)*
15 ml/1 tbsp tomato purée (paste)
300 ml/½ pt/1¼ cups red wine
225 g/8 oz green lentils, rinsed
1 bay leaf
2 courgettes (zucchini), sliced
5 ml/1 tsp caster (superfine) sugar
Salt and freshly ground black pepper
Crusty bread and green salad, to serve

Brown the fish in the olive oil in a
flameproof casserole dish (Dutch
oven). Remove and keep to one side.
Add the onion and carrot to the
casserole and fry (sauté) for
2 minutes. Add the garlic, passata,
tomato purée, wine and lentils. Stir
and add the bay leaf. Bring to the
boil, cover and cook in a preheated
oven at 180°C/350°F/gas mark 4 for
45 minutes. Stir in the courgettes
and sugar and season well. Add the
fish, cover and continue cooking for
15 minutes until tender. Transfer the
fish and lentils to warm plates,
discarding the bay leaf. Serve with
crusty bread and a green salad.

Normandy matelote

SERVES 4

*900 g/2 lb fresh mussels in their shells,
cleaned (page 13)*
150 ml/¼ pt/⅔ cup water
1 large onion, finely chopped
15 g/½ oz/1 tbsp butter or margarine
*450 g/1 lb cod fillet, skinned and
cubed*
*225 g/8 oz monkfish fillet, skinned
and cubed*
225 g/8 oz shelled scallops, quartered
300 ml/½ pt/1¼ cups dry cider
1 bay leaf
Salt and freshly ground black pepper
*25 g/1 oz/¼ cup plain (all-purpose)
flour*
60 ml/4 tbsp milk
30 ml/2 tbsp chopped parsley
*100 g/4 oz cooked peeled prawns
(shrimp)*
Lemon juice
Warm French bread, to serve

Place the mussels in a large
saucepan with the water. Cover with
a lid and cook over a high heat for
5 minutes, shaking the pan
occasionally, until the mussels have
opened. Strain the liquid into a
bowl. When cool enough to handle,
remove the mussels from their shells
and reserve. Discard any that remain
closed. Cook the onion in the butter
or margarine in the mussel saucepan
for 2 minutes, stirring, until softened
but not browned. Add the cod,
monkfish and scallops. Pour on the
mussel cooking liquid and the cider
and add the bay leaf, a little salt and
a good grinding of pepper. Bring to
the boil, cover with a lid, reduce the
heat and cook for about 5 minutes
until the fish is just cooked.
    Blend the flour with the milk until
smooth and stir into the pot. Bring
to the boil and cook for 2 minutes,
stirring very gently until thickened,

taking care not to break up the fish.
Remove the bay leaf. Add the
parsley, mussels and prawns and
season to taste with a little lemon
juice, salt and pepper. Ladle into
warm bowls and serve with lots of
French bread.

Tuna and vegetable mornay

SERVES 4

*20 g/¾ oz/3 tbsp plain (all-purpose)
flour*
300 ml/½ pt/1¼ cups milk
A knob of butter or margarine
75 g/3 oz/¾ cup Cheddar cheese, grated
Salt and freshly ground black pepper
5 ml/1 tsp made English mustard
*350 g/12 oz cooked leftover vegetables,
chopped, or cooked frozen vegetables*
*185 g/6½ oz/1 small can of tuna,
drained*
30 ml/2 tbsp cornflakes, crushed
3 tomatoes, sliced

Put the flour in a saucepan and
gradually blend in the milk. Add the
butter or margarine, bring to the boil
and cook for 2 minutes, stirring all
the time. Stir in 50 g/2 oz/½ cup of
the cheese, some salt and pepper
and the mustard. Mix in the
vegetables and tuna and heat
through for about 3 minutes until
piping hot. Turn into a flameproof
serving dish. Sprinkle with the
remaining cheese and the crushed
cornflakes and arrange the tomato
slices over the top. Place under a
preheated grill (broiler) until golden
and bubbling. Serve hot.

Old English mussel stew

SERVES 4

In days gone by, this would be served followed with hunks of strong cheese and more bread.

1.75 kg/4 lb mussels in their shells, cleaned (page 13)
90 ml/6 tbsp water
30 ml/2 tbsp dry Madeira or sherry
75 g/3 oz/⅓ cup unsalted (sweet) butter
225 g/8 oz field mushrooms, sliced
20 ml/1½ tbsp plain (all-purpose) flour
150 ml/¼ pt/⅔ cup single (light) cream
150 ml/¼ pt/⅔ cup double (heavy) cream
Salt and freshly ground black pepper
Juice of ½ lemon
30 ml/2 tbsp chopped parsley
Coarse wholegrain bread and green salad, to serve

Put the mussels in a large pan with the water and sherry. Cover with a lid and cook over a high heat, shaking the pan occasionally, for 4–5 minutes until the mussels have opened. Remove the mussels from their shells and discard the shells and any mussels that have not opened. Strain the mussel cooking juices and reserve.

Melt the butter in a large saucepan. Add the mushrooms and cook, stirring, for 3 minutes until softened. Stir in the flour and cook for 1 minute, stirring. Blend in the strained mussel stock and the creams. Return to the heat, bring to the boil and simmer for 2 minutes. Add the mussels and heat through. Season to taste, sharpen with lemon juice and add the parsley. Spoon into warm bowls and serve with wholegrain bread and a green salad.

Smoked haddock Florentine

SERVES 4

700 g/1½ lb smoked haddock fillet, skinned and cut into 4 portions
300 ml/½ pt/1¼ cups milk
450 g/1 lb spinach, thoroughly washed
Salt and freshly ground black pepper
A good pinch of grated nutmeg
25 g/1 oz/2 tbsp butter or margarine
20 g/¾ oz/3 tbsp plain (all-purpose) flour
2.5 ml/½ tsp made English mustard
50 g/2 oz/½ cup Cheddar cheese, grated
Plain potatoes and stewed fresh or canned tomatoes, to serve

Put the fish in a shallow pan and cover with the milk. Bring to the boil, reduce the heat, cover and cook gently for about 6 minutes or until the fish flakes easily with a fork. Meanwhile, cook the spinach with no extra water in a covered saucepan for about 5 minutes until tender. Drain in a colander, snip with scissors to chop, then season with salt and pepper and the nutmeg. Turn into a flameproof serving dish and dot with 15 g/½ oz/1 tbsp of the butter or margarine. Lift the fish out of the cooking liquid and lay on top of the spinach.

Melt the remaining butter or margarine in a saucepan. Blend in the flour and cook for 1 minute. Remove from the heat and stir in the fish cooking liquid. Return to the heat, bring to the boil and cook for 2 minutes, stirring. Blend in the mustard and cheese and season to taste. Pour over the fish. Flash under a hot grill (broiler) to brown the top. Serve hot with plain potatoes and stewed fresh or canned tomatoes.

Scottish-style haddock and eggs

SERVES 4

Traditionally, you should use whole Finnan Haddies, then skin and bone after cooking and before flaking. Dunlop is a Scottish cheese, but if you can't get it, Cheddar is a good substitute.

450 g/1 lb smoked haddock fillet
300 ml/½ pt/1¼ cups milk
75 g/3 oz/⅓ cup butter or margarine
50 g/2 oz button mushrooms, sliced
4 slices of wholemeal bread, crusts
    removed
45 ml/3 tbsp plain (all-purpose) flour
45 ml/3 tbsp water
30 ml/2 tbsp double (heavy) cream
15 ml/1 tbsp grated Dunlop cheese
Salt and freshly ground black pepper
15 ml/1 tbsp lemon juice
4 eggs

Put the fish in a shallow pan with the milk and 25 g/1 oz/2 tbsp of the butter or margarine. Bring to the boil, reduce the heat, cover and cook gently for about 6 minutes or until tender. Lift out of the pan and flake the fish, discarding the skin.

Fry (sauté) the mushrooms in 15 g/½ oz/1 tbsp of the butter or margarine in a frying pan (skillet) until golden. Remove from the pan. Spread the bread on both sides with the remaining butter or margarine. Fry in the same pan until golden on both sides. Transfer to individual ovenproof dishes, top with the mushrooms and keep warm in a low oven.

Blend the flour with the water and stir into the fish milk. Bring to the boil and cook for 2 minutes, stirring. Add the cream and cheese. Fold in the fish and season to taste. Heat through and keep hot.

Heat about 2.5 cm/1 in water in the frying pan. Add the lemon juice. When simmering, break the eggs, one at a time, into a cup and slide into the water. Cover and cook gently for 3 minutes or until cooked to your liking. Quickly spoon the haddock mixture on to the toast, top each with an egg and serve straight away.

Fireside fish pot

SERVES 4

1 onion, sliced
1 carrot, thinly sliced
2 large potatoes, diced
¼ small cabbage, shredded
25 g/1 oz/2 tbsp butter or margarine
400 g/14 oz/1 large can of chopped
    tomatoes
300 ml/½ pt/1¼ cups chicken or fish
    stock
225 g/8 oz white fish fillet, skinned
    and cubed
225 g/8 oz smoked haddock fillet,
    skinned and cubed
Salt and freshly ground black pepper
Snipped chives, to garnish

Place all the prepared vegetables in a very large saucepan with the butter or margarine. Cook, stirring, for 5 minutes. Add the tomatoes and stock. Bring to the boil, reduce the heat, cover and simmer gently for 15 minutes. Add the fish, re-cover and simmer for a further 5 minutes until the fish and vegetables are tender. Season to taste. Ladle into warm bowls and serve sprinkled with snipped chives.

Smoked haddock with spinach and poached eggs

SERVES 4

Prepare as for Smoked Haddock Florentine (page 167), but poach the fish in water instead of milk. Omit the cheese sauce. Lay the fish on the cooked spinach and top each portion with a poached egg.

Sweet and sour monkfish

SERVES 4

¼ cucumber, chopped
2 spring onions (scallions), chopped
225 g/8 oz/1 small can of pineapple chunks
225 g/8 oz/1 small can of chopped tomatoes
450 g/1 lb monkfish, cubed
20 ml/1½ tbsp cornflour (cornstarch)
30 ml/2 tbsp soy sauce
Caster (superfine) sugar (optional)
Plain Rice for Fish (page 392), to serve

Put the cucumber, spring onions, the contents of the can of pineapple and the tomatoes in a saucepan. Bring to the boil and simmer for 3 minutes. Add the monkfish and simmer for a further 6 minutes until the fish is tender. Blend the cornflour with the soy sauce and stir into the mixture. Bring to the boil and cook for 2 minutes, stirring gently. Taste and add a little caster sugar, if liked. Spoon on to a bed of rice and serve.

Sweet and sour scallops

SERVES 4

Prepare as for Sweet and Sour Monkfish, but substitute shelled queen scallops for the monkfish and serve on a bed of Egg Fried Rice (page 393).

Seville scallops

SERVES 4

When you can't get Seville oranges, use a sweet one and add the juice of half a small lemon.

16 shelled scallops
150 ml/¼ pt/⅔ cup dry white wine
150 ml/¼ pt/⅔ cup fish stock
5 ml/1 tsp white wine vinegar
1 small piece of cinnamon stick
2 cloves
15 g/½ oz/1 tbsp butter or margarine, softened
15 ml/1 tbsp plain (all-purpose) flour
Finely grated rind and juice of 1 Seville orange
Salt and freshly ground black pepper
A little caster (superfine) sugar (optional)
15 ml/1 tbsp snipped chives, to garnish
Plain Rice for Fish (page 392) and buttered spinach, to serve

Remove the corals from the scallops and halve the white flesh. Put the wine, stock, wine vinegar, cinnamon and cloves in a saucepan. Bring to the boil, reduce the heat, cover and simmer for 10 minutes. Strain the stock into a clean pan. Add the scallops and simmer for about 3 minutes until just firm. Lift out the scallops with a draining spoon. Boil the liquid rapidly until reduced by a third.

Mash together the butter or margarine and flour. Gradually whisk into the cooking liquid, whisking all the time, until thickened and smooth. Stir in the orange rind and juice and season to taste with salt, pepper and a little sugar, if liked. Return the scallops briefly to the sauce to heat through. Spoon on to a bed of rice, sprinkle with a little of the orange rind and the chives and serve with buttered spinach.

Russian cod cubat

SERVES 4

4 pieces of cod fillet, about 175 g/6 oz
  each, skinned
Salt and freshly ground black pepper
15 ml/1 tbsp lemon juice
600 ml/1 pt/2½ cups milk
65 g/2½ oz/generous ¼ cup butter or
  margarine, plus extra for greasing
2 large flat mushrooms, finely chopped
10 ml/2 tsp chopped parsley
10 ml/2 tsp chopped thyme
A good pinch of ground mace
75 ml/5 tbsp plain (all-purpose) flour
30 ml/2 tbsp grated Gruyère (Swiss)
  cheese
30 ml/2 tbsp grated Parmesan cheese
Rye bread, to serve

Put the fish in a saucepan and
season with a little salt and pepper.
Pour the lemon juice and half the
milk over. Bring just to the boil,
reduce the heat, cover and cook
gently for 5 minutes or until the fish
is just cooked. Meanwhile melt
15 g/½ oz/1 tbsp of the butter or
margarine in a separate pan and fry
(sauté) the mushrooms, stirring,
until no liquid is left. Add the herbs,
mace and a little salt and pepper.
Stir in 45 ml/3 tbsp of the flour and
cook for 1 minute. Remove from the
heat and blend in the remaining
milk. Return to the heat, bring to the
boil and cook for 2 minutes, stirring.
Turn into a greased, shallow,
ovenproof dish. Lift the fish fillets
out of the milk with a fish slice and
lay on the mushrooms.

Melt the remaining butter or
margarine in the rinsed-out
saucepan. Stir in the remaining flour
and cook for 1 minute, then remove

from the heat. Blend in the fish
cooking milk. Return to the heat,
bring to the boil and cook for
2 minutes, stirring. Add the Gruyère
and half the Parmesan and season to
taste. Pour over the fish. Sprinkle
with the remaining Parmesan. Place
under a moderate grill (broiler) for
about 5 minutes until lightly golden
and hot through. If necessary, cover
the top with foil to prevent over-
browning. Serve with rye bread.

Poached cod with fennel

SERVES 4

4 cod steaks
Salt and freshly ground black pepper
2 fennel bulbs, cut into matchsticks
2 carrots, cut into matchsticks
150 ml/¼ pt/⅔ cup white wine
150 ml/¼ pt/⅔ cup water
1 bay leaf
30 ml/2 tbsp chopped parsley
1 quantity of Hollandaise Sauce
  (page 371)

Wipe the fish with kitchen paper
(paper towels) and season with salt
and pepper. Put the fennel and
carrots in a pan with the wine, water
and bay leaf and simmer for
5 minutes until just tender. Lift out
the vegetables with a draining
spoon. Lay the fish in the pan,
cover and poach gently for about
10 minutes or until tender. Lift out of
the pan and transfer to warm plates.
Pile the vegetables to one side and
keep warm. Boil the cooking liquid
until reduced by half. Season to taste
and add the parsley. Spoon over the
fish and serve with Hollandaise
Sauce.

Truite au bleu

SERVES 4

You must use the freshest trout you can buy for this recipe.

75 ml/5 tbsp white wine vinegar
15 ml/1 tbsp coarse sea salt
4 fresh rainbow trout, cleaned but not washed
Horseradish Creme (page 381) and parsley sprigs, to garnish
Plain potatoes and mangetout (snow peas), to serve

Put 2 litres/3½ pts/8½ cups of water in a large, shallow pan and add the vinegar and salt. Bring to the boil. Carefully add the trout, cover, reduce the heat and cook gently for 7 minutes or until just cooked. Gently lift out with a fish slice and drain on kitchen paper (paper towels). The fish will turn a beautiful blue colour if very fresh. Transfer to warm plates. Put a spoonful of Horseradish Creme and a sprig of parsley to one side and serve with plain potatoes and mangetout.

Stewed tuna and beans

SERVES 4

400 g/14 oz/1 large can of chopped tomatoes
1 garlic clove, crushed
2 × 425 g/15 oz/large cans of mixed pulses, drained
185 g/6½ oz/1 small can of tuna, drained and flaked
1.5 ml/¼ tsp chilli powder
10 ml/2 tsp red wine vinegar
2.5 ml/½ tsp caster (superfine) sugar
30 ml/2 tbsp snipped chives
Salt and freshly ground black pepper

Put everything except half the chives into a pan. Bring to the boil and simmer for 4 minutes. Stir and

season to taste if necessary. Spoon into bowls, sprinkle with the remaining chives and serve with crusty bread.

Cod Provençal

SERVES 4

15 ml/1 tbsp olive oil
1 large onion, finely chopped
1 large garlic clove, crushed
1 green (bell) pepper, diced
400 g/14 oz/1 large can of chopped tomatoes
15 ml/1 tbsp tomato purée (paste)
30 ml/2 tbsp white or red wine
450 g/1 lb cod fillet, skinned and cubed
Salt and freshly ground black pepper
30 ml/2 tbsp sliced stuffed olives
Plain Rice for Fish (page 392), to serve

Heat the oil in a saucepan. Add the onion, garlic and green pepper and cook gently for 3 minutes, stirring. Add the tomatoes, tomato purée and wine. Bring to the boil, reduce the heat and simmer for 5 minutes. Add the fish and a little salt and pepper and continue cooking for about 5 minutes or until the fish is tender. Add the olives and spoon on to a bed of rice to serve.

Smoked haddock and cheese Provençal

SERVES 4

Prepare as for Cod Provençal, but substitute smoked haddock for the cod. When cooked, spoon over the rice and sprinkle liberally with grated Cheddar cheese before serving.

Haddock in asparagus cream sauce

SERVES 4

225 g/8 oz/1 cup long-grain rice
1 onion, finely chopped
15 g/½ oz/1 tbsp butter or margarine
295 g/10½ oz/1 medium can of
  condensed celery soup
4 haddock fillets, about 175 g/6 oz
  each
150 ml/¼ pt/⅔ cup double (heavy)
  cream
425 g/15 oz/1 large can of cut
  asparagus, drained
Freshly ground black pepper
Paprika, for dusting

Cook the rice in plenty of lightly salted, boiling water for 10 minutes. Drain and keep warm. Meanwhile, fry (sauté) the onion in the butter or margarine in a flameproof casserole dish (Dutch oven) until soft but not brown. Stir in the celery soup. Add the fish, cover and cook gently for about 8 minutes or until the fish is tender. Carefully lift the fish out on to warm plates. Stir the cream and asparagus into the casserole and heat through. Season with pepper and spoon over the fish. Pile the rice to one side and dust with paprika before serving.

Cod in broccoli cream sauce

SERVES 4

Prepare as for Haddock in Asparagus Cream Sauce, but substitute cod for the haddock and 175 g/6 oz broccoli, cut into small florets and cooked in lightly salted, boiling water for 4 minutes, for the canned asparagus.

Poached cod with tomatoes

SERVES 4

4 cod fillets, about 175 g/6 oz each
300 ml/½ pt/1¼ cups milk
1 bay leaf
1 onion slice
Salt and freshly ground black pepper
30 ml/2 tbsp cornflour (cornstarch)
45 ml/3 tbsp single (light) cream
30 ml/2 tbsp chopped parsley
8 tomatoes
45 ml/3 tbsp water

Put the fish in a pan with the milk, bay leaf, onion and a little salt and pepper. Bring to the boil, cover and simmer gently for about 5 minutes or until tender. Transfer the fish to a warm serving dish and keep warm. Strain the cooking liquid and return to the pan. Blend the cornflour with the cream and add to the pan. Bring to the boil and cook for 1 minute, stirring. Stir in the parsley and season to taste. Meanwhile, cut a cross in the top of each tomato. Place in a separate pan with the water. Cover and cook gently until just tender but still holding their shape. Spoon the sauce over the fish and put the tomatoes to one side. Serve hot.

Crunchy-topped salmon and borlotti casserole

SERVES 4

200 g/7 oz/1 small can of pink or red salmon, drained
425 g/15 oz/1 large can of borlotti beans, drained
295 g/10½ oz/1 medium can of condensed celery soup
60 ml/4 tbsp milk
75 g/3 oz/¾ cup Cheddar cheese, grated
3 tomatoes, sliced
2 × 25 g/1 oz/small packets of cheese and onion or plain potato crisps (chips)

Discard the bones and any skin from the fish and roughly flake in an ovenproof dish. Spoon the beans over. Blend the soup with the milk and cheese and pour over. Top with the tomato slices, then crush the crisps over the surface. Bake in the oven at 180°C/350°F/gas mark 4 for about 25 minutes or until piping hot and the top is well browned.

Crunchy-toppped tuna and corn casserole

SERVES 4

Prepare as for Crunchy-topped Salmon and Borlotti Casserole but substitute tuna for the salmon and 320 g/12 oz/1 medium can of sweetcorn (corn) for the beans. Use bacon-flavoured crisps (chips) for the topping.

Polynesian-style cod

SERVES 4

40 g/1½ oz/3 tbsp butter or margarine
1 green (bell) pepper, thinly sliced
1 red pepper, thinly sliced
2 celery sticks, thinly sliced
1 carrot, thinly sliced
1 onion, thinly sliced
700 g/1½ lb cod fillet, skinned and cut into 4 pieces
2 ripe tomatoes, skinned and quartered
225 g/8 oz/1 small can of pineapple pieces in natural juice
300 ml/½ pt/1¼ cups chicken stock
Salt and freshly ground black pepper
250 g/9 oz Chinese egg noodles
15 ml/1 tbsp cornflour (cornstarch)
30 ml/2 tbsp water
Torn coriander (cilantro) leaves, to garnish

Melt 25 g/1 oz/2 tbsp of the butter or margarine in a saucepan. Add the peppers, celery, carrot and onion. Cover and cook over a gentle heat for 10 minutes, stirring occasionally. Add the fish, tomatoes, pineapple and juice, the stock and seasoning to taste. Bring to the boil, reduce the heat, cover and cook gently for 10 minutes until the fish and vegetables are tender.

Meanwhile, cook the noodles according to the packet directions. Drain and toss in the remaining butter or margarine. Pile on to warm plates. Carefully lift the pieces of fish out of the pan and put on the noodles. Keep warm. Blend the cornflour with the water and stir into the vegetables. Bring to the boil and cook for 1 minute, stirring, until thickened. Taste and re-season if necessary. Spoon over the fish and scatter a few torn coriander leaves over.

Bean and anchovy stew with prawn dumplings

SERVES 4–6

225 g/8 oz/1⅓ cups dried flageolet
  beans
225 g/8 oz/1⅓ cups dried black-eyed
  beans
50 g/2 oz/¼ cup butter or margarine,
  diced
15 ml/1 tbsp olive oil
3 carrots, sliced
2 celery sticks, sliced
1 green (bell) pepper, sliced
1 red pepper, sliced
1 onion, sliced
1 garlic clove, crushed
1.2 litres/2 pts/5 cups chicken or
  vegetable stock
50 g/2 oz/1 small can of anchovy
  fillets, drained and chopped
1 bouquet garni sachet
15 ml/1 tbsp tomato purée (paste)
Freshly ground black pepper
100 g/4 oz/1 cup self-raising (self-
  rising) flour
A pinch of salt
50 g/2 oz cooked peeled prawns
  (shrimp), chopped
5 ml/1 tsp anchovy essence (extract)
Grated Parmesan cheese, to serve

Soak the flageolet and black-eyed
beans in cold water for several hours
or overnight. Drain. Melt 15 g/
½ oz/1 tbsp of the butter or
margarine with the oil in a large
saucepan. Add the carrots, celery,
peppers, onion and garlic and fry
(sauté) for 2 minutes, stirring. Add
the beans and stock. Bring to the
boil and boil rapidly for 10 minutes.
Reduce the heat, add the anchovies,
bouquet garni, tomato purée and a
good grinding of pepper and simmer
gently for 1¼ hours until the beans
are really tender.

Meanwhile, mix the flour and salt
in a bowl. Dice the remaining butter
or margarine and rub in. Stir in the
prawns and anchovy essence and
add enough cold water to form a
soft but not sticky dough. Shape into
six or eight small balls and arrange
around the top of the stew. Cover
and simmer for 15 minutes until
fluffy.

Lift out the dumplings with a
draining spoon. Discard the bouquet
garni, taste and re-season if
necessary. Ladle into warm bowls,
top with the dumplings and serve
with grated Parmesan handed
separately.

Chinese curried fishballs

SERVES 4

450 g/1 lb white fish fillet, minced
  (ground)
10 ml/2 tsp curry powder
1.5 ml/¼ tsp Chinese five-spice powder
5 ml/1 tsp soy sauce
5 ml/1 tsp ground ginger
1 egg, beaten
450 ml/¾ pt/2 cups fish stock
1 quantity of Curried Coconut Sauce
  (page 389)
175 g/6 oz Chinese egg noodles, cooked
Lime wedges, to garnish

Mix the fish with the curry and five-
spice powders, the soy sauce and
ginger. Mix with the egg to bind.
Bring the stock to the boil in a
saucepan, then reduce to a simmer.
Shape the fish mixture into small
balls. Drop into the simmering stock
and cook for 5 minutes. Heat the
Curried Coconut Sauce. Lift the balls
out of the pan and place on a bed of
Chinese egg noodles. Drizzle the
sauce over and serve straight away,
garnished with lime wedges.

Thai-style prawn and cucumber curry

SERVES 4

1 cucumber, quartered lengthways and
cut into bite-sized chunks
Salt
15 g/½ oz/1 tbsp butter or margarine
2 garlic cloves, finely chopped
15 ml/1 tbsp grated fresh root ginger
1 lemon grass stem, finely chopped
1 bunch of spring onions (scallions),
finely chopped
5 ml/1 tsp ground turmeric
10 ml/2 tsp garam masala
2.5 ml/½ tsp ground cloves
2.5 ml/½ tsp ground cinnamon
2 green chillies, seeded and chopped
5 ml/1 tsp caster (superfine) sugar
30 ml/2 tbsp plain (all-purpose) flour
300 ml/½ pt/1¼ cups coconut milk
300 ml/½ pt/1¼ cups fish stock
225 g/8 oz raw peeled king prawns
(jumbo shrimp), split in half
lengthways
Thai Fragrant Rice (page 392),
to serve

Put the cucumber in a pan with just
enough water to cover. Add a good
pinch of salt. Bring to the boil,
reduce the heat and cook for
5 minutes. Drain. Heat the butter or
margarine and fry (sauté) the garlic,
ginger, lemon grass, spring onions,
turmeric, garam masala, cloves and
cinnamon for 1 minute, stirring. Stir
in the chillies, sugar and flour and
cook for a further 1 minute. Remove
from the heat and blend in the
coconut milk and half the stock.
Return to the heat, bring to the boil
and cook for 2 minutes, stirring. Add
the prawns and cucumber and
simmer for 5 minutes. Taste and
re-season. Thin with a little more of
the stock, if necessary, then serve on
a bed of Thai fragrant rice.

Thai-style monkfish and courgette curry

SERVES 4

Prepare as for Thai-style Prawn and
Cucumber Curry, but substitute
3 courgettes (zucchini) for the
cucumber, and cubed monkfish for
the prawns (shrimp).

Country fish and rice stew

SERVES 4

1 onion, thinly sliced
2 carrots, thinly sliced
1 small swede (rutabaga), diced
2 potatoes, diced
¼ small green cabbage, shredded
25 g/1 oz/2 tbsp butter or margarine
400 g/14 oz/1 large can of tomatoes
450 ml/¾ pt/2 cups fish stock
Salt and freshly ground black pepper
100 g/4 oz/½ cup long-grain rice
350 g/12 oz cod or other white fish
fillet, skinned and cubed
15 ml/1 tbsp chopped parsley

Fry (sauté) the prepared vegetables
in the butter or margarine in a large
flameproof casserole dish (Dutch
oven), stirring, for 10 minutes. Add
the tomatoes, stock and a little salt
and pepper. Bring to the boil and
simmer for 10 minutes. Add the rice
and fish, cover and simmer for a
further 10 minutes, stirring
occasionally, until the rice, fish and
vegetables are tender. Taste and re-
season if necessary. Ladle into bowls
and serve garnished with parsley.

Deep South fish stew

SERVES 6

225 g/8 oz/1 cup long-grain rice
900 ml/1½ pts/3¾ cups fish stock
1 onion, sliced
1 green (bell) pepper, sliced
1 red pepper, sliced
50 g/2 oz/¼ cup unsalted (sweet)
   butter
15 ml/1 tbsp plain (all-purpose) flour
1 green chilli, seeded and chopped
400 g/14 oz/1 large can of chopped
   tomatoes
100 g/4 oz/1 cup frozen peas
100 g/4 oz French (green) beans, cut
   into short lengths
15 ml/1 tbsp cider vinegar
15 ml/1 tbsp light brown sugar
450 g/1 lb firm white fish such as cod
   or haddock, skinned and cubed
225 g/8 oz cooked peeled prawns
   (shrimp)
30 ml/2 tbsp medium-dry sherry
Tabasco sauce

Cook the rice in 600 ml/1 pt/
2½ cups of the stock for about
15 minutes until tender and all the
stock is absorbed. Press into a ring
mould and keep warm. Fry (sauté)
the onion and peppers in the butter
for 5 minutes until soft. Stir in the
flour and gradually blend in the
remaining stock. Bring to the boil,
stirring until thickened. Add the
chilli, tomatoes, peas, beans, cider
vinegar and sugar. Bring to the boil
and cook for about 10 minutes until
pulpy. Add the white fish and cook
for 5 minutes. Add the prawns,
sherry and Tabasco to taste. Heat
through. Turn the rice out on to a
large serving dish, spoon the stew
into the centre and any remaining
stew around the edge. Serve hot.

Lisbon mussels

SERVES 4

If you can't get the lovely smoky-
flavoured pimenton, use sweet
paprika instead.

450 g/1 lb mussels in their shells,
   cleaned (page 13)
150 ml/¼ pt/⅔ cup chicken stock
1 large onion, finely chopped
60 ml/4 tbsp olive oil
4 ripe tomatoes, skinned and chopped
1 garlic clove, crushed
5 ml/1 tsp pimenton
1 bay leaf
2.5 ml/½ tsp caster (superfine) sugar
Salt and freshly ground black pepper
450 g/1 lb pork tenderloin, cut into
   small cubes
30 ml/2 tbsp chopped parsley

Put the prepared mussels in a
saucepan with the stock. Cover and
cook for 5 minutes. Remove the lid
and discard any mussels that have
not opened. Fry (sauté) the onion in
half the oil for 3 minutes, stirring.
Add the tomatoes, garlic, pimenton,
bay leaf and sugar. Strain in the
mussel liquid. Bring to the boil,
reduce the heat slightly but cook
fairly rapidly for about 10 minutes
until pulpy. Taste and season with
salt and pepper. Remove the bay
leaf.

In a separate pan, heat the
remaining oil and fry the pork until
golden and tender. Add to the
tomato sauce and stir in. Break off
the top mussel shells and add the
mussels nestling in their bottom
shells to the sauce. Toss gently over
the heat until piping hot. Sprinkle
with the parsley and serve.

Fruity curried cod

SERVES 4

350 g/12 oz haddock fillet, skinned
300 ml/½ pt/1¼ cups fish or chicken
*   stock*
30 ml/2 tbsp dried milk powder (non-
*   fat dry milk)*
25 g/1 oz/2 tbsp butter or margarine
2 onions, thinly sliced
30 ml/2 tbsp mild curry powder
25 g/1 oz/¼ cup plain (all-purpose)
*   flour*
150 ml/¼ pt/⅔ cup apple juice
1 eating (dessert) apple, chopped
50 g/2 oz/⅓ cup ready-to-eat dried
*   apricots, chopped*
25 g/1 oz/3 tbsp sultanas (golden
*   raisins)*
5 ml/1 tsp caster (superfine) sugar
100 g/4 oz cooked peeled prawns
*   (shrimp)*
Salt and freshly ground black pepper
Plain Rice for Fish (page 392), to serve
15 ml/1 tbsp chopped coriander
*   (cilantro) and 30 ml/2 tbsp*
*   desiccated (shredded) coconut,*
*   to garnish*

Poach the haddock in the stock for
6–8 minutes or until it flakes easily
with a fork. Lift out of the liquid and
roughly break up. Stir the milk
powder into the stock and reserve.
Meanwhile, melt the butter or
margarine in a saucepan. Add the
onion and cook for 3 minutes,
stirring, until lightly golden. Add the
curry powder and flour and cook for
1 minute, stirring. Remove from the
heat and blend in the reserved stock
and the apple juice. Return to the
heat, bring to the boil and cook for
2 minutes, stirring. Add all the
remaining ingredients except the fish
and prawns and simmer for
10 minutes. Add the fish and prawns
and heat through. Spoon on to a bed

of rice and sprinkle with the
coriander and coconut before
serving.

Whiting and mushroom curry

SERVES 4

295 g/10½ oz/1 medium can of
*   condensed mushroom soup*
90 ml/6 tbsp water
30 ml/2 tbsp tomato purée (paste)
1 garlic clove, crushed
5 ml/1 tsp dried onion granules
15 ml/1 tbsp curry paste
5 ml/1 tsp garam masala
5 ml/1 tsp ground turmeric
30 ml/2 tbsp mango chutney
50 g/2 oz creamed coconut, cut into
*   pieces*
50 g/2 oz sliced mushrooms
4 whiting fillets, about 175 g/6 oz each
Plain Rice for Fish (page 392), to serve

Put all the ingredients except the
mushrooms and fish in a saucepan.
Heat through, stirring, until blended
and the coconut melts. When
bubbling, add the mushrooms and
stir gently. Add the fish, bathe in the
sauce, cover and simmer for about
5 minutes or until the fish is tender.
Transfer to warm plates and serve
on a bed of rice.

Cod and egg curry

SERVES 4

Prepare as for Whiting and
Mushroom Curry, but substitute
celery soup for mushroom soup and
omit the sliced mushrooms. Use
4 small cod fillets instead of the
whiting and add 3 quartered hard-
boiled (hard-cooked) eggs to the
mixture for the last 2 minutes of
cooking time.

Bourride

SERVES 4

2 small cooked lobsters
900 ml/1½ pts/3¾ cups fish stock
1 thick lemon slice
1 large leek, chopped
1 carrot, chopped
1 celery stick, chopped
1 bouquet garni sachet
4 fillets of monkfish, about
    150 g/5 oz each
150 ml/¼ pt/⅔ cup double (heavy)
    cream
2 quantities of Aioli (page 372)
Salt and freshly ground black pepper.
French bread, to serve

Halve the lobsters lengthways and remove the black vein and stomach sac (page 15). Put the stock in a pan and add the slice of lemon, the vegetables and bouquet garni. Bring to the boil, reduce the heat and simmer for 30 minutes. Strain the stock into a clean pan. Add the monkfish and poach for 8 minutes or until tender. Carefully lift out of the stock and transfer to a warm platter. Cover and keep warm.

Add the lobsters and simmer for 3 minutes until piping hot. Transfer to the dish with the monkfish and keep warm. Boil the stock until well reduced and slightly thickened. Stir in the cream. Over a gentle heat, gradually whisk in one quantity of the Aioli, a little at a time, whisking well after each addition until the sauce is lightly thickened. Season to taste. Pour over the fish and serve with the remaining Aioli and lots of French bread.

Cod in spicy yoghurt

SERVES 4

30 ml/2 tbsp sunflower oil
2 onions, thinly sliced
700 g/1½ lb cod fillet, skinned and cut
    into thick strips
15 ml/1 tbsp lemon juice
Salt and freshly ground black pepper
350 ml/12 fl oz/1⅓ cups plain yoghurt
5 ml/1 tsp caster (superfine) sugar
1 green chilli, seeded and finely
    chopped
5 ml/1 tsp ground cumin
2.5 ml/½ tsp garam masala
5 ml/1 tsp grated fresh root ginger
25 g/1 oz/2 tbsp unsalted (sweet)
    butter, cut into chunks
Torn coriander (cilantro) leaves, to
    garnish
Mango chutney and naan breads,
    to serve

Heat the oil in a large, flameproof dish. Add the onion rings and fry (sauté), stirring, for 3 minutes until softened and lightly golden. Remove from the heat. Lay the fish on top and sprinkle with the lemon juice and some salt. Mix together all the remaining ingredients except the butter and pour over the fish. Cover with foil and cook in a preheated oven at 190°C/375°F/gas mark 5 for 30 minutes until the fish is tender. Carefully pour off the cooking juices into a saucepan (they will look curdled). Bring to the boil and boil until reduced by half. Whisk in the butter a piece at a time until blended. Season to taste. Pour over the fish and sprinkle with the coriander. Serve with mango chutney and naan breads.

Balti prawns

SERVES 4

450 g/1 lb tomatoes, roughly chopped
1 large green (bell) pepper, chopped
2 green chillies, seeded and chopped
45 ml/3 tbsp sunflower oil
6 cardamom pods, split
5 ml/1 tsp light brown sugar
1.5 ml/¼ tsp ground turmeric
2.5 ml/½ tsp coarsely ground black
   pepper
Salt
150 ml/¼ pt/⅔ cup fish stock
2.5 cm/1 in piece of cinnamon stick
450 g/1 lb raw shelled tiger prawns
   (jumbo shrimp)
Plain Rice for Fish (page 392), to serve

Purée the tomatoes, green pepper
and chillies in a blender or food
processor. Heat the oil in a
flameproof casserole dish (Dutch
oven), add the cardamom pods and
fry (sauté) for 2 minutes. Add the
tomato and pepper mixture and stir
in the sugar, turmeric, pepper and a
little salt. Bring to the boil and
simmer for 15 minutes, stirring
occasionally, until the oil rises to the
surface. Stir in the stock and add the
cinnamon and prawns. Simmer
gently for 15 minutes until the
prawns are bathed in a rich sauce.
Discard the cinnamon stick. Heat a
balti dish until really hot and tip in
the curry; it should sizzle. Serve
straight away with rice.

Fish korma

SERVES 4

4 large onions
2 green chillies, seeded and chopped
5 ml/1 tsp grated fresh root ginger
1 garlic clove, crushed
5 ml/1 tsp ground turmeric
15 ml/1 tbsp black mustard seeds
100 g/4 oz creamed coconut, roughly
   chopped
45 ml/3 tbsp sunflower oil
5 cm/2 in piece of cinnamon stick
2 cardamom pods, split
2 cloves
Salt and freshly ground black pepper
300 ml/½ pt/1¼ cups plain yoghurt
900 g/2 lb hake, skinned and cut into
   large chunks
1 lemon, cut into 5 wedges
Plain Rice for Fish (page 392), to serve

Roughly chop two of the onions and
purée in a blender or food processor
with the chillies, ginger, garlic,
turmeric, mustard seeds and
creamed coconut. Slice the
remaining onions. Heat the oil in a
saucepan, add the sliced onions and
fry (sauté) for 3 minutes, stirring.
Add the spice purée and stir for
3 minutes. Add the cinnamon,
cardamom and cloves, season with
some salt and pepper and stir in the
yoghurt. Bring to the boil. Add the
fish, reduce the heat and simmer
very gently for 15 minutes. Lift out
the fish and boil the sauce rapidly
for a few minutes if necessary, to
thicken. Spoon over the fish.
Squeeze one of the lemon wedges
over the surface and serve hot with
rice, garnished with the remaining
lemon wedges.

Cheat prawn dhansak

SERVES 4

100 g/4 oz/⅔ cup green lentils, soaked
  overnight
1 garlic clove, crushed
385 g/13½ oz/1 large can of curry
  cook-in sauce
350 g/12 oz cooked peeled prawns
  (shrimp)
225 g/8 oz/1 cup long-grain rice
2.5 ml/½ tsp ground turmeric
2.5 ml/½ tsp salt
3 cardamom pods, split (optional)
2 hard-boiled (hard-cooked) eggs,
  sliced
2 bananas
Lemon juice
2 tomatoes, sliced
½ cucumber, sliced
Minted Yoghurt and Cucumber (page
  378), to serve

Drain the lentils and place them in a casserole dish (Dutch oven). Stir in the garlic and curry sauce. Cover and cook in a preheated oven at 180°C/350°F/gas mark 4 for 50 minutes or until the lentils are tender. Add the prawns, stir, cover and cook for a further 5 minutes.

Meanwhile, cook the rice in plenty of boiling water, to which the turmeric, salt and cardamom pods, if using, have been added, for about 10 minutes until just tender. Drain and fluff up with a fork. Spoon the rice in a ring on four warm plates. Top with the egg slices. Spoon the prawns and sauce in the centre. Slice the bananas and toss in the lemon juice. Arrange the banana, tomato and cucumber slices attractively around the edge and serve with Minted Yoghurt and Cucumber.

Swiss cod with spinach casserole

SERVES 4

1 large onion, finely chopped
2 celery sticks, chopped
25 g/1 oz/2 tbsp butter or margarine
15 ml/1 tbsp sunflower oil
450 g/1 lb spinach, thoroughly washed
  and drained
4 pieces of cod fillet, about 175 g/6 oz
  each, skinned
Salt and freshly ground black pepper
150 ml/¼ pt/⅔ cup fish stock
15 ml/1 tbsp plain (all-purpose) flour
150 ml/¼ pt/⅔ cup double (heavy)
  cream
50 g/2 oz/½ cup Gruyère (Swiss)
  cheese, grated
Baked Tomatoes with Herbs and
  Stuffed Olives (page 396), to serve

Fry (sauté) the onion and celery in the butter or margarine and oil for 2 minutes in a flameproof casserole dish (Dutch oven), stirring, until softened. Add the spinach and cook, stirring, until it wilts slightly. Lay the fish on top, season well and pour on the stock. Cover and bake in a preheated oven at 180°C/350°F/gas mark 4 for 20 minutes. Lift out the fish and keep warm. Blend the flour with the cream and stir into the casserole. Bring to the boil and cook for 2 minutes, stirring. Return the fish to the pot and sprinkle with the cheese. Cover and return to the oven for 5–10 minutes, uncovered, until the cheese melts. Serve hot with Baked Tomatoes with Herbs and Stuffed Olives.

Prawn dhansak

SERVES 4

50 g/2 oz/⅓ cup brown lentils, soaked
  overnight
50 g/2 oz/⅓ cup green spilt peas,
  soaked overnight
50 g/2 oz/⅓ cup red lentils
2 onions, roughly chopped
2 potatoes, roughly chopped
1 aubergine (eggplant), roughly
  chopped
1 large courgette (zucchini), roughly
  chopped
Salt
30 ml/2 tbsp sunflower oil
4 spring onions (scallions), chopped
3 garlic clove, crushed
5 ml/1 tsp fenugreek seeds
10 ml/2 tsp grated fresh root ginger
5 ml/1 tsp ground cumin
5 ml/1 tsp ground coriander (cilantro)
2.5 ml/½ tsp ground turmeric
15 ml/1 tbsp water
450 g/1 lb raw peeled tiger prawns
  (jumbo shrimp)
15 ml/1 tbsp chopped coriander
Quick Pilau Rice (page 393), lime
  pickle and chopped cucumber,
  tomato and banana, to serve

Drain the brown lentils and split
peas and place in a saucepan with
the red lentils, onions, potatoes,
aubergine and courgette. Add just
enough water to cover and sprinkle
with salt. Bring to the boil, cover,
reduce the heat and simmer for
1 hour or until the vegetables are
really tender.

Meanwhile, heat the oil in a frying
pan (skillet). Fry (sauté) the spring
onions and garlic until lightly
softened and golden. Take out half
and reserve for garnish. Add the
fenugreek seeds to the pan and fry
until they 'pop'. Stir in the remaining
spices and the water and fry for
2 minutes, stirring. Purée the

vegetables in a blender or food
processor. Return to the saucepan,
add the spice mixture and stir well.
Stir in the prawns, bring to the boil
and simmer for 10 minutes. Sprinkle
with the reserved spring onions and
garlic and the chopped coriander.
Serve with Quick Pilau Rice, lime
pickle and chopped cucumber,
tomato and banana.

Fish moghlai

SERVES 4

2 large onions, chopped
1 green (bell) pepper, chopped
2 green chillies, seeded and chopped
25 g/1 oz/2 tbsp butter or margarine
15 ml/1 tbsp sunflower oil
60 ml/4 tbsp plain yoghurt
60 ml/4 tbsp double (heavy) cream
4 garlic cloves, crushed
30 ml/2 tbsp cashew nut butter
Salt and freshly ground black pepper
900 g/2 lb any white fish fillets
1 lime
Torn coriander (cilantro) leaves, to
  garnish
Plain Rice for Fish (page 392), to serve

Fry (sauté) the onions, green pepper
and chillies in the butter or
margarine and oil for 3 minutes,
stirring. Blend together the yoghurt,
cream, garlic and cashew nut butter
and stir into the pan. Season with a
little salt and pepper. Simmer for
15 minutes, stirring occasionally,
until the mixture forms a thick
sauce. Add the fish, cover and
simmer gently for 10 minutes until
tender. Cut half the lime into thin
slices and reserve. Squeeze the juice
from the other half and stir into the
curry. Taste and re-season if
necessary. Spoon on to warm plates,
garnish with the lime slices and
coriander leaves and serve with rice.

Prawn sag

SERVES 4

2.5 ml/½ tsp ground cinnamon
2.5 ml/½ tsp ground cumin
2.5 ml/½ tsp ground coriander
  (cilantro)
2.5 ml/½ tsp chilli powder
1 garlic clove, crushed
30 ml/2 tbsp water
30 ml/2 tbsp sunflower oil
2 onions, halved and thinly sliced
60 ml/4 tbsp chopped coriander
1 large tomato, finely chopped
Salt
5 ml/1 tsp caster (superfine) sugar
175 g/6 oz frozen leaf spinach, thawed
225 g/8 oz cooked peeled prawns
  (shrimp)
4 cooked potatoes, cut into small
  chunks
Naan breads, to serve

Put the spices and garlic in a small
bowl and mix with the water. Heat
the oil and fry (sauté) the onions for
3 minutes, stirring. Add the spices
from the cup, the chopped coriander
and tomato and season lightly with
salt. Fry for 1 minute. Add the sugar,
spinach, prawns and potatoes, stir
well, cover and cook gently for
5 minutes. Serve with naan breads.

Prawn and lentil curry

SERVES 4

45 ml/3 tbsp sunflower oil
1 large onion, finely chopped
1 garlic clove, crushed
1 carrot, finely chopped
1 green (bell) pepper, finely chopped
5 ml/1 tsp chilli powder
5 ml/1 tsp ground turmeric
5 ml/1 tsp grated fresh root ginger
10 ml/2 tsp ground cumin
5 ml/1 tsp salt
15 ml/1 tbsp tomato purée (paste)
450 ml/¾ pt/2 cups fish stock
225 g/8 oz/1⅓ cups green lentils,
  soaked overnight in cold water
350 g/12 oz cooked peeled prawns
  (shrimp)
Lime pickle and naan breads, to serve

Heat the oil and brown the onion,
garlic, carrot and green pepper for
2 minutes, stirring. Stir in all the
spices and cook for 30 seconds,
stirring. Blend in the salt, tomato
purée and stock. Drain the lentils
and stir in. Bring to the boil, stir
again, cover and simmer for
50 minutes or until tender. Add the
prawns and stir well. Cover and
simmer for a further 5 minutes, then
stir again. Serve with lime pickle
and lots of naan bread.

Prawn vindaloo

SERVES 4

10 ml/2 tsp chilli powder
10 ml/2 tsp ground cumin
5 ml/1 tsp ground turmeric
10 ml/2 tsp ground mustard seeds
5 ml/1 tsp ground coriander (cilantro)
2.5 cm/1 in piece of fresh root ginger,
*   peeled and grated*
2.5 ml/½ tsp salt
60 ml/4 tbsp white wine vinegar
1 large onion, finely chopped
l large garlic clove, crushed
450 g/1 lb raw peeled tiger prawns
*   (jumbo shrimp)*
50 g/2 oz/¼ cup butter or margarine
Quick Pilau Rice (page 393) and
*   Minted Yoghurt and Cucumber*
*   (page 378), to serve*

Mix the spices with the salt and
wine vinegar in a large, shallow
dish. Stir in the onion and garlic.
Add the prawns and toss in the
mixture to coat completely. Cover
well and chill overnight to marinate.
Melt the butter or margarine in a
flameproof casserole dish (Dutch
oven). Add the prawn mixture, bring
to the boil, reduce the heat and
simmer for 15 minutes, stirring once
or twice, until the prawns are
cooked and the sauce is thick. Serve
with Quick Pilau Rice and Minted
Yoghurt and Cucumber.

Thai fish curry

SERVES 4

700 g/1½ lb monkfish fillet, cut into
*   bite-sized pieces*
60 ml/4 tbsp lime juice
10 ml/2 tsp curry powder
175 ml/6 fl oz/¾ cup canned coconut
*   milk*
75 g/3 oz/⅓ cup peanut butter
30 ml/2 tbsp white wine vinegar
15 ml/1 tbsp soy sauce
10 ml/2 tsp cornflour (cornstarch)
1 small green chilli, seeded and finely
*   chopped*
Light brown sugar
30 ml/2 tbsp sunflower oil
Torn coriander (cilantro) leaves, to
*   garnish*
Thai Fragrant Rice (page 392),
*   shredded Chinese leaves (stem*
*   lettuce) and fresh mango slices,*
*   to serve*

Place the fish in a shallow dish and
sprinkle with the lime juice and half
the curry powder. Leave to marinate
for at least 1 hour, stirring
occasionally. Put the coconut milk,
peanut butter, wine vinegar, soy
sauce, cornflour, chilli and the
remaining curry powder in a
saucepan. Heat gently, stirring, until
the peanut butter has melted, then
bring to the boil and simmer for
3 minutes, stirring. Sweeten to taste
with light brown sugar.

Thread the fish on to soaked,
wooden skewers, brush with the oil
and grill (broil) for 8–10 minutes
until tender and cooked through.
Transfer to warm plates, spoon a
little sauce over and sprinkle with
torn coriander leaves. Serve with
rice, shredded Chinese leaves,
mango slices and the remaining
sauce.

Spicy prawns and cod with courgettes

SERVES 4

2 courgettes (zucchini), cut into short fingers
Salt and freshly ground black pepper
60 ml/4 tbsp sunflower oil
1 large onion, halved and sliced
3 garlic cloves, finely chopped
1 green chilli, seeded and chopped
2.5 ml/½ tsp ground coriander (cilantro)
4 cardamom pods, split
2.5 ml/½ tsp grated fresh root ginger
225 g/8 oz/1 small can of chopped tomatoes
225 g/8 oz raw peeled tiger prawns (jumbo shrimp)
225 g/8 oz cod fillet, skinned and cut into chunks
45 ml/3 tbsp chopped coriander
Lemon juice, to taste
Plain Rice for Fish (page 392), to serve

Sprinkle the courgettes with salt and leave to stand for 15 minutes. Meanwhile, heat the oil in a saucepan. Add the onion, garlic and chilli and fry (sauté) for 3 minutes until golden. Add the spices and tomatoes and bring to the boil. Rinse the courgettes and add. Simmer gently, stirring, for 4 minutes. Add the prawns and cod, cover and simmer for 5 minutes until everything is tender. Season to taste, stir in nearly all the coriander and sprinkle with lemon juice. Spoon on to a bed of rice, discarding the cardamom pods if preferred, and sprinkle with the remaining coriander.

Spicy scallops and mackerel with aubergines

SERVES 4

Prepare as for Spicy Prawns and Cod with Courgettes, but substitute 1 large aubergine (eggplant) for the courgettes, mackerel fillets for the cod and shelled scallops for the tiger prawns (jumbo shrimp). Omit the cardamom pods and use a 5 cm/2 in piece of cinnamon stick instead.

Oriental prawn curry

SERVES 4

75 g/3 oz creamed coconut, cut into chunks
300 ml/½ pt/1¼ cups boiling water
45 ml/3 tbsp curry powder
5 ml/1 tsp Chinese five-spice powder
10 ml/2 tsp grated fresh root ginger
450 g/1 lb raw peeled tiger prawns (jumbo shrimp)
60 ml/4 tbsp sunflower oil
2 garlic cloves, crushed
Salt
30 ml/2 tbsp chopped coriander (cilantro)
Plain Rice for Fish (page 392), to serve

Put the coconut in a bowl and stir in the boiling water. When dissolved, stir in the spices and leave to cool. Add the prawns and leave to marinate for 1 hour. Heat the oil in a wok or large frying pan (skillet). Add the garlic and stir-fry for 1 minute. Lift the prawns out of the marinade and stir-fry for 5 minutes. Add the marinade and cook for a further 5 minutes, stirring. Season with salt to taste and stir in the coriander. Spoon on to a bed of rice and serve.

Mild curried banana fish

SERVES 6

6 pieces of hake fillet, about 175 g/
   6 oz each
30 ml/2 tbsp mild curry paste
50 g/2 oz/¼ cup unsalted (sweet)
   butter
30 ml/2 tbsp sunflower oil
2 onions, thinly sliced
1 large garlic clove, crushed
45 ml/3 tbsp plain (all-purpose) flour
600 ml/1 pt/2½ cups chicken stock
4 slightly green bananas
Salt and freshly ground black pepper
350 g/12 oz/1½ cups brown rice
45 ml/3 tbsp currants
15 ml/1 tbsp paprika
15 ml/1 tbsp desiccated (shredded)
   coconut

Rub the hake all over with half the
curry paste. Cover and leave in a
cool place to marinate for 2 hours.
Melt half the butter and half the oil
in a large, flameproof casserole dish
(Dutch oven). Add the onions and
garlic and fry (sauté) for 3 minutes,
stirring, until lightly golden. Add the
remaining curry paste and fry for
1 minute. Stir in the flour and cook
for a further 1 minute. Remove from
the heat and gradually blend in the
stock. Return to the heat, bring to
the boil and cook for 2 minutes,
stirring. Peel and thinly slice one of
the bananas and add to the sauce.
Bring to the boil, reduce the heat
and simmer for 35 minutes. Add the
fish and simmer for a further
10–15 minutes until tender. Season
to taste.
   Meanwhile, cook the rice in
plenty of lightly salted, boiling water
for about 35 minutes or until cooked
but still 'nutty'. Drain and stir in the
currants. Heat the remaining butter

and oil in a frying pan (skillet). Peel
the remaining bananas, cut into
halves, then split the halves to make
12 pieces. Fry in the butter and oil
for 1–2 minutes on each side until
lightly golden but still holding their
shape. Spoon the rice on to six
warm plates and make into nests.
Put the fish and sauce in the centre
and arrange two pieces of banana on
each plate. Mix the paprika with the
coconut and sprinkle over. Serve hot.

Steamed cod with asparagus

SERVES 4

4 pieces of cod fillet, about 175 g/6 oz
   each
5 ml/1 tsp dried mixed herbs
Salt and freshly ground black pepper
15 g/½ oz/1 tbsp butter or margarine
225 g/8 oz short asparagus spears,
   trimmed
Green Hollandaise (page 371), to serve
Watercress or parsley sprigs, to garnish

Lay the fish in a steamer or colander
and sprinkle with the herbs and a
little salt and pepper. Dot with the
butter or margarine. Cover and
steam for 8–10 minutes until the fish
is tender. Meanwhile, lay the
asparagus in a shallow pan and add
just enough boiling water to cover.
Add 2.5 ml/½ tsp salt. Cover and
simmer gently for 5 minutes, then
turn off the heat and leave for a
further 3 minutes. Carefully lift the
asparagus out of the pan with a fish
slice and lay on warm plates. Lay a
piece of fish on top and spoon the
Green Hollandaise over. Garnish
with watercress or parsley sprigs and
serve hot.

Cod steaks in cider

SERVES 4

1 carrot, cut into short matchsticks
2 celery sticks, cut into short
  matchsticks
1 onion, halved and thinly sliced
25 g/1 oz/2 tbsp butter or margarine
4 cod steaks
Salt and freshly ground black pepper
300 ml/½ pt/1¼ cups medium-sweet
  cider
25 g/½ oz/2 tbsp plain (all-purpose)
  flour
120 ml/4 fl oz/½ cup crème fraîche
15 ml/1 tbsp chopped parsley
Speciality Creamed Potatoes
  (page 391), to serve

Cook the vegetables in 15 g/½ oz/
1 tbsp of the butter or margarine for
3 minutes, stirring, until slightly
softened. Lay the cod steaks in a
flameproof casserole dish (Dutch
oven) and spoon the vegetables in
the centre. Season with salt and
pepper and pour the cider around.
Cover and bake in a preheated oven
at 180°C/350°F/gas mark 4 for
about 20 minutes or until the fish is
tender. Carefully transfer the fish
and vegetables to warm plates and
keep warm.
    Mash the remaining butter or
margarine and flour together. Whisk
into the fish cooking juices a piece
at a time over a gentle heat, then
bring to the boil, whisking all the
time, and cook for 1 minute. Stir in
the crème fraîche and re-season.
Spoon over the fish, sprinkle with
the parsley and serve with Speciality
Creamed Potatoes.

Spicy coconut fish

SERVES 4

10 ml/2 tsp tamarind pulp
250 ml/8 fl oz/1 cup water
30 ml/2 tbsp sunflower oil
2 large onions, finely chopped
1 green (bell) pepper, finely chopped
10 ml/2 tsp ground cumin
10 ml/2 tsp ground coriander
  (cilantro)
5 ml/1 tsp chilli powder
5 ml/1 tsp ground turmeric
2.5 ml/½ tsp ground cardamom
50 g/2 oz creamed coconut
4 pieces of hake fillet, about 175 g/
  6 oz each
2 large tomatoes, skinned and chopped
30 ml/2 tbsp chopped coriander, to
  garnish
Plain Rice for Fish (page 392) and
  curried fruit chutney, to serve

Infuse the tamarind pulp in the
water while starting to prepare the
remaining ingredients. Heat the oil
in a pan. Add the onions and green
pepper and fry (sauté) for 3 minutes.
Add the spices and fry for 1 minute,
stirring. Add the tamarind mixture
and the creamed coconut and stir
until the coconut melts. Simmer for
5 minutes. Add the fish and
tomatoes and continue cooking for
10–15 minutes until the fish is
tender and bathed in a rich sauce.
Transfer to warm plates, sprinkle
with the chopped coriander and
serve with rice and curried fruit
chutney.

Cod palak

SERVES 4

2 large onions, finely chopped
40 g/1½ oz/3 tbsp butter or margarine
2 garlic cloves, crushed
2.5 cm/1 in piece of cinnamon stick
10 ml/2 tsp ground coriander
   (cilantro)
5 ml/1 tsp grated fresh root ginger
2 beefsteak tomatoes, skinned and
   chopped
350 g/12 oz young leaf spinach,
   thoroughly washed
Salt and freshly ground black pepper
900 g/2 lb cod fillet, skinned and cut
   into large chunks
Plain Rice for Fish (page 392) and
   Minted Yoghurt and Cucumber
   (page 378), to serve

Fry (sauté) the onions in the butter
or margarine in a saucepan for
2 minutes, stirring. Add the garlic
and spices and fry for a further
1 minute. Add the tomatoes and
spinach and season lightly. Cook,
stirring, for 5 minutes until the
spinach wilts. Lay the fish on top,
cover and cook gently for about
15 minutes or until everything is
tender. Taste and re-season if
necessary. Serve with rice and
Minted Yoghurt and Cucumber.

Caribbean curried prawns

SERVES 4

350 g/12 oz raw peeled tiger prawns
   (jumbo shrimp)
Juice of 1 lime
30 ml/2 tbsp sunflower oil
1 bunch of spring onions (scallions),
   chopped
2 tomatoes, skinned and chopped
30 ml/2 tbsp curry paste
300 ml/½ pt/1¼ cups water
25 g/1 oz/¼ cup plain (all-purpose)
   flour
25 g/1 oz/2 tbsp unsalted (sweet)
   butter, softened
2 small pineapples, halved lengthways
Salt and freshly ground black pepper
Torn coriander (cilantro) leaves, to
   garnish
Plain Rice for Fish (page 392), to serve

Put the prawns in a dish and
sprinkle with the lime juice. Heat
the oil in a saucepan, add the spring
onions and cook, stirring, for
3 minutes. Stir in the tomatoes and
curry paste and cook, stirring, for
1 minute. Add the prawns and any
juice and the water. Bring to the
boil, reduce the heat, cover and
simmer gently for 5 minutes. Mash
the flour and butter together. Stir
into the pan, a piece at a time,
stirring well after each addition,
until thickened. Simmer gently for
3 minutes.

Plunge the pineapple halves in
boiling water for 4 minutes. Drain
and place on warm plates. Scoop out
some of the flesh, chop and stir into
the sauce. Taste and season with salt
and pepper. Spoon the sauce over
the pineapples and sprinkle with a
few coriander leaves. Serve with
rice.

Curried tomato salmon steaks

SERVES 4

4 salmon steaks
5 ml/1 tsp salt
2.5 ml/½ tsp ground turmeric
5 ml/1 tsp ground cumin
1.5 ml/¼ tsp chilli powder
5 ml/1 tsp paprika
90 ml/6 tbsp sunflower oil
1 large onion, thinly sliced
1 garlic clove, crushed
1 green (bell) pepper, thinly sliced
400 g/14 oz/1 large can of chopped
 tomatoes
15 ml/1 tbsp chopped coriander
 (cilantro)
2.5 ml/½ tsp garam masala
Plain Rice for Fish (page 392), to serve

Put the fish in a shallow dish. Mix together the salt and spices and sprinkle over both sides. Leave to stand for 1 hour. Heat half the oil in a saucepan. Add the onion, garlic and green pepper and fry (sauté) for 3 minutes, stirring. Add the tomatoes and simmer for 5 minutes until pulpy. Heat the remaining oil in a flameproof casserole dish (Dutch oven). Add the fish and brown on both sides for 2 minutes. Pour the tomato sauce over and bake in a preheated oven at 180°C/350°F/gas mark 4 for 15 minutes until the fish is tender. Transfer to warm plates. Stir the coriander and garam masala into the sauce, taste and add more salt if necessary. Spoon over the fish and serve with rice.

Monday tuna curry

SERVES 4

1 onion, chopped
1 garlic clove, crushed
30 ml/2 tbsp sunflower oil
175 g/6 oz button mushrooms, halved
15 ml/1 tbsp curry paste
450 ml/¾ pt/2 cups chicken stock
100 g/4 oz creamed coconut, cut into
 pieces
45 ml/3 tbsp raisins
185 g/6½ oz/1 small can of tuna,
 drained
175 g/6 oz cooked leftover or thawed
 frozen vegetables, chopped if
 necessary
Salt and freshly ground black pepper
30 ml/2 tbsp chopped coriander
 (cilantro)
Naan breads, to serve

Cook the onion and garlic in the oil for 3 minutes until lightly golden. Add the mushrooms and cook for 1 minute. Add the curry paste and stock. Bring to the boil and stir in the creamed coconut and raisins. Cook until the coconut dissolves. Add the tuna and vegetables and simmer very gently for 10 minutes. Season to taste and stir in the coriander. Serve with naan breads.

Dry fish curry

SERVES 4

5 ml/1 tsp fenugreek seeds, crushed
15 ml/1 tbsp ground coriander
(cilantro)
15 ml/1 tbsp ground cumin
5 ml/1 tsp ground turmeric
2 red chillies, seeded and finely
chopped
40 g/1½ oz/3 tbsp butter or margarine
1 onion, thinly sliced
5 ml/1 tsp black mustard seeds
15 ml/1 tbsp desiccated (shredded)
coconut
5 ml/1 tsp tamarind pulp
120 ml/4 fl oz/½ cup water
Salt and freshly ground black pepper
900 g/2 lb thick white fish fillet, cut
into 4 pieces
Bombay Puréed Potatoes (page 391)
and mango chutney, to serve

Mix the spices and chillies together.
Melt the butter or margarine in a
saucepan and add the onion. Fry
(sauté) for 3 minutes until lightly
browned. Add the spices and fry for
1 minute, stirring. Add the mustard
seeds and cook until they 'pop'. Add
all the remaining ingredients except
the fish and cook very gently for
about 30 minutes until pulpy. Add
the fish and cook for a further 10
minutes until tender. Serve with
Bombay Puréed Potatoes and mango
chutney.

Mild haddock curry

SERVES 4

2 potatoes, quartered
900 g/2 lb haddock fillet, cut into
8 pieces
2 onions, roughly chopped
90 ml/6 tbsp plain yoghurt
2.5 ml/½ tsp ground ginger
2.5 ml/½ tsp ground cumin
5 ml/1 tsp ground turmeric
A pinch of chilli powder
25 g/1 oz/2 tbsp butter or margarine,
melted
Salt
Naan breads and mango chutney, to
serve

Boil the potatoes in lightly salted
water for 6 minutes until almost
tender. Drain. Wipe the fish with
kitchen paper (paper towels) and
place in a shallow dish. Purée the
onions in a blender or food
processor with the yoghurt and
spices. Pour over the fish and turn
the pieces over to coat completely.
Leave to marinate for 30 minutes.
Heat half the butter or margarine in
a flameproof casserole dish (Dutch
oven). Add the fish mixture and fry
(sauté) for 3 minutes. Arrange the
potato pieces over and season with a
little salt. Brush with the remaining
butter or margarine. Cover and cook
in a preheated oven at 180°C/
350°F/gas mark 4 for 30 minutes.
Serve with naan breads and mango
chutney.

North Country mussel pudding

SERVES 4–6

275 g/10 oz/2½ cups self-raising (self-rising) flour
Salt and freshly ground black pepper
150 g/5 oz/1¼ cups shredded (chopped) suet
1.75 kg/4 lb mussels in their shells, cleaned (page 13)
1 large onion, finely chopped
4 smoked streaky bacon rashers (slices), rinded and diced
75 ml/5 tbsp chopped parsley
175 g/6 oz/¾ cup unsalted (sweet) butter, plus extra for greasing
15 ml/1 tbsp chopped thyme

Sift the flour and a pinch of salt in a bowl. Stir in the suet and mix with enough cold water to form a soft but not sticky dough. Cover and chill while you prepare the mussels. Place the cleaned mussels in a large saucepan with 200 ml/7 fl oz/scant 1 cup water. Cover and bring to the boil. Cook for 5 minutes, shaking the pan occasionally, until the mussels open. Discard any that remain shut. Drain, reserving the cooking liquid. Remove the fish from the shells and reserve.

Roll out the dough on a lightly floured surface to a rectangle about 5 mm/¼ in thick. Place on a large double thickness of buttered greaseproof (waxed) paper, laid over a large sheet of foil. Scatter the onion, bacon, 45 ml/3 tbsp of the parsley and some pepper over the surface. Top with the mussels. Dampen the edges, then roll up. Wrap in the greaseproof paper and foil loosely, to allow for rising, and seal the edges together well. Place on a trivet or old saucer in a fish kettle or roaster baster, half-full of boiling water. Bring back to the boil, cover, reduce the heat and simmer for 2 hours, topping up with boiling water as necessary.

Carefully lift the parcel out of the pan, unwrap, pouring any juices into the reserved mussel cooking liquid, and turn on to a warm, ovenproof serving dish. Place in a hot oven at 200°C/400°F/gas mark 6 for 10 minutes to crisp the crust, if liked. Meanwhile, melt the butter in a saucepan with the remaining parsley, the thyme and a little pepper. Reheat the mussel cooking water. Slice the pudding and serve with the herb butter and the mussel liquid.

Oyster pudding

SERVES 4–6

Prepare as for North Country Mussel Pudding, but substitute 36 oysters for the mussels. To prepare them for the pudding, open them (page 13) and tip them and their juices into a small pan. Heat gently just until the fish firm up, then continue as for mussel pudding.

Turbot with crab in green peppercorn sauce

SERVES 4–6

1 kg/2¼ lb piece of turbot
600 ml/1 pt/2½ cups water
250 ml/8 fl oz/1 cup dry white wine
1 small onion, quartered
1 celery stick, chopped
1 carrot, chopped
1 bouquet garni sachet
10 ml/2 tsp pickled green peppercorns
Salt
40 g/1½ oz/3 tbsp butter or margarine
170 g/6 oz/1 small can of white
    crabmeat, drained
40 g/1½ oz/1 very small can of dressed
    crab
45 ml/3 tbsp fresh white breadcrumbs
90 ml/6 tbsp crème fraîche
A pinch of cayenne
20 ml/¾ oz/3 tbsp plain (all-purpose)
    flour
15 ml/1 tbsp grated Parmesan cheese
New potatoes and mangetout (snow
    peas), to serve

Wipe the fish with kitchen paper (paper towels). Place in a saucepan with the water, half the wine, the onion, celery, carrot, bouquet garni and six of the peppercorns. Add a good pinch of salt. Bring almost to the boil, when small bubbles rise quite fast to the surface, reduce the heat, cover and cook very gently for 20 minutes or until the fish is just tender. Do not boil rapidly.

Meanwhile, melt 15 g/½ oz/1 tbsp of the butter or margarine in a separate saucepan. Add both cans of crab, the breadcrumbs, 30 ml/2 tbsp of the crème fraîche and the cayenne. Heat through gently, stirring. Spoon into a shallow flameproof dish and keep warm. When the fish is cooked, gently lift it out of the cooking liquid and place it on the crab mixture. Keep warm.

Strain the cooking liquid and measure out 150 ml/¼ pt/⅔ cup. Melt the remaining butter or margarine in a saucepan. Add the flour and cook for 1 minute, stirring. Remove from the heat and blend in the remaining wine and the measured stock and the remaining crème fraîche. Return to the heat, bring to the boil and cook for 1 minute, stirring. Add the remaining peppercorns and cook for a further 1 minute. Add the Parmesan and season with salt to taste. Spoon over the fish to coat completely. Place under a preheated grill (broiler), to set and lightly brown the top. Serve straight away with new potatoes and mangetout.

Poached skate au gratin

SERVES 4

900 g/2 lb skate wings
600 ml/1 pt/2½ cups water
30 ml/2 tbsp white wine vinegar
1½ quantities of Cheese Sauce
    (page 376)
25 g/1 oz/¼ cup Cheddar cheese, grated
45 ml/3 tbsp fresh white breadcrumbs
15 g/½ oz/1 tbsp butter or margarine,
    melted

Cut the skate into wide strips. Place in a saucepan with the water and wine vinegar. Bring to the boil, reduce the heat, cover and cook gently for 20 minutes. Leave in the liquid while preparing the Cheese Sauce. Lift out the skate with a fish slice, remove the skin and place in a flameproof serving dish. Pour the hot sauce over, sprinkle with the cheese and breadcrumbs and drizzle the butter or margarine over. Place under a preheated grill (broiler) until golden and bubbly. Serve hot.

Stewed eels

SERVES 4 OR 5

1 kg/2¼ lb eels
1 large onion, finely chopped
1 thick lemon slice
750 ml/1¼ pts/3 cups fish or chicken
stock
Salt and freshly ground black pepper
40 g/1½ oz/3 tbsp butter or margarine,
softened
20 g/¾ oz/3 tbsp plain (all-purpose)
flour
30 ml/2 tbsp chopped parsley

Wash the eels in running water.
Drain, then cut into 5 cm/2 in
pieces. Place in a large saucepan
with the onion, slice of lemon, stock
and seasoning. Bring to the boil,
reduce the heat, part-cover and
simmer gently for 30 minutes until
the eels are really tender. Lift out the
eels with a draining spoon and
transfer to large soup plates. Keep
warm. Mash the butter or margarine
with the flour. Whisk this mixture, a
piece at a time, into the stock over a
moderate heat until blended. Bring
to the boil, whisking all the time.
Squeeze the lemon slice against the
side of the pan to extract the juice,
then discard. Taste and re-season.
Pour over the eels and sprinkle with
the parsley.

Poached brill with caramelised onions

SERVES 4

450 g/1 lb onions, thinly sliced
50 g/2 oz/¼ cup butter or margarine
5 ml/1 tsp caster (superfine) sugar
Salt and freshly ground black pepper
700 g/1½ lb brill fillet
300 ml/½ pt/1¼ cups milk
1 small bay leaf
20 g/¾ oz/3 tbsp plain (all-purpose)
flour
150 ml/¼ pt/⅔ cup single (light) cream
5 ml/1 tsp Dijon mustard
30 ml/2 tbsp grated Cheddar cheese

Fry (sauté) the onions in the butter
or margarine in a saucepan for
3 minutes, stirring. Turn down the
heat, cover and cook for 10 minutes.
Remove the lid, add the sugar and
some salt and pepper, turn up the
heat again and cook, stirring, for a
further 5 minutes until a rich golden
brown. Transfer to a shallow,
flameproof serving dish and keep
warm.
 Meanwhile, put the fish in a
separate pan with the milk and bay
leaf. Bring to the boil, reduce the
heat, cover and poach for about
5 minutes until tender. Carefully lift
the fish out of the pan with a fish
slice and lay on top of the onions.
Cover and keep warm. Blend the
flour with the cream and mustard
and stir into the cooking milk. Bring
to the boil and cook for 2 minutes,
stirring. Season to taste and discard
the bay leaf. Pour the sauce over the
fish, sprinkle with the cheese and
place under a hot grill (broiler) to
brown the top. Serve hot.

Plaice Sylvie

SERVES 4

50 g/2 oz/¼ cup butter or margarine,
  plus extra for greasing
1 onion, finely chopped
1 carrot, finely chopped
1 turnip, finely chopped
½ celeriac, finely chopped
50 g/2 oz shelled fresh or frozen baby
  broad (fava) beans
2 beefsteak tomatoes, skinned and
  chopped
30 ml/2 tbsp apple juice
Salt and freshly ground black pepper
8 plaice fillets, skinned if black
150 ml/¼ pt/⅔ cup dry white wine
1 bay leaf
20 g/¾ oz/3 tbsp plain (all-purpose)
  flour
5 ml/1 tsp ground cumin
120 ml/4 fl oz/½ cup milk
30 ml/2 tbsp double (heavy) cream

Melt half the butter or margarine in
a casserole dish (Dutch oven). Add
the onion, carrot, turnip, celeriac
and beans and cook, stirring, for
3 minutes. Add the tomatoes and
apple juice and season to taste.
Bring to the boil, cover and transfer
to a preheated oven at 180°C/
350°F/gas mark 4 for 20 minutes or
until tender.
  Meanwhile, roll up the fish and
place in a lightly greased, ovenproof
dish. Add the wine, bay leaf and a
little salt and pepper. Cover and
cook in the oven for 15 minutes.
Transfer the vegetable mixture to a
warm serving dish. Remove the fish
fillets, reserving the cooking liquid
but discarding the bay leaf, and lay
on top of the vegetables. Cover and
keep warm in a very low oven.
  Melt the remaining butter or
margarine in a saucepan. Blend in
the flour and cumin and cook for
1 minute. Remove from the heat and
blend in the milk and fish cooking
liquid. Return to the heat, bring to
the boil and cook for 2 minutes,
stirring. Season to taste and stir in
the cream. Spoon over the fish and
serve.

Somerset sole

SERVES 4

700 g/1½ lb sole fillets
200 ml/7 fl oz/scant 1 cup medium-
  sweet cider
100 ml/3½ fl oz/scant ½ cup fish stock
50 g/2 oz/¼ cup butter or margarine,
  softened
20 g/¾ oz/3 tbsp plain (all-purpose)
  flour
30 ml/2 tbsp crème fraîche
Salt and freshly ground black pepper
2 eating (dessert) apples, cored and
  each sliced into 4 rings
15 ml/1 tbsp chopped parsley

Fold the fillets in three and place in
a shallow pan. Add the cider and
stock. Bring to the boil, cover with a
lid or foil, reduce the heat and
poach for about 8 minutes until
tender. Lift out of the pan and keep
warm. Mash half the butter or
margarine and flour together and
whisk into the liquid, a piece at a
time, over a gentle heat. Bring to the
boil and simmer for 1 minute. Stir in
the crème fraîche and season to
taste. Meanwhile, fry (sauté) the
apple slices in the remaining butter
or margarine until golden on both
sides and just tender. Spoon the
sauce over the fish, sprinkle with the
parsley and garnish with the apple
rings.

Sole bonne femme

SERVES 4

4 Dover sole fillets, skinned if black
120 ml/4 fl oz/½ cup dry white wine
120 ml/4 fl oz/½ cup water
6 peppercorns
1 bouquet garni sachet
1 small onion, quartered
1 lemon slice
25 g/1 oz/2 tbsp butter or margarine,
* plus extra for greasing*
15 g/½ oz/2 tbsp plain (all-purpose)
* flour*
90 ml/6 tbsp single (light) cream
Salt and white pepper
50 g/2 oz button mushrooms, sliced
5 ml/1 tsp lemon juice
1 quantity of Hollandaise Sauce
* (page 371)*

Fold the fish in halves lengthways and lay in a large, greased, flameproof serving dish. Pour the wine and water over and add the peppercorns, bouquet garni, onion and lemon slice. Cover with foil and bring to the boil. Reduce the heat and cook very gently for 10 minutes or until the fish is tender. Carefully strain off the cooking liquid and reserve. Discard the bouquet garni, peppercorns, onion and lemon slice. Keep the fish warm.

Melt the butter or margarine in a saucepan, add the flour and cook for 1 minute. Remove from the heat and stir in the reserved cooking liquid. Return to the heat, bring to the boil and cook for 2 minutes, stirring. Stir in the cream and season to taste. Pour over the fish. Quickly cook the mushrooms in the lemon juice and 15 ml/1 tbsp water for 2 minutes, stirring, (or cook briefly in the microwave) until softened. Scatter the mushrooms over the sauce, then put a spoonful of Hollandaise Sauce on each fillet. Place under a preheated grill (broiler) briefly to glaze the top. Serve straight away.

Steamed oriental sea bream

SERVES 4

1 large sea bream, about 900 g/2 lb,
* cleaned and scaled*
2.5 cm/1 in piece of fresh root ginger,
* peeled and grated*
1 green chilli, seeded and finely
* chopped*
½ bunch of spring onions (scallions),
* finely chopped*
30 ml/2 tbsp oyster sauce
30 ml/2 tbsp soy sauce
5 ml/1 tsp light brown sugar
2.5 ml/½ tsp ground coriander
* (cilantro)*
Salt and freshly ground black pepper
A few torn coriander leaves, to garnish
Thai Fragrant Rice (page 392),
* to serve*

Rinse the fish and pat dry with kitchen paper (paper towels). Lay on a large heatproof plate and place over a large pan of gently simmering water. Cover the fish with the saucepan lid, or another plate inverted over the top, and steam for 10 minutes. Mix together all the remaining ingredients and spoon over the fish. Re-cover and steam for a further 10 minutes or until the fish is cooked through. Garnish with a few torn coriander leaves and serve hot with Thai Fragrant Rice.

Sole Véronique with potato cake

SERVES 4

450 g/1 lb potatoes, scrubbed
2 small onions
Salt and freshly ground black pepper
30 ml/2 tbsp olive oil
700 g/1½ lb sole fillets
120 ml/4 fl oz/½ cup dry white wine
120 ml/4 fl oz/½ cup water
White pepper
1 thyme sprig
1 parsley sprig
25 g/1 oz/2 tbsp butter or margarine
20 g/¾ oz/3 tbsp plain (all-purpose) flour
120 ml/4 fl oz/½ cup single (light) cream
175 g/6 oz seedless green grapes, halved
Lemon juice, to taste
15 ml/1 tbsp chopped parsley

Grate the potatoes into a bowl. Grate one of the onions and mix in. Season with salt and black pepper. Heat the oil in a frying pan (skillet), add the potato mixture and press down firmly. Fry (sauté) for 10 minutes. Tip the cake out of the pan on to a plate, then slide back in the pan, browned-side up. Cover and continue to fry for a further 20 minutes until cooked through. Transfer to a serving plate.

Meanwhile, fold the fillets in three, and place in a casserole dish (Dutch oven). Quarter the remaining onion and add with the wine, water, seasoning and sprigs of herbs. Cover and poach in the oven at 180°C/ 350°F/gas mark 4 for 10 minutes. Carefully lift out the fish, cover and keep warm. Melt the butter or margarine in a saucepan, stir in the flour and cook for 1 minute. Remove from the heat and blend in the strained cooking liquid. Return to the heat, bring to the boil and cook for 2 minutes, stirring. Blend in the cream, grapes, seasoning and lemon juice. Put the fish on the potatoes, spoon the sauce over the fish and serve sprinkled with the parsley.

Pollack Alsace

SERVES 4

1 onion, thinly sliced
30 ml/2 tbsp sunflower oil
25 g/1 oz/2 tbsp butter or margarine
1 garlic clove, crushed
1 small green cabbage, shredded
15 ml/1 tbsp caraway seeds
Salt and freshly ground black pepper
2.5 ml/½ tsp dried mixed herbs
150 ml/¼ pt/⅔ cup fish stock
4 pollack fillets, about 175 g/6 oz each, skinned
60 ml/4 tbsp Cantal or Cheddar cheese, grated
30 ml/2 tbsp crème fraîche

Fry (sauté) the onion in the oil and half the butter or margarine in a flameproof casserole dish (Dutch oven) for 3 minutes, stirring, until softened but not browned. Add the garlic and cabbage and toss until the cabbage is glistening and beginning to shrink a little. Sprinkle with the caraway seeds, a little salt and pepper and the herbs. Pour on the stock and bring to the boil. Lay the fish fillets on top. Dot with the remaining butter or margarine and season lightly. Return to the boil, cover and transfer to a preheated oven at 180°C/350°F/gas mark 4 for 30 minutes or until the fish and cabbage are tender.

Mix the cheese and crème fraîche with a little salt and pepper. Spread over the top of the fish and flash under a hot grill (broiler) to brown.

Indian-style mussels

SERVES 4–6

3 large garlic cloves, crushed
15 ml/1 tbsp grated fresh root ginger
2.5 ml/½ tsp ground turmeric
5 ml/1 tsp ground cumin
5 ml/1 tsp ground coriander (cilantro)
375 ml/13 fl oz/1½ cups water
60 ml/4 tbsp sunflower oil
1 large onion, finely chopped
2 green chillies, seeded if preferred and finely chopped
100 g/4 oz creamed coconut, cut into chunks
Salt and freshly ground black pepper
1.5 kg/3 lb mussels, cleaned (page 13)
Chopped coriander, to garnish
Plain Rice for Fish (page 392), to serve

Pound the garlic with the ginger to a paste in a mortar with a pestle or in a bowl with the end of a rolling pin. Stir in the spices and mix with 120 ml/4 fl oz/½ cup of the water. Heat the oil in a large saucepan. Add the onion and fry (sauté) for 3 minutes until lightly golden. Add the spice mixture and chillies and bubble for 1 minute. Stir in the remaining water, the coconut and seasoning and cook, stirring, until the coconut melts. Add the mussels, stir well, cover and cook over a gentle heat for about 5 minutes or until the mussels open. Discard any that remain closed. Stir again, sprinkle with chopped coriander and serve with rice.

Casseroled cod with lentils

SERVES 4

1 onion, finely chopped
1 large carrot, finely chopped
1 celery stick, finely chopped
30 ml/2 tbsp olive oil
1 garlic clove, crushed
225 g/8 oz/1⅓ cups green lentils, soaked overnight
150 ml/¼ pt/⅔ cup medium-sweet cider
450 ml/¾ pt/2 cups water
1 bay leaf
Salt and freshly ground black pepper
4 pieces of cod fillet, about 175 g/6 oz each
30 ml/2 tbsp chopped parsley
Crusty bread, to serve

Fry (sauté) the onion, carrot and celery in the oil in a flameproof casserole dish (Dutch oven) for 3 minutes. Add the garlic, drained lentils, cider, water, bay leaf and seasoning and stir well. Cover and cook in a preheated oven at 180°C/ 350°F/gas mark 4 for about 1 hour until the lentils are tender. Lay the fish on top and season with salt and pepper. Cover and return to the oven for about 20 minutes or until the fish is tender. Discard the bay leaf. Spoon the lentils and fish on to warm plates and sprinkle with the parsley. Serve with crusty bread.

Any-night fish pot

SERVES 4

*400 g/14 oz/1 large can of chopped
tomatoes*
*275 g/10 oz/1 medium can of new
potatoes, drained and quartered*
*275 g/10 oz/1 medium can of baby
carrots, drained*
*275 g/10 oz/1 medium can of garden
peas, drained*
*300 ml/½ pt/1¼ cups fish, vegetable or
chicken stock*
5 ml/1 tsp anchovy essence (extract)
15 ml/1 tbsp tomato purée (paste)
A pinch of caster (superfine) sugar
Salt and freshly ground black pepper
*350 g/12 oz frozen white fish fillets,
thawed, skinned and cut into small
chunks*
15 ml/1 tbsp chopped parsley

Put all the ingredients except the
fish and parsley in a large saucepan.
Bring to the boil and simmer for
3 minutes. Add the fish and cook for
5 minutes or until the fish flakes
easily with the point of a knife. Taste
and re-season if necessary. Ladle
into warm bowls and sprinkle with
the parsley before serving.

Pollack poached in milk

SERVES 4

Use the milk in a fish soup, if liked.

4 pollack fillets, about 175 g/6 oz each
600 ml/1 pt/2½ cups milk
1 small bay leaf
*100 g/4 oz/½ cup unsalted (sweet)
butter*
*Finely grated rind and juice of ½ large
lemon*
30 ml/2 tbsp capers, roughly chopped
2 gherkins (cornichons), chopped
Salt and freshly ground black pepper

Lay the pollack in a shallow pan.
Add the milk and bay leaf. Bring to

the boil, reduce the heat, cover and
poach for 8 minutes or until the fish
is tender. Carefully lift out of the pan
with a fish slice, draining well, and
transfer to warm plates. Meanwhile,
melt the butter in a small saucepan.
Add the lemon rind and juice, the
capers, gherkins and a little salt and
pepper and allow to bubble for
30 seconds. Pour over the fish and
serve very hot.

Poached scallops with cream

SERVES 4

24 queen scallops
300 ml/½ pt/1¼ cups milk
150 ml/¼ pt/⅔ cup dry white wine
1 bouquet garni sachet
30 ml/2 tbsp cornflour (cornstarch)
60 ml/4 tbsp double (heavy) cream
Salt and white pepper
1 red (bell) pepper, finely diced
1 green pepper, finely diced
*Speciality Creamed Potatoes
(page 391), to serve*

Put the scallops in a saucepan with
the milk, wine and bouquet garni.
Bring to the boil, reduce the heat
and simmer for 4 minutes. Lift the
scallops out of the pan with a
draining spoon, transfer to a shallow
serving dish and keep warm. Blend
the cornflour with the cream and stir
into the cooking liquid. Bring to the
boil and cook for 2 minutes, stirring.
Season to taste and discard the
bouquet garni. Meanwhile, boil the
peppers in lightly salted water for
2 minutes until slightly softened.
Drain. Pour the sauce over the
scallops, scatter with the peppers
and serve with Speciality Creamed
Potatoes.

Parayemista (stuffed squid)

SERVES 4

450 g/1 lb baby squid, cleaned (page 14)
1 onion, finely chopped
120 ml/4 fl oz/½ cup olive oil
50 g/2 oz/¼ cup long-grain rice
120 ml/4 fl oz/½ cup tomato juice
Salt and freshly ground pepper
120 ml/4 fl oz/½ cup dry white wine
5 cloves
5 cm/2 in piece of cinnamon stick

Chop the squid tentacles and fry (sauté) with the onion in a little of the oil for about 3 minutes until the onion is soft but not brown. Stir in the rice and tomato juice. Bring to the boil, reduce the heat and simmer until the rice has absorbed the liquid. Season to taste and spoon into the squid. Heat the remaining oil in a large, flameproof casserole dish (Dutch oven). Fry the squid gently until turning golden, carefully turning once. Add the wine, spices and enough water to cover the squid completely. Bring to the boil, reduce the heat, cover with a plate that sits on top of the squid, then the lid, and transfer to a preheated oven at 180°C/350°C/gas mark 4 and cook for about 50–60 minutes or until the squid are tender. Transfer the squid to a serving dish and boil the liquid rapidly until well reduced and syrupy. Discard the spices and spoon over the squid.

Poached salmon with vegetable medley

SERVES 4

1 bunch of spring onions (scallions)
2 carrots, cut into thin diagonal slices
1 red (bell) pepper, cut into diamonds
8 waxy potatoes, thinly sliced

25 g/1 oz/2 tbsp butter or margarine
4 salmon tail fillets, about 175 g/6 oz each
300 ml/½ pt/1¼ cups fish stock
1 bay leaf
100 g/4 oz mangetout (snow peas)
30 ml/2 tbsp brandy
60 ml/4 tbsp crème fraîche
Salt and freshly ground black pepper

Trim the spring onions and cut into 10 cm/4 in lengths from the bulb end. Place in a flameproof casserole dish (Dutch oven) with the carrots, red pepper and potatoes and fry (sauté) in the butter or margarine for 2 minutes. Lay the fish on top, pour the stock over and add the bay leaf. Bring to the boil, cover and simmer gently for 3 minutes. Add the mangetout and simmer for a further 2 minutes or until the fish and vegetables are tender but still holding their shape. Carefully lift the fish and vegetables out of the pan and transfer to a warm, shallow dish. Boil the liquid until reduced by half. Discard the bay leaf. Warm the brandy in a soup ladle. Ignite and stir into the pan with the crème fraîche and salt and pepper to taste. Bring to the boil and simmer for 1 minute. Spoon over the fish and serve.

Poached cod with orange and vegetables

SERVES 4

Prepare as for Poached Salmon with Vegetable Medley, but substitute cod for the salmon. Scatter the thinly pared and shredded rind of an orange over the fish before cooking and use Cointreau or another orange liqueur instead of brandy.

Pies, tarts, flans and pizzas

Fish in all its guises can be used in a phenomenal range of pastry (paste) dishes, from a simple quiche to a coulibiac. Glorious combinations of cheese, eggs and vegetables blend beautifully with the delicate texture of fish and also complement the stronger flavours of smoked and salted varieties. As well as the pastry dishes you'd expect, this chapter includes other recipes where the fish is cooked in or on an edible crust, such as a stunning Neapolitan pizza and a whole crusty loaf baked with a tuna and mushroom stuffing.

Cod and prawn valentines

SERVES 2

225 g/8 oz/2 cups plain (all-purpose) flour
Salt and freshly ground black pepper
125 g/4½ oz/generous ½ cup butter or margarine, diced
100 g/4 oz cod fillet
105 ml/7 tbsp milk
1 small bay leaf
15 ml/1 tbsp tomato purée (paste)
15 ml/1 tbsp cornflour (cornstarch)
50 g/2 oz cooked peeled prawns (shrimp)
15 ml/1 tbsp chopped parsley
Beaten egg, to glaze
Parsley sprigs, halved cherry tomatoes and lemon wedges, to garnish
Avocado Cream (page 372) and mangetout (snow peas), to serve

Sift the flour and a pinch of salt into a bowl. Add 100 g/4 oz/½ cup of the butter or margarine and rub in with your fingertips until the mixture resembles breadcrumbs. Mix with enough cold water to form a firm dough. Wrap and chill while making the filling.

Put the cod in a saucepan with 75 ml/5 tbsp of the milk and the bay leaf. Bring to the boil, reduce the heat, part-cover and simmer for about 5 minutes until the fish flakes easily with a fork. Lift out of the milk, discard the skin and any bones and break up the flesh.

Discard the bay leaf, then whisk the remaining butter or margarine and the tomato purée into the fish cooking milk. Blend the cornflour with the reserved milk and whisk into the saucepan. Bring to the boil and cook for 2 minutes, stirring all the time. Stir in the cod, prawns, parsley and some salt and pepper and leave to cool.

Meanwhile, roll out the pastry (paste) and knead it gently on a lightly floured surface. Cut into four pieces and roll out each to an 18 cm/7 in round. Put them on top of each other and cut out four identical heart shapes. Put two hearts on a baking (cookie) sheet, spoon the filling on top and spread out, leaving a 1 cm/½ in border all round. Brush the edges with a little beaten egg and top with the remaining hearts. Press the edges well together, then knock up and flute with the back of a knife. Make your and your loved one's initials out of the trimmings and lay one set on top of each heart. Brush with beaten egg. Bake in a preheated oven at 200°C/400°F/gas mark 6 for 30 minutes. Transfer to warm plates, garnish each with parsley sprigs, halved cherry tomatoes and lemon wedges and serve with Avocado Cream and mangetout.

Salmon torte

SERVES 6

225 g/8 oz/2 cups plain (all-purpose) flour
100 g/4 oz/1 cup wholemeal flour
Salt and freshly ground black pepper
75 g/3 oz/⅓ cup butter or margarine, diced
75 g/3 oz/¾ cup white vegetable fat , diced
30 ml/2 tbsp caraway seeds
100 g/4 oz/½ cup long-grain rice
3 hard-boiled (hard-cooked) eggs, chopped
425 g/14½ oz/1 large can of artichoke hearts, cut into small pieces
15 ml/1 tbsp chopped parsley
15 ml/1 tbsp chopped dill (dill weed)
2 eggs, beaten
700 g/1½ lb salmon tail fillets, skinned
Pickled dill cucumbers and mixed salad, to serve

Sift the flours and a good pinch of salt into a bowl. Add the fats and rub in with your fingertips until the mixture resembles breadcrumbs. Stir in the caraway seeds, then mix with enough cold water to form a firm dough. Wrap in foil and chill until ready to use.

Cook the rice in plenty of lightly salted, boiling water for 10 minutes or until tender. Drain, rinse with cold water and drain again. Mix with the chopped eggs, artichokes, the herbs and a little salt and pepper. Stir in one of the beaten eggs. Reserve a quarter of the pastry (paste) to use as a 'lid'. Roll out the remainder and use to line a 20 cm/8 in springform tin (pan) or loose-bottomed cake tin. Spoon half the rice mixture into the tin, then lay the fish on top and season with a little more salt and pepper. Top with the remaining rice mixture. Roll out the remaining pastry and use to top the pie. Press the edges well together to seal, then trim. Use the trimmings to make leaves to decorate the top of the pie. Brush with beaten egg and put the leaves in position. Brush again.

Bake in a preheated oven at 200°C/400°F/gas mark 6 for 30 minutes, then reduce the heat to 180°C/350°F/gas mark 4 and continue cooking for 15–20 minutes until cooked through and golden brown. Leave to cool slightly, then remove from the tin. Serve warm or cold with pickled dill cucumbers and a mixed salad.

Mushroom, onion and prawn quiche

SERVES 4

175 g/6 oz/1½ cups plain (all-purpose) flour
Salt and freshly ground black pepper
75 g/3 oz/⅓ cup hard block margarine, diced
100 g/4 oz button mushrooms, sliced
1 onion, sliced
15 ml/1 tbsp sunflower oil
100 g/4 oz cooked peeled prawns (shrimp)
50 g/2 oz/½ cup Cheddar cheese, grated
300 ml/½ pt/1¼ cups milk or mixed milk and single (light) cream
2 eggs

Sift the flour and a pinch of salt into a bowl. Add the margarine and rub in with your fingertips until the mixture resembles fine breadcrumbs. Mix with enough cold water to form a firm dough. Knead gently on a lightly floured surface, roll out and use to line a 20 cm/8 in flan dish (pie pan). Prick the base with a fork. Place on a baking (cookie) sheet. Fry (sauté) the mushrooms and onion in the oil for 3 minutes, stirring, until softened. Turn into the flan case (pie shell). Top with the prawns, then the cheese. Beat the milk or mixed milk and cream with the egg and season with some salt and pepper. Pour into the flan and bake in a preheated oven at 190°C/375°F/gas mark 5 for about 30 minutes until the filling is set and golden brown. Serve hot or cold.

Tuna and sweetcorn quiche

SERVES 4

Prepare as for Mushroom, Onion and Prawn Quiche, but omit the mushrooms and prawns (shrimp). Add 200 g/7 oz/1 small can of sweetcorn (corn), drained, and 185 g/6½ oz/1 small can of tuna, drained, after putting the onions in the flan case (pie shell).

Tuna and courgette quiche

SERVES 4

Prepare as for Mushroom, Onion and Prawn Quiche, but omit the mushrooms and prawns (shrimp). Add 1 large, grated courgette (zucchini) when frying (sautéing) the onion and add 185 g/6½ oz/ 1 small can of tuna, drained. Use grated Gruyère (Swiss) cheese instead of Cheddar and add 2.5 ml/½ tsp dried thyme.

South Mediterranean quiche

SERVES 4

Prepare as for Mushroom, Onion and Prawn Quiche, but use 2 onions and omit the prawns (shrimp). Use grated Parmesan cheese instead of Cheddar (or half and half) and top with a ring of sliced tomatoes, then a lattice of canned anchovy fillets, first soaked in milk for 10 minutes. Scatter a few torn basil leaves over the surface before baking.

Salmon and green pepper quiche

SERVES 4

Prepare as for Mushroom, Onion and Prawn Quiche, but substitute 200 g/ 7 oz/1 small can of pink salmon, skin removed and flaked, for the prawns (shrimp), and top with a sliced green (bell) pepper.

Cod and bacon quiche

SERVES 4

Prepare as for Mushroom, Onion and Prawn Quiche but omit the mushrooms and prawns (shrimp). Add smoked streaky bacon rashers (slices), rinded and diced, and 175 g/6 oz cod fillet, skinned and cut into small pieces, when you fry (sauté) the onion.

Smoked haddock quiche

SERVES 4

Prepare as for Mushroom, Onion and Prawn Quiche, but omit the mushrooms, if preferred, and the prawns (shrimp). Add 175 g/6 oz smoked haddock fillet, skinned, poached in a little milk and flaked, to the flan case (pie shell) after adding the cooked onions.

Smoked salmon and spinach quiche

SERVES 4

Prepare as for Smoked Haddock Quiche, but substitute 100 g/4 oz chopped smoked salmon for the poached haddock and put 225 g/ 8 oz cooked, chopped spinach, thoroughly drained, in the base of the flan before adding the cooked onion. Use cottage cheese instead of Cheddar.

Ricotta and smoked salmon tart

SERVES 4

175 g/6 oz/1½ cups plain (all-purpose) flour
Salt and freshly ground black pepper
50 g/2 oz/¼ cup white vegetable fat, diced
25 g/1 oz/2 tbsp butter or margarine, diced
275 g/10 oz/1¼ cups Ricotta cheese
3 eggs, beaten
75 g/3 oz smoked salmon pieces, finely chopped
15 ml/1 tbsp chopped parsley
2.5 ml/½ tsp finely grated lemon rind
50 g/2 oz Gruyère or Emmental (Swiss) cheese, thinly sliced

Sift the flour and a pinch of salt into a bowl. Add the fats and rub in with your fingertips until the mixture resembles fine breadcrumbs. Mix with enough cold water to form a firm dough. Knead gently on a lightly floured surface. Roll out and use to line a 20 cm/8 in flan dish (pie pan). Beat the Ricotta with the eggs, fish and some salt and pepper. Mix in the parsley and lemon rind. Turn into the flan case (pie shell) and cover with the slices of cheese. Place the flan dish on a baking (cookie) sheet and bake in a preheated oven at 190°C/375°F/gas mark 5 for about 30 minutes until set and golden. Serve hot or cold.

Tomato, leek and sardine gougère

SERVES 4

120 g/4½ oz/1 small can of sardines
3 leeks, sliced
1 garlic clove, crushed
4 tomatoes, chopped
75 g/3 oz/⅓ cup butter or margarine
15 ml/1 tbsp chopped basil
A pinch of caster (superfine) sugar
Salt and freshly ground black pepper
65 g/2½ oz/scant ¾ cup plain
  (all-purpose) flour
150 ml/¼ pt/⅔ cup water
2 eggs, beaten
25 g/1 oz/¼ cup Parmesan cheese,
  grated

Drain and mash the sardines, discarding the bones if preferred. Cook the leeks, garlic and tomatoes in 25 g/1 oz/2 tbsp of the butter or margarine for 2 minutes, stirring. Add the sardines, basil, sugar and some salt and pepper, cover and cook gently for 4 minutes.

Sift the flour and a pinch of salt together. Melt the remaining butter or margarine in the water in a small saucepan. Add the flour all in one go and beat with a wooden spoon until the mixture leaves the sides of the pan clean. Beat in the eggs, a little at a time, until smooth and glossy but the mixture still holds its shape. Spoon round the edge of a lightly greased 23 cm/9 in shallow baking dish. Spoon the leek mixture into the centre and sprinkle all over with the Parmesan. Bake in a preheated oven at 220°C/425°F/gas mark 7 for 30 minutes until puffy and golden brown. Serve hot.

Crab and cucumber gougère

SERVES 4

Prepare as for Tomato, Leek and Sardine Gougère, but for the filling use 1 quantity of Béchamel Sauce (page 376). Mix with half a small cucumber, diced, 170 g/6 oz/1 small can of white crabmeat, drained, 5 ml/1 tsp anchovy essence (extract), 15 ml/1 tbsp chopped dill (dill weed) and lemon juice and salt and pepper to taste, then bake as before.

Cheesy cod gougère

SERVES 4

Prepare as for Tomato, Leek and Sardine Gougère, but for the filling use 1 quantity of Cheese Sauce (page 376) and add 175 g/6 oz cod fillet, skinned and diced, 50 g/2 oz sliced mushrooms and 15 ml/1 tbsp chopped parsley, then continue as before.

Tuna, tomato and onion gougère

SERVES 4

Prepare as for Tomato, Leek and Sardine Gougère, but substitute 2 large onions, sliced, for the leeks and 185 g/6½ oz/1 small can of tuna, drained, for the sardines. Flavour with 2.5 ml/½ tsp dried basil and top the filling with a few sliced black olives before baking.

Prawn and mushroom vol-au-vents

SERVES 4

225 g/8 oz puff pastry (paste), thawed
  if frozen
Beaten egg, to glaze
75 g/3 oz button mushrooms, chopped
30 ml/2 tbsp water
1 quantity of Béchamel Sauce
  (page 376)
175 g/6 oz cooked peeled prawns
  (shrimp)
A pinch of dried mixed herbs
Salt and freshly ground black pepper
Tomato and cucumber slices and salad
  leaves, to garnish

Roll out the pastry and cut out eight
vol-au-vents using a 5 cm/2 in
cutter. Place on a dampened baking
(cookie) sheet. Mark a 2 cm/¾ in
round in the centre of each round,
using a bottle top as a guide. Take
care not to cut right through the
pastry. Brush with beaten egg. Bake
in a preheated oven at 220°C/
425°F/gas mark 7 for 15–20 minutes
until risen, golden and crisp.
Carefully remove the centre rounds
and scoop out any uncooked pastry.
  Meanwhile, cook the mushrooms
in the water for 2 minutes, stirring,
until softened. Boil rapidly, if
necessary, to evaporate any water.
Stir into the sauce with the prawns,
herbs and salt and pepper to taste.
Heat through. Spoon the filling into
the vol-au-vents and replace the
pastry 'lids'. Return to the oven for
4–5 minutes until piping hot and
crisp. Serve two per person,
garnished with a few tomato and
cucumber slices and salad leaves.

Prawn and egg vol-au-vents

SERVES 4

Prepare as for Prawn and Mushroom
Vol-au-vents, but omit the
mushrooms and water and add
2 hard-boiled (hard-cooked) eggs,
chopped, and 15 ml/1 tbsp chopped
parsley with the prawns (shrimp).

Cod and parsley vol-au-vents

SERVES 4

Prepare as for Prawn and Mushroom
Vol-au-vents, but substitute 225 g/
8 oz cod fillet, skinned and poached
in a little milk (page 19) then flaked,
for the prawns (shrimp) and omit
the mushrooms cooked in water, if
preferred. Add 15 ml/1 tbsp chopped
parsley to the sauce instead of the
mixed herbs and add 5 ml/1 tsp
anchovy essence (extract) to
enhance the flavour, if liked.

Smoked salmon and watercress vol-au-vents

SERVES 4

Prepare as for Prawn and Mushroom
Vol-au-vents, but omit the mushrooms
cooked in water and the prawns
(shrimp). Stir 100 g/4 oz smoked
salmon trimmings, chopped, into the
sauce with half a bunch of
watercress, trimmed and finely
chopped. Add lemon juice to taste.
Use the remaining watercress to
garnish the dish.

Haddock puff pie with citrus

SERVES 4

350 g/12 oz haddock fillet, skinned
and cut into small cubes
15 ml/1 tbsp chopped parsley
Finely grated rind and juice of ½ lemon
Finely grated rind and juice of
½ orange
Salt and freshly ground black pepper
25 g/1 oz/¼ cup plain (all-purpose)
flour
300 ml/½ pt/1¼ cups milk
25 g/1 oz/2 tbsp butter or margarine
2 hard-boiled (hard-cooked) eggs,
chopped
225 g/8 oz puff pastry (paste), thawed
if frozen
Beaten egg, to glaze
Peas and Speciality Creamed Potatoes
(page 391), to serve

Mix the fish with the parsley, citrus
rinds and juices and some salt and
pepper. Leave to stand. Blend the
flour with the milk in a saucepan.
Add the butter or margarine, bring to
the boil and cook for 2 minutes,
stirring all the time. Fold in the fish
and chopped eggs and season to taste.
    Roll out the pastry to a round the
size of a large dinner plate. Spoon the
filling over one half. Dampen the
edges with water, fold the other half
over and press the edges together to
seal. Knock up and flute with the
back of a knife. Transfer to a
dampened baking (cookie) sheet and
brush with beaten egg to glaze. Make
leaves out of the trimmings and
arrange on top. Brush with a little
more egg. Make a small hole to allow
steam to escape. Bake in a preheated
oven at 220°C/425°F/gas mark 7 for
15 minutes. Reduce the heat to
180°C/350°F/gas mark 4, cover
loosely with foil and cook for a
further 25 minutes. Serve with peas
and Speciality Creamed Potatoes.

Plaice and prawn puff pie

SERVES 4

8 plaice fillets, halved lengthways and
skinned if black
100 g/4 oz cooked peeled prawns
(shrimp)
50 g/2 oz button mushrooms, thinly
sliced
295 g/10½ oz/1 medium can of
condensed mushroom soup
5 ml/1 tsp dried oregano
2.5 ml/½ tsp finely grated lemon rind
(optional)
225 g/8 oz puff pastry (paste), thawed
if frozen
Beaten egg, to glaze
Baby corn cobs and baby carrots,
to serve

Roll up the halved plaice fillets and
place in a 1.2 litre/2 pt/5 cup pie
dish. Add the prawns, mushrooms
and soup and sprinkle with the
oregano and lemon rind, if using.
Roll out the pastry to a round just
larger than the pie dish. Cut off a
strip all round. Brush the pie dish
rim with water and lay the strip
round it. Top with the pastry lid.
Trim to fit, then knock up and flute
the edges with the back of a knife.
Make a hole in the centre to allow
steam to escape. Make some leaves
out of pastry trimmings and arrange
round the hole. Brush with beaten
egg to glaze.
    Bake in a preheated oven at
220°C/425°F/gas mark 7 for
15 minutes, then reduce the heat to
190°C/375°F/gas mark 5 and
continue to cook for a further
30 minutes until golden brown and
the fish is cooked through. Serve hot
with baby corn cobs and baby
carrots.

Sardine stargazy pie

SERVES 6

350 g/12 oz/3 cups plain (all-purpose)
  flour
Salt and freshly ground black pepper
100 g/4 oz/½ cup white vegetable fat or
  lard (shortening), diced
50 g/2 oz/¼ cup hard block margarine,
  diced
12 large sardines, cleaned and boned
2 onions, finely chopped
15 ml/1 tbsp chopped parsley
15 ml/1 tbsp chopped thyme
60 ml/4 tbsp milk
1.5 ml/¼ tsp saffron powder
12 streaky bacon rashers (slices),
  rinded and diced

Sift the flour and a pinch of salt into
a bowl. Add the fats and rub in with
your fingertips until the mixture
resembles fine breadcrumbs. Mix
with enough cold water to form a
firm dough. Wrap and chill while
making the filling.

Rinse the sardines and pat dry on
kitchen paper (paper towels). Season
with salt and pepper. Mix the onions
with the herbs and put a little inside
the fish, then fold the fish sides back
together. Mix together the milk and
saffron powder, bring to the boil and
leave to cool. Halve the pastry
(paste). Roll out one half and use to
line a 23 cm/9 in pie plate. Brush
the edge with a little of the saffron
milk. Lay the sardines on the pastry
in a starburst pattern, with the
heads poking out from the rim all
round. Brush with the saffron milk.
Sprinkle the remaining onion
mixture and the bacon between the
fish. Season all over with pepper.
Roll out the remaining pastry and
cover the pie. Fold back the edge all
round to reveal the fish heads. Press
the pastry firmly between each fish

head to seal the edges. Brush all
over with saffron milk.

Place the pie on a baking (cookie)
sheet) and bake in a preheated oven
at 220°C/ 425°F/gas mark 7 for
12 minutes. Reduce the heat to
180°C/350°F/gas mark 4 and cook
for a further 30 minutes. Cover
loosely with foil if over-browning.
Serve hot.

Saucy cod pies

SERVES 4

350 g/12 oz puff pastry (paste),
  thawed if frozen
4 mushrooms, chopped
2 tomatoes, chopped
2.5 ml/½ tsp dried thyme
Salt and freshly ground black pepper
4 frozen cod steaks in parsley sauce
Beaten egg, milk or plain yoghurt, to
  glaze
Speciality Creamed Potatoes (page 391)
  and French (green) beans,
  to serve

Cut the pastry into four and roll out
each piece to a thin square. Trim the
edges. Divide the mushrooms and
tomatoes between the centres of the
pastry and sprinkle with the thyme
and a little salt and pepper. Carefully
remove the frozen cod steaks and
sauce from their bags and place on
top of the mushrooms and tomatoes.
Brush the edges of the pastry with
water and wrap over the filling to
encase completely, pressing the
edges well together to seal. Invert on
a dampened baking (cookie) sheet,
sealed-side down. Brush with beaten
egg, milk or yoghurt to glaze. Bake
in a preheated oven at 220°C/
425°F/gas mark 7 for 15–20 minutes
until golden brown and cooked
through. Serve hot with Speciality
Creamed Potatoes and French beans.

Herring stargazy pie

SERVES 6

6 herrings
225 g/8 oz/2 cups plain (all-purpose)
  flour
Salt and freshly ground black pepper
75 g/3 oz/⅓ cup beef dripping, diced
1 onion, very finely chopped
2 large hard-boiled (hard-cooked) eggs,
  chopped
15 ml/1 tbsp chopped parsley
10 ml/2 tsp chopped thyme
Beaten egg, to glaze

Bone the herrings, leaving the heads on and reshape. Sift the flour and a good pinch of salt into a bowl. Add the dripping and rub in with your fingertips until the mixture resembles breadcrumbs. Mix with enough cold water to form a firm dough. Knead gently on a lightly floured surface.

Cut the pastry (paste) in half. Roll out one half and use to line a 23 cm/ 9 in pie plate. Put the herrings on top with the heads towards the centre. Scatter the onion, eggs and herbs over and season with salt and pepper. Brush the edges of the pastry with water. Roll out the remaining pastry to use as a lid. Lay over the pie and press the edges well together to seal. Trim, knock up and flute with the back of a knife. Cut a fairly large cross in the centre of the pastry. Fold back the points and carefully draw the herring heads up through the centre so they point upwards. Brush all over the pastry with beaten egg and place on a baking (cookie) sheet.

Bake in a preheated oven at 200°C/400°F/gas mark 6 for 20 minutes until golden, then reduce the heat to 180°C/350°F/gas mark 4 and cook for a further 10 minutes or until everything is cooked through. Serve hot.

Salmon wraps

SERVES 4

4 sheets of filo pastry (paste)
15 ml/1 tbsp melted butter or
  margarine
4 small pieces of salmon fillet, about
  150 g/5 oz each, skinned
4 mushrooms, finely chopped
2 tomatoes, finely chopped
Salt and freshly ground black pepper
30 ml/2 tbsp chopped basil
300 ml/½ pt/1¼ cups passata (sieved
  tomatoes)
Lemon wedges and basil sprigs,
  to garnish
Baby new potatoes and mangetout
  (snow peas), to serve

Lay the filo sheets on a work surface. Brush very lightly with a little of the butter or margarine, then fold in halves. Place a salmon fillet on each piece and top with the mushrooms and tomatoes. Sprinkle with salt and pepper and add half the basil. Wrap up the fish in the pastry and lay, sealed-side down, on a non-stick baking (cookie) sheet. Brush with the remaining butter or margarine. Bake in a preheated oven at 200°C/400°F/gas mark 6 for 10–15 minutes until golden brown and the fish is cooked through.

Meanwhile, heat the passata in a small saucepan with the remaining basil and a little salt and pepper. Spoon on to warm plates. Top each with a salmon parcel, garnish with lemon wedges and basil sprigs and serve with potatoes and mangetout.

Any-day salmon wraps

SERVES 4

Prepare as for Salmon Wraps, but substitute 425 g/15 oz/1 large can of salmon for the fresh salmon. Divide it into four portions and remove the skin and any bones, if preferred.

Haddock and oyster mushroom wraps

SERVES 4

Prepare as for Salmon Wraps, but substitute pieces of haddock fillet, skinned, for the salmon. Use 100 g/ 4 oz oyster mushrooms, sliced, instead of the button mushrooms and tomatoes, and add a few drops of mushroom ketchup (catsup). Flavour with chopped thyme instead of basil, then continue as before. Serve with Cheese Sauce (page 376) instead of passata (sieved tomatoes).

Whiting and spinach wraps with orange

SERVES 4

Prepare as for Salmon Wraps, but substitute small whiting fillets for the salmon, tucking the tails underneath to give a small, neat shape. Use 225 g/8 oz cooked, very well-drained and chopped spinach instead of the mushrooms and tomatoes. Season with a pinch of grated nutmeg, salt and pepper and the finely grated rind of 1 orange. Omit the basil. Garnish with the orange segments and serve with All-year Tomato Sauce (page 379), instead of passata (sieved tomatoes).

Salmon and tomato puffs

SERVES 4

425 g/15 oz/1 large can of pink or red salmon, drained
350 g/12 oz puff pastry (paste), thawed if frozen
2 large tomatoes, chopped
5 ml/1 tsp dried oregano
Freshly ground black pepper
15 ml/1 tbsp milk, plus extra for brushing
170 g/6 oz/1 small can of creamed mushrooms
Lemon wedges and parsley sprigs, to garnish
New potatoes and peas, to serve

Empty the fish into a shallow dish. Carefully split into four portions, discarding the black skin and bones, if preferred. Cut the pastry into four pieces and roll out each to a thin square. Trim. Divide the tomatoes between the centres of the pastry and sprinkle with the oregano and some pepper. Top with the fish. Brush the edges with water and fold over the fish to cover completely. Invert on to a dampened baking (cookie) sheet and brush with milk. Make leaves out of the trimmings, put in place and brush again. Cook in a preheated oven at 200°C/ 400°F/gas mark 6 for about 15 minutes until puffy and golden brown.

Meanwhile, heat the mushrooms with the milk in a saucepan. Transfer the puffs to warm plates and put a spoonful of the mushroom mixture to one side of each. Garnish the plates with lemon wedges and parsley sprigs and serve with new potatoes and peas.

Piquant pilchard flan

SERVES 4–6

200 g/7 oz/1¼ cups plain (all-purpose) flour
Salt and freshly ground black pepper
40 g/1½ oz/3 tbsp white vegetable fat
65 g/2½ oz/scant ⅓ cup hard block margarine, diced
225 g/8 oz/1 medium can of pilchards in tomato sauce
300 ml/½ pt/1¼ cups milk
6 gherkins (cornichons), chopped
5 ml/1 tsp lemon juice
15 ml/1 tbsp tomato purée (paste)
A good pinch of cayenne
2 gherkins, cut into fans, and tomato wedges, to garnish
Pickled beetroot (red beets) and mixed salad, to serve

Sift 175 g/6 oz/1½ cups of the flour and a pinch of salt into a bowl. Add the white fat and 40 g/1½ oz/3 tbsp of the margarine and rub in with your fingertips until the mixture resembles breadcrumbs. Mix with enough cold water to form a firm dough. Knead gently on a lightly floured surface, roll out and use to line a 20 cm/8 in flan dish (pie pan). Prick the base with a fork and fill with crumpled foil. Bake in a preheated oven at 200°C/400°F/gas mark 6 for 10 minutes. Remove the foil and return the flan to the oven for 5 minutes to dry out.

Meanwhile, mash the pilchards thoroughly, discarding the bones, if preferred (but they are very good for you). Mix the remaining flour with the milk in a saucepan and add the remaining margarine. Bring to the boil and cook for 2 minutes, stirring all the time. Season with salt and pepper and stir in the chopped gherkins, lemon juice, tomato purée and cayenne. Mix in the fish and turn the mixture into the pastry case (pie shell). Leave to cool. Garnish with gherkin fans and tomato wedges and chill until ready to serve with pickled beetroot and a mixed salad.

Cottage cheese and salmon flan

SERVES 4

175 g/6 oz/1½ cups plain (all-purpose) flour
Salt and freshly ground black pepper
75 g/3 oz/⅓ cup hard margarine, diced
200 g/7 oz/1 small can of pink salmon
10 ml/2 tsp mayonnaise
2.5 ml/½ tsp dried dill (dill weed)
5 ml/1 tsp capers, chopped
1 egg
150 ml/¼ pt/⅔ cup milk
100 g/4 oz/½ cup cottage cheese
15 ml/1 tbsp snipped chives
Coleslaw, to serve

Sift the flour and a pinch of salt into a bowl. Add the margarine and rub in with your fingertips until the mixture resembles breadcrumbs. Mix with enough cold water to form a firm dough. Knead gently on a lightly floured surface. Roll out and use to line a 20 cm/8 in flan tin (pie pan).

Drain the salmon. Discard any bones (if preferred) and skin, then flake and mix with the mayonnaise, dill and capers. Spread in the base of the flan case (pie shell). Beat together the egg, milk and cheese and season lightly. Pour into the flan and sprinkle with the chives. Bake in a preheated oven at 180°C/350°F/gas mark 4 for about 40 minutes until set. Leave to cool, then chill. Serve cold with coleslaw.

Cottage haddock flan

SERVES 6

175 g/6 oz/1½ cups plain (all-purpose)
flour
A pinch of salt
5 ml/1 tsp paprika
100 g/4 oz/½ cup butter or margarine,
diced
900 g/2 lb potatoes, cut into chunks
30 ml/2 tbsp milk
1 egg yolk
30 ml/2 tbsp grated Parmesan cheese
450 g/1 lb smoked haddock fillet,
skinned
150 ml/¼ pt/⅔ cup water
100 g/4 oz button mushrooms, sliced
1 leek, thinly sliced
2 hard-boiled (hard-cooked) eggs,
sliced
1 quantity of Béchamel Sauce
(page 376)

Sift the flour, salt and paprika in a
bowl. Add 75 g/3 oz/⅓ cup of the
butter or margarine and rub in with
your fingertips until the mixture
resembles breadcrumbs. Mix with
enough cold water to form a firm
dough. Knead gently on a lightly
floured surface. Roll out and use to
line a 20 cm/8 in flan dish (pie
pan). Prick the base with a fork, fill
with crumpled foil and bake in a
preheated oven at 200°C/400°F/gas
mark 6 for 10 minutes. Remove the
foil and bake for a further 5 minutes
to dry out.

Boil the potatoes in lightly salted
water until tender. Drain and mash
with the milk and remaining butter
or margarine. Add the egg yolk and
half the cheese and beat until fluffy.
Put the fish in a saucepan with the
water, mushrooms and leek. Cover
and cook gently for 8 minutes until
tender. Drain and flake the fish,
discarding any bones. Put the fish
mixture in the flan case (pie shell).
Cover with the sliced eggs, then the
Béchamel Sauce. Spoon or pipe the
potato attractively over the top and
sprinkle with the remaining cheese.
Return to the oven and cook for
about 20–25 minutes until hot
through and golden on top.

Curried haddock and sweet potato flan

SERVES 4

Prepare as for Cottage Haddock
Flan, but use ground turmeric
instead of paprika in the pastry
(paste). Use white haddock instead
of smoked and flavour the sauce
with 15 ml/1 tbsp mild curry paste.
Use half ordinary and half sweet
potatoes for the topping.

Cod and tomato flan

SERVES 4

175 g/6 oz/1½ cups plain (all-purpose)
flour
Salt and freshly ground black pepper
100 g/4 oz/½ cup butter or margarine,
diced
15 ml/1 tbsp fennel or caraway seeds
(optional)
350 g/12 oz cod fillet, skinned
200 ml/7 fl oz/scant 1 cup milk
2 large onions, thinly sliced
15 ml/1 tbsp cornflour (cornstarch)
A good pinch of grated nutmeg
30 ml/2 tbsp chopped parsley
1 large egg, beaten
3 tomatoes, skinned, halved and
seeded
50 g/2 oz/½ cup Cheddar cheese, grated

Sift the flour and a pinch of salt into
a bowl. Add 75 g/3 oz/⅓ cup of the
butter or margarine and rub in with
your fingertips until the mixture
resembles breadcrumbs. Stir in the
seeds, if using, then mix with
enough cold water to form a firm
dough. Knead gently on a lightly
floured surface. Roll out and use to
line a 20 cm/8 in flan dish (pie
pan). Prick the base with a fork, fill
with crumpled foil and bake in a
preheated oven at 200°C/400°F/gas
mark 6 for 10 minutes. Remove the
foil and bake for a further 5 minutes
to dry out.

Meanwhile, put the fish in a pan
with the milk. Bring to the boil,
reduce the heat, cover and cook
gently for about 6 minutes or until
the fish flakes easily with a fork.
Drain off the milk and reserve. Flake
the fish, discarding any bones.
Meanwhile, cook the onions gently
in the remaining butter or margarine
in a saucepan for about 5 minutes
until soft but not brown. Stir in the
cornflour. Remove from the heat and

gradually blend in the fish milk.
Return to the heat and bring to the
boil, stirring, until thick. Cook for
1 minute. Season to taste with the
nutmeg and salt and pepper. Fold in
the parsley, then the egg. Put the
cooked fish in the base of the flan
case (pie shell) and cover with the
tomatoes, rounded-sides up. Pour
the sauce over, then sprinkle with
the cheese. Bake in the oven at
190°C/375°F/gas mark 5 for about
30 minutes until golden brown and
set. Serve warm.

Salmon and pimiento flan

SERVES 4

175 g/6 oz/1½ cups wholemeal flour
Salt and freshly ground black pepper
50 g/2 oz/¼ cup white vegetable fat,
diced
25 g/1 oz/2 tbsp hard block margarine,
diced
300 ml/½ pt/1¼ cups milk
45 ml/3 tbsp cornflour (cornstarch)
200 g/7 oz/1 small can of pink or red
salmon, drained
15 ml/1 tbsp tomato purée (paste)
200 g/7 oz/1 small can of pimientos,
drained and chopped
50 g/2 oz/1 small can of anchovy
fillets, drained
3 stuffed olives, halved
Mixed salad, to serve

Sift the flour and a pinch of salt into
a bowl. Add the fats and rub in with
your fingertips until the mixture
resembles breadcrumbs. Mix with
enough cold water to form a firm
dough. Knead gently on a lightly
floured surface. Roll out and use to
line a 20 cm/8 in flan dish (pie
pan). Prick the base with a fork,
then fill with crumpled foil. Bake in
a preheated oven at 200°C/400°F/

gas mark 6 for 10 minutes. Remove the foil and bake for a further 5–10 minutes to dry out. Remove from the oven and leave to cool.

Meanwhile, blend a little of the milk with the cornflour in a saucepan. Add the remaining milk and bring to the boil. Cook for 1 minute, stirring, until thickened. Remove from the heat. Discard any skin and the bones, if preferred, from the salmon and stir into the sauce with the tomato purée and salt and pepper to taste. Stir in the pimientos. Turn into the flan case (pie shell). Arrange the anchovies in a lattice pattern over the top and garnish with the sliced olives. Serve cold with a mixed salad.

Crab and spinach oatie tart

SERVES 6

100 g/4 oz/1 cup rolled oats
50 g/2 oz/½ cup wholemeal flour
Salt and freshly ground black pepper
5 ml/1 tsp baking powder
85 g/3½ oz/scant ½ cup butter or margarine
1 small onion, finely chopped
225 g/8 oz frozen leaf spinach, thawed
170 g/6 oz/1 small can of white crabmeat, drained
Finely grated rind of 1 small lemon
40 g/1½ oz/⅓ cup Parmesan cheese, grated
2 eggs
150 ml/¼ pt/⅔ cup skimmed milk
Tomato and spring onion salad, to serve

Mix the oats and flour in a bowl with a pinch of salt and the baking powder. Add all but 15 g/½ oz/ 1 tbsp of the butter or margarine and rub in with your fingertips. Mix with enough cold water to form a firm dough. Wrap and chill for 30 minutes. Knead gently on a lightly floured surface, then roll out and use a 23 cm/9 in flan dish (pie pan). Prick the base with a fork, then line with crumpled foil and bake in a preheated oven at 220°C/ 425°F/gas mark 7 for 10 minutes. Remove the foil and bake for a further 5 minutes to dry out.

Meanwhile, melt the remaining butter or margarine in a saucepan. Add the onion and fry (sauté) for 3 minutes, stirring. Squeeze the spinach to remove excess moisture and add to the onion. Cook, stirring, for 3 minutes. Snip with scissors to chop. Turn into the flan case (pie shell) and spread out. Top with the crabmeat, sprinkle with the lemon rind, then the cheese and a good grinding of pepper. Whisk together the eggs, milk and pour into the flan. Bake in the oven at 190°C/ 375°F/gas mark 5 for 35 minutes until set and golden. Serve warm with a tomato and spring onion salad.

Salmon coulibiac

SERVES 6

100 g/4 oz/½ cup long-grain rice
2 eggs, scrubbed under cold running
  water
Salt and freshly ground black pepper
450 g/1 lb salmon fillet, skinned
75 g/3 oz/⅓ cup butter or margarine
4 spring onions (scallions), chopped
100 g/4 oz button mushrooms, sliced
5 ml/1 tsp paprika
30 ml/2 tbsp soured (dairy sour)
  cream, plus extra for glazing
Lemon juice, to taste
350 g/12 oz puff pastry (paste),
  thawed if frozen
Hollandaise Sauce (page 371), to serve

Bring a saucepan of water to the
boil. Add the rice, eggs and a good
pinch of salt. Bring to the boil and
boil for 5 minutes. Add the fish and
cook for a further 5 minutes. Lift out
the fish. Drain the rice and eggs,
rinse with cold water and drain
again. Shell and chop the eggs and
add to the rice. Flake the fish and
add to the rice.

Meanwhile, melt the butter or
margarine in a frying pan (skillet).
Add the spring onions and
mushrooms and fry (sauté) for
3 minutes, stirring. Add to the rice
and season with salt, pepper and the
paprika. Fold in the cream and spike
with a dash of lemon juice. Roll out
the pastry and trim to a large
rectangle. Cut off a third. Place the
larger piece on a dampened baking
(cookie) sheet. Spoon the fish
mixture in the centre. Fold the edges
over and brush with a little soured
cream. Top with the remaining piece
of pastry. Press the edges together to
seal. Brush all over with soured
cream. Make shapes out of the
trimmings and arrange around the
pie. Brush again with cream.

Bake in a preheated oven at
200°C/400°F/ gas mark 6 for about
30 minutes until risen, golden and
piping hot. Serve sliced with the
Hollandaise Sauce.

Tuna and fennel coulibiac

SERVES 4–6

1 fennel bulb, chopped
1 onion, chopped
15 g/½ oz/1 tbsp butter or margarine
185 g/6½ oz/1 small can of tuna,
  drained
200 g/7 oz/1 small can of sweetcorn
  (corn) with (bell) peppers, drained
45 ml/3 tbsp mayonnaise
15 ml/1 tbsp chopped parsley
Salt and freshly ground black pepper
375 g/13 oz ready-rolled puff pastry
  (paste), thawed if frozen
Beaten egg, to glaze
10 ml/2 tsp fennel or poppy seeds
Cucumber salad, to serve

Fry (sauté) the fennel and onion
in the butter or margarine for
3 minutes, stirring, until softened
and slightly golden. Remove from
the heat and stir in the tuna,
sweetcorn, mayonnaise, parsley and
seasoning. Unroll the pastry on to a
dampened baking (cookie) sheet.
Spoon the filling down the centre.
Make horizontal cuts in the pastry at
2 cm/¾ in intervals down each side,
to within 2.5 cm/1 in of the filling.
Fold the pastry ends over the filling,
then lift the strips of pastry up over
the filling from alternate sides to
form a plait. Brush with the egg and
sprinkle with the seeds. Bake in a
preheated oven at 220°C/425°F/gas
mark 7 for about 25 minutes until
golden brown. Serve hot or cold
with a cucumber salad.

Tuna and sun-dried tomato tart

SERVES 4–6

100 g/4 oz/1 cup plain (all-purpose)
    flour
100 g/4 oz/1 cup wholemeal flour
15 ml/1 tbsp sesame seeds
Salt and freshly ground black pepper
100 g/4 oz/½ cup hard block
    margarine, diced
2 large onions, thinly sliced
1 garlic clove, crushed
30 ml/2 tbsp olive oil
400 g/14 oz/1 large can of chopped
    tomatoes
2 sun-dried tomatoes in oil, chopped
15 ml/1 tbsp tomato purée (paste)
15 ml/1 tbsp chopped basil
A good pinch of caster (superfine)
    sugar
185 g/6½ oz/1 small can of tuna,
    drained
1 basil sprig, to garnish

Mix the two flours together in a
bowl with the sesame seeds and a
good pinch of salt. Add the fat and
rub in with your fingertips until the
mixture resembles breadcrumbs. Mix
with enough cold water to form a
firm dough. Knead gently on a
lightly floured surface. Roll out and
use to line a 23 cm/9 in flan tin (pie
pan). Reserve the trimmings. Fill
with crumpled foil and bake in a
preheated oven at 200°C/400°F/
gas mark 6 for 10 minutes. Remove
the foil and return to the oven for
5 minutes to dry out.
    Meanwhile, fry (sauté) the onions
and garlic in the oil for 3 minutes
until softened and lightly browned.
Add the can of tomatoes, the sun-
dried tomatoes, tomato purée, basil,
sugar and some salt and pepper.
Bring to the boil and simmer for
5 minutes until pulpy. Stir in the
tuna, taste and re-season if
necessary. Turn into the pastry case
(pie shell). Roll out the reserved
trimmings. Cut into strips and
arrange in a lattice pattern over
the surface. Return to the oven for
20 minutes until the pastry is golden
brown and the filling is piping hot.
Garnish with a sprig of basil and
serve warm.

Cod coulibiac

SERVES 6

Prepare as for Salmon Coulibiac
(page 214), but substitute cod fillet
for the salmon. Add 50 g/2 oz/
½ cup cooked frozen peas to the
mixture, omit the paprika and add
30 ml/2 tbsp chopped parsley
instead. Use single (light) cream
instead of soured (dairy sour) cream.

Curried haddock coulibiac

SERVES 6

Prepare as for Salmon Coulibiac
(page 214), but substitute haddock
fillet for the salmon. Add 15 ml/
1 tbsp curry paste and 15 ml/1 tbsp
sultanas (golden raisins) to the
cooked spring onions (scallions).
Use 15 ml/1 tbsp chopped coriander
(cilantro) instead of half the parsley.
Serve with Curried Hollandaise
(page 371).

Seafood millefeuille

SERVES 6

*375 g/13 oz ready-rolled puff pastry
(paste), thawed if frozen*
350 g/12 oz cooked seafood cocktail
150 ml/¼ pt/⅔ cup mayonnaise
*2 spring onions (scallions), finely
chopped*
Salt and freshly ground black pepper
Lemon juice, to taste
*200 g/7 oz/scant 1 cup medium-fat soft
cheese*
30 ml/2 tbsp tomato purée (paste)
*200 g/7 oz/1 small can of pimientos,
drained and chopped*
6 cooked unpeeled prawns (shrimp)
6 stoned (pitted) olives, halved
30 ml/2 tbsp finely chopped parsley
*Mixed leaf salad and thinly sliced
peeled cucumber, dressed with cider
vinegar and black pepper, to serve*

Unroll the pastry and cut into three
equal rectangles. Place on a
dampened baking (cookie) sheet.
Bake in a preheated oven at 220°C/
425°F/gas mark 7 for 10–15 minutes
until risen and golden brown.
Remove from the oven and leave to
cool.

Dry the seafood cocktail on
kitchen paper (paper towels). Mix
with all but 30 ml/2 tbsp of the
mayonnaise and the spring onions,
then season and add lemon juice to
taste. Mash the cheese with the
remaining mayonnaise and the
tomato purée. Stir in the pimientos.

Carefully split each piece of pastry
in half horizontally. Place one sheet
of pastry on a serving plate and
spread a third of the seafood filling
over. Spread a second piece of pastry
with a third of the tomato mixture
and place on top of the seafood. Top
with a third piece of pastry and half
the remaining seafood mixture.
Spread a fourth piece of pastry with
half the remaining tomato mixture
and place on top. Repeat these
layers so you finish with a layer of
tomato mixture. Lay the prawns
down the centre and arrange the
olive halves in a line down each
side. Finish with a line of chopped
parsley along both outside edges.
Chill until ready to slice and serve
with a mixed leaf salad and thinly
sliced peeled cucumber, dressed
with cider vinegar and lots of black
pepper.

Pizza Napoletana

SERVES 4

You can, of course, add any other pizza toppings you like before adding the cheese.

275 g/10 oz/1 packet of pizza base mix
45 ml/3 tbsp tomato purée (paste)
2.5 ml/½ tsp dried oregano
4 ripe tomatoes, sliced
30 ml/2 tbsp olive oil, plus extra for greasing
Freshly ground black pepper
100 g/4 oz Mozzarella cheese, sliced
50 g/2 oz/1 small can of anchovy fillets, drained
8 basil leaves, torn
A few black olives

Make up the pizza base mix according to the packet directions and knead gently on a lightly floured surface. Roll out to a thin 23 cm/9 in round and place on an oiled baking (cookie) sheet. Spread with the tomato purée and sprinkle with the oregano. Top with the tomato slices and drizzle with half the oil. Add a good grinding of pepper. Bake in a preheated oven at 220°C/425°F/gas mark 7 for 10 minutes. Top with the cheese, then the anchovies, laid attractively over the surface. Drizzle with the remaining oil and scatter the basil and olives over. Bake for a further 10 minutes or until golden round the edges and the cheese is melted and bubbling. Serve hot.

Pizza primavera

SERVES 4

Prepare as for Pizza Napoletana, but omit the olives and, once cooked, pile 50 g/2 oz rocket leaves on top before serving.

Cosa nostra

SERVES 2

275 g/10 oz/1 packet of pizza base mix
2 tomatoes, chopped
1 canned pimiento, chopped
A few cooked French (green) beans, cut into small pieces
100 g/4 oz cooked peeled prawns (shrimp)
5 ml/1 tsp capers
1.5 ml/¼ tsp dried oregano
30 ml/2 tbsp grated Mozzarella cheese
Salt and freshly ground black pepper
Olive oil, for brushing and greasing
200 ml/7 fl oz/scant 1 cup passata (sieved tomatoes)
A good pinch of dried basil
Grated Parmesan cheese, to garnish

Make up the pizza base mix according to the packet directions and knead on a lightly floured surface. Cut in half and roll out each half to a fairly thin round. Divide the tomatoes, pimiento, beans, prawns, capers, oregano and Mozzarella between the centres of the rounds. Season lightly. Brush the edges with water and draw the dough up over the filling to cover completely. Press the edges together to seal. Place, sealed-side down, on a lightly oiled baking (cookie) sheet. Brush with olive oil. Bake in a preheated oven at 200°C/ 400°F/gas mark 6 for about 20 minutes until golden brown and cooked through. Meanwhile, warm the passata with the basil. Transfer the stuffed pizzas to warm plates, spoon the sauce over the centre and sprinkle with Parmesan before serving.

Quick tuna pan pizza

SERVES 2

Add other toppings of your choice before adding the cheese, if you like.

100 g/4 oz/1 cup self-raising (self-rising) flour
A pinch of salt
45 ml/3 tbsp sunflower or olive oil
225 g/8 oz/1 small can of chopped tomatoes, drained
1.5 ml/¼ tsp dried oregano
185 g/6½ oz/1 small can of tuna, drained
50 g/2 oz/½ cup Cheddar cheese, grated

Mix the flour and salt in a bowl. Add 30 ml/2 tbsp of the oil and mix with enough cold water to form a soft but not sticky dough. Knead gently on a lightly floured surface, then roll out to a round the size of a medium frying pan (skillet). Heat the remaining oil in the frying pan and add the base. Cook for 3 minutes until golden brown underneath. Turn over and top with the tomatoes, oregano, tuna and cheese. Cook for 2–3 minutes, then transfer the pan to a preheated grill (broiler) and cook for about 3 minutes or until the cheese is melted and bubbling. Serve hot.

Quick prawn pan pizza

SERVES 2

Prepare as for Quick Tuna Pan Pizza, but substitute 100 g/4 oz cooked peeled prawns (shrimp) for the tuna.

Sizzling seafood pizza

SERVES 4

175 g/6 oz cooked seafood cocktail
275 g/10 oz/1 packet of pizza base mix
Olive oil, for greasing
60 ml/4 tbsp tomato purée (paste)
100 g/4 oz/1 cup Mozzarella cheese, grated
2.5 ml/½ tsp dried oregano
A dash of lemon juice
1 black olive, to garnish

Drain the seafood cocktail on kitchen paper (paper towels). Make up the pizza mix according to the packet directions and knead gently on a lightly floured surface. Roll out to a thin round and place on a lightly oiled baking (cookie) sheet. Blend the tomato purée with a little water to form a smooth sauce. Spread over the pizza base to within 1 cm/½ in of the edge all round. Top with half the cheese, then the seafood, then the remaining cheese and sprinkle with the oregano and lemon juice. Put the olive in the centre. Bake in a preheated oven at 200°C/400°F/gas mark 6 for about 20 minutes until sizzling and the base is brown round the edges. Serve hot.

Sizzling tomato and anchovy pizza

SERVES 4

Prepare as Sizzling Seafood Pizza, but substitute 50 g/2 oz/1 small can of anchovy fillets, drained, for the seafood cocktail. Arrange them in a starburst pattern on top of all the cheese and garnish with sliced tomatoes all round the edge before placing the olive in the centre.

Sizzling sild pizza

SERVES 4

Prepare as for Sizzling Seafood Pizza, but substitute 120 g/4½ oz/ 1 small can of sild, drained, for the seafood cocktail. Arrange in a starburst pattern over half the cheese, top with the remaining cheese and sprinkle with 5 ml/1 tsp chopped capers. Omit the oregano.

Blushing tuna pizza

SERVES 4

Prepare as for Sizzling Seafood Pizza, but substitute 185 g/6½ oz/ 1 small can of tuna, drained, for the seafood cocktail and scatter 2 diced, cooked baby beetroot (red beets) over before topping with the remaining cheese.

Saucy sardine pizza

SERVES 4

23 cm/9 in ready-made pizza base
45 ml/3 tbsp tomato purée (paste)
1 quantity of Cheese Sauce (page 376), made using only 250 ml/8 fl oz/ 1 cup milk
120 g/4½ oz/1 small can of sardines, drained
50 g/2 oz/½ cup Cheddar cheese, grated
Freshly ground black pepper
15 ml/1 tbsp chopped parsley

Put the pizza base on a baking (cookie) sheet. Spread with the tomato purée to within 1 cm/½ in of the edge. Cover with the Cheese Sauce. Arrange the sardines in a starburst pattern on top. Sprinkle with the cheese and a grinding of pepper. Bake in a preheated oven at 220°C/425°F/gas mark 7 for 20 minutes or until golden. Sprinkle with the parsley and serve hot.

Seafood speciality pizza

SERVES 4

225 g/8 oz/2 cups self-raising (self-rising) flour
5 ml/1 tsp baking powder
2.5 ml/½ tsp salt
30 ml/2 tbsp olive oil, plus extra for greasing
45 ml/3 tbsp passata (sieved tomatoes)
30 ml/2 tbsp tomato purée (paste)
100 g/4 oz/1 cup Mozzarella cheese, grated
185 g/6½ oz/1 small can of tuna, drained and flaked
50 g/2 oz cooked peeled prawns (shrimp)
50 g/2 oz/1 small can of anchovy fillets, drained
5 ml/1 tsp dried oregano
A few black olives

Sift the flour, baking powder and salt in a bowl. Stir in the oil and add enough water to form a soft but not sticky dough. Knead gently on a lightly floured surface. Roll out fairly thinly to a 20–23 cm/8–9 in round. Transfer to a lightly greased baking (cookie) sheet. Blend the passata with the tomato purée and spread over the surface to within 1 cm/½ in of the edge. Sprinkle with half the cheese. Scatter the tuna and prawns over, then sprinkle with the remaining cheese. Arrange the anchovies attractively on top, sprinkle the oregano over and decorate with the olives. Bake in a preheated oven at 200°C/400°F/gas mark 6 for about 20 minutes or until the edge is golden and crisp and the topping bubbling and just beginning to brown.

Pissaladière

SERVES 6

2 × 50 g/2 oz/small cans of anchovy
fillets, drained
45 ml/3 tbsp milk
175 g/6 oz/1½ cups plain (all-purpose)
flour
Salt and freshly ground black pepper
5 ml/1 tsp ground cinnamon
75 g/3 oz/⅓ cup butter or margarine,
diced
1 egg, beaten
4 large onions, thinly sliced
2 large garlic cloves, crushed
90 ml/6 tbsp olive oil
400 g/14 oz/1 large can of chopped
tomatoes
15 ml/1 tbsp tomato purée (paste)
7.5 ml/1½ tsp caster (superfine) sugar
5 ml/1 tsp dried mixed herbs
1 small bay leaf
12 stoned (pitted) black olives

Soak the anchovies in the milk until
needed. Sift the flour, a pinch of salt
and the cinnamon into a bowl. Add
the butter or margarine and rub in
with your fingertips until the
mixture resembles breadcrumbs. Mix
with the egg and enough cold water
to form a firm dough. Knead gently
on a lightly floured surface. Roll out
and use to line a 25 cm/10 in flan
dish (pie pan). Prick the base with a
fork. Fill with crumpled foil and
bake in a preheated oven at 200°C/
400°F/gas mark 6 for 10 minutes.
Remove the foil and cook for a
further 5 minutes to dry out.

Cook the onions and garlic in
75 ml/5 tbsp of the oil in a
saucepan, stirring, for 2 minutes.
Cover, reduce the heat and cook
very gently for a further 20 minutes
until soft. Add the tomatoes, tomato
purée, sugar, mixed herbs, bay leaf
and a little salt and pepper. Bring to
the boil and boil rapidly until thick
and pulpy. Discard the bay leaf.
Spread in the pastry case (pie shell).
Drain the anchovies and arrange in a
criss-cross pattern over the top.
Scatter the olives over and drizzle
with the remaining oil. Bake in the
oven at 200°C/400°F/gas mark 6 for
about 20 minutes until piping hot.
Serve straight away.

Pissaladière with cheese

SERVES 6

Prepare as for Pissaladière, but cover
the tomato mixture with 25 g/1 oz/
¼ cup Gruyère (Swiss) cheese,
grated, 25 g/1 oz/¼ cup Mozzarella
cheese, grated, and 30 ml/2 tbsp
grated Parmesan cheese before
adding the anchovies and olives.

Calzone

SERVES 4

400 g/14 oz/3½ cups strong plain
  (bread) flour
15 ml/1 tbsp light brown sugar
1 sachet of easy-blend dried yeast
Salt and freshly ground black pepper
100 g/4 oz/½ cup butter or margarine
250 ml/8 fl oz/1 cup hand-hot milk
60 ml/4 tbsp olive oil, plus extra for
  greasing and brushing
2 spring onions (scallions), finely
  chopped
1 garlic clove, crushed
225 g/8 oz frozen chopped spinach,
  thawed and squeezed dry
350 g/12 oz/1½ cups Ricotta cheese
1.5 ml/¼ tsp grated nutmeg
2 beefsteak tomatoes, skinned and
  chopped
50 g/2 oz/1 small can of anchovy
  fillets, drained and chopped
15 ml/1 tbsp chopped parsley

Mix the flour, sugar, yeast and 5 ml/
1 tsp salt in a bowl. Rub in the
butter or margarine and mix with
the milk to form a firm dough.
Knead gently on a lightly floured
surface until smooth and elastic.
Place in an oiled plastic bag and
leave in a warm place while
preparing the filling.
  Fry (sauté) the spring onions and
garlic in the measured oil for
2 minutes, then stir in the remaining
ingredients. Knock back (punch
down) the dough and cut into four.
Roll out each to a fairly thin round.
Divide the filling between one half
of each of the rounds. Spread out to
a semi-circle, not right to the edges.
Brush the edges with water. Fold the
dough over the filling and press
together to seal. Use the floured
prongs of a fork to make an
attractive pattern round the edge.
Transfer to a lightly oiled baking
(cookie) sheet and brush with a little
oil. Bake in a preheated oven at
200°C/400°F/gas mark 6 for 20
minutes or until golden and cooked
through. Serve warm.

Wheaty potato pizza

SERVES 2

225 g/8 oz/1 cup mashed potato
75 g/3 oz/¾ cup wholemeal flour
2.5 ml/½ tsp salt
Milk
Oil, for shallow-frying
45 ml/3 tbsp tomato purée (paste)
2.5 ml/½ tsp dried oregano
75 g/3 oz/¾ cup Cheddar cheese, grated
50 g/2 oz/1 small can of anchovy
  fillets, drained

Mix the potato with the flour, salt
and enough milk to form a firm
dough. Roll out on a lightly floured
surface to a round the size of the
base of your frying pan (skillet).
Heat a little oil in the pan and fry
(sauté) the pizza base until golden
underneath. Slide out on to a plate,
heat a little more oil in the pan, then
invert the pizza base into the pan,
browned-side up. Spread with the
tomato purée, sprinkle with oregano,
then the cheese. Arrange the
anchovies attractively on top. Fry for
2 minutes or until golden on the
other side, then place under a hot
grill (broiler) until the cheese melts
and bubbles.

Tuna, chicken and mushroom Coburg

SERVES 4–6

1 Coburg or round crusty loaf
50 g/2 oz/¼ cup butter or margarine, melted
350 g/12 oz small flat mushrooms, peeled if necessary
1 onion, finely chopped
5 ml/1 tsp dried mixed herbs
20 g/¾ oz/3 tbsp plain (all-purpose) flour
250 g/8 fl oz/1 cup chicken stock
175 g/6 oz/1½ cups cooked chicken, chopped
185 g/6½ oz/1 small can of tuna, drained
15 ml/1 tbsp chopped parsley
Salt and freshly ground black pepper

Cut a thick slice off the top of the loaf and scoop out the soft bread from the loaf and the lid. Brush the base and the lid inside and out with some of the butter or margarine. Place on a baking (cookie) sheet and bake in a preheated oven at 180°C/350°F/gas mark 4 for 10 minutes until crisp. Fry (sauté) the mushrooms in the remaining butter or margarine until soft. Remove from the pan. Add the onion and herbs to the pan and cook for 2–3 minutes, stirring. Add the flour and cook, stirring, for 1 minute. Remove from the heat and blend in the stock. Return to the heat and bring to the boil, stirring. Cook for 2 minutes. Add the chicken, tuna and parsley to the sauce and heat through for 3 minutes. Season to taste. Lay the mushrooms in the bread case and spoon in the tuna mixture. Top with the lid. Return to the oven at 200°C/400°F/gas mark 6 for 5 minutes until piping hot. Serve cut into thick slices.

Salt cod tart

SERVES 6

450 g/1 lb salt cod, soaked and cooked (page 8)
225 g/8 oz/2 cups plain (all-purpose) flour
Salt and freshly ground black pepper
2.5 ml/½ tsp ground cinnamon
100 g/4 oz/½ cup butter or margarine, diced
2 onions, chopped
30 ml/2 tbsp olive oil
1 garlic clove, crushed
5 ml/1 tsp caster (superfine) sugar
700 g/1½ lb tomatoes, skinned and chopped
1 bay leaf
1 small red chilli, seeded and finely chopped
30 ml/2 tbsp sliced black olives
2 hard-boiled (hard-cooked) eggs, sliced
1 parsley sprig

Drain and flake the cooked cod, discarding the skin.

Mix together the flour, a pinch of salt and the cinnamon in a bowl. Add the butter or margarine and rub in with your fingertips until the mixture resembles fine breadcrumbs. Mix with enough cold water to form a firm dough. Knead gently on a lightly floured surface, then roll out and use to line a 25 cm/10 in flan dish (pie pan). Prick the base with a fork and chill while preparing the filling.

Cook the onions gently in the oil in a saucepan for 5 minutes until soft but not brown. Add the garlic and sugar, then turn up the heat slightly and cook, stirring, for 5 minutes until lightly golden all over. Add the tomatoes, bay leaf, chilli and some salt and pepper. Bring to the boil, reduce the heat and simmer for 10 minutes, stirring occasionally, until pulpy. Remove the bay leaf. Spoon half the tomato mixture into the pastry case (pie shell). Top with the fish, then the remaining tomato mixture. Scatter the olives over. Bake in a preheated oven at 200°C/400°F/gas mark 6 for 30 minutes until the pastry (paste) is golden round the edges. Put a ring of chopped egg round the edge of the flan and serve hot, garnished with a sprig of parsley.

English cod tart

SERVES 6

Prepare as for Salt Cod Tart, but substitute cooked white cod for the salt cod. Finish the flan with a lattice of anchovy fillets and 10 ml/ 2 tsp capers instead of the olives.

Marjolaine tart

SERVES 4

200 g/7 oz/1¾ cups plain (all-purpose) flour
Salt and freshly ground black pepper
125 g/4½ oz/generous ½ cup butter or margarine, diced
150 ml/¼ pt/⅔ cup water, plus extra for mixing
2 eggs, beaten
300 ml/½ pt/1¼ cups milk
1 bay leaf
100 g/4 oz/1 cup Cheddar cheese, grated
100 g/4 oz cooked peeled prawns (shrimp)

Put 100 g/4 oz/1 cup of the flour in a bowl with a good pinch of salt. Add 50 g/2 oz/¼ cup of the butter or margarine and rub in with your fingertips until the mixture resembles breadcrumbs. Mix with enough cold water to form a firm dough. Roll out and use to line an 18 cm/7 in flan dish (pie pan).

Sift 65 g/2½ oz/generous ½ cup of the remaining flour with a good pinch of salt. Put the water in a saucepan with 50 g/2 oz/¼ cup of the remaining butter or margarine. Heat until melted, then bring to the boil. Add the flour all in one go and beat with a wooden spoon until the mixture leaves the sides of the pan clean. Remove from the heat. Beat in the eggs a little at a time, beating well after each addition, until smooth and glossy but the mixture still holds its shape. Spoon the pastry (paste) round the edge of the flan case (pie shell), leaving a large hole in the centre.

Whisk the remaining flour with the milk in a saucepan. Add the remaining butter or margarine and the bay leaf. Bring to the boil and cook for 2 minutes, whisking all the time. Remove the bay leaf. Stir in half the cheese and season to taste with salt and pepper. Stir in the prawns. Spoon into the centre of the flan. Sprinkle the remaining cheese over the choux pastry border. Bake in a preheated oven at 200°C/400°F/ gas mark 6 for 30–35 minutes until the choux pastry is risen, crisp and golden. Serve hot.

Oven bakes

O ven cooking is suitable for large, whole fish and any pieces bathed in a sauce or coated to prevent them drying out. The bonus about baking is you can leave the food to cook itself, although not for very long as fish cooks so quickly. Here you'll find everything from golden-topped gratins to fluffy soufflés, from fish baked *en papillote* to crunchy crumbles. Many make ideal, nutritious family meals: others are rather more ambitious for that extra-special dinner.

Cauliflower, broccoli and tuna cheese

SERVES 4

This makes a good lunch or supper dish, served plain or with grilled (broiled) bacon.

½ small cauliflower, cut into small
  florets
175 g/6 oz broccoli, cut into small
  florets
185 g/6½ oz/1 small can of tuna,
  drained
225 g/8 oz/1 small can of chopped
  tomatoes
1 quantity of Cheese Sauce (page 376)
30 ml/2 tbsp crushed cornflakes

Boil the cauliflower and broccoli in lightly salted water for about 4 minutes until just tender but still with some 'bite'. Drain well and turn into an ovenproof dish. Add the tuna and tomatoes. Pour the Cheese Sauce over and top with the crushed cornflakes. Bake in a preheated oven at 190°C/375°F/gas mark 5 for about 25 minutes until golden and bubbling.

Golden prawn bake

SERVES 4

225 g/8 oz cooked peeled prawns
  (shrimp)
295 g/10½ oz/1 medium can of
  condensed mushroom soup
15 ml/1 tbsp tomato ketchup (catsup)
50 g/2 oz/1 cup fresh white
  breadcrumbs
100 g/4 oz/1 cup Cheddar cheese,
  grated
Oven Pilaff (page 393), to serve

Mix the prawns with the soup and ketchup in a flameproof serving dish. Stir in half the breadcrumbs and half the cheese. Mix together

the remaining breadcrumbs and cheese and sprinkle over the top. Bake in a preheated oven at 200°C/400°F/gas mark 6 for 20–25 minutes until golden and bubbling. Serve hot with Oven Pilaff.

Easy prawn supper

SERVES 4

225 g/8 oz cooked peeled prawns
  (shrimp)
295 g/10½ oz/1 medium can of
  condensed celery soup
15 ml/1 tbsp tomato purée (paste)
15 ml/1 tbsp Worcestershire sauce
A few drops of Tabasco sauce
15 ml/1 tbsp chopped parsley
50 g/2 oz/1 cup fresh wholemeal
  breadcrumbs
100 g/4 oz/1 cup Cheddar cheese,
  grated
1 tomato, sliced, and 6 cucumber
  slices, to garnish
Crusty bread and mixed leaf salad, to
  serve

Mix the prawns with the soup, tomato purée, Worcestershire and Tabasco sauces, the parsley, half the breadcrumbs and half the cheese. Turn into an ovenproof serving dish. Mix together the remaining breadcrumbs and cheese and sprinkle over. Bake in a preheated oven at 200°C/400°F/gas mark 6 for 25 minutes until bubbling and golden. Arrange the tomato and cucumber slices attractively on top and serve with a mixed leaf salad.

Easy crab supper

SERVES 4

Prepare as for Easy Prawn Supper, but substitute chopped crab sticks for the prawns (shrimp) and spike with a dash of lemon juice.

Simple sardine bake

SERVES 4

2 × 120 g/4½ oz/small cans of
sardines, drained
Salt and freshly ground black pepper
45 ml/3 tbsp olive oil
15 ml/1 tbsp chopped parsley
15 ml/1 tbsp snipped chives
15 ml/1 tbsp chopped thyme
45 ml/3 tsp chopped capers
6 large tomatoes, thinly sliced
25 g/1 oz/½ cup fresh white
breadcrumbs
15 ml/1 tbsp grated Parmesan cheese

Lay the fish in a shallow ovenproof
dish. Season lightly and trickle
15 ml/1 tbsp of the oil over. Mix the
herbs with the capers and scatter
over, then top with the tomato
slices. Mix together the breadcrumbs
and cheese and sprinkle all over.
Drizzle with the remaining oil.
Bake in a preheated oven at
180°C/350°F/gas mark 4 for about
25 minutes until golden and
bubbling.

Simple tuna bake

SERVES 4

Prepare as for Simple Sardine Bake,
but substitute 185 g/6½ oz/1 small
can of tuna for the sardines. Use
chopped gherkins (cornichons)
instead of the capers and 50 g/2 oz/
½ cup Cheddar cheese, grated,
instead of the Parmesan.

Halibut parcels

SERVES 4

15 ml/1 tbsp olive oil
2 courgettes (zucchini), thinly sliced
50 g/2 oz button mushrooms, thinly
sliced
25 g/1 oz/2 tbsp butter or margarine
4 halibut steaks
Finely grated rind and juice of 1 small
lemon
Freshly ground black pepper
50 g/2 oz/1 small can of anchovy
fillets, drained
30 ml/2 tbsp chopped parsley
1 hard-boiled (hard-cooked) egg, finely
chopped
New potatoes and mangetout (snow
peas), to serve

Brush four large squares of foil with
the oil. Arrange the courgettes over
the centre of each in a single layer.
Lay the mushrooms on top. Dot with
half the butter or margarine, then
place a fish steak on top of each.
Sprinkle with the lemon rind and
juice and a good grinding of pepper.
Lay the anchovies in a criss-cross
pattern over each fish steak and dot
with the remaining butter or
margarine. Loosely wrap in the foil,
sealing the edges together well.

Transfer to a baking (cookie)
sheet and bake in a preheated oven
at 190°C/375°F/gas mark 5 for
about 30 minutes until tender.

Carefully open up each parcel,
slide on to warm serving plates and
sprinkle with the chopped parsley
and egg. Serve hot with new
potatoes and mangetout.

Baked sole with mustard sauce

SERVES 4

50 g/2 oz/1 cup fresh white
breadcrumbs
50 g/2 oz button mushrooms, chopped
2 spring onions (scallions), finely
chopped
4 black stoned (pitted) olives, chopped
15 ml/1 tbsp chopped parsley
50 g/2 oz/½ cup strong Cheddar cheese,
grated
5 ml/1 tsp lemon juice
50 g/2 oz/¼ cup butter or margarine,
melted, plus extra for greasing
Salt and freshly ground black pepper
4 sole fillets, skinned
1 small onion, finely chopped
10 ml/2 tsp mustard powder
25 g/1 oz/¼ cup plain (all-purpose)
flour
300 ml/½ pt/1¼ cups milk
120 ml/4 fl oz/½ cup crème fraîche
Parsley sprigs, to garnish
New potatoes and mangetout (snow
peas), to serve

Mix the breadcrumbs with the
mushrooms, spring onions, olives,
chopped parsley, cheese and lemon
juice. Stir in half the butter or
margarine and a little salt and
pepper. Pile on to the skinned side
of each fillet and roll up. Grease four
squares of foil and place a fish roll
on each. Wrap up and place on a
baking (cookie) sheet. Bake in a
preheated oven at 200°C/400°F/gas
mark 6 for 30 minutes.

Meanwhile, fry (sauté) the onion
in the remaining butter or margarine
for 3 minutes until soft but not
brown. Stir in the mustard and flour
and cook for 1 minute. Remove from
the heat and gradually blend in the
milk. Return to the heat and bring to
the boil, stirring. Cook for 2 minutes.

Stir in the crème fraîche and reheat.
Season to taste. Carefully open the
fish parcels and transfer to warm
plates. Spoon the sauce over and
garnish with parsley sprigs. Serve
with new potatoes and mangetout.

Baked plaice with Dijon mustard sauce

SERVES 4

Prepare as for Baked Sole with
Mustard Sauce, but substitute plaice
fillets for the sole and Dijon mustard
for the mustard powder.

Crab and celery bake

SERVES 4

1 large cooked crab, all meat removed
(page 16)
1½ quantities of Béchamel Sauce
(page 376)
4 celery sticks, thinly sliced
Salt and freshly ground black pepper
20 g/¾ oz/1½ tbsp butter or margarine,
melted, plus extra for greasing
60 ml/4 tbsp fresh wholemeal
breadcrumbs
30 ml/2 tbsp grated Parmesan cheese

Mix the dark and white crabmeat
with the sauce and the celery and
season to taste. Turn into a greased
shallow ovenproof dish. Mix
together the breadcrumbs and
cheese and sprinkle over. Drizzle
with the melted butter or margarine.
Bake in a preheated oven at 180°C/
350°F/gas mark 4 for 20–25 minutes
until golden brown and bubbling.
Serve hot.

Family fish pot

SERVES 4

700 g/1½ lb potatoes, cut into bite-
sized pieces
350 ml/12 fl oz/scant 1½ cups milk
50 g/2 oz/½ cup strong Cheddar cheese,
grated
100 g/4 oz button mushrooms, sliced
225 g/8 oz frozen mixed vegetables
1 bay leaf
450 g/1 lb white fish fillet
Salt and freshly ground black pepper
45 ml/3 tbsp plain (all-purpose) flour
30 ml/2 tbsp chopped parsley

Cook the potatoes in lightly salted, boiling water until really tender. Drain and mash with 25 ml/1½ tbsp of the milk and half the cheese.

Meanwhile, put the mushrooms in a saucepan with the vegetables, bay leaf, fish and all but 25 ml/1 tbsp of the remaining milk. Season with salt and pepper. Bring to the boil, reduce the heat, part-cover and simmer gently for 8–10 minutes until the fish and vegetables are cooked. Carefully lift the fish out of the saucepan. Remove any skin and bones and roughly flake the flesh. Blend the flour with the remaining milk until smooth. Stir into the saucepan with the parsley, bring to the boil and cook for 2 minutes, stirring, until thickened. Discard the bay leaf and season with more pepper, if liked. Stir the fish into the sauce. Turn the mixture into a flameproof serving dish, top with the cheesy potato and sprinkle with the remaining cheese.

If serving immediately, grill (broil) for about 5 minutes until golden and piping hot. If not, leave to cool and store in the fridge. When ready to cook, bake in a preheated oven at 190°C/375°F/gas mark 5 for about 35 minutes until golden and piping hot. Serve straight away.

Nutty garlic and herb stuffed mackerel

SERVES 4

80 g/3¼ oz/1 small packet of garlic
and herb soft cheese
100 g/4 oz/2 cups fresh wholemeal
breadcrumbs
Grated rind and juice of 1 lime
25 g/1 oz/¼ cup chopped mixed nuts
1 large egg, beaten
Salt and freshly ground black pepper
4 mackerel, cleaned and boned
Butter or margarine, for greasing
Lime wedges, to garnish

Mash the cheese with the breadcrumbs, lime rind and juice, nuts and egg. Season with a little salt and lots of pepper. Spread along one side of the fish and fold over the other side. Wrap each in greased foil. Place on a baking (cookie) sheet and bake in the oven at 190°C/375°F/gas mark 5 for 30 minutes or until the fish are cooked through. Unwrap and serve garnished with lime wedges.

Jansson's temptation

SERVES 4

50 g/2 oz/¼ cup butter or margarine,
   melted
4 potatoes, thinly sliced
2 onions, thinly sliced
50 g/2 oz/1 small can of anchovy
   fillets, drained and chopped
Freshly ground black pepper
150 ml/¼ pt/⅔ cup milk
40 g/1½ oz/¾ cup fresh white
   breadcrumbs
50 g/2 oz/½ cup Emmental (Swiss)
   cheese, grated
Chopped parsley, to garnish
French (green) bean and tomato salad,
   to serve

Grease a 1.2 litre/2 pt/5 cup
ovenproof dish with some of the
butter or margarine. Layer the
potatoes, onions and anchovies in
the dish, sprinkling with pepper as
you go and finishing with a layer of
potatoes. Pour the milk over. Cover
with foil and bake in a preheated
oven at 180°C/350°F/gas mark 4 for
40 minutes. Toss the breadcrumbs
with the remaining butter or
margarine and the cheese and
scatter over the potatoes. Return to
the oven, uncovered, for a further
30 minutes or until golden brown
and the potatoes and onions are
tender. Sprinkle with chopped
parsley before serving with a green
bean and tomato salad.

Camembert and crab puff

SERVES 4

A knob of butter or margarine
6 slices of white bread, crusts removed
50 g/2 oz ripe Camembert cheese,
   thinly sliced
170 g/6 oz/1 small can of white
   crabmeat, drained
30 ml/2 tbsp chopped parsley
2 eggs
250 ml/8 fl oz/1 cup skimmed milk
Salt and freshly ground black pepper
Parsley sprigs, to garnish
Tomato and spring onion (scallion)
   salad, to serve

Grease a 1.2 litre/2 pt/5 cup shallow
ovenproof dish with a little of the
butter or margarine. Spread the rest
on the bread. Put three of the slices
of bread in the base of the dish.
Cover with the cheese, then the
crabmeat and sprinkle with the
parsley. Top with the remaining
bread. Beat the eggs with a little of
the milk, then whisk in the
remainder. Season well. Pour over
the bread and leave to soak for
30 minutes. Bake in a preheated
oven at 180°C/350°F/gas mark 4 for
about 30 minutes until puffy and
golden brown. Garnish with parsley
sprigs and serve straight away with
a tomato and spring onion salad.

Crunchy smoked mackerel bake

SERVES 4

1 onion, finely chopped
25 g/1 oz/2 tbsp butter or margarine
100 g/4 oz button mushrooms, sliced
20 g/¾ oz/3 tbsp plain (all-purpose)
  flour
300 ml/½ pt/1¼ cups milk
20 ml/1½ tbsp horseradish relish
15 ml/1 tbsp chopped parsley
Salt and freshly ground black pepper
4 smoked mackerel fillets
4 tomatoes, skinned and chopped
50 g/2 oz cheese and onion flavoured
  crisps (chips), crushed
New potatoes and French (green)
  beans, to serve

Fry (sauté) the onion in the butter or margarine for 2 minutes, stirring. Add the mushrooms and cook for a further 2 minutes. Stir in the flour. Remove from the heat and gradually blend in the milk. Return to the heat, bring to the boil and cook for 2 minutes, stirring. Add the horseradish and parsley and season to taste. Pull the skin off the mackerel fillets and cut the fish into neat pieces. Place in an ovenproof serving dish and top with the tomatoes. Pour the mushroom sauce over and sprinkle with the crisps. Bake in a preheated oven at 190°C/375°F/gas mark 5 for about 30 minutes until bubbling and golden. Serve with new potatoes and French beans.

Moroccan mackerel

SERVES 4

225 g/8 oz/1⅓ cups couscous
450 ml/¾ pt/2 cups boiling fish stock
4 mackerel, cleaned
Salt and freshly ground black pepper
Juice of ½ lemon or 1 lime
30 ml/2 tbsp olive oil
2 red onions, finely chopped
1 red (bell) pepper, cut into thin strips
1 green pepper, cut into thin strips
1 yellow pepper, cut into thin strips
3 ripe tomatoes, skinned, seeded and
  quartered
1 garlic clove, crushed
10 ml/2 tsp hot paprika
15 ml/1 tbsp coarsely chopped
  coriander (cilantro)
Lemon or lime wedges, to garnish

Put the couscous in a bowl and pour over just enough of the fish stock to cover. Leave to soak for 5 minutes. Tip into a steamer or sieve (strainer) and place over a pan of boiling water, taking care the base of the sieve does not come in contact with the water. Cover and steam for 15 minutes until the grains are fluffy and tender. Fluff up with a fork.
  Meanwhile, rinse the fish and pat dry with kitchen paper (paper towels). Make several slashes on each side of the fish. Season with salt and pepper and sprinkle with the lemon juice. Heat the oil in a large, flameproof casserole dish (Dutch oven). Add the onions, peppers, tomatoes, garlic and paprika and fry (sauté), stirring, for 5 minutes. Lay the fish on top. Cover and bake in a preheated oven at 180°C/350°F/gas mark 4 for 20 minutes. Spoon the couscous on to warm plates. Top with a fish and the vegetable mixture. Scatter the coriander over and garnish with lemon or lime wedges.

Baked stuffed mackerel

SERVES 4

4 small mackerel, cleaned and boned
2 small onions, grated
50 g/2 oz button mushrooms, chopped
75 g/3 oz/1½ cups fresh white
  breadcrumbs
45 ml/3 tbsp milk
Salt and freshly ground black pepper
2.5 ml/½ tsp dried tarragon
300 ml/½ pt/1¼ cups passata (sieved
  tomatoes)
1 small green cabbage, finely shredded
30 ml/2 tbsp butter or margarine, plus
  extra for greasing
15 ml/1 tbsp black mustard seeds
Plain potatoes, to serve

Lay the fish flesh-side up on a
board. Mix the onions, mushrooms
and breadcrumbs with the milk, a
little salt and pepper and the
tarragon. Spread over the fish and
roll up. Secure with cocktail sticks
(toothpicks). Place in a lightly
greased ovenproof dish. Pour the
passata around and season with a
little salt and pepper. Cover with
foil and bake in a preheated oven
at 190°C/375°F/gas mark 5 for
50 minutes.
  Meanwhile, cook the cabbage in a
little lightly salted, boiling water for
about 4 minutes until just tender but
still with some 'bite'. Drain and toss
in the butter or margarine. Pile on to
warm plates and sprinkle with the
mustard seeds. Top with the
mackerel, remove the cocktail sticks,
and pour a little of the cooking
liquid over each. Serve straight away
with plain potatoes.

Cod and broccoli crumble

SERVES 4

225 g/8 oz broccoli, cut into very small
  florets
75 g/3 oz/¾ cup plain (all-purpose)
  flour
10 ml/2 tsp paprika
40 g/1½ oz/3 tbsp butter or margarine
50 g/2 oz/½ cup Edam cheese, grated
450 g/1 lb cod fillet, skinned and
  cubed
295 g/10½ oz/1 medium can of
  condensed celery soup
2.5 ml/½ tsp dried thyme
15 ml/1 tbsp snipped chives
Baked Tomatoes with Herbs and
  Stuffed Olives (page 396), to serve

Cook the broccoli in lightly salted,
boiling water for 3 minutes only.
Drain. Put the flour in a bowl with
the paprika. Add the butter or
margarine and rub in with your
fingertips or a fork until the mixture
resembles breadcrumbs. Stir in the
cheese. Put the fish and broccoli in
an ovenproof dish and add the soup,
thyme and chives. Spoon the
crumble mixture over and press
down lightly. Bake in a preheated
oven at 200°C/400°F/gas mark 6 for
about 30 minutes until golden brown
and cooked through. Serve with
Baked Tomatoes with Herbs and
Stuffed Olives.

Smoked haddock, cauliflower and tomato crumble

SERVES 4

Prepare as for Cod and Broccoli Crumble (page 231), but substitute smoked haddock for the cod and cauliflower for the broccoli. Use condensed tomato soup instead of the celery soup and dried basil instead of thyme.

Speedy seaside crumble

SERVES 4

75 g/3 oz/¾ cup plain (all-purpose) flour
A pinch of salt
40 g/1½ oz/3 tbsp soft tub margarine
50 g/2 oz/½ cup Cheddar cheese, grated
450 g/1 lb white fish fillets, skinned and diced
100 g/4 oz frozen diced mixed vegetables
295 g/10½ oz/1 medium can of condensed celery soup
5 ml/1 tsp dried chives

Put the flour and salt in a bowl and work in the margarine with a fork. Stir in the cheese. Put the fish in an ovenproof dish. Add the vegetables, then spoon the soup over. Sprinkle with the chives, then the crumble mixture. Bake in a preheated oven at 200°C/400°F/gas mark 6 for 30 minutes or until golden and cooked through. Serve hot.

Grey mullet with pancetta and sage

SERVES 6

3 grey mullet, cleaned, scaled and filleted
100 g/4 oz pancetta, diced
10 sage leaves
1 small onion, quartered
1 thick slice of bread, torn into pieces
75 g/3 oz/⅓ cup unsalted (sweet) butter, melted
150 ml/¼ pt/⅔ cup dry white wine
150 ml/¼ pt/⅔ cup crème fraîche
Salt and freshly ground black pepper
Small sage sprigs, to garnish

Rinse the fillets and pat dry on kitchen paper (paper towels). With the machine running, drop the pancetta, sage, onion and bread into a food processor or blender. Add 30 ml/2 tbsp of the butter. Brush a baking tin (pan) liberally with half the remaining butter. Lay the fish in this and top with the stuffing, shaping it neatly to fit on the fillets. Drizzle the remaining butter over and add half the wine to the dish.

Bake in a preheated oven at 200°C/400°F/gas mark 6 for 15–20 minutes. Carefully lift out the fillets and transfer to warm plates. Place the tin on top of the stove and add the remaining wine. Boil rapidly until reduced by half. Add the crème fraîche and salt and pepper to taste and boil until thickened. Spoon round the fish and serve garnished with small sage sprigs.

Grey mullet with fennel and pernod

SERVES 2

1 fennel bulb, thinly sliced, fronds
  reserved
25 g/1 oz/2 tbsp unsalted (sweet)
  butter, plus extra for greasing
Salt and freshly ground black pepper
2 grey mullet, cleaned and scaled
1 lemon, thinly sliced
15 ml/1 tbsp olive oil
45 ml/3 tbsp Pernod

Boil the fennel slices in lightly salted water for 5 minutes until almost tender. Drain and lay in the base of a buttered flameproof serving dish. Season the mullet inside and out and stuff with the lemon slices. Make several slashes in the flesh on each side. Dot with the butter and sprinkle with the oil. Bake in a preheated oven at 190°C/375°F/gas mark 5 for 20 minutes until the fish is almost cooked. Baste well with the juices and place under a preheated grill (broiler) for a few minutes to crisp the skin. Transfer to two warm plates. Warm the Pernod in a soup ladle and ignite. Pour into the juices and shake the dish until the flames subside. Spoon on to the fish and serve garnished with the fennel fronds.

Cod with sorrel sauce

SERVES 4

900 g/2 lb cod fillet, skinned and cut
  into 4 pieces
30 ml/2 tbsp soy sauce
10 ml/2 tsp lemon juice
Salt and freshly ground black pepper
75 g/3 oz sorrel leaves, well washed
120 ml/4 fl oz/½ cup dry white wine
150 ml/¼ pt/⅔ cup double (heavy)
  cream
New potatoes and baked fresh or hot
  canned tomatoes, to serve

Wipe the cod with kitchen paper (paper towels) and lay in a shallow dish. Sprinkle with the soy sauce, lemon juice and a good grinding of pepper and leave to marinate for 1 hour. Lay the sorrel leaves in the base of a baking tin (pan). Top with the fish and any juices. Pour the wine around. Cover with foil and bake in a preheated oven at 190°C/375°F/gas mark 5 for 30 minutes. Lift out the fish with a fish slice and place on a serving platter. Keep warm. Boil the contents of the pan until most of the liquid has evaporated. Stir in the cream and season to taste. Spoon over the fish and serve with new potatoes and baked fresh or hot canned tomatoes.

Mushroom-stuffed plaice

SERVES 4

100 g/4 oz button mushrooms, finely
   chopped
25 g/1 oz/2 tbsp butter or margarine
50 g/2 oz/1 cup fresh white
   breadcrumbs
15 ml/1 tbsp chopped parsley
10 ml/2 tsp chopped thyme
Salt and freshly ground black pepper
4 plaice fillets, skinned if black
150 ml/¼ pt/⅔ cup crème fraîche
4 small parsley sprigs, to garnish
Plain potatoes and Baked Tomatoes
   with Herbs and Stuffed Olives
   (page 396), to serve

Cook the mushrooms in the butter
or margarine for 2 minutes, stirring.
Add the breadcrumbs, parsley and
thyme and season with a little salt
and pepper. Halve the plaice fillets
lengthways. Divide the stuffing
between the centres of the fillets and
fold the two ends over to form
parcels. Transfer to four individual
ovenproof dishes and spoon the
crème fraîche over. Season very
lightly again with pepper and bake
in a preheated oven at 180°C/
350°F/gas mark 4 for 20 minutes
until cooked through. Garnish each
with a small sprig of parsley and
serve with plain potatoes and Baked
Tomatoes with Herbs and Stuffed
Olives.

Plaice with orange and vegetables

SERVES 4

4 plaice fillets, skinned if black
1 carrot, grated
1 turnip, grated
5 ml/1 tsp paprika
5 ml/1 tsp ground coriander (cilantro)
Finely grated rind and juice of
   1 orange
Salt and freshly ground black pepper
Orange slices and chopped parsley, to
   garnish
New potatoes and mangetout (snow
   peas), to serve

Wipe the fish with kitchen paper
(paper towels) and fold each fillet
into three. Place in a flameproof
casserole dish (Dutch oven). Scatter
the carrot and turnip over and
sprinkle with the paprika and
coriander. Make the orange rind and
juice up to 150 ml/¼ pt/⅔ cup with
water and pour over the fish. Add a
little salt and a good grinding of
pepper. Cover and bake in a
preheated oven at 180°C/350°F/gas
mark 4 for 40 minutes until cooked
through. Carefully transfer the fish
to a warm serving dish using a fish
slice. Boil the juices rapidly for
5 minutes until reduced by half.
Spoon over the fish, garnish with
orange slices and chopped parsley
and serve with new potatoes and
mangetout.

Crusted cod with poached leeks

SERVES 4

A knob of butter or margarine
4 pieces of cod fillet, about 175 g/6 oz
* each*
100 g/4 oz/2 cups fresh wholemeal
* breadcrumbs*
5 ml/1 tsp grated fresh root ginger
30 ml/2 tbsp chopped parsley
30 ml/2 tbsp snipped chives
Finely grated rind and juice of 1 small
* lemon*
Salt and freshly ground black pepper
8 baby leeks
150 ml/¼ pt/⅔ cup chicken stock
2.5 ml/½ tsp ground cumin

Grease a shallow baking dish large enough to take the fish in a single layer. Lay the fish in the dish. Mix together the breadcrumbs, ginger, parsley, chives, lemon rind and some salt and pepper, then moisten with the lemon juice. Press the mixture on top of each fish fillet. Bake in a hot oven at 220°C/425°F/gas mark 7 for 20 minutes until the fish is cooked and the crumb mixture is crisp and browning.

Meanwhile, trim the leeks and wash thoroughly. Place in a frying pan (skillet) with the stock and cumin. Add a pinch of salt and a good grinding of pepper. Bring to the boil, cover with a lid or foil, reduce the heat and simmer for 10 minutes or until just tender but still holding their shape. Transfer the fish to warm plates. Lay the leeks to the side and serve hot.

Plaice with grapes

SERVES 4

4 plaice fillets, halved lengthways
150 ml/¼ pt/⅔ cup chicken stock
150 ml/¼ pt/⅔ cup dry white wine
1 small bay leaf
1 small piece of cinnamon stick
150 ml/¼ pt/⅔ cup buttermilk or crème
* fraîche*
50 g/2 oz seedless green grapes, halved
30 ml/2 tbsp chopped parsley
A pinch of salt
White pepper

Remove any black skin from the fillets (white skin can be left on). Roll up the fillets, skin-side in, and place in a single layer in a large, shallow, flameproof dish. Pour the stock and wine over and add the bay leaf and cinnamon. Cover with foil and bake in a preheated oven at 190°C/375°F/gas mark 5 for 15–20 minutes until the fish is cooked through. Carefully lift out the plaice rolls and keep warm. Boil the cooking liquid on top of the stove until it has reduced by half. Discard the bay leaf and cinnamon stick. Add the buttermilk or crème fraîche, grapes, parsley, salt and pepper to taste and heat through. Carefully transfer the fish to warm serving plates and spoon the sauce over.

Baked carp stuffed with field mushrooms

SERVES 4

1 carp, about 1 kg/2¼ lb
1 onion, quartered
2 large field mushrooms, peeled and
   quartered
1 slice of wholemeal bread, torn into
   pieces
50 g/2 oz/¼ cup butter or margarine,
   plus extra for greasing
30 ml/2 tbsp chopped parsley
15 ml/1 tbsp chopped thyme
Finely grated rind and juice of ½ small
   lemon
Salt and freshly ground black pepper
75 ml/5 tbsp crème fraîche
Plain potatoes, to serve

Remove the head, clean the fish from the head end and scale the skin. Rinse thoroughly and dry as much as possible inside with kitchen paper (paper towels) without tearing the flesh. With the machine running, drop the onion quarters, then the mushrooms, then the pieces of bread into a food processor or blender.

Melt half the butter or margarine in a frying pan (skillet). Add the mushroom mixture and fry (sauté), stirring gently, for 3 minutes. Add half the parsley and the thyme, the lemon rind and juice and a little salt and pepper. Stuff the fish with as much of the mixture as possible. If there is any left over, spread it in the base of a greased roasting tin (pan). Lay the fish on top. Spread the remaining butter or margarine over. Cover with foil and bake in a preheated oven at 180°C/350°F/gas mark 4 for 25 minutes.

Spoon the crème fraîche over and return, uncovered, to the oven for a further 10 minutes. Carefully lift the fish out on to a serving dish. Stir the juices well, taste and re-season if necessary. Spoon over, sprinkle with the remaining parsley and serve with plain potatoes.

Garfish Diana Marina

SERVES 4

900 g/2 lb garfish, skinned and cut
   into 5 cm/2 in lengths
90 ml/6 tbsp olive oil
15 ml/1 tbsp red wine vinegar
15 ml/1 tbsp chopped thyme
3 red onions, thinly sliced
2 garlic cloves, crushed
450 g/1 lb plum tomatoes, skinned
   and chopped
Salt and freshly ground black pepper
4 slices of ciabatta bread, halved
A few torn basil leaves
Green salad, to serve

Put the fish in a shallow ovenproof dish. Whisk 30 ml/2 tbsp of the oil with the wine vinegar and thyme and pour over. Toss gently and leave to marinate for 2 hours. Heat 30 ml/2 tbsp of the remaining oil in a frying pan (skillet). Add the onions and garlic and fry (sauté) for 3 minutes, stirring. Add the tomatoes, season to taste and cook for 1 minute. Spoon over the fish and turn gently to cover well. Place in a preheated oven at 190°C/ 375°F/gas mark 5 for 30 minutes. Meanwhile, fry (sauté) the bread in the remaining oil until golden on both sides. Taste the fish and re-season if necessary. Arrange the fried bread around, sprinkle with the basil and serve very hot with a green salad.

Baked bream stuffed with field mushrooms

SERVES 4

Prepare as for Baked Carp Stuffed with Field Mushrooms (page 236), but substitute bream, prepared in the same way, for the carp.

Welsh trout with bacon

SERVES 4

2 leeks, thinly sliced
25 g/1 oz/2 tbsp butter or margarine, plus extra for greasing
4 trout, cleaned
12 streaky bacon rashers (slices), rinded
Freshly ground black pepper
30 ml/2 tbsp chopped parsley
Speciality Creamed Potatoes (page 391) and creamed turnips, to serve

Cook the leeks in the butter or margarine gently for about 5 minutes, stirring, until softened. Rinse the trout under cold water and dry on kitchen paper (paper towels). Fill with the leeks, then wrap each in three of the bacon rashers. Lay in a lightly greased roasting tin (pan) and season with lots of pepper. Cover with foil and bake in a preheated oven at 180°C/350°F/gas mark 4 for about 20 minutes, removing the foil after 10 minutes to brown the bacon. Transfer to warm serving dishes, sprinkle with the parsley and serve with Speciality Creamed Potatoes and creamed turnips.

Tandoori fish with red rice

SERVES 4

450 g/1 lb cod fillet, skinned
150 ml/¼ pt/⅔ cup plain yoghurt
15 ml/1 tbsp lemon juice
5 ml/1 tsp ground coriander (cilantro)
5 ml/1 tsp ground cumin
2.5 ml/½ tsp ground turmeric
Salt and freshly ground black pepper
175 g/6 oz/¾ cup brown rice
400 g/14 oz/1 large can of chopped tomatoes
300 ml/½ pt/1¼ cups water
1 vegetable stock cube, crumbled
6 green cardamom pods, split (optional)
2 spring onions (scallions), chopped

Cut the fish into four equal pieces and place in a shallow dish in a single layer. Mix the yoghurt with the lemon juice, spices, a pinch of salt and a grinding of pepper. Spoon over the fish and turn gently to coat completely. Cover and leave in a cool place to marinate for 1 hour. Remove the cover and bake in a preheated oven at 180°C/350°F/gas mark 4 for 20 minutes, basting occasionally.

Meanwhile, wash the rice and place in a pan with all the remaining ingredients except the spring onions. Bring to the boil, reduce the heat and simmer for 35 minutes, adding a little extra water if necessary, until the rice is tender but 'nutty' and has absorbed all the liquid. Pile the rice on to warm plates, top with the fish and garnish with the spring onions.

Anchovy and pancetta-stuffed peppers

SERVES 4

4 large green (bell) peppers
2 large onions, finely chopped
100 g/4 oz pancetta, finely diced
90 ml/6 tbsp olive oil
100 g/4 oz/1 cup medium oatmeal
50 g/2 oz/1 small can of anchovy fillets
50 g/2 oz/1 cup fresh white breadcrumbs
2 tomatoes, skinned and chopped
Freshly ground black pepper
15 ml/1 tbsp chopped basil
100 g/4 oz/1 cup Mozzarella cheese, grated
Ciabatta bread and mixed salad, to serve

Cut the tops off the peppers and remove the seeds. Place in a pan of boiling water and cook for 5 minutes. Drain, rinse with cold water and drain again. Stand them in a shallow roasting tin (pan). Fry (sauté) the onions and pancetta in the oil, stirring, for 5 minutes. Sprinkle in the oatmeal and cook, stirring, until the oil is absorbed. Remove from the heat. Drain the anchovies, reserving the oil. Chop the fish and add to the mixture. Stir in the breadcrumbs, tomatoes, lots of pepper and the basil. Moisten with the anchovy oil to taste. Spoon into the peppers and add enough boiling water to the tin to come 5 mm/¼ in up the sides of the peppers.

Cover with foil and bake in a preheated oven at 180°C/350°F/gas mark 4 for 30 minutes. Baste with the water in the tin after 15 minutes. Remove the foil and top each pepper with the Mozzarella cheese. Return to the oven for 10 minutes until the cheese melts. Serve hot with ciabatta bread and a mixed salad.

Honey soused mackerel

SERVES 4

4 small mackerel, cleaned and boned
Salt and freshly ground black pepper
1 small onion, thinly sliced and separated into rings
30 ml/2 tbsp chopped coriander (cilantro)
300 ml/½ pt/1¼ cups malt vinegar
300 ml/½ pt/1¼ cups water
15 ml/1 tbsp clear honey
1 bay leaf
New potatoes and mixed salad, to serve

Cut the fins and tails off the fish. Season the flesh with salt and pepper and sprinkle with the onion and coriander. Roll up, starting from the head ends, and place in a shallow ovenproof dish. Mix the vinegar with the water and honey and pour over. Add the bay leaf. Cover with foil or a lid and cook in a preheated oven at 180°C/350°F/gas mark 4 for about 45 minutes until cooked through. Leave to cool in the liquid, then chill before serving with new potatoes and a mixed salad.

Hake majestic

SERVES 4

4 large waxy potatoes, scrubbed and diced
450 g/1 lb hake fillet, skinned
Juice of ½ small lemon
Salt and freshly ground black pepper
300 ml/½ pt/1¼ cups mayonnaise
2 spring onions (scallions), finely chopped
30 ml/2 tbsp olive oil
Parsley sprigs, to garnish

Boil the potatoes in lightly salted water for about 4 minutes until just tender. Drain. Lay the fish down the centre of a shallow ovenproof dish. Arrange the diced potatoes around. Sprinkle the fish with the lemon juice, salt and a good grinding of pepper. Spoon the mayonnaise over the fish. Sprinkle the potatoes with the spring onions and drizzle the olive oil all over. Bake in a preheated oven at 190°C/375°F/gas mark 5 for about 30 minutes until the fish is tender and the top is lightly golden. Serve garnished with parsley sprigs.

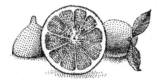

Portuguese country-style salt cod

SERVES 4–6

450 g/1 lb salt cod, soaked and cooked (page 8)
4 large potatoes, cut into chunks
2 large carrots, sliced
25 g/1 oz/2 tbsp butter or margarine
30 ml/2 tbsp milk
4 hard-boiled (hard-cooked) eggs, sliced
15 ml/1 tbsp capers
300 ml/½ pt/1¼ cups mayonnaise
Freshly ground black pepper
30 ml/2 tbsp grated hard cheese
1 parsley sprig, to garnish

Drain the cooked cod, remove the skin and flake the fish. Meanwhile, cook the potatoes and carrots separately in lightly salted, boiling water until tender. Drain. Mash the potatoes with three-quarters of the butter or the margarine and the milk. Grease a shallow 1.5 litre/ 2½ pt/6 cup ovenproof dish with the remaining butter or margarine. Put the fish in the dish and cover with the carrots, then the eggs. Sprinkle with the capers and spread the mayonnaise over. Add a good grinding of pepper over the top, then cover with the mashed potato. Sprinkle with the cheese and bake in a preheated oven at 190°C/375°F/ gas mark 5 for about 30–35 minutes until hot through and lightly golden. Garnish with the sprig of parsley and serve hot.

Swedish fish pudding

SERVES 6

350 g/12 oz cod or haddock fillet,
    skinned
150 g/5 oz/⅔ cup unsalted (sweet)
    butter, softened, plus extra for
    greasing
2 large eggs, separated
15 g/½ oz/2 tbsp plain (all-purpose)
    flour
150 ml/¼ pt/⅔ cup milk
150 ml/¼ pt/⅔ cup whipping cream
7.5 ml/1½ tsp salt
5 ml/1 tsp caster (superfine) sugar
Freshly ground black pepper
15 ml/1 tbsp chopped dill (dill weed)
30 ml/2 tbsp dried breadcrumbs
20 ml/2 tbsp chopped parsley
1 parsley sprig, to garnish
Creamy Whole Prawn Sauce
    (page 383), to serve

Cut the fish into pieces and place in
a blender or food processor with the
butter and egg yolks. Add the flour,
milk, cream, salt, sugar, a good
grinding of pepper and the dill. Run
the machine until the mixture is
smooth. Whisk the egg whites until
stiff and fold into the mixture with a
metal spoon. Grease a 1.2 litre/2 pt/
5 cup soufflé dish and dust with the
breadcrumbs and parsley. Spoon in
the fish mixture. Cover with buttered
foil and place in a roasting tin (pan)
containing 2.5 cm/1 in boiling water.
Cook in a preheated oven at 180°C/
350°F/gas mark 4 for about 1 hour
or until firm to the touch. Remove
the foil, loosen gently with a knife
and turn out. Garnish with a sprig of
parsley and serve with Creamy
Whole Prawn Sauce.

Crab soufflé

SERVES 4

25 g/1 oz/2 tbsp butter or margarine,
    plus extra for greasing
15 ml/1 tbsp grated Parmesan cheese
15 ml/1 tbsp dried breadcrumbs
1 small onion, finely chopped
5 ml/1 tsp curry powder
5 ml/1 tsp paprika
10 ml/2 tsp tomato purée (paste)
25 g/1 oz/¼ cup plain (all-purpose)
    flour
150 ml/¼ pt/⅔ cup milk
30 ml/2 tbsp single (light) cream
2 × 170 g/6 oz/small cans of white
    crabmeat
Salt and freshly ground black pepper
3 eggs, separated

Grease a 15 cm/6 in soufflé dish
with a little butter or margarine.
Dust with the Parmesan and
breadcrumbs. Gently fry (sauté) the
onion in the measured butter or
margarine for 2 minutes, stirring,
until softened but not browned. Stir
in the curry powder and paprika and
fry for a further 30 seconds. Blend in
the tomato purée and flour and cook
for 1 minute.

Remove from the heat and blend
in the milk. Return to the heat and
bring to the boil, stirring, until
thickened. Stir in the cream and
crabmeat and season well. Beat in
the egg yolks. Whisk the egg whites
until stiff. Beat 30 ml/2 tbsp into the
sauce to slacken it, then fold in the
remainder with a metal spoon. Turn
into the prepared dish. Mark a
10 cm/4 in circle in the centre of the
soufflé with a knife (this helps it rise
evenly). Bake in a preheated oven at
190°C/375°F/gas mark 5 for about
25 minutes or until risen, golden
and just set. Serve straight away.

Fish soufflé with tuna sauce

SERVES 4

25 g/1 oz/2 tbsp butter or margarine, plus extra for greasing
45 ml/3 tbsp dried breadcrumbs
450 g/1 lb white fish fillets such as cod, haddock, whiting or pollack, skinned
175 ml/6 fl oz/¾ cup milk, plus a little extra
1 bay leaf
1 onion slice
Salt and freshly ground black pepper
15 g/½ oz/2 tbsp plain (all-purpose) flour
1.5 ml/¼ tsp grated nutmeg
3 eggs, separated
185 g/6½ oz/1 small can of tuna, drained
60 ml/4 tbsp crème fraîche
60 ml/4 tbsp mayonnaise
15 ml/1 tbsp chopped parsley
Lemon juice

Grease an 18 cm/7 in soufflé dish and coat with the breadcrumbs. Remove any bones from the fish, then place in a saucepan with 150 ml/¼ pt/⅔ cup of the milk, the butter or margarine, bay leaf, onion slice and a little salt and pepper. Bring to the boil, reduce the heat, cover and poach for 5–6 minutes until really tender. Discard the bay leaf and onion. Mash the fish well in the cooking milk. Blend the remaining milk with the flour and stir into the fish and milk. Bring to the boil and cook for 2 minutes, stirring, until thick. Beat well with a spoon, then beat in the nutmeg, a little more salt and pepper and the egg yolks. Whisk the egg whites until stiff. Beat 30 ml/2 tbsp of them into the fish mixture, then fold in the remainder with a metal spoon.

Turn into the prepared soufflé dish. Mark a 15 cm/6 in circle in the centre of the soufflé with a knife (this helps it rise evenly). Bake in a preheated oven at 190°C/375°F/gas mark 5 for about 30 minutes or until risen, golden and just set.

Meanwhile, put the tuna in a small saucepan and flake with a fork. Beat in the crème fraîche, mayonnaise and parsley. Season with salt and pepper and add lemon juice to taste. Heat through but do not boil. Thin with a little milk to give a pourable consistency and reheat. Serve the soufflé straight from the oven with the tuna sauce.

Quick prawn and asparagus soufflé

SERVES 4

295 g/10½ oz/1 medium can of condensed asparagus soup
4 eggs, separated
75 g/3 oz/¾ cup Cheddar cheese, grated
295 g/10½ oz/1 medium can of cut asparagus spears, drained
175 g/6 oz cooked peeled prawns (shrimp)
Butter or margarine, for greasing

Empty the soup into a bowl and beat in the egg yolks and cheese. Whisk the egg whites until stiff and fold into the mixture with a metal spoon. Put the asparagus pieces and prawns in a lightly greased 18 cm/7 in soufflé dish. Spoon in the egg mixture. Bake in a preheated oven at 200°C/400°F/gas mark 6 for about 25 minutes or until risen, golden and just set. Serve straight away.

Miami cod

SERVES 4

15 g/½ oz/1 tbsp butter or margarine,
  melted
1 orange
1 grapefruit
4 cod fillets, about 175 g/6 oz each
1 onion, thinly sliced and separated
  into rings
A pinch of ground cinnamon
Salt and freshly ground black pepper
Watercress, to garnish
New potatoes and sugar snap peas, to
  serve

Brush four sheets of foil with a little
of the butter or margarine. Finely
grate the rind from half of the
orange and half of the grapefruit and
scatter half over the foil. Cut off all
the pith and the remaining peel from
the fruit and separate into segments.
Reserve for garnish. Lay the fish on
the foil and brush with the
remaining butter or margarine.
Scatter the onion rings over, then the
remaining fruit rind and a very fine
dusting of cinnamon. Season with
salt and pepper. Close the foil
parcels and seal the edges firmly.
Place on a baking (cookie) sheet
and bake in a preheated oven at
180°C/350°F/gas mark 4 for
25 minutes until the fish is tender.
Unwrap on to warm plates, garnish
with watercress and the fruit
segments and serve with new
potatoes and sugar snap peas.

Tarragon lemon trout

SERVES 4

Put the potatoes in the top of the
oven before you start preparing the
fish.

4 trout, cleaned
15 g/½ oz/1 tbsp butter or margarine
Salt and freshly ground black pepper
2 lemons, thinly sliced
60 ml/4 tbsp chopped tarragon
25 g/1 oz/2 tbsp caster (superfine)
  sugar
Small jacket potatoes and peas,
  to serve

Brush the fish inside and out with
the butter or margarine and season
with salt and pepper. Put four large
squares of foil on the work surface.
Lay two slices of lemon on each
sheet of foil and sprinkle with half
the tarragon and sugar. Put a fish on
top of each. Sprinkle with the
remaining tarragon and sugar. Wrap
up securely and place on a baking
(cookie) sheet. Bake in a preheated
oven at 190°C/375°F/gas mark 5 for
30 minutes. Carefully open the
parcels and transfer to warm plates.
Serve straight away with small
jacket-baked potatoes and peas.

Oven-baked fish and chips

SERVES 4

450 g/1 lb potatoes, scrubbed and cut
  into fingers
25 g/1 oz/2 tbsp butter or margarine,
  melted
100 g/4 oz/2 cups fresh wholemeal
  breadcrumbs
4 white fish fillets, about 175 g/6 oz
  each
1 egg white
Lemon wedges and parsley sprigs,
  to garnish
Peas, to serve

Boil the potato fingers in water for
3 minutes. Drain and dry on kitchen
paper (paper towels). Brush a
baking (cookie) sheet with half the
butter or margarine. Spread out the
chips (fries) on the baking sheet and
brush with the remaining butter or
margarine. Meanwhile, dry-fry or
bake the breadcrumbs in a hot oven
at 200°C/400°F/gas mark 6 until
golden brown. Dip the fish in the
egg white, then coat in the toasted
breadcrumbs. Lay on a second
baking sheet. Place the chips on the
top shelf of the oven and the fish
just below and bake at 200°C/
400°F/gas mark 6 for 30 minutes
until golden and cooked through.
Garnish with lemon wedges and
parsley sprigs and serve with peas.

Stuffed cucumber

SERVES 4

2 cucumbers
350 g/12 oz smoked haddock fillet,
  skinned
100 g/4 oz/½ cup long-grain rice
400 ml/14 fl oz/1¾ cups water
5 ml/1 tsp ground turmeric
Salt and freshly ground black pepper
1 large egg, beaten
45 ml/3 tbsp single (light) cream
30 ml/2 tbsp chopped parsley
8 streaky bacon rashers (slices), rinded
Parsley sprigs, to garnish

Halve the cucumbers lengthways,
then cut each in half widthways.
Scoop out the seeds to form shells.
Cook in lightly salted, boiling water
for 3 minutes. Drain, rinse with cold
water and drain again. Put the fish
in a saucepan with the rice, water,
turmeric and some salt and pepper.
Bring to the boil, reduce the heat
and simmer for 10 minutes until the
fish and rice are tender and all the
liquid has been absorbed. Break up
the fish with a fork. Allow to cool
slightly, then stir in the egg, cream
and parsley. Taste and re-season if
necessary. Spoon the mixture into
the cucumber shells. Stretch the
bacon rashers with the back of a
knife and wrap one around each
boat.
  Place in a baking tin (pan)
containing 1 cm/½ in boiling water.
Cover with foil and bake in a
preheated oven at 180°C/350°F/
gas mark 4 for 20 minutes. Remove
the foil and cook for a further
20 minutes until the bacon is turning
golden. Transfer to warm plates,
garnish with parsley sprigs and
serve.

Cidered perch

SERVES 4

4 perch, cleaned
25 g/1 oz/2 tbsp butter or margarine,
  plus extra for greasing
1 bunch of spring onions (scallions),
  finely chopped
4 tomatoes, skinned and chopped
1 eating (dessert) apple, skinned and
  finely chopped
5 ml/1 tsp dried thyme
30 ml/2 tbsp chopped parsley
Salt and freshly ground black pepper
100 g/4 oz soft cod's or herring's roe
50 g/2 oz/1 cup fresh white
  breadcrumbs
450 ml/¾ pt/2 cups dry cider
15 ml/1 tbsp cornflour (cornstarch)
30 ml/2 tbsp water
Speciality Creamed Potatoes (page 391)
  and peas, to serve

Rinse the fish and pat dry on
kitchen paper (paper towels). Melt
the butter or margarine in a
saucepan. Add the spring onions,
tomatoes, apple, thyme, half the
parsley and a little salt and pepper
and cook gently, stirring
occasionally, for 10 minutes. Mash
the roes with the breadcrumbs in a
bowl. Add 30 ml/2 tbsp of the
tomato mixture and stuff inside the
fish. Grease a shallow ovenproof
dish, large enough to hold the fish in
a single layer. Spoon the remaining
tomato mixture in the dish and top
with the fish. Pour the cider over.

Cover with foil and bake in a
preheated oven at 180°C/350°F/gas
mark 4 for 40 minutes until cooked
through. Carefully lift the fish out of
the dish and transfer to warm
serving plates. Keep warm. Blend
the cornflour with the water in a
saucepan and stir in the cooking
juices. Bring to the boil and cook
for 1 minute, stirring. Taste and
re-season if necessary. Pour over the
fish and sprinkle with the remaining
parsley. Serve with Speciality
Creamed Potatoes and peas.

Prawns, oyster mushrooms and asparagus au gratin

SERVES 4

450 g/1 lb thin asparagus
25 g/1 oz/2 tbsp butter or margarine
75 g/3 oz oyster mushrooms, sliced
75 g/3 oz cooked peeled prawns
  (shrimp)
45 ml/3 tbsp crème fraîche
75 g/3 oz/¾ cup Cheddar cheese, grated
Salt and freshly ground black pepper

Trim the stalks of the asparagus. Tie
in a bundle. Bring a large pan of
lightly salted water to the boil and
stand the asparagus upright in the
pan. Cover with a lid or foil and
cook for 5 minutes. Turn off the heat
and leave to stand for 5 minutes.
The stems should be tender but the
heads still intact. Remove the
asparagus, untie and lay in an
ovenproof dish.

Meanwhile, melt the butter or
margarine in a saucepan. Add the
mushrooms and fry (sauté) gently,
stirring, for 3–4 minutes until
cooked. Stir in the prawns, crème
fraîche, half the cheese and salt and
pepper to taste. Pour over the
asparagus, then sprinkle with the
remaining cheese. Bake in a
preheated oven at 200°C/400°F/
gas mark 6 for 15 minutes or until
lightly golden. Serve hot.

Cumberland roast pike

SERVES 6

1 pike, about 1.5 kg/3 lb, cleaned and
*   scaled*
175 g/6 oz/¾ cup butter or margarine
1 large onion, finely chopped
100 g/4 oz/2 cups fresh white
*   breadcrumbs*
30 ml/2 tbsp chopped parsley
10 ml/2 tsp chopped sage
10 ml/2 tsp chopped marjoram
Finely grated rind and juice of 1 lemon
15 ml/1 tbsp anchovy essence (extract)
10 ml/2 tsp tomato purée (paste)
Salt and freshly ground black pepper
1 large egg, beaten
150 ml/¼ pt/⅔ cup brown ale
150 ml/¼ pt/⅔ cup water
15 ml/1 tbsp rum
Parsley sprigs, to garnish
Plain potatoes and Caper Sauce
*   (page 377), to serve*

Remove the head, then wash the
pike and dry on kitchen paper
(paper towels). Melt 50 g/2 oz/
¼ cup of the butter or margarine in
a saucepan. Add the onion and cook
gently, stirring, for 3 minutes until
softened. Remove from the heat.
Add the breadcrumbs, herbs, lemon
rind and juice, anchovy essence and
tomato purée. Season well with a
little salt and lots of pepper and mix
with the egg to bind. Pack into the
pike and secure with cocktail sticks
(toothpicks) or small skewers.

Thoroughly grease a roasting tin
(pan) with some of the remaining
butter or margarine. Bend the pike
round to fit in the tin and spread
with most of the remaining butter or
margarine. Use the rest to grease a
large sheet of foil. Add the ale, water
and rum to the tin. Cover with the
greased foil and bake in a preheated
oven at 190°C/375°F/gas mark 5 for
30 minutes. Remove the foil and
cook for a further 20–30 minutes
until golden and cooked through,
basting frequently with the cooking
juices. Carefully transfer to a warm
serving dish and spoon the juices
over. Garnish with parsley sprigs and
serve with plain potatoes and Caper
Sauce.

Baked scallops for lunch

SERVES 4

8 shelled scallops
20 g/¾ oz/1½ tbsp butter or margarine
1 small onion, finely chopped
20 g/¾ oz/3 tbsp plain (all-purpose)
*   flour*
150 ml/¼ pt/⅔ cup fish stock
150 ml/¼ pt/⅔ cup milk
Salt and freshly ground black pepper
1 bay leaf
50 g/2 oz/½ cup Cheddar cheese, grated
50 g/2 oz/1 cup fresh white
*   breadcrumbs*
Green salad, to serve

Quarter the scallops and put in a
shallow ovenproof dish. Melt the
butter or margarine in a saucepan.
Add the onion and fry (sauté) gently
for 3 minutes until soft but not
brown. Add the flour and cook for
1 minute, stirring. Remove from the
heat and blend in the stock, milk
and a little salt and pepper. Add the
bay leaf. Bring to the boil and cook
for 2 minutes, stirring. Add half the
cheese, taste and re-season. Discard
the bay leaf and pour the sauce over
the scallops. Mix the remaining
cheese with the breadcrumbs and
sprinkle over the surface. Cook in a
preheated oven at 190°C/375°F/gas
mark 5 for about 30 minutes until
golden, bubbling and the scallops
are cooked. Serve hot with a green
salad.

Baked stuffed pike with mixed mushrooms

SERVES 6

1 pike, about 1.5 kg/3 lb, cleaned and
  scaled
Salt and freshly ground black pepper
50 g/2 oz/1 cup fresh wholemeal
  breadcrumbs
30 ml/2 tbsp milk
1 garlic clove, crushed
100 g/4 oz mixed mushrooms such as
  chanterelles, oyster and chestnut,
  finely chopped
30 ml/2 tbsp chopped basil
10 ml/2 tsp anchovy essence (extract)
Freshly ground black pepper
100 g/4 oz/½ cup unsalted (sweet)
  butter, softened, plus extra for
  greasing
Finely grated rind and juice of ½ lemon
15 ml/1 tbsp chopped parsley
Buttered new potatoes in their skins, to
  serve

Rinse the fish and pat dry with
kitchen paper (paper towels). Season
inside and out with salt and pepper.
Mix the breadcrumbs with the milk,
garlic, mushrooms, basil, anchovy
essence and pepper. Work in half the
butter. Use to stuff the pike and
secure the opening with cocktail
sticks (toothpicks). Grease a roasting
tin (pan) with a little butter. Lay the
fish in it and smear the remaining
butter over the surface. Cover with
foil and bake in a preheated oven at
220°C/425°F/gas mark 7 for about
30 minutes or until the fish pulls
easily away from the bones. Transfer
to a large serving platter. Sprinkle
with the lemon juice. Mix the lemon
rind and parsley and sprinkle over
the fish. Serve hot with buttered
new potatoes in their skins.

Smoked cod and egg bake

SERVES 4

40 g/1½ oz/3 tbsp butter or margarine
450 g/1 lb smoked cod, skinned and
  cut into neat pieces
20 g/¾ oz/3 tbsp plain (all-purpose)
  flour
300 ml/½ pt/1¼ cups milk
75 g/3 oz/¾ cup Cheddar cheese, grated
Salt and freshly ground black pepper
3 hard-boiled (hard-cooked) eggs,
  sliced
25 g/1 oz/½ cup fresh white
  breadcrumbs

Grease a shallow 1.2 litre/2 pt/
5 cup ovenproof dish with a little of
the butter or margarine. Lay the fish
in the dish. Whisk the flour with a
little of the milk in a saucepan. Add
the remaining milk and 20 g/¾ oz/
1½ tbsp of the remaining butter or
margarine. Bring to the boil and
cook for 2 minutes, whisking all the
time, until thick and smooth. Stir in
the cheese and season to taste.
Arrange the egg slices over the fish
and top with the sauce. Sprinkle the
breadcrumbs over and dot with the
remaining butter or margarine. Bake
in a preheated oven at 190°C/
375°F/gas mark 5 for 45 minutes
until golden and the fish is cooked
through. Serve hot.

Smoked cod and egg Florentine

SERVES 4

Prepare as for Smoked Cod and Egg
Bake, but put a layer of 350 g/12 oz
chopped, cooked spinach in the base
of the dish before adding the fish.

Gratin of lobster

SERVES 4

2 cooked lobsters
1 small onion, very finely chopped
50 g/2 oz/¼ cup unsalted (sweet) butter
30 ml/2 tbsp olive oil
200 ml/7 fl oz/scant 1 cup dry white wine
20 g/¾ oz/3 tbsp plain (all-purpose) flour
250 ml/8 fl oz/1 cup milk
1 bouquet garni sachet
Salt and freshly ground black pepper
45 ml/3 tbsp double (heavy) cream
60 ml/4 tbsp dried breadcrumbs
30 ml/2 tbsp grated Parmesan cheese
Parsley sprigs, to garnish
New potatoes and green salad, to serve

Prepare the lobster, removing all the meat (page 15). Clean the shells and slice the tail meat. Cook the onion gently in 25 g/1 oz/2 tbsp of the butter and the oil for 2 minutes, stirring, until soft but not brown. Add the wine and boil rapidly until reduced by half. In a separate pan, melt 20 g/¾ oz/1½ tbsp of the remaining butter. Stir in the flour and cook for 1 minute, stirring. Remove from the heat and blend in the milk. Add the bouquet garni. Return to the heat, bring to the boil and cook for 2 minutes, stirring. Squeeze the bouquet garni sachet to extract as much flavour as possible, then discard. Season to taste. Stir in the cream and the onion mixture.

Mix the picked-out meat, the coral and tomalley with 60 ml/4 tbsp of the sauce (keep the sliced meat separately). Spoon this mixture into the heads of the lobster shells and place on a baking (cookie) sheet. Pour a little of the remaining sauce in the shell bodies and top with the sliced lobster. Spoon the rest of the sauce over and sprinkle with the breadcrumbs and Parmesan. Dot with the remaining butter. Bake in a preheated oven at 200°C/400°F/gas mark 6 for about 20 minutes or until hot through and lightly golden. Garnish with parsley sprigs and serve hot with new potatoes and a green salad.

Smoked haddock ring

SERVES 4

1 bunch of watercress
450 g/1 lb smoked haddock, skinned and roughly chopped
2 streaky bacon rashers (slices), rinded and finely chopped
150 g/5 oz/2½ cups fresh white breadcrumbs
170 g/6 oz/1 small can of evaporated milk
1 bunch of spring onions (scallions), finely chopped
10 ml/2 tsp lemon juice
15 ml/1 tbsp horseradish relish
Freshly ground black pepper
2 eggs, beaten
Sunflower oil, for greasing
Tomato salad, to serve

Trim the feathery stalks off the watercress. Reserve half the watercress sprigs for garnish and finely chop the remainder. Mix the chopped watercress with all the remaining ingredients. Spoon into a lightly oiled 900 ml/1½ pt/3¾ cup ring mould and level the surface. Bake in a preheated oven at 190°C/375°F/gas mark 5 for about 40 minutes or until the mixture feels firm to the touch. Allow to cool slightly, then turn out on to a warm serving plate. Garnish with the remaining watercress and serve warm with a tomato salad.

Lobster thermidor

SERVES 4

2 cooked lobsters
65 g/2½ oz/generous ¼ cup unsalted
  (sweet) butter
1 small onion, very finely chopped
150 ml/¼ pt/⅔ cup dry white wine
15 ml/1 tbsp brandy
1 bouquet garni sachet
25 g/1 oz/¼ cup plain (all-purpose)
  flour
250 ml/8 fl oz/1 cup milk
1 bay leaf
A good pinch of celery salt
Freshly ground black pepper
30 ml/2 tbsp double (heavy) cream
2.5 ml/½ tsp Dijon mustard
30 ml/2 tbsp grated Parmesan cheese
60 ml/4 tbsp fresh white breadcrumbs
Watercress, to garnish
Crusty bread, to serve

Halve the lobsters and remove all
the meat (page 15). Clean the shells
and reserve. Melt 25 g/1 oz/2 tbsp
of the butter in a saucepan. Add the
onion and fry (sauté) gently for
2 minutes until softened but not
browned. Add the wine, brandy and
bouquet garni. Bring to the boil and
boil rapidly until reduced by half.
  Meanwhile, melt 25 g/1 oz/2 tbsp
of the remaining butter in a separate
pan. Stir in the flour and cook for
1 minute. Remove from the heat,
blend in the milk and add the bay
leaf. Bring to the boil and cook for
2 minutes, stirring all the time.
Discard the bay leaf. Beat in the
tomalley and any coral. Season with
the celery salt and pepper and stir in
the cream, mustard and half the
Parmesan. Mix in the onion mixture,
discarding the bouquet garni. Chop
the lobster meat and fold in. Spoon
back into the shells. Mix the
remaining Parmesan with the
breadcrumbs and sprinkle over.

Place on a baking (cookie) sheet.
Melt the remaining butter and
drizzle over. Bake in a preheated
oven at 200°C/400°F/gas mark 6 for
about 20 minutes until golden and
hot through. Garnish with
watercress and serve with crusty
bread.

Cod baked with peppers and mushrooms

SERVES 4

25 g/1 oz/2 tbsp butter or margarine
350 g/12 oz button mushrooms, sliced
Salt and freshly ground black pepper
4 cod steaks
400 g/14 oz/1 large can of chopped
  tomatoes
10 ml/2 tsp cornflour (cornstarch)
15 ml/1 tbsp water
15 ml/1 tbsp tomato purée (paste)
1 green (bell) pepper, thinly sliced into
  rings
5 ml/1 tsp dried oregano

Grease a shallow ovenproof dish
with the butter or margarine. Lay
the mushrooms in the base and
season lightly. Top with the fish.
Empty the tomatoes into a saucepan.
Blend the cornflour with the water
and tomato purée and stir into the
pan. Bring to the boil, stirring, until
thickened. Pour over the fish. Top
with the pepper rings and sprinkle
with the oregano and a little more
salt and pepper. Bake in the oven
at 180°C/350°F/gas mark 4 for
30 minutes until the fish and
mushrooms are cooked through.

Whiting San Remo

SERVES 4

350 g/12 oz whiting fillet
300 ml/½ pt/1¼ cups milk
Salt and freshly ground black pepper
25 g/1 oz/2 tbsp butter or margarine,
* plus extra for greasing*
25 g/1 oz/¼ cup plain (all-purpose)
* flour*
2.5 ml/½ tsp Dijon mustard
50 g/2 oz/½ cup strong Cheddar cheese,
* grated*
2 eggs, separated
320 g/12 oz/1 medium can of
* sweetcorn (corn) with (bell) peppers,*
* drained*
30 ml/2 tbsp crushed cornflakes
8 back bacon rashers (slices), rinded
300 ml/½ pt/1¼ cups passata (sieved
* tomatoes)*
5 ml/1 tsp dried basil

Put the fish in a saucepan with the milk and a little salt and pepper. Bring to the boil, reduce the heat, cover and poach gently for about 5 minutes or until the fish flakes easily with a fork. Lift out, discard the skin and any bones and flake. Pour off the milk and reserve. Melt the butter or margarine in the rinsed-out pan. Stir in the flour and cook for 1 minute, stirring. Remove from the heat and blend in the fish milk. Return to the heat, bring to the boil and cook for 2 minutes, stirring. Beat in the mustard, half the cheese and the egg yolks, then the sweetcorn. Whisk the egg whites until stiff and fold into the sauce with a metal spoon.

Grease a 1.2 litre/2 pt/5 cup ovenproof dish. Spoon a third of the sauce into the dish, then top with a layer of half the fish. Repeat the layers, finishing with a layer of sauce. Sprinkle with the cornflakes and the remaining cheese. Bake in a preheated oven at 180°C/350°F/gas mark 4 for about 25 minutes until puffy, golden brown and cooked through. Meanwhile, grill (broil) the bacon and heat the passata with the basil and a little salt and pepper. Spoon a pool of the passata on to four warm plates. Top with a portion of the fish mixture, then add two bacon rashers to each. Serve hot.

Red mullet envelopes

SERVES 4

75 g/3 oz/⅓ cup unsalted (sweet)
* butter*
4 red mullet, cleaned and scaled
Salt and freshly ground black pepper
Juice of 1 lemon
4 thyme sprigs

Cut four ovals of greaseproof (waxed) paper, large enough to wrap the fish in generously. Spread the centres liberally with the butter. Lay a fish on each and season well with salt and pepper. Sprinkle with the lemon juice and lay a sprig of thyme on each. Fold the paper over the fish, folding and pleating the edges to seal. Transfer to a baking (cookie) sheet. Bake in a preheated oven at 180°C/350°F/gas mark 4 for 20 minutes. Transfer to warm plates and open at the table.

Baked cod with olives and potatoes

SERVES 4

4 potatoes, cut into eight pieces
30 ml/2 tbsp olive oil
4 cod fillets, about 175 g/6 oz each, skinned
10 ml/2 tsp chopped oregano
10 ml/2 tsp chopped parsley
Finely grated rind and juice of ½ lemon
Freshly ground black pepper
1 red onion, chopped
2 ripe beefsteak tomatoes, skinned and chopped
1 garlic clove, crushed
16 stoned (pitted) green olives, halved
Green salad, to serve

Boil the potatoes in lightly salted water for 4 minutes until almost tender. Drain. Pour half the oil into a roasting tin (pan) and add the potatoes. Toss gently and place on the top shelf of a preheated oven at 200°C/400°F/gas mark 6. Cook for 10 minutes. Lay the fish in a single layer in a separate baking dish. Sprinkle with the herbs, lemon rind and juice and pepper. Cover with foil and place on the shelf just below the middle of the oven. Cook for about 30 minutes until the potatoes are turning golden and the fish is tender.

Meanwhile, heat the remaining oil in a small pan. Add the onion and fry (sauté), stirring, for 3 minutes. Add the tomatoes, garlic, olives and a good grinding of pepper. Simmer, stirring occasionally, for about 5 minutes or until pulpy. When the potatoes and fish are cooked, pour off any juices from the fish into the tomato mixture. Arrange the fish and potatoes on warm serving plates and spoon the tomato sauce over the fish. Serve straight away with a green salad.

Mediterranean red mullet

SERVES 4

4 red mullet, cleaned and scaled
30 ml/2 tbsp olive oil
1 large garlic clove, crushed
1 sun-dried tomato in oil, drained and finely chopped
10 ml/2 tsp tomato purée (paste)
120 ml/4 fl oz/½ cup dry white wine
1 bouquet garni sachet
A pinch of cayenne
A pinch of paprika
Salt and freshly ground black pepper
A good pinch of caster (superfine) sugar
100 g/4 oz stoned (pitted) black olives
225 g/8 oz thin French (green) beans, topped and tailed
Lemon wedges and parsley sprigs, to garnish
Coarse crusty bread, to serve

Wash the fish and pat dry on kitchen paper (paper towels). Place in a large casserole dish (Dutch oven). Mix together all the remaining ingredients except the olives and beans and pour over the fish. Cover and cook in a preheated oven at 180°C/350°F/gas mark 4 for 20 minutes, basting occasionally. Add the olives and heat through for a further 5 minutes. Taste and re-season if necessary.

Meanwhile, cook the beans in lightly salted, boiling water for about 4–5 minutes until just tender but still with some bite. Drain. Spoon the beans on to warm serving plates. Top each with a fish and spoon the juices over. Garnish with lemon wedges and parsley sprigs and serve with coarse crusty bread.

Baked salmon parcels

SERVES 6

The French term for cooking in paper or foil parcels is *en papillote*.

25 g/1 oz/2 tbsp butter or margarine
6 salmon fillets, about 175 g/6 oz
each, skinned
Finely grated rind and juice of 1 small
lemon
A pinch of salt
Freshly ground black pepper
175 g/6 oz button mushrooms, sliced
1 bunch of spring onions (scallions),
chopped
30 ml/2 tbsp capers
30 ml/2 tbsp chopped parsley
5 ml/1 tsp dried marjoram
New potatoes and mixed salad,
to serve

Smear six sheets of foil with half the butter or margarine. Lay a salmon fillet on each. Sprinkle with the lemon rind and juice, the salt, a good grinding of pepper, the mushrooms, onions, capers, parsley and marjoram. Dot with the remaining butter or margarine, fold the foil over the ingredients and roll the edges together to seal tightly. Place on a baking (cookie) sheet. Cook in a preheated oven at 200°C/400°F/gas mark 6 for 15 minutes or until the fish is cooked through. Open the foil on warm plates and serve with new potatoes and a mixed salad.

Baked cod, olive and gherkin parcels

SERVES 4

Prepare as for Baked Salmon Parcels, but substitute cod fillets for the salmon and half chopped gherkins (cornichons) and half chopped stoned (pitted) black olives for the capers.

Smoked haddock parcels

SERVES 4

Prepare as for Baked Salmon Parcels, but substitute fillets of smoked haddock for the salmon and omit the marjoram.

Baked red mullet and vegetable parcels

SERVES 4

20 ml/4 tsp butter or margarine
2 tomatoes, thinly sliced
1 courgette (zucchini), thinly sliced
2 shallots, finely chopped
4 red mullet, cleaned and scaled
1 large garlic clove, cut into thin slivers
1 lemon, sliced
4 parsley sprigs
4 thyme sprigs
Salt and freshly ground black pepper
New potatoes and baby carrots, to serve

Grease four large squares of double-thickness greaseproof (waxed) paper with the butter or margarine. Put the tomato and courgette slices in a thin layer on the centre of each sheet, sprinkle with the shallot and lay a mullet on top. Make three slashes in each fish and push a sliver of garlic into each slash. Push a slice of lemon and a parsley and thyme sprig into the body cavity of each. Add 15 ml/1 tbsp water to each pile and season with salt and pepper. Draw up the paper and pleat over the top, then fold in the sides to seal.

Put the parcels on a baking (cookie) sheet and bake in a preheated oven at 180°C/350°F/gas mark 4 for 30 minutes until the fish is cooked through and the vegetables are tender. Transfer to warm plates and open at the table. Serve with new potatoes and baby carrots.

Baked mullet with mushrooms

SERVES 4

25 g/1 oz/2 tbsp unsalted (sweet)
  butter
8 flat mushrooms, peeled
2 garlic cloves, finely chopped
Salt and freshly ground black pepper
4 red mullet, cleaned and scaled
120 ml/4 fl oz/½ cup red wine
120 ml/4 fl oz/½ cup fish stock
5 ml/1 tsp tomato purée (paste)
30 ml/2 tbsp crème fraîche
30 ml/2 tbsp torn flatleaf parsley
Crusty bread and green salad, to serve

Smear the butter over the base of a
large ovenproof dish that can hold
the mushrooms in a single layer. Lay
the mushrooms in the dish in pairs,
gills uppermost. Sprinkle with the
garlic and some salt and pepper.
Make several slashes in each side of
the fish. Lay a fish on top of each
pair of mushrooms, season again
and pour the wine and stock over.

Cover with foil and bake in a
preheated oven at 180°C/350°F/gas
mark 4 for 20 minutes or until the
fish and mushrooms are tender.
Carefully lift out the fish on their
mushrooms and transfer to warm
plates. Keep warm. Pour the juices
into a small saucepan. Add the
tomato purée and crème fraîche and
bring to the boil, stirring. Simmer for
2 minutes. Taste and re-season.
Spoon over the fish and garnish with
the flatleaf parsley. Serve hot with
crusty bread and a green salad.

Sea port herrings

SERVES 4

4 herrings, cleaned and boned,
  reserving any roes
25 g/1 oz/2 tbsp butter or margarine
1 onion, finely chopped
1 garlic clove, crushed
50 g/2 oz button mushrooms, finely
  chopped
15 ml/1 tbsp chopped thyme
15 ml/1 tbsp chopped parsley
1 large hard-boiled (hard-cooked) egg,
  finely chopped
25 g/1 oz/½ cup fresh white breadcrumbs
Finely grated rind of ½ small lemon
45 ml/3 tbsp milk
Salt and freshly ground black pepper
1 quantity of Sweet Mustard Sauce
  (page 383)
Parsley sprigs, to garnish
Plain potatoes, to serve

Wipe the fish with kitchen paper
(paper towels). Melt half the butter
or margarine in a frying pan
(skillet), add the onion, garlic and
mushrooms and cook gently,
stirring, for 3 minutes until softened.
Remove from the heat and stir in the
herbs, egg, breadcrumbs and lemon
rind. Stir in the milk to moisten and
season with salt and pepper. Put into
the fish, then reshape.

Use a little of the remaining butter
or margarine to grease a large,
shallow ovenproof dish. Lay the fish
in the dish and dot with the
remaining butter or margarine.
Cover with foil and bake in a
preheated oven at 180°C/350°F/gas
mark 4 for 25 minutes or until the
fish is cooked through. Meanwhile,
make the mustard sauce and pour in
a pool on four plates. Top each with
a stuffed herring, garnish with a
parsley sprig and serve with plain
potatoes.

Smoked haddock roulade

SERVES 4

225 g/8 oz smoked haddock fillet,
  skinned and any loose bones removed
1½ quantities of Béchamel Sauce
  (page 376)
4 eggs, separated
60 ml/4 tbsp grated Parmesan cheese
10 ml/2 tsp anchovy essence (extract)
2 large hard-boiled (hard-cooked) eggs,
  chopped
Salt and freshly ground black pepper
Parsley sprigs, to garnish

Poach the haddock in a saucepan
with just enough water to cover for
5 minutes or until it flakes easily
with a fork. Drain and flake the fish.
Meanwhile, make up the Béchamel
Sauce. Beat 45 ml/3 tbsp of the
sauce into the fish, then beat in the
egg yolks and half the cheese. Whisk
the egg whites until stiff and fold in
with a metal spoon. Turn into a
dampened 18 × 28 cm/7 × 11 in
Swiss roll tin (jelly roll pan), lined
with non-stick baking parchment to
come at least 2.5 cm/1 in above the
rim all round. Level the surface and
bake in a preheated oven at 200°C/
400°F/gas mark 6 for about
15 minutes until firm and golden.
  Meanwhile, add the anchovy
essence to the remaining sauce and
stir in the hard-boiled eggs. Season
with salt and pepper and heat
through. Lay a clean sheet of baking
parchment on a clean tea towel
(dish cloth) and dust with the
remaining cheese. Turn the roulade
out on to the paper and remove the
cooking paper. Spoon the hot sauce
over. Roll up, using the paper as a
guide, transfer to a warm dish and
garnish with parsley sprigs. Serve hot.

Smoked haddock and spinach roulade

SERVES 4

Prepare as for Smoked Haddock
Roulade, but omit the hard-boiled
(hard-cooked) eggs and add 225 g/
8 oz chopped, cooked spinach to the
sauce for the filling instead. Flavour
the spinach with 1.5 ml/¼ tsp grated
nutmeg.

Crab roulade

SERVES 4

Prepare as for Smoked Haddock
Roulade, but substitute 170 g/6 oz/
1 small can of white crabmeat,
drained, for the cooked haddock and
add 5 ml/1 tsp tomato purée (paste)
to the sauce.

Salmon roulade

SERVES 4

Prepare as for Smoked Haddock
Roulade, but substitute salmon tail
fillet for the haddock. Add 10 ml/
2 tsp tomato purée (paste) to the
fish with the 45 ml/3 tbsp sauce
before adding the egg yolks.
Substitute 100 g/4 oz cooked peeled
prawns (shrimp), roughly chopped,
for the hard-boiled (hard-cooked)
eggs, if preferred.

Tuna roulade

SERVES 4

Prepare as for Smoked Haddock
Roulade, but substitute 185 g/6½ oz/
1 small can of tuna, drained, for the
cooked haddock. Replace the eggs
with 200 g/7 oz/1 small can of
sweetcorn (corn), drained, if
preferred.

Smoked mackerel roulade

SERVES 4

Prepare as for Smoked Haddock Roulade (page 253), but substitute cooked smoked mackerel fillets, skinned and flaked, for the haddock. Use only 1 hard-boiled (hard-cooked) egg for the filling and add 3 tomatoes, skinned, seeded and chopped, and 10 ml/2 tsp horseradish relish to the sauce.

Baked bream

SERVES 4

1 bream, about 1 kg/2¼ lb, cleaned
  and scaled
Salt and freshly ground black pepper
1 small onion, thinly sliced
1 parsley sprig
1 thyme sprig
1 lemon balm or lemon mint sprig
30 ml/2 tbsp olive oil
250 ml/8 fl oz/1 cup dry white wine
15 ml/1 tbsp brandy
25 g/1 oz/2 tbsp unsalted (sweet)
  butter, diced
30 ml/2 tbsp chopped parsley

Wipe the fish and season inside and out. Stuff with the onion slices and herbs. Lay in an oiled ovenproof dish and pour in the rest of the oil. Cover the dish and bake in a preheated oven at 200°C/400°F/gas mark 6 for 15 minutes. Add the wine, re-cover and bake for a further 15 minutes or until the fish is cooked through. Carefully transfer the fish to a serving dish and keep warm. Strain the cooking liquid into a saucepan and add the brandy. Bring to the boil. Gradually whisk in the butter, a piece at a time, until slightly thickened. Stir in the parsley and season to taste. Spoon over the fish and serve.

Baked mackerel with rhubarb

SERVES 4

4 sticks of rhubarb, cut into short
  lengths
600 ml/1 pt/2½ cups fish stock
4 mackerel, cleaned
25 g/1 oz/2 tbsp butter or margarine
Salt and freshly ground black pepper
150 ml/¼ pt/⅔ cup double (heavy)
  cream
A little light brown sugar
Parsley sprigs, to garnish

Put the rhubarb in a saucepan with 90 ml/6 tbsp of the stock. Bring to the boil, reduce the heat, cover and cook for about 8 minutes or until the rhubarb is pulpy, depending on the thickness of the sticks. Meanwhile, put the fish in a flameproof dish, well-greased with half the butter or margarine. Season well and pour the remaining stock over. Cover and bake in a preheated oven at 200°C/400°F/gas mark 6 for about 20 minutes or until cooked through. Transfer the fish to a warm serving dish. Purée the rhubarb in a blender or food processor. Add the remaining butter or margarine and the cream and blend again. Season with sugar, salt and pepper to taste. Spoon over the fish and garnish with parsley sprigs.

Brill with oyster mushrooms, tomatoes and cucumber

SERVES 4

4 large brill fillets
100 g/4 oz oyster mushrooms, sliced
200 ml/7 fl oz/scant 1 cup dry white
    wine
1 bouquet garni sachet
Salt and freshly ground black pepper
4 tomatoes, skinned and thinly sliced
40 g/1½ oz/3 tbsp butter or margarine
1 small onion, finely chopped
½ cucumber, skinned and finely diced
20 ml/¾ oz/3 tbsp plain (all-purpose)
    flour
150 ml/¼ pt/⅔ cup milk
150 ml/¼ pt/⅔ cup single (light) cream

Put the brill in a flameproof dish with the mushrooms, wine, bouquet garni and some salt and pepper. Cover and bake in a preheated oven at 180°C/350°F/gas mark 4 for 15 minutes. Meanwhile, lay the tomato slices in a large, fairly shallow, ovenproof serving dish. Dot with 15 g/½ oz/1 tbsp of the butter or margarine and add a good grinding of pepper. Cover with foil and bake on the shelf under the fish for 6 minutes. Carefully lift the brill and mushrooms out of the cooking liquid and lay on top of the tomatoes. Discard the bouquet garni, cover with foil and keep warm. Boil the fish cooking liquid rapidly until reduced to 45 ml/3 tbsp. Melt the remaining butter or margarine in a saucepan, add the onion and cook gently, stirring, for 3 minutes. Add the cucumber and cook for 1 minute. Stir in the flour and cook for 1 minute. Remove from the heat and blend in the milk, then the cream and the fish stock. Return to the heat, bring to the boil and cook for 1 minute, stirring all the time. Season to taste and pour over the fish. Return to the oven at 220°C/425°F/gas mark 7 for a few minutes to set the top, then serve straight away.

Baked plaice with Stilton and celery

SERVES 4

4 large plaice fillets, each cut into
    4 pieces
30 ml/2 tbsp cornflour (cornstarch)
2.5 ml/½ tsp celery salt
Freshly ground black pepper
15 ml/1 tbsp olive oil
15 g/½ oz/1 tbsp butter or margarine
1 celery stick, very finely chopped
1 quantity of White Sauce (page 376)
75 g/3 oz/¾ cup blue Stilton cheese,
    crumbled
30 ml/2 tbsp crushed cornflakes
Crusty bread and green salad, to serve

Toss the fish in the cornflour mixed with the celery salt and some pepper. Heat the oil and butter or margarine in a flameproof serving dish. Add the fish and fry (sauté) quickly for 2–3 minutes to brown, turning once. Drain on kitchen paper (paper towels). Add the celery and fry for 1 minute to soften. Return the fish to the pan. Make up the sauce and stir in the Stilton until melted. Spoon over the fish and sprinkle with the cornflakes. Bake in a preheated oven at 190°C/375°F/gas mark 5 for about 20 minutes until golden and bubbling. Serve hot with crusty bread and a green salad.

Grey mullet paprikash

SERVES 4

50 g/2 oz/¼ cup unsalted (sweet)
  butter, plus extra for greasing
1 large onion, finely chopped
2 red (bell) peppers, finely chopped
15 ml/1 tbsp paprika
1 grey mullet, about 1 kg/2¼ lb,
  cleaned and scaled
Salt and freshly ground black pepper
1 large oregano sprig or 5 ml/ 1 tsp
  dried oregano
Juice of ½ lemon
8 smoked streaky bacon rashers
  (slices), rinded
200 ml/7 fl oz/scant 1 cup crème
  fraîche
5 ml/1 tsp Dijon mustard
Buttered Noodles for Fish (page 394),
  to serve

Melt half the butter in a frying pan
(skillet). Add the onion and peppers
and fry (sauté) stirring, for 2 minutes.
Stir in the paprika, then tip into a
large, lightly buttered baking dish.
Wipe the fish and season inside and
out with salt and pepper. Push the
oregano inside. Sprinkle with the
lemon juice and lay the fish on the
onion and peppers. Lay the bacon
rashers over the top and dot with
the remaining butter. Cover and
bake in a preheated oven at 220°C/
425°F/gas mark 7 for 15 minutes.
Baste well, leave the lid off and cook
for a further 5–10 minutes until the
fish is tender and the bacon is
lightly browned. Carefully transfer
the fish to a warm serving platter
and keep warm. Tip the remaining
contents of the baking dish into the
frying pan. Stir in the crème fraîche
and mustard. Bring to the boil,
stirring, taste and re-season if
necessary. Spoon around the fish
and serve hot with Buttered Noodles
for Fish.

Baked cod with bacon

SERVES 4

25 g/1 oz/2 tbsp unsalted (sweet)
  butter
4 cod steaks
4 streaky bacon rashers (slices), rinded
  and finely chopped
50 g/2 oz/½ cup frozen peas, thawed
5 ml/1 tsp dried mint
100 g/4 oz button mushrooms, sliced
60 ml/4 tbsp single (light) cream
Salt and freshly ground black pepper
New potatoes, to serve

Grease a shallow baking dish, large
enough to hold the fish in a single
layer, with half the butter. Lay the
steaks in the dish. Mix the bacon
with the peas and mint and spoon
into the cavities in the cutlets,
securing the flaps of fish with
cocktail sticks (toothpicks) if
necessary to keep in place. Arrange
the mushroom slices on top and
spoon the cream over. Season with
salt and pepper and dot with the
remaining butter. Cover tightly with
foil and bake in a preheated oven
at 180°C/350°F/gas mark 4 for
25 minutes. Remove the foil and
bake for a further 10–15 minutes to
lightly brown the surface. Serve hot
with new potatoes.

Baked mackerel with herb and onion butter

SERVES 4

4 mackerel, cleaned
50 g/2 oz/¼ cup butter or margarine,
   melted
15 ml/1 tbsp chopped parsley
15 ml/1 tbsp chopped sage
2 spring onions (scallions), finely
   chopped
Salt and freshly ground black pepper
Plain potatoes and peas, to serve

Lay each fish on a large square of foil, shiny side up. Spoon the butter or margarine over each and sprinkle with the herbs and spring onions. Season. Wrap loosely, sealing the edges well. Place on a baking (cookie) sheet and bake in a preheated oven at 190°C/375°F/gas mark 5 for 20 minutes or until the fish is cooked through and tender. Unwrap on to warm plates and serve hot with plain potatoes and peas.

Simple cod puff

SERVES 4

2 large potatoes, cut into small pieces
450 g/1 lb cod fillet
150 ml/¼ pt/⅔ cup milk
25 g/1 oz/2 tbsp butter or margarine
3 eggs, separated
Salt and freshly ground black pepper
300 ml/½ pt/1¼ cups passata (sieved
   tomatoes)
2.5 ml/½ tsp dried basil
Peas, to serve

Cook the potatoes in lightly salted, boiling water until tender. Meanwhile, poach the fish in the milk in a shallow pan for about 5 minutes or until tender. Drain and flake, reserving the milk. Drain the potatoes and mash with the butter or margarine. Beat the fish into the mashed potato, add two of the egg yolks, 60 ml/4 tbsp of the fish cooking milk and some salt and pepper. Turn into a shallow baking dish and bake in a preheated oven at 190°C/375°F/gas mark 5 for 20 minutes.

Meanwhile, whisk all the egg whites until stiff. Beat the remaining egg yolk with 15 ml/1 tbsp of the remaining fish milk and fold in the egg whites and some salt and pepper. Spoon over the fish mixture and return to the oven for a further 10 minutes until risen, set and golden. Meanwhile, heat the passata with the basil and a little salt and pepper. Serve the cod puff with the hot passata and peas.

Cheesy haddock puff

SERVES 4

Prepare as for Simple Cod Puff, but substitute haddock for the cod. Add 15 ml/1 tbsp sweet pickle to the potato mixture and 50 g/2 oz/½ cup finely grated Cheddar cheese to the whisked egg whites with the egg yolk.

Fish and tomato puff

SERVES 4

Prepare as for Simple Cod Puff, but add 15 ml/1 tbsp chopped basil to the fish mixture and lay 3 sliced tomatoes over the surface before baking. Add 30 ml/2 tbsp grated Parmesan cheese to the egg yolk before folding in the whisked egg whites.

Roasted monkfish joint with garlic and rosemary

SERVES 4–6

1.25 kg/2½ lb piece of monkfish,
  skinned and central bone removed
30 ml/2 tbsp olive oil
2 garlic cloves, cut into slivers
3 large rosemary sprigs, broken into
  short lengths
Juice of ½ lemon
Salt and freshly ground black pepper
25 g/1 oz/2 tbsp unsalted (sweet)
  butter
4 tomatoes, skinned, seeded and
  chopped
A pinch of caster (superfine) sugar
Rosemary sprigs, to garnish
Game Chips (page 390) and green
  salad, to serve

Tie the monkfish into a joint with
string as if it were meat. Heat 15 ml/
1 tbsp of the oil in a frying pan
(skillet), add the monkfish and
brown all over. Transfer to a baking
tin (pan). Make several small slits all
over the surface and insert a sliver
of garlic and a small sprig of
rosemary in each. Sprinkle with the
remaining oil, the lemon juice and
some salt and pepper.

Roast in a preheated oven at
220°C/425°F/gas mark 7 for
25–30 minutes until the fish feels
tender throughout when pierced
with a skewer. Transfer to a carving
dish and keep warm. Add the butter
to the juices in the pan and stir until
melted. Season to taste and stir in
the tomatoes and sugar. Simmer for
2 minutes. Remove the baked pieces
of rosemary and the string from the
fish. Cut into thick slices and lay on
warm plates. Spoon the sauce over,
garnish with rosemary sprigs and
serve with Game Chips and a green
salad.

Roasted monkfish joint with tomatoes, mushrooms and basil

SERVES 4–6

Prepare as for Roasted Monkfish
Joint with Garlic and Rosemary, but
omit the rosemary. Add 175 g/6 oz
button mushrooms, sliced, and pour
300 ml/½ pt/1¼ cups passata
(sieved tomatoes) round the fish in
the roasting tin (pan) when cooking.
Baste the fish twice during cooking.
Continue as before, but add
15 ml/1 tbsp chopped basil to the
sauce and 15 ml/1 tbsp tomato
purée (paste) as well as the
tomatoes and seasoning.

Scalloped cod

SERVES 4

450 g/1 lb cod fillet, skinned and cut
  into 4 pieces
30 ml/2 tbsp cornflour (cornstarch)
Butter or margarine, for greasing
1 quantity of Cheese Sauce (page 376)
100 g/4 oz/2 cups fresh wholemeal
  breadcrumbs
5 ml/1 tsp celery salt
50 g/2 oz/½ cup Red Leicester cheese,
  grated
2 tomatoes, thinly sliced

Dust the cod with the cornflour and
place in a greased, shallow,
ovenproof dish. Pour the sauce over.
Mix the breadcrumbs with the celery
salt and cheese and sprinkle over
the fish. Arrange the tomatoes round
the edge. Bake in a preheated oven
at 190°C/375°F/gas mark 5 for
40 minutes until the top is golden
brown and the fish feels tender
when a knife is inserted down
through the centre.

Country stuffed cod

SERVES 4

85 g/3½ oz/1 small packet of parsley,
thyme and lemon stuffing mix
1 small onion, finely chopped
25 g/1 oz/2 tbsp butter or margarine,
melted
2 pieces of cod fillet, about 350 g/12 oz
each, skinned
3 large tomatoes, sliced
Salt and freshly ground black pepper
White Sauce or Béchamel Sauce
(page 376), mixed root vegetables
and cauliflower, to serve

Make up the stuffing mix according
to the packet directions and stir in
the onion. Brush a large, shallow
baking dish with some of the butter
or margarine. Lay one fish fillet in
the dish, skinned-side down. Spread
the stuffing over and top with the
second fillet, skinned-side down. Lay
the tomatoes on top and season with
salt and pepper. Pour the remaining
butter or margarine over. Cover with
foil and bake in a preheated oven at
180°C/350°F/gas mark 4 for
40 minutes or until the fish flakes
easily with a fork. Serve with the
sauce and mixed root vegetables and
cauliflower.

Golden-topped ratatouille with cod

SERVES 4

4 pieces of cod fillet, about 175 g/6 oz
each
390 g/14 oz/1 large can of ratatouille
15 ml/1 tbsp red wine
75 g/3 oz/¾ cup Cheddar cheese, grated
Crusty bread, to serve

Lay the cod in a large, shallow
ovenproof dish. Mix the ratatouille
with the wine and spoon over. Top
with the cheese and bake in a

preheated oven at 190°C/375°F/gas
mark 5 for 15–20 minutes until
golden and bubbling and the fish is
cooked through. Serve straight away
with crusty bread.

Baked trout with lemon, garlic and rosemary

SERVES 4

50 g/2 oz/¼ cup butter or margarine,
softened
4 rainbow trout, cleaned
1 large lemon, thinly sliced
4 rosemary sprigs
Salt and freshly ground black pepper
2 garlic cloves, finely chopped
120 ml/4 fl oz/½ cup white wine
30 ml/2 tbsp chopped parsley
Sauté Potatoes (page 389) and
mangetout (snow peas), to serve

Smear the shiny side of four large
squares of foil with the butter or
margarine. Rinse the fish and dry
with kitchen paper (paper towels).
Stuff the cavities with the lemon
slices and rosemary sprigs. Place
one fish on each piece of foil and
sprinkle with salt and pepper and
the garlic. Spoon the wine over and
wrap loosely but securely in the foil.
Transfer to a baking (cookie) sheet.
Bake for about 20 minutes at 180°C/
350°F/gas mark 4 or until the fish
feels tender when pierced with the
point of a knife. Unwrap on warm
plates and sprinkle with the parsley
before serving with Sauté Potatoes
and mangetout.

Grills and barbecues

All fish that can be grilled (broiled) are also suitable for barbecuing. On the whole, the firm-fleshed and oily varieties cook best by these methods. Slash whole, round fish to the bone in several places to ensure even cooking. If cooking whole fish or fillets on the barbecue, hinged wire racks make life a lot easier as you can turn the fish without fear of them breaking up. If you don't have one, wrapping the fish in foil parcels will prevent accidents. Fillets are best cooked through from one side only and only require a few minutes. Check frequently and baste with any marinade, oil, butter or margarine and/or lemon juice (especially for oily fish) to prevent drying.

All the recipes in this chapter are suitable for both indoor and outdoor cooking, so you can enjoy them any time of the year, whatever the weather!

Spiced monkfish and mango kebabs with curried yoghurt dressing

SERVES 4

If you prefer your vegetables cooked until soft, blanch the courgettes (zucchini) and onion in boiling water for 3 minutes before threading them on the skewers.

5 ml/1 tsp ground cumin
5 ml/1 tsp ground coriander (cilantro)
5 ml/1 tsp ground turmeric
30 ml/2 tbsp lemon juice
350 g/12 oz monkfish, cubed
1 mango
2 courgettes, cut into chunks
1 small red onion, quartered and separated into layers
8 cherry tomatoes
For the dressing:
150 ml/¼ pt/⅔ cup plain yoghurt
15 ml/1 tbsp curry powder
2.5 cm/1 in piece of cucumber, very finely chopped
Plain Rice for Fish (page 392), to serve
Lemon wedges, to garnish

Mix the spices with the lemon juice in a shallow dish. Add the monkfish and toss gently to coat. Leave to marinate for 1 hour. Peel the mango and cut the flesh off the stone (pit) in cubes. Thread the fish, mango, courgettes and onion on eight kebab skewers and push a cherry tomato on the end of each. Place on foil on the grill (broiler) rack and grill (broil) for 10 minutes, turning occasionally and brushing with any juices left in the fish dish, until cooked through.

To make the dressing, mix the yoghurt with the curry powder and cucumber. Serve the kebabs on a bed of rice, garnished with lemon wedges with the dressing handed separately.

Fresh tuna, sweetcorn and red pepper kebabs

SERVES 4

450 g/1 lb tuna steak, cubed
30 ml/2 tbsp olive oil
1.5 ml/¼ tsp chilli powder
15 ml/1 tbsp lemon juice
5 ml/1 tsp dried oregano
5 ml/1 tsp light brown sugar
Salt and freshly ground black pepper
4 corn cobs, each cut into 4 pieces
1 red (bell) pepper, cut into chunks
Fiery Cucumber Salsa (page 379), to serve

Put the tuna in a shallow dish. Whisk together the oil, chilli powder, lemon juice, oregano, sugar and salt and pepper and pour over. Toss and leave to marinate for 2 hours. Meanwhile, blanch the corn cobs for 3 minutes in lightly salted, boiling water. Add the pepper for the last 40 seconds. Drain, rinse with cold water and drain again. Thread the fish, corn cobs and peppers on to skewers and brush with any remaining marinade. Place on foil on the grill (broiler) rack and grill (broil) for about 8 minutes, turning occasionally, until golden and cooked through. Serve with Fiery Cucumber Salsa.

Monkfish and bacon kebabs

SERVES 4

450 g/1 lb monkfish tail, cubed
30 ml/1 tbsp lemon juice
60 ml/4 tbsp olive oil
Salt and freshly ground black pepper
1 garlic clove, chopped
15 ml/1 tbsp chopped parsley
15 ml/1 tbsp snipped chives
4 streaky bacon rashers (slices), rinded
   and cut into squares
8 cherry tomatoes

Place the fish in a shallow dish. Pour the lemon juice and oil over and add a little salt and pepper, the garlic and herbs. Toss well and leave to marinate for 2 hours. Thread on to eight skewers with the bacon and tomatoes. Place on foil on the grill (broiler) rack and brush with the marinade. Grill (broil) for 8–10 minutes until cooked through, turning and basting with the marinade from time to time.

Swordfish, sun-dried tomato and courgette kebabs

SERVES 4

8 sun-dried tomatoes, soaked in
   boiling water for 30 minutes
4 small swordfish steaks, cubed
30 ml/2 tbsp olive oil
10 ml/2 tsp red wine vinegar
15 ml/1 tbsp chopped basil
A good pinch of caster (superfine)
   sugar
Salt and freshly ground black pepper
4 small courgettes (zucchini), cut into
   chunks
Avocado Cream (page 372), to serve

Drain the tomatoes and place them in a shallow dish with the fish. Whisk together the oil, wine vinegar, basil, sugar and a little salt and pepper and pour over. Leave to marinate for 2 hours. Meanwhile, blanch the courgettes in lightly salted, boiling water for 3 minutes. Drain, rinse with cold water and drain again. Thread the fish, tomatoes and courgettes on to four skewers and brush with any remaining marinade. Place on foil on the grill (broiler) rack and grill (broil) for about 8 minutes, turning and brushing occasionally with any remaining marinade, until golden and cooked through. Serve with Avocado Cream.

Smoked haddock, bacon, and mushroom kebabs

SERVES 4

8 streaky bacon rashers (slices), rinded
16 small chestnut mushrooms
450 g/1 lb thick smoked haddock fillet,
   skinned and cut into 16 chunks
8 cherry tomatoes
25 g/1 oz/2 tbsp butter or margarine,
   melted
Cheese Sauce (page 376), to serve

Halve the bacon rashers and stretch them with the back of a knife. Blanch the mushrooms in a little water for 2 minutes to soften slightly. Drain. Wrap each piece of fish in a piece of bacon. Thread a tomato, then the mushrooms and fish rolls alternately on to eight skewers. Place on foil on the grill (broiler) rack. Brush with the butter or margarine and grill (broil), turning occasionally and brushing with more butter or margarine, until cooked through. Serve with Cheese Sauce.

Halloumi cheese, bacon and prawn kebabs

SERVES 4

*8 smoked streaky bacon rashers
(slices), rinded*
*225 g/8 oz/1 block of Halloumi cheese,
cut into large cubes*
*16 raw peeled tiger prawns (jumbo
shrimp), tails left on*
8 bay leaves
8 stoned (pitted) black olives
30 ml/2 tbsp olive oil
A few drops of Tabasco sauce
10 ml/2 tsp lemon juice
Salt and freshly ground black pepper
*Rainbow Pepper Salsa (page 375), to
serve*

Halve the bacon rashers and stretch
them with the back of a knife, then
roll each up. Thread on to eight
skewers with the cheese and
prawns, adding a bay leaf half-way
down the skewers. End each kebab
with an olive. Whisk the oil with the
Tabasco, lemon juice and a little salt
and pepper. Brush all over the
kebabs. Place on foil on the grill
(broiler) rack and grill (broil),
turning occasionally, for about
4–5 minutes until the prawns are
pink all over and the bacon and
cheese are turning golden. Serve
with Rainbow Pepper Salsa.

Grilled tuna with lentils

SERVES 4

175 g/6 oz/1 cup green lentils
60 ml/4 tbsp sunflower oil
1 red onion, finely chopped
1 bouquet garni sachet
Finely grated rind and juice of 1 lemon
*About 600 ml/1 pt/2½ cups vegetable
stock*
Salt and freshly ground black pepper
*50 g/2 oz/¼ cup butter or margarine,
softened*
30 ml/2 tbsp chopped parsley
4 tuna steaks
Tomato and onion salad, to serve

Cover the lentils with boiling water
and leave to soak for 2 hours. Drain.
Heat half the oil in a saucepan. Add
the onion and cook gently for
3 minutes until softened but not
browned. Add the lentils, bouquet
garni, lemon rind and juice and
enough of the stock to cover. Bring
to the boil, reduce the heat and
simmer for 25–30 minutes until
tender and most of the liquid has
been absorbed. Season to taste.

Meanwhile, mash the butter or
margarine with the parsley and a
little pepper and reserve. Place the
tuna on foil on the grill (broiler)
rack. Brush with the remaining oil
and season lightly. Grill (broil) for
about 3 minutes on each side until
cooked through and tender. Do not
overcook. Spread the parsley butter
over the steaks and return to the
grill until it starts to melt, then
immediately remove from the heat.
Spoon the lentils on to warm serving
plates, top with the tuna and serve
straight away with a tomato and
onion salad.

Grilled tuna with lime and kiwi fruit

SERVES 4

4 tuna steaks
1 onion, sliced and separated into rings
30 ml/2 tbsp olive oil
Finely grated rind and juice of 1 lime
5 ml/1 tsp light brown sugar
Salt and freshly ground black pepper
2 kiwi fruit, peeled and sliced
Guacamole Dip (page 382)
Sauté Potatoes (page 389) and green salad, to serve

Lay the fish in a shallow dish, and scatter the onion rings over. Mix the oil with the lime rind and juice, the sugar and a little salt and pepper. Pour over and turn to coat. Leave to marinate for 2 hours. Lift out of the marinade and place on foil on a grill (broiler) rack. Grill (broil) for only 2–3 minutes on one side . Turn the fish over and lay the kiwi slices on top. Grill for a further 2–3 minutes, brushing with the marinade, until the fish is tender and just cooked and the kiwi is turning golden. Take care not to overcook or it will dry out. Transfer to warm plates and serve with Guacamole Dip, Sauté Potatoes and a mixed salad.

Gulf of Mexico cod

SERVES 4

100 g/4 oz okra (ladies' fingers), trimmed
1 onion, finely chopped
1 garlic clove, crushed
10 g/¼ oz/2 tsp butter or margarine
1 green (bell) pepper, chopped
12 green olives, stoned (pitted)
1 red chilli, seeded and chopped
400 g/14 oz/1 large can of chopped tomatoes
15 ml/1 tbsp tomato purée (paste)
2.5 ml/½ tsp caster (superfine) sugar
Salt and freshly ground black pepper
4 pieces of cod fillet, about 175 g/6 oz each, skinned
15 ml/1 tbsp olive oil
Plain Rice for Fish (page 392) and mixed leaf salad, to serve

Boil the okra in lightly salted water for 5 minutes until just tender. Drain. Fry (sauté) the onion and garlic in the butter or margarine for 2 minutes, stirring, in a large frying pan (skillet). Add the green pepper, olives, chilli, tomatoes, tomato purée, sugar, salt and lots of pepper and simmer for 5 minutes. Gently fold in the okra. Meanwhile, brush the cod on both sides with oil and season lightly. Place on foil on the grill (broiler) rack and grill (broil), skin-side up, for 3 minutes. Turn over and grill for a further 3 minutes, until golden and cooked through. Place on a bed of rice, spoon the okra mixture over and serve with a mixed leaf salad.

Bacon cod steaks

SERVES 4

4 cod steaks
25 g/1 oz/2 tbsp butter or margarine,
  melted
Salt and freshly ground black pepper
4 smoked back bacon rashers (slices),
  rinded
400 g/14 oz/1 large can of chopped
  tomatoes, drained
15 ml/1 tbsp chopped parsley
15 ml/1 tbsp chopped thyme
A good pinch of caster (superfine)
  sugar
50 g/2 oz/½ cup Cheddar cheese, grated
French (green) beans and crusty bread,
  to serve

Wipe the cod with kitchen paper
(paper towels) and place on foil on
the grill (broiler) rack. Brush with a
little of the butter or margarine and
season lightly. Lay the bacon
alongside. Grill (broil) for 3 minutes,
then turn the fish over and place on
top of the bacon. Meanwhile, mix the
tomatoes with the herbs, sugar and a
little salt and pepper. Spoon into the
cavities in the fish steaks. Grill for 3
minutes. Cover with the cheese and
grill for a further 2 minutes or until
the cheese melts and bubbles. Serve
the fish immediately with French
beans and crusty bread.

Rustic tuna steaks with garlic and parsley

SERVES 4

4 tuna steaks
Salt and freshly ground black pepper
60 ml/4 tbsp olive oil
Juice of 1 lemon
2 garlic cloves, finely chopped
60 ml/4 tbsp chopped parsley
Crusty French bread and green salad,
  to serve

Wipe the fish with kitchen paper
(paper towels) and lay each on a
sheet of foil, shiny side up. Season
lightly with salt and pepper. Whisk
together the oil and lemon juice and
pour over the fish. Sprinkle with the
garlic and parsley. Wrap in the foil
and seal well. Grill (broil) for about
12 minutes, turning once, until the
fish is cooked through. Carefully
transfer the fish and its juices to
warm plates and serve with crusty
bread and a green salad.

Thai grilled sole

SERVES 4

4 lemon sole fillets
Coarse sea salt
Juice of 2 limes
1 lemon grass stem, bruised
3 basil leaves, torn
90 ml/6 tbsp light brown sugar
Lime wedges, to garnish
Thai Fragrant Rice (page 392) and
  green salad, to serve

Lay the fish in a shallow dish and
sprinkle with coarse sea salt.
Sprinkle the lime juice over and add
the lemon grass and basil. Leave to
marinate for 1 hour. Remove the
basil and lemon grass. Lay the fillets
on foil on a grill (broiler) rack and
sprinkle the sugar over. Grill (broil)
for about 5 minutes until tender and
the sugar has caramelised. Garnish
with lime wedges and serve with
Thai Fragrant Rice and a green
salad.

Grilled hake with prawns

SERVES 4

4 pieces of hake fillet, about 175 g/
6 oz each
45 ml/3 tbsp sunflower oil
50 g/2 oz/¼ cup butter or margarine
30 ml/2 tbsp soy sauce
15 ml/1 tbsp chopped tarragon
15 ml/1 tbsp chopped parsley
1 garlic clove, crushed
Salt and freshly ground black pepper
100 g/4 oz cooked peeled prawns
(shrimp)
Potato Croquettes for Fish (page 390),
to serve

Wipe the hake with kitchen paper
(paper towels) and place, skin-side
up, on foil on the grill (broiler) rack.
Heat the oil and butter or margarine
with the soy sauce, herbs, garlic and
a little salt and pepper. Brush over
the fish. Grill (broil) for 3 minutes.
Turn the fish over, brush again and
grill for a further 3 minutes. Add the
prawns, brush again and cook for a
further 2 minutes. Transfer to warm
plates and keep warm. Pour the
juices into the remaining oil mixture,
heat through, spoon over the fish
and serve with Potato Croquettes for
Fish.

Trout with horseradish and almond butter

SERVES 4

4 trout, cleaned
75 g/3 oz/⅓ cup unsalted (sweet)
butter
20 ml/4 tsp horseradish relish
30 ml/2 tbsp flaked (slivered) almonds
20 ml/4 tsp chopped parsley
Salt and freshly ground black pepper
Lemon wedges, to garnish
New potatoes, cold cooked French
(green) beans, French dressing and
very finely chopped onion, to serve

Slash the fish several times on each
side. Mash the butter and
horseradish together. Spread a little
over four sheets of foil, shiny side
up, and sprinkle with half the
almonds. Lay a fish on top of each
and spread with the remaining
butter mixture. Sprinkle with the
remaining nuts, the parsley and a
little salt and pepper. Wrap loosely
but securely and grill (broil) for
12–15 minutes, turning once, until
the fish is cooked through. Open on
to plates and garnish with lemon
wedges. Serve with new potatoes
and a French bean salad, tossed in
French dressing and sprinkled with
chopped onion.

Mackerel with lemon and coriander

SERVES 4

4 mackerel, cleaned, heads removed and boned
Finely grated rind and juice of 1 lemon
60 ml/4 tbsp chopped coriander (cilantro)
1 green chilli, seeded and finely chopped
Salt and freshly ground black pepper
30 ml/2 tbsp sunflower oil
Anchovy Butter (page 384), to serve

Lay the fish in a large, shallow dish. Mix the lemon rind and juice with the coriander and chilli and sprinkle over the fish. Leave to marinate for 30 minutes. Season with salt and pepper. Lay the fish, skin-side up, on foil on the grill (broiler) rack (two at a time, if necessary). Brush with some of the oil. Grill (broil) for 4 minutes until the skin is golden and crispy. Turn over, brush with a little more oil and grill for a further 3–4 minutes until cooked through. Transfer to warm plates and serve with Anchovy Butter.

Mackerel with gooseberries

SERVES 4

450 g/1 lb gooseberries, topped and tailed
45 ml/3 tbsp apple juice
Sugar, to taste
50 g/2 oz/¼ cup butter or margarine, melted
4 mackerel, cleaned and heads removed
15 ml/1 tbsp chopped parsley
Salt and freshly ground black pepper
Finely grated rind of ½ lemon
Sauté Potatoes (page 389) and peas, to serve

Put the gooseberries in a pan with the apple juice and sugar. Bring to the boil, reduce the heat, cover and simmer gently for about 10 minutes until the gooseberries are pulpy. Purée in a blender or food processor, then pass through a sieve (strainer), if preferred, to remove the pips. Beat in 15 g/½ oz/1 tbsp of the butter or margarine. Return to the pan and keep warm.

Meanwhile, rinse the fish and wipe with kitchen paper (paper towels). Make several slashes on each side. Place on foil on a grill (broiler) rack. Melt the remaining butter or margarine with the parsley, some salt and pepper and the lemon rind. Brush over the fish. Grill (broil) for 5 minutes. Turn over and grill the other sides until cooked through, brushing with more butter mixture as the fish cooks. Spoon a pool of gooseberry sauce on to each of four serving plates. Lay a fish on top and serve hot with Sauté Potatoes and peas.

Sizzling lobster with citrus fire butter

SERVES 4

350 g/12 oz spring (collard) greens, finely shredded
Oil, for deep-frying
Coarse sea salt and freshly ground black pepper
100 g/4 oz/½ cup butter
Finely grated rind and juice of 1 large orange
1 red chilli, seeded and finely chopped
1 green chilli, seeded and finely chopped
2 cooked lobsters, about 700 g/1½ lb each
30 ml/2 tbsp sunflower oil
1 lemon and 1 orange, cut into wedges, to garnish
Jacket potatoes with soured (dairy sour) cream and chives, to serve

Wash the greens and dry thoroughly on kitchen paper (paper towels). Deep-fry a little at a time in hot oil for 2–3 minutes until crisp (be careful because it will spit). Drain on kitchen paper. Sprinkle with a little sea salt and toss gently. Keep warm. Mash the butter with the orange rind and chillies. Season with a little pepper. Cut the lobsters into halves lengthways and remove the stomach sac and the black vein that runs the length of the body (page 15). Brush all over with the sunflower oil and drizzle the flesh with the orange juice.

Place on foil on the grill (broiler) rack. Cover with more foil and grill (broil) for 5 minutes. Remove the foil cover. Spread the butter mixture over the flesh and grill until the butter is melted and sizzling. Put the crispy greens in a layer on four serving plates. Top each with half a lobster and garnish with orange and lemon wedges. Serve hot with jacket potatoes with soured cream and chives.

Ocean beach crab cakes with lemon mayo

SERVES 4

120 ml/4 fl oz/½ cup mayonnaise
Finely grated rind and juice of 1 large lemon
2 × 170 g/6 oz/small cans of white crabmeat, drained
100 g/4 oz/2 cups fresh white breadcrumbs
200 g/7 oz/1 small can of pimientos, drained and chopped
30 ml/2 tbsp snipped chives
15 ml/1 tbsp chopped parsley
1.5 ml/¼ tsp cayenne
Salt and freshly ground black pepper
A little milk, if necessary
45 ml/3 tbsp soured (dairy sour) cream
30 ml/2 tbsp sunflower oil

Put 90 ml/6 tbsp of the mayonnaise in a bowl with half the lemon juice. Add the crabmeat, half the breadcrumbs, the pimientos and herbs. Mix thoroughly and season to taste with the cayenne and salt and pepper. Moisten with a little milk, if necessary. Shape into eight small cakes and coat in the remaining breadcrumbs. Chill until ready to cook.

Mix the remaining mayonnaise with the lemon rind and remaining juice, the soured cream and seasoning to taste. Chill. Lay a sheet of foil on the grill (broiler) and brush with some of the oil. Add the crab cakes, brush with oil and turn over. Brush again. Cook for about 4 minutes on each side until browned and cooked through. Serve with the chilled lemon mayo.

Ginger-lime salmon fillet with fresh pineapple

SERVES 6

3 limes
30 ml/2 tbsp sesame oil
15 ml/1 tbsp olive oil
10 ml/2 tsp grated fresh root ginger
1 small garlic clove, crushed
30 ml/2 tbsp clear honey
15 ml/1 tbsp light soy sauce
6 small salmon fillets, about 150 g/
    5 oz each, skinned
1 small pineapple
30 ml/2 tbsp sesame seeds
15 ml/1 tbsp snipped chives
Small bunch of chives
Freshly ground black pepper
Thai Fragrant Rice (page 392),
    to serve

Finely grate the rind from one of the limes and squeeze the juice from two. Cut the remaining one into six slices, discarding both ends. Put the lime rind and juice in a large, shallow container. Mix in the oils, ginger, garlic, honey and soy sauce. Lay the salmon in the dish and turn to coat with the marinade. Cover and chill for 1 hour, turning once.

Meanwhile, cut all the skin off the pineapple and cut the flesh into six slices. Discard the tough central core. Toast the sesame seeds and mix with the snipped chives. Make a hole in the centre of each reserved lime slice and push a few long chives through so the lime is like a ring round the centre. Lay the fish, skinned-side up, and the pineapple slices in a single layer on foil on the grill (broiler). Cook for 6 minutes, brushing the fish with the remaining marinade during cooking and turning the pineapple once, until the fish is tender and the pineapple is turning golden.

Transfer the fish to serving plates. Top each with a slice of pineapple and a sprinkling of sesame seeds and snipped chives. Lay one of the chive and lime garnishes to one side of each and serve straight away with Thai Fragrant Rice.

Crunchy sardines with lemon

SERVES 4-6

1 kg/2¼ lb fresh sardines, cleaned and
    heads removed
Finely grated rind and juice of 1 small
    lemon
Salt and freshly ground black pepper
50 g/2 oz/1 cup oat bran
50 g/2 oz/1 cup cornflakes, crushed
30 ml/2 tbsp sesame seeds
30 ml/2 tbsp olive oil
Lemon wedges and parsley sprigs, to
    garnish

Rinse the sardines and pat dry on kitchen paper (paper towels). Lay on a baking (cookie) sheet, sprinkle with the lemon rind and juice and season with salt and pepper. Mix the oat bran with the cornflakes and sesame seeds. Brush the sardines with the oil, then coat completely in the oat bran mixture. Lay the fish in an oiled, hinged wire rack (two at a time, if necessary). Grill (broil) for 5-6 minutes on each side until golden and cooked through. Garnish with lemon wedges and parsley sprigs and serve.

Grilled salmon with dill

SERVES 4

45 ml/3 tbsp chopped dill (dill weed)
40 g/1½ oz/3 tbsp light brown sugar
Salt and freshly ground black pepper
4 salmon steaks
45 ml/3 tbsp cider vinegar
15 g/½ oz/1 tbsp butter or margarine,
  melted
Mixed lettuce leaves and lemon
  wedges, to garnish

Mix the dill with the sugar and some salt and pepper. Rub all over the salmon and leave to marinate for 2 hours. Place on foil on a grill (broiler) rack. Mix together the cider vinegar and butter or margarine and brush all over the salmon. Grill (broil) for about 6–8 minutes, brushing frequently with the vinegar mixture, until golden and cooked through. Transfer to warm plates and garnish with mixed lettuce leaves and lemon wedges.

Salmon with pesto and wine sauce

SERVES 4

4 salmon steaks
1 quantity of Pesto (page 377, or use
  bought)
150 ml/¼ pt/⅔ cup red wine
Buttered Noodles for Fish (page 394)
  and mixed salad, to serve

Place the salmon in a shallow dish. Mix together the Pesto and wine and spoon over the salmon. Marinate for 1 hour. Lift out of the dish and place on foil on a grill (broiler) rack. Grill (broil) for about 6–8 minutes or until tender. Heat the marinade until bubbling. When the fish is cooked, transfer to plates and spoon the marinade over. Serve with Buttered Noodles for Fish and a mixed salad.

Coriander pesto mullet

SERVES 4

Prepare as for Salmon with Pesto and Wine Sauce, but substitute red mullet fillets for the salmon steaks, Coriander Pesto (page 377) for the Pesto and use white wine instead of red.

Grilled salmon with rocket hollandaise

SERVES 4

25 g/1 oz rocket leaves
4 salmon tail fillets, about 175 g/6 oz
  each
Salt and freshly ground black pepper
2 eggs
30 ml/2 tbsp lemon juice
100 g/4 oz/½ cup butter or margarine,
  melted
30 ml/2 tbsp chopped parsley
New potatoes and mangetout (snow
  peas), to serve

Reserve a few rocket leaves for garnish and finely chop the remainder. Put the salmon on foil on the grill (broiler) rack and season lightly. Grill (broil) for about 5–6 minutes until cooked through. Do not overcook. Meanwhile, whisk the eggs in a saucepan with the lemon juice. Place over a gentle heat and gradually whisk in the butter or margarine, whisking all the time, until thick and creamy. Do not allow to boil. Remove from the heat and stir in the chopped rocket, the parsley and salt and pepper to taste. Transfer the fish to warm plates. Spoon a little of the sauce over and garnish with the reserved rocket leaves. Serve with new potatoes and mangetout.

Cod with prawns and parsley pesto

SERVES 4

4 cod steaks
100 g/4 oz cooked peeled prawns
  (shrimp), chopped
60 ml/4 tbsp fresh white breadcrumbs
5 ml/1 tsp anchovy essence (extract)
5 ml/1 tsp tomato purée (paste)
Salt and freshly ground black pepper
15 ml/1 tbsp milk
15 g/½ oz/1 tbsp butter or margarine
1 quantity of Parsley Pesto (page 377)

Wipe the fish with kitchen paper (paper towels) and place on foil on a grill (broiler) rack. Mix the prawns with the breadcrumbs, anchovy essence, tomato purée and a little salt and pepper. Moisten with the milk to form a firm stuffing. Pack into the cavities in the cod steaks. Dot with the butter or margarine and grill (broil) for 5 minutes. Carefully turn the fish and stuffing over, using a fish slice. Spread the Parsley Pesto over. Grill for a further 10 minutes until cooked through and bubbling. Serve with all the juices spooned over.

Red snapper with red almond pesto

SERVES 4

4 red snapper, cleaned and scaled
1 quantity of Red Almond Pesto
  (page 378)
15 ml/1 tbsp olive oil
15 ml/1 tbsp lemon juice
Coarse sea salt
30 ml/2 tbsp toasted flaked (slivered)
  almonds
Rocket salad, to serve

Rinse the fish inside and out. Spoon the pesto inside each fish. Mix together the oil and lemon juice. Lay the fish on foil on the grill (broiler) rack and brush with the oil and lemon juice. Grill (broil) for about 7 minutes on each side until cooked through and golden, brushing with oil and lemon juice during cooking. Transfer to warm plates. Scatter coarse sea salt and the toasted almonds over and serve with a rocket salad.

Grilled sweet peppers with king prawns, olives and sunflower seeds

SERVES 4

2 red (bell) peppers, quartered
1 yellow pepper, quartered
1 green pepper, quartered
Olive oil, for brushing
225 g/8 oz raw peeled tiger prawns
  (jumbo shrimp), tails left on
30 ml/2 tbsp sliced stoned (pitted)
  black olives
30 ml/2 tbsp sunflower seeds
5 ml/1 tsp coarse sea salt
Lemon wedges, to garnish
Aioli (page 372), to serve

Place the pepper quarters on foil on a grill (broiler) rack and brush liberally with olive oil until glistening. Grill (broil) for about 6 minutes, turning once, until slightly charred and soft. Add the prawns to the grill after 3 minutes, brush with oil and turn once during cooking. Transfer to a serving platter and scatter the olives, sunflower seeds and salt over. Garnish with lemon wedges and serve with Aioli.

Scallops with bacon and parsley pesto

SERVES 4

16 large shelled scallops
4 back bacon rashers (slices), rinded
15 ml/1 tbsp olive oil
15 ml/1 tbsp lemon juice
Salt and freshly ground black pepper
2 carrots, pared into thin ribbons with
  a potato peeler
2 courgettes (zucchini), pared into thin
  ribbons with a potato peeler
1 quantity of Parsley Pesto (page 377)
15–30 ml/1–2 tbsp hot water

Rinse the scallops and dry on kitchen paper (paper towels). Leave them whole and lay on foil on a grill (broiler) rack with the bacon. Whisk together the oil, lemon juice and a little salt and pepper and brush over the scallops. Grill (broil) for 2 minutes. Turn the scallops and bacon over and grill for a further 2 minutes or until the scallops are opaque and just turning lightly golden and the bacon is golden.

Meanwhile, blanch the carrot and courgette ribbons in lightly salted, boiling water for 2 minutes. Drain. Heat the pesto in a small saucepan with enough of the hot water to thin to a thick pouring sauce. Put a pile of carrot and courgette in the centre of four warm plates. Arrange the scallops on top and lay a rasher of bacon to the side of each. Trickle the sauce round the edge and serve.

Red mullet with fennel

SERVES 4

1 lemon
4 red mullet, cleaned and scaled
60 ml/4 tbsp olive oil
1 small onion, finely chopped
Salt and freshly ground black pepper
2 fennel bulbs, thickly sliced
25 g/1 oz/2 tbsp butter or margarine,
  melted
15 ml/1 tbsp chopped parsley
Plain potatoes, to serve

Grate the rind from the lemon. Cut off all the pith and separate the fruit into slices. Cut the slices in half. Wipe the fish with kitchen paper (paper towels) and make several slashes on each side with a sharp knife. Place in a shallow dish. Pour the oil over and sprinkle with the lemon rind, the onion and seasoning. Turn over in the oil and leave to marinate while preparing the rest of the dish.

Cook the fennel slices in lightly salted, boiling water for 3 minutes. Drain. Lay a sheet of foil on the grill (broiler) rack. Brush with some of the butter or margarine. Lay the fennel slices on this and brush with more butter or margarine. Grill (broil) for about 5 minutes, turning once, until golden brown. Top with the lemon pieces, brush again and grill until turning golden. Wrap in the foil and keep warm in a low oven.

Put a clean sheet of foil on the grill. Lay the fish on this and grill for 5 minutes on each side until golden and cooked through. Transfer the fennel with lemon and the mullet to warm plates. Sprinkle the fennel with the parsley and serve straight away with plain potatoes.

Santa Rosa salmon

SERVES 6

50 g/2 oz/¼ cup butter, softened
6 salmon fillets, about 175 g/6 oz
  each, skinned
Finely grated rind and juice of 1 small
  lemon
Salt and freshly ground black pepper
175 g/6 oz button mushrooms, sliced
1 bunch of spring onions (scallions),
  chopped
30 ml/2 tbsp capers
30 ml/2 tbsp chopped parsley
5 ml/1 tsp dried marjoram
150 ml/¼ pt/⅔ cup soured (dairy sour)
  cream
50 g/2 oz/1 small jar of red lumpfish
  roe

Smear six sheets of foil with some of
the butter. Lay a salmon fillet on
each. Sprinkle with the lemon rind
and juice, some seasoning, the
mushrooms, onions, capers, parsley
and marjoram. Dot with the
remaining butter. Fold the foil over
the ingredients and roll the edges
tightly together to seal. Cook under
a preheated grill (broiler) for
12–15 minutes, turning once.
Transfer the parcels to individual
plates. Open at the table and top
each with a good dollop of soured
cream, then a spoonful of lumpfish
roe.

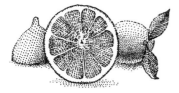

Barbie-stewed striped bass with herbs

SERVES 6

You can use any firm-fleshed fish
fillets for this recipe and, despite its
name, you can of course cook it
under the grill (broiler) or on top of
the stove if you prefer.

2 shallots, finely chopped
15 g/½ oz/1 tbsp butter or margarine
1 kg/2¼ lb striped bass fillets, skinned
  and boned
120 ml/4 fl oz/½ cup dry white wine
150 ml/¼ pt/⅔ cup chicken stock
1 small lemon, sliced
15 ml/1 tbsp finely chopped sage
15 ml/1 tbsp finely chopped parsley
Salt and freshly ground black pepper
15 ml/1 tbsp cornflour (cornstarch)
30 ml/2 tbsp water
Small sage sprigs, to garnish

Fry (sauté) the shallots in the butter
or margarine in a shallow,
flameproof dish or frying pan
(skillet) suitable for putting on the
barbecue for
2 minutes, stirring, to soften.
Remove from the heat. Lay the fish
fillets, just overlapping, on top. Pour
the wine and stock over. Lay the
lemon slices on top and sprinkle
with the herbs, a little salt and some
pepper. Cover loosely with foil and
cook on the barbecue for about
30 minutes until the fish is tender
and cooked through. Carefully
transfer to individual plates. Blend
together the cornflour and water, stir
into the juices and boil for 1 minute,
stirring. Taste and re-season if
necessary. Spoon over the fish and
serve garnished with small sage
sprigs.

Tropical stuffed trout

SERVES 4

4 large spring (collard) green leaves
4 rainbow trout, cleaned
Juice of 1 small lime
15 ml/1 tbsp light soy sauce
15 ml/1 tbsp medium-dry sherry
1 ripe avocado, peeled, stoned (pitted)
* and sliced*
1 slightly green banana, sliced
Oil, for greasing
Freshly ground black pepper
Lime wedges, to garnish
Wild Rice Mix for Fish (page 394),
* green salad and a few cooked peeled*
* prawns (shrimp), to serve*

Cut out any thick central base stalk from the leaves. Blanch the leaves in boiling water for 3 minutes. Drain, rinse with cold water and drain again. Rinse the fish and pat dry with kitchen paper (paper towels). Cut off the heads, if preferred. Mix the lime juice with the soy sauce and sherry and use to brush the fish inside and out. Stuff the body cavities with the avocado and banana slices. Oil the shiny side of four large pieces of foil and lay a leaf on each. Put a fish on each leaf and drizzle with any remaining lime juice mixture. Add a good grinding of pepper. Wrap up in the leaves, then foil to form secure parcels. Grill (broil) for 25 minutes, turning once after 15 minutes. Transfer the parcels to plates, unwrap and serve hot with Wild Rice Mix and a green salad topped with a few prawns.

Sharp prawn and scallop kebabs

SERVES 4

15 ml/1 tbsp cumin seeds
Finely grated rind and juice of 1 lemon
1 small onion, grated
15 ml/1 tbsp chopped coriander
* (cilantro)*
15 ml/1 tbsp chopped parsley
5 ml/1 tsp caster (superfine) sugar
25 g/1 oz/2 tbsp butter or margarine,
* melted*
Salt and freshly ground black pepper
225 g/8 oz raw peeled tiger prawns
* (jumbo shrimp)*
225 g/8 oz shelled scallops
Rice salad, to serve

Toss the cumin seeds in a dry frying pan (skillet) until lightly browned. Tip into a bowl and crush lightly with a pestle or the end of a rolling pin. Mix with the lemon rind and juice, onion, herbs, sugar, butter or margarine and a little salt and pepper. Add the seafood and toss well to coat completely. Leave to marinate for 2 hours. Thread on to soaked wooden skewers and place on foil on the grill (broiler) rack. Grill (broil) for about 5 minutes, turning occasionally, until cooked through. Serve with a rice salad.

Citrus seafood kebabs

SERVES 4

8 large shelled scallops
1 orange, ends discarded, cut into
   8 slices
8 raw peeled king prawns (jumbo
   shrimp)
1 lemon, ends discarded, cut into
   8 slices
175 g/6 oz monkfish, cut into 8 cubes
15 g/½ oz/1 tbsp butter or margarine,
   melted
15 ml/1 tbsp balsamic vinegar
15 ml/1 tbsp stoned (pitted) black
   olives, finely chopped
1 small onion, finely chopped
15 ml/1 tbsp chopped parsley
Garlic Bread (page 395) and melon,
   cucumber and tomato salad, to serve

Thread a scallop on to each of four
soaked wooden skewers, then add a
slice of orange to each. Slide on a
prawn, then a slice of lemon, then a
cube of monkfish. Repeat the
threading. Mix together the butter or
margarine and vinegar and brush
over the kebabs. Grill (broil) for
4–6 minutes, turning once, until
cooked through and lightly golden,
brushing with the mixture during
cooking. Mix together the olives,
onion and parsley. Transfer the
kebabs to four plates and sprinkle
with the olive mixture before serving
with Garlic Bread and a melon,
cucumber and tomato salad.

Santa Barbara seafood kebabs

SERVES 4

8 large shelled scallops
4 thin slices of pancetta or streaky
   bacon rashers (slices), halved
1 orange, ends discarded, cut into
   8 slices
8 raw peeled king prawns (jumbo
   shrimp)
2 kiwi fruit, peeled and cut into
   8 slices
175 g/6 oz tuna steak, cut into 8 cubes
15 ml/1 tbsp olive oil
15 ml/1 tbsp balsamic vinegar
15 ml/1 tbsp finely chopped capers
1 small onion, finely chopped
15 ml/1 tbsp chopped parsley
Plain Rice for Fish (page 392), to serve

Roll each scallop in half a slice of
pancetta or bacon. Thread one on
each of four soaked wooden
skewers, then add a slice of orange
to each. Slide on a prawn, then a
slice of kiwi, then a cube of tuna.
Repeat the threading. Mix together
the oil and vinegar and brush over
the kebabs. Place on foil on the grill
(broiler) rack and grill (broil) for
4–6 minutes until cooked through
and lightly golden, brushing with
more oil and vinegar during cooking.
Mix together the capers, onion and
parsley. Transfer the kebabs to
serving plates and sprinkle with the
caper mixture before serving with
Plain Rice for Fish.

Fresh tuna, lime and coriander kebabs

SERVES 4

450 g/1 lb tuna, cubed
Finely grated rind and juice of 1 lime
30 ml/2 tbsp chopped coriander
  (cilantro)
15 g/½ oz/1 tbsp butter or margarine,
  melted
15 ml/1 tbsp clear honey
Salt and freshly ground black pepper
Sauté Potatoes (page 389) and mixed
  leaf salad, to serve

Put the tuna in a shallow dish. Whisk together the remaining ingredients and pour over. Toss and leave to marinate for 2 hours. Thread the tuna on to soaked wooden skewers. Place on foil on the grill (broiler) rack. Grill (broil) for about 6 minutes, turning and basting occasionally, until cooked through. Serve with Sauté Potatoes and a mixed leaf salad.

Prawn and artichoke kebabs

SERVES 4

425 g/15 oz/1 large can of artichoke
  hearts, drained
16 raw peeled king prawns (jumbo
  shrimp), tails left on
30 ml/2 tbsp olive oil
15 ml/1 tbsp lemon juice
10 ml/2 tsp paprika
Freshly ground black pepper
Lemon wedges, to garnish
Avocado Cream (page 372) and mixed
  salad, to serve

Halve the artichoke hearts and pat dry with kitchen paper (paper towels). Thread alternately on soaked wooden skewers with the prawns. Place on foil on the grill

(broiler) rack. Whisk together the oil, lemon juice, paprika and a little pepper. Brush over the kebabs. Grill (broil) for 4–6 minutes, turning occasionally and brushing with the oil and lemon juice, until golden and the prawns are cooked through. Garnish with lemon wedges and serve with Avocado Cream and a mixed salad.

Jack Daniels swordfish

SERVES 4

175 ml/6 fl oz/¾ cup bourbon
175 ml/6 fl oz/¾ cup fish or chicken
  stock
25 g/1 oz/2 tbsp butter or margarine,
  melted
1 large garlic clove, crushed
Salt and freshly ground black pepper
4 swordfish steaks
30 ml/2 tbsp chopped parsley
Perfect Potato Wedges for Fish
  (page 389) and crisp green salad,
  to serve

Mix together the bourbon and stock with the butter or margarine, garlic and a little salt and pepper. Add the fish, turn to coat completely and leave to marinate for 2 hours. Lift out of the marinade and place on the grill (broiler) rack. Grill (broil) for about 10–15 minutes, turning once, until browned and cooked through. Meanwhile, boil the remaining marinade until reduced and thickened. Stir in the parsley. Transfer the steaks to warmed plates, spoon the sauce over and serve with Perfect Potato Wedges for Fish and a crisp green salad.

Summer waters swordfish steaks

SERVES 4

4 swordfish steaks
15 ml/1 tbsp Chinese five-spice powder
15 ml/1 tbsp sesame oil
45 ml/3 tbsp sunflower oil
30 ml/2 tbsp lemon juice
100 g/4 oz beansprouts
1 red (bell) pepper, finely shredded
2 spring onions (scallions), finely sliced
30 ml/2 tbsp light soy sauce
Jacket potatoes and Prawn Mayonnaise (page 376), to serve

Wipe the fish with kitchen paper (paper towels) and remove the skin. Mix the five-spice powder with half of each of the oils and half the lemon juice. Brush all over the fish and leave to marinate for 2 hours. Mix the beansprouts with the pepper and spring onion. Whisk together the soy sauce and the remaining oils and lemon juice. Grill (broil) for 3–4 minutes on each side, turning once and brushing with any remaining marinade, until cooked through. Add the soy dressing to the beansprout mixture and toss gently. Spoon on to plates. Transfer the swordfish to the plates and serve with jacket potatoes topped with Prawn Mayonnaise.

Mackerel with buttery horseradish

SERVES 4

4 mackerel, cleaned
4 thyme sprigs
30 ml/2 tbsp sunflower oil
30 ml/2 tbsp horseradish relish
5 ml/1 tsp lemon juice
A pinch of salt
Freshly ground black pepper
50 g/2 oz/¼ cup butter or margarine
30 ml/2 tbsp chopped parsley
New potatoes and green salad, to serve

Wash the fish inside and out and pat dry with kitchen paper (paper towels). Make several slashes in the fish on each side. Push a sprig of thyme inside the body cavity of each. Lay in a shallow dish. Mix the oil with half the horseradish, the lemon juice, salt and lots of pepper. Pour over the fish, turn to coat completely and leave to marinate in a cool place for at least 2 hours. Remove from the marinade and lay on foil on the grill (broiler) rack. Grill (broil) for 10–15 minutes, turning once, until cooked through, brushing with any remaining marinade during cooking.

Meanwhile, put the butter or margarine in a small saucepan with the remaining horseradish, the parsley and a good grinding of pepper. Heat until melted, stirring to blend. Transfer the cooked fish to plates and spoon the horseradish sauce over. Serve with new potatoes and a green salad.

Grilled mackerel with sweet mustard sauce

SERVES 4

4 equal-sized mackerel, cleaned
Salt and freshly ground black pepper
1 quantity of Sweet Mustard Sauce
(page 383)
10 ml/2 tsp black mustard seeds
Plain potatoes and broccoli, to serve

Make several slashes in the mackerel on each side. Place on foil on a grill (broiler) rack and season with salt and pepper. Grill (broil) for about 5 minutes on each side until cooked through and golden brown.

Meanwhile, make the Sweet Mustard Sauce. Transfer the mackerel to warm plates, spoon the sauce over and sprinkle with the mustard seeds. Serve with plain potatoes and broccoli.

Grilled mackerel with tomatoes and horseradish mayo

SERVES 4

4 equal-sized mackerel, cleaned
Salt and freshly ground black pepper
4 tomatoes
30 ml/2 tbsp mayonnaise
30 ml/2 tbsp fromage frais
10 ml/2 tsp horseradish relish
New potatoes and French (green)
beans, to serve

Make several slashes in the mackerel on each side and season with salt and pepper. Place on foil on the grill (broiler) rack. Grill (broil) for about 5 minutes on each side until cooked through and golden. Meanwhile, cut a cross in the rounded end of each tomato and add to the grill pan for the last 4 minutes of cooking. Mix the mayonnaise with the fromage frais and horseradish. Season to taste with salt and pepper. Transfer the mackerel and tomatoes to warm serving plates. Put a spoonful of the horseradish mayo to the side of each and serve with new potatoes and French beans.

Grilled cod with grainy mustard

SERVES 4

4 pieces of cod fillet, about 175 g/6 oz
each
50 g/2 oz/¼ cup butter or margarine
30 ml/2 tbsp wholegrain mustard
15 ml/1 tbsp chopped parsley
5 ml/1 tsp light brown sugar
Salt and freshly ground black pepper
Lemon wedges, to garnish
Sauté Potatoes (page 389) and peas,
to serve

Lay the cod, skin-side up, on foil on the grill (broiler) rack. Dot with 15 g/½ oz/1 tbsp of the butter or margarine and grill (broil) for 3 minutes. Turn the fish over. Mash the remaining butter or margarine with the mustard, parsley, sugar and a little salt and pepper. Spread over the flesh and grill for about 4–5 minutes until sizzling, golden and cooked through. Transfer to warm plates, garnish with lemon wedges and serve with Sauté Potatoes and peas.

Mackerel with chick peas

SERVES 4

4 equal-sized mackerel, cleaned
Salt and freshly ground black pepper
425 g/15 oz/1 large can of chick peas
   (garbanzos), drained
60 ml/4 tbsp passata (sieved tomatoes)
15 ml/1 tbsp tomato purée (paste)
1 garlic clove, crushed
5 ml/1 tsp dried thyme
15 ml/1 tbsp chopped parsley
Lemon wedges, to garnish
Crusty French bread, to serve

Make several slashes on each side of
the mackerel, then season with salt
and pepper. Grill (broil) for about
5 minutes on each side until cooked
through and golden brown.
Meanwhile, put the chick peas in a
saucepan with all the remaining
ingredients. Bring to the boil and
cook for about 3 minutes until the
chick peas are bathed in sauce.
Season to taste. Spoon on to warm
plates and top with the mackerel.
Garnish with lemon wedges and
serve with lots of crusty French
bread.

Scallops with bacon

SERVES 4

12 shelled scallops
6 streaky bacon rashers (slices), rinded
   and halved
425 g/15 oz/1 large can of artichoke
   hearts, drained and halved
30 ml/2 tbsp olive oil
15 ml/1 tbsp lemon juice
Freshly ground black pepper

Halve the scallops and wrap each
half in half a bacon rasher. Thread
with the artichokes on four skewers.
Mix together the oil, lemon juice and
a little pepper and brush all over the
kebabs. Lay the kebabs on foil on
the grill (broiler) rack. Grill (broil)
just until the bacon is cooked,
turning and brushing with the oil
and lemon juice. Serve hot.

Chinese-style marlin steaks

SERVES 4

4 marlin steaks
15 ml/1 tbsp sesame seeds
15 ml/1 tbsp grated fresh root ginger
1 garlic clove, crushed
15 ml/1 tbsp dry sherry
15 ml/1 tbsp sesame oil
45 ml/3 tbsp sunflower oil
30 ml/2 tbsp lemon juice
100 g/4 oz beansprouts
1 green (bell) pepper, finely shredded
2 spring onions (scallions), finely
   sliced
1 carrot, grated
30 ml/2 tbsp light soy sauce
30 ml/2 tbsp toasted sesame seeds

Wipe the fish with kitchen paper
(paper towels) and remove the skin.
Mix the sesame seeds with the
ginger, garlic, sherry and half the
oils and half the lemon juice. Brush
all over the fish and leave to
marinate for 2 hours. Mix the
beansprouts with the green pepper,
spring onions and carrot. Whisk
together the soy sauce and the
remaining oils and lemon juice.
Place on foil on the grill (broiler)
rack. Grill (broil) the fish for
3–4 minutes on each side, turning
once and brushing with any
remaining marinade, until cooked
through. Add the soy dressing to the
beansprout mixture and toss gently.
Spoon on to four plates. Transfer the
marlin to the plates and sprinkle
with the toasted sesame seeds.

Mackerel with horseradish

SERVES 4

4 mackerel, cleaned
4 thyme sprigs
30 ml/2 tbsp sunflower oil
30 ml/2 tbsp horseradish relish
5 ml/1 tsp lemon juice
Salt and freshly ground black pepper
50 g/2 oz/¼ cup butter or margarine
30 ml/2 tbsp chopped parsley
Plain potatoes and French (green) beans, to serve

Wash the fish inside and out and pat dry with kitchen paper (paper towels). Make several slashes in each side of the fish. Push a sprig of thyme inside the body cavity of each. Lay in a shallow dish. Mix the oil with half the horseradish, the lemon juice, a pinch of salt and lots of pepper. Pour over the fish, turn to coat completely and leave to marinate in a cool place for 2 hours. Place on foil on the grill (broiler) rack. Grill (broil) for 10–15 minutes, turning once and brushing with any remaining marinade, until cooked through.

Meanwhile, put the butter or margarine in a small saucepan with the remaining horseradish, the parsley and a good grinding of pepper. Heat until melted, stirring to blend. Transfer the cooked fish to serving plates and spoon the horseradish sauce over. Serve with plain potatoes and French (green) beans.

Leicestershire cod

SERVES 4

40 g/1½ oz/3 tbsp butter or margarine, softened
4 pieces of cod fillet, about 175 g/6 oz each, skinned
75 g/3 oz/⅓ cup red Leicester cheese, grated
15 ml/1 tbsp milk
30 ml/2 tbsp snipped chives
Salt and freshly ground black pepper
1.5 ml/¼ tsp cayenne
3 tomatoes, sliced
Sauté Potatoes (page 389) and peas, to serve

Grease a shallow flameproof dish, large enough to hold the fish in a single layer, with 15 g/½ oz/1 tbsp of the butter or margarine. Lay the fish, skinned-side up, in the dish and grill (broil) for 3 minutes. Turn the fish over. Mash the remaining butter or margarine with the cheese, milk and chives and season with a little salt and pepper and the cayenne. Spread over the fish and arrange the tomato slices round the edge. Grill for a further 8–10 minutes until bubbling, golden and cooked through. Serve hot with Sauté Potatoes and peas.

Creech pollack

SERVES 4

Prepare as for Leicestershire Cod, but substitute pollack for the cod and Cheddar for Leicestershire cheese and add 30 ml/2 tbsp sweet chutney to the mixture. Use parsley instead of chives and a dash of Tabasco sauce instead of the cayenne.

Italian grilled prawns

SERVES 4

8 thin slices of Parma ham
24 raw peeled tiger prawns (jumbo shrimp)
A good pinch of cayenne
15 ml/1 tbsp lemon juice
Freshly ground black pepper
30 ml/2 tbsp olive oil
Sun-dried Tomato and Basil Butter (page 386)
Lemon wedges and rocket leaves, to garnish
Crispy Noodle Cake (page 395), to serve

Cut each slice of ham into three strips lengthways. Toss the prawns in the cayenne, lemon juice and lots of black pepper. Roll up each in a piece of ham. Thread on four soaked wooden skewers. Place on foil on the grill (broiler) rack and brush with the oil. Grill (broil) for 5 minutes, turning occasionally and brushing with a little more oil, until just cooked through. Meanwhile, make the Sun-dried Tomato and Basil Butter, but melt it in a saucepan instead of rolling and chilling it. Transfer the kebabs to warm plates. Pour the flavoured butter over. Garnish with lemon wedges and rocket leaves and serve with Crispy Noodle Cake.

English grilled prawns

SERVES 4

Prepare as for Italian Grilled Prawns but use 12 smoked streaky bacon rashers (slices), rinded, instead of the Parma ham. Stretch them with the back of a knife and cut in halves. Serve the kebabs with melted Tarragon Butter (page 384) instead of Sun-dried Tomato and Basil Butter and serve with Plain Rice for Fish (page 392) instead of the Crispy Noodle Cake.

Plaice with creamed mushroom sauce

SERVES 4

100 g/4 oz mushrooms, sliced
2 spring onions (scallions), chopped
50 g/2 oz/¼ cup butter or margarine
15 g/½ oz/2 tbsp plain (all-purpose) flour
150 ml/¼ pt/⅔ cup milk
150 ml/¼ pt/⅔ cup single (light) cream
Salt and freshly ground black pepper
30 ml/2 tbsp chopped parsley
4 small whole plaice
Parsley sprigs, to garnish
Speciality Creamed Potatoes (page 391) and sautéed courgettes (zucchini), to serve

Fry (sauté) the mushrooms and spring onions in half the butter or margarine for 5 minutes, stirring, until soft but not brown. Remove four of the mushroom slices and reserve for garnish. Stir in the flour and cook for 1 minute, stirring. Remove from the heat and gradually blend in the milk and cream. Return to the heat, bring to the boil and cook for 2 minutes, stirring. Season to taste. Stir in the chopped parsley. Put the plaice on foil on the grill (broiler) rack, dot with the remaining butter or margarine and season lightly. Grill (broil) for 3 minutes on each side until cooked through. Transfer to warm plates, spoon the sauce over and garnish with the reserved mushrooms and the parsley sprigs. Serve hot with Speciality Creamed Potatoes and sautéed courgettes.

Lemon-tabasco whiting

SERVES 4

4 whiting fillets, about 175 g/6 oz each
5 ml/1 tsp Tabasco sauce
Finely grated rind and juice of 1 lemon
15 g/½ oz/1 tbsp butter or margarine
Salt and freshly ground black pepper
12 spring onions (scallions), trimmed
   but left whole
Crispy Noodle Cake (page 394),
   to serve

Lay the fish in a shallow dish.
Sprinkle with the Tabasco sauce and
the lemon rind and juice. Leave to
marinate for at least 30 minutes.
Place on foil on a grill (broiler) rack
and dot with half the butter or
margarine. Add the spring onions to
the grill and dot with the remaining
butter or margarine. Grill (broil) for
about 6 minutes, turning the onions
half-way through cooking, until the
fish is cooked and the onions are
browning. Serve hot with Crispy
Noodle Cake.

Lemon-barbecue whiting

SERVES 4

4 whiting fillets, about 175 g/6 oz each
Finely grated rind of ½ lemon
30 ml/2 tbsp bottled barbecue sauce
¼ cucumber
10 g/¼ oz/2 tsp butter or margarine
Perfect Potato Wedges for Fish
   (page 389) and baby corn cobs,
   to serve

Put the whiting in a shallow dish
and sprinkle with the lemon rind.
Brush with half the sauce and leave
to marinate for at least 30 minutes.
Place on foil on a grill (broiler) rack
and brush with the remaining sauce.
Cut the cucumber lengthways into
quarters and dot with the butter or
margarine. Grill (broil) for about
6 minutes until the fish is cooked.
Transfer the fish and cucumber to
warm plates and serve with Perfect
Potato Wedges for Fish and baby
corn cobs.

Lyme Regis grill

SERVES 4

900 g/2 lb mussels, cleaned (page 13)
1 onion, finely chopped
120 ml/4 fl oz/½ cup dry cider
60 ml/4 tbsp water
4 pieces of cod fillet, about 175 g/6 oz
  each
Juice of ½ lemon
Salt and freshly ground black pepper
40 g/1½ oz/3 tbsp butter or margarine
15 g/½ oz/2 tbsp plain (all-purpose)
  flour
90 ml/6 tbsp crème fraîche
A little milk (optional)
100 g/4 oz cooked peeled prawns
  (shrimp)
15 ml/1 tbsp chopped parsley
30 ml/2 tbsp grated Cheddar cheese
30 ml/2 tbsp crushed bran flakes

Put the mussels in a large pan with the onion, cider and water. Cover, bring to the boil, reduce the heat and cook for 5 minutes, shaking the pan until the mussels open. Remove from the shells, discarding any that have not opened. Strain the liquid into a measuring jug.

Meanwhile, lay the cod on foil on a grill (broiler) rack. Sprinkle with the lemon juice and season. Dot with half the butter or margarine. Grill (broil) for 5 minutes or until cooked through. Do not turn over.

Meanwhile, melt the remaining butter or margarine in a saucepan. Blend in the flour and cook for 1 minute. Remove from the heat and blend in the reserved mussel liquid and the crème fraîche. Bring to the boil and cook for 1 minute, stirring. Thin with a little milk, if necessary, to give a thick coating consistency.

Stir in the mussels and prawns and heat through. Season to taste and stir in the parsley. Lay the fish in a flameproof dish, pour the sauce over and cover with the cheese and branflakes. Grill for about 3–5 minutes until golden and bubbling. Serve straight away.

Grilled herrings with parsnip chips

SERVES 4

4 large herrings, cleaned and scaled
Juice of 1 small lemon
Salt and freshly ground black pepper
4 sprigs of fresh thyme
4 parsnips, cut into thin matchsticks
Oil, for deep-frying
Coarse sea salt
Lemon wedges and parsley sprigs, to
  garnish

Wash the fish in cold water and pat dry with kitchen paper (paper towels). Make several slashes in each side of the herrings. Season the insides with salt and pepper and tuck a sprig of thyme in each. Place on a grill (broiler) rack and grill (broil) for about 3 minutes on each side until golden and crisp on the outside and the flesh is tender. Meanwhile, heat the oil until a cube of day-old bread browns in 30 seconds. Add the parsnips and fry (sauté) for about 5 minutes until golden brown and crisp. Remove with a draining spoon and drain on kitchen paper. Transfer the herrings and parsnip chips (fries) to warm plates, garnish with lemon wedges and parsley sprigs and serve.

Nutty cheese cod

SERVES 4

40 g/1½ oz/3 tbsp butter or margarine
4 pieces of cod fillet, about 175 g/
  6 oz each, skinned
Freshly ground black pepper
50 g/2 oz/½ cup Cheddar cheese, grated
15 ml/1 tbsp plain yoghurt
30 ml/2 tbsp chopped walnuts
2 spring onions (scallions), finely
  chopped
3–4 tomatoes, sliced
Plain potatoes and peas, to serve

Grease a large flameproof dish with
a little of the butter or margarine
and lay the fish in a single layer in
the dish, skinned-sides up. Dot with
15 g/½ oz/1 tbsp of the butter or
margarine and sprinkle with pepper.
Grill (broil) for 2 minutes. Turn over.
Mash the remaining butter or
margarine with the cheese, yoghurt,
walnuts and onions and add a little
pepper. Spread all over the fish and
return to the grill (broiler), reduce
the heat and grill for a further
5 minutes. Arrange the tomatoes all
round the edge and return to the
grill for 5 minutes or until bubbling,
golden and cooked through. Serve
hot with plain potatoes and peas.

Hake dolcelatte

SERVES 4

75 g/3 oz/⅓ cup butter or margarine
4 pieces of hake fillet, about 175 g/
  6 oz each, skinned
10 ml/2 tsp lemon juice
225 g/8 oz Dolcelatte cheese
60 ml/4 tbsp single (light) cream
15 ml/1 tbsp chopped parsley
Salt and freshly ground black pepper

Use a little of the butter or
margarine to grease a large piece of
foil on the grill (broiler) rack. Lay
the hake, skinned-sides up, on the
foil. Dot with a third of the
remaining butter or margarine and
sprinkle with the lemon juice. Grill
(broil) for 5 minutes until almost
cooked. Meanwhile, mash the
remaining butter or margarine with
the Dolcelatte, cream and parsley.
Season with a little salt and lots of
pepper. Carefully turn the fish over
and spread with the Dolcelatte
mixture. Grill for a further
5–8 minutes or until the cheese has
melted and is turning golden brown.

Pasta and rice

All types of pasta and rice make wonderful foundations for fish dishes. Here you'll find recipes from all over the world, from voluptuous Italian specialities to the spicy creations of the Middle and Far East. Again, none take very long to prepare and all fish need only a few minutes' cooking to become tender. The trick with any of these recipes is not to overcook them or your pasta will become soggy and limp and your rice stodgy and sticky.

Prawn pilau

SERVES 4

175 g/6 oz/¾ cup long-grain rice
Salt and freshly ground black pepper
25 g/1 oz/¼ cup flaked (slivered)
* almonds*
15 g/½ oz/1 tbsp butter or margarine
2 onions, thinly sliced
1 large tomato, chopped
1 green (bell) pepper, chopped
50 g/2 oz/⅓ cup sultanas (golden
* raisins)*
2.5 ml/½ tsp curry powder
A good pinch of ground turmeric
225 g/8 oz cooked peeled prawns
* (shrimp)*

Cook the rice in plenty of boiling salted water for 10 minutes until just tender. Drain, rinse with boiling water and drain again. Brown the almonds in a large non-stick frying pan (skillet), stirring all the time. Remove from the pan and reserve. Heat the butter or margarine in the pan and fry (sauté) the onions for 3 minutes until lightly golden. Add the tomato, green pepper, sultanas and spices and fry for 1 minute. Stir in the rice and prawns and toss over a gentle heat for 5 minutes. Season with pepper and serve very hot.

Monkfish and mushroom pilau

SERVES 4

Prepare as for Prawn Pilau, but substitute 175 g/6 oz monkfish and 100 g/4 oz button mushrooms, quartered, for the prawns (shrimp) and add them with the tomato and spices.

Hake byriani

SERVES 4

1 onion, sliced
10 ml/2 tsp sunflower oil
10 ml/2 tsp ground turmeric
1 garlic clove, crushed
2.5 ml/½ tsp ground ginger
2.5 ml/½ tsp ground cumin
2.5 ml/½ tsp ground coriander
* (cilantro)*
150 ml/¼ pt/⅔ cup plain yoghurt
Salt and freshly ground black pepper
6 pieces of hake fillet, about 175 g/
* 6 oz each*
225 g/8 oz/1 cup long-grain rice
30 ml/2 tbsp currants
30 ml/2 tbsp flaked (slivered) almonds
Lettuce, sliced tomatoes and cucumber,
* to serve*

Fry (sauté) the onion in the oil for 3 minutes. Add 7.5 ml/1½ tsp of the turmeric and all the remaining ingredients except the hake, rice, currants and almonds. Bring to the boil, then reduce the heat and simmer for 15 minutes, stirring occasionally (the mixture will curdle at first). Add the hake and cook for a further 5 minutes until the mixture is almost dry and the fish is just cooked.

Meanwhile, cook the rice in plenty of boiling salted water, to which the remaining turmeric has been added, for 10 minutes or until the grains are just tender but still have some 'bite'. Drain. Dry-fry the currants and almonds in a frying pan (skillet) until the nuts are golden, stirring all the time, then remove from the heat immediately to prevent over-browning. Spoon the rice on to warm plates. Pile the hake mixture on top and sprinkle with the nuts and currants. Serve with a side salad of lettuce, tomatoes and cucumber.

Riviera cod and rice

15 ml/1 tbsp olive oil
1 onion, chopped
2 garlic cloves, crushed
1 red (bell) pepper, sliced
*600 ml/1 pt/2½ cups passata (sieved
  tomatoes)*
15 ml/1 tbsp tomato purée (paste)
150 ml/¼ pt/⅔ cup water
225 g/8 oz/1 cup long-grain rice
Salt and freshly ground black pepper
*450 g/1 lb cod fillet, skinned and
  cubed*
30 ml/2 tbsp chopped parsley
Black olives, to garnish

Heat the oil in a saucepan. Add the onion, garlic and red pepper and fry (sauté), stirring, for 2 minutes. Stir in the passata, tomato purée, water, rice and a little salt and pepper. Cover and cook gently, stirring occasionally, for 10 minutes. Add the fish and, if the mixture is getting dry, a little more water. Season with salt and pepper and cook for a further 5 minutes until all the liquid has been absorbed and the rice and fish are cooked. Serve sprinkled with the chopped parsley and garnished with a few black olives.

Sunshine mountains

*350 g/12 oz golden cutlets (smoked
  whiting) or smoked cod*
150 ml/¼ pt/⅔ cup milk
225 g/8 oz/1 cup long-grain rice
5 ml/1 tsp ground turmeric
*320 g/12 oz/1 large can of sweetcorn
  (corn) with (bell) peppers, drained*
Salt and freshly ground black pepper
4 eggs
Oil, for shallow-frying

Put the fish in a saucepan. Add the milk, cover and simmer gently for about 10 minutes until the fish is tender. Drain, reserving the liquid. Flake the fish, discarding the skin and any bones. Cook the rice in plenty of lightly salted, boiling water, to which the turmeric has been added, for 10 minutes or until tender. Drain, rinse with boiling water and drain again. Return to the pan Add the sweetcorn, fish and some salt and pepper. Add 60 ml/ 4 tbsp of the fish cooking milk and stir gently until piping hot. Meanwhile, fry (sauté) the eggs in a little hot oil. Pile the rice mixture on to four warm plates, top each with an egg and serve.

Cod piri piri

SERVES 4

450 g/1 lb cod fillet, skinned and diced
45 ml/3 tbsp plain (all-purpose) flour
Salt and freshly ground black pepper
30 ml/2 tbsp olive oil
1 large onion, chopped
1 green (bell) pepper, finely chopped
1 garlic clove, crushed
6 streaky bacon rashers (slices), rinded and diced
1 bay leaf
A pinch of ground mace
1 green chilli, seeded and chopped
200 ml/7 fl oz/scant 1 cup of milk
225 g/8 oz/1 cup long-grain rice
225 g/8 oz/1 small can of chopped tomatoes
300 ml/½ pt/1¼ cups chicken stock

Toss the cod in the flour, seasoned with a little salt and pepper. Fry (sauté) in half the oil in a flameproof casserole dish (Dutch oven) for 3 minutes, stirring, until lightly golden. Remove from the pan with a draining spoon. Add the remaining oil and fry the onion, pepper and garlic for 3 minutes. Add the bacon and fry for 1 minute, stirring. Add any remaining flour from the fish dish and the bay leaf, mace and chilli and stir in enough of the milk to form a thick sauce, stirring all the time. Discard the bay leaf. Gently fold in the fish. Season well and bake uncovered at 200°C/ 400°F/gas mark 6 for about 30 minutes until brown and bubbling. Put the rice in a separate flameproof casserole. Make the tomatoes up to 450 ml/¾ pt/ 2 cups with the stock. Bring to the boil, season lightly, cover and cook in the oven with the fish for 20–30 minutes until tender and the rice has absorbed all the liquid.

South of the border casserole

SERVES 4

350 g/12 oz/1½ cups long-grain rice
50 g/2 oz/¼ cup butter or margarine
3 celery sticks, chopped
2 onions, chopped
1 small red (bell) pepper, chopped
295 g/10½ oz/1 medium can of condensed cream of celery soup
150 ml/¼ pt/⅔ cup milk
450 g/1 lb raw peeled king prawns (jumbo shrimp)
30 ml/2 tbsp chopped coriander (cilantro)
Cayenne
Salt and freshly ground black pepper

Cook the rice in plenty of boiling salted water for 10 minutes until just tender. Drain, rinse with boiling water and drain again. Meanwhile, melt the butter or margarine in a saucepan and fry (sauté) the celery, onions and red pepper for 4 minutes until soft and lightly golden. Blend the soup with the milk, add to the pan and bring to the boil. Reduce the heat, add the prawns, cover and simmer gently for 15 minutes. Add the coriander and rice and heat through, stirring. Season to taste with cayenne, salt and pepper, pile on to warm serving plates and serve straight away.

Tangy monkfish with saffron rice

SERVES 4

*50 g/2 oz/¼ cup unsalted (sweet)
butter*
*1 bunch of spring onions (scallions),
chopped*
225 g/8 oz/1 cup long-grain rice
*600 ml/1 pt/2½ cups hot fish or
chicken stock*
2.5 ml/½ tsp saffron powder
*100 g/4 oz French (green) beans,
chopped*
*450 g/1 lb monkfish, cut into bite-sized
pieces*
300 ml/½ pt/1¼ cups milk
2 limes
30 ml/2 tbsp cornflour (cornstarch)
*300 ml/½ pt/1¼ cups single (light)
cream*
Salt and freshly ground black pepper
Watercress sprigs, to garnish

Melt 15 g/½ oz/1 tbsp of the butter
in a saucepan. Add the spring
onions and fry (sauté) for 2 minutes,
stirring. Add the rice and cook for
1 minute, stirring. Add the stock and
saffron, bring to the boil and simmer
for 5 minutes. Add the beans and
continue cooking for a further
5 minutes or until the rice is tender.
Drain off any excess stock. Press the
rice into a lightly greased ring
mould, press down well, cover
with foil and keep warm.

Meanwhile, cook the fish in the
milk for 5–10 minutes until just
tender. Drain off the milk into a
clean saucepan. Grate the rind and
squeeze the juice of one of the
limes. Blend the cornflour with a
little water, stir into the milk and
add the cream. Bring to the boil and
simmer for 1 minute. Add the
remaining butter in small flakes,
stirring, until melted. Stir in the lime
rind and juice and season lightly.
Fold in the fish. Turn the rice ring
out on to a serving dish and pile the
fish into the centre. Cut the
remaining lime into wedges and use
with watercress sprigs to garnish the
ring.

Golden kedgeree

SERVES 4

225 g/8 oz/1 cup long-grain rice
5 ml/1 tsp ground turmeric
*225 g/8 oz smoked cod, haddock or
whiting fillet, skinned*
*3 hard-boiled (hard-cooked) eggs,
roughly chopped*
45 ml/3 tbsp evaporated milk
Salt and white pepper
Grated nutmeg
30 ml/2 tbsp chopped parsley

Cook the rice in plenty of lightly
salted, boiling water, to which the
turmeric has been added, for
10 minutes or until just cooked.
Drain and return to the saucepan.
Meanwhile, poach the fish in water
for 5–10 minutes until it flakes easily
with a fork. Drain and break up,
discarding any bones. Stir the fish
into the rice with all the remaining
ingredients except the parsley. Heat
through, stirring gently. Serve
garnished with the parsley.

Poached egg and mushroom kedgeree

SERVES 4

350 g/12 oz undyed smoked haddock
  fillet
75 g/3 oz/⅓ cup butter or margarine
1 onion, sliced
100 g/4 oz button mushrooms, sliced
225 g/8 oz/1 cup long-grain rice
1.5 ml/¼ tsp cayenne
Salt and freshly ground black pepper
10 ml/2 tsp lemon juice
300 ml/½ pt/1¼ cups water
2.5 ml/½ tsp grated nutmeg
4 eggs
20 ml/4 tsp single (light) cream
10 ml/2 tsp chopped coriander
  (cilantro)

Skin and dice the fish, discarding
any bones. Melt the butter or
margarine in a large frying pan
(skillet) and fry (sauté) the onion for
2 minutes, stirring, until lightly
softened. Add the mushrooms and
fry for a further 2 minutes, stirring.
Stir in the rice, fish, cayenne, salt
and pepper, lemon juice and water.
Bring to the boil, reduce the heat,
cover and cook gently for
20 minutes or until the rice has
absorbed nearly all the water. Stir in
the nutmeg. Make four wells in the
rice mixture. Break an egg into each
and top each with 5 ml/1 tsp of the
cream. Cover and cook gently for
10–15 minutes, depending on how
well-cooked you like your eggs.
Sprinkle with the coriander and
serve straight from the pan.

Salmon and dill kedgeree

SERVES 4–6

450 g/1 lb salmon tail fillet
900 ml/1½ pts/3¾ cups water
30 ml/2 tbsp sunflower oil
1 bunch of spring onions (scallions),
  diagonally sliced
350 g/12 oz/1½ cups long-grain rice
4 hard-boiled (hard-cooked) eggs,
  quartered
1 dill pickle, chopped
30 ml/2 tbsp single (light) cream
25 g/1 oz/2 tbsp butter or margarine,
  flaked
15 ml/1 tbsp chopped dill (dill weed)
Salt and freshly ground black pepper
15 ml/1 tbsp chopped parsley

Cook the fish in the water for
10 minutes or until just tender.
Drain, reserving the cooking liquid.
Remove the skin and any bones
from the fish and break into biggish
chunks. Heat the oil in a large pan
and fry (sauté) the spring onions for
3 minutes, stirring. Add the rice and
cook for 1 minute, stirring. Add the
fish cooking liquid, bring to the boil,
reduce the heat, cover and simmer
for 15–20 minutes or until the rice is
cooked and has absorbed all the
liquid. Add the fish, eggs, dill pickle,
cream, butter or margarine, chopped
dill, a little salt and a good grinding
of pepper. Stir gently, then heat
through for 3–4 minutes. Sprinkle
with the parsley and serve hot.

White fish kedgeree

SERVES 4

225 g/8 oz white fish fillet
225 g/8 oz/1 cup long-grain rice
3 hard-boiled (hard-cooked) eggs,
  roughly chopped
15 ml/1 tbsp chopped parsley
45 ml/3 tbsp single (light) cream
Salt and freshly ground black pepper

Put the fish in a pan with just
enough water to cover. Cook gently
for 10 minutes until the fish is
tender. Drain and flake, discarding
the skin and any bones. Meanwhile,
cook the rice in plenty of boiling
salted water until just tender. Drain,
rinse with boiling water, drain again
and return to the pan. Add the eggs
and fish to the rice and stir in the
parsley and cream. Season to taste,
heat through and serve hot.

Quick party paella

SERVES 4

120 g/4½ oz/1 packet of savoury
  vegetable rice
450 ml/¾ pt/2 cups boiling water
100 g/4 oz/1 cup cooked chicken, diced
250 g/9 oz/1 medium can of mussels
  in brine, drained
100 g/4 oz cooked peeled prawns
  (shrimp)
15 ml/1 tbsp chopped parsley

Put the rice in a saucepan with the
boiling water. Stir, cover and simmer
for 12 minutes. Add all the
remaining ingredients except the
parsley, cover and simmer gently for
a further 8 minutes until the liquid
has been absorbed and the rice is
tender. Fluff up with a fork and
sprinkle with the parsley before
serving.

Smoked haddock and mushroom rice soufflé

SERVES 4

225 g/8 oz smoked haddock fillet
Sunflower oil, for brushing
100 g/4 oz button mushrooms, chopped
25 g/1 oz/2 tbsp butter or margarine
25 g/1 oz/¼ cup plain (all-purpose)
  flour
150 ml/¼ pt/⅔ cup milk
2.5 ml/½ tsp made English mustard
5 ml/1 tsp ground turmeric
1.5 ml/¼ tsp dried mixed herbs
Salt and freshly ground black pepper
75 g/3 oz/¾ cup cooked long-grain rice
3 eggs, separated

Brush the fish with oil and grill
(broil) until just tender, turning
once. Flake the fish, discarding the
skin and any bones. Fry (sauté) the
mushrooms in the butter or
margarine for 2 minutes, stirring.
Stir in the flour and cook for
1 minute. Remove from the heat and
blend in the milk. Return to the
heat, bring to the boil and cook for
2 minutes, stirring, until thick. Stir
in the mustard, turmeric, herbs and
a little salt and pepper. Stir in the
rice and beat in the egg yolks. Stir in
the fish. Whisk the egg whites until
stiff and fold in with a metal spoon.
Pour into a greased 1.2 litre/2 pt/5
cup soufflé dish and bake at 190°C/
375°F/gas mark 5 for 35 minutes
until risen and golden brown. Serve
straight away.

Paella Valencia

SERVES 6

3 chicken portions, each cut into
  2 pieces
60 ml/4 tbsp olive oil
1 onion, finely chopped
1 red (bell) pepper, diced
1 green pepper, diced
350 g/12 oz/1½ cups paella, risotto or
  long-grain rice
450 g/1 lb mussels in their shells,
  cleaned (page 13)
About 1 litre/1¾ pts/4¼ cups chicken
  stock
5 ml/1 tsp saffron powder
4 tomatoes, skinned, seeded and
  chopped
100 g/4 oz/1 cup frozen peas
Salt and freshly ground black pepper
1 bay leaf
1 marjoram sprig
100 g/4 oz chorizo sausage, sliced
100 g/4 oz cooked peeled prawns
  (shrimp)
425 g/15 oz/1 large can of artichoke
  hearts, drained and halved
Lemon wedges and 6 cooked unpeeled
  prawns, to garnish

Brown the chicken pieces in the oil
in a paella pan or large frying pan
(skillet). Remove from the pan. Fry
(sauté) the onion in the oil until soft
and lightly golden. Stir in the peppers
and rice and cook, stirring, for
2 minutes. Return the chicken to the
pan, add the mussels and enough
stock to cover the ingredients. Stir in
the saffron, tomatoes, peas and a
little salt and pepper and add the bay
leaf and marjoram. Bring to the boil,
reduce the heat, cover and simmer
gently for 20 minutes or until the rice
is cooked and has absorbed nearly all
the liquid. Add a little more stock
during cooking if necessary.

Remove the mussels, snap off the
top shells and keep the mussels

warm in the bottom shells. Discard
any mussels that have not opened,
and the bay leaf and marjoram. Stir
the chorizo, peeled prawns and
artichokes into the rice mixture and
heat through. Return the mussels in
their shells to the paella and garnish
with lemon wedges and the unpeeled
prawns before serving.

Creamy squid risotto

SERVES 4

450 g/1 lb baby squid, cleaned (page 14)
15 g/½ oz/1 tbsp butter or margarine
1 onion, finely chopped
1 leek, finely chopped
1 beefsteak tomato, skinned and finely
  chopped
1 large garlic clove, crushed
150 ml/¼ pt/⅔ cup dry white wine
450 ml/¾ pt/2 cups water
175 g/6 oz/¾ cup risotto rice
5 ml/1 tsp tomato purée (paste)
Salt and freshly ground black pepper
15 ml/1 tbsp chopped parsley

Cut the squid into rings and chop
the tentacles. Heat the butter or
margarine in a wide, shallow pan.
Add the onion and leek and fry
(sauté) gently, stirring, for 2 minutes
to soften. Add the squid, chopped
tomato and garlic and fry gently for
1 minute, stirring. Add the wine and
150 ml/¼ pt/⅔ cup of the water.
Bring to the boil, reduce the heat,
cover and simmer gently for
20 minutes. Add the rice and stir in
the tomato purée and a little salt and
pepper. Simmer, uncovered, until the
liquid is absorbed, stirring regularly.
Add a little more of the remaining
water and simmer again until
absorbed. Repeat, adding the water
a little at a time until the rice is just
tender and creamy (this will take
about 20 minutes). Stir in the
parsley and serve.

Seafood pilau

SERVES 4

900 g/2 lb mussels, cleaned (page 13)
120 ml/4 fl oz/½ cup dry white wine
300 ml/½ pt/1¼ cups water
1 small bay leaf
1 celery stick, chopped
About 300 ml/½ pt/1¼ cups fish stock
50 g/2 oz/¼ cup butter or margarine
1 onion, finely chopped
225 g/8 oz/1 cup long-grain rice
100 g/4 oz button mushrooms, sliced
225 g/8 oz raw peeled tiger prawns
    (jumbo shrimp), tails left on
8 raw unpeeled prawns (shrimp)
15 ml/1 tbsp chopped fresh parsley

Put the mussels in a pan with the wine, water, bay leaf and celery. Bring to the boil, cover, reduce the heat and cook for 5 minutes, shaking the pan occasionally until the mussels open. Remove half the mussels from their shells and break off the top shell of the remainder. Discard any that have not opened. Strain the cooking liquid through a piece of kitchen paper (paper towel) in a sieve (strainer). Make up to 600 ml/1 pt/2½ cups with stock.

 Melt the butter or margarine in a large, flameproof casserole dish (Dutch oven) and fry (sauté) the onion for 2 minutes, stirring. Stir in the rice and mushrooms and cook for 1 minute, stirring, until every grain of rice is coated. Add the tiger prawns and pour on the stock. Bring to the boil, cover and place in a preheated oven at 190°C/375°F/gas mark 5 for 15 minutes. Stir in the mussels and unpeeled prawns, add a little more stock if necessary and season to taste. Return to the oven for 5 minutes or until the rice has absorbed the liquid and is tender. Fluff up with a fork, sprinkle with parsley and serve.

Seafood risotto

SERVES 6

You can use four baby octopus if you prefer. They are usually sold ready-prepared.

45 ml/3 tbsp olive oil
1 large garlic clove
1 small onion, finely chopped
450 g/1 lb squid, cleaned (page 14),
    sliced and tentacles chopped
1 small cleaned octopus, sliced and
    tentacles chopped
225 g/8 oz raw peeled prawns
    (shrimp)
50 g/2 oz/½ cup chopped parsley
Salt and freshly ground black pepper
250 ml/8 fl oz/1 cup dry white wine
1.2 litres/2 pts/5 cups boiling chicken
    stock
450 g/1 lb/2 cups risotto rice
Lemon wedges, to garnish

Heat the oil in a large, flameproof casserole dish (Dutch oven). Add the whole garlic clove and the onion and fry (sauté) gently for 2 minutes. Add the seafood, parsley, a little salt and pepper, the wine and 250 ml/ 8 fl oz/1 cup of the chicken stock. Bring to the boil, reduce the heat and simmer gently for about 6 minutes or until the liquid has evaporated. Remove the garlic clove. Stir in the rice and cook for 1 minute. Add a quarter of the remaining stock and simmer, stirring, until it has been absorbed. Repeat the process until the rice is just tender and all the stock has been absorbed (this will take about 20 minutes). Remove from the heat, taste and re-season if necessary. Serve garnished with lemon wedges.

Creamy prawn risotto

SERVES 4

Prepare as for Creamy Squid Risotto (page 292), but substitute raw, peeled tiger prawns (jumbo shrimp) for the squid.

Chinese prawn fried rice

SERVES 4–6

30 ml/2 tbsp sunflower oil
½ bunch of spring onions (scallions), chopped
100 g/4 oz mushrooms, chopped
1 small red (bell) pepper, chopped
1 small green pepper, chopped
450 g/1 lb/4 cups cooked long-grain rice
100 g/4 oz cooked peeled prawns (shrimp)
100 g/4 oz/1 cup cooked ham, diced
2.5 ml/½ tsp ground ginger
1.5 ml/¼ tsp cayenne
Salt

Heat the oil in a large frying pan (skillet) or wok. Add the onions, mushrooms and peppers. Fry (sauté) for 2 minutes, stirring. Add the rice and fry, stirring, for 3 minutes. Add the remaining ingredients, adding salt to taste, and cook, stirring, for about 4 minutes until piping hot.

Black risotto with squid

SERVES 4–6

700 g/1½ lb squid, cleaned (page 14), reserving the ink sacs
30 ml/2 tbsp olive oil
1 garlic clove
1 small onion, finely chopped
Salt and freshly ground black pepper
375 ml/13 fl oz/1½ cups dry white wine
450 g/1 lb/2 cups risotto rice
900 ml/1½ pts/3¾ cups boiling water
15 g/½ oz/1 tbsp unsalted (sweet) butter
100 g/4 oz/1 cup Parmesan cheese, grated

Empty the ink sacs into a bowl. Slice the squid bodies into rings and chop the tentacles. Heat the oil in a large, flameproof casserole dish (Dutch oven). Add the whole garlic clove and the onion and fry (sauté) for 3 minutes until golden. Remove the garlic and discard. Add the squid to the pan and fry for 2 minutes, stirring. Season with salt and pepper, add the wine and simmer very gently for about 20 minutes until the squid is tender.

Add the rice and stir for 1 minute. Stir in a quarter of the water and simmer, stirring occasionally, until it has been absorbed. Add the ink and some more water and simmer, stirring until absorbed. Repeat this process until the rice is just tender (this will take about 20 minutes). Remove from the heat and stir in the butter and cheese. Serve straight away.

At-home seafood thermidor

SERVES 6

2 celery sticks, chopped
1 bunch of spring onions (scallions), chopped
1 small green (bell) pepper, chopped
100 g/4 oz/½ cup butter or margarine
30 ml/2 tbsp plain (all-purpose) flour
250 ml/8 fl oz/1 cup single (light) cream
60 ml/4 tbsp white wine
1 bay leaf
200 g/7 oz/1 small can of pimientos, drained and chopped
50 g/2 oz/½ cup strong Cheddar cheese, grated
A good pinch of cayenne
5 ml/1 tsp Worcestershire sauce
170 g/6 oz/1 small can of white crabmeat
175 g/6 oz cooked peeled prawns (shrimp)
250 g/9 oz/1 medium can of mussels in brine, drained
185 g/6½ oz/1 small can of tuna, drained
Salt and freshly ground black pepper
50 g/2 oz/1 cup fresh white breadcrumbs
350 g/12 oz/1½ cups long-grain rice
5 ml/1 tsp ground turmeric
15 ml/1 tbsp chopped parsley

Fry (sauté) the celery, spring onions and green pepper in half the butter or margarine for 3 minutes, stirring, until softened but not browned. Blend in the flour and cook for 1 minute. Stir in the cream, wine and bay leaf. Bring to the boil and simmer for 2 minutes until thickened, stirring all the time. Stir in the pimientos, cheese, cayenne, Worcestershire sauce and the seafood. Season to taste. Remove the bay leaf and turn the mixture into an ovenproof dish. Sprinkle with the breadcrumbs and dot with the remaining butter or margarine. Bake at 160°C/325°F/gas mark 3 for 40 minutes or until the top is golden.

Meanwhile, cook the rice in plenty of boiling water, to which the turmeric has been added, for 10 minutes or until just tender. Drain and fluff up with a fork. Sprinkle with the parsley and serve with the seafood.

Scallop stir-fry

SERVES 4

225 g/8 oz/1 cup long-grain rice
8 spring onions (scallions), cut into diagonal pieces
225 g/8 oz beansprouts
2 carrots, cut into matchsticks
1 celery stick, cut into matchsticks
60 ml/4 tbsp sunflower oil
16 queen scallops
15 ml/1 tbsp dry sherry
1.5 ml/¼ tsp grated fresh root ginger
10 ml/2 tsp light soy sauce
Juice of 1 lime
Salt and freshly ground black pepper

Cook the rice in plenty of boiling salted water until just tender. Drain, rinse with boiling water, drain again and cover with a clean cloth. Keep hot.

Meanwhile, stir-fry the spring onions, beansprouts, carrots and celery in 45 ml/3 tbsp of the sunflower oil in a wok or large frying pan (skillet) for 3 minutes. Push to one side. Add the remaining oil, heat, then add the scallops and stir-fry for 2 minutes. Add the sherry, ginger, soy sauce, lime juice and a little salt and pepper and cook, stirring, for 1 minute. Spoon the rice into small bowls, top with the scallops and vegetables and serve straight away.

Nashville baked seasoned trout

SERVES 4

175 g/6 oz/¾ cup brown rice
50 g/2 oz/½ cup pine nuts
100 g/4 oz button mushrooms, chopped
4 stoned (pitted) black olives, chopped
5 ml/1 tsp lime juice
Salt and freshly ground black pepper
5 ml/1 tsp paprika
1.5 ml/¼ tsp cayenne
4 trout, cleaned
Olive oil, for brushing
Lime wedges, to garnish

Cook the rice in plenty of boiling salted water for about 40 minutes until tender. Drain well. Mix with the pine nuts, mushrooms, olives, lime juice, a little salt and pepper, the paprika and cayenne. Use to stuff the trout, then lay them in an oiled roasting tin (pan). Brush with oil, cover with foil and bake at 180°C/ 350°F/gas mark 4 for 20–25 minutes until cooked through. Serve garnished with lime wedges.

Southern states shrimp

SERVES 4

225 g/8 oz/1 cup long-grain rice
50 g/2 oz/¼ cup butter or margarine
30 ml/2 tbsp sunflower oil
2 onions, chopped
1 garlic clove, crushed
2 celery sticks, chopped
15 ml/1 tbsp plain (all-purpose) flour
2 × 400 g/14 oz/large cans of chopped tomatoes
1 bay leaf
1.5 ml/¼ tsp dried thyme
1 red chilli, seeded and chopped
100 g/4 oz mushrooms, chopped
200 g/7 oz/1 small can of pimientos, drained and diced
450 g/1 lb raw peeled prawns (shrimp)
Salt and freshly ground black pepper

Cook the rice in plenty of boiling salted water until tender. Drain, rinse with boiling water, drain again and return to the pan. Cook over a gentle heat for 1 minute to dry out, then stir in the butter or margarine and fluff up with a fork. Meanwhile, heat the oil in a saucepan. Add the onions, garlic and celery and fry (sauté) for 3 minutes, stirring, until golden. Add the flour and cook for 1 minute. Stir in the tomatoes, bay leaf, thyme, chilli, mushrooms and pimientos and simmer for 5 minutes, stirring occasionally. Add the prawns and cook for a further 5 minutes. Season to taste. Spoon the rice into bowls and spoon the prawn mixture over.

New Orleans seafood gumbo

SERVES 6

25 g/1 oz/2 tbsp butter or margarine
175 g/6 oz okra (ladies' fingers), cut
    into 1 cm/½ in pieces
1 bunch of spring onions (scallions),
    chopped
1 garlic clove, crushed
1 small green (bell) pepper, diced
15 ml/1 tbsp plain (all-purpose) flour
100 g/4 oz/½ cup passata (sieved
    tomatoes)
30 ml/2 tbsp tomato purée (paste)
450 ml/¾ pt/2 cups chicken stock
1 bay leaf
15 ml/1 tbsp chopped parsley
Salt and freshly ground black pepper
1.5 ml/¼ tsp chilli powder
6–12 oysters in their shells
225 g/8 oz cooked peeled prawns
    (shrimp)
225 g/8 oz fresh crabmeat
350 g/12 oz/1½ cups long-grain rice

Melt the butter or margarine in a
large pan. Add the okra, spring
onions, garlic and green pepper and
fry (sauté) for 3 minutes until
softened. Stir in the flour and cook
for 1 minute. Blend in the passata,
tomato purée and stock. Add the
herbs and seasonings and simmer
very gently for 20 minutes. Carefully
shuck the oysters, reserving the juice
(page 00). Add to the pan with the
prawns and crabmeat. Simmer for a
further 20 minutes until thick and a
rich colour. Discard the bay leaf.
    Meanwhile, cook the rice in
plenty of boiling salted water until
tender. Drain, rinse with boiling
water and drain again. Fluff up with
a fork. Spoon the rice into large
bowls and spoon the gumbo on top.

Plaice with tomato and corn rice

SERVES 4

175 g/6 oz/¾ cup long-grain rice
400 g/14 oz/1 large can of chopped
    tomatoes
300 ml/½ pt/1¼ cups water
Salt and freshly ground black pepper
200 g/7 oz/1 small can of sweetcorn
    (corn)
15 ml/1 tbsp chopped parsley
8 plaice fillets, skinned if black
2 eggs, beaten
100 g/4 oz/1 cup cornmeal
Oil, for shallow-frying
Parsley sprigs and lemon wedges, to
    garnish

Put the rice in a saucepan with the
tomatoes, water and some salt and
pepper. Bring to the boil, reduce the
heat, cover and simmer gently for
20 minutes until the rice is tender
and has absorbed all the liquid. Stir
in the sweetcorn and chopped
parsley and heat through.
    Meanwhile, dip the fish fillets in
the egg, and then the cornmeal,
seasoned with a little salt and
pepper, to coat completely. Repeat, if
necessary, to give a good coating.
Heat a little sunflower oil in a large
frying pan (skillet) and fry the plaice
fillets, in batches if necessary, for
2–3 minutes on each side until
golden brown and cooked through.
Drain on kitchen paper (paper
towels) and keep warm while
cooking the remaining fish. Pile the
rice on to warm plates, top with the
fish and garnish with parsley sprigs
and lemon wedges before serving.

American shrimp with almonds

SERVES 6

120 ml/4 fl oz/½ cup sunflower oil
1 large green (bell) pepper, diced
1 onion, chopped
4 celery sticks, chopped, including leaves
120 ml/4 fl oz/½ cup bottled hot chilli sauce
75 g/3 oz/½ cup raisins
2.5 ml/½ tsp dried thyme
Salt and freshly ground black pepper
2.5 ml/½ tsp curry paste
1 bay leaf
400 g/14 oz/1 large can of chopped tomatoes
100 g/4 oz/1 cup toasted blanched almonds
700 g/1½ lb cooked peeled prawns (shrimp)
350 g/12 oz/1½ cups long-grain rice
50 g/2 oz/¼ cup butter or margarine
1 bunch of spring onions (scallions), cut into short lengths

Heat the oil in a large frying pan (skillet). Add the green pepper, onion and celery. Fry (sauté) for 2 minutes until softened but not browned. Add the chilli sauce, raisins, thyme, a little salt and pepper, the curry paste, bay leaf and tomatoes. Simmer very gently for 1 hour. Stir in the almonds and prawns and heat through.

Meanwhile, cook the rice in plenty of boiling salted water for about 10 minutes until tender. Drain, rinse with boiling water and drain again. Melt the butter or margarine in the rice saucepan, add the spring onions and fry for 2 minutes until slightly softened. Add the rice and toss well. Pile on to a serving dish and make a large nest in the centre. Spoon in the prawn and almond mixture and serve hot.

Prawn risotto

SERVES 4

20 raw unpeeled prawns (shrimp)
750 ml/1¼ pts/3 cups hot fish or chicken stock
45 ml/3 tbsp olive oil
1 onion, finely chopped
450 g/1 lb/2 cups risotto rice
450 ml/¾ pt/2 cups dry white wine
25 g/1 oz/2 tbsp unsalted (sweet) butter
Salt and freshly ground black pepper
100 g/4 oz/1 cup Parmesan cheese, grated

Cook the prawns in the stock for 3 minutes. Remove with a draining spoon, allow to cool slightly, then peel and remove the black thread down their backs (page 16). Heat the oil in a flameproof casserole dish (Dutch oven). Add the onion and fry (sauté) for 2 minutes, stirring. Stir in the rice and cook for 1 minute. Add two ladlefuls of the hot stock and simmer until it has been absorbed. Repeat until all the stock is used. Stir in the prawns and wine. Simmer for about 5 minutes until the wine is absorbed. Remove from the heat, stir in the butter, a little salt and pepper and the cheese. Serve straight away.

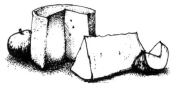

Rice with king prawn sauce

SERVES 4–6

25 g/1 oz/2 tbsp unsalted (sweet)
  butter
30 ml/2 tbsp olive oil
1 onion, finely chopped
1 celery stick, finely chopped
1 large carrot, finely chopped
120 ml/4 fl oz/½ cup brandy
250 ml/8 fl oz/1 cup dry white wine
12 raw peeled king prawns (jumbo
  shrimp)
Salt and freshly ground black pepper
1.2 litres/2 pts/5 cups chicken or fish
  stock
450 g/1 lb/2 cups risotto rice
Lemon twists

Heat half the butter with the oil in a
saucepan. Add the onion, celery and
carrot and fry (sauté) for 3 minutes,
stirring. Add the brandy, wine and
prawns. Season with salt and pepper
and simmer very gently for
15 minutes until slightly thickened.
Meanwhile, bring the stock to the
boil. Add the rice and simmer for
15–20 minutes until the rice is
tender and has absorbed the liquid.
Stir in the remaining butter and
spread out on a hot serving dish.
Spoon the prawn sauce on top and
serve straight away, garnished with
lemon twists.

Coriander mackerel with rice

SERVES 6

100 g/4 oz/2 cups fresh wholemeal
  breadcrumbs
15 ml/1 tbsp chopped coriander
  (cilantro)
6 large mackerel fillets, cut into wide
  strips
1–2 eggs, beaten
120 ml/4 fl oz/½ cup sunflower oil,
  plus extra for shallow-frying
50 g/2 oz/¼ cup butter or margarine
45 ml/3 tbsp pine nuts
450 g/1 lb/2 cups long-grain rice
1 litre/1¾ pts/4¼ cups boiling water
Salt and freshly ground black pepper
5 ml/1 tsp saffron powder
Coriander leaves and lemon wedges,
  to garnish

Mix together the breadcrumbs and
chopped coriander. Dip the mackerel
strips in the egg, then in the
breadcrumbs mixture. Chill while
preparing the rice. Heat the measured
oil in a saucepan with the butter or
margarine. Add the pine nuts and fry
(sauté) until brown. Remove from the
pan with a draining spoon and drain
on kitchen paper (paper towels). Add
the rice to the oil and butter or
margarine and fry for 1 minute. Stir
in the boiling water, a little salt and
pepper and the saffron. Bring to the
boil, reduce the heat, cover and
simmer for 20 minutes or until the
rice is tender and has absorbed the
liquid.
   Meanwhile, shallow-fry the
mackerel strips in oil until crisp and
golden. Remove from the pan with a
draining spoon. Fluff up the rice and
pile on to a serving dish, top with the
fish and drizzle with any oil left in
the pan. Garnish with coriander
leaves and lemon wedges.

Plaice goujons with turnip, orange and basil

SERVES 4

1 orange
225 g/8 oz/1 cup long-grain rice
450 ml/¾ pt/2 cups chicken stock
1 onion, finely chopped
15 g/½ oz/1 tbsp butter or margarine
1 turnip, cut into thin matchsticks
30 ml/2 tbsp orange juice
6 basil leaves, torn into small pieces
450 g/1 lb ready-crumbed plaice
  goujons

Grate the rind from the orange, then peel and separate the fruit into segments. Wash the rice well. Drain and place in a pan with the stock and orange rind. Bring to the boil, cover, reduce the heat and cook gently for 20 minutes until the stock is absorbed and the rice is tender.
   Meanwhile, fry (sauté) the onion in the butter or margarine for 2 minutes until soft but not brown. Add the turnip and cook for 1 minute. Add the orange juice, cover and simmer gently for 3–4 minutes until the turnip is almost tender but still has 'bite'. Grill (broil) the goujons, turning once. Spoon the orange rice on to serving plates and arrange the goujons to one side. Pile a little of the turnip, scattered with the basil leaves, at one side of the plates and garnish with the orange segments.

Scotch lobster

SERVES 2–4

225 g/8 oz/1 cup wild rice mix
75 g/3 oz/⅓ cup unsalted (sweet)
  butter
1 good-sized cooked lobster
60 ml/4 tbsp Scotch whisky
150 ml/¼ pt/⅔ cup double (heavy)
  cream
Salt and freshly ground black pepper

Cook the rice according to the packet directions. Drain, rinse with boiling water, drain again and return to the pan. Add 25 g/1 oz/2 tbsp of the butter and toss over a gentle heat. Pile on to warm plates. Meanwhile, remove all the meat from the lobster (page 15) and cut into chunks. Melt the remaining butter in a frying pan (skillet), add the lobster and cook gently for 2 minutes, stirring. Add the whisky and ignite. Shake the pan until the flames subside. Add the cream, a little salt and a good grinding of pepper. Bubble rapidly for 2 minutes until reduced by half. Spoon over the rice and serve straight away.

Chirashizushi (Japanese fish with rice)

SERVES 6

2 dried shiitake mushrooms
250 ml/8 fl oz/1 cup warm water
450 g/1 lb/2 cups round-grain rice
600 ml/1 pt/2½ cups cold water
45 ml/3 tbsp white wine vinegar or
  rice vinegar
60 ml/3 tbsp caster (superfine) sugar
Salt and freshly ground black pepper
30 ml/2 tbsp soy sauce
50 g/2 oz/½ cup canned bamboo
  shoots, chopped
1 small carrot, finely chopped
90 ml/6 tbsp dashi or ordinary fish
  stock
25 g/1 oz/1 cup frozen peas
5 ml/1 tsp sunflower oil
1 large egg, beaten
75 g/3 oz cooked peeled prawns
  (shrimp)
½ sheet nori (dried seaweed) or 50 g/
  2 oz spring (collard) greens,
  shredded and deep-fried until crisp

Soak the mushrooms in the warm water for 15 minutes. Rinse the rice in several changes of cold water. Drain and place in a saucepan with the cold water. Bring to the boil, cover, reduce the heat and cook gently for 15–20 minutes. Turn off the heat and leave undisturbed for 10 minutes.

Mix together the vinegar, half the sugar and 2.5 ml/½ tsp salt. When the rice is ready, add this mixture and fluff up with a fork. Meanwhile, cut off the stems from the mushrooms and discard, slice the caps and place with half the soaking water in a saucepan. Bring to the boil, add the remaining sugar and simmer for 3 minutes. Stir in half the soy sauce. Simmer until nearly all the liquid has evaporated and the mushrooms are tender. Add to the rice.

In a separate pan, simmer the bamboo shoots and carrot for 10 minutes in the remaining mushroom soaking water with the dashi or fish stock and the remaining soy sauce. Add the peas and simmer for a further 5 minutes. Drain off any excess stock and add the vegetables to the rice. Brush a frying pan (skillet) with the oil. Add the egg, sprinkle with salt and cook gently until set but not brown. Slide out of the pan and cut into fine shreds. Pile the rice on to a serving plate, top with the shredded egg and the prawns and finally the crisp nori or greens. Serve warm.

Cheesy prawns on rice

SERVES 4

225 g/8 oz cooked peeled prawns
  (shrimp)
295 g/10½ oz/1 medium can condensed
  mushroom soup
15 ml/1 tbsp tomato ketchup (catsup)
50 g/2 oz/1 cup fresh white breadcrumbs
100 g/4 oz/1 cup Cheddar cheese, grated
225 g/8 oz/1 cup long-grain rice
225 g/8 oz broccoli, cut into tiny florets
50 g/2 oz/½ cup toasted flaked
  (slivered) almonds

Mix the prawns with the soup, ketchup, half the breadcrumbs and half the cheese in a shallow, ovenproof serving dish. Sprinkle with the remaining breadcrumbs and cheese. Bake at 200°C/400°F/gas mark 6 for 20–25 minutes until golden and bubbling. Meanwhile, cook the rice in plenty of boiling salted water for 10 minutes, adding the broccoli for the last 6 minutes. Drain and mix in the almonds. Serve the rice mixture with the prawns.

Prawns in garlic butter with basil rice

SERVES 4

225 g/8 oz/1 cup long-grain rice
50 g/2 oz button mushrooms, chopped
15 ml/1 tbsp olive oil
15 ml/1 tbsp chopped basil
350 g/12 oz/1½ cups unsalted (sweet)
  butter
2 garlic cloves, crushed
150 ml/¼ pt/⅔ cup dry white wine
30 ml/2 tbsp chopped parsley
Salt and freshly ground black pepper
1 small onion, chopped
24 raw peeled king prawns (jumbo
  shrimp)
50 g/2 oz/1 cup fresh white
  breadcrumbs

Cook the rice in plenty of boiling
salted water until just tender. Drain,
rinse with boiling water, drain again
and return to the pan. Meanwhile,
fry (sauté) the mushrooms in the oil
for about 3 minutes until tender.
Add to the cooked rice with the basil
and toss thoroughly. Turn into a
serving dish and keep warm.

Meanwhile, purée the butter,
garlic, wine, parsley, a little salt and
pepper and the onion in a blender or
food processor. Spread half this
mixture in the base of a shallow
ovenproof dish. Top with the
prawns, then the remaining butter
mixture. Sprinkle with the
breadcrumbs and bake at 200°C/
400°F/gas mark 6 for 15 minutes
until golden and bubbling. Serve hot
with the basil rice.

Tiger prawns with cinnamon rice

SERVES 4

225 g/8 oz/1 cup long-grain rice
5 cm/2 in piece of cinnamon stick
30 ml/2 tbsp sunflower oil
1 garlic clove, chopped
2 leeks, sliced
3 tomatoes, skinned and chopped
60 ml/4 tbsp tomato purée (paste)
600 ml/1 pt/2½ cups fish or chicken
  stock
700 g/1½ lb raw peeled tiger prawns
  (jumbo shrimp)
Salt and freshly ground black pepper
30 ml/2 tbsp chopped parsley
Ground cinnamon, for dusting

Cook the rice in plenty of boiling
salted water, with the cinnamon
stick added, for 10 minutes or until
just tender. Drain. Meanwhile, heat
the oil in a pan, add the garlic and
leeks and fry (sauté) for 4 minutes,
stirring. Add the tomatoes and cook
for a further 3 minutes. Add the
tomato purée and stock, bring to the
boil, reduce the heat and boil rapidly
for 30 minutes or until reduced and
thickened. Add the prawns and cook
gently for a further 5–8 minutes
until cooked. Season to taste. Add
the parsley to the rice, spoon on to
serving plates and form into a nest
on each plate. Dust with cinnamon.
Spoon the prawn mixture in the
centre of each and serve straight
away.

Arabian sayadieh

SERVES 4–6

700 g/1½ lb white fish fillets, skinned
  and cubed
Grated rind and juice of 1 lemon
Salt and freshly ground black pepper
30 ml/2 tbsp plain (all-purpose) flour
120 ml/4 fl oz/½ cup sunflower oil
1 onion, chopped
225 g/8 oz/1 cup long-grain rice
450 ml/¾ pt/2 cups fish stock
2.5 ml/½ tsp ground cumin
A pinch of saffron powder
50 g/2 oz/½ cup toasted pine nuts

Put the fish in a bowl. Add the
lemon rind and juice and season
with salt. Leave to stand for
30 minutes. Drain and pat dry on
kitchen paper (paper towels). Season
the flour with a little salt and pepper
and use to coat the fish.

Heat the oil in a frying pan
(skillet) and fry (sauté) the fish until
lightly golden. Remove from the pan
with a draining spoon and drain on
kitchen paper. Add the onion to the
pan and fry until golden. Put the
fish and onion in a flameproof
casserole dish (Dutch oven). Add
the rice, stock, cumin and saffron.
Bring to the boil and simmer for
10 minutes until the rice has
absorbed nearly all the liquid, then
reduce the heat to as low as
possible, cover and simmer very
gently for about 10 minutes until the
rice is tender. Leave undisturbed for
5 minutes, then turn out on to a
serving dish and sprinkle with the
toasted pine nuts.

Prawn byriani

SERVES 6

450 g/1 lb/2 cups basmati rice
45 ml/3 tbsp sunflower oil
2 onions, thinly sliced
600 ml/1 pt/2½ cups canned coconut
  milk
300 ml/½ pt/1¼ cups chicken stock
10 curry leaves
2 green chillies, seeded and chopped
450 g/1 lb cooked peeled prawns
  (shrimp)
Salt and freshly ground black pepper

Wash and drain the rice, then soak
in cold water for 30 minutes. Drain
again. Heat the oil in a saucepan
and fry (sauté) the onions for
3 minutes until softened and golden.
Add the coconut milk and the stock.
Stir, then add the rice, curry leaves
and chillies. Bring to the boil, reduce
the heat, cover tightly and cook over
a gentle heat for 20 minutes. Quickly
stir in the prawns and re-cover. Cook
for a further 5 minutes or until the
rice is tender and has absorbed all
the liquid. Fluff up with a fork and
season to taste. Serve straight away.

Lobster byriani

SERVES 4

Prepare as for Prawn Byriani, but
substitute the meat from a 450 g/
1 lb cooked lobster for the prawns
(shrimp).

Spinach cod bake

SERVES 4

175 g/6 oz/¾ cup brown rice
1 onion, finely chopped
1 celery stick, chopped
50 g/2 oz/¼ cup butter or margarine,
*   plus extra for greasing*
450 g/1 lb frozen chopped spinach
Salt and freshly ground black pepper
A pinch of grated nutmeg
4 pieces of cod fillet, about 175 g/6 oz
*   each*
60 ml/4 tbsp boiling water
1 fish stock cube
300 ml/½ pt/1¼ cups single (light)
*   cream*
100 g/4 oz/1 cup Leerdammer cheese,
*   grated*

Cook the rice according to the
packet directions. Meanwhile, fry
(sauté) the onion and celery in the
butter or margarine for 3 minutes,
stirring. Add the spinach and cook,
stirring, for 4 minutes. Season to
taste with salt, pepper and the
nutmeg. Drain the rice and place in
a greased ovenproof dish. Spoon the
spinach mixture over the rice and
top with the fish. Blend the water
with the stock and mix in the cream.
Pour over the fish and sprinkle with
the cheese. Bake at 180°C/350°F/
gas mark 4 for about 30 minutes
until cooked through and the top is
golden and bubbling.

Salmon rice fish cakes

SERVES 4

200 g/7 oz/1 small can of pink salmon
5 ml/1 tsp anchovy essence (extract)
1 potato, boiled and mashed
100 g/4 oz/1 cup cooked long-grain rice
15 ml/1 tbsp snipped chives
15 ml/1 tbsp chopped parsley
2 eggs, beaten
Salt and freshly ground black pepper
Plain (all-purpose) flour, for dusting
50 g/2 oz/1 cup fresh white
*   breadcrumbs*
Oil, for shallow-frying
Lemon wedges, to garnish

Drain the salmon and flake the flesh,
removing the skin and bones if
preferred. Mix the fish with the
anchovy essence, potato, rice and
herbs. Add enough of one beaten
egg to bind the mixture. Season
lightly and mix again. Shape into
round cakes with floured hands.
Coat in the remaining beaten egg,
then the breadcrumbs. Shallow-fry
in hot oil until golden brown on
both sides. Drain on kitchen paper
(paper towels) and garnish with
lemon wedges.

Friday plaice with buttery rice

SERVES 4

225 g/8 oz/1 cup long-grain rice
100 g/4 oz/½ cup unsalted (sweet) butter
30 ml/2 tbsp single (light) cream
4 plaice fillets, skinned if black
30 ml/2 tbsp seasoned flour
Juice of ½ lemon
15 ml/1 tbsp chopped parsley

Cook the rice in plenty of boiling salted water until just tender. Drain and rinse with boiling water, then drain again. Return to the pan, add 50 g/2 oz/¼ cup of the butter and the cream and toss gently until well combined. Spoon into a warmed, shallow serving dish. Meanwhile, coat the plaice in seasoned flour and fry (sauté) in half the remaining butter until golden and cooked through. Lay on top of the rice. Melt the remaining butter and fry until nut brown. Add the lemon juice and parsley and spoon over the fish. Serve straight away.

Smokies supper

SERVES 4

1 onion, chopped
50 g/2 oz/¼ cup butter or margarine
225 g/8 oz/2 cups Cheddar cheese, grated
275 g/10 oz smoked trout fillets, skinned and diced
4 large tomatoes, skinned, seeded and chopped
225 g/8 oz/2 cups cooked long-grain rice
2.5 ml/½ tsp dried mixed herbs
Juice of 1 lemon
Salt and freshly ground black pepper

Fry (sauté) the onion in the butter or margarine for 2 minutes, stirring.

Mix with half the cheese and all the remaining ingredients. Pack into four individual ovenproof dishes and sprinkle with the remaining cheese. Bake at 200°C/400°F/gas mark 6 for about 20 minutes until bubbling and golden on top.

Ray in black butter with wild rice

SERVES 4

225 g/8 oz/1 cup wild rice mix
15 ml/1 tbsp chopped parsley
2 large ray wings
120 ml/4 fl oz/½ cup white wine vinegar
2 garlic cloves, crushed
1 bunch of spring onions (scallions), finely chopped
100 g/4 oz/½ cup butter or margarine
30 ml/2 tbsp capers

Cook the rice mix according to the packet directions. Drain and stir in the parsley. Meanwhile, wipe the fish with kitchen paper (paper towels). Heat the wine vinegar, garlic and spring onions in a large frying pan (skillet). Add the fish, cover and cook for 10 minutes, turning two or three times, until cooked through. Remove from the pan, reserving the juices. Scrape off the thin membrane covering the wings. Scrape the flesh off the bone into a bowl and keep warm. Melt the butter or margarine in a clean pan and heat until nut brown but do not allow to burn. Add the fish cooking juices and boil rapidly for 30 seconds. Return the fish to the pan with the rice. Toss quickly and pile on to a warm serving dish. Scatter a few capers over to garnish.

Bacon-stuffed grey mullet

SERVES 4

4 grey mullet, cleaned and scaled
8 smoked streaky bacon rashers
  (slices), rinded and finely chopped
  or minced (ground)
15 ml/1 tbsp chopped sage
50 g/2 oz/½ cup cooked long-grain rice
Salt and freshly ground black pepper
50 g/2 oz/¼ cup butter or margarine
150 ml/¼ pt/⅔ cup dry white wine
120 ml/4 fl oz/½ cup single (light)
  cream

Wipe the fish inside and out with kitchen paper (paper towels). Make several slashes on each side of the fish. Mix together the bacon and sage. Use half to spread in the slits. Mix the remainder with the rice and season well with salt and pepper. Pack into the body cavities of the fish and lay them in a baking dish, well-greased with the butter or margarine. Pour the wine over. Cover with foil and bake at 200°C/400°F/gas mark 6 for 15 minutes. Remove the foil and bake for a further 15 minutes. Pour the cream over and cook for a further 5 minutes. Serve straight away.

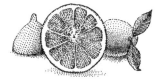

Mackerel with gooseberries and ginger rice

SERVES 4

225 g/8 oz/1 cup Thai fragrant rice
450 ml/¾ pt/2 cups boiling water
10 ml/2 tsp grated fresh root ginger
Salt and freshly ground black pepper
4 mackerel fillets
50 g/2 oz/¼ cup butter or margarine
450 g/1 lb gooseberries, topped and
  tailed
45 ml/3 tbsp water
Sugar, to taste
15 ml/1 tbsp chopped parsley
5 ml/1 tsp lemon juice

Wash the rice well, drain and place in a pan. Add the boiling water, ginger and a little salt and pepper. Bring to the boil again, cover tightly, reduce the heat to as low as possible and cook for 20 minutes. Turn off the heat and leave for 5 minutes. Meanwhile, fry (sauté) the mackerel in the butter or margarine, turning once, for about 5 minutes until cooked through. Meanwhile, cook the gooseberries in the water until they 'pop'. Stir in sugar to taste. Purée in a blender or food processor and pass through a sieve (strainer). Fluff up the ginger rice with a fork. Pile on to serving plates and lay a mackerel fillet on each. Add the parsley and lemon juice to the butter or margarine in the pan and spoon over the fish. Serve with the gooseberry purée on the side.

Summer paella

SERVES 6

450 g/1 lb mussels in their shells,
cleaned (page 13)
1.2 litres/2 pts/5 cups chicken stock
1.25 kg/2¾ lb chicken, jointed into
6 pieces
Salt and freshly ground black pepper
90 ml/6 tbsp olive oil
1 Spanish onion, finely chopped
1 garlic clove, crushed
4 baby squid, cleaned and sliced into
rings (page 14)
450 g/1 lb/2 cups risotto rice
15 ml/1 tbsp paprika
5 ml/1 tsp saffron powder
1 bay leaf
1 red (bell) pepper, sliced
1 green pepper, sliced
4 tomatoes, skinned and chopped
100 g/4 oz/1 cup shelled fresh or
frozen peas
12 cooked unpeeled prawns (shrimp)
6 black olives
Lemon wedges and chopped parsley,
to garnish
Focaccia bread and green salad, to serve

Place the mussels in a saucepan with half the stock. Bring to the boil, cover and cook for 5 minutes, shaking the pan occasionally, until the mussels have opened. Leave to cool. Wipe the chicken and season with a little salt and pepper. Heat the oil in a large paella pan or frying pan (skillet). Fry (sauté) the chicken on all sides to brown. Reduce the heat and cook for a further 10 minutes. Remove from the pan. Add the onion and garlic and fry for 2 minutes until slightly softened. Add the squid and cook for 1 minute. Stir in the rice and cook, stirring, for 1 minute until coated with oil. Strain the mussel liquor into the pan and add the remaining stock. Stir in the paprika, saffron and bay leaf. Return the chicken to the pan. Bring to the boil, cover with a lid or foil, reduce the heat and simmer gently for 15 minutes. Add the peppers, tomatoes and peas and cook for a further 10 minutes until the rice has absorbed nearly all the liquid and is just tender and the chicken is cooked through. Season to taste and stir gently. Remove from the heat. Leave to cool, then add the mussels still in their shells (or break off the top shells if preferred), discarding any unopened ones. Add the prawns and olives. Cover and chill. Garnish with lemon wedges and parsley and serve with focaccia and a green salad.

Okra and prawn pilaff

SERVES 4

1 onion, chopped
4 streaky bacon rashers (slices), rinded
and diced
15 ml/1 tbsp sunflower or olive oil
225 g/8 oz okra (ladies' fingers),
thickly sliced
225 g/8 oz/1 cup long-grain rice
5 ml/1 tsp ground cumin
600 ml/1 pt/2½ cups water
1 chicken stock cube
Salt and freshly ground black pepper
225 g/8 oz cooked peeled prawns
(shrimp)
Chopped parsley, to garnish

In a large saucepan, fry (sauté) the onion and bacon in the oil, stirring, until softened. Stir in the okra, rice and cumin and cook for about 1 minute until coated in the oil. Add all the remaining ingredients except the prawns, cover and simmer for 15 minutes. Add the prawns, cover and cook for a further 5 minutes or until the rice is tender and has absorbed the liquid. Taste and re-season if necessary. Sprinkle with chopped parsley and serve.

Bucatini tonnata

SERVES 4–6

450 g/1 lb bucatini (long macaroni)
1 onion, finely chopped
2 garlic cloves, crushed
30 ml/2 tbsp olive oil
250 ml/8 fl oz/1 cup fish or chicken
  stock
45 ml/3 tbsp dry vermouth
185 g/6½ oz/1 small can of tuna,
  drained
Salt and freshly ground black pepper
25 g/1 oz/2 tbsp butter or margarine
30 ml/2 tbsp snipped chives

Cook the bucatini according to the
packet directions. Meanwhile, fry
(sauté) the onion and garlic in the
oil for 3 minutes until soft but not
brown. Add the stock and vermouth,
bring to the boil and boil rapidly
until reduced by half. Stir in the
tuna, a little salt and lots of pepper.
Drain the pasta, return to the
saucepan and toss in the butter or
margarine. Add the fish mixture to
the pasta and toss gently. Serve
sprinkled with the chives.

Oriental tuna casserole

SERVES 6

100 g/4 oz Chinese egg noodles
2 × 185 g/6½ oz/small cans of tuna,
  drained
295 g/10½ oz/1 medium can of cream
  of mushroom soup
60 ml/4 tbsp water
15 ml/1 tbsp soy sauce
2 celery sticks, chopped
100 g/4 oz/1 cup cashew nuts
4 spring onions (scallions), chopped
100 g/4 oz button mushrooms,
  quartered

Cook the noodles according to the
packet directions. Drain. Mix with
all the remaining ingredients in an
ovenproof dish. Bake at 190°C/
375°F/gas mark 5 for about
30 minutes until golden and
bubbling.

Pasta with tuna and pesto

SERVES 4

350 g/12 oz rotelli (pasta wheels)
225 g/8 oz/2 cups frozen peas
185 g/6½ oz/1 small can of tuna,
  drained
1 quantity of Pesto (page 377 or use
  bought)
15 ml/1 tbsp olive oil
Basil leaves, to garnish

Cook the pasta according to the
packet directions, adding the peas
for the last 5 minutes. Drain, rinse
with boiling water and drain again.
Return to the pan. Stir in the tuna
and Pesto and toss over a gentle
heat. Pile on to serving plates and
drizzle with the olive oil. Serve
garnished with a few basil leaves.

Fish pot

SERVES 4

600 ml/1 pt/2½ cups fish stock
5 ml/1 tsp anchovy essence (extract)
100 g/4 oz conchiglie (pasta shells)
2 carrots, diced
100 g/4 oz French (green) beans, cut
into short lengths
350 g/12 oz white fish fillet, skinned
and cut into chunks
400 g/14 oz/1 large can of chopped
tomatoes with herbs
Salt and freshly ground black pepper
Crusty bread, to serve

Put the stock in a saucepan with the
anchovy essence, pasta and carrots.
Bring to the boil and simmer for
10 minutes. Add the remaining
ingredients and cook for about
6 minutes or until the pasta,
vegetables and fish are tender. Taste
and re-season if necessary. Serve
with lots of crusty bread.

Quick herby tuna pasta

SERVES 4

225 g/8 oz rigatoni (pasta tubes)
185 g/6½ oz/1 small can of tuna in oil
30 ml/2 tbsp olive oil
15 ml/1 tbsp lemon juice
15 ml/1 tbsp chopped parsley
15 ml/1 tbsp chopped marjoram
Salt and freshly ground black pepper
Grated Parmesan cheese, to serve

Cook the rigatoni according to the
packet directions. Drain and return
to the saucepan. Add the undrained
contents of the can of tuna, the olive
oil, lemon juice, herbs, a little salt
and lots of pepper. Toss over a
gentle heat until well combined and
hot through. Serve straight away
with grated Parmesan.

Oriental seafood hotpot

SERVES 6

3 plaice fillets, skinned if black and
cut into strips
4 mackerel fillets, skinned and cut into
strips
6 raw peeled king prawns (jumbo
shrimp)
6 shelled scallops, sliced
4 small squid, cleaned and cut into
rings (page 14)
1.2 litres/2 pts/5 cups chicken stock
5 ml/1 tsp chopped fresh root ginger
4 spring onions (scallions), chopped
50 g/2 oz cellophane noodles, soaked
in warm water for 5 minutes
450 g/1 lb spring cabbage, shredded
Hoisin sauce, to taste

Place all the seafood in a large,
flameproof casserole dish (Dutch
oven) with the stock, ginger and
spring onions. Bring to the boil,
reduce the heat, cover and simmer
for 5 minutes. Add all the remaining
ingredients except the hoisin sauce
and simmer for 5–10 minutes until
the fish and cabbage are tender. Stir
in a little hoisin sauce to taste and
serve ladled into warm bowls.

Tuna and mushroom gnocchi

SERVES 4

600 ml/1 pt/2½ cups milk
Salt and freshly ground black pepper
1 bay leaf
1.5 ml/¼ tsp ground mace
150 g/5 oz/scant 1 cup semolina
  (cream of wheat)
2 eggs, beaten
100 g/4 oz/1 cup Cheddar cheese,
  grated
185 g/6½ oz/1 small can of tuna,
  drained
100 g/4 oz button mushrooms, sliced
295 g/10½ oz/1 medium can of
  condensed mushroom soup
10 g/¼ oz/2 tsp butter or margarine,
  melted
15 ml/1 tbsp chopped parsley
Green salad, to serve

Put the milk, a little salt and pepper, the bay leaf and mace in a saucepan. Stir in the semolina. Bring to the boil and cook for 10 minutes, stirring all the time, until really thick. Discard the bay leaf. Stir the eggs into the semolina with three-quarters of the cheese. Turn into a dampened baking tin (pan), lined with non-stick baking parchment and spread out the mixture with a wet palette knife to a square about 2 cm/¾ in thick. Leave to cool, then chill for at least 1 hour.

Meanwhile, put the tuna in a 1.2 litre/2 pt/5 cup ovenproof serving dish. Add the mushrooms and soup and mix gently. Cut the tray of gnocchi into 4 cm/1½ in squares and arrange on top of the dish. Brush with the butter or margarine and sprinkle with the remaining cheese. Bake in a preheated oven at 200°C/400°F/gas mark 6 for 30 minutes until golden and bubbling. Sprinkle with the parsley and serve hot with a green salad.

Salmon and celery gnocchi

SERVES 4

Prepare as for Tuna and Mushroom Gnocchi, but substitute canned salmon, skin and bones removed, for the tuna, celery soup for the mushroom soup and 2 celery sticks, very finely chopped and boiled for 2 minutes in water, then drained, for the mushrooms.

Pasta with tuna and beans

SERVES 4

250 ml/8 fl oz/1 cup olive oil
100 ml/3½ fl oz/scant ½ cup lemon
  juice
2 garlic cloves, crushed
425 g/15 oz/1 large can of black-eyed
  beans, drained
30 ml/2 tbsp chopped parsley
185 g/6½ oz/1 small can of tuna, drained
Salt and freshly ground black pepper
175 g/6 oz short-cut macaroni
Black olives and snipped chives, to
  garnish

Mix together the oil, lemon juice, garlic, black-eyed beans and parsley in a saucepan. Cook for 5 minutes, stirring occasionally, until hot through. Gently fold in the tuna and a little salt and pepper and heat through, taking care to keep the tuna in chunks. Meanwhile, cook the macaroni according to the packet directions. Drain. Add to the sauce, toss gently and garnish with a few black olives and some snipped chives.

Midweek macaroni munch

SERVES 4

225 g/8 oz short-cut macaroni
1 onion, finely chopped
50 g/2 oz/¼ cup butter or margarine
50 g/2 oz/½ cup plain (all-purpose) flour
600 ml/1 pt/2½ cups milk
1 bay leaf
5 ml/1 tsp made English mustard
Salt and freshly ground black pepper
185 g/6½ oz/1 small can of tuna, drained
4 hard-boiled (hard-cooked) eggs, sliced
12 stuffed olives, sliced
75 g/3 oz/¾ cup Gouda cheese, grated

Cook the pasta according to the packet directions. Meanwhile, fry (sauté) the onion in the butter or margarine for 3 minutes until soft and lightly golden. Stir in the flour, then blend in the milk until smooth. Add the bay leaf, bring to the boil and cook for 2 minutes, stirring all the time, until thickened. Remove the bay leaf. Stir in the mustard and season to taste. Drain the macaroni and stir in, then add all the remaining ingredients except two-thirds of the cheese. Taste and re-season if necessary. Pile into an ovenproof dish. Top with the remaining cheese and bake in the oven at 200°C/400°F/gas mark 6 for about 25 minutes until bubbling and golden.

Tuna, sweetcorn and tomato pasta

SERVES 4

225 g/8 oz pasta shapes
185 g/6½ oz/1 small can of tuna, drained
200 g/7 oz/1 small can of sweetcorn (corn), drained
450 ml/¾ pt/2 cups passata (sieved tomatoes)
5 ml/1 tsp dried oregano
Freshly ground black pepper
50 g/2 oz/½ cup strong Cheddar cheese, grated
2 tomatoes, sliced
Mixed leaf salad, to serve

Cook the pasta according to the packet directions. Drain and return to the saucepan. Add the tuna, sweetcorn, passata, oregano and lots of pepper and heat through, stirring gently. Turn into a flameproof serving dish. Top with the cheese and arrange the tomato slices around the edge. Place under a hot grill (broiler) until the cheese melts and bubbles. Serve hot with a mixed leaf salad.

Rigatoni with tuna and sweetcorn

SERVES 4

225 g/8 oz rigatoni (pasta tubes)
20 g/³⁄₄ oz/3 tbsp plain (all-purpose) flour
300 ml/½ pt/1¼ cups milk
A knob of butter or margarine
75 g/3 oz/³⁄₄ cup Cheddar cheese, grated
185 g/6½ oz/1 small can of tuna, drained
200 g/7 oz/1 small can of sweetcorn (corn) drained
Salt and freshly ground black pepper
Paprika, for dusting
30 ml/2 tbsp chopped parsley

Cook the pasta according to the packet directions until just tender. Drain and return to the saucepan. Meanwhile, blend the flour with a little of the milk in a saucepan. Add the remaining milk and the butter or margarine. Bring to the boil and cook for 2 minutes, stirring. Stir in the cheese, tuna and sweetcorn and heat through. Season to taste. Add to the pasta and toss over a gentle heat until well mixed and piping hot. Spoon on to plates. Dust with paprika, sprinkle with the parsley and serve.

Tuna and tomato temptation

SERVES 4

350 g/12 oz any ribbon pasta
1 garlic clove, crushed
150 ml/¼ pt/⅔ cup chicken stock
225 g/8 oz/1 small can of chopped tomatoes
15 ml/1 tbsp tomato purée (paste)
30 ml/2 tbsp snipped chives
45 ml/3 tbsp dry vermouth
185 g/6½ oz/1 small can of tuna, drained
10 ml/2 tsp cornflour (cornstarch)
15 ml/1 tbsp water
Salt and freshly ground black pepper
15 ml/1 tbsp olive oil
30 ml/2 tbsp single (light) cream

Cook the pasta according to the packet directions. Meanwhile, place the garlic, stock, tomatoes, tomato purée, chives and vermouth in a saucepan. Bring to the boil, reduce the heat and simmer for 5 minutes or until reduced by half. Add the tuna and heat through, stirring. Blend the cornflour with the water. Add to the sauce, bring to the boil and simmer for 1 minute, stirring. Season to taste and stir in the olive oil. Drain the pasta and toss in the cream. Add a good grinding of black pepper and pile on to warm plates. Spoon the tuna sauce on top and serve straight away.

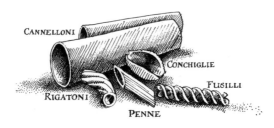

CANNELLONI
CONCHIGLIE
FUSILLI
RIGATONI
PENNE

Fishy pasta grill

SERVES 4

225 g/8 oz pasta shapes
225 g/8 oz/1 medium can of pilchards
  in tomato sauce, mashed
30 ml/2 tbsp olive oil
30 ml/2 tbsp snipped chives
A dash of lemon juice
60 ml/4 tbsp passata (sieved tomatoes)
Salt and freshly ground black pepper
75 g/3 oz/¾ cup Cheddar cheese, grated
2 tomatoes, sliced

Cook the pasta according to the
packet directions. Drain and return
to the saucepan. Add all the
remaining ingredients except the
cheese and tomato slices. Toss over
a gentle heat until well combined.
Season to taste and add a little more
passata to moisten if necessary. Turn
into a flameproof dish. Cover with
the cheese and garnish with the
tomato slices. Grill (broil) until the
cheese melts and bubbles. Serve
straight away.

Spaghetti with clams

SERVES 4

350 g/12 oz spaghetti
1 large onion, finely chopped
1 large garlic clove, crushed
15 g/½ oz/1 tbsp butter or margarine
400 g/14 oz/1 large can of chopped
  tomatoes
15 ml/1 tbsp tomato purée (paste)
2 × 295 g/10½ oz/medium cans of
  baby clams, drained
Salt and freshly ground black pepper
15 ml/1 tbsp chopped parsley
Dressed green salad, to serve

Cook the spaghetti according to the
packet directions. Meanwhile, fry
(sauté) the onion and garlic in the
butter or margarine for 2 minutes,
stirring, until softened but not
browned. Add the tomatoes and
tomato purée. Bring to the boil,
reduce the heat and boil rapidly for
5 minutes until pulpy. Stir in the
clams and season with salt and
pepper. Heat for 2 minutes. Drain
the spaghetti and return to the pan.
Add the clam mixture and toss well.
Pile on to warm plates and sprinkle
with the parsley before serving with
a dressed green salad.

Spaghettini alle vongole

SERVES 4–6

40 g/1½ oz/3 tbsp unsalted (sweet)
  butter
15 ml/1 tbsp olive oil
3 garlic cloves, crushed
100 ml/3½ fl oz/scant ½ cup dry white
  wine
2 × 295 g/10½ oz/medium cans of
  baby clams, drained and juice
  reserved
Freshly ground black pepper
350 g/12 oz spaghettini
15 ml/1 tbsp chopped parsley

Melt the butter with the oil in a
saucepan. Add the garlic and cook
gently for 2 minutes until lightly
golden but not too brown. Add the
wine, bring to the boil and simmer
for 2 minutes until slightly reduced.
Add the clams and 45 ml/3 tbsp of
their juice to the saucepan. Heat
through gently until piping hot.
Meanwhile, cook the spaghettini
according to the packet directions.
Drain and pile on to warm plates.
Spoon the sauce over and sprinkle
with the parsley before serving.

Smoked salmon and broccoli pappardelle

SERVES 4

250 g/9 oz pappardelle (wide ribbon noodles)
175 g/6 oz broccoli, cut into tiny florets
175 g/6 oz smoked salmon pieces, cut up if necessary
150 ml/¼ pt/⅔ cup crème fraîche
2 eggs
60 ml/4 tbsp milk
Salt and freshly ground black pepper
Lemon juice
20 ml/4 tsp grated Parmesan cheese

Cook the pasta according to the packet directions, adding the broccoli for the last 5 minutes. Drain and return to the saucepan. Add the salmon and crème fraîche. Toss gently. Beat together the eggs and milk and add to the pan with some salt and pepper. Cook over a gentle heat until creamy but not totally scrambled. Taste and add lemon juice and a little more seasoning to taste. Pile on to warm plates, sprinkle with the Parmesan cheese and serve.

Smoked salmon, prawn and broccoli vermicelli

SERVES 4

Prepare as for Smoked Salmon and Broccoli Pappardelle, but use half smoked salmon and half cooked peeled prawns (shrimp). Add 5 ml/ 1 tsp anchovy essence (extract) to the mixture and use vermicelli instead of pappardelle (it is quicker to cook, so check the directions on the packet before adding the broccoli).

Crab tetrazzini

SERVES 4

100 g/4 oz short ribbon noodles
20 g/¾ oz/3 tbsp plain (all-purpose) flour
20 g/¾ oz/1½ tbsp butter or margarine, plus extra for greasing
150 ml/¼ pt/⅔ cup chicken stock
150 ml/¼ pt/⅔ cup single (light) cream
Salt and freshly ground black pepper
A pinch of grated nutmeg
170 g/6 oz/1 small can of white crabmeat, drained
295 g/10½ oz/1 medium can of asparagus spears, drained
120 ml/4 fl oz/½ cup soured (dairy sour) cream
50 g/2 oz/½ cup Parmesan cheese, grated

Cook the pasta according to the packet directions. Drain. Meanwhile, blend the flour with the butter or margarine and stock in a saucepan. Stir in the cream. Bring to the boil and cook for 2 minutes, stirring. Season to taste with salt, pepper and the nutmeg. Stir in the crabmeat. Grease a shallow ovenproof dish and lay the asparagus spears in the base. Mix the cooked noodles with the soured cream and a little salt and pepper. Spoon over the asparagus. Sprinkle with some of the Parmesan. Spoon the crab and sauce over and sprinkle with more Parmesan. Bake at 180°C/350°F/gas mark 4 for about 30 minutes until golden and bubbling.

Fusilli with clams and bacon

SERVES 4

1 bunch of spring onions (scallions), chopped
1 carrot, finely diced
150 ml/¼ pt/⅔ cup olive oil
2 garlic cloves, crushed
4 streaky bacon rashers (slices), rinded and finely diced
2 × 295 g/10½ oz/medium cans of baby clams, drained
A pinch of cayenne
10 ml/2 tsp chopped thyme
Freshly ground black pepper
350 g/12 oz fusilli (thick spiral pasta)
30 ml/2 tbsp chopped parsley

Fry (sauté) the spring onions and carrot in 60 ml/4 tbsp of the oil for 3 minutes until softened but not browned. Add the garlic and bacon and continue cooking for a further 3 minutes, stirring. Add the remaining oil with the clams, cayenne, thyme and a good grinding of pepper. Heat through gently, stirring, until piping hot. Meanwhile, cook the fusilli according to the packet directions. Drain, add the sauce and toss well. Garnish with the parsley before serving.

Conchiglie con cozze

SERVES 4

2 garlic cloves, chopped
15 ml/1 tbsp olive oil
450 g/1 lb tomatoes, skinned, seeded and chopped
15 ml/1 tbsp chopped parsley
15 ml/1 tbsp chopped basil
1 kg/2¼ lb mussels in their shells, cleaned (page 13)
75 ml/5 tbsp dry white wine
225 g/8 oz conchiglie (pasta shells)
Salt and freshly ground black pepper
Lemon juice, to taste

Fry (sauté) the garlic gently in the oil for 1 minute. Add the tomatoes and herbs and bring just to the boil, then reduce the heat and cook very gently for 5 minutes.

Meanwhile, put the mussels in a large pan with the wine. Cover and cook over a moderate heat, shaking the pan occasionally, for 5 minutes until the mussels have opened. Discard any that remain closed. When cooked, strain the liquid into the tomato mixture and continue simmering for about 20 minutes until pulpy. Remove the mussels from their shells. Cook the conchiglie according to the packet directions. Drain and turn into a warm serving dish. Stir the mussels into the tomato sauce, season with salt and pepper and add lemon juice to taste. Spoon over the pasta and serve hot.

Fiery mussels

SERVES 4

30 ml/2 tbsp olive oil
1 onion, finely chopped
1 garlic clove, crushed
1–2 red chillies, seeded and chopped
2 canned pimiento caps, chopped
400 g/14 oz/1 large can of chopped
  tomatoes
15 ml/1 tbsp tomato purée (paste)
250 g/9 oz/1 medium can of mussels
  in brine, drained
Salt and freshly ground black pepper
350 g/12 oz spaghettini

Heat the oil in a saucepan. Add the onion and garlic and cook gently for 2 minutes until softened but not browned. Add the chillies, pimientos, tomatoes and tomato purée. Bring to the boil, reduce the heat and simmer gently for 10 minutes until pulpy. Stir in the mussels. Season to taste and heat through gently until piping hot. Meanwhile, cook the spaghettini according to the packet directions. Drain and pile on to warm plates. Spoon the sauce over and serve straight away.

Vermicelli marina

SERVES 4–6

120 ml/4 fl oz/½ cup olive oil
3 garlic cloves, crushed
2 kg/4½ lb mussels in their shells,
  cleaned (page 13)
150 ml/¼ pt/⅔ cup chicken stock
450 g/1 lb vermicelli
15 ml/1 tbsp brandy
Salt and freshly ground black pepper
30 ml/2 tbsp chopped parsley

Heat 45 ml/3 tbsp of the oil in a large pan. Add the garlic and fry (sauté) gently until golden. Add the mussels and stock. Cover and cook gently, shaking the pan occasionally, for 3–4 minutes or until the mussels open. Drain, reserving the liquid. Carefully remove the mussels from their shells and return to the liquid. Discard any that have not opened. Meanwhile, cook the vermicelli according to the packet directions. Drain and return to the saucepan. Add the mussels in their liquid and the brandy. Season to taste, add the parsley and toss well before serving.

Country cod bake

SERVES 6

300 ml/½ pt/1¼ cups fish or vegetable
  stock
60 ml/4 tbsp tomato ketchup (catsup)
30 ml/2 tbsp mayonnaise
350 g/12 oz/3 cups frozen mixed
  country vegetables
Salt and freshly ground black pepper
450 ml/1 lb cod fillet, skinned and
  cubed
2.5 ml/½ tsp dried mixed herbs
350 g/12 oz fettuccine (ribbon noodles)
75 g/3 oz/¾ cup Cheddar cheese, grated

Mix together the stock, ketchup and mayonnaise in a saucepan. Add the vegetables and a little seasoning, cover and simmer for 10 minutes or until tender. Add the fish and herbs and simmer for 5 minutes.

Meanwhile, cook the pasta according to the packet directions. Drain and turn into a flameproof dish. Spoon the sauce over. Top with the cheese and place under a hot grill (broiler) until the cheese is melted, bubbling and turning golden.

Cidered prawns with lumachi

SERVES 4–6

50 g/2 oz/¼ cup butter or margarine
1 bunch of spring onions (scallions),
  cut into short lengths
2 courgettes (zucchini), sliced
450 ml/¾ pt/2 cups fish stock
150 ml/¼ pt/⅔ cup dry cider
30 ml/2 tbsp cornflour (cornstarch)
225 g/8 oz cooked peeled prawns
  (shrimp)
Salt and freshly ground black pepper
150 ml/¼ pt/⅔ cup single (light) cream
15 ml/1 tbsp chopped parsley
225 g/8 oz lumachi (snail-shaped
  pasta)

Melt the butter or margarine in a saucepan. Add the spring onions and courgettes and fry (sauté) gently for 2 minutes. Cover and cook for 5 minutes until softened but not browned, stirring occasionally. Add the stock and bring to the boil. Simmer for 2 minutes. Blend the cider with the cornflour and stir into the mixture. Bring to the boil and simmer for 1 minute, stirring all the time. Stir in the prawns, a little salt and pepper, the cream and parsley. Heat through gently until piping hot. Meanwhile, cook the pasta according to the packet directions. Drain, add to the sauce, toss gently and serve.

Speciality crab conchiglie

SERVES 4–6

Prepare as for Cidered Prawns with Lumachi, but substitute diced crab sticks for the prawns (shrimp), white wine for the cider and conchiglie (pasta shells) for the lumachi (snail-shaped pasta).

Cod ragu

SERVES 4–6

1 onion, chopped
1 garlic clove, crushed
15 ml/1 tbsp olive oil
100 g/4 oz button mushrooms, sliced
400 g/14 oz/1 large can of chopped
  tomatoes
15 ml/1 tbsp tomato purée (paste)
50 g/2 oz/½ cup frozen peas
15 ml/1 tbsp chopped fresh basil
Salt and freshly ground black pepper
450 g/1 lb cod fillet, skinned and
  cubed
350 g/12 oz pappardelle (wide ribbon
  noodles)
Basil leaves, to garnish
50 g/2 oz/½ cup Cheddar cheese,
  grated, to serve

Fry (sauté) the onion and garlic in the oil for 2 minutes until softened but not browned. Add all the remaining ingredients except the cod and pasta. Bring to the boil, reduce the heat and simmer for 10 minutes until pulpy. Add the fish and cook for a further 5 minutes, stirring gently occasionally, until the fish is cooked. Meanwhile, cook the papardelle according to the packet directions. Drain. Pile on to a warm serving dish, spoon the cod ragu over, garnish with a few basil leaves and sprinkle with the grated cheese.

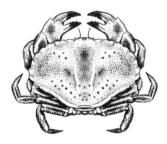

Chinese-style prawns with cucumber

SERVES 4

1 cucumber, diced
50 g/2 oz/¼ cup butter or margarine
175 g/6 oz button mushrooms, sliced
15 ml/1 tbsp plain (all-purpose) flour
150 ml/¼ pt/⅔ cup chicken stock
15 ml/1 tbsp medium-dry sherry
5 ml/1 tsp grated fresh root ginger
90 ml/6 tbsp single (light) cream
175 g/6 oz cooked peeled prawns
(shrimp)
Salt and freshly ground black pepper
250 g/9 oz Chinese egg noodles

Boil the cucumber in lightly salted water for 3 minutes. Drain, rinse with cold water and drain again. Melt the butter or margarine in the same saucepan, add the mushrooms and cook for 2 minutes, stirring. Add the cucumber, cover and cook for a further 3 minutes. Stir in the flour, then the stock, sherry, ginger and cream. Bring to the boil and cook for 2 minutes, stirring. Add the prawns, heat through until piping hot and season to taste. Meanwhile, cook the noodles according to the packet directions. Drain and pile into warm bowls. Spoon the prawn mixture over and serve.

Prawn and cucumber lu mein

SERVES 4

Prepare as for Chinese-style Prawns with Cucumber, but omit the flour. Add 250 g/9 oz soaked cellophane noodles with the stock, sherry and ginger but do not add the cream at this stage. Simmer the noodles until cooked, adding a little more stock if necessary. Then add the cream and prawns (shrimp), heat through and season to taste. Omit the egg noodles.

Quick curried prawn and pasta supper

SERVES 4

225 g/8 oz any pasta shapes
295 g/10½ oz/1 medium can of
condensed cream of chicken soup
15 ml/1 tbsp curry paste
225 g/8 oz cooked peeled prawns
(shrimp)
15 ml/1 tbsp chopped coriander
(cilantro) or parsley
50 g/2 oz/1 cup fresh white
breadcrumbs
15 g/½ oz/1 tbsp butter or margarine,
melted

Cook the pasta according to the packet directions. Drain and return to the saucepan. Mix in all the remaining ingredients except the breadcrumbs and butter or margarine. Heat gently, stirring, until piping hot and well mixed. Turn into a flameproof dish. Mix the breadcrumbs with the butter and sprinkle over. Place under a hot grill (broiler) until crisp and golden. Serve straight away.

Lasagne di mare

SERVES 4

1 onion, finely chopped
1 garlic clove, crushed
100 g/4 oz mushrooms, finely chopped
400 g/14 oz/1 large can of chopped
    tomatoes
15 ml/1 tbsp tomato purée (paste)
2.5 ml/½ tsp dried oregano
450 g/1 lb cod fillet, skinned and
    cubed
Salt and freshly ground black pepper
50 g/2 oz/½ cup plain (all-purpose)
    flour
50 g/2 oz/¼ cup butter or margarine
600 ml/1 pt/2½ cups milk
100 g/4 oz/1 cup Cheddar cheese,
    grated
8 no-need-to-precook lasagne sheets

Put the onion, garlic, mushrooms,
tomatoes, tomato purée and oregano
in a saucepan. Bring to the boil,
reduce the heat and simmer for
5 minutes until pulpy. Stir in the fish
and cook for a further 5 minutes.
Season to taste. Blend the flour with
the butter or margarine and a little
of the milk in a saucepan. Stir in the
remaining milk. Bring to the boil
and cook for 2 minutes, stirring,
until thickened. Season to taste and
add half the cheese. Spoon a thin
layer of the cheese sauce in the base
of a 2.25 litre/4 pt/10 cup ovenproof
dish. Cover with a layer of lasagne,
breaking it to fit. Cover with a third
of the fish sauce, then a little more
cheese sauce. Repeat the layers twice
more, making sure you have plenty
of cheese sauce left for the top.
Sprinkle with the remaining cheese
and bake at 190°C/375°F/gas mark
5 for about 35–40 minutes until the
pasta feels tender when a knife is
inserted down through the centre.

Macaroni with fresh clams

SERVES 4

1 large onion, finely chopped
2 celery sticks, chopped
25 g/1 oz/2 tbsp unsalted (sweet)
    butter
1 kg/2¼ lb clams in their shells,
    cleaned (page 17)
300 ml/½ pt/1¼ cups chicken stock
225 g/8 oz short-cut macaroni
5 ml/1 tsp saffron powder
Salt and freshly ground black pepper
50 g/2 oz/½ cup frozen peas
15 ml/1 tbsp chopped parsley

Cook the onion and celery in the
butter in a large saucepan, stirring,
for 3 minutes until soft but not
brown. Add the clams and stock.
Cover, bring to the boil and cook for
about 4 minutes, shaking the pan
occasionally, until the clams open.
Discard any that remain closed.
Meanwhile, cook the macaroni in
plenty of boiling, lightly salted water
for about 8 minutes until almost
tender. Drain and return to the pan.
Strain the clam cooking liquid into
the macaroni and stir in the saffron,
some salt and pepper and the peas.
Simmer until nearly all the liquid
has been absorbed and the peas are
tender. Mix in the clams. Pile on to
warm plates and serve sprinkled
with the parsley.

Portuguese fishermen's friend

SERVES 4

450 g/1 lb salt cod, soaked and cooked
  (page 8)
50 g/2 oz/½ cup plain (all-purpose) flour
Oil, for shallow frying
15 ml/1 tbsp olive oil
1 garlic clove, crushed
1 onion, chopped
400 g/14 oz/1 large can of chopped
  tomatoes
15 ml/1 tbsp tomato purée (paste)
5 ml/1 tsp caster (superfine) sugar
12 stuffed green olives
6 gherkins (cornichons), halved
  lengthways
10 ml/2 tsp capers
225 g/8 oz short-cut macaroni
15 ml/1 tbsp chopped parsley

Remove the skin and any bones from the cooked cod and break the fish into bite-sized pieces. Dust with the flour. Shallow-fry in oil until golden brown. Drain on kitchen paper (paper towels). Heat the olive oil in a saucepan. Fry (sauté) the garlic and onion for 3 minutes until soft but not brown. Add the tomatoes, tomato purée and sugar. Bring to the boil, reduce the heat and simmer for 10 minutes until pulpy. Stir in the cod, olives, gherkins and capers. Simmer gently for 3 minutes. Meanwhile, cook the pasta according to the packet directions. Drain and spoon into a warm serving dish. Spoon the sauce over and sprinkle with the parsley. Serve piping hot.

Delicate cod pie

SERVES 4

225 g/8 oz farfalle (pasta bows)
450 g/1 lb cod fillet, skinned and
  cubed
450 ml/¾ pt/2 cups milk
25 g/1 oz/¼ cup plain (all-purpose)
  flour
25 g/1 oz/2 tbsp butter or margarine
Salt and freshly ground black pepper
2 hard-boiled (hard-cooked) eggs,
  roughly chopped
30 ml/2 tbsp chopped parsley
150 ml/¼ pt/⅔ cup single (light) cream
2 eggs, beaten
50 g/2 oz/½ cup Cheddar cheese, grated

Cook the pasta according to the packet directions. Meanwhile, cook the cod in the milk for about 5 minutes until just tender. Drain, reserving the milk. Whisk the flour into a little of the milk. Add the remaining milk and the butter or margarine and bring to the boil, whisking all the time, until thickened. Cook for 2 minutes. Season to taste. Drain the pasta and gently fold into the sauce with the fish, chopped eggs and parsley. Turn into an ovenproof dish. Whisk together the cream and eggs with a little salt and pepper. Pour over and sprinkle on the cheese. Bake at 190°C/375°F/gas mark 5 for about 25 minutes or until the top is set and golden. Serve hot.

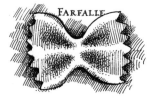

FARFALLE

Crab ravioli

SERVES 4

225 g/8 oz/2 cups plain (all-purpose)
flour, plus extra for dusting
1.5 ml/¼ tsp salt
2 large eggs, beaten
75 g/3 oz/⅓ cup butter or margarine
2 × 170 g/6 oz/small cans of white
crabmeat
15 ml/1 tbsp mayonnaise
20 ml/4 tsp lemon juice
A pinch of cayenne
Salt and freshly ground black pepper
1 small egg, beaten
150 ml/¼ pt/⅔ cup milk
20 ml/4 tsp cornflour (cornstarch)
300 ml/½ pt/1¼ cups single (light)
cream
15 ml/1 tbsp tomato purée (paste)
Freshly grated Parmesan cheese

Sift the flour and salt into a bowl.
Make a well in the centre and add
the large eggs. Melt half the butter
or margarine and add to the bowl.
Mix well to form a firm dough,
adding a little cold water if
necessary. Knead gently on a lightly
floured surface until shiny and
elastic. Wrap in a plastic bag and
leave to rest for at least 30 minutes.
  Meanwhile mix the crabmeat with
the mayonnaise, 5 ml/1 tsp of the
lemon juice, and cayenne, salt and
pepper to taste. Roll out the dough
as thinly as possible on a floured
surface to a large square. Spoon the
crab mixture at 4 cm/1½ in intervals
across half the dough. Brush
between the filling with the beaten
small egg. Fold the other half of the
dough over and press down between
each pile of filling. Using a pastry
wheel or sharp knife, cut between
the filling piles to make little
cushions. Dust with flour and leave
to rest while making the sauce.

Blend the milk and cornflour in a
saucepan. Add the cream and the
remaining butter or margarine, cut
into small pieces, and the tomato
purée and bring to the boil, stirring
all the time. Add the remaining
lemon juice, and cayenne, salt and
pepper to taste. Drop the ravioli, one
after the another, into a large pan of
lightly salted, boiling water. When
they are all in the pan, cook for
about 7 minutes until just tender.
Remove from the pan with a
draining spoon and transfer to a
warm serving dish. Spoon the hot
sauce over and sprinkle with
Parmesan before serving.

Prawn ravioli

SERVES 4

Prepare as for Crab Ravioli, but
substitute 350 g/12 oz cooked peeled
prawns (shrimp), chopped, for the
crabmeat. Serve with All-year
Tomato Sauce (page 379) instead of
the cream sauce, if you prefer.

Cod and spinach ravioli

SERVES 4

Prepare as for Crab Ravioli, but
substitute 175 g/6 oz cooked
spinach, chopped, and 175 g/6 oz
poached cod (page 19), flaked, for
the crabmeat. Mix with medium-fat
soft cheese or fromage frais instead
of the mayonnaise, and flavour with
a good pinch of grated nutmeg.

Quick conchiglie cod casserole

SERVES 4

15 g/½ oz/1 tbsp butter or margarine
175 g/6 oz conchiglie (pasta shells)
450 g/1 lb cod fillet, skinned and diced
300 ml/½ pt/1¼ cups milk
425 g/15 oz/1 large can of crab bisque
Salt and freshly ground black pepper
30 ml/2 tbsp chopped parsley

Thoroughly grease a casserole dish (Dutch oven) with the butter or margarine and put the dry pasta in the base. Put the fish in a layer over the top. Blend together all the remaining ingredients and pour over. Cover and bake in the oven at 180°C/350°F/gas mark 4 for about 50 minutes until the pasta is cooked.

Crab creation

SERVES 4

225 g/8 oz green tagliatelle
225 g/8 oz crab sticks, diced
425 g/15 oz/1 large can of crab bisque
Salt and freshly ground black pepper
30 ml/2 tbsp single (light) cream
30 ml/2 tbsp chopped parsley
Lemon juice, to taste
4 lemon twists, to garnish

Cook the pasta according to the packet directions. Drain and return to the pan. Put the crab sticks, soup, a little salt and pepper, the cream and parsley in a separate pan and heat through gently, stirring. Spike with lemon juice to taste. Add to the cooked pasta and toss gently. Pile on to plates and serve hot, garnished with a twist of lemon on each plate.

Brandied crab crisp

SERVES 4–6

25 g/1 oz/¼ cup plain (all-purpose) flour
25 g/1 oz/2 tbsp butter or margarine
300 ml/½ pt/1¼ cups milk
30 ml/2 tbsp single (light) cream
50 g/2 oz/½ cup Cheddar cheese, grated
5 ml/1 tsp Dijon mustard
2.5 ml/½ tsp dried thyme
Salt and freshly ground black pepper
15 ml/1 tbsp brandy
2 × 170 g/6 oz/small cans of white crabmeat
225 g/8 oz farfalle (pasta bows)
50 g/2 oz/1 cup fresh white breadcrumbs
15 ml/1 tbsp melted butter or margarine

Whisk together the flour, butter or margarine and milk in a saucepan until the flour is blended in. Bring to the boil and cook for 2 minutes, stirring all the time. Stir in the cream, cheese, mustard and thyme. Season with a little salt and pepper. Add the brandy and the contents of the cans of crabmeat, including the juice. Stir in gently and heat through until piping hot. Taste and re-season if necessary. Meanwhile, cook the pasta according to the packet directions. Drain and turn half into a flameproof dish, then half the sauce. Repeat the layers. Mix the breadcrumbs with the melted butter or margarine. Sprinkle over and place the dish under a hot grill (broiler) until crisp and golden on top.

Tagliatelle alla rustica

SERVES 4

2 garlic cloves, crushed
90 ml/6 tbsp olive oil
50 g/2 oz/1 small can of anchovy
  fillets, chopped, reserving the oil
5 ml/1 tsp dried oregano
45 ml/3 tbsp roughly chopped parsley
Salt and freshly ground black pepper
225 g/8 oz tagliatelle (preferably fresh)
Thin slivers of Parmesan cheese

Fry (sauté) the garlic in the oil until
golden brown. Remove from the heat
and add the anchovies and their oil.
Return to the heat and cook gently,
stirring, until the anchovies form a
paste. Stir in the oregano, parsley, a
very little salt and lots of black
pepper. Meanwhile, cook the
tagliatelle according to the packet
directions. Drain and return to the
pan. Add the sauce, toss well and
serve garnished with thin slivers of
Parmesan.

Squid and radicchio euphoria

SERVES 4

450 g/1 lb baby squid, cleaned (page 14)
1 small head of radicchio
60 ml/4 tbsp olive oil
2 garlic cloves, crushed
1 red onion, chopped
½ green (bell) pepper, chopped
Salt and freshly ground black pepper
30 ml/2 tbsp lemon juice
30 ml/2 tbsp chopped parsley
225 g/8 oz any ribbon noodles

Slice the squid into rings and chop
the tentacles. Separate the radicchio
into leaves and tear into bite-sized
pieces. Heat the oil in a large frying
pan (skillet) and fry (sauté) the
garlic, onion and green pepper for
3 minutes, stirring, until softened

but not browned. Add the squid,
season well with salt and pepper and
add the lemon juice. Stir-fry for
1 minute, then cover and cook gently
for 5 minutes. Add the radicchio and
cook, stirring, for 2 minutes until
slightly wilted. Sprinkle with half the
parsley and heat through for a
further 1 minute. Meanwhile, cook
the noodles according to the packet
directions. Drain and return to the
pan. Add the sauce, toss quickly and
serve garnished with the remaining
parsley.

Queen scallop and bacon tagliatelle

SERVES 4–6

2 small leeks, sliced
25 g/1 oz/2 tbsp butter or margarine
90 ml/6 tbsp fish stock
3 streaky bacon rashers (slices), rinded
  and chopped
175 g/6 oz queen scallops
50 g/2 oz/¼ cup fromage frais
Salt and freshly ground black pepper
350 g/12 oz green tagliatelle
15 ml/1 tbsp chopped parsley

Fry (sauté) the leeks in half the
butter or margarine for 2 minutes
until softened but not browned. Add
the stock, cover and simmer gently
for 5 minutes until tender. Purée in a
blender or food processor, then
return to the saucepan. Meanwhile,
dry-fry the bacon until the fat runs.
Add the scallops and cook quickly,
tossing, for 2 minutes. Stir the
fromage frais into the leek purée.
Add the bacon and scallops and stir
in gently. Season to taste and heat
through until piping hot. Meanwhile,
cook the tagliatelle according to the
packet directions. Pile on to warm
plates, spoon the scallop mixture
over and sprinkle with the parsley.

Smoked haddock macaroni cheese

SERVES 4

225 g/8 oz smoked haddock fillet
450 ml/¾ pt/2 cups milk
1 bay leaf
25 g/1 oz/2 tbsp butter or margarine
100 g/4 oz button mushrooms, sliced
25 g/1 oz/¼ cup plain (all-purpose)
  flour
100 g/4 oz/1 cup Cheddar cheese,
  grated
Salt and white pepper
225 g/8 oz elbow macaroni
300 ml/½ pt/1¼ cups passata (sieved
  tomatoes), warmed

Poach the fish in the milk, with the bay leaf added, for 5 minutes or until it flakes easily with a fork. Lift out the fish, reserving the milk. Discard the skin and any bones from the fish and break the flesh into bite-sized pieces. Melt the butter or margarine in the saucepan and add the mushrooms. Cook gently, stirring for 1 minute. Add the flour and cook for a further 1 minute. Remove from the heat and gradually blend in the reserved milk, discarding the bay leaf. Return to the heat, bring to the boil and cook for 2 minutes, stirring. Stir in 75 g/3 oz/¾ cup of the cheese and season to taste. Gently fold in the fish and reheat until piping hot.

Meanwhile, cook the macaroni according to the packet directions. Drain. Fold gently into the fish mixture, then turn into a flameproof dish. Top with the remaining cheese and place under a hot grill (broiler) to brown. Serve straight away with warm passata.

Macaroni cheese brunch

SERVES 4–6

Prepare as for Smoked Haddock Macaroni Cheese, but substitute kipper fillets for the haddock and 3 hard-boiled (hard-cooked) eggs, quartered, for the mushrooms. Omit the passata (sieved tomatoes), if preferred.

Smoked salmon and asparagus centrepiece

SERVES 6

225 g/8 oz asparagus spears, cut into
  short lengths
100 g/4 oz smoked salmon, cut into
  small pieces
300 ml/½ pt/1¼ cups crème fraîche
15 ml/1 tbsp chopped dill (dill weed)
2 hard-boiled (hard-cooked) eggs,
  roughly chopped
Salt and freshly ground black pepper
225 g/8 oz tagliatelle al pomodoro
  (pasta ribbons flavoured with
  tomato)
A good knob of butter or margarine
Small dill sprigs, to garnish

Steam the asparagus or boil in a little salted water until just tender. Drain and return to the pan. Add all the remaining ingredients except the pasta and butter or margarine and heat through gently, stirring lightly, until piping hot. Meanwhile, cook the pasta according to the packet directions. Drain and return to the pan. Toss in the butter or margarine and pile on to warm plates. Spoon the sauce over and garnish with small dill sprigs.

Golden creamy cannelloni

SERVES 4–6

450 g/1 lb smoked haddock fillet
600 ml/1 pt/2½ cups milk
1 bouquet garni sachet
90 ml/6 tbsp double (heavy) cream
Salt and freshly ground black pepper
15 ml/1 tbsp chopped parsley
40 g/1½ oz/3 tbsp butter or margarine
25 g/1 oz/¼ cup plain (all-purpose) flour
100 g/4 oz/1 cup Leerdammer or Gruyère (Swiss) cheese, grated
12 no-need-to-precook cannelloni (pasta tubes)
320 g/12 oz/1 large can of sweetcorn (corn), drained

Poach the haddock in the milk, with the bouquet garni added, for about 10 minutes until it flakes easily with a fork. Drain, reserving the milk. Discard the bouquet garni. Remove any skin and bones from the fish and mash well. Stir in the cream, season with salt and pepper and add the parsley. Melt 25 g/1 oz/2 tbsp of the butter or margarine in a saucepan. Blend in the flour, then the reserved milk. Bring to the boil and cook for 2 minutes, stirring. Season to taste and stir in half the cheese.

Put the fish mixture in a piping bag and pipe it (or spoon it) into the cannelloni tubes. Grease an ovenproof dish with the remaining butter or margarine. Spread the sweetcorn in the base of the dish and spoon a little of the cheese sauce over. Lay the cannelloni on top and cover with the remaining cheese sauce. Sprinkle with the remaining cheese and bake in the oven at 190°C/375°F/gas mark 5 for about 35 minutes until golden and cooked through.

Fresh salmon and pimiento wheels

SERVES 4

225 g/8 oz salmon fillet, skinned and cut into thin strips
Grated rind and juice of ½ lemon
90 ml/6 tbsp olive oil
8 spring onions (scallions), chopped
400 g/14 oz/1 large can of pimientos, drained and chopped
15 ml/1 tbsp chopped basil
Salt and freshly ground black pepper
225 g/8 oz wholemeal ruote (pasta wheels)
50 g/2 oz/1 cup fresh wholemeal breadcrumbs
15 g/½ oz/1 tbsp butter or margarine

Put the salmon in a dish with the lemon rind and juice and leave to marinate while preparing the rest of the sauce. Heat 60 ml/4 tbsp of the oil in a saucepan and fry (sauté) the spring onions for about 3 minutes until softened but not browned. Add the pimientos and toss in the oil for 2 minutes. Add the salmon with any juices and cook gently for 2 minutes until just cooked. Do not overcook. Add the basil and the remaining oil and season well with salt and pepper. Heat through until piping hot.

Meanwhile, cook the pasta according to the packet directions. Drain and return to the pan. Add the hot sauce and toss well. Fry the breadcrumbs in the butter or margarine until golden. Pile the pasta on to warm plates and sprinkle with the buttered crumbs.

Savoury egg and tuna pasta

SERVES 4

225 g/8 oz any pasta shapes
1 large onion, finely chopped
1 garlic clove, crushed
75 g/3 oz/⅓ cup butter or margarine
225 g/8 oz spring (collard) greens,
  shredded
400 g/14 oz/1 large can of chopped
  tomatoes
5 ml/1 tsp caster (superfine) sugar
A good pinch of dried basil
Salt and freshly ground black pepper
185 g/6½ oz/1 small can of tuna,
  drained
2 hard-boiled (hard-cooked) eggs,
  roughly chopped
30 ml/2 tbsp plain (all-purpose) flour
300 ml/½ pt/1¼ cups milk
1 large bay leaf
50 g/2 oz/1 cup fresh white
  breadcrumbs

Cook the pasta according to the
packet directions until just tender.
Drain. Cook the onion and garlic in
40 g/1½ oz/3 tbsp of the butter or
margarine for 2 minutes, stirring.
Add the greens, tomatoes, sugar,
basil and a little salt and pepper.
Cover and simmer for 5 minutes,
stirring occasionally. Stir in the pasta
and tuna.
    Use a little of the remaining butter
or margarine to grease a 1.2 litre/
2 pt/5 cup ovenproof dish. Spoon
half the pasta into the dish. Cover
with a layer of the eggs, then add
the remaining pasta. Blend the flour
with a little of the milk in a
saucepan. Blend in the remaining
milk and add 15 g/½ oz/1 tbsp of
the remaining butter or margarine
and the bay leaf. Bring to the boil
and simmer for 2 minutes, stirring
all the time. Season to taste and

discard the bay leaf. Pour over
the pasta. Sprinkle with the
breadcrumbs and dot with the
remaining butter or margarine.
Bake in a preheated oven at 190°C/
375°F/gas mark 5 for about
20 minutes until hot through and
turning golden on top.

Simple salmon supper

SERVES 4

25 g/1 oz/¼ cup plain (all-purpose)
  flour
300 ml/½ pt/1¼ cups milk
25 g/1 oz/2 tbsp butter or margarine
200 g/7 oz/1 small can of pink or red
  salmon
A few drops of anchovy essence
  (extract)
Salt and freshly ground black pepper
225 g/8 oz short-cut macaroni
100 g/4 oz/1 cup Cheddar cheese,
  grated
Lemon wedges, to garnish

Whisk the flour with the milk in a
saucepan until smooth. Add the
butter or margarine, bring to the boil
and cook for 2 minutes, stirring.
Discard the skin and any bones from
the fish. Stir into the sauce with the
juice. Add a few drops of anchovy
essence and salt and pepper to taste.
Meanwhile, cook the macaroni
according to the packet directions.
Drain and stir into the fish sauce.
Turn into a flameproof dish. Sprinkle
the cheese over and brown under a
hot grill (broiler). Garnish with
lemon wedges before serving.

Japanese-style crab stick ravioli with lime sauce

SERVES 4

100 g/4 oz/1 cup strong plain (bread)
  flour
1 large egg
Salt and freshly ground black pepper
15 ml/1 tbsp olive oil
5 ml/1 tsp sesame oil
30 ml/2 tbsp semolina (cream of
  wheat)
175 g/6 oz crab sticks, chopped
45 ml/3 tbsp single (light) cream
1 small egg, beaten
200 ml/7 fl oz/scant 1 cup vegetable
  stock
A few drops of anchovy essence
  (extract)
3 kaffir lime leaves or the pared rind
  of ½ lime
2.5 ml/½ tsp dried lemon grass
5 ml/1 tsp grated fresh root ginger
15 ml/1 tbsp soy sauce
15 ml/1 tbsp cornflour (cornstarch)
30 ml/2 tbsp water

Put the flour, egg, a pinch of salt,
the oils and semolina in a food
processor. Run the machine to form
a firm dough. (Alternatively, work
all the ingredients together by hand.)
Knead on a lightly floured surface
until smooth and elastic. Wrap in a
plastic bag and leave to rest for
30 minutes.

Meanwhile, mix together the crab
sticks, cream and a little salt and
pepper. Roll out the dough thinly
and cut into 16 rounds using a
6 cm/2½ in cutter. Place the crab
filling in the centre of eight of the
rounds. Brush the edges with egg
and place the other eight rounds on
top. Press the edges well together
and crimp between finger and
thumb to seal. Put the stock,
anchovy essence, lime leaves, lemon
grass, ginger and soy sauce in a
saucepan. Bring to the boil and
simmer for 5 minutes. Blend the
cornflour with the water, stir into
the sauce and simmer for 2 minutes.
Meanwhile, drop the ravioli into a
pan of boiling salted water and cook
for 5 minutes until just tender.
Drain. Place two ravioli on each of
four warm plates. Strain the sauce
over and serve.

Tiger prawn and artichoke adventure

SERVES 4

45 ml/3 tbsp olive oil
1 onion, finely chopped
45 ml/3 tbsp dry white vermouth
425 g/15 oz/1 large can of artichoke
  hearts, drained and chopped
225 g/8 oz raw peeled tiger prawns
  (jumbo shrimp)
6 stoned (pitted) green olives, halved
Salt and freshly ground black pepper
150 ml/¼ pt/⅔ cup crème fraîche
225 g/8 oz farfalle (pasta bows)
30 ml/2 tbsp snipped chives
25 g/1 oz/1 tbsp Danish lumpfish roe

Heat the oil in a saucepan. Add the
onion and fry (sauté) gently for
3 minutes until softened but not
browned. Add the vermouth, bring
to the boil and simmer for 1 minute.
Add the artichokes, prawns, olives
and a good grinding of pepper.
Cook, stirring gently, for about
3 minutes until the prawns are pink.
Stir in the crème fraîche and season
to taste with salt and pepper.
Meanwhile, cook the farfalle
according to the packet directions.
Drain, return to the saucepan and
add the chives and the sauce and
toss well. Spoon on to plates and top
each with a spoonful of lumpfish
roe.

Speedy seafood lasagne

SERVES 4

400 g/14 oz/1 large can of chopped
    tomatoes
2.5 ml/½ tsp dried basil
1 garlic clove, crushed
185 g/6½ oz/1 small can of tuna,
    drained
170 g/6 oz/1 small can of prawns
    (shrimp), drained
250 g/9 oz/1 medium can of mussels
    in brine, drained
Freshly ground black pepper
6–8 no-need-to-precook lasagne sheets
225 g/8 oz frozen chopped spinach,
    thawed
295 g/10½ oz/1 medium can of
    condensed celery soup
25 g/1 oz/¼ cup Cheddar cheese, grated
Green salad, to serve

Empty the contents of the can of
tomatoes into a pan and add the
basil and garlic. Bring to the boil
and boil rapidly for 3 minutes until
pulpy. Stir in the tuna, prawns and
mussels. Season with pepper. Spoon
a little of the seafood mixture in the
base of a fairly shallow 1.2 litre/
2 pt/5 cup ovenproof dish. Cover
with a layer of lasagne sheets,
breaking them to fit, then half the
remaining seafood mixture, then half
the thawed spinach. Repeat the
layers and finish with a layer of
lasagne. Spoon the soup over the top
and sprinkle with the cheese. Bake
in a preheated oven at 190°C/
375°F/gas mark 5 for 40 minutes
until golden on top and cooked
through. Serve hot with a green
salad.

Aubergine and anchovy tagliatelle

SERVES 4

1 large aubergine (eggplant), halved
    and thinly sliced
60 ml/4 tbsp olive oil
1 large red onion, thinly sliced
1 garlic clove, crushed
1 red (bell) pepper, thinly sliced
1 green pepper, thinly sliced
4 ripe tomatoes, skinned, seeded and
    chopped
4 canned anchovy fillets, drained and
    finely chopped
150 ml/¼ pt/⅔ cup dry white wine
15 ml/1 tbsp chopped basil
Salt and freshly ground black pepper
350 g/12 oz tagliatelle
100 g/4 oz/1 cup Mozzarella cheese,
    grated

Fry (sauté) the aubergine in half the
oil in a saucepan for 3 minutes until
lightly browned. Add the remaining
oil, the onion, garlic and peppers
and fry for 5 minutes, stirring. Add
the tomatoes, anchovies and wine
and cook, stirring occasionally, for
about 5 minutes until pulpy. Stir in
the basil and season to taste.
Meanwhile, cook the tagliatelle in
lightly salted, boiling water for about
10 minutes until just tender but still
with some bite. Drain and pile on to
warm plates. Top with the aubergine
mixture and sprinkle with the
Mozzarella. Serve piping hot.

Salads

This is an area where fish lovers can really experiment. Any fish can be cooked, then eaten cold, and many, of course, can be eaten raw as well as cooked. This makes just about all fish and shellfish ideal for salads and other cold dishes – and not just in the summer. For instance, on a chilly evening there is nothing nicer than enjoying a rich, hearty fish soup (see pages 24–52), then tucking into some soused herrings or other pickled fish and a crisp salad. The variety of recipes in this chapter is almost endless: some are light and simple, others rich and sophisticated, but there are salads here to suit every occasion. And most can be prepared ahead of time, then just finished, if necessary, when you are ready to eat.

Vitello tonnato

SERVES 4

This is, of course, traditionally a veal dish, but I give you the option of using pork instead as I prefer it.

4 veal or pork escalopes
150 ml/¼ pt/⅔ cup olive oil
1 bay leaf
5 ml/1 tsp dried oregano
A good pinch of celery salt
Salt and freshly ground black pepper
85 g/3½ oz/1 very small can of tuna,
  drained
50 g/2 oz/1 small can of anchovy
  fillets, drained
30 ml/2 tbsp lemon juice
2 egg yolks
15 ml/1 tbsp capers
4 gherkin (cornichon) fans
Rice salad, to serve

Place the meat a piece at a time in a plastic bag and beat with a rolling pin or meat mallet until flattened. Place in a shallow dish and add 30 ml/2 tbsp of the oil, the bay leaf, oregano, celery salt and some pepper. Leave to marinate for 2 hours.

Meanwhile, put the tuna in a blender or food processor with half the anchovies and the lemon juice. Blend until smooth. Add the egg yolks and blend again. With the machine running, add the remaining oil, a drop at a time, until thick and glossy. Season to taste. Turn into a container and chill overnight. Heat a large frying pan (skillet), add the meat and cook quickly for 2–3 minutes on each side until golden brown and cooked through. Remove from the pan, place on a cold platter and leave until cold. Chill overnight. When ready to serve, spoon the sauce over the meat and sprinkle with the capers. Garnish with gherkin fans and serve with a rice salad.

Salade niçoise

SERVES 4

8 baby new potatoes, boiled and
  halved
225 g/8 oz French (green) beans,
  cooked
3 hard-boiled (hard-cooked) eggs,
  quartered
8 cherry tomatoes, halved
5 cm/2 in piece of cucumber, diced
1 little gem lettuce, cut into bite-sized
  pieces
185 g/6½ oz/1 small can of tuna,
  drained
8 black olives
45 ml/3 tbsp olive oil
15 ml/1 tbsp white wine vinegar
2.5 ml/½ tsp dried mixed herbs
A good pinch of caster (superfine)
  sugar
2.5 ml/½ tsp Dijon mustard
Salt and freshly ground black pepper
1 small onion, thinly sliced and
  separated into rings
15 ml/1 tbsp chopped parsley

Put the potatoes, beans, eggs, tomatoes, cucumber, lettuce, tuna and olives in a salad bowl. Whisk together the oil, wine vinegar, herbs, sugar, mustard and some salt and pepper. Pour over the salad and toss gently. Scatter the onion rings on top and sprinkle with the parsley.

Monkfish tabbouleh

SERVES 4

*225 g/8 oz/2 cups bulghar (cracked
wheat)*
600 ml/1 pt/2½ cups boiling water
*350 g/12 oz monkfish, cut into large
cubes*
Salt and freshly ground black pepper
*1 bunch of spring onions (scallions),
trimmed, reserving the trimmings,
finely chopped*
60 ml/4 tbsp chopped parsley
*30 ml/2 tbsp chopped coriander
(cilantro)*
30 ml/2 tbsp chopped mint
60 ml/4 tbsp olive oil
Finely grated rind and juice of ½ lemon
30 ml/2 tbsp white wine vinegar
1 garlic clove, crushed
5 cm/2 in piece of cucumber, chopped
100 g/4 oz cherry tomatoes, halved

Put the bulghar in a large bowl. Add
the boiling water, stir and leave to
stand for 30 minutes or until swollen
and soft and the water has been
absorbed. Drain and leave to cool.
Put the monkfish in a saucepan.
Cover with water and add a little
salt and pepper and the spring onion
trimmings. Bring to the boil, reduce
the heat, cover and simmer gently
for 5 minutes until just tender.
Drain, discarding the onion
trimmings, and leave to cool. Tip the
bulghar into a large salad bowl. Add
all the remaining ingredients except
the fish and toss well. Add the fish
and gently toss in the salad. Season
to taste. Cover and chill for at least
2 hours before serving.

Tuna and flageolet tabbouleh

SERVES 4–6

Prepare as for Monkfish Tabbouleh,
but omit the monkfish. Add 185 g/
6½ oz/1 small can of flaked tuna to
the soaked bulghar (cracked wheat)
with 425 g/15 oz/1 large can of
flageolets, drained, then continue as
before.

Mediterranean pasta salad

SERVES 4

175 g/6 oz any pasta shapes
*100 g/4 oz French (green) beans, cut
into short lengths*
90 ml/6 tbsp olive oil
45 ml/3 tbsp white wine vinegar
2.5 ml/½ tsp dried oregano
2.5 ml/½ tsp Dijon mustard
5 ml/1 tsp caster (superfine) sugar
Salt and freshly ground black pepper
8 cherry tomatoes, halved
12 anchovy-stuffed green olives
*120 g/4½ oz/1 small can of sardines,
drained and cut into small chunks*
½ iceberg lettuce, shredded
*50 g/2 oz/1 small can of anchovy
fillets, drained*

Cook the pasta according to the
packet directions, adding the beans
for the last 4 minutes. Drain and tip
into a bowl. Whisk together the oil,
wine vinegar, oregano, mustard,
sugar and some salt and pepper.
Pour a quarter of this dressing into
the pasta and beans, toss and leave
to cool. Add all the remaining
ingredients except the lettuce and
anchovies. Toss well. Pile on to a
bed of lettuce and garnish with the
anchovies before serving.

Mixed bean and tuna salad

SERVES 4

425 g/15 oz/1 large can of mixed
pulses, drained
185 g/6½ oz/1 small can of tuna,
drained and roughly flaked
1 onion, chopped
170 g/6 oz/1 small can of pimiento
caps, drained and sliced
4 gherkins (cornichons), chopped
30 ml/2 tbsp olive oil
15 ml/1 tbsp red wine vinegar
A pinch of caster (superfine) sugar
Salt and freshly ground black pepper
5 ml/1 tsp dried chives

Drain the pulses, rinse them and
drain again. Mix with the tuna,
onion, pimientos and gherkins.
Whisk together the remaining
ingredients and pour over the salad.
Toss and chill for at least 1 hour to
allow the flavours to develop.

Smoked eel and pancetta salad

SERVES 4

16 baby new potatoes, scrubbed and
sliced
20 ml/1½ tbsp cider vinegar
Salt and freshly ground black pepper
45 ml/3 tbsp olive oil
100 g/4 oz pancetta, diced
450 g/1 lb smoked eel fillet
5 ml/1 tsp caster (superfine) sugar
30 ml/2 tbsp crème fraîche
1 round lettuce, finely shredded
4 hard-boiled (hard-cooked) eggs,
sliced
Horseradish Creme (page 381), to serve

Boil the potatoes in lightly salted
water for about 3–4 minutes until
just tender but still holding their
shape. Drain and tip into a bowl.
Immediately sprinkle in half the
vinegar, some salt and pepper and
15 ml/1 tbsp of the oil and toss
gently. Dry-fry the pancetta in a
frying pan (skillet) until crisp and
golden, stirring all the time. Remove
from the pan with a draining spoon.
Drain on kitchen paper (paper
towels). Slice the eel thinly. Stir the
remaining vinegar and oil in the
frying pan with the pancetta fat.
Heat, stirring, until blended, then
stir in the sugar, crème fraîche and
some salt and pepper. Put the lettuce
on four plates. Top with the
potatoes, then the eel slices, then
the eggs. Spoon the dressing over
and top with the pancetta. Serve
straight away with Horseradish
Creme.

Seafood pasta salad

SERVES 4

175 g/6 oz conchiglie (pasta shells)
225 g/8 oz cooked seafood cocktail
1 small onion, finely chopped
1 green (bell) pepper, finely chopped
60 ml/4 tbsp olive oil
30 ml/2 tbsp lemon juice
5 ml/1 tsp caster (superfine) sugar
1 garlic clove, crushed
Salt and freshly ground black pepper
Lettuce leaves

Cook the pasta according to the
packet directions, Drain, rinse with
cold water and drain again. Place in
a bowl. Drain the seafood and add
to the pasta with the onion and
green pepper. Whisk together the oil
and lemon juice with the sugar,
garlic and a little salt and pepper.
Pour over the salad, toss and chill
until ready to serve on a bed of
lettuce.

Sicilian prawn salad

SERVES 4

175 g/6 oz/¾ cup wild rice mix
30 ml/2 tbsp olive oil
10 ml/2 tsp red wine vinegar
5 ml/1 tsp paprika
Salt and freshly ground black pepper
A good pinch of caster (superfine)
  sugar
50 g/2 oz/½ cup toasted flaked
  (slivered) almonds
150 ml/¼ pt/⅔ cup mayonnaise
75 ml/5 tbsp extra-thick double
  (heavy) cream
Finely grated rind and juice of
  ½ orange
Finely grated rind and juice of ½ lemon
5 ml/1 tsp tomato purée (paste)
200 g/7 oz/1 small can of pimiento
  caps, drained
1 spring onion (scallion), very finely
  chopped
2 sun-dried tomatoes, very finely
  chopped
175 g/6 oz cooked peeled prawns
  (shrimp)
1 small round lettuce, finely shredded

Cook the rice in plenty of lightly
salted, boiling water for 10 minutes
or until tender. Drain, rinse with
cold water and drain again. Whisk
together the oil, wine vinegar,
paprika, a little salt and pepper and
the sugar in a bowl. Add the rice
and almonds and toss well. Pack
into four individual moulds and chill
until ready to serve.

Mix the mayonnaise with the
cream, lemon and orange rinds and
juices, the tomato purée and a little
salt and pepper. Cut one of the
pimientos into thin strips and chop
the remainder. Mix the chopped
pimiento into the mayonnaise
mixture with the spring onion and
sun-dried tomatoes. Fold in the
prawns, taste and re-season if
necessary. Put the shredded lettuce
on four plates. Turn out a rice mould
in the centre of each plate and
spoon the prawn mixture all round.
Garnish with strips of pimiento and
serve.

Cooling conger salad

SERVES 4

4 conger eel cutlets
600 ml/1 pt/2½ cups fish stock
100 g/4 oz baby asparagus spears
100 g/4 oz baby corn cobs
15 ml/1 tbsp olive oil
5 ml/1 tsp lemon juice
Salt and freshly ground black pepper
½ lollo rosso lettuce, torn into small
  pieces
1 quantity of Gorgeous Green Sauce
  (page 375)
4 tomatoes, skinned and quartered
¼ cucumber, peeled and finely chopped
2 hard-boiled (hard-cooked) eggs, cut
  into small wedges

Poach the eel in the stock for
15 minutes or until tender. Leave to
cool in the stock, then drain.
Meanwhile, cook the asparagus and
corn cobs in lightly salted boiling
water for just 3 minutes. Drain, rinse
with cold water and drain again.
Toss in the oil, lemon juice and a
little salt and pepper. Arrange the
lettuce on four plates and top each
with a drained eel cutlet. Spoon the
sauce over. Arrange the asparagus
and corn cobs around, interspersed
with the tomato quarters. Pile the
cucumber on top of the green sauce
and arrange the egg wedges around
the edge of the plates.

Melon and prawn salad with hot herb loaf

SERVES 4

2 small round melons such as galia,
  ogen or chanterais
450 g/1 lb tomatoes, skinned and
  quartered
1 large cucumber, peeled and cubed
225 g/8 oz cooked peeled prawns
  (shrimp)
30 ml/2 tbsp white wine vinegar
90 ml/6 tbsp olive or sunflower oil
Salt and freshly ground black pepper
5 ml/1 tsp caster (superfine) sugar
75 g/3 oz/⅓ cup unsalted (sweet)
  butter, softened
10 ml/2 tsp dried mixed herbs
5 ml/1 tsp lemon juice
1 small French stick
5 ml/1 tsp chopped mint
5 ml/1 tsp snipped chives

Halve the melons and discard the seeds. Scoop out the flesh using a melon baller or cut it out and dice it. Reserve the shells. Place the flesh in a bowl and mix with the tomatoes, cucumber and prawns. Whisk together the wine vinegar, oil, some salt and pepper and the sugar. Pour over the salad, toss gently and chill for at least 1 hour but no longer than 3 hours.

To make the loaf, mash the butter with the dried mixed herbs, lemon juice and a little salt and pepper. Cut the loaf into 12 slices, not quite through the bottom crust. Spread the butter mixture between each slice and any remainder over the top. Wrap in foil and grill (broil), turning frequently, for about 8 minutes, until the bread is piping hot and the butter melted. Open the foil and grill briefly to brown the top. Take care it doesn't burn. Put the melon shells in serving bowls. Stir the mint and chives into the salad and spoon into the shells. Serve with the hot bread.

Oriental salad

SERVES 4

225 g/8 oz/1 small can of pineapple
  rings, drained, reserving the juice
1 green (bell) pepper, diced
2 spring onions (scallions), chopped
175 g/6 oz beansprouts
175 g/6 oz cooked peeled prawns
  (shrimp)
15 ml/1 tbsp soy sauce
15 ml/1 tbsp sunflower oil
A pinch of ground ginger

Cut the pineapple into small pieces and mix with the green pepper, spring onions, beansprouts and prawns. Whisk together the remaining ingredients with 15 ml/ 1 tbsp of the pineapple juice. Pour over the salad, toss and serve.

Mimosa egg salad

SERVES 4

225 g/8 oz/1 cup wild rice mix
45 ml/3 tbsp olive oil
15 ml/1 tbsp white wine vinegar
15 ml/1 tbsp chopped coriander
(cilantro)
Salt and freshly ground black pepper
4 large hard-boiled (hard-cooked) eggs,
halved
175 g/6 oz cooked peeled prawns
(shrimp)
300 ml/½ pt/1¼ cups mayonnaise
5 ml/1 tsp hot chilli sauce
15 ml/1 tbsp milk
Watercress, to garnish
Tomato salad and wholemeal bread, to
serve

Cook the rice according to the
packet directions. Drain, rinse with
cold water and drain again. Whisk
together the oil, wine vinegar,
coriander and some salt and pepper
and add to the rice. Toss well.
Spread out on a large serving platter.
Remove the yolks from the eggs. Put
the whites, cut-side up, on the bed
of rice. Pile the prawns into the
cavities. Blend the mayonnaise with
the chilli sauce and milk. Spoon
over the prawns to coat completely.
Push the yolks through a sieve
(strainer) so that they scatter all over
the tops of the stuffed eggs. Garnish
the dish with watercress and serve
with a large tomato salad and
wholemeal bread.

Tuna egg salad

SERVES 4

225 g/8 oz thin French (green) beans,
cut into short lengths
4 large hard-boiled (hard-cooked) eggs
185 g/6½ oz/1 small can of tuna,
drained
150 ml/¼ pt/⅔ cup mayonnaise
150 ml/¼ pt/⅔ cup crème fraîche
Salt and freshly ground black pepper
A good pinch of cayenne
Lemon juice
4 tomatoes, skinned and quartered
100 g/4 oz black olives
45 ml/3 tbsp olive oil
15 ml/1 tbsp balsamic vinegar
15 ml/1 tbsp chopped basil
5 ml/1 tsp caster (superfine) sugar

Cook the beans in lightly salted,
boiling water for about 4 minutes
until just tender but still with some
'bite'. Drain, rinse with cold water
and drain again. Halve the eggs and
scoop out the yolks into a bowl. Cut
a small slice off the base of each
half so the whites will not slide
around. Chop the slices and add to
the yolks. Mash with a fork, then
mash in the tuna until fairly smooth.
Beat in 45 ml/3 tbsp of the
mayonnaise. Season with salt,
pepper and the cayenne and sharpen
slightly with lemon juice.
  Spoon the mixture into the eggs
and arrange in a cluster on a serving
platter. Mix the beans with the
tomatoes, and olives. Whisk together
the remaining ingredients, including
the remaining mayonnaise and
adding a little salt and pepper to
taste. Add to the beans mixture and
toss gently. Spoon round the eggs
and serve cold.

Mussel and rice salad

SERVES 4

½ head of celery
1.75 kg/4 lb mussels, cleaned (page 13)
1 onion, quartered
120 ml/4 fl oz/½ cup dry vermouth
150 ml/¼ pt/⅔ cup water
1 bay leaf
Salt and freshly ground black pepper
About 300 ml/½ pt/1¼ cups chicken or
  fish stock
45 ml/3 tbsp sunflower oil
2 spring onions (scallions), finely
  chopped
175 g/6 oz/¾ cup long-grain rice
2 carrots, cut into very small
  matchsticks
100 g/4 oz baby button mushrooms,
  sliced
15 ml/1 tbsp lemon juice
30 ml/2 tbsp mayonnaise
30 ml/2 tbsp single (light) cream
15 ml/1 tbsp chopped parsley

Discard the outer sticks from the
celery and cut the remainder into
short, thin matchsticks. Put the
mussels in a large saucepan with the
onion, vermouth, water, bay leaf and
a good grinding of pepper. Bring to
the boil, cover and cook for
5 minutes, shaking the pan
occasionally, until the mussels open.
Drain in a colander over a bowl and
allow the cooking liquid to settle.
Leave the mussels to cool. Carefully
strain the mussel liquid into a
measuring jug, leaving any gritty
sediment behind. Make up to
450 ml/¾ pt/2 cups with the stock.

Heat the oil in the rinsed-out
saucepan, add the spring onions and
rice and cook, stirring, until every
grain of rice is coated in oil. Pour on
the stock, bring to the boil, cover,
reduce the heat and cook gently for
15 minutes. Add the celery and
carrot and continue cooking for a
further 5 minutes until the
vegetables are softened but still
slightly crunchy, the rice is just
tender and the stock is absorbed.

Meanwhile, mix the mushrooms
and lemon juice with a little salt and
pepper. Remove all the mussels from
their shells, discarding any that have
remained closed. When the rice is
cooked, tip it into a large, shallow
bowl, spread it out and leave until
cold. Stir in the mushrooms and
mussels. Blend the mayonnaise with
the cream and fold in. Taste and
re-season if necessary. Spoon into
serving bowls and sprinkle with the
parsley.

Tuscan beans

SERVES 4

2 × 425 g/15 oz/large cans of
  cannellini beans
100 g/4 oz conchiglie (pasta shells)
185 g/6½ oz/1 small can of tuna,
  drained
1 onion, thinly sliced and separated
  into rings
1 green (bell) pepper, diced
50 g/2 oz stoned (pitted) black olives
30 ml/2 tbsp lemon juice
15 ml/1 tbsp olive oil
15 ml/1 tbsp water
1 garlic clove, crushed
15 ml/1 tbsp chopped parsley
Salt and freshly ground black pepper
Lettuce leaves

Drain the beans, rinse and drain
again. Cook the pasta according to
the packet directions. Drain, rinse
with cold water and drain again.
Place in a bowl and add the beans,
tuna, onion, green pepper and
olives. Whisk together the lemon
juice, oil, water, garlic, parsley and
some salt and pepper and pour over.
Toss gently. Pile on a bed of lettuce
on four plates and serve cold.

Prawn and rice salad

SERVES 4

125 g/5 oz/⅔ cup long-grain rice
100 g/4 oz/1 cup frozen peas
1 red (bell) pepper, chopped
100 g/4 oz cooked peeled prawns
(shrimp)
30 ml/2 tbsp olive oil
10 ml/2 tsp lemon juice
Salt and freshly ground black pepper
2.5 ml/½ tsp dried summer savory
50 g/2 oz/1 small can of anchovy fillets

Cook the rice in plenty of lightly salted, boiling water for 5 minutes. Add the peas and continue cooking for about 5 minutes until the rice is tender. Drain, rinse with cold water and drain again. Place in a salad bowl with the red pepper and prawns. Whisk together all the remaining ingredients except the anchovies and pour into the bowl. Toss well. Arrange the anchovies over and chill until ready to serve.

Prawn, mushroom and rice salad

SERVES 4

Prepare as for Prawn and Rice Salad, but add 50 g/2 oz thinly sliced mushrooms to the salad and use a green (bell) pepper instead of red. Flavour the dressing with oregano instead of summer savory.

Tuna, mushroom and wild rice salad with anchovy olives

SERVES 4

Prepare as for Prawn and Rice Salad, but substitute wild rice mix for the long-grain rice, cooked according to the packet directions. Use 185 g/ 6½ oz/1 small can of tuna, drained, instead of the prawns and add 12 olives stuffed with anchovies, halved, to the mixture.

Caesar salad

SERVES 4

2 garlic cloves, halved
1 small cos (romaine) lettuce, coarsely
shredded
100 ml/3½ fl oz/scant ½ cup olive oil
4 slices of white bread, crusts removed,
cubed
1 egg
Juice of ½ lemon
50 g/2 oz/1 small can of anchovy
fillets, drained and halved
25 g/1 oz/¼ cup Parmesan cheese,
grated
Salt and freshly ground black pepper

Rub a salad bowl with one of the halved garlic cloves. Add the lettuce to the bowl. Put all the garlic in a frying pan (skillet) with 60 ml/ 4 tbsp of the oil. Fry (sauté) the bread until golden. Drain on kitchen paper (paper towels) and discard the garlic. Drizzle the remaining oil over the lettuce and toss. Boil the egg for 1 minute, then break into a bowl. Whisk in the lemon juice and add to the lettuce with the anchovies, Parmesan and a little salt and pepper. Toss gently and add the croûtons just before serving.

Pompeii salad

SERVES 4

Prepare as for Caesar Salad, but substitute 100 g/4 oz smoked salmon trimmings, cut into neat pieces, for the anchovies, and shave the Parmesan into small slivers instead of grating it. Throw in a handful of sliced, stoned (pitted) black olives as well.

Lemon sole with rémoulade sauce

SERVES 4

4 large or 8 small lemon sole fillets
Juice of ½ small lemon
Salt and freshly ground black pepper
Butter or margarine, for greasing
1 small green (bell) pepper
150 ml/¼ pt/⅔ cup mayonnaise
1 spring onion (scallion), finely
  chopped
5 ml/1 tsp chopped parsley
5 ml/1 tsp chopped tarragon
5 ml/1 tsp chopped thyme
2.5 ml/½ tsp Tabasco sauce
Lettuce leaves
Parsley sprigs, to garnish
Jacket potatoes and tomato and red
  pepper salad, to serve

Season the sole with the lemon juice and salt and pepper and roll up with the skins inside. Place in a greased ovenproof dish. Cover with foil and bake in a preheated oven at 190°C/375°F/gas mark 5 for 15 minutes or until the fish is tender. Leave to cool. Meanwhile, mix together all the remaining ingredients except the lettuce leaves. Transfer the fish to a bed of lettuce leaves on serving plates. Spoon the sauce over, garnish with parsley sprigs and serve with jacket potatoes and a tomato and red pepper salad.

Monkfish with rémoulade sauce

SERVES 4

Prepare as for Lemon Sole with Rémoulade Sauce, but use 450 g/ 1 lb monkfish, cut into thick strips, and bake for 20 minutes or until tender. Omit the tarragon and add 5 finely chopped green olives, stuffed with anchovies, to the sauce.

Marinated plaice tartare

SERVES 4

This also makes a delicious starter for eight people.

4 plaice fillets, skinned if black, halved
  lengthways
1 small garlic clove, crushed (optional)
30 ml/2 tbsp single (light) cream
10 ml/2 tsp lemon juice
15 ml/1 tbsp chopped gherkins
  (cornichons)
15 ml/1 tbsp chopped capers
15 ml/1 tbsp chopped parsley
Salt and freshly ground black pepper
45 ml/3 tbsp mayonnaise
Lettuce leaves, lemon twists and
  parsley sprigs, to garnish
Mixed salad, to serve

Lay the fish in a shallow, ovenproof dish. Mix together all the remaining ingredients except the mayonnaise and pour over. Leave in a cool place for 2 hours to marinate. Lift the fillets out of the marinade, roll each one up and secure with a cocktail stick (toothpick). Return to the marinade. Cover with foil and bake in a preheated oven at 180°C/350°F/gas mark 4 for 20 minutes. Leave to cool in the liquid. Remove the cocktail sticks and transfer the fish to a bed of lettuce. Mix the marinade with the mayonnaise and spoon over. Garnish with lemon twists and parsley sprigs and serve with a mixed salad.

Warm summer seafood

SERVES 4

450 g/1 lb baby squid, cleaned and
  sliced into rings (page 14)
225 g/8 oz raw peeled tiger prawns
  (jumbo shrimp)
100 g/4 oz queen scallops
15 ml/1 tbsp olive oil
15 g/½ oz/1 tbsp butter or margarine
1 garlic clove, crushed
5 ml/1 tsp chopped dill (dill weed)
15 ml/1 tbsp chopped parsley
15 ml/1 tbsp lemon juice
Salt and freshly ground black pepper
1 lollo rosso lettuce, torn
½ cucumber, peeled, seeded and cut
  into matchsticks
8 cherry tomatoes, halved
Dill sprigs, 4 green olives and lemon
  wedges, to garnish

Put the squid, prawns and scallops
in a frying pan (skillet) with the oil
and butter or margarine and the
garlic and cook gently, stirring, for
about 5 minutes until pink and
tender. Stir in the herbs, lemon juice
and some salt and pepper. Turn into
a large salad bowl and add the
remaining ingredients. Toss and
re-season if necessary. Serve straight
away, garnished with dill sprigs,
olives and lemon wedges.

Warm salad of with pancetta

2 oranges
175 g/6 oz mixed salad leaves
8 cherry tomatoes, halved
5 cm/2 in piece of cucumber, diced
1 green (bell) pepper, thinly sliced
1 red onion, thinly sliced
100 g/4 oz pancetta, finely diced
24 queen scallops
90 ml/6 tbsp olive oil
30 ml/2 tbsp lemon juice
15 ml/1 tbsp Worcestershire sauce
Salt and freshly ground black pepper

Thinly pare the rind of one orange
and cut into thin shreds. Boil in a
little water for 3 minutes. Drain,
rinse with cold water and drain
again. Cut all the rind off both fruit
and, holding the fruit over a bowl to
catch the juice, segment the flesh.
Squeeze the membranes over the
bowl to extract the last of the juice
and discard.
  Arrange the salad leaves on four
plates. Scatter the tomatoes,
cucumber, green pepper and onion
over. Dry-fry the pancetta until the
fat runs and continue to cook until
crisp. Add the scallops and toss for
2 minutes or until opaque and
tender. Place on the salads. Pour in
the oil, lemon juice, reserved orange
juice and Worcestershire sauce and
add a little salt and pepper. Bring to
the boil and pour over the salads.
Sprinkle with the orange rind and
serve.

Devilled tuna fish salad

SERVES 4

45 ml/3 tbsp olive oil
15 ml/1 tbsp red wine vinegar
30 ml/2 tbsp tomato ketchup (catsup)
2.5 ml/½ tsp made English mustard
5 ml/1 tsp Worcestershire sauce
A few drops of Tabasco sauce
5 ml/1 tsp clear honey
185 g/6½ oz/1 small can of tuna,
   drained
350 g/12 oz flat green beans, cut
   diagonally into 2.5 cm/1 in pieces
¼ cucumber, thinly sliced
50 g/2 oz/1 small can of anchovy
   fillets, drained and halved
   lengthways
6 stoned (pitted) olives, halved

Whisk together the oil, wine vinegar, ketchup, mustard, Worcestershire and Tabasco sauces and honey. Stir in the tuna, breaking it up well with a fork. Chill while preparing the remainder of the dish. Cook the beans in lightly salted, boiling water for 4 minutes until just tender. Drain, rinse with cold water and drain again. Put a thin layer of half the beans in the base of a shallow serving dish and top with half the tuna mixture. Repeat the layers. Top with a layer of cucumber slices, then a lattice of anchovies. Dot the olives in between and chill for at least 1 hour before serving.

Tomato, egg and anchovy cooler

SERVES 4

50 g/2 oz/1 small can of anchovy
   fillets, drained and halved
   lengthways
45 ml/3 tbsp milk
6 hard-boiled (hard-cooked) eggs,
   sliced
6 gherkins (cornichons), finely
   chopped
15 ml/1 tbsp capers, chopped
15 ml/1 tbsp chopped parsley
8 tomatoes, skinned and halved
Salt and freshly ground black pepper
10 ml/2 tsp caster (superfine) sugar
90 ml/6 tbsp olive oil
30 ml/2 tbsp red wine vinegar
5 ml/1 tsp Dijon mustard
30 ml/2 tbsp tomato ketchup (catsup)
15 ml/1 tbsp chopped mint
15 ml/1 tbsp snipped chives
Hot French bread, to serve

Soak the anchovies in the milk while preparing the rest of the dish. Lay the egg slices in four shallow dishes. Sprinkle with the gherkins, capers and parsley. Put the tomato halves on top, rounded-side up, and sprinkle with salt, pepper and the sugar. Drain and dry the anchovy fillets on kitchen paper (paper towels) and lay them attractively over the tomatoes. Thoroughly whisk together the remaining ingredients and pour over the salads. Chill for 30 minutes before serving to allow the flavours to develop. Serve with lots of hot French bread to mop up the juices.

Light tuna mousse

SERVES 6–8

15 ml/1 tbsp powdered gelatine
30 ml/2 tbsp water
425 g/15 oz/1 large can of tuna,
drained
45 ml/3 tbsp mayonnaise
15 ml/1 tbsp tomato purée (paste)
30 ml/2 tbsp lemon juice
Salt and freshly ground black pepper
300 ml/½ pt/1¼ cups whipping cream,
whipped
Lettuce leaves and lemon twists,
to garnish
New potatoes and mixed salad,
to serve

Sprinkle the gelatine over the water
in a small bowl and leave to soften
for 5 minutes, then stand the bowl
in a pan of hot water and stir until
the gelatine completely dissolves)or
heat briefly in the microwave). Mash
the tuna thoroughly in a large bowl.
Stir in the mayonnaise, tomato
purée, lemon juice and salt and
pepper to taste. Mix in the gelatine,
then fold in the cream. Turn into an
attractive serving dish and chill until
set. Spoon on to lettuce leaves,
garnish with lemon twists and serve
with new potatoes and a mixed
salad.

Light salmon mousse

SERVES 6–8

Prepare as for Light Tuna Mousse,
but substitute 400 g/14 oz/1 large
can of salmon for the tuna and
remove the skin and bones before
use.

Tuna and minted cucumber mousse

SERVES 6

425 g/15 oz/1 large can of tuna,
drained and flaked
2 quantities of Béchamel Sauce
(page 376), cooled completely
300 ml/½ pt/1¼ cups mayonnaise
25 g/1 oz/2 tbsp powdered gelatine
75 ml/5 tbsp water
75 ml/5 tbsp dry white wine
Salt and freshly ground black pepper
2 egg whites
Oil, for greasing
½ cucumber, finely diced
60 ml/4 tbsp plain yoghurt
15 ml/1 tbsp chopped mint
Small mint sprigs, to garnish
Tomato, celery and French (green)
bean salad, to serve

Beat the tuna into the cold Béchamel
Sauce until the mixture is as smooth
as possible. Beat in the mayonnaise.
Sprinkle the gelatine over the water
in a small bowl. Leave to soften for
5 minutes, then stand the bowl in a
pan of hot water and stir until
completely dissolved or heat briefly
in the microwave. Stir in the wine,
then stir this into the fish mixture.
Season to taste. Whisk the egg
whites until stiff and fold into the
mixture with a metal spoon. Turn
into an oiled 1.5 litre/2½ pt/6 cup
ring mould. Chill until set.
   Meanwhile, mix the cucumber
with the yoghurt, mint and a little
salt and pepper. Turn the set mousse
out on to a serving plate and fill the
centre with the cucumber mixture.
Garnish with small mint sprigs and
serve with a tomato, celery and
French bean salad.

Cod with egg and lemon dressing

SERVES 4

4 pieces of cod fillet, about 175 g/6 oz
  each, skinned
3 onions, thinly sliced
300 ml/½ pt/1¼ cups water
Juice of 2 lemons
Salt and freshly ground black pepper
2 eggs
10 ml/2 tsp caster (superfine) sugar
1 bunch of watercress, trimmed
225 g/8 oz young spinach leaves
12 cherry tomatoes, halved
Lemon twists, to garnish
New potatoes, to serve

Put the fish in a saucepan with the onions, water, 10 ml/2 tsp of the lemon juice and a little salt and pepper. Bring to the boil, reduce the heat, part-cover and simmer gently for about 10 minutes until the fish is tender. Carefully lift out the fish and onions with a fish slice and leave to cool.

Break the eggs into a bowl and whisk in the strained cooking liquid and the remaining lemon juice. Place the bowl over a pan of simmering water and whisk until thick. Do not allow to boil. Remove from the heat and whisk in the sugar and some salt and pepper to taste. Arrange the watercress and spinach on four plates. Top with a piece of fish and the onions. Spoon the dressing over and garnish with the tomatoes and lemon twists. Chill before serving with new potatoes.

Warm grilled salmon salad

SERVES 4

4 small salmon tail fillets, about
  150 g/5 oz each
Juice of 1 lime
15 ml/1 tbsp chopped dill (dill weed)
Freshly ground black pepper
225 g/8 oz mixed salad leaves
100 g/4 oz cherry tomatoes, halved
5 cm/2 in piece of cucumber, quartered
  and sliced
1 small red onion, thinly sliced and
  separated into rings
45 ml/3 tbsp Worcestershire sauce
45 ml/3 tbsp white wine vinegar
15 ml/1 tbsp clear honey
45 ml/3 tbsp water
Lime wedges, to garnish
New potatoes, to serve

Place the salmon fillets on foil on a grill (broiler) rack and brush with the lime juice. Sprinkle with the dill and season with pepper. Grill (broil) for 6–8 minutes until cooked through and golden. Meanwhile arrange the salad leaves, tomatoes, cucumber and onion rings on serving plates. Mix together the remaining ingredients in a small saucepan. When the fish is cooked, carefully transfer to the piles of salad. Strain the juices into the ingredients in the saucepan and heat through, stirring. Spoon over the fish, garnish with lime wedges and serve straight away with new potatoes.

Warm grilled red mullet and grapefruit salad

SERVES 4

Prepare as for Warm Grilled Salmon Salad (see page 342), but substitute red mullet fillets for the salmon and add a segmented grapefruit to the salad ingredients.

Swedish potato salad

SERVES 4

450 g/1 lb baby new potatoes, scrubbed and halved
4 rollmop herrings, sliced
1 red eating (dessert) apple, diced but not peeled
5 cm/1 in piece of cucumber, diced
200 g/7 oz/1 small can of sweetcorn (corn), drained
5 ml/1 tsp caraway seeds
150 ml/¼ pt/⅔ cup soured (dairy sour) cream
30 ml/2 tbsp milk
Salt and freshly ground black pepper
1 onion, sliced and separated into rings
4 gherkins (cornichons), sliced

Cook the potatoes in lightly salted boiling water until tender. Drain, rinse with cold water, drain again and turn into a bowl. Add the herrings, apple, cucumber, sweetcorn and caraway seeds and toss gently. Blend together the cream and milk and add a little salt and pepper. Pour over the salad and toss gently. Pile on to serving plates and garnish with the onion rings and sliced gherkins.

Around-the-world warm salad

SERVES 4

225 g/8 oz French (green) beans, cut into 3 pieces
4 eggs
1 Spanish onion, halved and thinly sliced
1 garlic clove, finely chopped
45 ml/3 tbsp olive oil
4 streaky bacon rashers (slices), rinded and finely chopped
100 g/4 oz cooked peeled prawns (shrimp)
15 ml/1 tbsp red wine vinegar
Salt and freshly ground black pepper
100 g/4 oz/1 cup Feta cheese, crumbled
Salad leaves, to garnish

Cook the beans in lightly salted, boiling water until just tender. Drain, rinse with cold water and drain again. Place in a bowl. Poach the eggs in water for 3–5 minutes until cooked to your liking. Drain and place in cold water to prevent further cooking. Meanwhile, fry (sauté) the onion and garlic in the oil for 3 minutes until soft but not brown. Add the bacon and fry for a further 2 minutes, stirring. Add the contents of the pan to the beans with the prawns, wine vinegar, a little salt and pepper and the cheese. Toss gently. Arrange the salad leaves on plates and top each with a poached egg. Serve straight away.

Red salmon and pasta plenty

SERVES 4

225 g/8 oz conchiglie (pasta shells)
200 g/7 oz/1 small can of red salmon,
  drained
50 g/2 oz button mushrooms, sliced
5 cm/2 in piece of cucumber, diced
8 cherry tomatoes, halved
For the dressing:
45 ml/3 tbsp olive oil
Finely grated rind and juice of 1 lime
5 ml/1 tsp caster (superfine) sugar
5 ml/1 tsp dried dill (dill weed)
20 ml/4 tsp single (light) cream
Watercress and 15 ml/1 tbsp snipped
  chives, to garnish

Cook the pasta according to the
packet directions. Drain, rinse with
cold water and drain again. Turn
into a bowl. Remove the skin and
any bones from the salmon. Break
the fish into chunky pieces and add
to the pasta. Add the remaining
ingredients and toss very gently.
  To make the dressing, whisk
together all the ingredients and pour
over the salad. Toss gently. Fill salad
bowls with some watercress. Pile the
salad on top and serve, sprinkled
with the chives.

Polish potato salad

SERVES 4

700 g/1½ lb baby new potatoes,
  scrubbed
30 ml/2 tbsp dry white wine or cider
1 plain cooked beetroot (red beet), grated
10 ml/2 tsp horseradish relish
45 ml/3 tbsp mayonnaise
45 ml/3 tbsp soured (dairy sour) cream
2.5 ml/½ tsp mustard powder
Salt and freshly ground black pepper
50 g/2 oz/1 small can of anchovy
  fillets, drained

Cook the potatoes in lightly salted,
boiling water until tender. Drain and
tip into a bowl. Sprinkle with the
wine or cider and leave to cool. Mix
together all the remaining
ingredients except the anchovies,
add to the bowl and toss gently. Pile
on to a serving dish and top with a
lattice of anchovy fillets.

Soused herrings with apple

SERVES 4

4 herrings, cleaned, heads removed
  and boned
2 small onions
1 eating (dessert), apple, finely
  chopped
5 ml/1 tsp dried dill (dill weed)
15 ml/1 tbsp pickling spices
1 bay leaf
120 ml/4 fl oz/½ cup cider vinegar
120 ml/4 fl oz/½ cup water
15 ml/1 tbsp light brown sugar
1.5 ml/¼ tsp salt
Hot Potato Salad (page 391), to serve

Rinse and dry the fish with kitchen
paper (paper towels). Finely chop
one of the onions. Scatter over the
fish with the apple and sprinkle with
the dill. Roll up and place in an
ovenproof dish. Slice the remaining
onion and scatter over with the
pickling spices. Add the bay leaf.
Mix together the remaining
ingredients and pour over. Cover
with foil and bake in a preheated
oven at 160°C/325°F/gas mark 3 for
1 hour until the fish is cooked
through. Leave to cool in the liquid,
then chill before serving with Hot
Potato Salad.

Lobster cordon bleu

SERVES 4

225 g/8 oz/1 cup long-grain rice or
  wild rice mix
10 ml/2 tsp paprika
45 ml/3 tbsp olive oil
15 ml/1 tbsp white wine vinegar
5 ml/1 tsp chopped fresh tarragon
Salt and freshly ground black pepper
2.5 ml/½ tsp caster (superfine) sugar
1 canned pimento cap
300 ml/½ pt/1¼ cups mayonnaise
10 ml/2 tsp tomato purée (paste)
5 ml/1 tsp Worcestershire sauce
A few drops of Tabasco sauce
5 ml/1 tsp lemon juice
2 cooked lobsters
30 ml/2 tbsp toasted flaked (slivered)
  almonds
Watercress sprigs and lemon wedges,
  to garnish
Green salad, to serve

Cook the rice in plenty of lightly
salted, boiling water for 10 minutes
or until just tender. Drain, rinse with
cold water and drain again. Place in
a bowl. Whisk together the paprika,
oil, wine vinegar, tarragon, a little
salt and pepper and the sugar and
pour over the rice. Toss well. Pass
the pimiento through a sieve
(strainer) or purée in a blender or
food processor. Beat in the
mayonnaise, tomato purée,
Worcestershire and Tabasco sauces
and lemon juice. Season lightly.

Halve the lobsters, leaving the
claws intact and remove the stomach
sac and black thread (page 15).
Arrange the lobster halves on a large
serving platter. Spoon the rice
around and sprinkle with the
almonds. Garnish with watercress
sprigs and lemon wedges and serve
with a green salad and the pimiento
mayonnaise.

Parisian lobster

SERVES 4

1 carrot, finely diced
1 turnip, finely diced
50 g/2 oz small French (green) beans,
  chopped
50 g/2 oz/½ cup petit pois
2 tarragon sprigs
2 parsley sprigs
2 mint sprigs
1 bunch of watercress
300 ml/½ pt/1¼ cups mayonnaise
Salt and freshly ground black pepper
2 cooked lobsters
Green salad, to serve

Cook the carrot and turnip in lightly
salted, boiling water for 2 minutes.
Add the beans and petit pois and
cook for a further 3 minutes until
they are all just tender. Drain, rinse
with cold water and drain again. Put
the herbs in a blender or food
processor. Cut off the stalks from the
watercress and add about a quarter
of the leaves to the herbs. Run the
machine to chop them. Scrape down
the sides and add the mayonnaise.
Run the machine again until well
blended and fairly smooth. Mix the
mayonnaise with the cooked
vegetables and season to taste.

Split the lobsters, remove all the
meat (page 15) and cut into neat
pieces. Spoon the lobster meat back
into the shells and spoon the
vegetable salad on top. Garnish with
the remaining watercress and serve
with a green salad.

Lobster frigador

SERVES 6

3 small cooked lobsters, prepared
(page 15)
45 ml/3 tbsp olive oil
1 bunch of spring onions (scallions),
chopped
150 ml/¼ pt/⅔ cup mayonnaise
150 ml/¼ pt/⅔ cup crème fraîche
30 ml/2 tbsp brandy
50 g/2 oz/½ cup strong Cheddar cheese,
grated
Salt and freshly ground black pepper
1.5 ml/¼ tsp cayenne
50 g/2 oz/½ cup Parmesan cheese,
grated
Paprika, for dusting
Parlsey sprigs and lemon wedges, to
garnish
Olive ciabatta, mixed leaf salad and
sliced avocado tossed in French
dressing, to serve

Put the green tomalley and the coral
from the lobsters in a fairly large
bowl. Cut all the lobster meat into
neat pieces. Wash and dry the shells.
Heat the oil in a frying pan (skillet)
and fry (sauté) the spring onions for
1 minute to soften slightly. Add to
the tomalley and coral. Add all the
remaining ingredients, except the
lobster meat, Parmesan and paprika,
and season to taste with the salt,
pepper and the cayenne. Mix well.

Fold in the lobster meat and pile
back into the shells. Sprinkle with
the Parmesan and dust with a little
paprika. Place on six plates, garnish
with parsley sprigs and lemon
wedges and serve with olive
ciabatta, a mixed leaf salad and
avocado slices tossed in French
dressing.

Far Eastern salad

SERVES 4

175 g/6 oz/¾ cup basmati rice
350 g/12 oz hake fillet
10 ml/2 tsp ground turmeric
1 green or under-ripe banana, sliced
15 ml/1 tbsp lemon juice
50 g/2 oz/⅓ cup sultanas (golden
raisins)
50 g/2 oz creamed coconut, grated
1 green (bell) pepper, finely chopped
200 g/7 oz/1 small can of sweetcorn
(corn), drained
1 green chilli, seeded and finely
chopped (optional)
1 mango or peach, peeled, stoned
(pitted) and diced
30 ml/2 tbsp sunflower oil
Salt and freshly ground black pepper

Cook the rice and hake in plenty of
boiling salted water, to which the
turmeric has been added, for
10 minutes or until just tender. Lift
out the fish. Drain the rice, rinse
with cold water and drain again.
Discard the skin and flake the fish.
Place the rice and fish in a bowl.
Toss the banana in the lemon juice
to prevent browning, then add to the
bowl with all the remaining
ingredients. Toss well and serve.

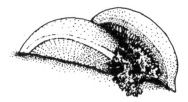

Valencian salad

SERVES 4

225 g/8 oz/1 cup long-grain rice
1.5 ml/¼ tsp saffron powder
2 oranges, all pith removed and
  segmented
1 small cucumber, finely diced
1 red (bell) pepper, finely diced
1 green pepper, finely diced
225 g/8 oz cherry tomatoes, quartered
Salt and freshly ground black pepper
2 cooked lobsters, prepared (page 15)
1 quantity of Romesco Sauce
  (page 378)
30 ml/2 tbsp toasted pine nuts

Cook the rice in plenty of boiling
water, to which the saffron has been
added, for 10 minutes or until
tender. Drain, rinse with cold water
and drain again. Tip into a bowl and
add the orange segments, cucumber,
peppers and tomatoes. Season with
salt and pepper. Cut the lobster tail
meat into neat pieces. Mix the rest
of the meat into the rice and spoon
into bowls. Top with the tail meat.
Spoon a little Romesco Sauce over
each portion and sprinkle with the
pine nuts before serving.

Dressed crab salad

SERVES 4

1 large cooked crab, about 1.5 kg/3 lb,
  prepared (page 16)
15 ml/1 tbsp fresh white breadcrumbs
Lemon juice
2.5 ml/½ tsp Dijon mustard
A pinch of cayenne
Salt and freshly ground black pepper
Chopped parsley and lemon wedges, to
  garnish
Crisp mixed salad and brown bread
  and butter, to serve

Mix the dark crabmeat with the
breadcrumbs, lemon juice to taste,
the mustard, cayenne, salt and a
good grinding of pepper. Season the
white meat with a little salt and
pepper. Wash the shell and put a
row of white meat at each side with
the dark meat in the centre. Put a
line of chopped parsley down each
side of the dark meat where it meets
the white. Place on a serving plate
and surround with lemon wedges.
Serve with a crisp mixed salad and
brown bread and butter.

Smoked mackerel and potato bowls

SERVES 4

450 g/1 lb baby new potatoes,
  scrubbed and halved
1 mint sprig
4 ready-to-eat smoked mackerel fillets,
  skinned and cut into bite-sized
  pieces
100 g/4 oz/1 cup shelled, fresh or
  cooked frozen peas
45 ml/3 tbsp mayonnaise
30 ml/2 tbsp sunflower oil
15 ml/1 tbsp lemon juice
10 ml/2 tsp horseradish relish
Salt and freshly ground black pepper
Lettuce leaves
12 cherry tomatoes, halved

Boil the potatoes in lightly salted
water, to which the mint has been
added, until just tender. Drain and
tip into a large bowl, discarding the
mint. Add the fish and peas and mix
gently. Whisk together the
mayonnaise, oil, lemon juice,
horseradish relish and a little salt
and pepper and add to the bowl.
Toss gently but thoroughly. Line four
large soup bowls with lettuce leaves
and spoon in the potato and fish
mixture. Scatter the cherry tomatoes
on top and serve.

Soused mackerel and potato salad

SERVES 4

4 small mackerel, boned
Salt and freshly ground black pepper
2 small onions, thinly sliced
5 ml/1 tsp dried dill (dill weed)
300 ml/½ pt/1¼ cups malt vinegar
300 ml/½ pt/1¼ cups water
10 ml/2 tsp light brown sugar
1 bay leaf
450 g/1 lb baby new potatoes, scraped
45 ml/3 tbsp mayonnaise
45 ml/3 tbsp plain yoghurt
4 large lettuce leaves
15 ml/1 tbsp snipped chives
15 ml/1 tbsp chopped parsley

Lay the mackerel skin-side down, season with salt and pepper and sprinkle with half the sliced onions and dill. Roll up and pack closely together in a shallow, ovenproof dish. Pour the vinegar and water over and sprinkle with the sugar. Add the bay leaf. Cover with foil and bake in a preheated oven at 180°C/350°F/gas mark 4 for 45 minutes until cooked through. Remove from the oven and leave to cool, then chill.

Meanwhile, boil the potatoes in plenty of lightly salted water until just tender. Drain and leave to cool. Mix the mayonnaise with the yoghurt, the remaining onion and a little salt and pepper and add to the potatoes. Toss gently. Pile on to lettuce leaves on four plates and sprinkle with the chives and parsley. Drain the mackerel, arrange alongside and serve.

Smoked mackerel boats with gooseberry mayo

SERVES 4

175 g/6 oz gooseberries, topped and tailed
15 ml/1 tbsp water
30 ml/2 tbsp granulated sugar
150 ml/¼ pt/⅔ cup mayonnaise
Salt and freshly ground black pepper
2 small baguettes, halved lengthways
Butter or margarine, softened, for spreading
4 smoked mackerel fillets
4 small parsley sprigs
½ lollo rosso lettuce
8 cherry tomatoes, halved
8 stoned (pitted) black olives, halved
12 gherkin (cornichon) fans and lemon wedges, to garnish

Put the gooseberries in a saucepan with the water and sugar. Bring to the boil, reduce the heat, cover and simmer for about 10 minutes or until the fruit is really tender (the time will depend on how ripe the gooseberries are). Purée in a blender or food processor or pass through a sieve (strainer). Taste and add more sugar, if liked. Leave to cool, then fold into the mayonnaise and season with salt and pepper. Turn into a small pot.

Spread the baguette halves with butter or margarine and top each with a mackerel fillet. Garnish each with a small sprig of parsley. Lay the boats on beds of lollo rosso leaves on four plates. Scatter the tomatoes and olives round and garnish with the gherkin fans and lemon wedges. Serve with the gooseberry mayonnaise.

Prawn and pasta bows

225 g/8 oz farfalle (pasta bows)
45 ml/3 tbsp mayonnaise
15 ml/1 tbsp single (light) cream
225 g/8 oz cooked peeled prawns
(shrimp)
Salt and freshly ground black pepper
15 ml/1 tbsp snipped chives
15 ml/1 tbsp chopped parsley
5 ml/1 tsp finely grated lemon rind

Cook the pasta according to the
packet directions. Drain, rinse with
cold water and drain again. Mix the
mayonnaise with the cream and add
to the pasta. Toss well and add the
prawns, salt and pepper to taste, the
herbs and lemon rind. Chill until
ready to serve.

Smoked trout and apple salad

4 smoked trout fillets, skinned
1 red eating (dessert) apple, sliced but
not peeled
1 green eating apple, sliced but not
peeled
Lemon juice
1 red (bell) pepper, sliced
1 green pepper, sliced
1 courgette (zucchini), thinly sliced
15 ml/1 tbsp chilli oil or olive oil
120 ml/4 fl oz/½ cup plain yoghurt
5 ml/1 tsp horseradish relish
Salt and freshly ground black pepper
1 bunch of watercress, trimmed

Break the fish into bite-sized pieces
and place in a bowl. Toss the apple
slices in a little lemon juice to
prevent browning and add to the
fish with the peppers and courgette.
Add the oil and toss gently until
glistening. Put the yoghurt in a
blender or food processor with the
horseradish and a little salt and
pepper. Reserve four watercress
sprigs for garnish and add the
remainder to the yoghurt. Run the
machine until well blended. Divide
the salad between four shallow
bowls. Spoon the watercress
dressing over and garnish with
watercress sprigs before serving.

Greek-style tuna and chick peas

1 onion, chopped
1 large garlic clove, crushed
30 ml/2 tbsp olive oil
2 × 425 g/15 oz/large cans of chick
peas (garbanzos), drained
400 g/14 oz/1 large can of chopped
tomatoes
150 ml/¼ pt/⅔ cup dry white wine
5 ml/1 tsp caster (superfine) sugar
Salt and freshly ground black pepper
5 ml/1 tsp dried marjoram
185 g/6½ oz/1 small can of tuna,
drained
8 stoned (pitted) black olives, sliced
Round lettuce leaves
30 ml/2 tbsp chopped fresh parsley

Fry (sauté) the onion and garlic in
the oil for 2 minutes, stirring. Add
the chick peas, tomatoes, wine,
sugar, some salt and pepper and the
marjoram. Bring to the boil, reduce
the heat and simmer for about
10–15 minutes until the chick peas
are bathed in a rich sauce. Turn into
a bowl and leave to cool. Gently fold
in the tuna and olives, taste, and
re-season if necessary and chill until
ready to serve. Spoon on to a bed of
lettuce leaves and garnish with the
parsley.

Trout Grenoble

SERVES 4

1 small lemon
4 trout, cleaned
60 ml/4 tbsp dry sherry
200 ml/7 fl oz/scant 1 cup water
6 peppercorns
1 small onion, quartered
10 ml/2 tsp horseradish relish
60 ml/4 tbsp crème fraîche
Salt and freshly ground black pepper
A good pinch of caster (superfine)
sugar
30 ml/2 tbsp snipped chives
15 ml/1 tbsp chopped parsley
Granary bread and tomato and onion
salad, to serve

Halve the lemon. Grate the rind and squeeze the juice from one half. Slice the other half thinly and reserve for garnish. Put the trout in an ovenproof dish. Add half the sherry, the water, lemon rind, peppercorns and onion. Cover and cook in a preheated oven at 180°C/350°F/gas mark 4 for 15 minutes or until tender. Leave to cool in the liquid. Lift out and place on individual plates. Pull off the skin.

Mix together the remaining sherry, 15 ml/1 tbsp of the lemon juice, the horseradish, crème fraîche and some salt and pepper in a small bowl, then sweeten to taste with the caster sugar. Stir in half the chives. Spoon over the trout and sprinkle with the remaining chives and the parsley. Garnish with the lemon slices and serve with granary bread and tomato and onion salad.

Canny tuna salad loaf

SERVES 4–6

15 ml/1 tbsp powdered gelatine
150 ml/¼ pt/⅔ cup chicken stock
425 g/15 oz/1 large can of tuna,
drained
425 g/15 oz/1 large can of potato
salad
295 g/10½ oz/1 medium can of diced
mixed vegetables, drained
30 ml/2 tbsp mayonnaise
Salt and freshly ground black pepper
30 ml/2 tbsp chopped parsley
Sunflower oil, for greasing
Parsley sprigs and lemon wedges, to
garnish
Crusty bread and green salad, to serve

Sprinkle the gelatine over the stock in a small bowl and leave to soften for 5 minutes. Place the bowl in a pan of hot water and stir until completely dissolved or heat briefly in a microwave. Leave to cool. Mix together the tuna, potato salad and mixed vegetables. Stir the mayonnaise into the cold, unset stock, then stir into the fish mixture. Season to taste and stir in the parsley. Turn the mixture into a lightly oiled 900 g/2 lb loaf tin (pan). Level the surface and chill until set. Turn out on to a serving plate, garnish with parsley sprigs and lemon wedges and serve with crusty bread and a green salad.

Aubergine, tuna and carrot terrine

SERVES 6

2 aubergines (eggplants)
4 large carrots, thinly sliced
25 g/1 oz/2 tbsp butter or margarine
5 ml/1 tsp caster (superfine) sugar
Salt and freshly ground black pepper
15 ml/1 tbsp plain (all-purpose) flour
4 large eggs, separated
300 ml/½ pt/1¼ cups crème fraîche
185 g/6½ oz/1 small can of tuna,
   drained
75 g/3 oz/¾ cup Cheddar cheese,
   grated
Crusty bread and spinach salad,
   to serve

Cut the stalks off the aubergines and discard. Boil in lightly salted water for about 10 minutes until tender. Drain, rinse with cold water and drain again. Meanwhile, boil the carrots separately in lightly salted water for about 5 minutes until tender. Drain and mash with half the butter or margarine, the sugar and some salt and pepper. Peel the skin off the aubergines, then mash the flesh.

Melt the remaining butter or margarine in a saucepan. Stir in the flour and cook for 1 minute, stirring. Remove from the heat and beat in two of the egg yolks and half the crème fraîche. Finally, beat in the aubergine and season to taste. Beat the remaining egg yolks and crème fraîche into the mashed carrots. Beat the tuna into the aubergine mixture and the cheese into the carrot mixture. Whisk the egg whites until really stiff. Fold half into each mixture.

Grease and line a 900 g/2 lb loaf tin (pan) or terrine with greased greaseproof (waxed) paper. Layer the mixtures alternately in the prepared tin. Bake in a preheated oven at 190°C/375°F/gas mark 5 for about 40 minutes until set. Leave to cool, then turn out on to a serving dish. Serve sliced with crusty bread and a spinach salad.

Jellied eels

SERVES 6

You can spoon the eels into individual, lightly oiled dishes, then turn them out to serve.

2 carrots, chopped
2 celery sticks, chopped
1 small onion, chopped
1.5 ml/¼ tsp grated nutmeg
1.5 ml/¼ tsp ground mace
15 ml/1 tbsp chopped parsley
5 ml/1 tsp chopped sage
5 ml/1 tsp chopped thyme
Finely grated rind and juice of 1 small
   lemon
600 ml/1 pt/2½ cups fish stock
900 g/2 lb eels, skinned and cut into
   short lengths
Salt and freshly ground black pepper
15 ml/1 tbsp powdered gelatine
Pickles and salads, to serve

Put everything except the eels, salt and pepper and gelatine in a large saucepan. Bring to the boil, add the eels, reduce the heat, part-cover and simmer gently for 30 minutes. Leave to cool, then season to taste. Using a draining spoon, transfer the eels to a bowl and remove the bones. Strain the liquid and return to the pan. Bring to the boil, skim, then stir in the gelatine until dissolved. Pour over the eels. Cool, then chill until set. Serve with pickles and salads.

Sardine crunch salad

SERVES 4

*8 slices of bread from a small sliced
loaf, crusts removed*
*75 g/3 oz/⅓ cup butter or margarine,
melted*
*225 g/8 oz shelled fresh or frozen
broad (fava) beans*
*120 g/4½ oz/1 small can of sardines,
drained*
10 ml/2 tsp lemon juice
A few drops of Tabasco sauce
Salt and freshly ground black pepper
*5 cm/2 in piece of cucumber, finely
chopped*
4 tomatoes, skinned and quartered
*4 spring onions (scallions), finely
chopped*
*100 g/4 oz button mushrooms, thinly
sliced*
*100 g/4 oz/½ cup medium-fat soft
cheese*
30 ml/2 tbsp milk
1.5 ml/¼ tsp celery salt
5 ml/1 tsp caster (superfine) sugar
Lettuce leaves
Parsley sprigs, to garnish

Dip the bread in the butter or
margarine until coated. Press one
slice into each section of a tartlet tin
(patty pan). Bake in a preheated
oven at 190°C/375°F/gas mark 5 for
about 20 minutes until crisp and
golden. Transfer to a wire rack to
cool.

Meanwhile, cook the broad beans
in lightly salted water until tender.
Drain, rinse with cold water and
drain again. Mash the sardines,
discarding the bones if preferred
(but they are good for you!). Add
the lemon juice, Tabasco and
seasoning to taste. Stir in the
cucumber. Mix the beans with the
tomatoes, spring onions and
mushrooms. Blend together the
cheese, milk, celery salt, sugar and a
little salt and pepper. Add to the
bean mixture and fold in gently.

Spoon the sardine mixture into
the bread cases and arrange on
lettuce leaves on serving plates. Pile
the bean mixture to one side and
serve garnished with parsley sprigs.

Potato and lentil salad with tuna

SERVES 4

*100 g/4 oz/⅔ cup green lentils, soaked
overnight*
900 ml/1½ pts/3¾ cups fish stock
1 bay leaf
8 small waxy potatoes, quartered
2 spring onions (scallions), chopped
4 celery sticks, chopped
*185 g/6½ oz/1 small can of tuna,
drained and roughly flaked*
90 ml/6 tbsp olive oil
30 ml/2 tbsp soy sauce
30 ml/2 tbsp white wine vinegar
1 small garlic clove, crushed
*2 streaky bacon rashers (slices), rinded
and finely chopped*

Drain the lentils and boil in the
stock with the bay leaf for
30–40 minutes until tender. Drain
and discard the bay leaf. Meanwhile,
boil the potatoes in lightly salted
water for about 5 minutes until just
tender. Drain. Place the lentils and
potatoes in a bowl and add the
onions, celery and tuna. Whisk
together all the remaining
ingredients except the bacon and
pour over. Toss gently. Dry-fry the
bacon pieces quickly until crisp.
Spoon over and serve.

Amber trout with baby vegetable salad

SERVES 6

6 even-sized trout
300 ml/½ pt/1¼ cups dry cider
15 ml/1 tbsp cider vinegar
300 ml/½ pt/1¼ cups water
1 onion, sliced
1 carrot, sliced
1 celery stick, sliced
1 bouquet garni sachet
1.5 ml/¼ tsp salt
8 peppercorns
A pinch of saffron powder
100 g/4 oz baby carrots, scrubbed
100 g/4 oz baby corn cobs
100 g/4 oz mangetout (snow peas)
8 baby turnips, halved
24 baby new potatoes
45 ml/3 tbsp olive oil
15 ml/1 tbsp lemon juice
Salt and freshly ground black pepper
A good pinch of caster (superfine) sugar
5 ml/1 tsp Dijon mustard
15 ml/1 tbsp chopped parsley

Clean and fillet the trout, reserving the heads, tails and bones. Put the cider, vinegar, water, onion, carrot, celery, bouquet garni, salt, peppercorns and fish scraps in a saucepan. Bring to the boil, reduce the heat, cover and simmer for 20 minutes. Halve the fish fillets and lay them in a shallow pan (I use a roasting tin) in which they will fit in a single layer. Strain the cooking liquid over. Reserve the vegetables with the fish bones.

Cover the pan with foil, bring to the boil, reduce the heat and simmer gently for 4–5 minutes or until the fish is just cooked. Gently lift the fish out of the liquid and leave to cool. Remove the skin and lay the fillets in a shallow serving dish.

Return the fish bones and vegetables to the stock and add the saffron. Bring back to the boil and boil until the stock is reduced to about 300 ml/½ pt/1¼ cups. Strain over the trout and leave to cool, then chill overnight until set.

The next day, cook all the vegetables in lightly salted water or steam separately until just tender. Drain and leave to cool. Arrange attractively on a serving platter. Whisk together all the remaining ingredients except the parsley. Drizzle over the vegetables and serve with the jellied fish, garnished with the parsley.

Savoy tuna salad

SERVES 4

1 red eating (dessert) apple, diced but not peeled
5 ml/1 tsp lemon juice, plus a little extra (optional)
¼ small savoy cabbage, all core removed, thinly shredded
1 red (bell) pepper, cut into thin strips
1 green pepper, cut into thin strips
1 leek, thinly sliced
185 g/6½ oz/1 small can of tuna, drained and broken into large chunks
15 ml/1 tbsp Dijon mustard
10 ml/2 tsp clear honey
30 ml/2 tbsp soy sauce
15 ml/1 tbsp apple juice

Toss the apple in the measured lemon juice to prevent browning. Plunge the cabbage in boiling water for 1 minute. Drain, rinse with cold water and drain again. Place in a large salad bowl with the peppers, apple, leek and the tuna chunks. Whisk together the remaining ingredients and sharpen with a little lemon juice, if liked. Pour over, toss very gently and serve.

Jellied salmon trout

SERVES 6

1.5 kg/3 lb salmon trout, cleaned
600 ml/1 pt/2½ cups fish stock
300 ml/½ pt/1¼ cups dry white wine
40 g/1½ oz/⅓ cup powdered gelatine
15 ml/1 tbsp white wine vinegar
2 egg whites
60 ml/4 tbsp medium-dry sherry
8 cooked unpeeled prawns (shrimp)
½ cucumber, thinly sliced
Parsley sprigs, to garnish
Prawn Mayonnaise (page 376) and
  new potatoes, to serve

Trim the fish and vandyke the tail (page 13). Wash well and pat dry on kitchen paper (paper towels). Bend round slightly so the fish sits upright (rather than on its side) in a fish kettle or ovenproof dish. Pour the stock and wine around. Cover with foil and bake in a preheated oven at 180°C/350°F/gas mark 4 for 35 minutes. Remove from the oven and leave to cool in the liquid. Lift out on to a board and carefully pull off the skin, leaving the head and tail intact.

While the fish is cooking, strain the stock through kitchen paper (paper towel) or a new, disposable kitchen cloth in a sieve (strainer) into a saucepan. Spoon a little of the stock into a small bowl and sprinkle the gelatine over. Leave to soften for 5 minutes, then either stand the bowl over a pan of hot water and stir until completely dissolved or heat briefly in the microwave. Heat the remaining stock and when hot, but not boiling, whisk in the vinegar, egg whites and sherry. Continue whisking until the mixture boils. Let it rise to the top of the pan, then take the pan off the heat. Let it settle for 5 minutes, then bring to the boil until it rises in the pan

again. Again, draw aside and leave to settle. Skim off as much scum as possible, then strain through a sieve, lined with a clean disposable cloth, into a bowl. Stir in the dissolved gelatine. Leave until cold but not set.

Pour a little of the cold, unset jelly on to a shallow serving dish and lay the fish on top. Brush with a little more of the cold, unset jelly. Lay the prawns along its back and brush again. Chill to set. Pour the remaining jelly into a shallow baking tin (pan) and chill to set. Chop the set jelly in the tin and spoon round the fish. Garnish with the cucumber slices and parsley sprigs and serve with Prawn Mayonnaise and new potatoes.

Smoked mackerel, chicory, orange and cashew nut salad

SERVES 4

2 heads of chicory (Belgian endive)
2 oranges
2 smoked mackerel fillets, cut into
  pieces
A few coriander (cilantro) leaves, torn
50 g/2 oz/½ cup cashew nuts
1 quantity of Scandinavian Caraway
  Dressing (page 373)

Cut a cone-shaped core out of the base of each head of chicory and discard. Cut the heads into three pieces and separate into leaves. Place in a salad bowl. Cut all the rind and pith off the oranges, slice the fruit and halve or quarter the slices, depending on size. Add to the bowl with the mackerel, coriander leaves and nuts. Add the dressing, toss and serve.

Mackerel terrine with golden gate salad

SERVES 4–6

5 small mackerel, skinned and boned
45 ml/3 tbsp lemon juice
5 ml/1 tsp dried mixed herbs
1.5 ml/¼ tsp ground mace
6 juniper berries, crushed
Salt and freshly ground black pepper
100 g/4 oz/½ cup long-grain rice
450 ml/¾ pt/2 cups chicken or fish
 stock
3 hard-boiled (hard-cooked) eggs,
 quartered
1 bunch of spring onions (scallions)
100 g/4 oz chestnut mushrooms,
 quartered
1 egg, beaten
175 g/6 oz/¾ cup unsalted (sweet)
 butter
For the salad:
1 small cos (romaine) lettuce, cut into
 chunks
320 g/12 oz/1 medium can of
 sweetcorn (corn), drained
2 nectarines, skinned, halved, stoned
 (pitted) and sliced
60 ml/4 tbsp olive oil
15 ml/1 tbsp balsamic vinegar

Lay the mackerel fillets in a shallow dish and sprinkle with 30 ml/2 tbsp of the lemon juice, the herbs, mace, juniper berries and a little salt and pepper. Leave to marinate while preparing the rest of the dish. Cook the rice in the stock for 10 minutes or until tender. Drain off any remaining stock and place in a blender or food processor with the hard-boiled eggs, one of the spring onions, roughly chopped, the mushrooms and a little salt and pepper. Run the machine until the mixture forms a paste. Stop the machine and scrape down the sides as necessary. Add the beaten egg and run the machine until blended to a paste.

Grease a 900 g/2 lb terrine with some of the butter. Spoon half the paste into the container and smooth the surface. Lay the marinated fillets on top, then spread with the remaining paste. Cover with greased foil and stand the container in a baking tin with enough boiling water to come halfway up its sides. Bake in a preheated oven at 180°C/ 350°F/gas mark 4 for 1 hour. Remove from the oven, lift out of the baking tin and leave to cool. Melt the remaining butter, pour over and cool, then chill until firm.

Meanwhile, to make the salad, put the lettuce in a salad bowl with the sweetcorn, the remaining spring onions, diagonally sliced, and the nectarine slices. Whisk the remaining lemon juice with the oil, vinegar and a little salt and pepper. Just before serving, whisk the dressing again, pour over the salad, toss and serve with the terrine, cut into slices.

Creamy rock salmon mayonnaise

SERVES 6

1 kg/2¼ lb rock salmon
1.2 litres/2 pts/5 cups fish stock
30 ml/2 tbsp white wine vinegar
1 bouquet garni sachet
1 bay leaf
3 thick slices of white bread
45 ml/3 tbsp water
75 ml/5 tbsp olive oil
1 small garlic clove, crushed
300 ml/½ pt/1¼ cups mayonnaise
300 ml/½ pt/1¼ cups crème fraîche
Lemon juice
Salt and freshly ground black pepper
Round lettuce leaves
15 ml/1 tbsp capers
15 ml/1 tbsp chopped parsley
Mixed salad and French bread,
   to serve

Put the fish in a saucepan with the stock, vinegar, bouquet garni and bay leaf. Bring to the boil, reduce the heat, cover and simmer gently for 8 minutes until the fish comes away from the bones easily. Leave to cool in the liquid. Lift out of the pan and remove the bones.

Break up the bread in a bowl and add the water and 15 ml/1 tbsp of the oil. Leave to soak for 5 minutes, then squeeze out the moisture. Place the bread in a bowl with the fish and work with a fork until well blended. Gradually work in the remaining oil, then the garlic. Blend together the mayonnaise and crème fraîche. Fold half into the fish. Add lemon juice, salt and pepper to taste to the remaining mayonnaise. Pile the fish in a mound on a bed of lettuce leaves. Spoon the remaining mayonnaise over and sprinkle with the capers and parsley. Chill. Serve with a mixed salad and crusty bread.

Marinated squid salad

SERVES 4

450 g/1 lb baby squid, cleaned and cut
   into rings (page 14)
90 ml/6 tbsp olive oil
Juice of 1 lemon
5 ml/1 tsp white wine vinegar
1 large garlic clove, crushed
30 ml/2 tbsp chopped parsley
15 ml/1 tbsp chopped basil
15 ml/1 tbsp stoned (pitted) black
   olives, sliced
Salt and freshly ground black pepper
100 g/4 oz rocket leaves
450 g/1 lb baby new potatoes,
   scrubbed and boiled
200 g/7 oz/1 small can of pimientos,
   drained and cut into small chunks
5 cm/2 in piece of cucumber, diced
Lemon wedges, to garnish

Drop the prepared squid into a pan of boiling water, reduce the heat and simmer for 15 minutes or until tender. Drain and dry with kitchen paper (paper towels). Place the oil, lemon juice, wine vinegar, garlic, herbs, olives and a little salt and pepper in a large plastic container with a sealable lid and shake to mix. Add the squid, toss and chill for 24 hours.

Arrange the rocket on four plates. Add the cooked potatoes, pimientos and cucumber. Spoon the squid and dressing over and serve garnished with lemon wedges.

The ultimate seafood platter

SERVES 4

You can enjoy this dish in the restaurants of Normandy and Brittany – and many other coastal regions of France. Alter the quantities according to your taste (and pocket!) – those given here are purely a guide. Follow the platter with a well-dressed green salad. Provide finger bowls and pickers, pins and nutcrackers to remove all the succulent meat from the shells.

A bed of well-washed seaweed or shredded lettuce
1 dressed crab (page 16)
8 oysters, shucked (page 15), but left in their shells with the juices
225 g/8 oz cooked whelks in their shells
225 g/8 oz cooked winkles in their shells
450 g/1 lb mussels, cleaned (page 13) and cooked (see Sole Meunière aux Moules, page 130)
450 g/1 lb cooked unpeeled prawns (shrimp) or cooked unpeeled Dublin Bay prawns (saltwater crayfish)
450 g/1 lb cooked clams in their shells or 175 g/6 oz shelled cockles
1 cooked lobster, halved lengthways and cleaned (page 15), then halved again lengthways
Parsley sprigs and lemon wedges, to garnish
Black pepper, Aioli (page 372), Rouille (page 374), plain mayonnaise and lots of crusty bread, to serve

Spread a layer of seaweed or lettuce on a very large platter or tray. Put the dressed crab in the centre and surround with the oysters. Put neat piles of whelks, winkles and mussels around and then the prawns.

Intersperse with little piles of clams or cooked cockles. Put a quarter lobster at the four sides of the platter round the edge. Garnish with parsley and lots of lemon wedges. Serve with black pepper, Aioli, Rouille and plain mayonnaise and lots of bread to nibble in between. A chilled dry white wine – preferably Chablis – is as essential as the finger bowls!

Spicy Japanese rice salad

SERVES 4

50 g/2 oz/1 small can of anchovy fillets
30 ml/2 tbsp milk
175 g/6 oz/¾ cup long-grain rice
120 g/4½ oz/1 small can of sardines, drained and broken into pieces
250 g/9 oz/1 medium can of mussels in brine, drained
15 ml/1 tbsp chilli sauce
30 ml/2 tbsp tomato relish
30 ml/2 tbsp soy sauce
A pinch of curry powder
45 ml/3 tbsp red wine vinegar
Lettuce leaves
12 stoned (pitted) black olives
A few flatleaf parsley leaves, torn

Soak the anchovies in the milk for 10 minutes. Drain and chop. Meanwhile, cook the rice in plenty of lightly salted, boiling water for about 10 minutes until tender. Drain, rinse with cold water and drain again. Tip into a bowl and add the anchovies, sardines and mussels. Whisk together all the remaining ingredients except the lettuce, olives and parsley and pour over the rice. Toss gently. Pile on to a bed of lettuce, scatter the olives over and garnish with a few torn parsley leaves.

Quinoa tabbouleh with prawns

SERVES 4

100 g/4 oz/1 cup quinoa, rinsed
750 ml/1¼ pts/3 cups water
2 tomatoes, chopped
5 cm/2 in piece of cucumber, finely chopped
1 garlic clove, crushed
5 ml/1 tsp dried mint
30 ml/2 tbsp olive oil
15 ml/1 tbsp lemon juice
Salt and freshly ground black pepper
100 g/4 oz cooked peeled prawns (shrimp)
30 ml/2 tbsp chopped parsley

Simmer the quinoa in the water for about 20 minutes until tender and the liquid is absorbed. Leave to cool. Add all the remaining ingredients except half the parsley and toss well. Leave to stand for 30 minutes, if possible, to allow the flavours to develop, then sprinkle with the remaining parsley before serving.

Salad bowls

The following are quick ideas for salads thrown together with what you might have to hand for a quick lunch or supper. The quantities are not vital. Just mix and match as you please, and make as little or as much as you like to feed one or an army!

Hawaiian tuna

Mix drained, canned tuna with drained, canned pineapple chunks, boiled rice and a diced green (bell) pepper. Moisten with mayonnaise and pile on to lettuce.

Golden corn and tuna delight

Mix drained, canned sweetcorn (corn) with drained, canned tuna. Add a few cubes of Cheddar cheese and a good grinding of black pepper and moisten with mayonnaise. Scatter a handful of chopped cucumber over.

Rollmop, potato and beetroot special

Slice a jar of rollmop herrings. Mix with sliced, canned new potatoes and toss in plain yoghurt, soured (dairy sour) cream or crème fraîche. Season well. Tip into a bowl and arrange diced beetroot (red beet) all round the edge. Sprinkle with chives or parsley, if available.

Russian pilchard salad

Mix drained, canned, diced, mixed vegetables with mayonnaise and some black pepper. Pile into a lettuce-lined bowl. Cut canned pilchards in tomato sauce into neat chunks and pile on top. Squeeze some lemon juice over and serve.

Salmon and cucumber pasta salad

Cook any pasta shapes you have to hand. Add flaked, canned salmon (skin removed but leave in the bones if you like), some diced cucumber and chopped tomato. Moisten with mayonnaise, tartare sauce or cream whisked with vinegar, mustard, a good pinch of sugar, salt and freshly ground black pepper.

Curried bean and tuna bowl

Mix baked beans with curry paste and mayonnaise to taste. Fold in some sultanas (golden raisins) or raisins, a flaked, drained can of tuna and some chopped cucumber. Pile on to crisp lettuce.

Apple, tuna and walnut crunch

Cut one or two eating (dessert) apples into cubes and toss in lemon juice. Mix with a handful of walnut halves, a chopped stick or two of celery and a few cubes of Cheddar cheese. Add a can of flaked, drained tuna. Thin some mayonnaise with a little milk and fold in. Season to taste.

Mixed bean and tuna lunch

Drain and rinse a can of mixed pulses. Add a can of tuna, drained and flaked, sliced hard-boiled (hard-cooked) eggs, a chopped green (bell) pepper and a dash of Tabasco sauce or cayenne. Toss in olive oil and vinegar and add seasoning to taste.

Prawn and egg magic

Mix cooked peeled prawns (shrimp), or a drained, rinsed can of prawns with quartered, hard-boiled (hard-cooked) eggs, sliced avocado and roughly chopped crisp lettuce. Thin some mayonnaise with a little lemon juice and milk and fold in. Season to taste.

Mackerel and pear munch

Drain a can of pear quarters and slice. Cut a can of mackerel steaks into chunks. Mix with the pears and arrange on lettuce leaves. Mix some mayonnaise with a little vinegar and milk, a very little dried tarragon and some salt and freshly ground black pepper. Spoon over the mackerel. Sprinkle with finely chopped onion or some snipped chives and arrange some tomato slices around.

Mussel salad supreme

Mix a jar of mussels in tomato sauce with a few drops of chilli sauce. Fold into cooked long-grain rice. Add chopped cucumber, celery or celeriac and pile the mixture on to lettuce leaves.

Sardine surprise

Mash some canned sardines and fold in chopped cucumber, dill pickles and cold, cooked peas. Season to taste with lemon juice, salt and freshly ground black pepper. Fry (sauté) some slices of French bread in butter or margarine until golden. Pile the sardine mixture into a lettuce-lined bowl. Top with a spoonful of mayonnaise or crème fraîche and eat with the crunchy bread.

Carrot creation

Grate as many carrots and courgettes (zucchini) as you like. Mix with a can of tuna, drained and flaked. Heat a little olive oil in a frying pan (skillet). Add some black mustard seeds and fry (sauté) until they 'pop'. Add some lemon juice and pour over the carrot mixture. Toss, season with salt and freshly ground black pepper and serve warm.

Fondues

You may not automatically think of fish for a fondue but it makes an ideal relaxed supper party – easy to prepare, fantastically tasty and a wonderful way to spend ages eating. All types of fish are perfect as they cook quickly and are always tender. If serving chunks of fish, use firm-fleshed varieties and don't cut them too small or they will fall apart during cooking. Shellfish is wonderful too, as everything from scallops to oysters sits very easily on a fork for a quick flash in the pot. Make sure your fish is very fresh and always have plenty of bread, new potatoes or even a bowl of perfectly cooked chips (fries) to serve alongside.

Thai sole and sherry fondue

SERVES 4–6

This is equally good using plaice fillets instead of sole. If you don't have Chinese wire strainers, roll up the fish fillets and cut them into thick slices. These can then be speared with fondue forks. Take care not to overcook.

3 lemon sole fillets, skinned
900 ml/1½ pts/3¾ cups fish stock
10 ml/2 tsp fresh root ginger, peeled and sliced
1 lemon grass stem, crushed
1.5 ml/¼ tsp chilli powder (optional)
45 ml/3 tbsp dry sherry
15 ml/1 tbsp chopped coriander (cilantro)
Ginger Dipping Sauce (page 381), Rouille (page 374) and Fiery Cucumber Salsa (page 379), to serve

Cut the sole fillets into strips and arrange on serving plates. Put the stock in a saucepan with the ginger, lemon grass and chilli powder, if using. Simmer for 10 minutes. Add the sherry and coriander and simmer for a further 5 minutes. Strain into a fondue pot and place on the table. Provide individual Chinese wire strainers for each person to cook their own fish, then dip in Ginger Dipping Sauce, Rouille or Fiery Cucumber Salsa.

Matzo fish balls

SERVES 6

Look out for bargains on your fish counter for this dish.

700 g/1½ lb white fish fillet, skinned and boned
1 onion, chopped
5 ml/1 tsp anchovy essence (extract)
100 g/4 oz/1 cup fine matzo meal
50 g/2 oz/1 cup fresh white breadcrumbs
30 ml/2 tbsp chopped parsley
Salt and freshly ground black pepper
2 eggs, beaten
Oil, for fondue cooking
Dill Cream (page 375), Rouille (page 374) and Rainbow Pepper Salsa (page 375), to serve

Place the fish and onion in a food processor and blend for 1 minute. Add the anchovy essence, matzo meal, breadcrumbs, parsley and salt and pepper. Add the eggs and blend until it is well mixed. Form the mixture into balls and chill for 1 hour. Heat the oil in a fondue pot until bubbling. Use fondue forks to spear the fish balls and cook in hot oil until golden. Serve with Dill Cream, Rouille and Rainbow Pepper Salsa.

Sweet spiced prawns

SERVES 4

450 g/1 lb raw peeled tiger prawns
(jumbo shrimp)
30 ml/2 tbsp sunflower oil
5 ml/1 tsp paprika
2.5 ml/½ tsp ground ginger
2.5 ml/½ tsp chilli powder
15 ml/1 tbsp lemon juice
60 ml/4 tbsp dry white wine
Oil, for fondue cooking
Guacamole Dip (page 382), Hot Chilli
Salsa (page 378) and Rouille
(page 374), to serve

Put the prawns in a bowl. Add the
oil, paprika, ginger, chilli powder,
lemon juice and wine and mix well.
Cover the bowl with clingfilm
(plastic wrap) and allow to marinate
for 1 hour in the fridge. Arrange on
four plates. Heat the oil in a fondue
pot until bubbling. Cook the prawns
and serve with Guacamole Dip,
Piquant Tomato Sauce and Rouille.

Lobster bisque fondue

SERVES 6–8 AS A STARTER

1 garlic clove, halved
425 g/15 oz/1 large can of lobster
bisque
100 g/4 oz/1 cup Emmental (Swiss)
cheese, grated
Freshly ground black pepper
30 ml/2 tbsp dry white wine
Cubes of French bread, to serve

Rub the garlic clove round the
fondue pot and discard. Add the
soup and cheese and heat, stirring,
until the cheese melts. Season with
pepper and stir in the wine. Stir
well. Serve with French bread cubes
to dip in.

Tuna cheese fondue

SERVES 4

225 g/8 oz/2 cups Cheddar cheese, grated
150 ml/¼ pt/⅔ cup single (light) cream
Milk
185 g/6½ oz/1 small can of tuna,
drained and flaked
60 ml/4 tbsp dry white wine
5 ml/1 tsp paprika
100 g/4 oz baby corn cobs
100 g/4 oz mangetout (snow peas)
Cubes of French bread, to serve

Put the cheese in a fondue pot and
heat until it begins to melt. Stir in the
cream and heat gently. When
thoroughly blended, stir in enough
milk to thin to the consistency of thick
cream. Stir in the tuna and wine and
heat again until bubbling. Sprinkle
with the paprika but do not stir again.
Arrange the corn cobs, mangetout and
bread on serving plates and use to dip
into the hot fondue.

Crunchy seafood fondue

SERVES 4

225 g/8 oz frozen scampi in
breadcrumbs
225 g/8 oz frozen scallops in
breadcrumbs
8 mini Chinese prawn (shrimp) spring
rolls
Thin carrot and celery matchsticks,
to garnish
Oil, for fondue cooking
Tartare Sauce (page 372) and Avocado
Cream (page 372), to serve

Arrange the frozen scampi and
scallops and the spring rolls on
serving plates and garnish with
the carrot and celery sticks. Heat the
oil in a fondue pot until bubbling.
Cook the fish and spring rolls until
golden and cooked through. Serve
with Tartare Sauce and Avocado
Cream.

Surf 'n' turf fondue

SERVES 4

2 large potatoes, fairly thickly sliced
225 g/8 oz raw peeled king prawns
  (jumbo shrimp), tails left on
Juice of 1 lemon
A few drops of Worcestershire sauce
450 g/1 lb fillet steak, cubed
15 ml/1 tbsp coarsely crushed black
  peppercorns or steak seasoning
Oil, for fondue cooking
Rouille (page 374) and Jalapeño Salsa
  (page 374), to serve

Parboil the potatoes in lightly salted, boiling water for 3 minutes until almost tender but still firm enough to spear without breaking. Drain. Put the prawns in a dish and sprinkle with the lemon juice and Worcestershire sauce. Put the meat in a separate dish and sprinkle with the peppercorns or steak seasoning. Toss thoroughly. Arrange the potato slices, prawns and meat attractively on serving plates. Heat the oil in a fondue until bubbling. Cook the potatoes, prawns and steak and serve with Rouille and Jalapeño Salsa.

Cornish crab fondue

SERVES 4

Serve this gorgeous concoction with glasses of chilled dry sherry, then follow with a crisp salad.

425 g/15 oz/1 large can of Cornish
  crab soup
½ soup can of milk
50 g/2 oz/½ cup Cheddar cheese, grated
170 g/6 oz/1 small can of white
  crabmeat
A good pinch of cayenne
30 ml/2 tbsp dry sherry
Cubes of French bread and canned
  smoked mussels, drained, to serve

Put the soup in a fondue pot with the milk. Add the cheese and heat through until it melts. Stir in the remaining ingredients, heat through and serve with lots of French bread cubes and smoked mussels.

Bagna cauda fondue with green vegetables

SERVES 4

100 g/4 oz small thin asparagus spears
3 garlic cloves, crushed
30 ml/2 tbsp milk
50 g/2 oz/¼ cup unsalted (sweet)
  butter, diced
120 ml/4 fl oz/½ cup walnut oil
120 ml/4 fl oz/½ cup sunflower oil
30 ml/2 tbsp anchovy essence (extract)
1 canned white truffle (optional),
  finely chopped
A good grinding of black pepper
A pinch of cayenne
1 bunch of spring onions (scallions),
  trimmed
1 large green (bell) pepper, cut into
  thin strips
4 celery sticks, cut into matchsticks
½ cucumber, cut into matchsticks

Blanch the asparagus for 1 minute in boiling water. Drain, rinse with cold water and drain again. Soak the garlic in the milk for 1 hour. Drain, discarding the milk. Put the butter in the fondue pot and heat until melted. Add the garlic. Whisk in the oils a trickle at a time, whisking continuously, until completely incorporated. Remove from the heat and whisk in the anchovy essence, the truffle if using, the pepper and cayenne. Return to the heat and keep hot but do not allow to boil. Arrange the asparagus and all the other vegetables on plates for dipping in the hot sauce.

Cod in beer batter fondue

SERVES 4

100 g/4 oz/1 cup plain (all-purpose)
   flour
Salt and freshly ground black pepper
5 ml/1 tsp olive oil
1 egg
250 ml/8 fl oz/1 cup beer
900 g/2 lb cod fillet, skinned and cut
   into bite-sized pieces
Oil, for fondue cooking
Lemon wedges, to garnish
Green Hollandaise (page 371) and
   Aioli (page 372), to serve

Sift the flour into a bowl. Add a
good pinch of salt and a good
grinding of pepper. Make a well in
the centre, add the oil and break in
the egg. Gradually beat in the beer
to form a smooth batter. Tip into
individual bowls. Arrange the fish
on individual plates with the lemon
wedges. Heat the oil in a fondue pot
until bubbling. Dip the cod, one
piece at a time, in the batter and
cook in the hot oil until crisp and
golden. Squeeze a little lemon juice
over and dip in either Green
Hollandaise or Aioli.

Ocean fondue

SERVES 4–6

295 g/10½ oz/1 medium can of clams
1 carrot, finely chopped
1 leek, finely chopped
1 celery stick, finely chopped
450 ml/¾ pt/2 cups dry white wine
450 ml/¾ pt/2 cups fish stock
1 bouquet garni sachet
Salt and freshly ground black pepper
225 g/8 oz raw peeled tiger prawns
   (jumbo shrimp)
225 g/8 oz queen scallops
350 g/12 oz sole fillets, cut into squares
Lemon wedges and parsley sprigs, to
   garnish
Sweet and Sour Sauce (page 374),
   Rouille (page 374), Jalapeño Salsa
   (page 374) and cubes of crusty
   bread, to serve

Empty the clams and their juice into
a blender or food processor and run
the machine until smooth. Tip into a
saucepan and add the carrot, leek,
celery, wine, stock and bouquet
garni. Bring to the boil, reduce
the heat, cover and simmer for
30 minutes. Strain into a fondue pot
and season to taste. Bring to a
simmer. Arrange the various fish on
serving plates and garnish with
lemon wedges and parsley sprigs.
Cook each piece individually in the
hot clam mixture and serve with the
sauces. Serve bread cubes to dip in
any remaining clam mixture when
all the fish is cooked.

Prawn, artichoke and parsley fondue

SERVES 4

450 g/1 lb raw peeled tiger prawns
  (jumbo shrimp)
2 × 425 g/15 oz/large cans of
  artichoke hearts, halved
1 large bunch of parsley
Lemon wedges, to garnish
Special Dip (page 386), to serve
Oil, for fondue cooking

Arrange the prawns and artichokes
on serving plates with large parsley
sprigs and lemon wedges. Spoon the
dip into individual pots. Heat the oil
in a fondue pot until bubbling. Cook
the prawns and artichokes a piece at
a time and sprigs of parsley too.
These should be cooked just for a
minute or two until frazzled and
crisp. Allow the parsley to drain well
before eating. Dip everything in the
Special Dip before eating.

Speedy clam fondue

SERVES 4

2 × 300 g/11 oz/medium cans of
  minced (ground) clams
350 g/12 oz/1 large jar of cheese
  spread
4 spring onions (scallions), very finely
  chopped
1 green (bell) pepper, very finely
  chopped
1 small garlic clove, crushed
5 ml/1 tsp Worcestershire sauce
A little milk
Cubes of French bread, to serve

Drain one of the cans of clams. Put
these and the whole contents of the
other can in a fondue pot with all
the remaining ingredients except the
milk. Heat gently, stirring all the
time, until the cheese melts and
everything is blended. Thin with

milk to a coating consistency. When
beginning to bubble, turn down the
heat as low as possible and serve
with French cubes of bread.

Scallop, avocado and Halloumi cheese fondue

SERVES 4

2 just-ripe avocados
Lemon juice
350 g/12 oz queen scallops
225 g/8 oz/2 cups Halloumi cheese,
  cubed
600 ml/1 pt/2½ cups chicken stock
150 ml/¼ pt/⅔ cup dry white wine
15 ml/1 tbsp brandy
Whipped Orange Mayonnaise (page
  382), Cooling Cheese and Onion Dip
  (page 382) and Jalapeño Salsa
  (page 374), to serve

Halve the avocados and remove the
stones (pits). Peel, then cut the flesh
into large cubes. Toss in lemon juice
to prevent browning. Arrange with
the scallops and cheese on serving
plates. Put the stock, wine and
brandy in a fondue pot and heat
until bubbling. Cook the pieces of
avocado and scallop for only about
1 minute per piece. Cook the
Halloumi cheese until softening and
lightly golden. Serve the scallops
with Whipped Orange Mayonnaise,
the avocado with Cooling Cheese
and Onion Dip and the cheese with
Jalapeño Salsa.

Mussel cheese fondue

SERVES 4

Use the mussel cooking liquid as a basis for any of the soups that call for fish stock.

1.5 kg/3 lb mussels, cleaned (page 13)
300 ml/½ pt/1¼ cups water
½ onion
100 g/4 oz/½ cup butter or margarine
40 g/1½ oz/⅓ cup plain (all-purpose)
  flour
750 ml/1¼ pts/3 cups milk
150 ml/¼ pt/⅔ cup dry white wine
2 egg yolks
100 g/4 oz/1 cup Emmental (Swiss)
  cheese, grated
100 g/4 oz/1 cup Cheddar cheese,
  grated
1.5 ml/¼ tsp grated nutmeg
Salt and freshly ground black pepper
Crusty bread, to serve

Put the mussels in a large saucepan with the water and onion. Bring to the boil, cover and cook for 5 minutes, shaking the pan occasionally, until the mussels open. Discard any that remain closed. Drain in a colander. When cool enough to handle, pull off the top shells, leaving the mussels in their bottom shells.

Meanwhile, melt half the butter or margarine in a saucepan. Add the flour and cook, stirring, for 2 minutes. Remove from the heat and gradually blend in the milk and wine. Return to the heat, bring to the boil and cook for 2 minutes, stirring. Beat in the egg yolks, then stir in the cheeses until melted. Do not allow to boil again. Season with nutmeg, salt and pepper. Pile the mussels on four plates.

When ready to serve, pour the hot fondue into warm individual bowls. Dip the mussels into the fondue, scooping a little into the shells, then eat. Serve with crusty bread.

Breton fondue

SERVES 4

Brittany is famous for its shellfish and this is a delicious way of serving it, combined with a little pork or chicken fillet.

225 g/8 oz raw peeled tiger prawns
  (jumbo shrimp)
175 g/6 oz shelled mussels
225 g/8 oz pork or chicken fillet, cubed
Juice of 2 lemons
Worcestershire sauce
Salt and freshly ground black pepper
5 ml/1 tsp brandy
2 garlic cloves, chopped
60 ml/4 tbsp chopped mixed herbs
30 ml/2 tbsp cornflour (cornstarch)
Lemon and cucumber twists, to
  garnish
Oil, for fondue cooking
Rainbow Pepper Salsa (page 375) and
  plain mayonnaise, to serve

Put the shellfish and pork or chicken in a bowl. Add all the ingredients except the cornflour and toss well. Chill for 10 minutes. Remove from the dish, toss in the cornflour and arrange on four plates, garnished with lemon and cucumber twists. Heat the oil in a fondue pot until bubbling. Cook the fish and meat and serve with Rainbow Pepper Salsa and mayonnaise.

Bouillabaisse fondue

SERVES 4

When you've cooked all the fish, add 15–30 ml/1–2 tbsp brandy to the stock and ladle into soup bowls.

225 g/8 oz monkfish, cubed
175 g/6 oz raw peeled king prawns (jumbo shrimp)
175 g/6 oz shelled mussels or oysters
8 shelled scallops
Lemon wedges and parsley sprigs, to garnish
1.2 litres/2 pts/5 cups fish or chicken stock
1 small onion, peeled
1 bouquet garni sachet
Freshly ground black pepper
Rouille (page 374) and Gorgeous Green Sauce (page 375), to serve

Arrange the fish attractively on serving plates with the lemon wedges and parsley sprigs. Simmer the stock in a fondue pot with the onion and bouquet garni for about 10 minutes, then remove the onion and bouquet garni. Season with pepper. Cook the fish in the stock and serve with Rouille and Gorgeous Green Sauce.

Japanese oyster and prawn fondue

SERVES 4

16 oysters in their shells
15 ml/1 tbsp salt
16 raw peeled tiger prawns (jumbo shrimp), tails left on
100 g/4 oz oyster mushrooms
1 bunch of spring onions (scallions)
2 large carrots
2 courgettes (zucchini)
45 ml/3 tbsp red miso
15 ml/1 tbsp mirim
750 ml/1¼ pts/3 cups fish stock
15 ml/1 tbsp soy sauce
15 cm/5 in piece of konbu seaweed (optional)
A little saki or dry sherry (optional)

Open (shuck) the oysters (page 13) and tip the fish into a bowl of cold water. Add the salt and stir well until the oysters turn opaque. Drain and dry on kitchen paper (paper towels). Arrange on individual plates with the prawns. Cut the oyster mushrooms into neat pieces. Trim and cut the spring onions into 2.5 cm/1 in lengths. Pare the carrots and courgettes into ribbons with a potato peeler, then roll up individually and secure with cocktail sticks (toothpicks). Arrange these attractively on serving plates too. Mix together the miso, mirim, 60 ml/4 tbsp of the fish stock and the soy sauce in a fondue pot. Gradually blend in the remaining stock. Add the seaweed, if using. Bring to the boil, then turn down the heat. Using chopsticks, cook the vegetables and prawns for about 2–3 minutes and the oysters for about 1 minute. If liked, strain the stock into small bowls, add a dash of saki or sherry and serve.

Ocean Bay scallop and prawn fondue

SERVES 4

225 g/8 oz queen scallops
100 g/4 oz Parma ham, cut into strips
225 g/8 oz raw peeled tiger prawns
(jumbo shrimp)
Parsley sprigs, to garnish
600 ml/1 pt/2½ cups chicken stock
150 ml/¼ pt/⅔ cup dry white wine
1 bay leaf
Pesto (page 377 or use bought) and
Romesco Sauce (page 378), to serve

Rinse the scallops, pat dry on kitchen paper (paper towels) and wrap each in a piece of Parma ham. Arrange on plates with the prawns and garnish with parsley sprigs. Heat the stock, wine and bay leaf in a fondue pot until bubbling. Cook the scallops and prawns individually. Serve with Pesto Sauce and Piquant Tomato Sauce.

Caribbean fondue

SERVES 4

225 g/8 oz plaice goujons in
breadcrumbs
225 g/8 oz chicken fingers in
breadcrumbs
4 slightly green bananas, cut into
2.5 cm/1 in pieces
Lemon juice
100 g/4 oz button mushrooms
Oil, for fondue cooking
Curried Coconut Sauce (page 389) and
Jalapeño Salsa (page 374), to serve

Arrange the fish and chicken on four serving plates. Toss the bananas in lemon juice and add to the plates with the mushrooms. Heat the oil in a fondue pot. Cook the fish and chicken pieces individually and dip in the Curried Coconut Sauce or Jalapeño Salsa before eating.

Fish and chip fondue

SERVES 4

This is an awfully long-drawn-out way of serving fish and chips (fries) – but fun! Use oven chips because they cook more quickly than completely raw ones.

450 g/1 lb breaded fish bites
450 g/1 lb oven chips
2 × 300 g/11 oz/medium cans of
mushy peas
Tomato ketchup (catsup)
Malt vinegar
Pickled eggs and pickled onions
Salt and freshly ground black pepper
Oil, for fondue cooking
Bread and butter, to serve

Arrange the fish bites and oven chips on serving plates. Heat the mushy peas in a saucepan or, ideally, in a separate fondue pot. Put bowls of ketchup, vinegar, pickled eggs and pickled onions on the table and have salt and pepper available. Heat the oil in the fondue pot until bubbling. Cook the fish and chips a piece at a time, then dip in the vinegar and mushy peas or ketchup. Nibble the pickled eggs and onions in between and eat with bread and butter.

Cheese, mushroom and prawn fondue

SERVES 6

1 garlic clove, halved
150 ml/¼ pt/⅔ cup dry white wine
5 ml/1 tsp lemon juice
225 g/8 oz/2 cups Cheddar cheese, grated
225 g/8 oz/2 cups Gruyère (Swiss) cheese, grated
15 ml/1 tbsp cornflour (cornstarch)
30 ml/2 tbsp kirsch
75 g/3 oz button mushrooms, finely chopped
75 g/3 oz cooked peeled prawns (shrimp), chopped
A pinch of ground mace
Freshly ground black pepper
Chunks of French bread, to serve

Rub the garlic all round the fondue pot, then discard. Add the wine and lemon juice and bring to the boil. When bubbling, stir in the cheeses, a little at a time, until smooth. Blend the cornflour with the kirsch and stir in. Cook until bubbling and thickened. Add the mushrooms and prawns and season with mace and pepper. When bubbling again, turn down the heat to really low, stir well and serve with lots of chunks of French bread to dip in.

Quick trawler fondue

SERVES 4

Choose fish that give a variety of colours and textures.

A selection of any fish, about 1.5 kg/ 3 lb in all, cut into bite-sized pieces
Plain (all-purpose) flour, seasoned with salt and pepper
Oil, for fondue cooking
Mayonnaise, Tartare Sauce (page 372), Honeyed Mustard Sauce (page 373) and Ginger Dipping Sauce (page 381), to serve

Arrange the fish attractively on serving plates. Put the seasoned flour into four small bowls. Heat the oil in a fondue pot until bubbling. Each guest spears a piece of fish, dips it in the seasoned flour, then cooks it in the oil for 1–3 minutes maximum until golden and just cooked. Serve with the sauces.

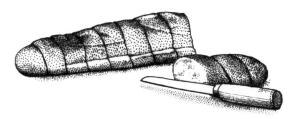

Sauces, dips, dressings and marinades

I n this chapter you will find everything you could want to enhance any plain-cooked fish. There are the classic sauces that every cook needs (made in the simplest way possible, of course!); dressings and marinades to moisten and flavour raw and cooked fish of all kinds; and a whole range of dips and salsas to serve with fondues and grilled (broiled), barbecued and fried (sautéed) fish. The quantities given will usually serve four people: if you are making a dish that serves more, simply increase the quantities accordingly.

Hollandaise sauce

SERVES 4

This is the easiest method I know.

2 eggs
30 ml/2 tbsp lemon juice
100 g/4 oz/½ cup butter or margarine,
  melted
Salt and white pepper
A pinch of cayenne

Whisk the eggs and lemon juice in a small saucepan. Gradually whisk in the butter or margarine. Cook over a gentle heat, whisking all the time, until thickened. Do not allow to boil or the mixture will curdle. Season to taste with salt, pepper and cayenne. Serve warm.

Green hollandaise

SERVES 4

Prepare as for Hollandaise Sauce, but stir a chopped, trimmed bunch of watercress, 4 chopped parsley sprigs and 8 chopped marjoram or tarragon leaves into the finished sauce.

Curried hollandaise

SERVES 4

Prepare as for Hollandaise Sauce, but whisk in 15 ml/1 tbsp mild curry paste with the egg yolks and lemon juice.

Mousseline sauce

SERVES 4

Prepare as for Hollandaise Sauce, but fold in 60 ml/4 tbsp whipped cream before serving.

White sauce with butter for fish

SERVES 4

The water must be boiling to cook the flour. Do not reboil the sauce or it will taste gluey!

50 g/2 oz/¼ cup unsalted (sweet)
  butter
15 ml/1 tbsp plain (all-purpose) flour
300 ml/½ pt/1¼ cups boiling water
Salt and white pepper
Lemon juice, to taste

Melt a quarter of the butter in a small saucepan. Remove from the heat and stir in the flour until smooth. Whisk in the water (it must be boiling), whisking all the time until smooth. Whisk in the remaining butter, a small piece at a time, whisking well after each addition. Season to taste with salt, pepper and the lemon juice.

Mock hollandaise

SERVES 4

Prepare as for Fish White Sauce with Butter, but whisk in 2 egg yolks after whisking in the boiling water, then continue as before.

Mustard mock hollandaise

SERVES 4

Prepare as for Mock Hollandaise, but whisk in 15 ml/1 tbsp Dijon mustard or 5 ml/1 tsp made English mustard with the egg yolks.

Caper mock hollandaise

SERVES 4

Prepare as for Mock Hollandaise, but stir 30 ml/2 tbsp chopped capers and 15 ml/1 tbsp chopped parsley into the finished sauce.

Genovaise sauce

SERVES 4

Prepare as for Mock Hollandaise, but substitute boiling fish stock for the water. Stir 15 ml/1 tbsp double (heavy) cream, 2 finely chopped anchovy fillets, 5 ml/1 tsp anchovy essence (extract) and 15 ml/1 tbsp chopped parsley into the finished sauce.

Ravigote sauce

SERVES 4

Prepare as for Mock Hollandaise, but add 1 finely chopped shallot, simmered for 3 minutes in 45 ml/ 3 tbsp white wine, and 5 ml/1 tsp Dijon mustard and 10 ml/2 tsp each of snipped chives, chopped parsley and chopped tarragon to the finished sauce.

Piquant dip

SERVES 6

6 stuffed green olives, finely chopped
1 spring onion (scallion), finely chopped
75 ml/5 tbsp mayonnaise
30 ml/2 tbsp tomato ketchup (catsup)
A few drops of Tabasco sauce
Salt and freshly ground black pepper

Mix together all the ingredients and chill until ready to serve.

Aioli

SERVES 4–6

300 ml/½ pt/1¼ cups mayonnaise
2 garlic cloves, crushed
2.5 ml/½ tsp lemon juice
A few drops of Tabasco sauce
Salt and freshly ground black pepper

Mix together all the ingredients and chill until ready to serve.

Avocado cream

SERVES 2

1 ripe avocado
30 ml/2 tbsp lemon juice
25 g/1 oz/2 tbsp butter or margarine, melted
75 ml/5 tbsp single (light) cream
A few drops of Tabasco sauce
A few drops of Worcestershire sauce
Salt and freshly ground black pepper

Halve the avocado and remove the stone (pit). Scoop out the flesh into a saucepan and mash well with the lemon juice. Beat in the butter or margarine and cream. Flavour to taste with the Tabasco and Worcestershire sauces and season with salt and pepper. Heat through but do not boil before serving.

Tartare sauce

SERVES 4

30 ml/2 tbsp mayonnaise
15 ml/1 tbsp double (heavy) cream
15 ml/1 tbsp chopped capers
2 gherkins (cornichons), chopped
15 ml/1 tbsp chopped parsley
1 shallot, finely chopped
Salt and freshly ground black pepper

Mix together all the ingredients and chill for at least 30 minutes to allow the flavours to develop.

Dill and mustard sauce

SERVES 8

This is good with pickled fish.

30 ml/2 tbsp Dijon mustard
10 ml/2 tsp light brown sugar
1 egg yolk
150 ml/¼ pt/⅔ cup sunflower oil
30 ml/2 tbsp white wine vinegar
15 ml/1 tbsp chopped dill (dill weed)
Salt and freshly ground black pepper

Mix together the mustard, sugar and egg yolk in a bowl, using an electric whisk. With the machine running, gradually add the oil, a drop at a time, until the mixture is thick and glossy and resembles mayonnaise. Whisk in the wine vinegar and dill and season to taste. Turn into a small pot and chill until required.

Yoghurt and apple dressing

SERVES 4

This is good with any pickled fish.

150 ml/¼ pt/⅔ cup plain yoghurt
150 ml/¼ pt/⅔ cup single (light) cream
30 ml/2 tbsp milk
1 pickled dill cucumber, finely chopped
2 spring onions (scallions), chopped
2.5 ml/½ tsp caster (superfine) sugar
Salt and freshly ground black pepper
1 bay leaf
A pinch of ground allspice
1 red eating (dessert) apple
1 green eating apple
5 ml/1 tsp lemon juice

Mix together everything except the apples and lemon juice. Leave to stand for at least 2 hours or overnight. Just before serving, finely chop the unpeeled apples and toss in lemon juice. Discard the bay leaf from the yoghurt mixture and fold in the apples. Serve cold.

Scandinavian caraway dressing

MAKES ABOUT 300 ML/½ PT/1¼ CUPS

Serve this with any oily or pickled fish.

15 ml/1 tbsp caraway seeds
150 ml/¼ pt/⅔ cup water
10 ml/2 tsp salt
90 ml/6 tbsp white wine vinegar
45 ml/3 tbsp light brown sugar
Freshly ground black pepper

Crush the caraway seeds with a pestle and mortar or in a bowl with the end of a rolling pin. Place in a small saucepan with the water. Bring to the boil, remove from the heat and leave to cool. Strain into a screw-topped jar with the remaining ingredients and shake well. Taste and add more salt if necessary.

Honeyed mustard sauce

SERVES 4

Very different from the English-style mustard-flavoured white sauce, this goes exceptionally well with oily fish.

150 ml/¼ pt/⅔ cup plain Greek yoghurt
150 ml/¼ pt/⅔ cup mayonnaise
15 ml/1 tbsp made English mustard
Juice of ½ lemon
A few drops of Worcestershire sauce
Clear honey
Salt and freshly ground black pepper
30 ml/2 tbsp snipped chives

Blend the yoghurt with the mayonnaise, mustard and lemon juice. Season with Worcestershire sauce, honey, salt and pepper to taste and fold in the chives. Chill, if time allows, before serving.

Curried coconut sauce

SERVES 4

Serve with any plain fish.

100 g/4 oz creamed coconut
20 ml/1½ tbsp curry paste
60 ml/4 tbsp plain yoghurt
60 ml/4 tbsp mayonnaise
90 ml/6 tbsp milk
15 ml/1 tbsp chopped coriander
  (cilantro) (optional)
Freshly ground black pepper

Melt the coconut in a saucepan over
a gentle heat with the curry paste
heat, stirring. Remove from the heat
and stir in the yoghurt, mayonnaise
and milk. Add the coriander, if
using, and season with pepper.

Jalapeño salsa

SERVES 4

1 jalapeño pepper, seeded
3 large ripe tomatoes, skinned
200 g/7 oz/1 small can of pimientos,
  drained
15 ml/1 tbsp tomato purée (paste)
15 ml/1 tbsp red wine vinegar
15 ml/1 tbsp chopped parsley
15 ml/1 tbsp clear honey
Salt and freshly ground black pepper

Put the chilli in a blender or food
processor with all the remaining
ingredients except the salt and
pepper. Run the machine until fairly
smooth, stopping and scraping down
the sides as necessary. Season to
taste. Serve hot or cold.

Sweet and sour sauce

SERVES 4–6

Serve with any seafood fondues.

10 ml/2 tsp cornflour (cornstarch)
15 ml/1 tbsp malt vinegar
250 g/9 oz/1 medium can of crushed
  pineapple
30 ml/2 tbsp tomato ketchup (catsup)
15 ml/1 tbsp soy sauce
¼ small cucumber, finely diced

Blend the cornflour with the vinegar
in a small pan. Stir in the remaining
ingredients, bring to the boil and
simmer for 5 minutes. Serve warm.

Rouille

SERVES 4

Rich and garlicky, this sauce is ideal
for fish fondues and soups.

1 slice of white bread, crusts removed
1 red chilli, seeded and chopped
1 small red (bell) pepper, chopped
2 garlic cloves, chopped
1 egg yolk
150 ml/¼ pt/⅔ cup olive oil
Salt

Soak the bread in water, then
squeeze dry and place in a blender
or food processor. Run the machine
and drop in the chilli, red pepper,
garlic and egg yolk. With the
machine running, add the oil a drop
at a time until the mixture is thick
and glossy and resembles
mayonnaise. Season with salt and
serve.

Thousand island dip

SERVES 4

Serve with fish fondues or pieces of fried (sautéed) fish.

250 ml/8 fl oz/1 cup mayonnaise
150 ml/¼ pt/⅔ cup plain yoghurt
10 ml/2 tsp lemon juice
30 ml/2 tbsp tomato ketchup (catsup)
10 ml/2 tsp Worcestershire sauce
A few drops of Tabasco sauce
Salt and freshly ground black pepper

Blend together the mayonnaise and yoghurt. Whisk in the remaining ingredients. Chill until ready to serve.

Gorgeous green sauce

SERVES 4

Use the rest of the watercress to garnish the fish on the serving plates.

½ bunch of watercress
150 ml/¼ pt/⅔ cup mayonnaise
90 ml/6 tbsp crème fraîche
15 ml/1 tbsp olive oil
10 ml/2 tsp chopped basil
15 ml/1 tbsp chopped parsley
Lemon juice
Salt and freshly ground black pepper

Put the watercress in a blender or food processor and run the machine briefly to chop it, or place in a bowl and snip with scissors until finely chopped. Add the mayonnaise, crème fraîche, oil and herbs and run the machine until well blended (or beat with a wooden spoon). Add lemon juice, salt and pepper to taste.

Dill cream

SERVES 4

This is particularly delicious with oily fish.

150 ml/¼ pt/⅔ cup soured (dairy sour)
*   cream*
Juice of 1 lime
1.5 ml/¼ tsp Worcestershire sauce
Salt and freshly ground black pepper
5 ml/1 tsp clear honey
30 ml/2 tbsp chopped dill (dill weed)
5 ml/1 tsp brandy

Whisk together all the ingredients except the brandy in a bowl. Chill. Stir in the brandy just before serving.

Rainbow pepper salsa

SERVES 4–6

This makes a perfect accompaniment to any fish.

25 g/1 oz/2 tbsp butter or margarine
1 large onion, chopped
1 small red (bell) pepper, chopped
1 small green pepper, chopped
1 small yellow pepper, chopped
1 garlic clove, crushed
300 ml/½ pt/1¼ cups chicken stock
Salt and freshly ground black pepper

Melt the butter or margarine and fry (sauté) the onion until soft but not brown. Stir in the peppers and garlic. Cook gently for 5 minutes. Pour in the stock and season to taste with salt and pepper. Simmer for 15 minutes or until pulpy. Serve hot.

Prawn mayonnaise

SERVES 4–6

100 g/4 oz cooked peeled prawns
  (shrimp)
90 ml/6 tbsp mayonnaise
90 ml/6 tbsp whipping cream, whipped
15 ml/1 tbsp chopped parsley
Lemon juice
Salt and freshly ground black pepper
A good pinch of cayenne

Reserve a few prawns for garnish and finely chop the remainder. Fold into the mayonnaise, then fold in the cream. Add lemon juice, salt, pepper and cayenne to taste. Spoon into a small pot, top with the reserved prawns and chill until ready to serve.

White sauce

SERVES 4

20 g/¾ oz/3 tbsp plain (all-purpose)
  flour
300 ml/½ pt/1¼ cups milk
A knob of butter or margarine
Salt and freshly ground black pepper

Blend the flour with a little of the milk in a saucepan. Stir in the remainder. Add the butter or margarine, bring to the boil and cook for 2 minutes, stirring until thickened and smooth. Season to taste.

Béchamel sauce

SERVES 4

300 ml/½ pt/1¼ cups milk
1 onion slice
1 bouquet garni sachet
A few black peppercorns
A good knob of butter or margarine
20 g/¾ oz/3 tbsp plain (all-purpose)
  flour
Salt

Put the milk, onion, bouquet garni and peppercorns in a saucepan. Bring to the boil and remove from the heat. Leave to infuse for 15 minutes, then strain. Melt the butter or margarine in a clean pan. Stir in the flour and cook for 1 minute, stirring. Remove from the heat and gradually blend in the infused milk. Return to the heat, bring to the boil and cook for 2 minutes, stirring. Season to taste with salt.

Mushroom sauce

SERVES 4

Stew 4–5 finely chopped button mushrooms in 30 ml/2 tbsp water in a covered pan for 3 minutes. Remove the lid and boil rapidly, if necessary, to evaporate any remaining liquid. Stir into either White Sauce or Béchamel Sauce and add a squeeze of lemon juice, if liked.

Cheese sauce

SERVES 4

Prepare as for either White Sauce or Béchamel Sauce, but stir 50 g/ 2 oz/½ cup strong Cheddar cheese, grated, into the sauce until melted.

Onion sauce

SERVES 4

Stew 2 finely chopped onions gently in a saucepan with 30 ml/2 tbsp water for 10 minutes until really soft. Stir into either White Sauce or Béchamel Sauce (page 376) and re-season, if liked.

Parsley sauce

SERVES 4

Prepare as for either White Sauce or Béchamel Sauce (page 376), but add 30 ml/2 tbsp chopped parsley before seasoning the sauce.

Caper sauce

SERVES 4

Prepare as for either White Sauce or Béchamel Sauce (page 376), but add 15 ml/1 tbsp chopped capers and 15 ml/1 tbsp caper vinegar before seasoning the sauce.

Cucumber and dill sauce

SERVES 4

Prepare as for either White Sauce or Béchamel Sauce (page 376), but add ¼ cucumber, finely chopped, and 5 ml/1 tsp dried dill (dill weed) to the sauce.

Blusher

SERVES 4

Prepare as for either White Sauce or Béchamel Sauce (page 376), but add 1 grated, cooked beetroot (red beet) and 5 ml/1 tsp white wine vinegar to the sauce.

Green cress sauce

SERVES 4

Prepare as for either White Sauce or Béchamel Sauce (page 376), but add 1 bunch of finely chopped watercress and a pinch of cayenne to the sauce.

Pesto

SERVES 4

20 basil leaves
1 large parsley sprig
50 g/2 oz/½ cup pine nuts
1 large garlic clove, halved
75 ml/5 tbsp olive oil
30 ml/2 tbsp grated Parmesan cheese
A pinch of salt
Freshly ground black pepper
15 ml/1 tbsp hot water

Put the herbs, pine nuts and garlic in a blender or food processor. Run the machine briefly to chop. With the machine running, gradually add the oil to form a thick paste. Stop the machine to scrape down the sides from time to time. Add the cheese, some pepper and the water and run the machine again to form a glistening paste. Store in a screw-topped jar in the fridge for up to 2 weeks.

Coriander pesto

SERVES 4

Prepare as for Pesto, but substitute coriander (cilantro) for the basil.

Parsley pesto

SERVES 4

Prepare as for Pesto, but substitute flatleaf parsley for the basil.

Red almond pesto

SERVES 4

1 large garlic clove, halved
50 g/2 oz/½ cup ground almonds
15 basil leaves
4 sun-dried tomatoes in olive oil, drained
30 ml/2 tbsp sun-dried tomato oil
30 ml/2 tbsp olive oil
30 ml/2 tbsp grated Parmesan cheese
15 ml/1 tbsp hot water
A pinch of salt
Freshly ground black pepper

Put the garlic, almonds, basil and tomatoes in a blender or food processor and run the machine briefly to chop. With the machine running, gradually add the oil to form a thick paste. Stop the machine to scrape down the sides from time to time. Add the cheese, water, salt and some pepper. Run the machine again to form a paste. Store in a screw-topped jar in the fridge for up to 2 weeks.

Romesco sauce

SERVES 4

4 ripe tomatoes, skinned, seeded and quartered
200 g/7 oz/1 small can of pimiento caps, drained
2 garlic cloves, crushed
45 ml/3 tbsp ground almonds
Salt and freshly ground black pepper
200 ml/7 fl oz/scant 1 cup olive oil
Red wine vinegar, to taste

Put the tomatoes, pimientos, garlic, almonds and a little salt and pepper in a blender or food processor and run the machine until smooth, stopping to scrape down the side if necessary. With the machine running, gradually add the oil, a drop at a time, until smooth and glistening. Add wine vinegar to taste

and chill until ready to serve. You may need to beat the sauce again just before serving.

Minted yoghurt and cucumber

SERVES 4

Use this as a dip or to top jacket potatoes or to serve with curries.

5 cm/2 in piece of cucumber, grated
5 ml/1 tsp dried mint
1 small garlic clove, crushed (optional)
150 ml/¼ pt/⅔ cup plain yoghurt
Freshly ground black pepper

Squeeze the cucumber to remove excess moisture. Place in a bowl. Add the remaining ingredients and mix thoroughly. Chill until ready to serve.

Hot chilli salsa

SERVES 4

1 small onion, very finely chopped
1 small red chilli, seeded and finely chopped
3 ripe tomatoes, skinned and finely chopped
30 ml/2 tbsp tomato ketchup (catsup)
15 ml/1 tbsp chopped parsley

Mix together all the ingredients and chill until ready to serve.

Fiery cucumber salsa

SERVES 4

¼ cucumber, grated
½ bunch of spring onions (scallions),
  finely chopped
1 green chilli, seeded and finely
  chopped
Grated rind and juice of ½ lime
2.5 ml/½ tsp ground cumin
15 ml/1 tbsp chopped coriander
  (cilantro)
7.5 ml/1½ tsp clear honey
Freshly ground black pepper

Squeeze the cucumber to remove
excess moisture. Place in a bowl.
Add the remaining ingredients and
mix thoroughly. Chill until ready to
serve.

Cucumber and dill salsa

SERVES 4

¼ cucumber, very finely chopped
1 shallot, very finely chopped
30 ml/2 tbsp chopped dill (dill weed)
15 ml/1 tbsp caster (superfine) sugar
15 ml/1 tbsp cider vinegar
Salt and freshly ground black pepper

Mix the cucumber and shallot in a
small bowl. Stir in the dill and sugar.
Moisten with the vinegar. Season to
taste and add a dash more vinegar,
if liked. Leave to stand for at least
30 minutes to allow the flavours to
develop.

Ravishing relish

MAKES 1 POT

5 ml/1 tsp pickling spice
450 g/1 lb ripe pears, finely chopped
50 g/2 oz/⅓ cup dried dates, stoned
  (pitted) and chopped
150 ml/¼ pt/⅔ cup malt vinegar
60 ml/4 tbsp apple juice
1 small ripe melon, seeded and chopped
1 small marrow (squash), seeded and
  chopped

Tie the pickling spice in a piece of
clean muslin (cheesecloth) or a new
disposable dish cloth. Put the pears
and dates in a saucepan with the
vinegar, bag of spice and apple juice.
Bring to the boil, reduce the heat and
simmer very gently for 1 hour. Add
the melon and marrow and simmer
for a further 30 minutes until really
soft, adding a little more apple juice
if the mixture is becoming too dry.
Remove the pickling spice. Spoon the
relish into a clean, warm jar. Cover
and seal. When cold, store in the
fridge. Serve with cold poached
salmon or smoked or pickled fish.

All-year tomato sauce

SERVES 4

1 onion, finely chopped
1 garlic clove, crushed (optional)
15 g/½ oz/1 tbsp butter or margarine
400 g/14 oz/1 large can of chopped
  tomatoes
15 ml/1 tbsp tomato purée (paste)
2.5 ml/½ tsp caster (superfine) sugar
Salt and freshly ground black pepper

Fry (sauté) the onion and garlic, if
using, in the butter or margarine in
a saucepan for 2 minutes, stirring.
Add the tomatoes, tomato purée and
sugar. Bring to the boil and boil
rapidly for about 5 minutes until
pulpy. Season to taste and serve hot.

Herby tomato sauce

SERVES 4

Prepare as for All-year Tomato Sauce (page 379), but add 2.5 ml/½ tsp dried, oregano, basil or mixed herbs when adding the tomatoes.

Barbecue sauce

SERVES 4–6

1 garlic clove, crushed
1 small onion, very finely chopped
10 ml/2 tsp butter or margarine
100 g/4 oz/½ cup tomato purée (paste)
300 ml/½ pt/1¼ cups fruity dry white wine
10 ml/2 tsp light soy sauce
30 ml/2 tbsp clear honey
30 ml/2 tbsp white wine vinegar
A few drops of Tabasco sauce
Salt and freshly ground black pepper

Put the garlic, onion and butter or margarine in a small saucepan. Cook for 2 minutes, stirring, until the onion is softened. Add the remaining ingredients, bring to the boil, reduce the heat and simmer for about 20 minutes until thick. Taste and re-season if necessary.

Speedy barbecue sauce

SERVES 4

This is made with the cooking juices after frying (sautéing) or grilling (broiling) fish.

10 ml/2 tsp plain (all-purpose) flour
200 ml/7 fl oz/scant 1 cup potato cooking water or vegetable stock
15 ml/1 tbsp soy sauce
A few drops of Worcestershire sauce
A few drops of Tabasco sauce
2 tomatoes, skinned, seeded and chopped

Sprinkle the flour into the fish cooking juices in the grill (broiler) pan or frying pan (skillet). Cook gently, stirring, for 2 minutes. Remove from the heat and gradually blend in the cooking water or stock. Return to the heat and bring to the boil, stirring. Add the flavourings and tomatoes. Simmer for about 3 minutes, stirring, until thick. Serve hot.

Fresh tomato sauce

SERVES 4

1 large onion, finely chopped
15 g/½ oz/1 tbsp butter or margarine
450 g/1 lb tomatoes, skinned and chopped
15 ml/1 tbsp tomato purée (paste)
A pinch of caster (superfine) sugar
15 ml/1 tbsp chopped basil or parsley
Salt and freshly ground black pepper

Fry (sauté) the onion in the butter or margarine in a large saucepan for 2 minutes, stirring. Add the tomatoes and tomato purée. Bring to the boil, reduce the heat, part-cover and simmer gently for 6–8 minutes, stirring occasionally, until pulpy. Stir in the caster sugar, parsley or basil and season to taste.

Sweet and sharp mustard sauce

SERVES 4

250 ml/8 fl oz/1 cup white wine vinegar
175 ml/6 fl oz/¾ cup made English mustard
½ onion, finely chopped
3 garlic cloves, crushed
75 ml/5 tbsp water
60 ml/4 tbsp tomato ketchup (catsup)
10 ml/2 tsp light brown sugar
15 ml/1 tbsp paprika
2.5 ml/½ tsp chilli powder
Salt and freshly ground black pepper

Put all the ingredients in a saucepan. Bring to the boil and simmer gently for 20 minutes until thick and pulpy. Serve warm or cold with grilled (broiled) fish.

Orange and mango salsa

SERVES 4–6

1 large just-ripe mango
4–6 spring onions (scallions), finely chopped
2 oranges
1 small red chilli, seeded and chopped
15 ml/1 tbsp chopped mint
2.5 ml/½ tsp grated fresh root ginger
A pinch of salt
Freshly ground black pepper
5 ml/1 tsp lemon juice

Peel the mango and cut all the fruit off the stone (pit). Cut the flesh into small dice and place in a bowl with the spring onions. Finely grate the rind from one of the oranges. Cut off all the peel and pith from both. Slice the fruit, then cut into small pieces. Add to the mango and onion. Add the remaining ingredients and mix well. Cover and chill for at least 1 hour to allow the flavours to develop. Serve with any fish.

Orange and pineapple salsa

SERVES 4

Prepare as for Orange and Mango Salsa, but substitute 250 g/9 oz/ 1 medium can of crushed pineapple, well-drained, for the mango.

Brown onion salsa

SERVES 4–6

450 g/1 lb onions, chopped
25 g/1 oz/2 tbsp butter or margarine
30 ml/2 tbsp light brown sugar
Salt and freshly ground black pepper
30 ml/2 tbsp chopped parsley

Cook the onions in the butter or margarine for 5 minutes, stirring, until softened. Add the sugar, turn up the heat and continue cooking until a rich golden brown. Purée in a blender or food processor and season to taste. Stir in the parsley. Reheat gently, if liked.

Horseradish creme

SERVES 4

90 ml/6 tbsp crème fraîche
15 ml/1 tbsp horseradish relish
A pinch of white pepper

Mix the crème fraîche with the horseradish and season with pepper. Chill until ready to serve.

Ginger dipping sauce

SERVES 4

20 ml/1½ tbsp grated fresh root ginger
45 ml/3 tbsp dry sherry
30 ml/2 tbsp soy sauce
45 ml/3 tbsp apple juice

Mix together all the ingredients. Serve in small individual bowls.

Cooling cheese and onion dip

SERVES 4

A simple sauce, good with any fish fondue. Try it as a topping for jacket potatoes too!

175 g/6 oz/¾ cup medium-fat soft cheese
75 ml/5 tbsp soured (dairy sour) cream
½ bunch of spring onions (scallions), finely chopped
A pinch of cayenne

Blend together all the ingredients and serve chilled.

Guacamole dip

SERVES 4

1 ripe avocado
15 ml/1 tbsp lemon juice
5 ml/1 tsp grated onion
30 ml/2 tbsp olive oil
30 ml/2 tbsp mayonnaise
5 ml/1 tsp Worcestershire sauce
A few drops of Tabasco sauce
Salt and freshly ground black pepper

Halve the avocado, remove the stone (pit) and scoop the flesh into a bowl. Mash well with the lemon juice and onion. Gradually beat in the oil, a little at a time, then beat in the mayonnaise. Flavour with the Worcestershire and Tabasco sauces and salt and pepper to taste.

Thai chilli ginger sauce

SERVES 6

This is delicious with any fried (sautéed) or grilled (broiled) fish. You can get sambal oelek – a hot chilli paste – in most good supermarkets.

200 g/7 oz/scant 1 cup light brown sugar
200 ml/7 fl oz/scant 1 cup water
2.5 cm/1 in piece of fresh root ginger, peeled and grated
30 ml/2 tbsp soy sauce
90 ml/6 tbsp red wine vinegar
5 ml/1 tsp sambal oelek
Salt and freshly ground black pepper
5 ml/1 tsp cornflour (cornstarch)

Warm the sugar and water together in a saucepan until the sugar has dissolved. Add all the remaining ingredients except the cornflour, seasoning to taste with salt and pepper. Bring to the boil, reduce the heat and simmer for 10 minutes. Blend the cornflour with 15 ml/ 1 tbsp water and stir into the sauce. Stir until slightly thickened. Leave to cool, then strain into a screw-topped jar and store in the fridge for up to 1 month.

Whipped orange mayonnaise

SERVES 4

150 ml/¼ pt/⅔ cup mayonnaise
Finely grated rind and juice of ½ orange
Celery salt
75 ml/5 tbsp double (heavy) cream, whipped

Put the mayonnaise in a bowl and stir in the orange rind and juice. Season to taste with celery salt and fold in the whipped cream.

Peanut sauce

SERVES 4–6

225 g/8 oz/1 cup peanut butter
5 ml/1 tsp chilli powder
250 ml/8 fl oz/1 cup chicken stock
7.5 ml/1½ tsp cornflour (cornstarch)
5 ml/1 tsp soy sauce

Blend the peanut butter with the chilli powder and stock in a saucepan and bring slowly to the boil. Mix the cornflour with a little water, stir into the peanut butter mixture and simmer for 2 minutes, stirring. Flavour with the soy sauce, then turn into a serving dish.

Sweet mustard sauce

SERVES 4

25 g/1 oz/¼ cup plain (all-purpose) flour
300 ml/½ pt/1¼ cups milk
1 bay leaf
A knob of butter or margarine
15 ml/1 tbsp made English mustard
30 ml/2 tbsp light brown sugar
30 ml/2 tbsp malt vinegar
Salt and freshly ground black pepper

Blend the flour with a little of the milk in a saucepan. Blend in the remaining milk. Add the bay leaf and butter or margarine. Bring to the boil and cook for 2 minutes, stirring, until very thick. Stir in the mustard, sugar and vinegar and season to taste. Taste and add a dash more vinegar or sugar, if liked, to suit your own taste. Remove the bay leaf before serving.

Creamy whole prawn sauce

SERVES 4–6

This is more fiddly than a basic sauce, but the flavour is fantastic!

225 g/8 oz cooked unpeeled prawns (shrimp)
50 g/2 oz/¼ cup butter or margarine
150 ml/¼ pt/⅔ cup water
25 g/1 oz/¼ cup plain (all-purpose) flour
150 ml/¼ pt/⅔ cup chicken or fish stock
150 ml/¼ pt/⅔ cup single (light) cream
30 ml/2 tbsp dry vermouth
Salt and white pepper

Peel the prawns (page 16). Put the shells in a frying pan and toss over a moderate heat until crisp and dry. Grind to a powder in a blender or food processor, or pound in a mortar with a pestle. Place in a saucepan with the butter or margarine and water and heat until the fat melts. Bring to the boil and simmer for 5 minutes. Strain through a fine sieve (strainer) and leave until cold and set.

Lift out the solidified butter or margarine and transfer to a saucepan. Heat until melted. Blend in the flour and cook for 1 minute, stirring. Remove from the heat and blend in the chicken or fish stock and the cream. Return to the heat, bring to the boil and cook for 2 minutes, stirring all the time, until thick. Stir in the vermouth and season to taste. Add the prawns and heat through.

Noisette butter

SERVES 4

50 g/2 oz/¼ cup butter or margarine
15 ml/1 tbsp lemon juice

Melt the butter or margarine in a pan until a golden, nut brown colour, but not burnt. Add the lemon juice and pour over cooked fish straight away while still foaming.

Maître d'hôtel butter

SERVES 4

50 g/2 oz/¼ cup butter or margarine,
softened
15 ml/1 tbsp chopped parsley
1.5 ml/¼ tsp lemon juice
Salt and freshly ground black pepper

Mash the butter or margarine with the remaining ingredients, seasoning to taste. Shape into a roll on a piece of greaseproof (waxed) paper. Wrap and chill until firm. Cut into slices and use to top cooked fish before serving.

Tarragon butter

SERVES 4

Prepare as for Maître d'Hôtel Butter, but substitute chopped tarragon for the parsley and sharpen with tarragon vinegar instead of lemon juice, if preferred.

Mixed herb butter

SERVES 4

Prepare as for Maître d'Hôtel Butter, but use 5 ml/1 tsp each of chopped parsley and thyme and snipped chives instead of all parsley.

Anchovy butter

SERVES 4

The remaining anchovies can be frozen until needed for another recipe.

4 anchovy fillets
30 ml/2 tbsp milk
50 g/2 oz/¼ cup unsalted (sweet)
butter, softened
5 ml/1 tsp anchovy essence (extract)
2.5 ml/¼ tsp tomato purée (paste)
Freshly ground black pepper

Soak the anchovies in the milk for 5 minutes, then drain. Place the fish in a bowl and snip with kitchen scissors until they almost form a paste. Mash in the butter, anchovy essence and tomato purée, then season to taste with pepper. Shape into a roll on a piece of greaseproof (waxed) paper. Wrap and chill until firm. Cut into slices and use to top cooked fish before serving.

Lime butter

SERVES 4

50 g/2 oz/¼ cup butter or margarine,
softened
Finely grated rind of 1 lime
5 ml/1 tsp lime juice
15 ml/1 tbsp chopped parsley
Salt and freshly ground black pepper

Mash the butter or margarine with the lime rind and juice and the parsley. Season to taste with salt and pepper. Shape into a roll on a piece of greaseproof (waxed) paper. Wrap and chill until firm. Cut into slices and use to top cooked fish before serving.

Orange butter

SERVES 4

50 g/2 oz/¼ cup butter or margarine, softened
Finely grated rind of ½ orange
5 ml/1 tsp orange juice
5 ml/1 tsp tomato purée (paste)
Salt and freshly ground black pepper

Mash the butter or margarine with the orange rind and juice. Work in the tomato purée until completely blended. Season to taste. Shape into a roll on a piece of greaseproof (waxed) paper. Wrap and chill until firm. Cut into slices and use to top cooked fish before serving.

Lemon and chive butter

SERVES 4

50 g/2 oz/¼ cup butter or margarine, softened
Finely grated rind of ½ lemon
5 ml/1 tsp lemon juice
30 ml/2 tbsp snipped chives
Salt and freshly ground black pepper

Mash the butter or margarine with the lemon rind and juice until well blended. Work in the chives and season to taste. Shape into a roll on a piece of greaseproof (waxed) paper. Wrap and chill until firm. Cut into slices and use to top cooked fish before serving.

Garlic butter

SERVES 4

50 g/2 oz/¼ cup butter or margarine, softened
1 garlic clove, crushed
15 ml/1 tbsp chopped parsley
Salt and freshly ground black pepper

Mash the butter or margarine with the garlic and parsley and season to taste. Shape into a roll on a piece of greaseproof (waxed) paper. Wrap and chill until firm. Cut into slices and use to top cooked fish before serving.

Chutney butter

SERVES 4

15 ml/1 tbsp sweet chutney
50 g/2 oz/¼ cup unsalted (sweet) butter, softened
15 ml/1 tbsp chopped parsley

Pound the chutney in a mortar with a pestle or in a bowl with the end of a rolling pin until smooth. Mash into the butter with the parsley. Shape into a roll on a piece of greaseproof (waxed) paper. Wrap and chill until firm. Cut into slices and use to top cooked fish before serving.

Tomato butter

SERVES 4

50 g/2 oz/¼ cup butter or margarine, softened
10 ml/2 tsp tomato purée (paste)
15 ml/1 tbsp snipped chives
A pinch of caster (superfine) sugar
Salt and freshly ground black pepper

Mash the butter or margarine with the tomato purée until well blended. Work in the chives and season to taste with the sugar and salt and pepper. Shape into a roll on a piece of greaseproof (waxed) paper. Wrap and chill until firm. Cut into slices and use to top cooked fish before serving.

Sun-dried tomato and basil butter

SERVES 4

1 sun-dried tomato in oil, chopped
5 ml/1 tsp sun-dried tomato oil
50 g/2 oz/¼ cup unsalted (sweet) butter
15 ml/1 tbsp chopped basil
Salt and freshly ground black pepper

Pound the tomato and tomato oil in a mortar with a pestle or in a bowl with the end of a rolling pin until it forms a paste. Work in the butter, basil and salt and pepper to taste. Shape into a roll on a piece of greaseproof (waxed) paper. Wrap and chill until firm. Cut into slices and use to top cooked fish before serving.

Boiled salad dressing for seafood

SERVES 4–6

15 ml/1 tbsp caster (superfine) sugar
10 ml/2 tsp plain (all-purpose) flour
5 ml/1 tsp celery salt
10 ml/2 tsp Dijon mustard
15 ml/1 tbsp water
150 ml/¼ pt/⅔ cup white wine vinegar
150 ml/¼ pt/⅔ cup water
15 g/½ oz/1 tbsp unsalted (sweet) butter
1 egg
30 ml/2 tbsp single (light) cream

Mix together all the ingredients except the butter, egg and cream in a saucepan. Heat gently, stirring, until the sugar melts, then bring to the boil and boil for 5 minutes. Whisk in the butter. Whisk the egg in a bowl. Gradually add the hot vinegar mixture, whisking all the time. Leave until cold, then whisk in the cream. Store in a screw-topped jar in the fridge.

Alabama dressing

SERVES 4–6

1 quantity of Boiled Salad Dressing for Seafood
1 small red (bell) pepper, finely chopped
1 small green pepper, finely chopped
2 celery sticks, finely chopped
1 spring onion (scallion), finely chopped
45 ml/3 tbsp double (heavy) cream, lightly whipped
15 ml/1 tbsp mild chilli relish
15 ml/1 tbsp tomato ketchup (catsup)
Salt and freshly ground black pepper

Put the boiled dressing in a bowl and fold in all the remaining ingredients, adding salt and pepper to taste. Chill until ready to serve.

Special dip

SERVES 4–6

This is gorgeous with fish fondues but also with cooked, peeled prawns (shrimp) as a starter.

120 ml/4 fl oz/½ cup mayonnaise
120 ml/4 fl oz/½ cup crème fraîche
10 ml/2 tsp curry paste
5 ml/1 tsp made English mustard
1 spring onion (scallion), very finely chopped
15 ml/1 tbsp curried fruit chutney
Salt and freshly ground black pepper

Mix together all the ingredients, seasoning to taste. Chill until ready to serve.

White wine marinade

ENOUGH FOR UP TO 900 G/2 LB FISH

150 ml/¼ pt/⅔ cup dry white wine
15 ml/1 tbsp lemon juice
15 ml/1 tbsp olive oil
1 onion, finely chopped
15 ml/1 tbsp chopped parsley
15 ml/1 tbsp chopped tarragon
1 small bay leaf
Salt and freshly ground black pepper

Whisk together all the ingredients and use as required.

Thai marinade

ENOUGH FOR UP TO 900 G/2 LB FISH

75 ml/5 tbsp sunflower oil
30 ml/2 tbsp sesame oil
Juice of 1 lime
1 large garlic clove, crushed
15 ml/1 tbsp peanut butter
15 ml/1 tbsp light brown sugar
1 lemon grass stem, crushed
1 small green chilli, seeded, if
  preferred, and chopped
15 ml/1 tbsp chopped coriander
  (cilantro)

Whisk together all the ingredients until smooth and use as required.

Yoghurt marinade for oily fish

ENOUGH FOR UP TO 700 G/1½ LB FISH

150 ml/¼ pt/⅔ cup plain yoghurt
15 ml/1 tbsp dried dill (dill weed)
15 ml/1 tbsp lemon juice
15 ml/1 tbsp Dijon mustard
15 ml/1 tbsp horseradish relish
30 ml/2 tbsp olive oil
Salt and freshly ground black pepper

Whisk together all the ingredients and use as required.

Lime sesame marinade

ENOUGH FOR UP TO 700 G/1½ LB FISH

120 ml/4 fl oz/½ cup sunflower oil
Finely grated rind and juice of 1 lime
15 ml/1 tbsp tahini paste
5 ml/1 tsp ground cumin
2.5 ml/½ tsp dried marjoram
1 garlic clove, crushed
15 ml/1 tbsp chopped coriander
  (cilantro) or parsley

Whisk together all the ingredients and use as required.

Italian marinade

ENOUGH FOR UP TO 700 G/1½ LB FISH

This is particularly good with shellfish.

120 ml/4 fl oz/½ cup olive oil
45 ml/3 tbsp balsamic vinegar
45 ml/3 tbsp lemon juice
1 large garlic clove, crushed
1 shallot, finely chopped
5 ml/1 tsp anchovy essence (extract)
5 ml/1 tsp dried basil

Whisk together all the ingredients and use as required.

Bajan marinade

ENOUGH FOR 900 G/2 LB FISH

2 passion fruit
120 ml/4 fl oz/½ cup pure orange juice
60 ml/4 tbsp sunflower oil
1 large garlic clove, crushed
Finely grated rind and juice of 1 lime
30 ml/2 tbsp dark rum
15 ml/1 tbsp dark brown sugar
1.5 ml/¼ tsp chilli powder

Scoop out the flesh from the passion fruit and place in a bowl. Whisk with all the remaining ingredients and use as required.

Accompaniments

It's not just a coincidence that we like chips (fries) with fried (sautéed) fish, or rice with curry. It's part of a properly balanced meal. The food value of fish (and other proteins) is best utilised by our bodies when mixed with vegetable foods at each meal and the starchy foods provide the carbohydrates necessary to ensure we get enough energy not only to rush around but also for our bodies to function properly. Here I have included the best ways to make all the classic 'fillers', plus some more elegant and unusual accompaniments. Where stock is used, I prefer it to be fish stock to add an extra dimension of flavour, but chicken will do as well.

Chips

SERVES 4

Use either a deep-fryer with a basket or a deep, heavy-based frying pan (skillet).

4 large potatoes, peeled and thickly sliced
Oil, for deep-frying
Salt

Cut the potato slices into fingers and place in a bowl of cold water until ready to cook. Drain well and dry in a clean tea towel (dish cloth). Heat the oil until a cube of day-old bread browns in 30 seconds. Add the potatoes and cook until they are tender but not brown. Remove from the pan, either in the basket or with a fish slice, and drain on kitchen paper (paper towels). Reheat the oil until smoking. Return half the chips (fries) to the pan and cook until crisp and golden. Drain on kitchen paper and keep warm while cooking the remainder. Season with salt before serving.

Sauté potatoes

SERVES 4

4 potatoes, diced
25 g/1 oz/2 tbsp butter or margarine
30 ml/2 tbsp sunflower oil

Boil the potatoes in water for about 3 minutes until almost tender. Drain and dry on kitchen paper (paper towels). Heat the butter or margarine and oil in a large frying pan (skillet). Add the potatoes and fry (sauté), turning gently occasionally, until golden brown and cooked through. Drain on kitchen paper before serving.

Sauté potatoes with garlic

SERVES 4

Prepare as for Sauté Potatoes, but add 2 halved garlic cloves to the butter and oil. Discard before serving.

Perfect potato wedges for fish

SERVES 4

4 large potatoes
30 ml/2 tbsp sunflower or olive oil
5 ml/1 tsp barbecue seasoning
1 fish stock cube, crumbled

Prick the potatoes and either boil in water for about 20 minutes or cook in the microwave according to the manufacturer's instructions until almost tender. Drain, if necessary. When cool enough to handle, halve the potatoes, then cut each half into wedges. Lay in a roasting tin (pan) and drizzle with the oil. Sprinkle with the barbecue seasoning and crumbled stock cube, then cook at the top of a preheated oven at 220°C/425°F/gas mark 7 for about 20–25 minutes until crisp and golden, turning once.

Garlic potato wedges

SERVES 4

Prepare as for Perfect Potato Wedges, but add 5 ml/1 tsp garlic powder to the barbecue seasoning.

Potato croquettes for fish

SERVES 4

450 g/1 lb potatoes
1 fish stock cube
A good knob of butter or margarine
30 ml/2 tbsp plain (all-purpose) flour
Salt and freshly ground black pepper
1 egg, beaten
75 g/3 oz/¾ cup dried breadcrumbs
Oil, for shallow frying

Boil the potatoes in water, to which the stock cube has been added, until tender. Drain and mash well with the butter or margarine. Beat in the flour and salt and pepper to taste. Shape into small sausage shapes, then brush with the egg and roll in the breadcrumbs. Chill until ready to cook. Shallow-fry in hot oil, turning occasionally, until golden brown all over. Drain on kitchen paper (paper towels) and serve hot.

Duchesse potatoes for fish

SERVES 4

Do not use a food processor for this – the potato shapes would collapse in the oven.

450 g/1 lb potatoes
1 fish stock cube
50 g/2 oz/¼ cup butter or margarine
1 large egg yolk
Salt and freshly ground black pepper

Boil the potatoes in water to which the stock cube has been added. Drain and pass the potatoes through a sieve (strainer). Beat in the butter or margarine, then the egg yolks. Pipe into whirls or spoon into mounds on a greased baking (cookie) sheet. Bake in a preheated oven at 180°C/350°F/gas mark 4 for about 20 minutes until golden.

Scalloped potatoes for fish

SERVES 4

450 g/1 lb potatoes, thinly sliced
50 g/2 oz/¼ cup butter or margarine, flaked, plus extra for greasing
Salt and freshly ground black pepper
5 ml/1 tsp anchovy essence (extract)
300 ml/½ pt/1¼ cups milk

Layer the potatoes in a greased ovenproof dish with a little salt and pepper and flakes of butter or margarine between each layer. Whisk the anchovy essence into the milk and pour over. Cover with foil and bake in a preheated oven at 190°C/375°F/gas mark 5 for 1½ hours or until really tender.

Game chips

Serve these with any roasted or grilled (broiled) fish.

Peel as many potatoes as you like (I usually allow a medium-sized one per person). Slice very thinly, either with a knife or using a mandolin cutter. Soak in cold water for at least 10 minutes. Drain and dry well on kitchen paper (paper towels). Heat oil for deep-frying until a cube of day-old bread browns in 30 seconds. Deep-fry the potato slices for about 3 minutes until crisp and golden brown. Drain on kitchen paper (paper towels) and sprinkle with salt before serving. Do not overload the pan; it is better to cook two small batches than one big one. Keep them warm in the oven while cooking the remainder.

Puréed potatoes

SERVES 4

Add a fish stock cube to the potatoes when boiling for added flavour.

700 g/1½ lb potatoes, peeled and cut into neat pieces
A large knob of butter or margarine
Freshly ground black pepper

Cook the potatoes in plenty of boiling salted water until really tender. Drain. Tip the potatoes into a blender or food processor and add the butter or margarine and pepper to taste. Run the machine until the mixture is smooth. Serve straight away.

Bombay puréed potatoes

SERVES 4

Prepare as for Puréed Potatoes, but add 5 ml/1 tsp garam masala with the butter or margarine. Top with a crumbled piece of grilled (broiled) Bombay duck before serving.

Speciality creamed potatoes

SERVES 4

Add a fish stock cube, if liked, when boiling the potatoes and omit the salt.

1 kg/2¼ lb potatoes, peeled and cut into chunks
25 g/1 oz/2 tbsp butter or margarine
30 ml/2 tbsp single (light) cream
Freshly ground black pepper

Boil the potatoes in plenty of lightly salted water until tender. Drain and return to the pan over a moderate heat. Shake the pan for 1 minute to dry out the potatoes. Mash the potatoes well, then beat in the butter or margarine and cream until soft and fluffy. Season to taste with pepper.

Hot potato salad

SERVES 6–8

1 kg/2¼ lb potatoes, scrubbed and halved, if large
1 fish stock cube
50 g/2 oz/1 small can of anchovy fillets, drained
250 ml/8 fl oz/1 cup crème fraîche
5 ml/1 tsp lemon juice
A pinch of caster (superfine) sugar
Freshly ground black pepper
Paprika, for dusting

Cook the potatoes in plenty of boiling water to which the stock cube has been added until just tender. Drain and when cool enough to handle, peel off the skins. Cut into chunks and return to the pan. Reserve four anchovies for decoration. Finely chop the remainder and mix with the crème fraîche, lemon juice, sugar and a little pepper. Add to the potatoes and toss lightly over a gentle heat. Turn into a warm serving dish. Halve the reserved anchovies lengthways and arrange attractively on top. Dust with paprika and serve hot.

Cheat game chips

SERVES 4

Heat any good-quality pan-fried crisps (chips) on a baking (cookie) sheet in a preheated oven at 150°C/300°F/gas mark 2 for 2–3 minutes. Serve with any roasted or grilled (broiled) fish.

Cheese potatoes

SERVES 4

Prepare as for Speciality Creamed Potatoes, but add 75 g/3 oz/¾ cup Cheddar cheese, grated, with the butter or margarine and continue as before.

Anchovy mustard seed potatoes

SERVES 4

You can cook these for a slightly shorter time in a hotter oven if that suits whatever else you are cooking.

700 g/1½ lb potatoes, scrubbed and halved or quartered, depending on size
1 quantity of Anchovy Butter (page 384)
30 ml/2 tbsp black mustard seeds

Boil the potatoes in water for 3 minutes. Drain and tip into a roasting tin (pan). Add the Anchovy Butter and toss to coat completely. Sprinkle with the mustard seeds. Roast towards the top of a preheated oven at 180°C/350°F/gas mark 4 for 1½ hours or until golden brown and tender, turning once during cooking.

Oven-sautéed potatoes with garlic

SERVES 4

700 g/1½ lb potatoes, scrubbed
45 ml/3 tbsp olive oil
40 g/1½ oz/3 tbsp butter or margarine
1–2 garlic cloves, finely chopped
Salt

Dice the potatoes and put in a bowl of cold water until ready to cook. Drain and dry on kitchen paper (paper towels). Heat the oil and butter or margarine in a baking tin (pan). Add the potatoes and toss to coat completely. Add the garlic and a little salt and toss again. Place towards the top of a preheated oven at 200°C/400°F/gas mark 6 for about 45 minutes, turning two or three times, until golden brown and cooked through. Drain on kitchen paper and serve hot.

Plain rice for fish

SERVES 4

175 g/6 oz/¾ cup long-grain rice, preferably basmati
1 fish stock cube

Wash the rice well until the water is no longer cloudy. Drain thoroughly. Dissolve the stock cube in a large pan of boiling water. Add the rice and stir to separate the grains. Bring back to the boil. Boil rapidly, uncovered, for 10 minutes. Test by lifting out a few grains and pinching them between your finger and thumb or by biting between the teeth. The grain should be almost soft but still with a little resistance – not crunchy – in the middle. Drain in a colander and rinse with boiling water. Set on top of the saucepan with water in it over a gentle heat for a few minutes to dry out. Fluff up with a fork and serve.

Buttered rice

SERVES 4

Cook the rice as for Plain Rice for Fish. Toss in 25 g/1 oz/2 tbsp butter or margarine and sprinkle with 30 ml/2 tbsp chopped parsley before serving.

Thai fragrant rice

SERVES 4

Cook as for Plain Rice for Fish, but use Thai fragrant rice. The rice will be slightly stickier than when using basmati or other long-grain rice.

Egg fried rice

SERVES 4

Cook one quantity of Plain Rice for Fish (page 392). Heat 30 ml/2 tbsp sunflower in a frying pan (skillet). Add the cooked rice and 50 g/2 oz/ ½ cup thawed, frozen peas and toss for 2 minutes. Push the rice to one side and tilt the pan. Pour in a beaten egg. Cook the egg, stirring, then gradually draw in the rice until it is scattered with tiny strands of egg. Add a pinch of Chinese five-spice powder and a sprinkling of soy sauce. Toss and serve.

Special egg fried rice

SERVES 4

Prepare as for Egg Fried Rice, but add 100 g/4 oz cooked, peeled prawns (shrimp) with the peas.

Quick pilau rice

SERVES 4

Prepare as for Plain Rice for Fish, but add 5 ml/1 tsp ground turmeric to the water, 4–6 split cardamom pods and a small piece of cinnamon stick. Cook a finely chopped onion in 15 ml/1 tbsp sunflower oil until golden brown and soft and fork through the rice before serving. Remove the spices before using if you wish.

Oven pilaff

SERVES 4–6

This is ideal to cook on a shelf below fish being roasted or casseroled.

1 onion, finely chopped
25 g/1 oz/2 tbsp butter or margarine
225 g/8 oz/1 cup long-grain rice, well-washed and drained
600 ml/1 pt/2½ cups fish stock
Salt and freshly ground black pepper
4 ready-to-eat dried apricots, finely chopped
4 ready-to eat prunes, finely chopped
50 g/2 oz button mushrooms, thinly sliced
50 g/2 oz/½ cup frozen peas

Fry (sauté) the onion in the butter or margarine for 2 minutes in a flameproof casserole dish (Dutch oven). Add the rice and stir until coated in the fat. Pour in the stock and add a little seasoning. Bring to the boil, cover and transfer to a low shelf in a preheated oven at 200°C/ 400°F/gas mark 6. Cook for 10 minutes. Add the chopped fruit, mushrooms and peas and fork through. Cover with foil and the lid and return to the oven on the lowest shelf for a further 10 minutes until the rice is cooked and has absorbed all the liquid. Fluff up and serve.

Wild rice mix for fish

SERVES 4

175 g/6 oz/¾ cup wild rice mix
1 fish stock cube
Freshly ground black pepper

Rinse the rice mix in several changes of cold water. Drain thoroughly. Bring a saucepan of water to the boil and add the stock cube. Stir until dissolved. Add the rice mix and stir well again. Bring back to the boil and boil for 20 minutes or according to the packet directions until the rice is tender but still has some 'bite'. Drain in a colander. Place the colander over the saucepan with a little water in it. Simmer for 2–3 minutes to dry out, stirring the rice occasionally. Fluff up and serve.

Buttered noodles for fish

SERVES 4

350 g/12 oz tagliatelle or other ribbon noodles
1 fish stock cube
25 g/1 oz/2 tbsp unsalted (sweet) butter, flaked

Cook the tagliatelle in plenty of boiling water to which the stock cube has been added for 10 minutes or until just tender, stirring occasionally to separate the strands. Drain and return to the pan. Add the butter and toss until every strand is coated. Serve straight away.

Anchovy pasta for fish

SERVES 4

225 g/8 oz pasta shapes
10 ml/2 tsp anchovy essence (extract)
25 g/1 oz/2 tbsp unsalted (sweet) butter, flaked
30 ml/2 tbsp crème fraîche
Freshly ground black pepper

Cook the pasta according to the packet directions. Drain and return to the pan. Add the anchovy essence and the butter. Toss until the butter melts, then stir in the crème fraîche and a good grinding of pepper.

Crispy noodle cake

SERVES 4

250 g/9 oz Chinese egg noodles
45 ml/3 tbsp sunflower oil

Cook the noodles according to the packet directions. Drain and dry thoroughly on kitchen paper (paper towels). Heat 30 ml/2 tbsp of the oil in a frying pan (skillet). Add the noodles and spread out in the pan in an even layer. Fry (sauté) until golden brown underneath. Lift out of the pan. Add the remaining oil. Turn the noodle cake over and return to the pan. Continue to fry until crisp and golden. Serve whole, cut into wedges, as an accompaniment to any of the Chinese-style dishes.

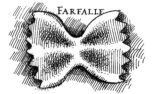
FARFALLE

Crisp fried noodles

SERVES 4

Other pasta shapes can also be deep-fried. They make a good garnish for oriental dishes and soups, too.

225 g/8 oz cooked ribbon noodles, cut into short lengths
Oil, for deep-frying
Coarse sea salt

Make sure the noodles are completely dry and that the strands are separate. Heat the oil to 190°C/375°F or until a cube of day-old bread browns in 30 seconds. Deep-fry the noodles in small batches in a wire basket until crisp and golden brown. Drain on kitchen paper (paper towels), then toss in coarse sea salt.

Garlic bread

SERVES 4

50 g/2 oz/¼ cup butter or margarine, softened
1–2 garlic cloves, crushed
30 ml/2 tbsp chopped parsley
1 small baguette or ciabatta loaf

Mash the butter or margarine with the garlic and parsley. Cut the baguette or ciabatta into 12 slices, not right through the bottom crust. Spread the butter or margarine between the slices, spreading any remainder over the top. Wrap in foil and bake in a preheated oven at about 200°C/400°F/gas mark 6 for 15 minutes or until the crust feels crisp when squeezed with an oven-gloved hand.

Hot herb bread

SERVES 4

Prepare as for Garlic Bread, but omit the garlic and mash 5 ml/1 tsp dried mixed herbs and the finely grated rind of half a lemon into the butter or margarine with the parsley.

Croûtons

SERVES 4

25 g/1 oz/2 tbsp butter or margarine
15 ml/1 tbsp sunflower oil
2 slices of white or wholemeal bread, crusts removed, cubed

Heat the butter or margarine and oil in a frying pan (skillet). Add the bread cubes and toss for 2–3 minutes until crisp and brown. Drain on kitchen paper (paper towels) and serve with soups or sprinkled over salads or pasta.

Cheese croûtons

SERVES 4

25 g/1 oz/2 tbsp butter or margarine
15 ml/1 tbsp sunflower oil
2 thick slices of white bread, crusts removed, cubed
15 ml/1 tbsp grated Parmesan cheese

Heat the butter or margarine and oil in a frying pan (skillet). Add the bread and toss for 2–3 minutes until crisp and brown. Drain on kitchen paper (paper towels) and toss immediately in the Parmesan. Serve with soups or sprinkled over salads or pasta.

Cheese and anchovy croûtes

SERVES 4

Serve these as an accompaniment to any fish soup.

4 slices cut from a ciabatta loaf
25 g/1 oz/2 tbsp unsalted (sweet)
  butter
5 ml/1 tsp anchovy essence (extract)
15 ml/1 tbsp grated Parmesan cheese
Freshly ground black pepper

Toast the bread on one side. Meanwhile, mash the butter with the anchovy essence, Parmesan and a good grinding of pepper. Spread on the untoasted sides of the bread. Place on foil on the grill (broiler) rack and grill (broil) until the topping is melted and bubbling.

Baked tomatoes with herbs and stuffed olives

SERVES 4

8 equal-sized tomatoes
30 ml/2 tbsp water
15 ml/1 tbsp chopped basil
15 ml/1 tbsp chopped parsley
A good pinch of caster (superfine)
  sugar
Salt and freshly ground black pepper
8 green olives stuffed with anchovies,
  chopped

Cut a cross in the rounded end of each tomato and place in a casserole dish (Dutch oven). Add the water, herbs, sugar and seasoning. Cover and bake in a preheated oven at 190°C/375°F/gas mark 5 for 10 minutes. Sprinkle the olives over and cook for a further 5 minutes until the tomatoes are just cooked but still hold their shape. Serve with the juices spooned over.

Index